PSYCHOLOGICAL MALTREATMENT OF
CHILDREN AND YOUTH
(PGPS-143)

Pergamon Titles of Related Interest

Mrazek/Kempe SEXUALLY ABUSED CHILDREN AND THEIR
FAMILIES
Plas SYSTEMS PSYCHOLOGY IN THE SCHOOLS
Roberts PEDIATRIC PSYCHOLOGY
Santostefano COGNITIVE CONTROL THERAPY WITH
CHILDREN AND ADOLESCENTS
Walker/Bonner/Kaufman THE PHYSICALLY AND SEXUALLY
ABUSED CHILD: Evaluation and Treatment
Wielkiewicz BEHAVIOR MANAGEMENT IN THE SCHOOLS:
Principles and Procedures

Related Journals
(Free sample copies available upon request)

CHILD ABUSE AND NEGLECT
CHILDREN AND YOUTH SERVICES REVIEW
CLINICAL PSYCHOLOGY REVIEW
JOURNAL OF CHILD PSYCHOLOGY AND PSYCHIATRY

PERGAMON GENERAL PSYCHOLOGY SERIES

EDITORS
Arnold P. Goldstein, *Syracuse University*
Leonard Krasner, *Stanford University and SUNY at Stony Brook*

Psychological Maltreatment of Children and Youth

Marla R. Brassard
University of Georgia

Robert Germain
Worthington, Ohio Public Schools

Stuart N. Hart
Indiana University

PERGAMON PRESS
New York   Oxford   Beijing   Frankfurt
São Paulo   Sydney   Tokyo   Toronto

Pergamon Press Offices:

U.S.A.	Pergamon Press, Maxwell House, Fairview Park, Elmsford, New York 10523, U.S.A.
U.K.	Pergamon Press, Headington Hill Hall, Oxford OX3 0BW, England
PEOPLE'S REPUBLIC OF CHINA	Pergamon Press, Qianmen Hotel, Beijing, People's Republic of China
FEDERAL REPUBLIC OF GERMANY	Pergamon Press, Hammerweg 6, D-6242 Kronberg, Federal Republic of Germany
BRAZIL	Pergamon Editora, Rua Eça de Queiros, 346, CEP 04011, São Paulo, Brazil
AUSTRALIA	Pergamon Press (Aust.) Pty., P.O. Box 544, Potts Point, NSW 2011, Australia
JAPAN	Pergamon Press, 8th Floor, Matsuoka Central Building, 1-7-1 Nishishinjuku, Shinjuku-ku, Tokyo 160, Japan
CANADA	Pergamon Press Canada, Suite 104, 150 Consumers Road, Willowdale, Ontario M2J 1P9, Canada

First printing 1987

Library of Congress Cataloging in Publication Data

Psychological maltreatment of children and youth.

(Pergamon general psychology series ; 143)
Includes index.
1. Child abuse--Psychological aspects. 2. Youth--Crimes against--Psychological aspects. I. Brassard, Marla R. II. Germain, Robert, 1952-   . III. Hart, Stuart N. IV. Series.
HV6626.5.P78   1987   362.7'044   86-22531
ISBN 0-08-032775-3

Printed & bound in Great Britain by Redwood Burn Limited, Trowbridge, Wiltshire.

We dedicate this book to our spouses, George, Susan, and Ginny
and to the late Calvin Catterall whose vision and leadership in regard to
children's psychological rights was an inspiration.

Contents

PART 3: INTERDISCIPLINARY PERSPECTIVES

Foreword

Rejection, isolation, humiliation, verbal assaults, being ignored, being terrorized—these are things that happen to children. These are the things that crush a child's self-esteem, taint a child's emotional well-being, and damage a child's potential to contribute fully in this world. These are the things that make up psychological maltreatment.

Sometimes verbal assaults and emotional neglect occur by themselves. All too often, they accompany physical and sexual abuse and physical neglect. Psychological maltreatment is at the core of all child maltreatment. Indeed, the long-term and most insidious consequences of all forms of maltreatment are emotional.

Despite the pervasiveness of psychological maltreatment in all forms of abuse, and even though for the past decade most state child abuse reporting laws include psychological maltreatment in their definitions of abuse, serious scientific inquiry into the causes, consequences, prevention and treatment of psychological maltreatment has been sparse. Only now is the public coming to understand that emotional abuse is a serious form of child abuse. And only now are numbers of child abuse professionals—researchers and clinicians alike—focusing their attention on emotional abuse.

This book heralds the increased attention we now see being paid to this problem. And, just as this book reflects pioneering and concrete thinking about a problem long regarded as too abstract to define, so this book will be a catalyst for efforts long needed to bring the problem into sharp focus and eventually under control.

Anne H. Cohn, DPH

Director, National Committee
for the Prevention of Child Abuse

Preface and Acknowledgments

"The majority of human suffering which has occurred throughout history may have been due to psychological abuse."

Psychological maltreatment is the core issue in child abuse and neglect.

The first statement was made by a county prosecutor in response to a questionnaire on psychological abuse. The second statement is a paraphrase of the positions taken by the physician who directed the American Medical Association's child abuse projects and by a leading biochemist who discussed the relationships between physical and psychological stress. Experts in the field of child abuse and neglect generally recognize that psychological maltreatment almost always accompanies other forms of child maltreatment, is the most prevalent form of maltreatment, and is often more destructive than other forms. Yet, very little consideration has been given to psychological maltreatment in research and intervention projects. It is the intention of the editors and authors of this book to change this situation by clarifying the nature of psychological maltreatment and suggesting directions for dealing with it.

While concern for the psychological needs, rights, and health of young people has a long history, the impetus for this book has its roots in several recent events. During the International Year of the Child, 1979, the International School Psychology Association enlisted the participation of school, educational, and child psychologists to produce the "Declaration of the Psychological Rights of the Child." To insure that the principles of that declaration would live outside the filing cabinets of the well-intentioned, the National Association of School Psychologists and the School of Education of Indiana University established a national leadership and clearinghouse center to assist, stimulate, and pursue projects which would clarify and promote children's psychological needs and rights. The center, named the Office for the Study of the Psychological Rights of the Child and directed by the editors of this book, determined through its review of issues that psychological maltreatment deserved first priority status.

The investigation of this issue had revealed that psychological maltreatment was a very serious problem, and was very probably the main precipitator of a wide range of destructive behaviors and conditions of life for individuals of all ages. It also revealed that the issue was very poorly understood and that it was not being dealt with in meaningful or powerful ways. A clear starting point for progress was needed.

The International Conference on Psychological Abuse of Children and Youth, Indianapolis, 1983, was chosen to be that starting point. As the first major conference devoted entirely to this topic, its major goals were to establish the present state of knowledge and to determine promising directions for research and intervention. It was a working conference, whose 200 participants from the United States and eight other countries represented helping professions, advocacy groups, organized religion, and victims/survivors of psychological maltreatment. With the guidance of 16 national and international experts, conference participants reviewed and debated definitions, causes, consequences, mediating variables, interventions and research issues. The conference produced a unanimously supported generic working definition (see chapter 1), a consensus that psychological maltreatment is the core issue in child abuse and neglect, a resolution encouraging professional and advocacy groups to join in coordinated efforts for further work, and over one hundred suggestions for activities to clarify and combat psychological maltreatment.

In many ways, this book is one of the products of the International Conference on Psychological Abuse of Children and Youth. During the conference, and through the follow-up activities it stimulated, it became increasingly clear that insufficient awareness of the nature of psychological maltreatment existed for helping professionals and researchers as well as for the general public. The base of knowledge established through the conference needed to be expanded and communicated to all interested parties if progress was to be made. The conference had produced issues papers which were the perfect starting point for approximately one-half of the book's chapters. The remaining chapters were selected to achieve comprehensiveness.

The book is divided into three main sections dealing with: basic perspectives, domains, and interdisciplinary perspectives associated with psychological maltreatment. The first section presents the challenge which psychological maltreatment represents to our children and society and deals in depth with issues which clarify the degree to which psychological maltreatment is the core concept or component in child maltreatment. They give particular attention to direct and indirect forms of psychological maltreatmnt and relationships between physical and psychological aspects of maltreatment.

The second section of the book deals with the domains of psychological maltreatment by concentrating specifically on psychological aspects of other forms of maltreatment (i.e., corporal punishment, sexual abuse, and substance abuse) and the characteristics of forms of maltreatment which are discretely psychological in nature (i.e., emotional neglect and stimulus deprivation, psychologically unavailable caretaking, influence by negative and limiting models, prejudice and cultural bias, racism, social system maltreatment, and dangerous and limiting models). In these chapters, examples of maltreatment are provided and attention is given to historical backgrounds, definitional and standards issues, research, correction, and prevention.

The third section of the book clarifies the present and potential contributions of expertise and practice embodied in professional and policy orientations. Coverage is specific to the law, legislative approaches, education and schooling, and psychology. Special emphasis is given to research issues and models relative to the contributions of psychology. This section closes the book by providing a chapter that identifies the themes, issues, and recommendations that represent convergence and divergence of findings and opinions in the book as a whole.

It is our belief that this book presents and differentiates between the solid ground of knowledge and potentially powerful speculation, expert opinion and belief. We hope that it makes clear the wide range of forms of psychological maltreatment, their destructive natures, and pervading presence. Our response to these conditions must be reasoned, sensitive, responsible, comprehensive, and systematic. The health of our most valuable resources, our children, and of our society is at stake.

We, the editors, are indebted to Mark Gelardo, research associate in school psychology (University of Georgia), Nancy Lubera, research assistant (Indiana University–Purdue University at Indianapolis), and Patricia Smith, school psychologist (Indiana), for editorial assistance; to Melinda Pass and Dora Ervin (University of Georgia), and Brenda Riley, Marge Marek, and Judy Hawley (IUPUI) for secretarial support; and to Jerry Frank of Pergamon who continually encouraged us. The chapter authors provided good initial drafts and were cooperative throughout the revision process. The University of Georgia and Indiana University–Purdue University at Indianapolis have been supportive throughout this project. The National Association of School Psychologists and Lilly Endowment, Inc., have provided support and encouragement in associated projects for many years.

PART 1

BASIC PERSPECTIVES

1

The Challenge:
To Better Understand and Combat
Psychological Maltreatment
of Children and Youth

Stuart N. Hart, Robert B. Germain, and Marla R. Brassard

INTRODUCTION

Child abuse and neglect has become a topic of major concern in the United States. Records kept by the American Humane Association (1986) indicate that over 1.7 million cases of child maltreatment were reported in the most recent year, 1984, for which statistics have been published. Most of the cases reported dealt with deprivation of necessities and major and/or minor physical injuries, while psychological maltreatment (e.g., emotional maltreatment, mental cruelty/injury) accounted for 10% of the cases. Although it is usually conceded that "reported maltreatment" may be only a small part of the different types of maltreatment that actually occur, this is likely to be particularly true for psychological maltreatment.

Experts generally believe that psychological maltreatment almost always accompanies other forms of abuse and neglect, is more prevalent than other forms of maltreatment, and is often more destructive in its impact on the lives of young people (Egeland, Sroufe, & Erickson, 1983; Garbarino, Guttman, & Seeley, 1986; Hart, Gelardo, & Brassard, 1986). Psychological maltreatment is a problem of major proportions which occurs under a variety of conditions of human interaction. However, even though opin-

ion and limited available data suggest this to be the case, little has been done to investigate or remedy the situation.

Little effort has been devoted to research and intervention focused on psychological maltreatment primarily because available definitions and standards for determining its existence and impact are inadequate. Under these conditions, the limited resources available for child maltreatment work have been devoted to forms of child abuse and neglect which are better understood.

Recent progress has been made. In August of 1983, the International Conference on Psychological Abuse of Children and Youth was held to clarify and consolidate the state of knowledge regarding psychological maltreatment and to provide directions for research and intervention (Hart, Germain, & Brassard, 1983). That conference has stimulated the development of plans to comprehensively and systematically deal with psychological maltreatment, has influenced intervention and research projects, and has provided the impetus for this book.

This chapter introduces and clarifies the major dimensions and issues of psychological maltreatment, as well as developments planned or underway which will contribute to our ability to understand and combat it. The major sections of this chapter will deal with the nature of psychological maltreatment as it is presently understood, the rationale for studying it, recommendations for its investigation, and directions for intervention. The information provided in this chapter should be of assistance in developing perspectives on the material presented in the other chapters of this book.

PSYCHOLOGICAL MALTREATMENT AS PRESENTLY CONCEIVED

Descriptions

Psychological maltreatment is the term used throughout this book to stand for all affective and cognitive aspects of child maltreatment, including both acts of omission and commission. This term seems to best subsume the many dimensions of such maltreatment and is now being used by specialists in the field (Garbarino, Guttman, & Seeley, 1986; Germain, Brassard, & Hart, 1985; Hart, Gelardo, & Brassard, 1986). Psychological maltreatment has historically been labeled as "mental cruelty" (Laury & Meerloo, 1967), "mental injury" (Public Law 93-247, 1974, detailed later in this chapter), "emotional abuse" (Lourie & Stefano, 1978), "emotional neglect" (Whiting, 1978), and "emotional maltreatment" (Lauer, Lourie, Salus, & Bradhurst, 1979). Attempts to describe psychological maltreatment under these labels have varied widely in their focus on its characteristics. The following examples verify this point. Emphasis has been given both to caretaker actions and to child behavior outcomes (Lourie & Stefano, 1978). The core of psychological maltreatment has been suggested, in a general way, to be caretaker acts which punish or deny development toward self-esteem and interpersonal skills (Garbarino, 1978). In more specific ways, it has been said to involve acts of rejection (Garbarino & Garbarino, 1980; Rohner & Rohner, 1980), inappropriate control, extreme inconsistency (Garbarino & Garbarino, 1980), and deliberately subjecting a child to traumatic experiences in the form of alternating patterns of repetitive and chronic overstimulation and emotional deprivation (Shengold, 1979). Refusing to provide help for a child who is emotionally disturbed has also been suggested as a form of psychological maltreatment (Whiting, 1978).

The International Conference on Psychological Abuse of Children and Youth dealt with eight major domains of psychological maltreatment.

These domains, covering psychological maltreatment associated with other forms of maltreatment as well as forms in which it stands alone, provided the organizing structures for conference presentations and work. They also provided the basis for the organization of the chapters in Part 2 of this volume. The eight domains are:

Mental cruelty: For example, verbal abuse and downgrading, psychological associates of physical abuse, setting of unreasonably high or low expectations for achievement, dramatic and open discrimination in the treatment of siblings.

Sexual abuse and exploitation: For example, the psychological aspects of incest, rape, pornography, prostitution, teenage pregnancy, and unjustified discriminatory practices regarding the sexes.

Living in dangerous and unstable environments: For example, the psychological aspects of living in environments of civil and international war, high crime and violence, and severe family instability.

Drug and substance abuse: For example, misuse of drugs and other potentially harmful substances as administered or encouraged by adults or peers.

Influence by negative and limiting models: For example, the effects of powerful models (peers and adults) in the home, school community, or media (television, movies, music) who encourage narrow, rigid, self-destructive, violent and/or antisocial behavior.

Cultural bias and prejudice: For example, conditions or actions outside or inside culturally different minority groups which unfairly limit expectations or opportunities for experience by members of such groups.

Emotional neglect and stimulation deprivation: For example, deprivation of essential love and attention experiences, interpersonal rejection, and deprivation of sensory stimulation and other physical needs supporting psychological development.

Institutional abuse: For example, institutional treatment or practices which result in the psychological maltreatment of children in their care.

This partial listing of labels, characteristics and domains of psychological maltreatment provides some indication of the range of meanings ascribed to it. One of the few points of agreement established among experts regarding psychological maltreatment is that there has not been agreement on its meanings (Garbarino,

1978; Hart, Germain, & Brassard, 1983). Attempts to define psychological maltreatment shed additional light on its meaning.

Definitions

The Child Abuse, Prevention and Treatment Act (Public Law 93-247), originally passed in 1974, defined child abuse and neglect as follows:

> The physical or mental injury, sexual abuse or exploitation, negligent treatment, or maltreatment of a child under the age of eighteen, or the age specified by the child protection law of the state in question, by a person who is responsible for the child's welfare under circumstances which indicate that the child's health or welfare is harmed or threatened thereby, as determined in accordance with regulations prescribed by the Secretary.

"Mental injury" is the single reference to psychological maltreatment in the statute. It is not defined by presentation of categories or example. Numerous attempts have been made to develop definitions for psychological maltreatment in the wake of the national imperative for dealing with it which was produced by the federal statute's inclusion of the mental injury category.

The Second National Conference on Child Abuse and Neglect addressed this issue through a workshop. Emphasis was given to psychological maltreatment which is produced through consistently expressed parental behaviors/characteristics. A list of examples was produced which included scapegoating, ridicule, and denigration; shaming; ambivalence; inappropriate expectations for behavior/performance; threatened withdrawal of love; exploitation; threats to safety/health; physical abuse; sexual abuse; substance abuse; and psychosis (Lourie & Stefano, 1978).

The National Center on Child Abuse and Neglect has recommended the following general definition of mental injury as a guide for developing state standards:

> "Mental injury" means an injury to the intellectual or psychological capacity of a child as evidenced by an observable and substantial impairment in the child's ability to function within a normal range of performance and behavior, with due regard to the child's culture. (Landau, Salus, Stiffarm, & Kalb, 1980, p. 2)

Both the National Center on Child Abuse and Neglect (NCCAN) and the American Humane Association have developed more specific definitions of psychological maltreatment for the purposes of gathering data to clarify the incidence of maltreatment nationally. In its National Study of the Incidence and Severity of Child Abuse and Neglect, NCCAN identified the following as categories of "emotional maltreatment": verbal and emotional assault, close confinement, inadequate nurturance/affection, and knowingly permitting maladaptive behavior (National Center on Child Abuse and Neglect, 1981). The American Humane Association, which has the responsibility of gathering national data on a yearly basis regarding child neglect and abuse, has developed definitions of both emotional abuse and emotional neglect as guides to states in organizing reports they receive. It defines emotional abuse as "active, intentional berating, disparaging or other abusive behavior toward the child which impacts upon the emotional well-being of the child," and emotional neglect as "passive or passive/aggressive inattention to the child's emotional needs, nurturing, or emotional well-being" (American Humane Association, 1980, pp. 3.36–3.37).

None of these attempts at definition has been found to be adequate. National concern has developed regarding the lack of sufficient definition and unclear standards of evidence associated with the mental injury category of the federal statute. Additionally, concerns have focused on the lack of guidance provided for state laws and child protective services, and the possibilities that application of the law could lead to unfair intrusions in family life and to remedies which might prove more destructive than the conditions they were meant to correct. States have found it difficult to define and apply the mental injury category. Corson and Davidson (see chapter 14 in this volume) have detailed some of the resistance to this category at the national level and the very limited progress states have made in developing legal definitions for it.

These problems were among the reasons the mental injury category was given special consideration during the April 1983 hearings on the statute conducted by the Subcommittee on Family and Human Services of the Committee on Labor and Human Resources of the United States Congress (Child Abuse Prevention and Treatment and Adoption Reform Act Amendments for 1983, 1983). The lack of agreement which has existed among experts regarding the adequacy of definitions of psychological maltreatment was exemplified in those hearings through the testimony of Wayne Holder, then Director of the Children's Division of the American Humane Association, and Eli Newberger, pediatrician at Children's Hospital, Boston. They were each given the opportunity to state their opinions regarding the general form of the definition recommended by the National Center on Child Abuse and Neglect. Holder spoke in favor of the definition, indicating that it adequately outlined the nature of the problem and gave sufficient direction to professionals charged with legal investigation. Newberger argued against the definition, stating that he believed "emphatically" that it was not adequate and that it created "enormous ambiguity and confusion" (Holder, Newberger, & Loken, 1983, p. 301).

The inadequacy of psychological maltreatment definitions has been a major stumbling block to progress in research and intervention. In recognition of this, the International Conference on Psychological Abuse of Children and Youth gave primary importance to developing a definition that would have strong support. This conference, with representatives from virtually all the major helping professions and child advocacy groups as well as eight countries, produced the following definition:

> Psychological maltreatment of children and youth consists of acts of omission and commission which are judged on the basis of a combination of community standards and professional expertise to be psychologically damaging. Such acts are committed by individuals, singly or collectively, who by their characteristics (e.g., age, status, knowledge, organizational form) are in a position of differential power that renders a child vulnerable. Such acts damage immediately or ultimately the behavioral, cognitive, affective, or physical functioning of the child. Examples of psychological maltreatment include acts of rejecting, terrorizing, isolating, exploiting, and mis-socializing. (Hart, Germain, & Brassard, 1983, p. 2)

This definition was given unanimous support as a generic working definition by those attending the conference. Clarification of the definition was provided in Hart, Germain, & Brassard (1983). Among the points included were the following: *Maltreatment* is used to stand for both acts of

abuse and neglect. *Acts of commission and omission* are identified as channels of maltreatment, again to emphasize both abuse and neglect dimensions. The combination of *community standards and professional expertise* is required to establish standards regarding maltreatment that will have a broad base of support, including endorsement of the general public. *Individuals and collections of individuals* (e.g., parents, peers, neighbors, teachers, families, groups, organizations, institutions, cultures) are capable of maltreating others. *Differential power* in relationships rendering the child/youth vulnerable to the influence of the action or inaction of the other(s) is necessary for the maltreatment to occur. The maltreatment must be known to be *immediately or ultimately psychologically damaging*, allowing for application of evidence of existing conditions of the individual's functioning and predictions of eventual changes in functioning in determining whether or not maltreatment has occurred or is occurring. Acts which are psychologically damaging immediately or ultimately affect one or more of the four areas of human functioning: *behavioral, cognitive, affective,* or *physical*. The acts of omission or commission take the form of *rejecting, terrorizing, isolating, exploiting, or mis-socializing the child*. The last form, mis-socializing, is intended to stand for situations in which a child is directly taught, influenced by models, or otherwise encouraged to develop self- or other-destructive orientations toward human relations, values, and strategies for living and pursuing goals.

This generic working definition is a more logical extension of psychological maltreatment than is the more general definition for maltreatment which was recommended previously by Garbarino and Gilliam. They defined maltreatment as

> acts of omission or commission by a parent or guardian that are judged by a mixture of community values and professional expertise to be inappropriate and damaging (Garbarino & Gilliam, 1980, p. 7).

The definition of psychological maltreatment produced by the International Conference has been submitted to a wide variety of parties and organizations to solicit recommendations for refinement. The few suggestions received for modifications have focused primarily on refinement and expansion of the list of acts of maltreatment. The list of acts has recently been given major emphasis in psychological maltreatment work because they are believed to provide the best direction for further clarifying the nature of such maltreatment (Garbarino, Guttman, & Seeley, 1986; Hart, Gelardo, & Brassard, 1986). The Office for the Study of the Psychological Rights of the Child (OSPRC, Indiana University), the national center which conducted the International Conference, has recently modified that list as a result of reviewing recommendations it has received. The modified list, accompanied by dictionary definitions and a few examples, follows.

- Rejecting. To refuse to acknowledge, believe, receive; to decline to accept, to refuse, to cast or throw away as useless, unsatisfactory. To discard; to relegate. To refuse to hear, receive. To repel. (Distinguished from the "denying emotional responsiveness" category below by expressing active rejecting as opposed to passive ignoring.) *Examples:* treating a child differently from siblings or peers in ways suggesting a dislike for the child; actively refusing to act to help or acknowledge a child's request for help.
- Degrading. To reduce from a higher to lower rank or degree; to deprive of dignity. To bring into disrepute or disfavor; to depreciate. *Examples:* calling a child "stupid"; labeling as inferior; publicly humiliating.
- Terrorizing. To impress with terror (a state or instance of extreme fear; violent dread; fright); to coerce by intimidation. *Examples:* threatening to physically hurt or kill; forcing a child to observe violence directed toward loved ones; leaving a young child unattended.
- Isolating. To place apart by one's self; to separate from all others; (medical) separate from persons not similarly infected. *Examples:* locking in a closet or, for extended time, in a room alone; refusing to allow interactions or relationships with peers or adults outside the family.
- Corrupting. To render antisocial or malsocialized; to maladapt to social needs or uses; to change from a state of uprightness, correctness, truth, etc., to a bad state; depraved; to make putrid; to change from good to bad; to debase. *Examples:* teaching and reinforcing acts that degrade those racially or ethnically different; teaching and reinforcing criminal behavior; providing antisocial and unrealistic models as normal, usual or appropriate via the public media.
- Exploiting. To utilize; to get the value out of. To make use of basely for one's own advantage or profit. *Examples:* sexually molesting a child; keeping a child at home in the role of a servant or surrogate parent in lieu of school attendance; encouraging a child to participate in the production of pornography.
- Denying Emotional Responsiveness. To fail to provide the sensitive, responsive caregiving necessary to facilitate healthy social/emotional development; to be detached and uninvolved; to interact only when necessary. *Examples:* ignoring a child's attempts to interact; mechanistic child handling which is void of hugs, stroking, kisses and talk.

These acts appear to cover all major forms of psychological maltreatment. They have not been operationalized. The definitions and examples given above are provided only for clarification purposes. Operational definitions must be developed and validated if progress is to be made in clarifying and combating psychological maltreatment. The importance of developing operational definitions and strategies for accomplishing this task will be discussed later in this chapter.

Though presently available definitions and standards for decision making are inadequate, attempts have been made to gather data regarding the incidence of psychological maltreatment. The status of work in this area is considered next.

Incidence

It is doubtful that any of us escape being victims or perpetrators of psychological maltreatment. The descriptions and definitions just presented cover such a wide range of human conditions as to lend credibility to this conclusion. Most of us probably experience psychological maltreatment under conditions which lack sufficient intensity, frequency, and duration to have lasting negative effects. However, in the absence of standards for determining levels of seriousness, one might justifiably predict that it would be difficult to determine the extent to which psychological maltreatment occurs. Efforts to acquire incidence data validate this prediction.

It appears that relatively few cases of psychological maltreatment are reported. Evidence for this exists in several forms. From May of 1979 through April of 1980, NCCAN gathered child maltreatment data through its National Study of Incidence and Severity of Child Abuse and Neglect (National Center on Child Abuse and Neglect, 1981). The very conservative estimates of the NCCAN study indicated that there were approximately 200,000 cases of emotional abuse and neglect during that period. During a similar period, 1980, the American Humane Association gathered incidence data from state reports, as it does annually. Its figures imply that approximately 103,000 (13% of 788,884) cases of emotional maltreatment were reported (American Humane Association, 1981). Combined, this information suggests that only half of those that might have been reported, according to rather narrow conceptualizations of psychological maltreatment, were reported. This discrepancy may be due to the differences in definitions used (see earlier section on definitions) and/or to differences in data-gathering procedures.

There is no way of knowing the degree to which these figures accurately represent the cases reported at local and state levels or the degree to which they represent the actual incidence of psychological maltreatment. The American Humane Association has no control over the manner in which states gather and organize data. Child protective service workers in some states do not formally accept reports of psychological maltreatment. In some of the areas where such reports are accepted, systems of recording are so erratic as to be completely undependable. These conditions were described to us by child protective service workers by telephone and at regional and national presentations on psychological maltreatment. Different definitions and categories are used in different states. Only seven of the states have produced definitions to cover the mental injury category of the national statute. (See Corson & Davidson, see chapter 14 in this volume, for a detailed description of state legal practices.)

The American Humane Association's published data for a more recent period, 1984, indicates that 11% of the reports analyzed for nature of maltreatment fell within its definitions of emotional maltreatment (American Humane Association, 1986). This implies that, for those two years, approximately 190,000 cases were reported.

Wayne Holder, while Director of the Children's Division of the American Humane Association, indicated that available data on the numbers of maltreated children represents only what has become known, probably a small percentage of those who are maltreated, and that these figures cannot be considered as incidence figures (Holder, Newberger, & Loken, 1983, p. 228). NCCAN recognized that the figures from its national incidence study could not be considered to accurately represent the true levels of occurrence of child maltreatment (National Center on Child Abuse and Neglect, 1981). The judgments expressed by Holder and NCCAN dealt with child maltreatment in general, which includes conditions much easier to identify and process (e.g., physical abuse, sexual abuse) than psychological maltreatment.

It appears that presently available estimates of the incidence of psychological maltreatment should be considered to be highly speculative in nature. Additionally, given the widely held opinion that other forms of child maltreatment embody psychological maltreatment (Holder et al., 1983; Navarre, chapter 3 in this volume; Hart, Germain, & Brassard, 1983), it seems likely that those estimates represent only a small portion of cases which occur. The true incidence of psychological maltreatment may never be known; however, we are likely to develop more accurate estimates when we have a clearer understanding of what we mean by the term.

The Nature of Psychological Maltreatment

Psychological maltreatment work is in an embryonic stage. At this time, for heuristic purposes, it is important to propose formulations of the nature of psychological maltreatment. We believe the existing state of knowledge supports the following position:

> Psychological maltreatment consists of acts which deny or frustrate efforts on the part of an individual to satisfy his/her basic psychological needs to the degree that the individual's functioning becomes maladaptively deviant.

This formulation relies on the credibility of the following positions: (a) psychological needs theory has power in explaining important aspects of human motivation and behavior; (b) acts of psychological maltreatment are in conflict with and impede fulfillment of basic psychological needs; (c) the frustration of fulfillment of basic psychological needs leads to functioning which is deviant and maladaptive.

It is logically supportable to hypothesize that psychological maltreatment is a direct attack on psychological need fulfillment, and that this is what produces its destructive power. The work of Maslow (1968, 1970) provides the theoretical foundations and most well-developed conceptualization of needs/motivational theory relevant to this position. The basic psychological needs as set forth by Maslow have been divided into two groups, and categorized as "deficiency" needs and "growth" needs. They are organized in hierarchical fashion because it is believed that needs at lower levels must be met before responsible pursuit of those at higher levels can occur. The deficiency needs include physiological needs, safety needs, belongingness and love needs, and esteem needs. The growth needs include the need for self-actualization, desire to know and understand, and aesthetic needs, with the group often referred to as simply "self-actualization" needs. The deficiency needs create disagreeable tension and, thereby, motivate the individual to act to reduce that tension. Growth needs are pursued because of the pleasurable tension accompanied by their satisfaction. The deficiency needs are most relevant to psychological maltreatment. From our point of view, psychological maltreatment tends to frustrate or distort efforts to fulfill these needs. Maslow (1968, 1970) and others (Biehler & Snowman, 1982; Glasser, 1965; Maddi, 1980) have indicated that failure to meet deficiency needs may produce maladaptive, ineffective, and destructive patterns of living. The empirical evidence for these needs and their influences continues to be debated (Fox, 1982, 1983; Goud, 1983; Wahba & Bridwell, 1976). While Maslow's Need Hierarchy has ". . . received little clear or consistent support from the available research findings" (Wahba & Bridwell, 1976, p. 233), the studies which have been reviewed have been judged to have substantial limitations which render conclusions about the power of the theory unjustifiable (Goud, 1983). Maslow indicated that his orientation to basic needs was shared "by most clinicians, therapists, and child psychologists" (1968, p. 21) whether or not they would phrase them as he did. It is our opinion that this continues to be a supportable position, and that the Needs Hierarchy clarifies the nature of psychological maltreatment.

The acts of psychological maltreatment which were presented in the lists of descriptions and definitions earlier in this chapter appear to be in direct conflict with, and likely to frustrate fulfillment of, basic psychological needs in precisely the manner in which Maslow (1970) has described the frustration of these needs. Terrorizing, verbal assault, and physical abuse would be in conflict with safety, and in some cases, physiological needs. Threatened withdrawal of love, inattention to nurturing, rejecting, and denying emotional responsiveness would be in conflict with belongingness and love needs, and would also interfere with fulfillment of physiological and safety needs. Scapegoating, exploiting, knowingly permitting maladaptive behavior, berating and disparaging would be in conflict with esteem needs. The Second National Conference on Child Abuse and Neglect, in its work on psychological maltreatment, identified for particular emphasis conditions which conflict with a healthy balanced approach to fulfillment of basic psychological needs. For example, emotional maltreatment was concluded to be present when parents provide, in the extreme, either too much or too little love, praise, acceptance, sense of self-worth, stability, and rewards for learning and mastery (Lourie & Stefano, 1978).

The state of knowledge regarding the impact of psychological maltreatment on child victims provides support for considering maladaptive deviancy to be the primary consequence. NCCAN documents state that "The behavior of emotionally maltreated and emotionally disturbed children is similar" (Lauer, Lourie, Salus, & Broadhurst, 1979). The list of indicators of emotional maltreatment produced at the Second National Conference on Child Abuse and Neglect (Lourie & Stefano, 1978) is made up entirely of symptoms and/or expressions of maladaptive deviancy (e.g., self-destructive behavior, pseudomaturity, excessive peer dependence, gender confusion). The maladaptive and destructive nature of the consequences suspected for psychological maltreatment provides the major justification for investigating this phenomenon. For that reason, more extensive consideration of the impact of psychological maltreatment will be provided in the next section.

RATIONALE FOR STUDYING PSYCHOLOGICAL MALTREATMENT

People, individually and collectively, are concerned about child maltreatment because of the damage it does to children. The national statute (Public Law 93-247), reviewed earlier, defines maltreatment in terms of acts which harm or threaten harm to the child's health or welfare. The major justification for investigating and combating child maltreatment is found in the potential for reducing or eliminating harm to children.

Much speculation and some research has focused on the consequences of psychological maltreatment. In this section we will present information regarding the suspected and known impact of psychological maltreatment on children, evidence which suggests that psychological maltreatment produces serious emotional/behavioral problems, and indicates that it is the "core" issue in child abuse and neglect.

The Known and Suspected Impact of Psychological Maltreatment

The present state of knowledge regarding the impact or consequences of psychological maltreatment for child victims falls into categories of speculation based on expert opinion and findings supported by research. At a different level of evidence, between these two and incorporating some of the characteristics of both, is knowledge in the form of opinions based on clinical case experiences. This section provides information from each of these categories.

Expert opinion has frequently been represented in efforts at state and national levels to provide direction to child service personnel. Virginia and Mississippi provide examples of such efforts at the state level. They have identified characteristics they consider to be potentially valuable as evidence of psychological maltreatment. Their combined sets of characteristics of mental abuse and mental neglect include excessive need for sucking; rocking; feeding and sleeping problems; excessive, age-inappropriate or unrealistic fears; enuresis; excessive masturbation; stuttering; intense symbiotic relationships; functional or social retardation; functional/organic disorders, such as failure-to-thrive syndrome and psychosocial dwarfism; inability to form trusting and mutual relationships; apathy; lethargy; depression; low self-esteem; self-denial; impaired memory; difficulty in concentrating; mental confusion and disorientation; psychological numbing; pseudomaturity; poor school performance; runaway behavior; stubborn or defiant activity; poor peer relationships; extensive denial; suicide threats or behavior; property destruction; and violent behavior towards others (Mississippi Department of Public Welfare, 1984, pp. 5, 8; Virginia Department of Social Services, 1985, pp. 6c, 6d). This list was developed through soliciting the opinions of professionals. Corson and Davidson (see chapter 14 in this volume)

describe conditions associated with the development and application of this list.

At the national level, the American Humane Association (Wald, 1961) and NCCAN (Broadhurst, 1984) publications have both identified the same list of possible consequences of psychological maltreatment. That list includes the following:

- *habit disorders*, such as sucking, biting, rocking, enuresis, or feeding disorders;
- *conduct disorders*, including withdrawal and antisocial behavior such as destructiveness, cruelty, and stealing;
- *neurotic traits*, such as sleep disorders and inhibition of play;
- *psychoneurotic reactions*, including hysteria, obsession, compulsion, phobias, and hypochondria;
- *behavior extremes*, such as appearing overly compliant, extremely passive or aggressive, very demanding or undemanding;
- *overly adaptive behaviors*, which are either inappropriately adult (parenting other children, for example) or inappropriately infantile (e.g., rocking, head-banging or thumbsucking);
- *lags* in emotional and intellectual development; and
- *attempted suicide* (Wald, 1961, pp. 6–7).

Another integration of expert opinion was produced by the workshop on defining emotional maltreatment held as a part of the Second National Conference on Child Abuse and Neglect (Lourie & Stefano, 1978). That workshop generated a list of child outcome indicators of emotional maltreatment similar to, though somewhat more extensive than, the two sets just presented. Appendix B presents this list and other lists of acts and suspected consequences of psychological maltreatment which have been proposed by major organizations.

Expert opinion seems generally in agreement that psychological maltreatment is potentially destructive to the quality of life of young people. Evidence somewhat stronger than opinion is available in findings from clinical case studies and empirical research. Our review of the literature found the following negative child conditions/characteristics to either be associated with or caused by psychological maltreatment broadly defined:

- *poor appetite* (Leonard, Rhymes, & Solnit, 1966; McCarthy, 1979; Spitz, 1946);

- *lying and stealing* (Pemberton & Benady, 1973);
- *encopresis and enuresis* (Hyman, 1985; McCarthy, 1979; Pemberton & Benady, 1973);
- *low self-esteem or negative self-concept* (Krugman & Krugman, 1984; Rohner & Rohner, 1980);
- *emotional instability or emotional maladjustment* (Dean, 1979; Hyman, 1985; Krugman & Krugman, 1984; Laury & Meerloo, 1967; Moore, 1974; Shengold, 1967, 1979);
- *reduced emotional responsiveness* (Fischoff, Whitten, & Petit, 1979; McCarthy, 1979; Shengold, 1979);
- *inability to become independent* (Egeland, Sroufe, & Erickson, 1983; Hyman, 1985; Rohner & Rohner, 1980);
- *incompetence and/or underachievement* (Dean, 1979; Moore, 1974; Pastor, 1981; Waters, Limpan, & Sroufe, 1979);
- *inability to trust others* (Densen–Gerber, 1979);
- *depression* (Krugman & Krugman, 1984);
- *prostitution* (Densen–Gerber, 1979);
- *failure to thrive* (Bullard, Glaser, Heagarty, & Pivchik, 1967; Brook, 1980; Egeland & Sroufe, 1981; Gardner, 1972; Powel, Brasel, & Blizzard, 1967);
- *withdrawal* (Hyman, 1985; Krugman & Krugman, 1984; Main & Goldwyn, 1984; Moore, 1974);
- *suicide* (Laury & Meerloo, 1967);
- *aggression* (Bandura, Ross, & Ross, 1961; Eron, Huesmann, Lefkowitz, & Walder, 1972; Main, 1973; Main & Goldwyn, 1984; Pemberton & Benady, 1973; Rohner & Rohner, 1980; Shengold, 1967);
- *homicide* (Hellsten & Katilla, 1965; Sendl & Blomgren, 1975).

The similarities between the sets of characteristics with some research support and those produced through expert opinion are readily apparent. These characteristics might be interpreted as symptoms of maladjustment. That point of view receives support from several sources.

Serious Emotional/Behavioral Disorders as the Major Consequence of Psychological Maltreatment

The Draft Model Child Protection Act developed and encouraged by NCCAN gave emphasis to four criteria to be applied in differentiating children who had been psychologically maltreated from those who had not. They indicated that "emotional maltreatment" (a) caused emotional or mental injury, (b) caused abnormal performance and behavior, (c) eroded the child's capacity to think, and (d) produced a "handicap" (Lauer, Lourie, Salus, & Broadhurst, 1979). Collectively, these criteria establish the existence of an emotional or behavioral disorder.

Opinion appears to be converging on this point of view. The focus is not new. Mulford (1958) and Whiting (1978) noted the relationships in early work on psychological maltreatment. Krugman & Krugman (1984), Hyman (1985), Corwin (1985), and Shultz (1985) have all concluded that psychological maladjustments and handicaps result from psychological maltreatment. The positions of many states (see Corson & Davidson, chapter 14 in this volume), the legal profession (American Bar Association Juvenile Justice Standards Project, 1980), and public policy experts (see Melton & Thompson, chapter 15 in this volume) emphasize the need to establish as a precondition for formal societal intervention that psychological maltreatment acts on the part of caretakers have produced documented emotional or behavioral disorders for the child.

Speculation, in the nature of informed expert opinion, supports the hypothesis that psychological maltreatment produces serious emotional/behavioral disorders. The strongest support for this position exists in empirical research and clinical case studies *directly* focused on psychological maltreatment. The relevant empirical studies include the cross-sectional controlled studies reported by Rohner and Rohner (1980), George and Main (1979), and Main & George (1985) which focused on parental rejection; and of Herrenkohl and Herrenkohl (1981) which focused on parental rejection, mental cruelty and terrorizing; and the longitudinal prospective research of Egeland and associates (Egeland & Sroufe, 1981; Egeland, Sroufe & Erickson, 1983) which discriminated differences in outcomes for four forms of physical and psychological maltreatment. The results of these studies are presented in abstract form in Tables 1.1 & 1.2. They are organized according to their fit within one or more of five criterion categories of emotional or behavioral disorders included within the standards for the "seriously emotionally disturbed" in The Education for All Handicapped Act (Public Law 94-142, 1975). The findings from these studies fit easily into the Public Law 94-142 structure. Clarification and further study of the relationships between

Table 1.1. Cross-Sectional Control Studies Linking Emotional/Behavioral Problems to Child Maltreatment by Parents/Caretakers

ED/BD Criteria	Rohner & Rohner (1980): Parental rejection evidenced by (a) active aggression toward the child, (b) physical/ emotional neglect	George & Main (1979), Main & George (1985): Parental rejection implied by physical maltreatment	Herrenkohl & Herrenkohl (1981): Psychological maltreatment defined as: parental rejection, mental cruelty, and terrorizing in cases of physical and sexual maltreatment and gross neglect
An inability to learn which cannot be explained by intellectual, sensory, or health factors.	*	*	*
An inability to build or maintain satisfactory interpersonal relationships with peers and teachers.	• excessive dependency on parents or other adults	• physically avoid caregivers and peers (i.e., isolation) • approach/avoidance behaviors in response to friendly overtures of caregivers and peers	*
Inappropriate types of behavior or feelings under normal circumstances.	• hostile and aggressive • emotionally unstable or unresponsive	• harass caregivers and peers (i.e., physically assault or threaten to physically assault) • respond with anger, fear, aggression to distress (e.g., crying) in peers	• low frustration tolerance, aggression
A general pervasive mood of unhappiness or depression.	• impaired self-esteem	*	*
A tendency to develop physical symptoms or fears associated with personal or school problems.	*	*	*

*Research data not available.

psychological maltreatment and emotional/behavioral child outcomes will be facilitated by application of recognized conceptual structures such as this. Corwin (1985) and Hyman (1985) have recommended the use of the syndrome categories of the *Diagnostic and Statistical Manual of Mental Disorders—Third Edition* (American Psychiatric Association, 1980), commonly referred to as the DSM-III, to deal with psychological maltreatment in the forms of sexual abuse and posttraumatic shock produced in educational processes, respectively. We have chosen to use the Public Law 94-142 categories in this context because they are more behaviorally oriented than the DSM-III syndromes, and less encumbered by esoteric language, and because a wealth of experience with their meanings and associated standards is being developed nationally through their widespread application in the public schools.

When clinical case study reports focused specifically on psychological maltreatment are added to the research results just presented, further support for the relationship between psychological maltreatment and emotional/behavioral disorder child outcomes is apparent. The recent work of Hyman (1985) and Krugman and Krugman (1984) dealing with psychological maltreatment perpetrated by teachers in a first-grade and a third-to-fourth-grade class, respectively, is instructive in this regard. These researchers found a wide range of behavioral and emotional symptoms of maladjustment, covering all the Public Law 94-142 categories with the exception of the one which deals with educational achievement. Table 1.2 presents their findings. All the criterion categories of Public Law 94-142 for the "seriously emotionally disturbed" would be filled, each with a variety of symptoms, if we were to include the findings from research relevant to psycholog-

Table 1.2. A Longitudinal Perspective Study Linking Emotional/Behavioral Problems to Child Maltreatment by Parents/Caretakers

ED/BD Criteria	Physically Abuse[a]	Hostile/Verbally Abuse[b]	Psychologically Unavailable[c]	Neglectful[d]
Egeland & Sroufe (1981): findings birth to 24 months of age				
An inability to learn which cannot be explained by intellectual, sensory, or health factors.	*	*	*	*
An inability to build or maintain satisfactory interpersonal relationships with peers and teachers.	• "anxiously attached" to mother	• "anxiously attached" to mother	• "anxiously attached" to mother	• "anxiously attached" to mother
Inappropriate types of behavior or feelings under normal circumstances.	• anger, frustration, noncompliance, aggression	• anger, frustration, noncompliance	• anger, frustration, noncompliance, whining, negative affect	• anger, frustration, noncompliance, negative affect
A general pervasive mood of unhappiness or depression.	*	*	*	*
A tendency to develop physical symptoms or fears associated with personal or school problems.	*	*	*	*
Egeland, Sroufe, & Erickson (1983): findings from 42 to 60 months of age				
An inability to learn which cannot be explained by intellectual, sensory, or health factors.	*	*	*	*
An inability to build or maintain satisfactory interpersonal relationships with peers and teachers.	• reliant on or avoidant of mother • school-related adjustment problems	• avoidant of mother, lack of affection	• avoidant of mother, lack of affection • dependent on teacher • school-related adjustment problems	• avoidant of mother, lack of affection • dependent on teacher • school-related adjustment problems
Inappropriate types of behavior or feelings under normal circumstances.	• hyperactive, distractible, noncompliant, express more negative emotions • less persistent during teaching tasks	• less persistent during teaching tasks • noncompliant, express more negative emotions	• less persistent during teaching tasks • noncompliant, express more negative emotions	• less persistent during teaching tasks • negative affect, apathetic noncompliant, withdrawn, hyperactive, distractible
A general pervasive mood of unhappiness or depression	• low self-esteem	*	*	• low self-esteem
A tendency to develop physical symptoms or fears associated with personal or school problems.	*	*	*	*

*Research data not available.
[a]Defined as unprovoked extrapunitive discipline.
[b]Defined as harsh criticism, child harassment.
[c]Defined as passively rejecting child; depressed, "flat" affect.
[d]Defined as failure to provide adequate physical care.

Table 1.3. Case Studies Linking Emotional/Behavioral Problems to
Psychological Maltreatment in the Schools

ED/BD Criteria	Krugman & Krugman (1984): Psychological maltreatment by 3rd/4th grade teacher as evidenced by terrorizing, rejecting, degrading, corrupting and exploiting	Hyman (1985): Psychological maltreatment by 1st grade teacher as evidenced by terrorizing, degrading, physical confinement
An inability to learn which cannot be explained by intellectual, sensory, or health factors.	*	*
An inability to build or maintain satisfactory interpersonal relationships with peers or teachers.	• decreased functioning in social relations outside of school • withdrawal behaviors	• excessive dependency • fear of strangers • withdrawn behavior
Inappropriate types of behavior or feelings under normal circumstances.	*	• thumbsucking • eyelash and hair pulling • crying • hyperactive/anxious
A general pervasive mood of unhappiness or depression.	• negative self-perception • negative perceptions of school • depression	*
A tendency to develop physical symptoms or fears associated with personal or school problems.	• excessive worry about school performance • fear teacher would hurt children • headaches, stomachaches, nightmares	• fear of dark, insomnia • vomiting, nausea, headaches, stomachaches, enuresis, encopresis

*Research data unavailable.

ical maltreatment more broadly defined, research not necessarily intentionally focused on psychological maltreatment. Additional support, obviously of a much more speculative nature, comes from lists of consequences we have reviewed which have been developed through acquiring and organizing expert opinion.

Sufficient evidence has been accumulated to suggest the strong likelihood that psychological maltreatment increases the risk for the development of emotional/behavioral disorders. This provides additional support for the conceptualization of the nature of psychological maltreatment we proposed earlier: psychological maltreatment frustrates the fulfillment of basic psychological needs and, thereby, produces deviancy which is maladaptive.

Psychological Maltreatment as the "Core" Issue in Child Maltreatment

One of the products of the International Conference on Psychological Abuse of Children and Youth was the agreement reached by participants that psychological maltreatment is the core issue in all forms of child abuse and neglect (Hart, Germain, & Brassard, 1983). This position was stated most emphatically by the keynote speaker representing the American Medical Association (Sargent, 1983).

There are many supports for this position. It is widely recognized that, while psychological maltreatment is sometimes expressed in forms unique to itself, it almost always accompanies other forms of maltreatment (Garbarino, Guttman, & Seeley, 1986; Holder, Newberger, & Loken, 1983). As stated in one of NCCAN's publications, "While emotional maltreatment may occur alone, it often accompanies physical abuse and sexual abuse. Emotionally maltreated children are not always physically abused, but physically abused children are almost always emotionally maltreated as well" (Lauer, Lourie, Salus, & Broadhurst, 1979, p. 16).

The psychological symptoms for each form of child maltreatment are extensive (Broadhurst, 1984, p. 12). The psychological consequences of child maltreatment are often the most destructive of the consequences experienced by child victims (Egeland, Sroufe, & Erickson, 1983;

Garbarino, Guttman, & Seeley, 1986). The prescriptions applied to other forms of child maltreatment testify to the fact that psychological variables are generally the major prescriptive targets, after separation/protection from perpetrators is accomplished. The literature on sexual abuse exemplifies this point (Brassard & McNeill, chapter 5 in this volume; Mrazek & Kempe, 1981).

There appear to be only two major categories of maltreatment, physical and psychological. Navarre and Hyman, each in this volume, have detailed the supports for this position. Garbarino and associates (Garbarino, Guttman, & Seeley, 1986; Garbarino & Vondra, chapter 2 in this volume) and others (Hart, Gelardo, & Brassard, 1986) have argued strongly that it is the psychological impact of treatment that defines it as abusive. It is the psychological impact of maltreatment that determines how the victim will view self, others, expectations for the nature of interactions between people, and the manner in which one must live one's own life. Clearly, the study of psychological maltreatment is justified and necessary.

HOW PSYCHOLOGICAL MALTREATMENT SHOULD BE INVESTIGATED

It is important for investigations of psychological maltreatment to be comprehensive in their consideration of influencing variables and systematic in focusing on targets which will add to presently available knowledge. This requires that ecological and developmental orientations be applied to develop and test operational definitions, determine the relationships between perpetrator acts and child outcomes, study variables which mediate the effects and occurrences of psychological maltreatment, and determine the relationships between different forms of child maltreatment and different patterns of child outcomes. The systematic pursuit of these directions will be assisted greatly if coordinated and cooperative relationships between researchers are established.

Ecological and Developmental Models

While child maltreatment may sometimes appear to occur in the isolated context of interactions between two people, a perpetrator and a victim, the conditions that produce the maltreatment and its results do not.

The human ecological model conceptualized and promoted for child development research by Bronfenbrenner (1979) has been judged by Garbarino (1977a, 1979) and others (Valentine, Freeman, Acuff, & Andreas, 1985) to be essential to understanding and dealing with the complex conditions associated with child maltreatment. That model stresses the importance of the interactive effects on behavior and meanings of (a) the child as a dynamic system within her/himself, (b) the microsystems experienced as day-to-day reality by the child (e.g., family, school, day-care center, church), and (c) the exosystems and macrosystems less directly experienced by the child (e.g., parent's workplace, city council, school board, courts, political units, culturally institutionalized patterns of belief and behavior). The conceptual works of Belsky (1984), Bittner and Newberger (1982), and Garbarino (1977a, 1977b) give specific attention to the nature and power of conditions associated with maltreatment, and possible causes of maltreatment, which fall within and across these ecological levels (e.g., psychological characteristics of perpetrators, social and economic stresses, characteristics of the child, cultural orientations and preparation for parenting, cultural sanctioning of extremes in family privacy and of violence). The recent works by Hyman (1985), Hart (1985) and Hart, Brassard, and Germain (chapter 16 in this volume) dealing with psychological maltreatment in schooling, provide evidence of the importance of influences from the broad societal/institutional level, the common practices level in the local community, and the individual teacher-to-student level.

The developmental characteristics of the child are highly relevant to the nature and impact of psychological maltreatment. It is, after all, the personal subjective meaning of maltreatment from the perspective of the victim which determines its power and focus of influence. The stage, phase or level of development of the victim in physical, cognitive and affective areas will provide context and standards for educing meaning. Theories of cognitive development (Piaget, 1928), moral development (Kohlberg, 1975), psychosexual development (Freud, 1964), and competency development (Havighurst, 1972; White, 1959) may all be of relevance. The psychosocial stages of development as conceptualized by Erikson (1968) seem to deserve particular consideration as major critical issues, or challenges, of development which place the child in a position of vulnerability to psychological maltreatment. This is the position taken by Egeland and associates in psychological maltreatment research (Egeland & Erickson, chapter 8 in this volume; Erickson & Egeland, in press).

Operational Definitions

A working generic definition with substantial support has been developed. Neither research nor intervention projects can be successful in the sense of being useful beyond the confines of their original context unless they are based on operational definitions considered to be valid and susceptible to reliable application. Sufficiently rigorous operational definitions do not presently exist and they therefore deserve first priority in psychological maltreatment work (Garbarino, 1978; Garbarino, Guttman, & Seeley, 1986; Hart, Germain, & Brassard, 1983).

However, some progress has recently been achieved toward development of operational definitions through a federal and five-state project devoted to that goal (Baily & Baily, 1986). The project, entitled "Operational Definitions of Child Emotional Maltreatment," directed and organized responses from protective service professionals, broadly defined, on seven opinion questionnaires. The process enabled the researchers to (a) develop statements of parental maltreatment behavior, (b) transform those statements into cluster categories of behaviors agreed upon to represent emotional maltreatment, and (c) evaluate on a four-point scale the seriousness of action required by each cluster category when combined with a range of child outcomes. Limited field testing by protective service workers, in combination with the opinion support of questionnaire respondents, indicated that the behavioral clusters were promising in regard to their potential for practical application in case handling. Our analysis of the cluster items found them to fall logically within the seven psychological maltreatment act categories given attention in previous sections (i.e., terrorizing, rejecting, degrading, isolating, exploiting, corrupting, and denying emotional responsiveness). Some agreement has developed in support of giving primary emphasis to operationalizing this set or a similar set of acts (Garbarino, Guttman, & Seeley, 1986; Office for the Study of the Psychological Rights of the Child, 1985). Further work on operational definitions should incorporate the recent research described here and the seven acts of maltreatment. The operational definitions which are developed should be both developmentally and ecologically specific for reasons previously discussed. This would mean that they would deal with the important contexts of child development stages/phases which would produce vulnerability to maltreatment and give direction to the meaning attributed to maltreatment by the child. For example, in the early years major emphasis might be given to the microsystem of the family involved in child nurturing, to the high level of dependence on caretakers for fulfilling physiological, safety and love and belongingness needs, and to the forming of primary and secondary attachments in relating to caretakers. During the school years attention might be given to the microsystems of schooling, to the development of esteem through school achievements, and the development of a sense of acceptance and belonging in relationships with teachers and peers. Regardless of the degree to which the primary focus is on relationships in microsystems at any particular stage of development, attention should also be given to the influence of interactions between microsystems (e.g., effects of interactions between father and his employer on interactions between father and his child), and the influences of exosystem institutional/organizational practices (e.g., school standards for advancement) and macrosystem principles, values, and beliefs (e.g., racial prejudice, supremacy of parental rights over children's rights).

Relationships Between Perpetrator Acts and Child Outcomes

Limited resources are available nationally and in the states for child maltreatment work. Those resources are being devoted to the perceived areas of greatest need and those areas in which standards are most clear. Psychological maltreatment has not yet been established in either regard, beyond the informed speculation of experts. Legal and social policy experts (Corson & Davidson, chapter 14 in this volume; Melton & Thompson, chapter 15 in this volume) have indicated that it is essential that the relationships between perpetrator acts of psychological maltreatment and negative child outcomes be established before social intervention is applied.

Therefore, the operationally defined acts of psychological maltreatment, when produced, should be investigated to determine their effects on child outcomes. Consistent with the evidence and positions presented earlier in this chapter, it is our opinion that child outcomes should be investigated in a manner which will reveal the degree to which serious emotional/behavioral disorders (maladaptive deviancy) occur. Acts perpetrated or stimulated through all levels of the human ecological system and their impact meanings for each developmental stage should be studied.

Mediating Variables that Modify Effects and Risk of Occurrence of Psychological Maltreatment

It is generally accepted that individual children may react differently to the same acts of maltreatment. The work of Garmezy (1981) and Anthony (1975) in their studies of "stress-resistant" children suggest that factors within the individual child and/or one or more levels of the human ecological system may produce the ability to withstand maltreatment. Pines' (1979) analysis of that work led her to judge that children who have certain of the basic psychological needs met sufficiently may be able to withstand rather severe forms of psychological stress. Werner (1985, 1986) has recently reported that a child's risk to serious problems in adolescence is reduced by experiencing "emotional support," positive responses from caretakers, and personal competence in the midst of high levels of psychological stress. Research projects should be pursued which will further clarify those factors which reduce or increase the negative impact of psychological maltreatment on child victims. The incorporation of ecological and developmental models in this work will promote sensitivity to the differential meanings of forms of maltreatment at different developmental stages, producing greater or lesser degrees of impact, and to the factors in and outside of the home which influence levels of stress resistance.

The risk that maltreatment will occur has been suggested to be influenced by the psychological characteristics of the caretaker, characteristics of the socio-cultural environment experienced by the perpetrator, and characteristics of the child victim (Smith, 1984; Starr, 1979; Wolfe, 1984). Differences in the forms and levels of factors within each of these areas should be studied to

determine the manner and degree to which they influence toward or away from psychological maltreatment. As an example, Garbarino (1977b) has emphasized the significance of family isolation in facilitating maltreatment. Its relevance for psychological maltreatment should be studied. The degree to which caretakers have had their own emotional needs met and have accurate expectations and constructive perspectives regarding child behavior have been identified as influencing the degree of risk for psychological maltreatment (Egeland & Erickson, chapter 8 in this volume). These factors deserve careful study. Speculation has focused on the influence on risk for maltreatment produced by characteristics of the child (e.g., temperament, handicaps, order of birth). Findings to date suggest that child characteristics are not related to psychological maltreatment but may be related to physical maltreatment (Herrenkohl, Herrenkohl, & Egolf, 1983). Recent research suggests the possibility that the influencing characteristics of the child may be learned in reaction to caretaker behaviors (Egeland & Erickson, chapter 8 in this volume; Main & Goldwyn, 1984). Further research is needed.

Most of the factors associated with risk which have been discussed here exist at the individual and microsystem level. However, economic and social stress influences may very well have their roots in training and employment policies, style and cost of living factors, political systems and values within the community, state or nation. Gil's analysis of major influences (chapter 12 in this volume) emphasizes exosystem and macrosystem factors such as these. The availability of home health visitors, respite care and day care at place of employment, all of which are speculated to reduce risk of maltreatment, may be determined by exosystem and macrosystem conditions.

Relationships Between Type of Maltreatment and Form of Child Outcomes

Research has only begun to focus on psychological maltreatment in ways which will reveal differential relationships between types of maltreatment and child outcomes. The research of Egeland and associates (Egeland, Sroufe, & Erickson, 1983; Egeland & Erickson, chapter 8 in this volume) provides direction in this regard. That work, described in detail in this volume, has investigated longitudinally the child outcome effects of four conditions of maltreatment: physically abusive, hostile/verbally abusive, psychologically unavailable, and neglectful. While outcomes for children from all maltreated groups were severe and varied, they were most dramatic for the children of psychologically unavailable mothers. These children displayed the most negative impact in areas of intellectual functioning, attachment disturbances and social/emotional competence. The findings draw attention to a form of child abuse which is presently least likely to come to the attention of child protective services. Research of this nature, covering the full range of developmental and ecological influences, is essential if we are to understand psychological maltreatment and responsibly develop priorities and strategies.

Coordination of Investigations of Psychological Maltreatment

There is a great deal to be done to investigate this many-faceted area of psychological maltreatment. The more general area of child abuse and neglect suffers from being provided with very limited resources (Garbarino & Vondra, chapter 2 in this volume; Holder, Newberger, & Loken, 1983). Available resources for psychological maltreatment work should be carefully directed to maximize increases in our knowledge in the areas just described. Research projects should be designed and supported which will systematically reveal the essential elements and relationships which create risk, determine nature and degree of expression, and influence impact. Major emphasis on prevention and correction would logically follow from such a base of understanding.

The systematic and comprehensive investigation of psychological maltreatment will be facilitated by coordination of resources and projects and cooperative relationships between researchers. These conditions will increase the likelihood for the following benefits to occur: (a) products of research will be used as the foundations for subsequent investigations, (b) the few longitudinal child-development projects pursued nationally/internationally will be solicited for meaningful inclusion of psychological maltreatment foci, (c) research design components too demanding for a single project will be coopera-

tively pursued through coordination of the necessary number of projects of several researchers, (d) multidisciplinary orientations will be incorporated in research, and (e) research projects which are unnecessarily redundant, or poorly focused, will be discouraged and modified to enhance their potential for contributions to the state of knowledge.

The Office for the Study of the Psychological Rights of the Child (OSPRC), Indiana University-Purdue University, Indianapolis is presently organized to coordinate and facilitate investigations of psychological maltreatment through relationships with researchers. This was one of the responsibilities the OSPRC assumed as an extension of its role in conducting the International Conference on Psychological Abuse of Children and Youth (Hart, Germain, & Brassard, 1983). The OSPRC undertakes research, pursues research cooperatively with other researchers, facilitates the acquisition of funding and collaborative relationships for other researchers, and provides information regarding psychological maltreatment research through its newsletter.

DIRECTIONS FOR INTERVENTION NOW

Relatively little progress has been made in the development of effective interventions, whether prevention or correction oriented, for child abuse and neglect broadly conceived (Holder, Newberger, & Loken, 1983; Rosenberg & Reppucci, 1985; Smith, 1984; Starr, 1979). Prevention strategies/programs have generally received less attention and are less well developed than correction strategies/programs, as is the case in our society for virtually every problem area dealt with by human services.

Among the categories of child abuse and neglect, psychological maltreatment has received the least attention and is generally considered the area presenting the most difficulties for intervention (Holder, Newberger, & Loken, 1983; Tower, 1984). However, some guidance is presently available. The International Conference on Psychological Abuse of Children and Youth (Hart, Germain, & Brassard, 1983) produced over 100 recommendations for correction and prevention which cut across the major levels of the human ecological system. Intervention strategies/projects which have focused on child maltreatment as broadly defined, or which were specifically intended to deal with other categories of child maltreatment, appear to be relevant to psychological maltreatment. The other chapters of this book offer suggestions for intervention which are specific to psychological maltreatment, in some cases dealing with particular forms of psychological maltreatment (e.g., sexual abuse, psychologically unavailable caretaking) and in other cases dealing with the potential of specific resources (e.g., schools, psychologists) for application in intervention. Therefore, it is probable that the best available set of suggestions for intervention will be found in the remaining chapters of this book.

In this section, a sample of recommendations for correction and prevention will be presented using the human ecological system categories (i.e., microsystem, exosystem and macrosystem). This is done to provide a sense of the nature of interventions falling within these categories and the breadth of forms interventions take. The work of the Office for the Study of the Psychological Rights of the Child, which is involved in psychological maltreatment projects which cut across all these levels, will be described briefly at the end of this section. Some generalizations regarding correction and prevention deserve attention first.

Regardless of the level of the human ecological system given attention, it is important to create awareness among those who might be perpetrators, victims, or interventionists regarding major dimensions of psychological maltreatment. This means that through education and the public media, attempts should be made to make people aware of (a) the major acts and suspected consequences of psychological maltreatment, (b) symptoms of psychological maltreatment, (c) the importance of basic psychological need fulfillment to healthy human development and functioning and its suspected relationships with psychological maltreatment, and (d) strategies for reducing and overcoming psychological maltreatment. Please see the other chapters of this book for more detailed and specific suggestions.

Microsystem Interventions

For child maltreatment in general, at the family level, corrective intervention in the form of caretaker involvement with parent aides or a parenting group in combination with caseworker

services appears to show the most promise (Starr, 1979). Kempe and Helfer (1972) indicated that primary emphasis should be given in intervention to work with the maltreating family. Family intervention has been strongly recommended for cases of sexual maltreatment (Brassard & McNeill, chapter 5 in this volume), for which one of the best models has been developed (Giaretto, 1976). Egeland and Erickson (see chapter 8 in this volume) have suggested that the major source of influence causing caretakers to psychologically maltreat is their own state of unmet needs. This logically directs corrective intervention toward fulfillment of the basic psychological needs of the caretakers. Egeland and Erickson suggest this be done through the development of problem-solving skills focused on practical living concerns.

Reviews of preventive strategies identify involvement in families by home visitors as one of the most promising strategies (Rosenberg & Reppucci, 1985; Starr, 1979). Strategies for preventing sexual abuse emphasize educating children to recognize risks and protect themselves, providing information to families, and supplying direct support to families at risk (Brassard & McNeill, chapter 5 in this volume). Egeland and Erickson (chapter 8 in this volume) indicate that preventive intervention should be directed at mothers during the last trimester of pregnancy to help them better understand the behavior of children, and develop readiness to more appropriately interpret and respond to the baby's state of need.

Exosystem Interventions

At this level, the focus is on structures and systems of interaction within the community/society which affect the experiences of the child but which are not contained within the regular and frequent direct experience of the child. Practices associated with schooling, legal intervention, cultural bias in media, and child care provide good examples for correction and prevention.

In schools maltreatment would be more likely to be identified and corrected if school practices encouraged greater personal interaction between teachers and students. Efforts to reduce class sizes might help. If schools gave curriculum emphasis to child development and hands-on child care experience, under the supervision and direction of good models, child maltreatment might be reduced for the children of today's students. If school boards and curriculum committees were to emphasize specifically the responsible meeting of basic psychological needs as a high priority in schooling, both present and future maltreatment might be reduced. Hart, Brassard, & Germain (chapter 16 in this volume) describe these and many other directions important to correction and prevention of maltreatment at the exosystem level.

Present legal practices generally ignore psychological maltreatment cases and limit the majority of their interventions to temporary or permanent separation of victims and perpetrators (Corson & Davidson, chapter 14 in this volume; Thomas, 1984). To encourage both corrective and preventive action at the child-protective-services and court levels, a "mental health neglect" model for intervention has been recommended (Hart, 1985). This model defines mental health neglect as the condition existing when a "child is found to be seriously emotionally/behaviorally disordered and his caretakers refuse to apply available and recommended corrective/therapeutic procedures" (p. 1). The intervention process is modeled after Public Law 94-142, the Education for All Handicapped Children Act (1975). It incorporates action by a team of mental health professionals who carry out evaluations, make diagnoses, and recommend prescriptive alternatives, all under due-process guidelines and with full opportunity for caretaker participation. Major emphasis in evaluation/diagnostic processes is given to determining whether the child is deviant from age-peers in areas which presently produce maladaptive functioning. If no such finding is made, the case is closed. If a finding of serious emotional/behavioral disorder is made, prescription alternatives are developed. If the caretakers agree with the findings and implement one or more of the prescriptions, the case is followed by the responsible community agency to determine accountability in carrying out the prescriptions and their effectiveness. If the caretakers do not agree with the findings and/or refuse to pursue a prescriptive alternative, they may request a due-process hearing. If the parents lose the due-process hearing and refuse to participate beyond that point, or refuse to participate in the process at any earlier point, the case is transferred to the court system for adjudication as a typical child maltreatment case. Emphasis throughout the

process, prior to any court system involvement, is on helping the child, not on determining blame for the child's condition. While the first priority of this model is the correction of existing problems which may have been produced by psychological maltreatment, the model could stimulate preventive orientations in a community, and it could serve as a base for prevention in cases at risk for the development of serious emotional/behavioral disorders. The mental health neglect model is included in Appendix C.

Other strategies applicable to the exosystem level have both corrective and preventive potential. Jones and Jones (chapter 11 in this volume) recommend that racial/ethnic stereotypes and degrading references be eliminated from textbooks, and Telzrow's findings (chapter 9 in this volume) support the same recommendation for public media (e.g., television). This would reduce the general climate of psychological maltreatment present in racial/ethnic prejudice in our communities and reduce the likelihood that people would model values and acts of prejudice in their interactions with others.

Recommendations have been made for child care to be provided by employers and at the site of employment of parents. This practice could reduce stress-stimulated psychological maltreatment for caretakers, provide models of good child care procedures for caretakers, and support a system of monitoring child development and reinforcing good parenting through the employing agency which could reduce and prevent maltreatment.

Macrosystem Interventions

The macrosystem level encompasses attitudes, principles, patterns of values and procedures within the political, economic, and social systems of the culture. At the macrosystem level the elimination of corporal punishment has been recommended to reduce child maltreatment (Starr, 1979). In this volume, Hyman has clarified relationships between corporal punishment and psychological maltreatment. Melton (1983) has judged that a positive ideology of children, valuing them for what they are and can become rather than for the manner in which they meet the needs of caretakers and/or others, does not presently exist for any culture. It is his opinion that such a positive ideology may be essential to providing for the welfare of children.

Gil (chapter 12 in this volume) has given specific attention to macrosystem intervention. He views psychological maltreatment as a dimension of violence, broadly conceived, which is tolerated, sanctioned, and promoted by the culture. Correction and prevention, in Gil's view, must be aimed at transforming the society toward nonviolence. To do this he recommends political action to redesign and reconstruct social, economic, political and cultural institutions to achieve cooperation as well as egalitarian and genuinely democratic values. Based on his conceptualizations of basic psychological needs, Gil recommends establishment of the unconditional right to meaningful work and that the concept of work be expanded to include child care by parents.

Jones and Jones, and Reschley and Graham-Clay (coauthor teams in this volume) have identified the need to overcome the negative and limiting attitudes which pervade our culture regarding racial and ethnic subgroups. Reschley and Graham-Clay recommend that an attitude change be attempted by presenting fair and accurate information which will create dissonance and require new adjustments in attitudes. National mass media would need to reflect commitments to these goals in the information it provides. Jones and Jones, with similar intent, recommend that school textbooks, which are generally developed to respect national perspectives, must be aimed at similar goals.

Projects of the Office for the Study of the Psychological Rights of the Child

The base for progress in correcting and preventing psychological maltreatment through all levels of the human ecological macrosystem level has been somewhat enhanced by the fact that the human rights movements of this century have recently focused on the rights of children, and, in particular, on the psychological rights of children (Hart, 1982). The Office for the Study of the Psychological Rights of the Child (OSPRC), at Indiana University–Purdue University at Indianapolis, as an expression of that movement was originally established to clarify and promote the psychological rights of children. Its major projects are now focused on psychological maltreatment issues. As indicated previously, OSPRC conducted the International Conference on Psychological Abuse of Children and Youth (Hart, Germain, & Brassard, 1983). It has begun to implement a five-year plan for a first phase of work to achieve the recommendations of the conference. OSPRC's goals cut across all levels of the human ecological system and emphasize the development of a knowledge and resource base as well as pursuit and facilitation of research and intervention projects. Uppermost among its priorities is the establishment of comprehensive and systematic planning and development which incorporate collaborative efforts with researchers, helping professions and advocacy groups. OSPRC is developing a national network of such groups; communicating developments, issues and opportunities via a newsletter; pursuing and promoting research; reviewing intervention programs; promoting awareness through presentations to a wide variety of groups and publications (e.g., professional journals, this book); and developing and promoting intervention strategies (e.g., the mental health neglect model, Appendix C). The staff of OSPRC is guided in its projects by a National Advisory Board representing leaders in the field of psychological maltreatment (see Appendix D for membership). OSPRC is jointly sponsored by Indiana University and the National Association of School Psychologists.

THE CONTRIBUTIONS OF THE REMAINING CHAPTERS OF THIS BOOK

In many ways this chapter provides an introduction to the remaining chapters of this book. The issues raised here in regard to major dimensions of psychological maltreatment, definitions, standards, and critical issues in research and intervention are expanded upon in those chapters.

REFERENCES

American Bar Association Juvenile Justice Standards Project/Institute of Judicial Administration. (1980). (Not officially published by the ABA.)

American Humane Association. (1980). *Definitions of the national study data items and response categories: Technical report #3.* Denver, CO: Author.

American Humane Association. (1981). *Annual Report, 1980: National analysis of official child neglect and abuse reporting.* Denver, CO: Author.

American Humane Association. (1986). *Highlights of the official child neglect and abuse reporting 1982*. Denver, CO: Author.

American Psychiatric Association. (1980). *Diagnostic and statistical manual of mental disorders* (3rd ed.). Washington, DC: Author.

Anthony, E. J. (1975). *Explorations in child psychiatry*. New York: Plenum.

Baily, T. F., & Baily, W. F. (1986). *Operational definitions of child emotional maltreatment: Final report*. Augusta, ME: EM Project, Bureau of Social Services, Maine Department of Human Services.

Bandura, A., Ross, D., & Ross, S. A. (1961). Transmission of aggression through imitation of aggressive models. *Journal of Abnormal Psychology, 63*, 575–582.

Belsky, J. H. (1984). The determinants of parenting: A process model. *Child Development, 55*, 83–86.

Biehler, R., & Snowman, F. (1982). *Psychology applied to teaching*. Boston: Houghton Mifflin.

Bittner, S., & Newberger, E. H. (1982). Child abuse: Current issues of etiology, diagnosis, and treatment. In J. Henning (Ed.), *The rights of children: Legal and psychological perspectives*. Springfield, IL: Charles C Thomas.

Broadhurst, D. D. (1984). *The educator's role in the prevention and treatment of child abuse and neglect*. Washington, DC: National Center on Child Abuse and Neglect, U.S. Department of Health and Human Services.

Bronfenbrenner, U. (1979). *The ecology of human development: Experiments by nature and design*. Cambridge: Harvard University Press.

Brook, C. G. D. (1980). Short stature. *Practitioner, 244*(1340), 131–138.

Bullard, D. M., Glaser, H. H., Heagarty, M. C., & Pivchik, E. C. (1967). Failure to thrive in the "neglected" child. *American Journal of Orthopsychiatry, 37*, 680–690.

Child Abuse Prevention and Treatment and Adoption Reform Act Amendments for 1983. (1983). *Hearings before the Subcommittee on Family and Human Services of the Committee on Labor and Human Resources of the United States Senate*. Washington, DC: U.S. Government Printing Office.

Corwin, D. (1985). *The sexually abused child disorder*. Paper presented at the National Summit Conference on Diagnosing Child Sexual Abuse, Los Angeles.

Dean, D. (1979, July–August). Emotional abuse of children. *Children Today*, pp. 18–21.

Densen-Gerber, J. (1979). Sexual and commercial exploitation of children: Legislative responses and treatment challenges. *Child Abuse and Neglect, 3*, 61–66.

Egeland, B., & Sroufe, L. A. (1981). Developmental sequelae of maltreatment in infancy. *New Directions for Child Development, 2*, 77–92.

Egeland, B., Sroufe, L. A., & Erickson, M. (1983). The developmental consequence of different patterns of maltreatment. *Child Abuse and Neglect, 7*, 459–469.

Erickson, M. F., & Egeland, B. (In press). A developmental view of the psychological consequences of maltreatment. *School Psychology Review*.

Erikson, E. (1968). *Identity: Youth and crisis*. New York: Norton.

Eron, L. D., Huesmann, L. R., Lefkowitz, M. M., & Walder, L. O. (1972). Does television violence cause aggression? *American Psychologist, 27*, 253–263.

Fischoff, J. K., Whitten, D. F., & Petit, M. G. (1979). A psychiatric study of mothers of infants with growth failure secondary to maternal deprivation. *Journal of Pediatrics, 79*, 209–215.

Fox, W. M. (1983). A reply to Goud's rebuttal. *Humanistic Education and Development, 22*, 2, 50.

Freud, S. (1964). New introductory essays on psychoanalysis. In J. Strachey (Ed.), *The standard edition of the complete psychological works of Sigmund Freud* (Vol. 22). London: Hogarth Press.

Garbarino, J. (1977a). The human ecology of child maltreatment. *Journal of Marriage and the Family, 39*, 721–736.

Garbarino, J. (1977b). The price of privacy in the social dynamics of child abuse. *Child Welfare, 56*(9), 565–575.

Garbarino, J. (1978). The elusive "crime" of emotional abuse. *Child Abuse and Neglect, 2*, 89–100.

Garbarino, J. (1979). The role of the school in the human ecology of child maltreatment. *School Review, 87*(2), 190–213.

Garbarino, J., & Garbarino, A. C. (1980). *Emotional maltreatment of children*. Chicago: National Committee for Prevention of Child Abuse.

Garbarino, J., & Gilliam, G. (1980). *Understanding abusive families*. Lexington, MA: Lexington Books.

Garbarino, J., Guttman, E., & Seeley, J. (1986). *The psychologically battered child: Strategies for identification, assessment and intervention*. San Francisco: Jossey-Bass.

Gardner, L. I. (1972). Deprivation dwarfism. *Scientific American, 227*, 76–82.

Garmezy, R. (1981). Children under stress: Perspectives on antecedents and correlates of vulnerability and resistance to psychopathology. In A. I. Rabin, J. Aronoff, A. M. Barclay, & R. A. Zucker (Eds.), *Further explorations in personality*. New York: Wiley.

George, C., & Main, M. (1979). Social interactions of young abused children: Approach, avoidance, and aggression. *Child Development,* 50, 306–318.

Germain, R., Brassard, M., & Hart, S. (1985). Crisis intervention for maltreated children. *School Psychology Review,* 14(3), 219–245.

Giaretto, H. (1976). Humanistic treatment of father-daughter incest. In R. E. Helfer & C. H. Kempe (Eds.), *Child abuse and neglect.* Cambridge, MA: Ballinger.

Glasser, W. (1965). *Reality therapy.* New York: Harper and Row.

Goud, N. (1983). The need for Maslow: A rebuttal to William M. Fox. *Humanistic Education and Development,* 22(2), 44–49.

Hart, S. (1982). The history of children's psychological rights. *Viewpoints in Teaching and Learning,* 158(1), 1–15.

Hart, S. (1985). *Psychological maltreatment and schooling.* Paper presented to the Annual Convention of the American Educational Research Association, Chicago.

Hart, S., Gelardo, M., & Brassard, M. (1986). Psychological maltreatment. In J. Jacobsen (Ed.), *The psychiatric sequelae of child abuse.* Springfield: Charles C Thomas.

Hart, S., Germain, B., & Brassard, M. (Eds.). (1983). *Proceedings Summary of the International Conference on Psychological Abuse of Children and Youth.* Indiana University: Office for the Study of the Psychological Rights of the Child.

Havighurst, R. (1972). *Developmental tasks and education.* New York: David McKay.

Hellsten, P., & Katila, O. (1965). Murder and other homicide by children under 15 years in Finland. *Psychiatric Quarterly,* 3, 54–74.

Herrenkohl, R. C., & Herrenkohl, E. C. (1981). Some antecedents and consequences in child maltreatment. In R. Rizley & D. Cicchetti (Eds.), *Developmental Approaches to Child Maltreatment.* San Francisco: Jossey-Bass.

Herrenkohl, R. C., Herrenkohl, E. C., & Egolf, B. P. (1983). Circumstances surrounding the occurrence of child maltreatment. *Journal of Consulting and Clinical Psychology,* 51, 424–431.

Holder, W., Newberger, E., & Loken, G. (1983). Child Abuse and Treatment and Adoption Reform Act Amendments of 1983. *Testimony in the Hearings before the Subcommittee on Family and Human Services of the Committee on Labor and Human Resources of the United States Senate* (pp. 219–304). Washington, DC: U.S. Government Printing Office.

Hyman, I. (1985). *Psychological abuse in the schools: A school psychologist's perspective.* Paper presented to the annual convention of the American Psychological Association, Los Angeles.

Kempe, C. H., & Helfer, R. E. (1972). *Helping the battered child and his family.* Philadelphia: Lippincott.

Kohlberg, L. (1975). The cognitive-developmental approach to moral education. *Phi Delta Kappan,* 56(10), 670–677.

Krugman, R. D., & Krugman, M. K. (1984). Emotional abuse in the classroom. *American Journal of Diseases of Children,* 138, 284–286.

Landau, H. R., Salus, M. K., Stiffarm, T., & Kalb, N. L. (1980). *Child protection: The role of the courts.* Washington, DC: U.S. Government Printing Office.

Lauer, J. W., Lourie, I. S., Salus, M. K., & Broadhurst, D. D. (1979). *The role of the mental health professional in the prevention and treatment of child abuse and neglect.* Washington, DC: U.S. Department of Health, Education, and Welfare.

Laury, G. V., & Meerloo, J. A. M. (1967). Mental cruelty and child abuse. *Psychiatric Quarterly,* 41(2), 203–254.

Leonard, M. F., Rhymes, J. P., & Solnit, A. J. (1966). Failure to thrive in infants. *American Journal of Diseases of Children,* 111, 600–612.

Lourie, M. D., & Stefano, L. (1978). On defining emotional abuse. Child abuse and neglect: Issues in innovation and implementation. *Proceedings of the Second Annual National Conference on Child Abuse and Neglect.* Washington, DC: Government Printing Office.

Maddi, S. R. (1980). *Personality theories: A comparative analysis.* Homewood, IL: Dorsey Press.

Main, M. (1973). *Play, exploration and competence as related to child-adult attachment.* Unpublished doctoral dissertation, Johns Hopkins University.

Main, M., & George, C. (1985). Responses of abused and disadvantaged toddlers to distress in age mates: A study in the daycare setting. *Developmental Psychology,* 21, 407–412.

Main, M., & Goldwyn, R. (1984). Predicting rejection of her infant from mother's representation of her own experience: Implications for the abused-abusing intergenerational cycle. *Child Abuse and Neglect,* 8, 203–217.

Maslow, A. (1968). *Toward a psychology of being.* New York: Van Nostrand Reinhold.

Maslow, A. (1970). *A theory of human motivation.* New York: Harper and Row.

McCarthy, D. (1979). Recognition of signs of emotional deprivation: A form of child abuse. *Child Abuse and Neglect,* 3, 423–428.

Melton, G. (1983). *Child advocacy: Psychological issues and interventions.* New York: Plenum.

Moore, J. G. (1974). Yo-yo children. *Nursing Times,* 70(49), 1888–1889.

Mrazek, P. B., & Kempe, C. H. (1981). *Sexually abused children and their families.* New York: Pergamon.

Mulford, R. M. (1958). Emotional neglect of children. *Child Welfare,* 37, 19–24.

National Center on Child Abuse and Neglect.

(1981). *Executive summary: National study of the incidence and severity of child abuse and neglect.* Washington, DC: Author.

Office for the Study of the Psychological Rights of the Child (February, 1985). *Advisory board minutes.* Indiana University–Purdue University at Indianapolis: Author.

Pastor, D. L. (1981). The quality of mother-infant attachment and its relationship to toddler's initial sociability with peers. *Developmental Psychology, 17,* 323–335.

Pemberton, D. A., & Benady, D. R. (1973). Consciously rejected children. *British Journal of Psychiatry, 123,* 575–578.

Piaget, J. (1928). *The language and thought of the child.* (M. Worden, translator.) New York: Harcourt, Brace & World.

Pines, M. (1979, January). Superkids. *Psychology Today,* pp. 52–63.

Powell, G. F., Brasel, J. A., & Blizzard, R. M. (1967). Emotional deprivation and growth retardation simulating idiopathic hypopituitarism. *New England Journal of Medicine, 276,* 1271–1278.

Public Law 93-247. (1974). Child abuse, prevention and treatment act of 1974. USC 5101.

Public Law 94-142. (1975). The Education for All Handicapped Children Act.

Rohner, R. P., & Rohner, E. C. (1980). Antecedents and consequences of parental rejection: A theory of emotional abuse. *Child Abuse and Neglect, 4,* 189–198.

Rosenberg, M. S., & Reppucci, N. D. (1985). Primary prevention of child abuse. *Journal of Consulting and Clinical Psychology, 5,* 576–585.

Sargent, D. (1983). *The role of medicine in psychological maltreatment work.* Presentation to the International Conference on Psychological Abuse of Children and Youth. Indianapolis: Indiana University–Purdue University at Indianapolis.

Sendl, I. B., & Blomgren, P. G. (1975). A comparative study of predictive criteria in the predisposition of homicidal adolescents. *American Journal of Psychiatry, 132,* 423–427.

Shengold, L. (1967). The effects of overstimulation: Rat people. *International Journal of Psychoanalysis, 48,* 403–415.

Shengold, L. (1979). Child abuse and deprivation: Soul murder. *Journal of the American Psychoanalytic Association, 27,* 533–599.

Shultz, R. (1985, October). *Creativity and the imaginary companion phenomenon: Prevalence and phenomenology in multiple personality disorder compared to major depression.* Presentation to the Second International Conference on Multiple Personality/Dissociative States, Chicago.

Smith, S. (1984). Significant research findings in the etiology of child abuse. *Social Casework: The Journal of Contemporary Social Work,* 337–346.

Spitz, R. A. (1946). Anaclitic depression. *The Psychoanalytic Study of the Child, 2,* 313–342.

Starr, R. H. (1979). Child abuse. *American Psychologist, 34,* 872–878.

Thomas, P. (1984). *Developments to the legal concept of emotional abuse.* Presentation to the Fifth International Congress on Child Abuse and Neglect, Montreal, Canada.

Tower, C. C. (1984). *Child abuse and neglect: A teacher's handbook for detection, reporting, and classroom management.* Washington, DC: National Education Association.

Valentine, D. P., Freeman, M. L., Acuff, S., & Andreas, T. (1985). Abuse and neglect: Identifying and helping school children at risk. *School Social Work Journal, 9*(2), 83–99.

Wahba, M. A., & Bridwell, L. G. (1976). Maslow reconsidered: A review of research on Need Hierarchy Theory. *Organizational Behavior and Human Performance, 15,* 212–245.

Wald, M. (1961). *Protective services and emotional neglect.* Denver: American Humane Association.

Waters, E., Lipman, J., & Sroufe, L. A. (1979). Attachment, positive affect, and competence in the peer group: Two studies in construct validation. *Child Development, 51,* 208–216.

Werner, E. E. (1985, May). *Longitudinal studies of vulnerability and resiliency among early adolescents.* Presented at the Symposium on Biological and Behavioral Research in Early Adolescence, American Association for the Advancement of Science Meeting. Los Angeles.

Werner, E. E. (1986). Resilient offspring of alcoholics. *Journal of Studies on Alcohol, 1.*

White, R. W. (1959). Motivation reconsidered: The concept of competence. *Psychological Review, 66,* 297–333.

Whiting, L. (1978). Emotional neglect of children. In M. Lauderdale, R. Anderson, & S. Cramer (Eds.), *Child abuse and neglect: Issues on innovation and implementation (Vol. 1).* Publication No. 78-30147, pp. 209–213. Washington, DC: U.S. Department of Health, Education, and Welfare.

Wolfe, D. A. (1985). Child-abusive parents: An empirical review and analysis. *Psychological Bulletin, 97*(3), 462–482.

2

Psychological Maltreatment: Issues and Perspectives

James Garbarino and Joan Vondra

THE ISSUES

For all the public and professional attention directed at the phenomenon of maltreatment, debate continues over whether it is a major or a minor social problem. On the one hand are those who argue that the incidence of "serious" or "severe" abuse and neglect (at least as conventionally defined) is low when compared with other social problems such as poverty (which touches the lives of more than one in five young children). Gil (1970) offered this view in his groundbreaking study, *Violence Against Children*:

> . . . the scope of physical abuse of children resulting in serious injury does not constitute a major social problem, at least in comparison with several more widespread and more serious social problems that undermine the developmental opportunities of many millions of children in American society, such as poverty, racial discrimination, malnutrition, and inadequate provisions for medical care and education. (p. 137)

Although the number of cases identified a decade and a half later is much higher, the point is still well taken.

Others have noted that the number of children who die because of abuse—while a tragedy for each individual, family, and community involved—is small when contrasted with the numbers who die from accidents: perhaps 2,000 per year as opposed to many times that figure for preventable accidents (e.g., infants who die because they are not protected by safety seats). Others note that public concern is mobilized by citing the details of the most severe cases (e.g., mutilations, burnings, savage beatings, and incestuous rape), not the incidence data for the total pool of possible cases contained within the broadest possible definition, the details of which usually do not elicit public shock and outrage (e.g., the routine bruises, lack of supervision, and genital fondling that comprise the bulk of all cases of physical abuse, neglect, and sexual misuse dealt with in survey research and protective services).

These issues must remain in the forefront of our minds as we wrestle with the meaning and significance of psychological maltreatment. There is already widespread political suspicion that our efforts to employ a broad definition of maltreatment are politically unwise, ethically unacceptable, administratively monstrous, and scientifically uncertain. In the current political climate, any efforts to broaden the "intrusion" of the state into family life will be met with suspicion. This suspicion comes from both the right and left ends of the political spectrum, although with different origins and motives. We must face up to the ethical issues inherent in efforts to employ a broad definition of maltreatment—one that includes psychological abuse and neglect—because the broader the definition, the easier it is to apply biased operational definitions to discriminate against the politically and economically weak, to violate constitutionally guaranteed freedoms essential to a pluralistic society, and to be guilty of "iatrogenesis" (where the treatment causes more damage than the illness itself).

In the current bureaucratic climate in which professional resources are strained to the limits and beyond, it is debatable whether or not a broad definition which seems humane in principle will, in reality, serve the best interests of children (let alone families). If a broad definition keeps professionals busy investigating and serving cases of marginal need, danger, and suitability to available methods of intervention, will not the result be *less* service to those in most indisputable and acute need? Finally, as the short history of research on maltreatment shows, there are many uncertainties involved in defining any form of maltreatment. These uncertainties undermine the credibility of efforts to extend the mission of protective intervention. History argues that we are on very shaky ground, concerning the long-term effects of the "wrong" we seek to "right," when we intervene in the broader realms of maltreatment beyond the most acute, life-threatening, and otherwise "serious" cases.

Having said all this about the broad versus the narrow definition of maltreatment as a public issue, what can we say about psychological maltreatment? The foregoing discussion suggests that before we countenance a massive expansion of the focus of public and professional concern from the already well-established domains of physical and sexual maltreatment—each of which applies to the issues discussed above—we must be sure that we can answer three questions in the affirmative: (a) Can we predict a genuine improvement of the quality of life for children by so doing? (b) Are we able to justify the diversion of resources and attention away from other child welfare programs (and more specifically from physical and sexual maltreatment, whether narrowly or broadly defined)? (c) Can we assure the public that our professional conceptions of psychological maltreatment stand on firm scientific ground and practical expertise? We think the answer to all three questions is "yes," and that we should proceed with our efforts to understand and intervene to prevent and treat cases of psychological maltreatment. But in arriving at this conclusion, we found it necessary first to travel a difficult and often circuitous route. In this chapter we chronicle that exploration.

Summing up the three critical considerations

just indicated, it becomes apparent that the broader question we must ask is this one: Is psychological maltreatment a peripheral or a central concept in understanding the welfare and developmental robustness of children and youth? Unless we know this to be true, we fear that efforts to deal with psychological maltreatment as a matter for professional activity, policy initiative, and public concern will be unjustified, and that the costs of movement in this direction will outweigh the benefits. We begin by addressing the "con" side to this question.

THE "CON" SIDE: AMBIGUITY AND IMPRECISION

The negative response to this question emphasizes the conceptual vagueness and ambiguity of the term *psychological maltreatment*, and further, questions our ability to define it operationally in ways that will allow us to use it in the field as child welfare and mental health professionals. We begin with the ambiguity issue.

What is psychological maltreatment? Researchers and theorists have offered several definitions. For example, a federally encouraged effort to define psychological maltreatment (Lourie & Stefano, 1978) concluded that a two-level definition was necessary. Mental health professionals need a broad definition; those involved in legal action "against" perpetrators need a more explicit and limited definition to avoid having legal actions dismissed on grounds of vagueness. Their clinical definition focuses on "mental injury" (defined as "an injury to the intellectual or psychological capacity of a child, as evidenced by an observable and substantial impairment in his or her ability to function within his or her normal range of performance and behavior with due regard to his or her culture," p. 203). Their legal definition is unspecified, but implicitly narrows the clinical definition to the most severe forms, in the absence of parental willingness or capacity to cooperate voluntarily in remediation. We have some official definitions at both the federal and state levels in the various child abuse and neglect laws. Furthermore, at the federal level, the *Glossary of Child Abuse and Neglect* (National Center on Child Abuse and Neglect, 1978) offers several definitions that have been incorporated in survey research on the incidence of child maltreatment. The federally funded National Incidence Study (Burgdorff, 1980) employed these definitions in its efforts to identify the incidence and prevalence of all forms of maltreatment across the United States through an intensive search in 26 representative counties. The definitions of emotional abuse included verbal or emotional assault, close confinement, and threatened harm. The definition of emotional neglect included inadequate nurturance/affection, allowance of maladaptive behavior (e.g., delinquency), and any other refusal to provide essential care. Using these definitions, the National Incidence Study reported a rate of 2.2 per 1,000 children for emotional abuse and 1.0 per 1,000 children for emotional neglect. These constituted the primary problems identified in about 39% of the abuse cases and 18% of the neglect cases.

Although the definitions employed by the National Incidence Study help quantify the problem of psychological maltreatment, there are objections. One objection is that the data bases underlying the assumption that psychological maltreatment exists are ambiguous. While we all "know" that poor parental treatment produces developmental damage to children, research has been slow to document this cause–effect relationship. As Lourie and Stefano (1978) recognized, children vary dramatically in how they respond to parental treatment, and the existence of "stress-resistant" children seems to suggest that harsh and even hostile environments can produce prosocial, competent children (Garmezy, 1983). What is more, it is very difficult to separate the distinctly "psychological" components of psychological abuse. How exactly do people commit psychological maltreatment? What are the behaviors, the operational definition that researchers must have? What is verbal and emotional assault? How close is "close confinement?" What is inadequate nurturance and affection? What is included in essential care? Beyond the surface, these can be profoundly difficult questions to answer in detail and in general.

Third, any observation of psychological abuse depends heavily upon social and cultural context. Behavior becomes psychologically abusive because it conveys a specific negative message or because it impairs a specific vital psychological process. Behavior becomes psychologically abusive if it conveys the message of rejection or if it prevents the development of a coherent positive self-concept – if it directly induces mental illness.

How can we understand these messages without the perceptual filter of cultural mediation? Granting this, how can we transcend cultural and ethnic differences when defining such maltreatment (Garbarino & Ebata, 1983)?

A second class of objections to the soundness of psychological maltreatment lies in its imprecise operational definition. Even if we can reach closure and consensus on the conceptual meaning of psychological maltreatment, how can we provide a generally accepted operational definition that is specific and explicit enough to permit its application in the field (and ultimately in courts of law)? Do we focus on parental action or consequences for the child? The former requires that we consider parental motivation – difficult enough in the case of physical and sexual maltreatment. The latter may force us into the tricky business of assessing causality – can we be sure that a particular problem is the direct result of parental behaviors? The scientific challenges here are staggering, and the answer, as we pointed out earlier, is that "no, we cannot, as scientists, guarantee that the specific cause–effect relation is present."

Furthermore, if we are to move to an operational definition of psychological maltreatment we must take into account a developmental perspective on the meaning and significance of behavior. Is the same behavior psychological maltreatment when it is expressed towards an infant versus a toddler? Towards a school-age child? Towards an adolescent? Clearly, the answer is not always "yes." We may need age- or stage-specific definitions here to the same extent that we do in assessing social competence and other developmental phenomena.

Also, are we to confine ourselves to the most severe forms of psychological maltreatment or adopt a broad definition? If we adopt a broad definition will we not establish a legally indefensible position for the practitioner in the field and cast so wide a net as to catch all parents at one time or another? This would be unacceptable on many grounds: political, ethical, and bureaucratic.

The preceding catalog of issues should demonstrate that the scientific, clinical, and policy challenges implicit in any effort to move psychological maltreatment to the forefront of mental health, child welfare, and protective service concerns are formidable. On the other hand, we believe the advantages of a central concept for psychological maltreatment transcend the conceptual and technical challenges. Interestingly, each advantage seems to convert a liability into a benefit, as shall become apparent as we proceed.

First, the very "problem" that the socioemotional consequences of acts go far toward determining their meaning implies that psychological maltreatment is the central issue in most considerations of child welfare. Preserving the physical organism is vital, of course. It is a necessary precondition for child welfare to exist. However, once we assure physical survival we must quickly recognize that the *subjective* reality of child development is our primary concern—how do children think and feel about themselves and their world? How do they define the treatment they receive at the hands of their parents? Bronfenbrenner goes so far as to define development in just such social-psychological terms.

> The developmental status of the individual is reflected in the substantive variety and structural complexity of the...activities which he imitates and maintains in the absence of instigation or direction by others. (1979, p. 55)

Rather than casting psychological maltreatment as an ancillary issue (subordinate to other forms of abuse and neglect), we should place it as the centerpiece of our efforts to understand family functioning and to protect children. In almost all cases, it is the psychological consequences of an act that define that act as abusive—be it physical abuse (e.g., the meaning to a child of an injury inflicted by a parent in rage versus the same "injury" inflicted by accident in the course of an athletic event, recreation, or even in the course of medical attention) or sexual abuse (since sexual acts have little or no intrinsic meaning apart from the social-psychological connotations—as the incredible variety of norms regarding sexual activity in childhood and adolescence across cultures suggests).

But are there *no* universal laws to which we can look for guidance in formulating a sound concept of psychological maltreatment? There are few, if any. What we do have, however, is a set of principles that has emerged from research grounded in cross-cultural observations. Rejection, for example, appears to be a general form of psychological maltreatment that comes close to meeting the criterion of universality (Rohner, 1975). Terrorizing is another. Isolating is a third. Rejecting

means telling or showing children that they are worthless. Terrorizing means telling or showing children that the world is hostile, dangerous, and capriciously pernicious. Isolating means telling or showing children that they are alone in the world. These are the basic threats to human development. Psychological maltreatment is the core issue in the broader picture of abuse and neglect, as it is in poverty and oppression of all kinds. It provides the unifying theme. However, it is the critical aspect in the overwhelming majority of what appear as physical and sexual maltreatment cases. The justification of this view is well established in the research on maltreatment of all forms. One source of support for this view derives from studies of what some have called "invulnerable" children or "superkids" or "stress-resistant children" (to use the preferred term). The research documents that such children are *not* impervious to psychological maltreatment. Quite to the contrary, this research suggests to us that such children are differentiated from other children exposed to stressful life events—such as sick parents and economically impoverished circumstances—precisely because the mistreatment or threat they experience at the hands of their environment is counterbalanced by compensatory doses of psychological nurturance and sustenance that enable them to develop social competence, that fortify their self-esteem, and that offer a positive social definition of self. This research highlights the centrality of psychological maltreatment. Where children are rejected, terrorized, or isolated from sources of social support, they are vulnerable to negative influences in the broader social environment. Thus, the key to stress resistance is the absence of psychological maltreatment. Thus, we see that psychological maltreatment *is* the central issue. While children can absorb and overcome the experience of physical assault and sexual misuse if they are psychologically strengthened, they rarely do if they are psychologically mistreated as part of the experience.

On the issue of operational definition, we must recognize the challenges of trying to specify actionable criteria for psychological maltreatment. We do not accept the implication that these challenges override the conceptual significance and soundness of the concept, however. Rather, we suggest that focusing on the need to specify the operational meaning of psychological maltreatment in context can only help us understand better the need to do so for all forms of maltreatment. This makes the concept not worse than others, but better. It is for this reason that we favor the following general definition of maltreatment:

> Acts of omission or commission by a parent or guardian that are judged by a mixture of community values and professional expertise to be inappropriate and damaging. (Garbarino & Gilliam, 1980, p. 7)

This conception provides the foundation for our discussion of specific domains of psychological maltreatment.

DOMAINS OF PSYCHOLOGICAL MALTREATMENT

There is considerable heuristic value in distinguishing two separate but not mutually exclusive pathways of psychological maltreatment—one direct, the other indirect. Unlike physical abuse, which occurs almost exclusively through a directed interchange between individuals (e.g., husband and wife, parent and child), abuse that is psychological in its content and consequences can occur as the by-product of behavior that has another subject entirely as its target. This is the case when a child is caught in the psychological crossfire between, for instance, parent and school. Antipathy and resentment provoked by actions on the part of parents and school officials could easily produce distress in the hapless school child who serves as the focal point of the conflict. To generate fruitful dialogue and conceptual alternatives, we examine both direct abuse—that is, acts of omission or commission which are directly targeted at the child as a psychological agent (e.g., verbal degradation), and indirect abuse—that is, behavior with a separate and distinct primary focus which has secondary effects on the mental health of the child (e.g., parental conflict). Therefore, we group domains of psychological maltreatment according to the focus and target of the perpetrated acts.

DIRECT PSYCHOLOGICAL MALTREATMENT

Mental Cruelty

The phrase "mental cruelty" is much bandied about among social scientists, service agents, and the lay public. Indeed, when we speak of emotional maltreatment, it is the most frequent

image conveyed. Yet even here there is a lack of clarity with regard to the specific behaviors belonging in this subcategory of psychological abuse. The boundaries become still more blurred when we begin to consider one of the fundamental manifestations of mental cruelty—the phenomenon of rejection.

Researchers Rohner and Rohner (1980) have investigated the construct of rejection from an ethnological perspective by comparing parenting behaviors that characterize several geographically and culturally disparate societies (using The Human Relations Area Files described in Rohner, 1975). From studies of the Colombian mestizo, the villagers of Tepoztlan, Mexico, and the Ik of Africa, among others, Rohner and Rohner conceptualized two distinct patterns of parental rejection. In the first, the mental attitude of hostility is converted into behavioral aggression toward one's offspring. In the second, the mental attitude of indifference is manifested behaviorally in neglect of the physical and/or emotional needs of children. While each pattern contains elements of other forms of abuse (i.e., physical abuse or neglect), the message conveyed to children is unambiguous: "You are neither valued nor loved." Mental cruelty is clearly implied in such a scenario.

For both lay and professional audiences, the natural response to the situation described above is to question the circumstances, the background, and the motives of parents who experience and who express such feelings toward their children. Inevitably, we seek an answer to the question that a popular abuse prevention slogan poses: "Who could do such a thing to a child?" To better understand the phenomenon of rejection as well as the broader issue of psychological maltreatment in its many other forms, it is instructive to briefly summarize the findings of the Rohners regarding both the parental antecedents and child consequences of rejection.

Despite the wide variability in society and culture, Rohner and Rohner were able to document a consistent set of factors which occurred in reports or observations of rejection of children by their parents. As is the case in nearly every form of child abuse, rejecting parents appear generally overwhelmed by a convergence of social and economic hardships: too many children, inadequate material resources, too much stress, and too little emotional support. Whatever characteristics individually describe such parents (in terms of personality attributes, attitudes, and values), a reliable set of situational variables identified cross-culturally those parents at risk for perpetrating this type of emotional maltreatment.

Specifically, these were the circumstances associated with increased risk for rejection: (a) restrictions against family planning alternatives sanctioned by the society (implying a greater incidence of unwanted pregnancies), (b) an absence of adults in the home other than the primary caregiver (preventing caregivers the opportunity for time alone or time away from home), (c) a lack of involvement on the part of fathers in the role as socializer of children, and (d) social and instrumental isolation of families in the community (i.e., families detached from friendship and assistance networks). These findings are hardly surprising, and probably apply whether the topic under scrutiny is rejection, neglect, physical abuse, or some other manifestation of psychological abuse. Unless parents feel materially and psychologically secure enough to move beyond concern for themselves to provide the attention, energy, and nurturance children demand, it is unlikely that such individuals will be able to function effectively as caregivers, as instructors, or as providers of emotional support for their children.

Given the defining characteristics of rejecting parents (i.e., aggression, indifferent neglect) and given the environmental deficiencies which tend to accompany such behavior, it is only to be expected that Rohner and Rohner should document a whole host of adverse outcomes for the personality and behavior of rejected children. Youngsters who are rejected physically and/or psychologically by their parents are likely to be noticeably hostile and aggressive, to have an impaired sense of self-esteem, and to exhibit either excessive dependency on parents and/or other adults, or a "defensive independence" that appears to derive more from a negativistic reaction to their experiences than from a secure, constructive sense of autonomy. Furthermore, these children and teens appear emotionally unstable or unresponsive, and come to perceive the world in which they live in negative terms. This last finding suggests that rejection wields a two-edged blade, eroding the confidence and self-esteem with which children view themselves, and distorting the perspective through which these children view their immediate and broader context.

We should note that the origins and outcomes of parental rejection are generally congruent with the details of other forms of maltreatment described by researchers and practitioners, very probably because either rejection or some comparable expression of psychological maltreatment almost invariably occurs with physical abuse and neglect, a point we mentioned earlier. The same identifying characteristics tend also to define both other acts of mental cruelty and other dimensions of direct emotional abuse. Hence, we should expect to find some of the same parental antecedents as well as child consequences whether we direct our attention to rejection per se, or to contradictory demands, emotional neglect, or stimulus deprivation. With these thoughts in mind, let us review some additional acts of mental cruelty, both within and beyond the family.

One class of behaviors which is closely related to and often a manifestation of rejection is parental scapegoating. This may involve overtly (and unjustly) attributing undesirable circumstances or events to a youngster (e.g., a conflicted marital relationship, problems in the neighborhood) or projecting personal dislikes and frustrations on a child who is essentially blameless (as when a child resembles an ex-spouse). It may mean placing severe restrictions on or being excessively critical of a child as a result of some personal neurosis (as when a child is instinctively and precipitately judged as one who will "come to a bad end" like his alcoholic grandfather or unfaithful mother, perhaps like the parent him or herself). Finally, it may simply consist of flagrantly preferential treatment of siblings: selectively remarking on the "good" behavior of sisters and brothers, while emphasizing the relative deficiencies and wrongdoings of the target child.

Regardless of the specific configuration of cause and deed, it is clear that scapegoating implies some type of rejection, if not of the child, then of some person or situation with which the child is inextricably related in the mind of the parent. Nevertheless, rejection need not assume so blatant a form. As we shall see throughout this discussion of direct psychological maltreatment, rejection is the theme which interweaves the many quite dissimilar instances of this type of abuse, at times in obvious ways, at times more subtly. In the following paragraphs, rejection is a topic unmentioned but not unimplicated.

Bateson (1972) has described a particular configuration of parental expectations and demands which place the child in what he has termed a "double bind." Behavior on the part of parents in this case is so inconsistent as to be contradictory, creating for the child or teen what is truly a "no-win" situation. In one case, as a mother and child walked down the hall, she moved close to the boy, thus eliciting his gesture of putting his arm up around her waist. She then subtly pulled away and he dropped his arm. She responded, "What's the matter, don't you love me anymore?". A double bind may be as flagrant a contradiction as this one, or, as in the case where pleasing one parent automatically implies rejecting a disputing spouse. On the other hand, it may be as subtle as intimating that praiseworthy achievement in the school and larger community must be bought at the cost of accepting a strict code of family values.

This type of double jeopardy has clear parallels to the experimental phenomenon of "learned helplessness" which Seligman (1975; Seligman, Maier, & Solomon, 1971) studied in laboratory animals. Helplessness can be experimentally induced by preventing animals any opportunity to escape repeated presentation of a noxious stimulus (e.g., an electrical shock). No matter what the animal attempts, it can neither terminate nor control the occurrence of some distressing event. This is only half the story when children are caught in a double bind, however, for they are confronted with inescapable conflict or censure in *each* of the several alternatives they would seek to pursue.

What are the consequences for a child of being raised in such an environment? Bateson proposed that this was the type of background which provided the breeding ground for adulthood schizophrenia. A child whose mental health may already be at risk due to biogenic factors is propelled into psychological disorder by constant exposure to the mental trap which is a double bind. It represents a clear case of psychological terrorism.

At another level, demands by parents may not be contradictory, but simply unreasonably high or low. When too much or too little is expected from children, their self-concepts and self-confidence are likely to suffer. Indeed, it is somewhat ironic that the parent who constantly places demands that cannot be met on a child should represent a similar developmental threat in terms of child ego strength as the parent who makes it clear that there are few, if any, expectations at all regarding the child. Related to or included in

these patterns of parenting are such actions as misinforming the children about their abilities, encouraging unrealistic goals or expectations, and attempting to reverse roles by seeking sympathy, encouragement, or counsel from children on adult matters. Behavior of this kind may simply stem from parental ignorance or misconceptions about child competencies. Alternatively or simultaneously, it may reflect attempts by parents to gratify their own real or perceived needs. In extreme cases, actions such as these may be indicative of parental psychopathology. In all such cases, rejection and isolation are implicated in the problem, whether the site be the home, the classroom, or the residential institution, and the perpetrator be a parent, a teacher, or a child care worker.

Emotional Neglect and Stimulation Deprivation

Just as social and economic circumstances were indicated in the case of rejection, so material poverty and social isolation have also been linked with both emotional neglect and stimulation deprivation. When meeting basic psychophysical needs is a daily struggle, the drain on parental resources may discourage nurturance of what appear to parents as more ancillary developmental needs. "I feed and clothe him, don't I?" may be the defensive parental retort. On the other hand, some parents are psychologically unfit to provide for their children's psychosocial development, regardless of the available socioeconomic resources. Mental illness may preclude the ability to furnish any but the most obvious physical necessities.

We cannot, however, ignore the potentially major contribution which children consciously or unconsciously make to their own care. When confronted with parental negligence stemming from some self-absorbing psychological disturbance, it may well be that assertive children act to promote their own care. In contrast, to a parent already overwhelmed by environmentally induced stress, the same characteristics may serve as a catalyst for more active forms of abuse. In this instance, attention-getting behavior and demands provide the impetus for violent parental reactions. Further consideration of the role children may play in eliciting extreme incompetence in parental behavior suggests that there are innumerable physical, behavioral, and personality traits which may evoke negative responses in the absence of any volition on the part of children. Excessive activity, a naturally shy disposition, some mental or physical handicap—any of these might generate the sorts of reactions which are easily translated into parental withdrawal, rejection, or neglect.

Kadushin and Martin (1981) provide extensive testimony by abusive parents to illustrate the important (and often inadvertent) role which children can play in provoking maltreatment at the hands of their parents. One parent recalls:

> And my oldest child [Steve] is the extreme opposite of Carl [the abused child]—very timid and quiet and . . . I like his sensitivity. I liked him better from day one. . . . And Carl, I just don't understand him at all. It's like he's not like me at all. He rarely shows feelings, he is bullheaded, strong, real aggressive. And when I first came home from the hospital with Carl, all I could think of was protecting Steve from this intruder. I felt that the baby [Carl] was an intruder between him and me. So I guess I'm very partial to the older boy. (p. 241)

How do parents neglect the psychosocial needs of their children? How is their lack of involvement or support made evident? For some, the emotional withdrawal accompanies more basic physical neglect. Indifference or hostility is transformed into a total disregard for the needs of the child, both physical and psychological. In other cases, the well-groomed, well-tended child is simply confronted with emotional coldness and distancing behavior by the parent: "Don't rumple your dress trying to climb into my lap"; "Well-behaved children don't get angry; good children don't cry"; "How many times have I told you not to touch *anything* in this house that isn't yours?"

Children learn by doing, by interacting with objects and with people. If parents or other adults severely restrict the opportunity for children to play, explore, make friends, visit neighbors, or participate in community organizations, they are thwarting the development of competence. If parents or other adults do not provide occasions for children to exercise responsibility, to generate solutions to problems, to enjoy the pride of accomplishment, they are denying the experiences which promote a sense of personal efficacy. Evidence in support of these observations derives from studies of maternal restric-

tions during infancy and their presumed consequences for child development. Negative associations between the amount of floor freedom children are allowed (Ainsworth & Bell, 1974), the frequency of physical and verbal prohibitions (Tulkin & Covitz, 1975), maternal limitations on her child's freedom to explore the environment (Wachs, 1976), and various indices of later cognitive development suggest the detrimental impact of excessive parental regulation on the development of the child.

With regard to more direct forms of social and emotional neglect, the renowned work of Rene Spitz (1945, 1946) on children raised in orphanages further chronicles the deleterious consequences for children reared in socioemotional deprivation. Illustrating the extreme in potential outcomes, Spitz documented an infant mortality rate of over 33% in their sample of 91 orphans "in spite of good food and meticulous medical care" (1945, p. 59). It is not surprising, given circumstances such as those described here, to find additional documentation of both physical and psychological deficits in children whose psychosocial needs are grossly ignored—mind and body are inextricably linked in the developing child.

Bullard, Glaser, Hagarty, and Pivchik (1967) have described in detail the confluence of traits which together define the medically recognized phenomenon of "nonorganic failure to thrive." Particularly evident in the period of late infancy and early childhood, children suffering from this "malady" are typically undernourished physically, apathetic and lethargic in nature, and developmentally delayed—often both physically and behaviorally. The diagnostic key is the child's responsivity to treatment. Under watchful, therapeutic hospital care, the failure-to-thrive baby or child rapidly gains weight and animation. Withdrawn, uncomplaining, and unconcerned youngsters begin to participate in the activity surrounding them, even seeking out attention and favor. Nevertheless, lingering psychological symptoms (tantrums, secrecy, petty theft) belie hasty and overly optimistic pronouncements on the efficacy of compensatory experiences. Doubts remain about the degree of plasticity available and necessary to rechart the developmental course of a child exposed to early and pervasive socioemotional neglect.

Physical anomalies beyond simple low weight and developmental delays have been linked to severe neglect during childhood (Powell, Brasel, & Blizzard, 1967). The phenomenon labeled "psychosocial dwarfism" or "deprivational dwarfism" is a case in point. Gardner (1972) elucidates some of the hypothesized precursors, possible biological processes, and physical and behavioral characteristics accompanying growth disorders of psychosocial origin. Abnormalities in sleeping, eating, and motor ability, as well as in physical growth and psychological functioning, were marked in his small sample of infants from "disordered" and neglectful family environments. It is worthwhile to present the observations of this researcher regarding the developmental outcome of the six "thin dwarfs" followed in this medical treatment study:

> In spite of . . . short-term gains [in weight, motor ability, and social responsiveness] few of the children recovered entirely from their experience of deprivation dwarfism. They tended to remain below average in height, weight, and skeletal maturation. Furthermore, the two we were able to follow until late childhood gave evidence of residual damage to personality structure and to intellect. (p. 78)

Finally, neglected children appear to be at risk for considerable interpersonal dysfunction as well (Polansky, Chalmers, Butten-Wieser, & Williams, 1979). The child who is raised in an environment devoid of warm, reciprocal interaction with at least one parental figure is unlikely to acquire the social skills and orientation with which to cultivate peer relationships. In support of this position is the work of Alan Sroufe (1983; Waters, Wippman, & Sroufe, 1979), for instance, who has related insecurity of attachment to one's primary caregiver at 12 months (thought to result from a deficiency of warm, intimate, reciprocal interaction throughout infancy) to less competent peer relations during the preschool years. Consequently, descriptions of the neglected child as "asocial," as "antisocial," and/or as "lacking in friends," are consistent with knowledge about the origins and characteristics of more general social incompetence. In view of the growing body of literature linking poor peer relations during childhood with social or psychological dysfunction in later years (see Robins, 1979; Van Hasselt, Hersen, Whitehill, & Bellack, 1979) there is a clear mandate for greater efforts aimed at preventing parental negligence of their children's psychological needs.

INDIRECT PSYCHOLOGICAL MALTREATMENT

Influence by Negative or Limiting Models

As we noted earlier, in contrast to physical or sexual maltreatment, psychological maltreatment may take place without specifically focusing on the child or adolescent as a target for psychological victimization. Thus, by simply modelling grossly inappropriate behavior, or by subordinating concern for child welfare to highly incompatible personal goals, adults indirectly engage in psychological maltreatment. Let us first review some of the potential enactments of inappropriate familial models before broadening our discussion in a consideration of extrafamilial patterns of mistreatment.

Several behavioral psychologists (e.g., Burgess & Conger, 1977; Patterson, 1979) have identified patterns of negative behavior between parents and children which progressively intensify inappropriate and injurious exchanges within the family. In becoming caught up into this so-called "cycle of coercion," parents lose their ability to control child behavior by means other than physical or verbal force. Aversive child behavior becomes the exclusive focus of social interchange, and by attending only to such misbehavior, parents consciously or unconsciously extinguish positive interpersonal behaviors, reinforcing instead those which are negative. Such youngsters quickly discover that whining or shouting or slamming things is the commonly acknowledged method to gain parental notice in their families. It is apparent that the eventual outcome of such socialization experiences is likely to be one of social maladjustment, social alienation, and/or delinquency. What is learned in the home is readily generalized to the peer group, the school, and the community. Inadvertently, parents may thus place their children at risk for developmental dysfunction in the realm of interpersonal relations outside the home. In this regard, inadequate behavioral responses by parents constitute indirect psychological maltreatment, a form of neglect if not outright abuse.

Egocentricism on the part of parents represents another opportunity for conscious or inadvertent psychological victimization. By putting their own self-interests before the well-being of their children, parents may be placing youngsters in psychosocial jeopardy. Consider the case of a power struggle in the family—marital or intergenerational (i.e., grandparents vs. parents). In order to gain the upper hand, parents may resort to manipulating their children as pawns in the power play. This becomes another example of a child trapped in the psychological crossfire of adults. Such a situation is hardly likely to promote either psychological well-being or socioemotional development. The children in effect become the psychological victims of adult self-interest.

Commercial or status-oriented exploitation of children is a more obvious and publicized version of ego-oriented victimization. The media delights in sensationalized accounts of the exploitative promotion of child models, child actors, and child personalities. Based on the lurid autobiographical tales told in retrospect by these same individuals, one wonders how they survived to psychologically intact adulthood (if they did so). Enumeration of the marital breakups, bouts of substance abuse, periods of mental disturbance, and sessions with the psychoanalyst is most revealing in this respect.

More subtle in its evolution, though not necessarily in its effects, is what we might term "socialization into intransigence." McCandless (1967) furnishes a rich account of the development of an authoritarian personality, characterized by progressive socialization of personality traits which include rigidity and conformity, intolerance of ambiguity, and unrealistic goal setting. Parenting practices which emphasize dichotomies of behavior and perception, which rely on extremes of punishment and reward, and which demand an orientation to power and status in order to earn adult recognition are thought to be instrumental in the genesis of the authoritarian personality. In view of the self-limiting and intolerant nature of the authoritarian adult, we may consider parenting practices which evoke such a configuration of traits to be an indirect form of psychological maltreatment. The parallels between authoritarian characteristics and the psychological outcomes of a childhood marked by consistently unreasonable parental demands (i.e., one form of mental cruelty) further warrant the inclusion of this pattern of parental functioning within the broad scheme of indirect maltreatment. Since parents who subscribe to such childrearing practices tend to exhibit similar attributes within their own psychological makeup, authoritarian traits may be considered a legacy of parents' own narrow, restricted, and

intolerant orientation. It is therefore reasonable to represent such a style of childrearing as a negative, ego-oriented form of psychological maltreatment.

We can readily extend the discussion of authoritarian personality development into a third model of negative and limiting parental influence, that of teaching children prejudice. Whether through active coaching or behavioral modelling, parents who communicate slanderous stereotypes to their children distort the manner in which youngsters perceive their world and simultaneously limit both their social experiences and psychological development. In transmitting their own frailties, such parents engage in a process of systematic closure in terms of their children's development. Depending on the cultural context in which this prejudice is nurtured, parents may be curtailing both normative and enriching socio-cultural experiences for their truly misguided offspring.

Let no one intimate, however, that the family is a solitary agent in the promotion of deleterious and debilitating psychosocial characteristics in children and youth. The mass media, as one example, are rife with images of damaging stereotypes and antisocial activities (e.g., in reinforcing sexist and racist stereotypes). The pioneer work of Bandura (1963, 1973) and investigations by other researchers (e.g., Eron, 1963; Lefkowitz, Eron, Walder, & Heusmann, 1972; Leifer & Roberts, 1972) on the effects of television violence on children, exposes but one unsavory by-product of media omnipresence. Cultural and sexual stereotypes dictate similarly biased attitudes and behaviors in children who might otherwise have assumed more tolerant postures.

The policies which we legislate on an institutional or governmental level may also exert subtle (and not so subtle) influences on the latitude and fair-mindedness of children's thinking. There are implicit messages in governmental policies which restrict access to resources on the basis of ethnicity, gender or religion; in public and federal support for corporal punishment in the home, the school, and the criminal justice system; and in political efforts to promote subversive activities on a national and international level. Through discriminatory practices, inflexible policies, and neglect of the needy, every government conveys its own prejudices, intolerances, and unconcern. As a result of increasingly sophisticated communication systems and diminishing personal contact, the transmission of social, cultural, and political dogma seems to grow simultaneously more potent and more pervasive.

It is meaningful at this point to ask whether cultural standards can be wrong. On the basis of our present discussion, we do not hesitate to respond in the affirmative. When socio-cultural mores and practices interfere with psychological and emotional development by restricting growth-promoting interactions or experiences, by preventing creative expression which is threatening only insofar as it violates strict socio-cultural codes, and by penalizing efforts to gain enlightened knowledge, then we feel justified in calling such standards ethically indefensible. The opportunities are already too great for closing oneself off from the experience and exchange of ideas, for curtailing one's personal development, to tolerate social and cultural sanctions which do the same. Yes, we believe, cultural mores can be wrong.

Living in Dangerous and Unstable Environments

We have briefly examined how parents, communities, and governments may constrict the experimental realm of the individual—what Lewin (1951) has termed the "life-space"—through what eventually becomes self-generated antipathy and fear. Needless to say, similar restrictions and often, more severe consequences result when danger and enmity are imposed by forces external to the individual. Most obvious in both their environmental disruption and their individual effects are macrolevel events such as war, riot, natural disaster, and widespread poverty. The often devastating consequences of these hazardous living conditions have been chronicled in research efforts as diverse as the situations they describe.

Little systematic research exists on war as a force in the psychological maltreatment of children. The topic has received significant journalistic attention (e.g., *Time* magazine's Roger Rosenblatt, January 11, 1982, explored "children of war" in Northern Ireland, Israel, Lebanon, Cambodia, and Vietnam and has since published a book by the same title—Rosenblatt, 1983). In studies of children of war we observe perhaps more clearly than anywhere else *both* the "stress resistance" and the "vulnerability" of children. Children who are well integrated into an effectively functioning system of social support tend to avoid severe psychological damage (although

temperamental sensitivity in combination with extreme trauma can overwhelm even these socially fortified individuals). Children without secure resources fall victim. Even transient adult support coupled with peer group stability can go a long way towards protecting children. Freud and Dann's (1951) classic study of children living in concentration camps during World War II showed that psychological survival is possible under perilous conditions, but that the costs to personal development are often high and long term. Research in progress on the life-course impact of concentration camp survivors should illuminate these costs.

However, in assessing the impact of war on children we must speculate that the causal relationship is not a simple one. For example, a psychiatric study of Catholic and Protestant children in Belfast, Northern Ireland (Rosenblatt, 1982) reported that the rate of clinical "emotional disturbance" is *not* very high because "the whole place is emotionally disturbed." As Heskin (1980) sees it, there is a high level of adaptive behavior that conforms to the craziness of the environment (but which would be seen as maladaptive and antisocial were it performed in a peaceful environment). For example, the children of Northern Ireland appear preoccupied with violence (Heskin, 1980)—even if they have little direct experience of "the troubles"—because it is the dominant motif in their environment (e.g., through the mass media). This finding reinforces concern about the psychological impact of the nuclear arms race (Reveron, 1982). (Sensitive children exposed to "duck-and-cover drills" in the 1950s, when the spectre of atomic war was vivid, report "fear" as a dominant childhood image associated with any bright flash in the sky.) Spencer (personal communication, 1983) reports that the Atlanta murders of the early 1980s seem to have been incorporated into the general "normal" level of threat perceived in the social environment by poor black youth. It seems that children can and do accommodate to living in a state of siege. That is both a reassuring and a chilling conclusion.

Moving from the crisis of war to the crisis of poverty, we may turn to the work of sociologist Glenn Elder. Elder's retrospective analysis of the effects of the Great Depression on two cohorts of children (248 who were preschoolers and 212 who were young teens from two urban regions in California at the outset of the Depression, ca. 1933) provides invaluable insight into some of the likely effects of widespread economic hardship on children and their families (Elder, 1974). With respect to this issue, it is noteworthy that one in four families slipped below the poverty line at least once. By comparing developmental outcomes of children whose families did or did not suffer substantial financial loss during the Depression, Elder was able to arrive at some provocative conclusions about the processes of influence as well as developmental risks for children of different ages. Particularly noteworthy was the fact that teenagers, unlike preschoolers, seemed able to derive certain growth-promoting experiences from this otherwise calamitous event. Specifically, by providing personal and material assistance to their needy families, teenagers appeared to gain a sense of efficacy, of responsibility, and of commitment. In terms of various social and economic indices, as well as more psychological measures, these teens were judged to be, on the whole, better off later on than their nondeprived peers but only if the pre-Depression marital relationship was positive and strong. This makes intuitive sense in the context of our discussion of psychological maltreatment. Material deprivation may be of considerably less importance (up to a point) than provision of supportive, mutually satisfying socioemotional experiences. Challenge, in the context of support, appears to be growth-inducing. As we pointed out in our discussion of mental cruelty, there is a fundamental human need to gain a sense of mastery and competence.

The psychosocial consequences of missing experiences which foster these self-perceptions become apparent when we review Elder's findings for children who were too young to make similar contributions during this period of hardship. As Bronfenbrenner and Crouter (1982) point out in their summary of Elder's findings:

> Alas, adversity was not so sweet for male children who were still preschoolers when their families suffered economic loss. The results were almost the opposite of those for the adolescent boys. . . . Compared to controls from non-deprived families, these youngsters subsequently did less well in school, showed less stable and successful work histories, and exhibited more emotional and social difficulties, some still apparent in middle adulthood. (p. 68)

Thus we find that even disruption on a macrolevel is qualified in its impact on children depending on the psychological experiences which are translated to them. It is intuitively sound to suppose that the same level of personal involvement also mediates turmoil and dissolution in the sphere of family functioning. In this regard, we may profit from consideration of three conditions of instability in the familial environment: marital discord, transient foster care, and the experiences of "latchkey" children.

In response to the surging statistics on divorce, researchers are increasingly devoting time and energy to understanding the effects of marital conflict on children. Whether an investigation of the precursors of delinquency (West, 1969, 1973), the situational determinants of competent parental functioning (Belsky, Gilstrap, & Rovine, 1984; Price, 1977), or the adjustment of children following a divorce, discord and disharmony in the marital relationship imply a less facilitating context and a poorer prognosis for child development (Bronson, 1966; see also Emery, 1982). Apparently, marital discord has a two-fold pathway of influence on the children involved: direct effects of witnessing conflict between father and mother, and/or indirect effects of experiencing diminished parental efficacy in the caregiving role.

In psychological terms, a conflicted marital relationship, especially one severe enough to culminate in divorce, may imply self-guilt to the child (Hetherington, 1980; Wallerstein & Kelly, 1975), may furnish inappropriate models of interpersonal behavior, and may deprive the child of the nurturance and support that is contingent on the parents' own well-being (Belsky, 1984). These are the conditions which make it admissible to label such a home environment as psychologically injurious for children. Regardless of the role which difficult children might play in occasioning such discord, they become the unwitting victims of the strained relations which ensue. Some of the possible consequences include antisocial, aggressive, and other problematic behaviors on the part of the children involved (e.g., see Emery, 1982).

The developmental risks which a conflicted marriage presents for children are paralleled and magnified in the case of familial transience. There is sufficient anecdotal evidence (e.g., see Goldstein, Freud, & Solnit, 1973, 1979) relating to what might be termed the "foster care shuttle" to suggest that instability and impermanence in family membership have potentially dire consequences on the present and future functioning of young people. Repeated associations between cases of child abuse, for example, and a history of foster care fluctuation among those parents involved reveal one possible outcome of familial transience. Psychological disturbance has also been linked to a background of family instability, marital conflict, and separation from parental figures (Rutter, 1971).

The likely mechanisms connecting unstable family situations and poor developmental prognoses include disruption in relationships to primary attachment figures and inconsistency in experiences of childrearing. The literature on parent–child attachment (e.g., see Ainsworth, Blehar, Waters, & Wall, 1978) indicates that a secure relationship with a least one adult *maintained over time* is a fundamental precursor and correlate of later competence in psychosocial functioning. If a child is shuttled from one home to the next or, comparably, is exposed to a continual flux in institutional caregivers, such a relationship has little opportunity to develop and less so to persist for any appreciable amount of time. Hence we find the deleterious outcomes for a subsample of repeatedly transplanted foster children and for the "maternally deprived" orphans Spitz followed.

Literature on parenting (see Belsky, 1984; Coopersmith, 1967; Patterson, 1978) suggests that, among other qualities, consistency in caregiving—in discipline, in warmth, and in sensitive responding—promotes psychological well-being (e.g., self-esteem, self-efficacy) and social adaptation (e.g., social competence, lower rates of delinquency) throughout the childhood years. One can surmise that periodic disruption or inconsistency in the family setting, therefore, whether a result of marital incompatibility or of alternating caregivers, will likewise jeopardize developmental outcomes. A child who was raised according to the "authoritative" or "permissive" standards of parenting identified by Baumrind (1971, 1972), will very likely undergo major upheaval if later confronted with an "authoritarian" model. Hetherington (1983) presents an illustrative situation of how child functioning can be so undermined in cases of postdivorce parenting. If, for example, stepfathers enter a new household with a goal of teaching unruly children or teens to mind, rather than of supporting existing maternal efforts to cope with postdivorce behavior problems, misbehavior or emotional problems will tend to be exacerbated rather than ameliorated. For these children, still engaged in the difficulties of adapting to familial disruption, the consequences of further alterations in parent–child relations can be highly detrimental.

The final instance of unreliable familial environments we will address here is that of latchkey children. This term refers to youngsters who are—out of necessity or merely neglect—regularly left to fend for themselves for substantial periods of the day. This includes children who are left unattended while parents go out shopping or visiting, as well as those who must let themselves into an empty home (via the ubiquitous latchkey) to entertain and care for themselves until parents return home after work. Estimates yield a figure of 7 million children 13 years of age or younger who fall under this description, including thousands who are 6 years or less. Although children so described do not experience family "instability" in the same sense as we have applied the term earlier to changes in caregivers or parenting practices, they *are* exposed to the real or imagined dangers which result from an unsupervised, unregulated situation. In this sense, with the uncertainty they experience in the absence of parents or other responsible adults, these youngsters may indeed dwell in an unstable home environment.

From media accounts and from research such as that conducted by Long and Long (1982) it has been shown that young latchkey children living in an urban area experience a very high level of fears and nightmares. Other evidence (Garbarino, 1980) ties the latchkey situation to greater risk of accidents and exploitation in dangerous urban environments. Children left unsupervised in this manner thus seem vulnerable to both objective dangers and subjective fears. Is it surprising that some of these children express feelings of insecurity and fearfulness? By placing children in this position without adequate preparation and safeguards, parents may create a threat to their youngsters' physical and psychological well-being—whether from ignorance, perceived economic necessity, false convictions about safety, or simply a lack of concern. It is this disregard for child welfare which warrants the label of psychological maltreatment.

Sexual Abuse and Exploitation

We may ask, in the same way we have in previous sections of this chapter, what causes a sexually exploitative relationship between adult and child or adult and teen to constitute psychological maltreatment. In essence, there are two characteristics which define such sexual relations or sexually related activities as psychological victimization of the children involved. The first is what Finkelhor (1979) calls the informed consent issue. Children and teens suffer an imbalance of social rank and power relative to adults and, at the same time, are handicapped by restricted information and experience as well as by cognitive limitations (depending upon age and maturity). Due to the power adults inherently possess, it is a facile and often subtle matter to tyrannize, cajole, or otherwise induce youngsters who are both less influential and more ignorant to conform to adult desires, even when these violate the strictest, most fundamental social and cultural standards. The issue of power is starkly apparent in the definition of sexual abuse adopted by the National Center on Child Abuse and Neglect (1978): "contacts or interactions between a child and an adult when the child is being used for the sexual stimulation of the perpetrator or another person *when the perpetrator is in a position of power or control over the victim*" (emphasis added).

In addition, sexual exploitation again pits adult self-interest against the developmental robustness of the children who become their victims. The developmental jeopardy, once more, is twofold. Densen-Gerber and Hutchinson (1979) eloquently attest to the emotional damage likely to ensue from what are clearly inappropriate sexual relations or activities. Role reversals, contradictory messages, psychological manipulation, unreasonable emotional demands, ineffectual models of parenthood (in the case of incest), all are permutations of the mentally cruel acts implicated earlier, and may become probable accompaniments to the physical acts which define sexual abuse. As if this were not enough, sexual abuse victims frequently experience emotional trauma resulting from shame, uncertainty, guilt, fear of breaking up the family (among victims of incest), and, for female teenagers, the fear of pregnancy. The psychological risks are evident in reports that incest victims are more likely than the general population to engage in substance abuse, to exhibit depressive, anxious, and/or psychosomatic symptomology, and to commit suicide (Garbarino & Gilliam, 1980).

Social development, too, is imperiled by adult behavior of this sort. Even viewing sexual relations as a purely contextual phenomenon — the creation of proscribed social roles amid previously established and socially sanctioned interpersonal or familial ones — indicts such relations as a threat to current or future social functioning (Kaus & Garbarino, 1984). In the case of incest, social roles within the family must become strained when parent and child effect a travesty of the spousal relationship. This is apparent, once again, in the approach taken by the National Center on Child Abuse and Neglect, which identifies five necessary ingredients for incest (enacted primarily between father and adolescent daughter): (a) the daughter's assumption (whether voluntary or forced) of a mother role; (b) relative sexual incompatibility between the parents; (c) the father's unwillingness to seek a partner outside the family unity; (d) family fear of disintegration; and (e) unconscious sanction by the mother. The belief that in many cases the noninvolved parent condones such behavior by sexual unavailability and/or by affected ignorance adds further credence to the postulated social and emotional turmoil the child undergoes (DeFrancis, 1969; Kaufman, Puck, & Tagiuri, 1954).

Whether within or outside the home, sexually exploitative relations will tend to interfere with the development and maintenance of normal social relationships. This is particularly true for adolescents, as are the problems attendant upon sexual abuse. Normative heterosexual experiences with peers (social interaction outside of school, dating, etc.) may be curtailed by an adult sexual partner who fears exposure or who experiences jealousy. Self-condemnation or denunciation by parents or friends often eventuates in the problematical action of leaving home prematurely. Of the projected 800,000 teenagers who run away annually, the federal government estimates that one-half to one-third were victims of mistreatment. Densen-Gerber and Hutchinson (1979) cite prostitution, pornography, and substance abuse as a subsample of the likely consequences for those who have fled their homes to escape sexually exploitative situations. Recognizing the social and emotional risks associated with being a runaway (including, ironically, the danger of further exploitation), such an outcome serves as additional confirmation of the psychosocial perils of sexual abuse or exploitation.

Drug and Substance Abuse

The final domain of indirect psychological mistreatment we considered is that which occurs when parents, physicians, or other adults inappropriately encourage, administer, or provide inadequate care while under the influence of drugs or alcohol. Although these behaviors may seem widely disparate, it is primarily the degree of intentionality on the part of the caregiver that ultimately distinguishes these acts. In the former case, responsible but often uninformed adults consciously condone, make available, or even administer substances whose use may be questionable among adults and indefensible among children or minors. In the latter, misuse of children by adults who are under the influence of alcohol or drugs becomes far less an issue of knowledge or intent than of individual psychology or psychopathology. Regardless of these distinctions, the topic of substance abuse is a fitting one to reserve until the end, since its analysis unites several points and issues discussed earlier in our consideration of other forms of psychological maltreatment.

The first parallels can be drawn between sexual abuse and substance abuse, since the two present similar criteria for determining the inappropriateness of adult behavior. Just as it was impossible, in theory, to obtain informed consent for adult–child sexual relations, so it is equally untenable to suppose that children and youth have the knowledge, the experience, and the understanding that makes their decision (if they are given one) to take psychotropic substances an informed one. Without firm evidence to show that a specific drug has a beneficial or, at the very least, a neutral effect on children, administration of such a drug violates the rights of children to a nurturant and protected context for development. This issue has been argued most persuasively in reference to the prescription and administration of inadequately tested drugs for treatment of hyperactivity and presumed "minimal brain damage" in children (McCoy & Koocher, 1976; Stewart, 1976). Beyond this argument, inasmuch as ("voluntary") substance misuse or abuse by youth may have social as well as psychological repercussions (e.g., academic problems, strained peer relations, social withdrawal, etc.), a lack of effort by responsible adults to attend to the problem may be interpreted as psychological neglect of children (i.e., as further evidence of the inappropriateness of adult behavior).

In situations where adults themselves are substance abusers, the theme of negative and limiting models comes into play. Whether parents or other guardians merely make available the substances they (mis)use or, in fact, mistreat their charges while under the influence of either drugs or alcohol, they are exhibiting and may indeed be promoting behavior which is especially unsuitable in children. Youngsters in these situations witness either one or both of two behavioral dictums: use (or misuse) of this substance is an acceptable practice, and/or mistreatment of children is not cause enough to warrant cessation of its use. Each message conveys its own set of damaging implications to the children involved.

Once more, we must recognize that individual adults are not the only models of substance use and abuse. Both obvious and more subtle pressures from peers as well as from the mass media reflect social attitudes which, if not condoning, are certainly not condemning substance abuse. Commercial emphasis on reactive and instinctive use of pharmaceutical drugs, on the sophistication attendant upon alcohol consumption, even on the bold individualism of cigarette smokers, promotes inappropriate use of these substances among the younger generation. Cognizant of the increasing desire for conformity during early and middle adolescence, we realize how much more potent such media images can appear at this age. In the absence of adult guidance or, worse yet, in the example set by presumably responsible adults, young people are just that much more vulnerable to the negative influence of others.

This matter of caregiver involvement or, more accurately, lack of involvement, brings to the fore questions relating to psychological neglect. Parental noninvolvement, or the abdication of responsibility on the part of school, social service, or health officials, all represent neglect of children's rights and needs for conscientious guidance and for demonstrations of concern by caring adults. Informed consent relies on some basic foundation of knowledge and awareness. In the case of children and teens, this implies an active role by those charged with their care and rearing. Inadequate fulfillment or partial neglect of this role indicates, at the very least, psychological neglect of children.

The final point we would highlight regarding connections between substance abuse and other facets of abuse and neglect derives from the knowledge that substance abuse by parents and other adults is often the companion to physically or sexually abusive or neglectful behavior toward children. Caregivers under the influence of alcohol or drugs are less likely to inhibit hostile, aggressive, or impulsive behavior toward children, and more likely to become too preoccupied to provide for their physical and emotional needs. Through their physical actions or their psychological unavailability, these caregivers thus create the very environments we labeled earlier as dangerous and unstable. In other words, we have travelled the full circuit of maltreatment within this model by linking substance use and abuse by adults to each of the identified forms of direct and indirect psychological mistreatment. In doing so, we have reaffirmed our cardinal point regarding the centrality of this latter phenomenon in any discussion of psychosocially induced developmental jeopardy. Despite the wide variability of abusive and neglectful acts which may be perpetrated against children, psychological maltreatment almost invariably surfaces as the common bond uniting and underlying all forms of injurious behavior toward children.

CORE ISSUES

Having laid out a scheme for understanding the major forms and types of psychological maltreatment, we are left with several core issues. First, we ask, can and should we differentiate between psychological maltreatment, on the one hand, and more general "negative influences," "risk factors," and "destructive social interactions" on the other? This issue contains two additional questions. For purposes of intervention, should we have a narrow or broad definition to sustain voluntary intervention? How does the definition differ for efforts associated with community mental health agencies versus legally mandated enforcement-oriented services? It is easy to be broad and all-encompassing with one's definitions when one's responsibilities are academic and intellectual in nature. We feel more compelled to be specific and narrowly focused when we know that we must live with the bureaucratic, legal, and financial implications of that definition. And yet, we are convinced that the driving engine of progress in child welfare is provided by a conception of maltreatment in which "our reach exceeds our grasp."

First, let us remember the importance of context in deciding what is and is not psychological maltreatment. Most behavior can be understood only in the social, economic, and political context in which it occurs; as examples, we have the following:

- Diana Baumrind's research on parenting concluded that an authoritative style was better than either an authoritarian or a permissive approach. However, there is reason to believe that an authoritarian approach may be necessary to protect children from delinquent influences in a socially dangerous environment (e.g., an inner-city black ghetto). In such circumstances is "overrestrictiveness" abusive?
- A. S. Neill's (1960) Summerhill school (an aggressively permissive institution if ever there was one) appeared to be very successful with English children who had been reared in repressive Victorian-style families. But it appeared to be developmentally irresponsible when addressed to already "liberated" American children. Knowing that, would it be psychologically neglectful to provide a permissive school to contemporary American youth?
- Recall Chaim Potok's novel *The Chosen* (1967). In it a father embarks (out of love) upon a campaign of silence with his genius son to teach the boy humility and to develop his character as a *mensch*, as a feeling person rather than an arrogant mind. Was this pattern of more than a decade a case of chronic emotional abuse?
- And what about parents who take a hard line with troublesome teenagers? For all that we have heard about runaways, a substantial number of youth on the streets are in fact throwaways, adolescents who have been expelled from their homes. How is this different from the "Toughlove" groups — collections of parents who band together to support each other in taking a tough stand toward their children's behavior — including throwing them out of the house (but sending them into the care of another member's home)? Is this a form of psychological maltreatment?

Second, let us remember that there is a difference between psychological maltreatment and growth-inducing challenge. Psychological abuse attacks character and self; neglect fails to nourish it in important ways. Challenge, when it occurs in the context of supportive relationships, can induce the growth of character and an enhanced sense of self. Some years ago, the following anonymous homily was posted in a cabin at a church camp. Despite its limitations as literature, it makes a pertinent statement:

Strong Words

Have you learned lessons only
from those who admired you
and were tender with you
and stood aside for you?

Have you not learned great lessons
from those who reject you and
brace themselves against you, or
who treat you with contempt, or
dispute the passage with you?

We should not protect children from growth-inducing challenges—things should not always be "nice." There's more to life than smiling faces with "have a good day" printed on them. That's not our goal here, of course. What we seek is a good society, one in which the institutional sources of psychological maltreatment are dismantled and replaced with justice and a humanly and environmentally sane and sustainable society.

The definition of maltreatment we presented earlier incorporates both community standards and scientific/professional expertise as criteria for judging the appropriateness and correctness of intervention on behalf of children (Garbarino & Gilliam, 1980). To fulfill the mission of pioneering advances in child welfare, we need to adopt broad definitions that we can justify on scientific grounds, and then use these definitions as a bargaining position in interactions with policy makers, with other practitioners, and with the general public. We view such a course as the engine of progress and consequently, do not see as threatening, short-term compromises that move steadily in the direction of greater protection of children, based on increasingly high standards of care, most notably within the family and the school.

Our second core question is this: How do we assess the processes and consequences of psychological maltreatment? This issue again reveals the tension between the researcher and practitioner, on the one hand, and the helper and the legal system on the other. The standards of evidence for all four groups differ. The methods available differ as well. Can we find a resolution? We conclude that the practitioner will rarely, if

ever, be able to use the kind of research orientation and techniques favored by the researcher; the cost per family is prohibitive, as is the investment of time. Likewise, the level of certainty needed to permit the delivery of services is not the same as that required for criminal prosecution or most other court-related procedures. This is a long-standing issue with regard to all forms of maltreatment, including physical abuse (is the injury inflicted?) and sexual abuse (can we believe the child's story?). In the case of psychological maltreatment, we must add the more subtle issues of interpretation to the simpler yet challenging task of documenting events.

Can we manage this? In our view, such a goal requires multiple sources of information and access to families. We see the need for some enduring intimate ties between families and the formal support systems of the community. The home health visitor program may provide a model for such relationships. When the home health visitor (perhaps a volunteer, likely to be a paraprofessional) establishes a relationship with a family during pregnancy and continues it postnatally through childhood, he or she becomes a source of information flow both into and from the family. We need such information to flow both ways to properly prevent psychological maltreatment. There are no two ways around it. We will not get very far simply looking for effects, if we do not have the ability to correlate those effects with causes in the interactional experience of children. We will not have that ability without enduring relationships such as those generated by home health visitors.

Our third question is this: How do we design and implement successful, cost-effective interventions which will not alienate those targeted for service? Here we face the psychosocial analog to the "uncertainty principle" in physics. Recall that the uncertainty principle asserts that we cannot simultaneously assess the position and direction of an electron because the very act of measurement disturbs and influences the electron. Similarly, we cannot overtly intervene in the family with any power without the process of intervention itself influencing events in the family—perhaps independently of the desired goals of the intervention, perhaps in contradiction of those goals. How then do we proceed? We think the logical course of action is to move along several lines at once, to adopt a course of multiple and converging "mini-interventions" (Belsky

& Vondra, 1985). The first is to do more to enhance the potential and actual connections between formal human services and the informal human services of the communities in which we seek to help (e.g., friends, neighbors, relatives, coworkers, church congregations; Whittaker & Garbarino, 1983). This would permit us to have the kind of multiple access to families we need. The second is to locate opportunities to enhance psychological functioning and prevent psychological maltreatment. These opportunities are seized most cost-effectively when they involve institutional policies and practices that structure and promote positive social interaction: those that can elicit counterforces to psychological maltreatment, reduce precipitating stresses, generate patterns of support, and generally suppress maltreatment and reinforce nonmaltreating patterns of interaction between children and their caregivers (Garbarino, 1982). To appreciate the range of opportunities for doing this we need to maintain an ecological perspective on human development, one that offers a map of social experience and thus provides the structure for our efforts to cope with the antecedents of psychological maltreatment, to divert situational forces that precipitate it, and to remediate its effects when we cannot prevent it from occurring (Garbarino, 1982).

REFERENCES

Ainsworth, M. D. S., & Bell, S. M. (1974). Mother–infant interaction and the development of competence. In K. J. Connolly & J. Bruner (Eds.), *The growth of competence*. London & New York: Academic Press.

Ainsworth, M. D. S., Blehar, M. C., Waters, E., & Wall, S. (1978). *Patterns of attachment*. Hillsdale, N.J.: Erlbaum.

Bandura, A. (1973). *Aggression: A social learning analysis*. Englewood Cliffs, NJ: Prentice-Hall.

Bandura, R., Ross, D., & Ross, S. (1963). Imitation of film-mediated aggressive models. *Journal of Abnormal and Social Psychology, 66*, 3–11.

Bateson, G. (1972). *Steps to an ecology of mind*. New York: Chandler.

Baumrind, D. (1971). Current patterns of parental authority. *Developmental Psychology Monographs, 4*(No. 1, Part 2).

Baumrind, D. (1972). Socialization and instrumental competence in young children. In W. W. Hartup (Ed.), *The young child: Reviews of*

research (Vol. 2). Washington, DC: National Association for Education of Young Children.

Belsky, J. (1984). The determinants of parenting: A process model. *Child Development, 55*, 83–96.

Belsky, J., Gilstrap, B., & Rovine, M. (1984). Stability and change in mother–infant and father–infant interaction in a family setting: One, three, and nine months. *Child Development, 55*, 692–705.

Belsky, J., & Vondra, J. (1985). Characteristics, consequences, and determinants of parenting. In L. L'Abate (Ed.), *Handbook of family psychology and therapy*. Homewood, IL: Dorsey Press.

Bronfenbrenner, U. (1979). *The ecology of human development: Experiments by nature and design*. Cambridge: Harvard University Press.

Bronfenbrenner, U., & Crouter, A. C. (1982). Work and family through time and space. In C. Hayes & S. Kamerman (Eds.), *Families that work: Children in a changing world*. Washington, DC: National Academy of Sciences.

Bronson, W. (1966). Early antecedents of emotional expressiveness and reactivity control. *Child Development, 37*, 793–810.

Bullard, D. M., Glaser, H. H., Hagarty, M. C., & Pivchik, E. C. (1967). Failure to thrive in the "neglected" child. *American Journal of Orthopsychiatry, 37*(1), 680–690.

Burgdorff, K. (1980). *Recognition and reporting of child maltreatment: Findings from the National Study of the Incidence and Severity of Child Abuse and Neglect*. Prepared for the National Center on Child Abuse and Neglect, Washington, DC, December.

Burgess, R., & Conger, R. (1977). Family interaction patterns related to child abuse and neglect. *Child Abuse and Neglect, 1*, 269–278.

Coopersmith, S. (1967). *The antecedents of self-esteem*. San Francisco: W. H. Freeman.

DeFrancis, V. (1969). *Protecting the child victim of sex crimes committed by adults*. Denver: American Humane Association.

Densen-Gerber, J., & Hutchinson, S. F. (1979). Sexual and commercial exploitation of children: Legislative responses and treatment challenges. *Child Abuse and Neglect, 3*, 61–66.

Elder, G. H. (1974). *Children of the Great Depression*. Chicago: University of Chicago Press.

Emery, R. E. (1982). Marital turmoil: Interparental conflict and the children of discord and divorce. *Psychological Bulletin, 92*, 310–330.

Eron, L. D. (1963). Relationship of TV viewing habits and aggressive behavior in children. *Journal of Abnormal and Social Psychology, 64*, 193–196.

Finkelhor, D. (1979). *Sexually victimized children*. New York: Free Press.

Freud, A., & Dann, S. (1951). An experiment in

group upbringing. In *The psychoanalytic study of the child* (Vol. VI, pp. 127–168). New York: International Universities.

Garbarino, J. (1980). Latchkey children. *Vital Issues, 30*(3), 1–4.

Garbarino, J. (1982). *Children and families in the social environment*. New York: Aldine.

Garbarino, J., & Ebata, A. (1983). On the significance of ethnic and cultural differences in child maltreatment. *Journal of Marriage and the Family, 45*, 773–783.

Garbarino, J., & Gilliam, G. (1980). *Understanding abusive families*. Lexington, MA: Lexington Books.

Gardner, L. I. (1972). Deprivation dwarfism. *Scientific American, 227*(1), 76–82.

Garmezy, N. (1983). Resilience to the development of psychological disorders. Colloquium presented at The Pennsylvania State University, April, 1983.

Gil, D. G. (1970). *Violence against children: Physical child abuse in the United States*. Cambridge, MA: Harvard University Press.

Goldstein, J., Freud, A., & Solnit, A. J. (1973). *Beyond the best interests of the child*. New York: The Free Press.

Goldstein, J., Freud, A., & Solnit, A. J. (1979). *Before the best interests of the child*. New York: The Free Press.

Heskin, K. (1980). *Northern Ireland: A psychological analysis*. New York: Basic Books.

Hetherington, E. M. (1980). Children and divorce. In R. Henderson (Ed.), *Parent–child interaction: Theory, research, and prospect*. New York: Academic Press.

Hetherington, E. M. (1983). Divorce and changing familial configurations: What effects might they have on children and how can they be ameliorated? Discussion session at the Biennial Meeting of the Society for Research in Child Development, Detroit, Michigan, April, 1983.

Kadushin, A., & Martin, J. A. (1981). *Child abuse: An interactional event*. New York: Columbia University Press.

Kaufman, I., Puck, A. L., & Tagiuri, C. K. (1954). The family constellation and overt incestuous relations between father and daughter. *American Journal of Orthopsychiatry, 24*, 266–277.

Kaus, C. R., & Garbarino, J. (1984). Sexuality and intimacy. In J. Garbarino (Ed.), *Adolescent development: An ecological perspective*. Columbus, OH: Charles E. Merrill.

Lefkowitz, M. M., Eron, L. D., Walder, L. O., & Huesmann, L. R. (1972). Television violence and child aggression: A follow-up study. In G. A. Comstock & E. A. Rubinstein (Eds.), *Television and social behavior, Vol. III: Television and adolescent aggressiveness* (pp. 35–135.) Washington, DC: U.S. Government Printing Office.

Leifer, A. D., & Roberts, D. F. (1972). Children's responses to television violence. In J. P. Murray, E. A. Rubinstein, & G. A. Comstock (Eds.), *Television and social behavior, Vol. II: Television and social learning* (pp. 43–180). Washington, DC: U.S. Government Printing Office.

Lewin, K. (1951). *Field theory in social science*. New York: Harper.

Long, T. J., & Long, L (1982). *Latchkey children: The child's view of self-care*. Unpublished manuscript, Loyola College.

Lourie, I., & Stefano, L. (1978). On defining emotional abuse. Child abuse and neglect: Issues in innovation and implementation. *Proceedings of the Second Annual National Conference on Child Abuse and Neglect*. Washington DC: Government Printing Office.

McCandless, B. R. (1967). *Children: Behavior and development* (2nd ed.). New York: Holt, Rinehart & Winston.

McCoy, R., & Koocher, G. P. (1976). Needed: A public policy for psychotropic drug use with children. In G. P. Koocher (Ed.), *Children's rights and the mental health professions*. New York: John Wiley & Sons.

National Center on Child Abuse and Neglect (1978). *Interdisciplinary glossary on child abuse and neglect*. Washington, DC: Department of Health, Education, and Welfare. (OHDS 78-30137)

Neill, A. S. (1960). *Summerhill*. New York: Hart.

Patterson, G. R. (1978). Mothers: The unacknowledged victims. In T. H. Stevens & R. U. Mathews (Eds.), *Mother–child, father–child relations*. Washington, DC: National Association for the Education of Young Children.

Patterson, G. R. (1979). A performance theory for coercive family interaction. In R. B. Cairns (Ed.), *The analysis of social interactions: Methods, issues, and illustrations*. Hillsdale, NJ: Erlbaum.

Polansky, N., Chalmers, M., Butten-Wieser, E. & Williams, D. (1979). The isolation of the neglectful family. *American Journal of Orthopsychiatry, 49*, 149–152.

Potok, C. (1967). *The chosen*. Greenwich, CT: Fawcett.

Powell, G. F., Brasel, J. A., & Blizzard, R. M. (1967). Emotional deprivation and growth retardation simulating idiopathic hypopituitorism. *New England Journal of Medicine, 276*(23), 1271–1278.

Price, G. (1977). *Factors influencing reciprocity in early mother–infant interaction*. Paper presented at the Biennial Meeting of the Society for Research in Child Development, New Orleans, March, 1977.

Reveron, D. (1982, April). Nuclear war: A make-believe world. *APA Monitor*, p. 3ff.

Robins, L. N. (1979). Follow-up studies. In H. C. Quay & J. S. Werry (Eds.), *Psychopathological disorders of childhood* (2nd ed.). New York: Wiley.

Rohner, R. (1975). *They love me, they love me not.* New Haven, CT: HRAF Press.

Rohner, R. P., & Rohner, E. C. (1980). Antecedents and consequences of parental rejection: A theory of emotional abuse. *Child Abuse and Neglect, 4*(3), 189–198.

Rosenblatt, R. (1982, January) Children of war. *Time*, p. 32ff.

Rosenblatt, R. (1983). *Children of war.* New York: Doubleday.

Rutter, M. (1971). Parent–child separation: Psychological effects on the children. *Journal of Child Psychology and Psychiatry, 12*, 233–260.

Seligman, M. E. P. (1975). *Helplessness.* San Francisco: W. H. Freeman.

Seligman, M. E. P., Maier, S. F., & Solomon, R. L. (1971). Unpredictable and uncontrollable aversive events. In F. R. Brush (Ed.), *Aversive conditioning and learning.* New York: Academic Press.

Spitz, R. (1945). Hospitalism: An inquiry into the genesis of psychiatric conditions in early childhood. *The Psychoanalytic Study of the Child, 1*, 53–74.

Spitz, R. (1946). Hospitalism: A follow-up report. *The Psychoanalytic Study of the Child, 2*, 113–117.

Sroufe, L. A. (1983). Infant–caregiver attachment and patterns of adaptation in preschool: The roots of maladaptation and competence. In M. Perlmutter (Ed.), *Minnesota Symposia in Child Psychology* (Vol. 16, pp. 41–83). Hillsdale, NJ: Lawrence Erlbaum.

Stewart, M. A. (1976). Treating problem children with drugs: Ethical issues. In G. P. Koocher (Ed.), *Children's rights and the mental health professions.* New York: John Wiley & Sons.

Tulkin, S., & Covitz, F. (1975). *Mother–infant interactions and intellectual functioning at age six.* Paper presented at the Biennial Meeting of the Society for Research in Child Development, Denver, April, 1975.

Van Hasselt, V. B., Hersen, M., Whitehill, M. B., & Bellack, A. S. (1979). Social-skill assessment and training for children: An evaluative review. *Behavior Research and Therapy, 17*, 413–437.

Wachs, T. (1976). Utilization of a Piagetian approach in the investigation of early experience effects: A research strategy and some illustrative data. *Merrill-Palmer Quarterly, 22*, 11–30.

Wallerstein, J. S., & Kelly, J. B. (1975). The effects of parental divorce: Experiences of the preschool child. *Journal of the American Academy of Child Psychiatry, 14*, 600–616.

Waters, E., Wippman, J., & Sroufe, L. (1979). Attachment, positive affect, and competence in the peer group: Two studies in construct validation. *Child Development, 50*, 821–829.

West, D. J. (1969). *Present conduct and future delinquency.* First Report of the Cambridge Study in Delinquent Development. New York: International Universities Press.

West, D. J. (1973). *Who becomes delinquent?* Second Report of the Cambridge Study in Delinquent Development. London: Heinemann Educational.

Whittaker, J., Garbarino, J., & associates (1983). *Social support networks in the human services.* New York: Aldine.

3

Psychological Maltreatment: The Core Component of Child Abuse

Elizabeth L. Navarre

In professional literature, the terms psychological abuse, emotional abuse and mental cruelty have been used interchangeably and without clear definition. The term *mental cruelty* as used in law has been a residual category and there has been an advantage in preserving its elasticity for this purpose. Perhaps because physical and sexual forms of abuse were defined first, psychological abuse has also tended to be used as a residual category (i.e., abuse that is not within the definitions of physical or sexual is "psychological"). A much more specific definition is necessary if psychological abuse is to be the subject of legislation, research, prevention, or judicial or therapeutic intervention. A definition that is sufficiently precise to sustain demonstration and measurement on the one hand and foster the development of an integrative theory on the other hand is needed. This chapter will attempt to provide a beginning.

DEFINING ABUSE

If parental behaviors that are aversive to child development in some degree were placed upon a continuum, the term abuse implies actions or outcomes that tend toward the more negative and severe end of that continuum. Before attempting to deal with the boundaries of "psychological" it is necessary to consider some of the questions that have confused efforts to define "abuse," whether it be physical, sexual, or psychological. Attempts to define such terms as

abuse, cruelty, assault, and so on have centered upon some combination of three dimensions—action, outcome, and intent.

Action

It is difficult to make lists of potentially aversive actions because the content and length of such lists are so varied. In general, an act is defined as aversive on the basis of the probability of an aversive outcome. Just as driving while under the influence of alcohol or drugs is forbidden because of the high probability of killing or maiming one's self or others, some actions can be shown to have a high probability of damaging children, and, in many cases, adults as well. Society does not have to wait until the drunken driver has damaged others before it may intervene. In the same way, society should be able to intervene without proving that another human being has already been harmed. Since the results of psychological or emotional damage are more difficult to observe than those of physical damage and, like some physical damage, may not be identifiable until long after the fact, research should be directed to identifying the probabilities of damage resulting from specific actions.

If abusive actions and outcomes are placed upon a continuum ranging from mildly aversive to fatal; "cruelty," "abuse," or "maltreatment" may be presumed to refer to the more aversive end of that continuum causing pain, suffering, and possibly irreversible damage. The typology subsumed under these headings must recognize the interacting dimensions of intensity, frequency, duration, context, and subjective meaning. Within each dimension, it is very difficult to define the dividing line between that which is tolerable or acceptable to the individual, the community, or the culture, and that which will not be tolerated. Both legal and public battles over definitions of abuse or maltreatment in recent years have raged over the "how much" question. Is pain and humiliation an effective way to control behavior and socialize either children or adults? If so, how much pain and/or humiliation is necessary? At what point does this become abusive? How many stitches are necessary for a family battle to become a court case? How much blood or how many broken bones differentiate "normal" punishment from maltreatment? If these questions have been difficult to answer in terms of physical abuse, how can they be addressed in terms of psychological attack, of cognitive or emotional damage that cannot be photographed or X-rayed, or even evaluated, in some cases, except in terms of very long-range outcomes? The task of resolving these questions is not simplified by attempting to define the continuum as a dichotomy by (a) denying the possible negative effects to be found even at the less severe end of the continuum, or (b) failing to subject to careful study the positive values popularly ascribed to milder forms of aversive behavior.

Logically, one would assume that if most actions and/or outcomes could be placed on a continuum ranging from mild to severe, then a severe action would lead to a severe outcome; however, frequent and/or repetitive mild acts could also lead to a severe outcome. In both cases, one would expect outcomes to be modified by other conditions, either positive or negative, that constitute the entire milieu. A few widely spaced, mildly aversive acts in an otherwise positive and supportive milieu may not have a noticeably aversive outcome. Indeed, the acts may be identified as positive because the specific negative effect is masked by the total effects of the positive situation. However, even mildly abusive acts may have strong negative consequences if there are few or no positive factors to dilute or offset them. It is unfortunate that so little research has been done in this area for it becomes difficult to assess the effect of any given factor accurately without a concept of varying strength of outcome related to the intensity, the duration, and the frequency of the stimulus and upon the

interaction of other system factors as catalysts or inhibitors. With the understanding that I will assume that all factors discussed later in this paper exist and interact upon the continuum just described, I shall attempt to define those elements that may constitute mental cruelty, psychological abuse, or psychological maltreatment rather than become lost in questions of degree.

Outcomes

Much attention has been paid to research on outcomes of physical abuse, with some attention to outcomes on sexual abuse. Even on these more readily definable situations, however, control of major intervening factors such as intensity and duration of the abuse, intent, and other factors which might intensify or mitigate long-term outcomes has been inadequate and research has not revealed enough information about the precise relationships among the variables to allow strong prediction. Numerous questions of definition and measurement remain. In dealing with children, especially, the outcome is relative to the age and condition of the child as well as to the nature of the act. The blow that bruises an adolescent may kill an infant. Is the blow more cruel to the infant than to the adolescent? Developmental theory suggests that children may be more vulnerable to certain types of negative experiences at one developmental stage than at another. Studies of child abuse, however, indicate that it tends to continue over a period of years and will probably escalate with time. Does an accumulation of negative experiences over several developmental periods predict differing outcomes or only more severe outcomes? Does the negative experience at one stage create conditions affecting the probability of negative experiences at a later stage? Research necessary to establish the relationship between a potentially aversive act and a negative outcome must provide adequate identification of differential physical, mental, and developmental vulnerabilities over the period of time covered by the maltreatment.

Both studies of outcomes of physical and/ or sexual abuse, and theories being developed around psychological abuse, strongly suggest that the degree of abuse (or negative consequences) of a given action may also be related to the subjective meaning that action has for the victim. It could be postulated, for example, that individuals whose self-esteem has been severely damaged by past abuse might make themselves increasingly vulnerable to continued damage by interpreting the actions of others as rejecting when they were not so intended and would not be so evaluated by objective observers. Such learned oversensitivity could also lead to defensive postures that would make the individual less acceptable to others and create a self-fulfilling prophecy. It is also possible that some individuals have a greater degree of resistance to stress than others, although, on a psychological level, it is difficult to determine whether the greater resistance is innate, conditioned or due to modifying factors in the environment.

Intent

Of the three dimensions, intent is the most difficult to measure objectively or demonstrate legally. Intent is not always clear even to the actor. Furthermore, even if it could be measured with some precision, intent is not a necessary or sufficient predictor of either benign or aversive outcomes. Many abusive acts are perpetrated with the best of intentions but have severely aversive outcomes because of the following factors:

1. The intensity and/or duration of the act is grossly out of proportion to the intended outcome.
2. The actor's understanding of the victim's needs or behavior is inaccurate and inappropriate, leading to overreaction in an attempt to control the perceived behavior.
3. The actor has a distorted view of reality that interferes with the actor's ability to predict the outcomes of his or her own actions accurately or to recognize his or her own involvement in the situation from which the action arises.
4. The actor's perceptions of both the interaction taking place and the intensity of the actor's own responses are distorted by personal emotional needs.
5. The abusive act is so common and acceptable in the culture or the community that the probability of a negative outcome is neither recognized nor believed.

In other cases, the adult and the child may be so enmeshed in a self-perpetuating pattern of interaction that the adult is incapable of perceiving or responding to some or many of the child's needs. These may be acts of omission more often than commission and labeled "neglect" rather

than "abuse," but the child is still damaged. An act of omission that is deliberate may be seen as equal to an act of commission. Again, the difficulty of establishing intent confuses the effort to define abuse.

Finally, the environment may be the source of the abuse. Children growing up in the center of a battlefield, as they are in Lebanon and other places in the world; children of oppressed groups growing up in the hostility of the external environment even when the intimate environment is supportive; and children who because of sex or age are punished or criticized for behavior or emotions that are approved or rewarded for others in the same personal environment may all exhibit forms of psychological damage to be discussed at a later point in this chapter.

Questions about the ultimate source of an abusive pattern, possible identification of the person or persons who bear responsibility, the degree of responsibility, the capacity of the abuser to perceive the needs of another or to alter their own responses represent important and complex facets of abusive situations. The very complexity of these questions suggests that they be addressed separately from the initial definition of abuse. However, a definition of abuse must exclude damage that results from accidental or random events (a stroke of lightning, a skidding bicycle, a remark not intended to be overheard, etc.). Rather, abuse is damage that arises from patterned behavior and is therefore subject to prediction and prevention. Patterning may arise without conscious planning from common interactions at any system level. Traffic patterns will be established in a community with or without a planning committee. Institutions have many carefully planned rules and regulations and numerous informal structures and patterns that are as powerful as the formal rules. However it may develop, for communities, organizations, families, or individuals, the pattern of behavior can be observed, and its continuance predicted and, hopefully, altered in positive directions when necessary.

At this point, then, abuse is defined as (a) damage to the individual's physical or psychological well-being, normal functioning, or potential development that is (b) nonaccidental or nonrandom and the result of (c) patterned behavior at some level.

Definitions are developed to serve a purpose. The concern for the safety of children who are at great risk has led to emphasis on definitions of the most aversive end of the continuum of any given action or outcome. This is perfectly appropriate for definitions that may underlie serious action by the state to punish the abusers or put the child into protective custody. No one would wish such action to be taken without clear necessity. If, on the other hand, the intent is not to punish abusers but to give each child the most positive development that can be provided, attention must be paid to the other end of the continuum. Even the "least aversive" end of the continuum does not imply a positive effect upon the child. The use of such emotional words as "abuse," "mental cruelty," "terrorizing," "corrupting," and so forth makes us all anxious that we do not define abusive actions in such a way that all child-rearing patterns are included. This leads to narrow definitions of abuse, but it also leads to a reluctance to recognize that a whole category of actions may need to be reevaluated, not in terms of how much is allowed, but in terms of what is going to contribute to the positive development of the child. The public acceptance of forms of physical punishment that are not "too severe," for example, is perceived as tacit encouragement by those whose questionable judgment leads them into actions that the public would consider abusive. It may also lead to the substitution of punishment for the positive discipline that all children need to learn. While I will continue to discuss the more aversive actions and outcomes, it is most important that the community understand that an action which is not severe enough to be labeled abuse is not necessarily desirable in human interaction, and especially in child rearing. Failure to meet the child's psychological and socialization needs may be one of the categories of psychological abuse. Finally, the question of the effect upon the community itself must be considered. Does the acceptance of actions at the milder end of the continuum make it more difficult to draw the line between what is or is not abusive? Does the acceptance of some forms of physical, sexual, or psychological violence increase the probability of acceptance of different or more severe forms of violence because it is difficult to draw the line between that which is acceptable and that which is only one step beyond?

The special concern for the child as a victim of abuse stems from (a) the greater defenselessness of the child and (b) the long-term consequences of impairment at the earlier stages of human development, possibly including impairment of the capacity for continued positive development. However, adults may be and often are targets of all kinds of abuse and may suffer consequences similar to those suffered by children. Adults also find themselves in situations from which escape is difficult, painful, or potentially fatal. Failing to recognize and to resolve problems of abuse of adults may intensify the risk of damage for abused children in four ways. (a) The child is deprived of the full protection of one of the adults upon whom the child depends if that protector is being abused. (b) The child has a model of adult life in which the adult is unable to protect herself or himself from abuse. (c) Children who witness one parent abusing the other are more likely, as adults, to exhibit violence toward the spouse, and spouses who exhibit marital violence are also more likely to abuse their children (Straus, Gelles, & Steinmetz, 1980, pp. 100–115). (d) Abuse of older children may receive less attention because "they are almost adults." Statistics indicate that adolescents have a higher incidence of abuse and neglect than any other age group. The National Study found adolescents overrepresented at every level of injury or impairment (National Center on Child Abuse and Neglect, 1980, pp. 6, 7).

DEFINING PSYCHOLOGICAL ABUSE

Rather than accept the implications of residual categorization (i.e., that psychological abuse is any abusive act that does not involve physical contact or leave observable bodily scars) let us explore the implications of an independent identification of psychological abuse as assaults upon the bases necessary to the cognitive, emotional, or interactive functioning and development of the individual.

A number of authors have attempted to list actions that are subsumed within the category of psychological abuse. However, without a theoretical formulation to provide a common structure it is not surprising that the lists are not consistent. The National Study of the Incidence and Severity of Child Abuse and Neglect (National Center on Child Abuse and Neglect, 1980) suggests scapegoating, belittling, denigrating, or other overly hostile treatment including threats of sexual or physical assault, overworking, close confinement, or the withholding of food, sleep or shelter as a form of punishment. Mayhall and Norgard (1983, p. 159) define emotional abuse as penalizing the child for positive normal behavior, discouraging the child from bonding with the caretaker, penalizing the child for showing self-esteem, and penalizing the child for using interpersonal skills that will be needed for interaction in the world outside the family. Garbarino and Vondra (chapter 2) list rejection, scapegoating, double bind, double jeopardy, and unreasonable expectations. Conversations with psychiatrists, psychologists, and social workers who are involved in treatment of abused children invariably emphasize damage to the child's self-esteem and sense of confidence, provision of an unpredictable and insecure environment or one that is so interpreted to the child, placement of blame for all occurrences upon the child, and the pain, fear, and downgrading that result from physical or sexual assault. The International Conference on Psychological Abuse of Children and Youth, which set the stage for the development of this book, produced a generic definition of psychological maltreatment (see chapter 1) which includes acts of rejecting, terrorizing, isolating, exploiting and missocializing. Through the work of the Office for the Study of the Psychological Rights of the Child (Indiana University), following the conference, that list was modified slightly. "Missocializing" was changed to "corrupting," and "denying emotional responsiveness" was added.

Inspection of these lists suggests an underlying pattern in which actions are related to possible outcomes that affect the importance of cognitive, emotional and interactional bases of the individual perception of the self in relation to others and to the demands of life. Whether delivered through physical, verbal or interactional vehicles, the messages of psychological abuse seem to be the same. The assault is not (or not only) upon the physical body but upon the following:

1. The individual's perception of the self as valuable.
2. The individual's perception of the self as being valued or potentially valued by others.
3. The individual's perception of the self as competent or potentially competent to perform necessary life tasks.
4. The individual's perception that other people and the general environment are responsive to the self.
5. The individual's perception that the world is beneficent or neutral rather than innately hostile.

6. The individual's ability to learn from and adjust to the environment through producing fear of interaction with the environment, through which learning might take place, or through producing a level of fear or pain that affects the ability to focus attention upon problem solving.
7. The ability to identify emotions of the self and others accurately, and the development of appropriate and differentiated responses to those emotions.
8. The ability to perceive and respond positively to the desires and needs of others.
9. The ability to form and maintain relationships through which learning may take place.

If this formulation is accurate, studies of the outcomes of abuse should show evidence of damage in the areas of cognitive and emotional development and/or functioning, self-denigration and destructive behaviors, lack of effective interaction skills and/or ineffective or self-defeating patterns of interaction, and an inability to maintain close long-term relationships.

Studies of the outcomes of abuse that do not contain physical or sexual abuse components are difficult to locate. Straus found a direct link between physical and verbal abuse: "People who hurt another family member verbally are also the ones most likely to hurt them physically" (Straus, 1980, p. 94). Bateson's studies of "double-bind" situations (1972) in which contradictory requirements create engineered failure for the child, and the studies of Seligman, Maier, and Solomon (1971) of laboratory animals who have no escape from noxious stimuli which cannot be controlled or avoided by their own responses, throw considerable light upon the possible dynamics of situations which may constitute a risk to mental well-being with or without the presence of physiological assault. Case histories and interviews with clinicians indicate, for both the abused and the abusers, a high incidence of low self-esteem frequently accompanied by perceptions that many elements of life are uncontrollable (or controllable only with violence) and that the world is generally hostile/aversive.

The Minnesota Mother–Child Interaction Project (Egeland & Erickson, chapter 8 in this volume) is the only longitudinal study known to the author that carefully divides its sample on the basis of types of abuse and neglect and provides an appropriate control group. The earliest subjects of this study are just now reaching school age. Within each maltreatment group, there is a division between those in which physical maltreatment is also present and those in which it is not. Current findings indicate differentiated relationships between specific actions and their outcomes. The samples of hostile/verbal abuse groups and psychologically unavailable groups are particularly interesting since no physical abuse has occurred in either group. Children of hostile/verbally abusive mothers were very similar to physically abused children, angry and noncompliant, while children with psychologically unavailable mothers were the most devastated. For the latter group, the study's authors state, "The sharp decline in the intellectual functioning of children, their attachment disturbances and subsequent lack of social/emotional competence in a variety of situations is a cause for great concern. The consequences of this form of maltreatment are particularly disturbing when considered in light of the fact that this is probably the least likely pattern of maltreatment to be detected" (Egeland & Erickson, chapter 8 in this volume). Additionally, it may be noted that these forms of psychological maltreatment may be relatively undetected among other family structures and other economic levels of society. Further research could clarify the extent to which these forms of maltreatment may fit with culturally accepted patterns of higher economic groups as well as delineate the effects of psychologically unavailable or hostile/verbally abusive fathers or other family members. It will also be interesting to see, as the study sample grows older, whether some of these children manage to locate significant others who are psychologically available to them. Some of the literature on children who have been labeled survivors suggests this as a possibility (Segal & Yahraes, 1979; Smith & Bohnstedt, 1981).

The paucity of research relating action to psychological outcome is partially due to the emphasis on physical trauma as the only provable type of abuse and partially to the difficulty of operationalizing and measuring either the acts or the outcomes in the absence of physical evidence. A third factor, however, may be the difficulty of separating the effects of physical and nonphysical assault conceptually. As we learn more about the mind, the body, the social environment, and their interaction, it becomes more and more clear that physical, psychological, and social survival are different faces of the same struggle. Severe risk to any of the three may bring about similar consequences for the individual.

DYNAMICS OF PSYCHOLOGICAL ABUSE

In this final section of the chapter, the objective is to develop hypothetical relationships between the variables established previously, which may be subjected to empirical investigation, and to clarify the relationships between abusive actions and potentially damaging outcomes.

Psychological Effects of Pain or Fear

Physical pain and bodily trauma are experienced mentally as well as physically. Intense or prolonged pain may produce such shock that cognitive functioning is reduced or disoriented (chapter 4, p. 59). The primal fear for bodily safety may be aroused, affecting both reactions and decisions. Even at lower levels of intensity, repetition and/or long-term experience of pain is physically exhausting and may induce a degree of attention to management or prevention of the repetition of pain that reduces the amount of attention available for investment in other necessary activities. This could affect learning activities of any kind as well as the initiation or maintenance of relationships. If intensity, duration, and frequency are all relatively high, fear of pain may continue to have these effects even when the physical source of the pain is absent or inactive. A little intimidation goes a long way. Since the fear may persist beyond the actual experience of pain, is it possible that the psychological damage could continue to mount from continued threat even in the absence of continued physical abuse? This form of intimidation may also explain the previously quoted findings (Straus, Gelles, & Steinmetz, 1980) that observance of the abuse of parents or siblings may have effects similar to the actual experience of abuse.

When pain (punishment) is associated with normal exploration of alternatives, with accidental circumstances, or is applied unpredictably without reference to the child's behavior or intent, the experience may set up mental barriers to or avoidance of new experiences and thus impair potential learning (Martin, 1980).

Psychological abuse may result from direct psychological assault upon cognitive, emotional, or interactional well-being or from the psychological effects of physical or sexual abuse. If so, similar psychological outcomes should be observed among children who have been physically or sexually abused. Since these areas have been studied more extensively, more evidence is available.

As a side note, this formulation raises questions for research. If several layers of abuse may exist simultaneously, is it necessary to recognize the relative intensities of the components and their interaction in order to measure accurately the relationship between actions and outcomes? If an incident involves physical, sexual, and psychological abuse, how does one measure the intensities? Answers to these questions may provide explanations for inconsistencies between observed levels of abuse and seemingly inconsistent outcomes.

Studies of physically or sexually abused children indicate, in comparison to control groups, a greater probability of impairment of cognitive functioning or development (Cohn, 1979; Dietrich, 1977; Elmer & Gregg, 1967; Johnson & Morse, 1968; Martin, 1972, 1976). Evidence of specific cognitive impairments include delayed language development (Blager, 1978; Blager & Martin, 1976; Oates, Davis, Ryan, & Stewart, 1978), reading disability (Hufton & Oates, 1977), and lower performance in tests of reasoning, hearing and speech, and personal–social skills (Van Staden, 1978). There is some evidence that these deficits may be lessened if the abusive situation is resolved and intensive remedial intervention is available, though the recovery may not be complete (Cohn, 1979; Kent, 1976; Martin, 1976). This suggests that genetic deficiency was not the primary causal factor of either the abuse or the impairment. In addition to cognitive deficits, abused children tend to exhibit behavioral, disciplinary, and school-attendance problems (Smith & Bohnstedt, 1981) and poor peer relations (Roberts, Lynch, & Duff, 1978).

Self-abusive behavior, including suicide, was found to be related to abuse even among very young children. Green (1968, 1978) found that 8.3% of abused children with a mean age of 8.5 years had attempted suicide and 20% exhibited other forms of self-mutilation. Silbert's Delancey Street Study (1982) found that almost two-thirds of the sample of prostitutes were victims of sexual abuse, mostly within their own home or primary group, from ages 3 to 16. Seventy-eight percent of the sample had started prostitution before reaching their majority. Ninety-eight percent were runaways before entering prostitution. Runaway centers suggest that a large number of runaways have been victimized physically or sexually or both within the family from which they ran. Since psychological abuse was not investigated, there are no statistics on the number of runaways whose abuse was on a psychological or emotional level only. Although economic necessity may place prostitution or crime among the few alternatives available for survival when the laws restrict freedom of choice and employment opportunities for those under 18, the specific choices also seem to be related to the child's own perception of his or her own self-esteem and perception of capability. As one teen-age girl said to her caseworker, "If I don't do this, there's nothing I can do."

Although more definitive work is needed, a preponderance of studies from several disciplines provide evidence that violence leads to violence. Kent (1976) and Reidy (1977) found a higher incidence of aggression in abused children as compared to neglected children or a normal control group. Numerous studies have found that a substantial proportion of people who commit violent crimes spent their childhood in abusive homes or violent situations (Cyriaque, 1982; Duncan, Frasier, Litin, Johnson, & Barron, 1958; Easson & Steinhelber, 1961; Lewis, Shanok, Pincus, & Glaser, 1979; Wolfgang, 1981). As stated previously, both studies and extensive practice experience suggest that a background of being abused as a child or witnessing violence directed by one family member to another leads to a higher probability of being an abusive parent, spouse, or sibling (Hunter, Kilstrom, Kraybill, & Loda, 1978; Straus, Gelles, & Steinmetz, 1980). A study done by the author's "Family Violence" class, which analyzed family homicides reported in the newspapers over a 2-year period found that the largest single group to be adult siblings, a group seldom studied in this respect. Lewis, Shanok, Pincus, and Glaser (1979) and Straus, Gelles, and Steinmetz (1980) found evidence that violence between family members not only increases the probability of later violent behavior for the victim but also for other family members. Experiencing violence within the family group possibly constitutes psychological abuse for other family members as well as for those who are victimized.

Psychological Effects of Sensory Maltreatment

Sensory assault has not been seen as a separate category in abuse. It clearly belongs under the heading of physical abuse, yet there is often no physical evidence of maltreatment and long-term damage may not be immediately recognizable.

Nevertheless, it is important to recognize that some responses to forms of abuse that have been seen as wholly psychological may include some physiological responses to forms of sensory assault.

Information input that is too rapid, too intense, or too contradictory to be handled by normal sensory processing will be experienced as painful by the organism. In extreme degrees, such overload may cause mental confusion, denial of some portions of the input, or a temporary cessation of processing. The senses constitute major elements of the communication system. Since the brain not only experiences information but interprets, stores, and uses that information to interpret new input, distortions or disfunctions in sensory processing may have very long-term effects. In some circumstances, sensory assault may also cause strong fear reactions. The fear of falling and of sudden loud noises are among the earliest fears noted in normal human development. Sensory assault may frequently combine with other forms of abuse. Verbal abuse often combines loud, possibly sudden, or continuous noise with denigration, contradictory commands, and verbal hostility. Enduring noxious odors, forcing down nauseating or inedible substances, enduring constant interruption of sleep or not being allowed sleep that would allow the organism to renew itself are all actions that have been used abusively.

Conditions like these are a part of the daily living pattern for some people. Consider, for example, the central-city tenement with little or no protection from extremes of heat or cold, with plumbing that does not work, and with a radio that plays full blast 24 hours a day because tenements have thin walls and the noise affords a tenuous kind of privacy. The radio must be very loud to mask the children's yells, the jackhammer in the street and the radios of the other apartments that are also radiating decibels. Both children and adults may be subjected to a sensory assault that is also their only means of defense, an environmental double bind. In some cases, the whole family suffers from abuse from the environment; in others, one or more family members deliberately uses these methods in an attempt to control the behavior of other members. In the latter case, not only is no attempt made to help the child develop defenses, but any defenses the child may develop will probably be defined as defiance and efforts to achieve absolute control will be redoubled.

Sensory assault may block or distort the developmental process of differentiation between noxious and benign stimuli, causing the person to avoid, ignore, or misinterpret benign and necessary levels of similar stimuli, (e.g., the child who has become enured to yells as a response to any and all behavior may ignore the yell that would save its life). Sensory assault may establish a pattern of contradictory stimuli so that any response will have negative outcomes and normal stimulus/response patterns lead only to frustration.

Either of these possibilities may bring about or contribute to a state of cognitive confusion that will interfere with the child's ability to learn and may interfere with the ability to perceive or act upon either an opportunity or a danger. For these reasons, prolonged sensory assault may contribute to inappropriate actions which are negatively defined by both the person and the environment, increasing the perception that the person is incompetent, unacceptable, and disvalued.

Faced with inescapable pain or injury or an impossible decision, both animals and humans may tend to "turn off the senses" and freeze both action and awareness. Yet the denial or withdrawal from sensory perception is a danger in itself. When that denial becomes an established defense mechanism, future risk may be enhanced. A very common psychological defense used by young children who are being sexually abused is to pretend, even to themselves, that they are sleeping, thus avoiding the double bind of disobeying and rejecting a parent or older relative or consenting to acts of which they are consciously aware (Armstrong, 1978). For some individuals, the confusion between sleeping and waking continues and feeds their feelings of guilt for having such "dreams." The degree to which sensory assaults contribute to emotional disturbance and impairment of cognitive functioning needs to be investigated more thoroughly.

Psychological Effects of Negative or Distorted Perceptions of the Self and the World

While we have noted that, to paraphrase Marshall McLuhan, in physical and sensory forms of assault the medium also carries a message, in many forms of mental cruelty, the message itself is the instrument of assault. Whether the medium was overtly physiological, expressed verbally or via symbolic action, the content of the messages at this level may be very similar. Whatever the medium, the attack is upon the value of the unique qualities of the individual, upon the probability of being accepted and valued by significant others, upon the expectation of ultimately being competent to survive, and upon the perception of the environment as reasonably benign and predictable. Verbal denigration, humiliation, engineered failure, the projection of inescapable and unwarranted guilt, the many forms of rejection, penalizing the child for showing self-esteem, curiosity, or positive interactions with the world outside the family, and placing the burden of unrealistic and unreachable expectations upon the child may all be forms of psychological abuse.

Assault upon the valuation of the self probably describes the most common conception of psychological abuse. The individual's self-valuation is based partially upon a personal interpretation of life experiences and partially upon the individual's perception of how he is valued by others. The interaction of personal and external validation would be expected to approach a perfect correlation. However, some degree of independence is indicated by the ability of persons with a high personal valuation to withstand a good deal of denigration by others, while those with a low personal valuation may be sustained by high external valuation though they question its substance and view its maintenance as precarious.

Human beings have a tendency to live up or down to their perception of themselves. Value judgments such as "I am bad," "I am stupid," or "No one could like me" may become self-fulfilling prophecies. All of the many forms of rejection send a message of devaluation. The psychologically unavailable parent goes even farther. The message is not just that "I don't love you" or "I don't care what happens to you," but that "You don't really exist in my world." Physical abuse, sexual abuse, verbal downgrading, unjustified and hostile criticism, unearned blame, the many forms of active rejection, and inequitable treatment in relation to other family members all carry the same message of devaluation, which are particularly likely to be internalized when occurring within close personal relationships.

Personal valuation may also be negative due to the almost universal self-blaming reaction of victims of abuse. The abuse is seen as punishment and therefore the victim must be guilty of something. The abuse then becomes both personal and an external assault upon self-esteem.

Without a minimal sense of competence, an individual feels at the mercy of random and possibly hostile forces. An environment that is so restrictive, so demanding, or so protective that the child has no opportunity to experience mastery over some portion of the tasks and experiences of everyday life may impair the development of this sense of competence. If, on the other hand, there are no expectations and no support for trials of competence, the message to the child is the same: "Maybe you can't do anything." Restriction that is too rigid and total freedom from demands may have the same effect upon the child's development of mastery and increase the profound distrust of personal control and ability that is noted as an outcome of physical and sexual as well as psychological maltreatment.

Some children experience more violent attacks on their sense of competence. Expectations of behavior that are irrational or unreasonable in relation to the age or level of development of the child or children involved; demands of behavior that require resources or authority that are not available to the child or a level of judgment which the child has not reached or has had no opportunity to develop; and expectations that are in conflict with other expectations all place the child in a no-win situation. Failure is not only inevitable but engineered by the parent or other adult who programmed the situation. When physical punishment, verbal denigration, or angry rejection is the response to failure to meet expectations and the situation is repeated frequently, the child may develop an overwhelming sense of helplessness, incompetence, and a need to avoid the possibility of future failures. Such conditions could set up a behavior pattern likely to increase the probability of future failure experiences.

Psychological Effects of Inadequate or Destructive Relations

Human relationships are the primary vehicle for the formation of self-esteem, trust, and security for everyone. For children, the relationships within the family are the base for personal development, whether through modeling, teaching, internalization of discipline, or the desire to please people who are loved. Disruption of necessary relationships is often cited as a possible outcome of abuse, but the disruption may also become abusive in itself as well as a factor intensifying aversive outcomes. Most theoretical formulations agree with wisdom gained through professional practice in hypothesizing that the probability of long-term damage is multiplied when the child is in a primary, dependent, and long-term relationship with the abuser. Such a relationship not only increases the direct impact of the action, but also increases the probability (a) that the action will be repeated in continued association, possibly escalating with time; (b) that important sources of protection, self-definition, and socialization will be parties to the aversive actions or, at least, tolerate them, thus deactivating or weakening normal familial sources of defense for the child; (c) that normal cultural and familial reinforcements of primary relationships may be interpreted as reinforcing the legitimacy of aversive actions, isolating the child and increasing the reactions of helplessness and self-blame; and (d) that the jeopardy of emotional ties with the abuser and other family members may add to the psychological pain and fear aroused by other factors. The fact that both children and adults have been known to defend and maintain emotional ties to the family and to the abusive members of that family in the face of terrible abuse indicates the strength of such ties and the potential for damage when they are breached.

When the disrupted relationships are within the primary group, the disruption may diminish the opportunity for the child to learn the interpersonal and/or emotional behaviors that will enable the child to meet his or her own needs for love and companionship on either a current or a long-term basis. Harlow's studies (Harlow, Harlow, Dodsworth, & Arling, 1967) indicate clearly that giving and receiving love and emotional support are acquired skills that can be learned only within the interactional process and may need to be initiated at an early stage of development (Main & Goldwyn, 1984). Evidence of the positive value of personal relationships in maintaining the psychological health of children is indicated by studies of those children who are popularly called "survivors," that is, children who seem to escape serious damage from extremely aversive living situations. Smith and Bohnstedt (1981) and Segal and Yahraes (1979) note that survivors had at least one person who provided a stable caring relationship, although that person may not have been a parent or even a relative.

It may be important to identify the extent to which the weakening or destruction of strong loving and positive relationships between parents and children may weaken or destroy the parents' ability to perform their functions. If the authority and influence of the parents is based upon the child's desire to please the loved parents, the child's trust that the parent knows what is best, and the child's secure knowledge that the parents will do their best to provide the child's basic needs, then abuse in any form will inevitably weaken or destroy the very basis of good child rearing. When the base is weakened or destroyed, the child is not only the target of destructive child-rearing practices but cannot learn the positive and effective child-rearing practices that would make him or her, eventually, an effective parent. Treatment for abuse must not only change destructive parental practices in the home but must rebuild the necessary relationships as well.

Some relationships are destructive in themselves. When a parent or sibling has a need to defend personal status by criticizing or controlling others, any independent behavior may be seen as defiance of authority. Extreme limitation upon independence of action may limit or destroy the potential for further development. The seductive parent who constantly promises wonderful things and constantly blames their total failure to deliver upon another parent (or a sibling, foster parent, etc.) is not just a negative role model. Such a parent leads the child to lose trust in others who could meet some needs. Most importantly, the child adds to the personal perception of self-blame and low self-esteem. The child cannot even deal with the constant rejection, because the parent never acknowledges it. Some children become suicidal in this situation. Finally, the psychologically unavailable parent, as defined by Egeland, may create one of the most destructive relationships by meeting physical needs with a total lack of emotional responsiveness that rejects the child's need of (or right to) the psychological and emotional relationships that have been identified as necessary to psychosocial development. The destructiveness of this type of relationship may be increased by the inability of people outside the family to recognize the abusive elements in the situation. External reinforcement of what appears to be a positive family system increases the child's confusion and perception that the fault is his or hers.

These forms of psychological abuse are not limited to the primary group. Denigration of whole groups of people through discrimination, loss of trust in security forces such as police or armed forces, or living in a totally hostile world (as children may be doing in areas of total war such as Lebanon or Northern Ireland) may create similar psychological damage on a very broad scale.

Psychological Effects of Inadequate Transmission of Social Knowledge, Skills, and Perception

The abusive family models maladaptive behavior (abuse) while failing to model values and behavior that would help the child to develop behavior patterns that would make them acceptable to other people. The child then becomes isolated and dependent upon the abuser to an even greater extent. The victim's low self-esteem becomes validated by the difficulties of developing relationships outside of the abusive situation. If the children use hostile, exploitative, or indifferent ways of relating to others which they have learned from abusive adults, they will be rejected by others. On the other hand, they have no knowledge (or sometimes, no appreciation) of behaviors that will achieve the recognition and attention they desire. Having been abused and rejected, these children may crave more attention than children whose needs have been met on a regular basis. Whether the acting-out of some abused children derives from socialization to hostility and self-centered patterns in interaction, from identification with the aggressor or from a conviction that they have nothing to lose because no one will like them anyway, without empathy or sympathy, their behaviors are self-defeating.

Some abused children may become withdrawn and fearful, avoiding relationships, fearful of any exploration of the world, and apparently fearful of any positive action. It is often suggested that abused children may grow up to become abusers, but therapists also note that abused children are more likely than nonabused children to accept abuse of themselves or their children in adulthood.

Abusers may model great emotional constriction, lack of emotional control, or inappropriate affect. They frequently project emotional confusion by combining verbal devotion with totally rejecting behavior, or by exploiting the child's emotions to meet the needs of the adult while proclaiming great self-sacrifice for the sake of the child whose needs are still not met. Not only are such situations abusive in themselves, but they create barriers to the child's development of an accurate interpretation of his/her own emotional states and those of others. The child is further constrained in the development of appropriate and differentiated responses to his/her own emotional needs and those of others. A child who is punished for the expression of normal emotions may become so emotionally constricted that continued emotional development is blocked and the emotional interaction necessary for long-term relationships is never learned. Finally, a self-perpetuating pattern may develop within the individual's life or across generations.

CONCLUSION

Psychological abuse has a number of interacting variables and multidimensional outcomes. Current evidence indicates that psychological factors are present in all types of abuse and resulting psychological damage may be independent of the degree of physical damage involved. Psychological abuse seems to distort, destroy or block the development of a positive sense of identity, self-esteem, and competence in a nonhostile environment; of knowledge and social skills needed to ensure acceptance within that environment; and of the relationships necessary to provide such learning and development. In addition, there may be direct blockage of cognitive functioning through pain, fear or emotional exhaustion that lessens the attention span. Emotional constriction, the inability to differentiate between emotions and/or emotional responses, may further limit personal development and the ability to form and maintain personal relationships. The psychological damage of psychological, physical, or sexual abuse may be more threatening over a longer period of time than some levels of physiological damage and must not be ignored.

REFERENCES

Armstrong, L. (1978). *Kiss daddy goodnight.* New York: Simon and Schuster.

Bateson, G. (1972). *Steps to an ecology of mind.* New York: Chandler.

Blager, F. (1978). Effect of intervention on speech and language of abused children. In A. White Franklin (Ed.), *Second international congress on child abuse and neglect: Abstracts.* London: Pergamon.

Cohn, A. H. (1979). An evaluation of three demonstration child abuse and neglect treatment programs. *Journal of the American Academy of Child Psychiatry, 18,* 283–291.

Cyriaque, J. (1982, February). *The chronic serious offender: How Illinois juveniles match up.* Illinois Department of Corrections.

Dietrich, K. M. (1977). *The abused infant: Develop-*

mental characteristics and maternal handling. Unpublished masters thesis, Wayne State University.

Duncan, G. M., Frasier, S. H., Litin, E. M., Johnson, A. M., & Barron, A. J. (1958). Etiological factors in first-degree murder. *Journal of the American Medical Association, 168*(13), 1755–1758.

Easson, W. M., & Steinhilber, R. M. (1961). Murderous aggression by children and adolescents. *Archives of General Psychiatry, 4*(1), 1–9.

Elmer, E., & Gregg, G. S. (1967). Developmental characteristics of abused children. *Pediatrics, 40*, 596–602.

Green, A. H. (1968). Self-destructive behavior in physically abused schizophrenic children: Report of cases. *Archives of General Psychiatry, 19*, 171–179.

Green, A. H. (1978). Self-destructive behavior in battered children. *American Journal of Psychiatry, 135*(5), 579–582.

Harlow, H. F., Harlow, M. K., Dodsworth, R. D., & Arling, G. L. (1967). Maternal behavior of rhesus monkeys deprived of mothering and peer association in infancy. *Proceedings of the American Philosophical Society, 110*, 329–335.

Hufton, I. W., & Oates, R. K. (1977). Non-organic failure to thrive: A long-term follow-up. *Pediatrics. 59*, 73–77.

Hunter, R. S., Kilstrom, N., Kraybill, E. N., & Loda, F. (1978). Antecedents of child abuse and neglect in premature infants: A prospective study in a newborn intensive care unit. *Pediatrics, 61*, 629.

Johnson, B., & Morse, H. (1968). *The battered child: A study of children with inflicted injuries.* Denver: Denver Department of Welfare.

Kent, J. T. (1976). A follow-up study of abused children. *Journal of Pediatric Psychology, 1*, 25.

Lewis, D. O., Shanok, S. S., Pincus, J. H., & Glaser, G. H. (1979). Violent juvenile delinquents: Psychiatric, neurological, psychological, and abuse factors. *Journal of American Academy of Child Psychiatry, 18*, 307.

Main, M., & Goldwyn, R. (1984). Predicting rejection of her infant from mother's representation of her own experience: Implications for the abused–abusing intergenerational cycle. *Child Abuse and Neglect, 8*, 203–217.

Martin, H. P. (1972). The child and his development. In C. H. Kempe and R. Helfer (Eds.), *Helping the battered child and his family.* Philadelphia: Lippincott.

Martin, H. P., Beezley, P., Conway, E. F., & Kempe, C. H. (1974). The development of abused children—Part I: A review of the literature; Part II: Physical, neurologic, and intellectual outcome. *Advanced Pediatrics, 21.*

Martin, H. P. (Ed.). (1976). *The abused child: An interdisciplinary approach to developmental issues and treatment.* Cambridge, MA: Ballinger.

Martin, P. (1980). The consequences of being abused and neglected: How the child fares. In C. H. Kempe & R. E. Helfer (Eds.), *The battered child* (3rd ed.). Chicago: University of Chicago Press.

Mayhall, P. D., & Norgard, K. E. (1983). *Child abuse and neglect: Sharing responsibility.* New York: John Wiley and Sons.

National Center on Child Abuse and Neglect. (1980). *Executive summary: National study of the incidence and severity of child abuse and neglect.* Washington, DC: Childrens Bureau, ACYF, OHDS, U.S. Department of Health and Human Services.

Oates, R. K., Davis, A. A., Ryan, M. G., & Stewart, L. F. (1978). Risk factors associated with child abuse. In A. White Franklin (Ed.), *Second international congress on child abuse and neglect: Abstracts.* London: Pergamon Press.

Reidy, T. J. (1977). The aggressive characteristics of abused and neglected children. *Journal of Clinical Psychology, 33*, 1140–1145.

Roberts, J., Lynch, M. A., & Duff, P. (1978). Abused children and their siblings: A teacher's view. *Therapeutic Education, 6*, 25.

Seligman, M. E. P., Maier, S. F., & Solomon, R. L. (1971). Unpredictable and uncontrollable aversive events. In F. R. Brush (Ed.), *Aversive conditioning and learning.* New York: Academic Press.

Segal, J., & Yahraes, H. (1979). *A child's journey: Forces that shape the lives of our young.* New York: McGraw-Hill.

Silbert, M. H. (1982). *Delancey Street study: Prostitution and sexual assault.* Summary of results, Delancey Street Foundation, Inc., San Francisco.

Smith, P., & Bohnstedt, M. (Draft, 1981). *Child victimization study highlights.* Social Research Center of the American Justice Institute, Sacramento (NCCAN).

Straus, M. A. (1980). Stress and child abuse. In C. H. Kempe & R. E. Helfer (Eds.), *The battered child* (3rd ed.). Chicago: University of Chicago Press.

Straus, M. A., Gelles, R. J., & Steinmetz, S. K. (1980). *Behind closed doors: Violence in the American family.* Garden City, NY: Anchor Books.

Van Staden, J. (1978). The mental development of abused children in South Africa. In A. White Franklin (Ed.), *Second international congress on child abuse and neglect: Abstracts.* London: Pergamon Press.

Wolfgang, M. E. (1981, June). *Delinquency in a birth cohort II: Some preliminary results.* Paper prepared for the Attorney General's Task Force on Violent Crime, Chicago.

PART 2

DOMAINS OF
PSYCHOLOGICAL MALTREATMENT

4

Psychological Correlates of Corporal Punishment

Irwin A. Hyman

On December 8, 1981, Shelly Gaspersohn made a mistake which would have long-lasting repercussions. Shelly was a senior high school student in Dunn, North Carolina. A deeply religious, compassionate young woman, she was a talented flutist, gifted debator, and honor student. She had an exemplary school record with no indications of any discipline problems. Her mistake was that she cut school with some friends. This was her first behavioral indiscretion. Raised in a closely knit, loving family where she had rarely been spanked or disciplined, she felt this lark in her senior year was, at the worst, a minor infraction for which she would be forgiven by both school and parents. She and her friends were caught, and even though this was her first infraction, she was assigned to 6 days of in-school suspension. She did not receive her school assignments for 3 days while sitting in the suspension room and decided to accept an alternative punishment suggested by the football coach and assistant principal, Glenn Varney. Varney, a strapping man with broad shoulders and thick arms, administered six licks with a wooden paddle. The pain was so intense that Shelly could only stand two swats at a time. She cried bitterly during the beating. The paddling resulted in terrible bruises and menstrual hemorrhaging. Her shocked parents took her to a physician, who was even more outraged. He reported Varney as a child abuser. To the physician's amazement, he learned that the child abuse

authorities have no jurisdiction over school personnel.

Two years following the incident, Shelly still had recurring nightmares, cried when discussing the event, and demonstrated an array of symptoms which was diagnosed as posttraumatic stress syndrome. She felt physically violated. Her descriptions of the event and related feelings resembled those of rape victims. However, the psychological correlates of the abuse had just begun. The Gaspersohns, finding no other recourse within the school, county, or state bureaucracies, sued Coach Varney and the school. Several years later, a jury in Harnett County, North Carolina, decided that the force used was not unreasonable (*Gaspersohn v. Harnett Board of Education and Glenn Varney*, 1983). At the time of this writing, the case is on appeal.

This incident illustrates the possible devastating personal and emotional ramifications of the use of corporal punishment on American children in both the school and the home. Common behavioral problems associated with the effects of corporal punishment, especially in young children, include sleep disturbances, enuresis, encopresis, temper tantrums, aggressive behavior, headaches, fear of school and school personnel, frequent crying, anger at parents, and withdrawal (Krugman & Krugman, 1984). These symptoms of stress are most likely to occur with vulnerable children, but do emerge in well-adjusted children (Hyman, 1985).

In order to understand why the public continues to support the use of corporal punishment for children both in the home and school, it is necessary to understand its historical context.

BACKGROUND

The year 1984 marked two events of some historical interest. Most people recognized the arrival of George Orwell's 1984; fewer noted the 110th anniversary of the Mary Ellen case in New York City. In 1874, since there was no other organized vehicle for seeking redress, the New York Society for the Prevention of Cruelty to Animals sought legal relief for Mary Ellen, a severely abused girl. One year later (and 10 years after the founding of the group to protect animals), the New York Society for the Prevention of Cruelty to Children was founded (Hyman, 1978b). This early movement against severe child abuse did not consistently sustain the public's interest. In fact, it did not have much impact on public policy until the medical recognition and labelling of the battered-child syndrome (Kempe, Silverman, Steele, Droegemueller, & Silver, 1962). Most adults cringe at the thought of severe sexual or physical abuse of children. Yet, it was not until 1975 that the country finally mobilized a significant effort against child abuse. At that time, the Child Abuse Prevention and Treatment Act was passed, the National Center on Child Abuse and Neglect was organized, and a group of citizens established the National Committee for the Prevention of Child Abuse. All states have enacted child abuse legislation to ensure proper reporting of abuse and have developed programs to protect abused children. The passage of child abuse legislation occurred because at some level Americans value social justice, fair play, and protection of the helpless.

If America wished to eliminate child abuse, would it not be reasonable to expect a well-coordinated, well-funded, effective program to deal with treatment and prevention of child abuse? Unfortunately, it would be naive to expect this to occur. Despite annual conferences on child abuse, efforts at treatment and prevention have been woefully inadequate.

The problem is related to our many myths concerning children and their value to society. If children were highly valued as torchbearers of democracy, education would be our nation's highest priority. Schools would be modern and air-conditioned. Teachers would be well-paid and

would have the highest academic credentials. Administrators would match their successful counterparts in corporations in terms of intelligence, creativity, flexibility, and leadership. Perhaps, as a result of some collective unconscious, we still believe that children are the "imps of darkness" described in earlier times. Perhaps, at some level, most Americans still subscribe to admonitions to beat the devil out of children. Why else would American school children be among the minority of students in the world who are still corporally punished? All of continental Europe, the entire Soviet bloc, China, Israel, Japan, Ireland, and many other countries have strictly forbidden the infliction of physical pain on school children (Hyman & Wise, 1979).

Do we still believe that children are inherently evil and that we must "beat the devil out of them"? Or, have we not yet fully mobilized our efforts to eliminate a poorly examined tradition which most Americans support? While the case of Shelly Gaspersohn is a rather dramatic example, it is a reflection of a widespread problem. It suggests that hitting (a) is an appropriate way to change behavior, (b) is seen as having limited or no negative psychological correlates, and (c) is acceptable as long as it is conducted in the name of discipline. Meanwhile millions of spankings received by American school children each year teach them that force, violence, and humiliation are legitimate ways to change another person's behavior. These beliefs are reinforced on television by the constant portrayal of violent solutions to personal and social problems. No wonder violence becomes ingrained in our national psyche.

DEFINING THE ISSUES

In the context of this chapter, corporal punishment is the purposeful infliction of pain upon the body of a child as the penalty for doing something which is disapproved of by the punisher. It is an attempt to reduce the reoccurrence of the undesirable behavior. When defined legally, it does not include physical action meant to prevent the child from hurting him/herself, others, or property, nor does it apply in cases of self-protection.

Surveys of press reports (Clarke, Erdlen, & Hyman, 1984; Clarke, Liberman-Lascoe, & Hyman, 1982) indicate that an assortment of techniques are used for the infliction of pain on school children. Students have been hit with paddles of various sizes, hands, fists, and instruments such as arrows, whips, ropes, rubber hoses, and belts. They have submitted to demeaning acts such as running the gauntlet, being strip-searched, and being forced to eat cigarettes. School and institutional personnel have developed an ingenious number of distortions of the behavioral concept of "time out" in order to confine children in uncomfortable places. Despite the specific details of acts of corporal punishment, each has some psychological correlates which are invariably negative (Hyman & Wise, 1979).

PSYCHOLOGICAL EFFECTS

There is a growing body of literature on the effects of corporal punishment (cf. Hyman & Wise, 1979). Ample evidence indicates that corporal punishment only temporarily suppresses undesirable behavior. It teaches aggressive behavior through the mechanism of modeling (Hyman & Wise, 1979).

Excessive corporal punishment is associated with humiliation, embarrassment, loss of dignity, reduced self-esteem and a lack of a sense of physical safety (Hyman & Wise, 1979). It promotes aggressive responses as an alternative to rational approaches to problem solving. Fear of infliction of physical pain by a parent or teacher promotes feelings of loss of freedom and dignity. Often the affected child cannot easily escape from the adult caregiver without actually running away. While excessive employment of corporal punishment is always associated with psychological maltreatment, even mild or moderate corporal punishment is linked with negative psychological concomitants (Hyman, 1985). Furthermore, witnessing the infliction of pain on peers and siblings often results in psychological effects similar to those felt by the child actually punished (Hyman & Wise, 1979). Widespread use of pain to change children's behavior results in society's dependence on punitiveness to solve problems. These general propositions are illustrated by the following example.

Alice Miller (1980), a psychoanalyst living in Switzerland, has written an interesting book entitled in German, *In the Beginning Was Education*. The English translation is *For Your Own Good*. Miller analyzes the effect of punitiveness on individuals and societies in lands with the kind of hidden cruelty that is so often rationalized in the time-honored phrase "this is for your own good" (Montague, 1983). The frequent association of corporal punishment with the demand for unquestioning and reflexive obedience has been described as a major contributor to the development of character in Adolf Hitler. Miller also discloses how "poisonous pedagogy" in the home and at school contributed to a self-destructive adolescence. She demonstrates through clinical evidence and case study "what happens to children who are physically punished, humiliated and demeaned by parents; who are expected, indeed commanded, to respect and love those who have abused them."

In discussing Hitler, Miller (1980) explains how a child who was once persecuted becomes a persecutor. She describes the dynamics of Hitler's family, and concludes it could well be characterized as "the prototype of a totalitarian regime" (Montague, 1983).

The case made by Miller is obviously extreme, but highly instructive. Reflexive obedience to authority enables the continuing existence of systems which depend upon a combination of physical and psychological abuse. In American schools, classes in social studies teach the *concepts* of democracy. But there is a palpable reluctance to institute developmentally appropriate democratic *processes* in schools. There is reluctance to teach the importance of and the need for legitimate debate, dissent and opposition to unjust practices and laws. The process of schooling in America stresses the need for conformity and obedience. Administrative procedures in schools too often exemplify a lack of due process that is endemic to the most authoritarian political systems (Hyman, 1970).

An example of the connection between the use of corporal punishment and emotional abuse, that of Shelly Gaspersohn, was presented at the beginning of this chapter. This case illustrates the effects of a single school paddling. A jury representing local community values in North Carolina said it was not unreasonable for a football coach to physically and psychologically damage a teenage girl (*Gaspersohn v. Harnett Board of Education and Glenn Varney*, 1983). When such abuse is sanctioned, a common pattern of parents' frustration and rage and children's fear and helplessness is apparent. This officially sanctioned form of child abuse, when administered in excess of what the parents themselves would administer, sometimes leads to counterviolence by parents and victims. In some cases bitterness and loss of faith in the system develop.

Despite the severity of some school beatings by educators, officials who would normally protect children are reluctant to act. Prosecutors, police, and judges typically refuse to intervene. Unless parents have adequate financial resources or are poor enough to obtain publicly funded legal services, there is little they can do. Even if they do go to litigation, the chances of winning appear poor (Clarke, Liberman-Lascoe, & Hyman, 1982). The lack of action by authorities and the attitudes of the public constitute an institutionalized form of mental cruelty. Corporally punished children are denied feelings of physical safety and dignity which are essential for mental health in a democratic society (Hyman & Wise, 1979).

Americans believe strongly in corporal punishment, yet the United States is not the only country which needs reform. The institutionalized use of shame and ridicule found in the Communist school systems, and the sexism inherent in the female infanticide which reportedly still occurs in Communist China, are no less ignominious. But criticism of America is relevant in relation to what should be expected in a democracy. We espouse equal protection under law and due process for all. Somehow, children have slipped through the cracks.

DEMOGRAPHIC AND ETIOLOGICAL CONSIDERATIONS

According to the Office of Civil Rights, approximately 1 million children are officially reported to have received corporal punishment each year in the schools (Farley, 1983). These figures constitute low estimates. In Hyman's estimation, the real incidence is probably closer to 2–3 million acts of corporal punishment per year (Hyman, 1985).

The use of corporal punishment is related to other variables, and is often discriminatory. Hyman and Wise (1979) report that corporal punishment is related to lower school achievement, is sexist since males are more often the recipients, and is racist in schools because blacks and Hispanics receive it disproportionately more often. Furthermore, its frequency is related to class, as poor urban and rural children are paddled more than their middle- and upper-middle-class peers. The infliction of pain occurs more often in schools in the south and southwest and least in the northeast. Excessive use of corporal punishment in the home and in institutions is

strongly associated with juvenile delinquency and adult commission of violent crimes (Hyman & Wise, 1979). In the home, corporal punishment is least likely to be used by Jews and devout Catholics and most frequently used by Baptists and those of lower socioeconomic status (Erlanger, 1974). Lower levels of education among parents and lack of domestic satisfaction are also related to increased use of corporal punishment in the home (Teichman, Engle, Heider, & Kleihpter, 1978). Teachers and parents under stress are more inclined to hit children (Feshback & Campbell, 1978).

Examination of any type of corporal punishment reveals emotional concomitants including feelings of denigration and humiliation. The inexorable conclusion is that there is no valid support for the infliction of pain as either a pedagogical or parenting tool. Yet, 60–80% of the public supports the use of corporal punishment on children, despite the overwhelming findings from learning theory, educational and experimental research, and clinical practice (cf. Hyman & Wise, 1979).

Studies by both Sofer (1983) and Lennox (1982) suggest that modelling may cause professionals to ignore theory and research which offer effective alternatives to corporal punishment. To resolve cognitive dissonance, some psychologists distort the theoretical bases for their beliefs. For instance, Sofer found that relatively equal percentages of psychologist respondents cited behaviorism to either support or reject the use of corporal punishment, this despite the fact that B. F. Skinner is adamantly against its use (Skinner, 1979).

Among the industrialized nations, the biblical belief of "spare the rod and spoil the child" is supported mostly in schools in English-speaking countries. However, within these countries interesting ethnic differences appear, as illustrated by a survey conducted in Canada. When asked if they agreed that teachers should be able to inflict corporal punishment, 60% of the respondents in English-speaking Ontario answered yes, while in French-speaking Quebec only 21% agreed (Hyman, 1983b). Sweden is the only known western society which has forbidden the use of corporal punishment by parents, although it is not used frequently in many nonindustrialized societies (Babcock, 1978).

As noted previously, the use of corporal punishment in schools is based, in part; on tradition and religious beliefs. Furthermore, in English-speaking countries its use in schools is supported by the legal precedent of *in loco parentis*, which allows teachers to use parental discretion in disciplining students. As a result, corporal punishment is allowed in 43 states and most school districts. Although the National Education Association Delegate Assembly voted against its use, most state education associations will not support that vote (National Education Association, 1972). In fact, it is difficult to elicit acknowledgment of this position from the central office of the National Education Association. The American Federation of Teachers maintains that teachers should be able to use corporal punishment. Their official stance is that the decision should be left to individual teachers. They claim that the threat of corporal punishment may be necessary to maintain proper discipline. Yet, research demonstrates that the elimination of corporal punishment has no substantive effect on the discipline climate (Farley, 1983; Hyman & Wise, 1979).

In the case of *Smith v. the West Virginia Board of Education* (1982), the State Supreme Court ruled against the use of any instrument for hitting children. The National Education Association affiliate West Virginia Education Association was enraged and lobbied the state legislature to allow the use of paddles. The legislature complied as a result of extensive political pressure. The sponsors of the bill to eliminate corporal punishment were pressured into backing down.

Putting aside historical, legal and religious considerations, the employment of corporal punishment may be understood from a reinforcement and modelling perspective. Corporal punishment usually results in the immediate cessation of the offending behavior, thereby reinforcing the punisher. Furthermore, studies by Lennox (1982) and Sofer (1983) indicate a strong modelling effect. Lennox found that teachers who were not hit as children were most unlikely to use corporal punishment. Sofer found that 50% of responding psychologists would favor the use of corporal punishment in limited situations. Of the sample, 30% would support its use in schools in specific situations. Compared to the public and other types of professionals, psychologists are more unfavorable toward corporal punishment. They also see a more restricted role for it. But, despite their training and the research available, those who are favorable are likely to base their beliefs on their own early experiences.

Bogacki (1981) found a strong association between authoritarian ideology and the use of corporal punishment by teachers. Rust and Kinnard (1983) also found that employment of corporal punishment was associated with dogmatism and neuroticism as measured by the Eysenck Scale. Frequent users of corporal punishment tended to be relatively inexperienced, close minded, neurotic, and impulsive compared to peers who used corporal punishment less.

Examination of the data leads to the inexorable conclusion that there is no valid support for the infliction of pain as either a pedagogical or parenting tool (Hyman, 1978a; Hyman, 1980; Hyman & Lally, 1981; Hyman & Lally, 1982; Hyman & Wise, 1979). Yet, with so many professionals still supporting the use of corporal punishment, despite its concomitant psychological traumas, it is not difficult to understand why change is difficult. While many child-related professional associations have issued official resolutions against corporal punishment in the schools, few have approached the problem in relation to parenting. Yet, the basic scientific findings about punishment remain constant across situations. If professionals can't agree, it is not hard to understand why it is so difficult to convince policy makers. Where change occurs, the moral imperatives of the politicians often are as influential as any research they have read.

It appears that we are all trapped by tradition and folkways regarding the disciplining of children. Our cultural values and the myths which surround them blind us to the realities of children's lives.

CULTURAL VALUES AND AMERICAN MYTHS

Americans believe that we highly value children and youth. The myth is that American children receive high-quality health, nutrition and educational services. However, an examination of policies reflecting concern and nurturance suggests a paradox. While many policy makers speak enthusiastically of their concern for children's welfare, it is obvious that they too often attend to social, political and economic factors which mitigate against children's welfare.

For instance, children in public schools have historically been victims of struggles between the political right and left. But, regardless of who is in political power, the value of children in schools can be gauged by low teacher salaries, lack of resources and a dearth of administrative talent. Currently, we are moving toward a fragmented society as private schools grow almost exponentially, leaving large numbers of poor and minority students attending meagerly supported public schools. Millions of inner-city children attend school in decaying buildings with "burned-out" teachers who struggle to teach using inadequate materials and supplies.

The dearth of adequate support for children might be understood historically if one were to examine the periodic portrayal of "the evil child" in the media. Do we share a view similar to some Victorian fundamentalists who considered children as "a swarm of little vipers" (Collins, 1963, p. 187)? Many still consciously believe that it is necessary to "beat the devil" out of children in order to instill appropriate character development.

Certainly, in many areas we have done well. Medical advances in the 20th century have been significant. We have reduced the devastating numbers of infant deaths resulting from childhood diseases (Coles, 1975). Education is universal, the ubiquitous use of flogging has been reduced, and the economic exploitation of children bears little resemblance to what occurred during the Industrial Revolution (Hyman & Wise, 1979). Unfortunately, however, contemporary analysis yields disturbing similarities to the past. For instance, the hunger documented by Charles Dickens (1981a) in *Oliver Twist* seems to have a modern sequel—perhaps not as dramatic but just as real to hungry children. While Nancy Reagan was publishing her second book, *To Love a Child*, "a tearful tribute to the joys of intergenerational affection, her husband's administration was pocketing the lunch money of 3 million American children and depriving millions more of subsidized snacks, dinners and breakfasts" (Ehrenreich & Nasaw, 1983, p. 597). Denying proper nutrition to poor children became public policy.

Dickens (1981b), in *Nicholas Nickleby*, described a world of childhood in which dirt and disorder caused much disease. Modern hygiene has reduced filth, yet chemical pollutants in the environment currently affect the lives of too many children "who are substantially more sensitive than adults to the toxic effects of many pollutants." Thus, many childhood cancers are related to environmental pollutants and now appear at rates of more than 6,000 per year (Freedman & Weir, 1983). Yet funding for research on the effects of environmental pollutants on the young has been discontinued.

The history of brutal floggings and denigra-

tion of children in 17th century English schools and in colonial America are well documented (Freedman & Weir, 1983). In 1669 and in 1698, the children of England unsuccessfully petitioned Parliament for redress from beatings and sadism. Contemporary efforts by those children's descendants are still largely unsuccessful in Parliament and at the federal level in America. Despite the many documented cases of child abuse by teachers, one suspects a conspiracy of silence. School boards and administrators ignore it, police and prosecutors refuse to take action, and the judicial system offers little relief (Clarke, Erdlin, & Hyman, 1984; Clarke, Liberman-Lasco, & Hyman, 1982). Almost every case of corporal punishment is associated with emotional trauma (Hyman, 1985).

Child labor laws, while well-meaning, set the stage for another type of abuse by disenfranchising children as economic assets for families. Most Americans, at some level, view children as economic liabilities. The American business establishment exacerbates the problem through manipulation of the kiddie and youth market. Television provides a perfect medium for catching young children and turning them into uncritical consumers (Rubenstein, 1983). Television executives contribute to psychological abuse as they continue to program excessive amounts of violence. The passive acceptance of violence adds to the climate of violence in which children readily accept the use of force to solve problems. Hundreds of thousands of children are constantly exposed to violence on television and learn to accept it as a way of life.

While the preceding may offer an overly pessimistic view, it is presented to emphasize our paradoxical views about children. Our stated values regarding children and youth are certainly at variance with the realities of life for large numbers of children who are psychologically abused. Belief that we really make good on our commitment to children is the real cause of lack of progress. Large numbers of children are in double jeopardy as we move towards a highly technological society. It is inevitable that many children who are poor, handicapped, or of low intelligence will be labeled, cataloged, and warehoused. These are the ones most likely to receive generous amounts of corporal punishment in home and school. They are further at risk because of the "get tough" emphasis in the schools. This law-and-order approach to education, promoted in a politically conservative climate, inevitably increases both psychological and physical abuse (Hyman & D'Allessandro, 1984). We need to change public policy and recognize the myths that perpetuate the abuses described.

Having framed the problem in a broad perspective, it is appropriate to turn to some considerations for change.

DIRECTIONS AND CONCLUSIONS

The concept of psychological abuse of children is just beginning to reach the public consciousness. A few conferences, some scholarly publications and infrequent media reporting will sustain interest for a while. It is unlikely that President Reagan's conservative administration will do much about the problem. It may be that the National Center for Child Abuse and Neglect will take more interest in this issue. Some states may set up commissions, but there will be little impact where it is really needed. For anything significant to happen, we will need a major effort by persistent citizens.

The professional community and many citizens readily recognize the relationship between early physical abuse and later disturbed behavior, especially in the commission of violent crimes which mirror early maltreatment. It is, however, important that the public becomes aware of the contribution made by daily acts of parental spanking and school paddling. When the educational establishment endorses the infliction of pain as a legitimate pedagogical tool, parents and the public have justification for a wide range of beliefs about the use of force to change behavior. Even a significant minority of psychologists, who should know better, endorse paddling in the schools (Sofer, 1983).

Perhaps the most frightening part of the scenario is the slow, but steady, movement towards the world of Orwell's 1984. This world stresses reflexive obedience, conformity, cooperation with authority, and sanctions against actions based on individual conscience. We are currently a country which is frightened by crime, angry at youth and willing to forgo civil liberties in order to mete out as much punishment as possible.

We know from the research on child abuse that there is a high correlation between family stress and abuse. Economic factors appear to be the most influential in creating family discord and the resulting physical and emotional abuse (Hyman, 1980).

There is a hierarchy of possible solutions to the problems of emotional maltreatment as a function of physical abuse. The following is a brief overview of an agenda for change. It starts with the most important approaches. While it is realized that this may be viewed as somewhat grandiose, it is nonetheless defensible from both theory and evidence available.

The Economy

Despite the romanticism of our beliefs, most parents understand the economic realities of raising children. It is probably inevitable that children and youth will, to some extent, be defined by their economic ability. However, the political system in America has been far from forthright in confronting the facts. We must find ways to eliminate the economic liabilities associated with family child-rearing and education. This involves a recognition of the realities of contemporary society. An unprecedented proportion of intact families function with both parents fully employed. The increasing number of single-parent families with mothers as the bread-earners raises the rate of children in the poverty or near-poverty level. In addition, there is the growing rate of blended families. The difficulties of latch-key children and the impossible costs of college education for middle-income families are just a few of the problems modern families face. Obvious answers lie in a policy of full employment, improved day care, incentives for education, and so forth, which are all programs which cost money. If we really want to prevent physical and psychological abuse of children, economic changes must be made.

Mythology and Reality

As a nation, we believe that we highly cherish children. However, most Americans are convinced that hitting children is an appropriate way to change behavior. Most adults think a good spanking never hurt anyone, and they believe that even nonrelatives in school buildings should be allowed the use of the paddle. The evidence is that hitting only produces aggression, hostility-laden ideation, humiliation, and so on. We need to consistently and graphically present the American public with the facts. This involves a campaign supported by corporate officials, professionals, citizens, and the media. The first step is to eliminate corporal punishment in the schools; the second is to blitz the public with information about positive methods of child-rearing. The final goal is to convince people that they should be ashamed to admit to the belief that force and the administration of physically painful procedures are appropriate methods to punish children.

The Schools

The schools will remain a bastion of mediocrity, conformity, and oppression of civil liberties. Despite court rulings in the 1970s, discipline in the typical high school is more similar to the education portrayed in Orwell's *1984* than to the paragon of democracy that some envision (Hyman, 1970; Hyman, Bilus, Dennehy, Feldman, Flanagan, Maital, & McDowell, 1979; Hyman, Stern, Lally, Kreutter, Berlinghof, & Prior, 1982). The Reagan administration's agenda for the 1980s is to eliminate those few constitutional rights that have been gained by students in the past few decades. Much of the emotional and physical abuse of students in schools can only be eliminated by changing the attitudes of school staffs. This must accompany any training in the theory, research and practice of effective discipline. The techniques for accomplishing this are extensive and beyond the scope of this paper (Hyman, Flanagan, & Smith, 1982).

We need to focus on school climate through extensive work in organizational development (Hyman, 1983a). But we also need to use school psychologists and other trained specialists to provide consultation to teachers to help them deal with the stresses of the contemporary classroom. An interesting 3-year effort based on a Teacher Improvement Model is reported elsewhere (Pokalo, Hyman, & Moore, 1983). Besides psychological consultation and training, teachers should receive periodic refresher courses in constitutional law. The American Constitution and Bill of Rights are instruments of unparalleled beauty and wisdom for *understanding* and preserving freedom and dignity. If teachers could, in developmentally appropriate ways, apply and teach the principles of the Constitution, we would significantly decrease physical and emotional abuse in the schools.

Prevention

Primary and secondary prevention are approaches which hold great potential for eliminating corporal punishment as a mainstay of discipline in America (Albee, 1982). Strategies for implementing prevention depend upon the extent of the goals. Surprisingly, local modest efforts have great potential. For example, at the National Center for the Study of Corporal Punishment and Alternatives in the Schools, a local discipline helpline was developed. The major goal is to offer the public effective alternatives to corporal punishment. This was accomplished with very modest funding. The program provides a free service for parents who want help in dealing with their children's problems. Evaluation research indicates that the service has helped parents to recognize and discontinue ineffective approaches to disciplining children (Fina, 1983).

In conclusion, the solutions suggested here are broad, but it is hoped that they will be useful in setting the stage for policy changes. Progress on behalf of children does not necessarily follow as a result of exemplary research, fine scholarship or well-attended conferences. Public policy regarding children is ultimately a political process, and as such, requires political action. The preceding offers ample evidence that any type of corporal punishment has negative psychological concomitants for all parties involved. The atmosphere of violence in our society supports the use of force to solve problems. This, in turn, takes its toll. It is clear that no significant change will take place until at least one generation of children learns to use rational methods to solve problems. This will only be accomplished when social scientists and politicians critically examine the data and reject traditions which they consciously or unconsciously support. A good start is to eliminate corporal punishment in the schools and convince the public that there are a wealth of effective alternatives to change children's behavior.

Acknowledgments—Literature reviews by Lou Delsoldo, Susan Jacobowitz, Marcia Minor, Claudia Rogers, and Marcie Ruberg contributed to the development of this chapter. Thanks are also extended to Susan Brown Eitel for editing and typing.

REFERENCES

Albee, G. (1982). Preventing psychopathology and promoting human potential. *American Psychologist, 37*(9), 1043–1050.

Babcock, A. (1978). A cross cultural examination of corporal punishment: An initial conceptualization. In J. Wise (Ed.), *Proceedings: Conference on corporal punishment in the schools.* Washington, DC: National Institute of Education (1979, NIE p77–0079).

Bogacki, D. (1981). *Attitudes toward corporal punishment: Authoritarian personality and pupil control ideology of school personnel.* Unpublished doctoral dissertation, Temple University.

Clarke, J., Erdlin, R., & Hyman, I. (1984, April). *Analysis of recent corporal punishment cases reported in national newspapers.* Paper presented at the Annual Convention of the National Association of School Psychologists, Philadelphia, PA.

Clarke, J., Liberman-Lasco, R., & Hyman, I. (1982). Corporal punishment as reported in nationwide newspapers. *Children and Youth Services, 4*(1–2), 47–56.

Coles, R. (1975, December). Growing up in American—Then and now. *Time,* 27–29.

Collins, D. (1963). *Dickens and education.* London: MacMillan & Co.

Dickens, C. (1981a). *Oliver Twist.* New York: Bantam Books.

Dickens, C. (1981b). *Nicholas Nickleby.* New York: Bantam Books.

Ehrenreich, B., & Nasaw, D. (1983). Kids as consumers and commodities. *The Nation, 283*(19), 597–599.

Erlanger, H. (1974). Social class and corporal punishment in child rearing: An assessment. *American Sociological Review, 34,* 68–85.

Farley, A. (1983). *National survey of the use and non-use of corporal punishment as a disciplinary technique in United States schools.* Unpublished doctoral dissertation, Temple University.

Feshback, N., & Campbell, M. (1978, March). *Teacher stress and disciplinary practices in schools.* Paper presented at the annual convention of the American Orthopsychiatric Association, San Francisco.

Fina, A. (1983, April). *Analysis of the discipline helpline.* Paper presented at the annual convention of the National Association of School Psychologists, Philadelphia.

Freedman, T., & Weir, D. (1983). Polluting the most vulnerable. *The Nation, 263*(19), 600–604.

Gaspersohn v. Harnett Board of Education and Glenn Varney, 82 CVS 421 (General Court of Justice, Supreme Court Division, North Carolina, 1983).

Hyman, I. (1970). Democracy, mental health and achievement: A modern educational mythology. *Annual Yearbook of the New Jersey Association of Secondary School Teachers.*

Hyman, I. (1978a). A social science review of evidence cited in litigation on corporal punishment in the schools. *Journal of Child Clinical Psychology, 7*(3), 195–200.

Hyman, I. (1978b). A bicentennial consideration of the advent of child advocacy. *Journal of Child Clinical Psychology, 161,* 15–20.

Hyman, I. (1980). Corporal punishment: America's officially sanctioned form of child abuse. In G. Williams & J. Money (Eds.), *Traumatic abuse and neglect of children at home.* Baltimore: Johns Hopkins Press.

Hyman, I. (1983a, March). *Are advocacy and organization consultation compatible: An example of a dilemma.* Paper presented at the annual convention of the National Association of School Psychologists, Detroit.

Hyman, I. (1983b). *Paddling, punishment and force in school and home: A contemporary dilemma.* Invited address presented at the thirty-sixth annual convention of the Ontario Psychological Association, Toronto.

Hyman, I. (1985, August). *Psychological abuse in the schools: A school psychologist's perspective.* Paper presented at the meeting of the American Psychological Association, Los Angeles.

Hyman, I., Bilus, F., Dennehy, N., Feldman, G., Flanagan, D., Maital, S., & McDowell, E. (1979). Discipline in American education: An overview and analysis. *Journal of Education, 2,* 51–70.

Hyman, I., & D'Allessandro, J. (1984). Good old fashioned discipline: The politics of punitiveness. *Phi Delta Kappan, 66*(1), 39–45.

Hyman, I., Flanagan, D., & Smith, K, (1982). Discipline in the schools. In C. Reynolds & T. Gutkin (Eds.), *The handbook of school psychology* (pp. 454–480). New York: John Wiley and Sons.

Hyman, I., & Lally, D. (1981). Corporal punishment in American education: An historical and educational dilemma. *Educational Comment.* Toledo, OH: University of Toledo College of Education.

Hyman, I., Lally, D. (1982). The effectiveness of staff development programs to improve school discipline. *Urban Review, 14*(3), 181–196.

Hyman, I., Stern, A., Lally, D., Kreutter, K., Berlinghof, M., & Prior, J. (1982). Discipline in the high school: Organizational factors and the role of the school's psychologist. *School Psychology Review, 11*(4), 409–416.

Hyman, I., & Wise, J. (Eds.) (1979). *Corporal punishment in American education.* Philadelphia: Temple University Press.

Kempe, C., Silverman, F., Steele, B., Droegemueller, W., & Silver, H. (1962). The battered child syndrome. *Journal of the American Medical Association, 181,* 17–24.

Krugman, R., & Krugman, M. (1984). Emotional abuse in classrooms: The pediatrician's role in diagnosis and treatment. *American Journal of Diseases of Children, 138,* 284–286.

Lennox, N. (1982). *Teacher use of punishment as a*

function of modeling behavior. Unpublished doctoral dissertation, Temple University.

Miller, A. (1980). *For your own good.* New York: Farer, Straus & Giroux.

Montague, A. (1983, May). Poisonous pedagogy (review of *For your own good*). *Psychology Today*, 80–81.

National Education Association. (1972). *Report of the task force on corporal punishment.* (Library of Congress No. 22-85743).

Pokalo, M., Hyman, I., & Moore, D. (1983, March). *The teacher improvement model for organization development.* Paper presented at the annual convention of the National Association of School Psychologists, Detroit.

Rubenstein, E. (1983). Television and behavior. *American Psychologist, 38*(7), 820–825.

Rust, J., & Kinnard, K. (1983). Personality characteristics of the users of corporal punishment. *Journal of School Psychology, 21*(2), 91–95.

Skinner, B. (1979). Corporal punishment. In I. Hyman & J. Wise (Eds.), *Corporal punishment in American education.* Philadelphia: Temple University Press.

Smith v. West Virginia Board of Education, West Virginia Superior Court (1982) (Case No. 15454).

Sofer, B. (1983). *Psychologists' attitudes toward corporal punishment.* Unpublished doctoral dissertation, Temple University.

Teichman, H., Engle, H., Heider, B., & Kleihpter, V. (1978). Attitude of mothers towards physical punishment as a counseling problem in small children with developmental disorders. *Psychiatric–Neurologic–Medical Psychologies, 30*(3), 173–174 (Medlars Document Reproduction Service No. BRS 78179365.7800).

5

Child Sexual Abuse

Marla R. Brassard and Linda E. McNeill

BACKGROUND

Public and professional awareness of child sexual abuse has risen dramatically in the last decade. Despite the fact that child sexual abuse is regarded by professionals and the public as harmful, there is surprisingly little well-researched empirical evidence concerning the cognitive, behavioral, and especially the emotional effect of the various forms of sexual abuse. The purpose of this chapter is to review the theory and research in the area of child sexual abuse, particularly as it relates to psychological maltreatment, and to provide direction for further research.

Garbarino and Vondra (chapter 2 of this volume) have suggested that psychological maltreatment is at the core of child maltreatment and is the unifying concept in these cases as the psychological consequences of the act defines the act as abuse. Navarre, in chapter 3 of this volume, agrees with this view, citing current evidence indicating that psychological maltreatment is present in all forms of abuse and that the resulting psychological damage is not necessarily related to the extent of physical damage. The major elements of psychological maltreatment are identified as rejection, terrorizing, degrading, isolation, exploitation, corruption, and emotional unresponsiveness (Hart, Germain, & Brassard, chapter 1 of this volume). This conceptualization of child abuse as psychological maltreatment based upon these identified factors helps address the difficult definitional issues that occur when these concepts are applied to different cultures. Moreover, this conceptualization may help clar-

ify the difficult issue of assessing damage on the basis of consequences to the child or upon the intention of the perpetrator (Fraser, 1981; Gelles, 1975, 1982).

Sexual abuse is psychologically abusive as children are not in a position to consent freely to sexual contact with adults; being under the legal and physical control of adults, they are trained to comply with adult wishes and behavior in spite of their own feelings of displeasure. Frequently, naive as to the societal sanctions concerning adult–child sexual activity, children are not in a position to understand the implications of their behavior regardless of their complicity.

In the case of caretaker–child relationships, an additional form of sexual abuse is the deprivation of normal parental affection and guidance. This pattern of emotional deprivation and sexual exploitation can become generalized by the victim to other social relationships (Herman & Hirschman, 1981) and later in life this pattern is frequently repeated by the victim to children (Cooper & Cormier, 1982; Spencer, 1978; Sroufe, Jacobvitz, Mangelsdorf, DeAngelo, & Ward, 1985; Sroufe & Ward, 1980). Another consequence of being deprived of parental affection and guidance is that the victim often adopts a pseudo-adult or contemporary role with the parent that further diminishes the opportunities for age-appropriate development. Finally, the extant evidence, based on clinical judgment, case reports, retrospective surveys, and comparison studies using objective measures, consistently indicates that there are short- and longer-term behavioral and psychological difficulties associated with a history of child sexual abuse (Briere & Runtz, 1985; Browne & Finkelhor, 1986; DeVine, 1980; Fromuth, 1986; Kaufman, Peck, & Tagiuri, 1954; Knittle & Tuana, 1980; Manarino & Cohen, 1986; Sedley & Brooks, 1984; Tufts, 1984).

DEFINITIONAL ISSUES

In reviewing the literature, a consistent definition of child sexual abuse does not develop. Attempts to define child sexual abuse are further complicated by the fact that although 42 states include the element of sexual molestation in their child abuse statues, 34 of these states do not attempt to define what actions constitute sexual molestation (Fraser, 1981). The phrase "child sexual abuse" can be broken down into its component parts to illustrate the definitional problems. For example, what is meant by "child"? Legally, the upper age limit that defines childhood varies from state to state (Navarre, 1983), country to country (Doek, 1981), and researcher to researcher (e.g., Finkelhor, 1979; National Center on Child Abuse and Neglect, 1981a, 1981b; Russell, 1983; Tyler & Brassard, 1984). The definition of a sexual act with a child varies in the clinical literature from "physical contact that was kept secret" (Herman & Hirschman, 1981, p. 967) to "an entire spectrum of acts from exhibitionism to intercourse including genital manipulation of the child, oral–genital sexual acts and fondling" (Johnston, 1979, p. 944). The third term in the phrase, "abuse," is the most widely used in the literature; however, it is sometimes interchanged with misuse, molestation, trauma, exploitation and assault. These terms appear to represent a conceptual consensus among professionals that the child has been acted upon in an inappropriate way. However, this judgment is based upon adult perceptions and not upon the actual reactions of the child to an abusive sexual act. The question can be posed, is an act abusive if it produces no evidence of harm to the child?

If we look at the phrase "child sexual abuse" in a more holistic sense, the literature does not provide a consistent definition. Sexual abuse has been defined most frequently in accordance with the definition used by the National Center on Child Abuse and Neglect. This definition states that contacts or interaction between a child and adult are abusive when the child is being used as an object of gratification for adult sexual needs or desires; it is an experience that interferes with, or has potential for interfering with, a child's nor-

mal healthy development (DeVine, 1980). It is important to note that the impact or potential impact on the child is a key component of this definition; however, the assessment of the impact often reflects adult perceptions, beliefs and values and not the actual consequences to the child.

An alternative definition with broad developmental implications is proposed by Brant and Tisza (1977). They define "sexual misuse" of the child as exposure of the child to sexual stimulation inappropriate for the child's age, level of psychosexual development, and role in the family. This definition does not specify a positive or negative outcome for the child or how the act impinges psychologically on the child.

Determining what actions are psychosexually harmful to a child is complicated as there is little professional agreement about optimal childhood sexual development and the family interactions that facilitate this development. Ideally, sexual abuse could be defined as any act of commission or omission which prevents a child from achieving healthy adult sexual functioning. Included in this ideal definition would be biological norms and social judgments concerning normative development of gender identity and sex role identification. In this ideal framework, even the omission of providing sex education to a child could be considered sexual abuse. A good definition of child sexual abuse should attempt to include some of these elements even if a comprehensive definition remains an ideal.

The psychological effects of sexual abuse are not necessarily directly related to the immediate sexual nature of the acts. There is theoretical agreement that specific factors impinging upon acts of sexual abuse, such as the relationship between the child and partner, the type of abuse, the length or duration of the relationship between participants, the age of the child, and the degree of violence affect the psychological outcomes for the child (DeVine, 1980; Jorne, 1979; MacVicar, 1979; Mrazek & Mrazek, 1981; Summit & Kryso, 1978). There are only a few empirical studies that have addressed these variables (see Browne & Finkelhor, 1986, for a recent review) but most of these studies have methodological limitations. In reviewing these studies, there does not appear to be a consistent contributing factor associated with negative outcomes for the child. However, these studies suggest that acts of sexual abuse by fathers or father substitutes, the occurrence of genital contact in acts of sexual abuse, and the use of force are associated with more negative psychological outcomes. There is not clear evidence that the age of the child at the time of the abuse is related to impact on the child. Evidence about the qualitative elements of the relationship between the child and the abusing adult is contradictory. Involvement with adolescent as opposed to adult perpetrators and female as opposed to male perpetrators appears to be less traumatic for victims of both sexes. The response of the victim's family seems to contribute to the psychological outcome for the child. Unsupportive families and the removal of the child from the home are related to negative outcomes for the victim. Further methodologically sound research is needed to determine the relationship of these variables to psychological harm.

A complete definition of child abuse would appear to combine elements of the previously mentioned definitions and results from objective studies. For the purposes of this chapter, sexual abuse of the child is defined as exposure of a child to sexual stimulation inappropriate for the child's age, level of psychosexual development, and role in the family. It is an experience that interferes with, or has potential for interfering with, a child's normal healthy development.

This proposed definition omits defining the perpetrator; the abuser can be an adult or an older child. Community values have traditionally castigated the adult perpetrator but no consensus has been reached about noncoercive child-to-child sexual play, especially when the children are of similar age. Finkelhor (1979) defined a perpetrator as someone at least 5 years older than the victim and could be an older child. Also, specific acts have not been included in this definition, as societal norms are often ambiguous about considering some behaviors as acts of sexual abuse (e.g., depriving a child of an age-appropriate sex education, or allowing a child free access to pornographic movies on cable television). Hopefully, further research will help clarify these definitional problems and ambiguity, especially as related to the identification of factors that promote or inhibit optimal psychosexual development.

DEMOGRAPHIC CHARACTERISTICS

National statistics documenting the sexual abuse of children do not exist. All states track child abuse but often do not include categories of victimization that are comparable to the categories used in other states (Navarre, 1983). Thus, the extent of child sexual abuse can only be estimated from limited data sources including retrospective surveys, estimates based upon clinical reports using small select populations, and the ambitious, flawed National Incidence Study (Finkelhor & Hotaling, 1984; National Center on Child Abuse and Neglect, 1981a, 1981b).

The National Center on Child Abuse and Neglect in Washington, DC, estimated in its 1981 report that 7% of the 652,000 reported child abuse cases met their strict criteria for sexual abuse (e.g., only cases of caretaker abuse were included). The report estimated that 44,700 cases of sexual abuse were known to professionals for the year May, 1979 to April, 1980. However, using estimates of the prevalence of child sexual abuse (both intra- and extrafamilial) based upon retrospective random surveys and a base figure of 60 million American children currently under the age of 18, it has been conservatively estimated that the National Incidence Study identified only a quarter to a third of actual cases (Finkelhor & Hotaling, 1984). This estimate by Finkelhor and Hotaling would indicate that at least 5–6% of all children will at some point in their childhood be victims of child sexual abuse.

A number of large retrospective surveys (Finkelhor, 1979; Fromuth, 1986; Gagnon, 1965; Kercher & McShane, 1984; Kinsey et al., 1953; Landis, 1956; Russell, 1983) have indicated that between 20% and 38% of all women have had a childhood sexual encounter with an adult male, that 4–12% of all women have had such an experience with a relative, and that approximately 1–4.5% of all women have been involved in father–daughter incest. Several of these studies included male victims, with prevalence figures of 2.5–8.7% being reported. These studies suggest that girls are sexually abused 2–3 times more than boys. As with girls, boys are also sexually abused predominantly by males (80–87% of the cases; see Finkelhor, 1984 for a review of the literature). For both sexes, sexual abuse tends to occur within a child's intimate social network. Seventy to 89% of child sexual abuse incidents involve a perpetrator known to the child (Finkelhor, 1979; Groth, 1979; Russell, 1983). Male victims, however, appear to be involved more often in extrafamilial abuse. In Finkelhor's nonrepresentative survey, 44% of the female experiences and 17% of the male experiences were with a family member.

Hitherto, there has been a commonly held

belief that female children constituted the major population at risk for sexual exploitation. Recent evidence indicates that males are also at risk; indeed, several authors have even suggested that males may constitute as many cases of sexual abuse as females (Swift, 1977; Walters, 1975). The higher percentage of male, as compared to female, victims reported by non-incarcerated sex offenders under conditions of strict confidentiality suggests that in cases of sexually abused boys, particularly in extrafamilial abuse, there is considerable underreporting of the sexual event (Abel, Mittelman, & Becker, 1985). Interestingly, some early studies of child sexual abuse found one third of the victims to have been boys (Bender & Blau, 1937; Landis, 1956). There appears to have been little attempt by these authors to further study the implication that a substantial proportion of sexual victims were young males.

The underreporting of male victims may be due to several factors: (a) boys report their deviant sexual experiences less frequently than girls (Finkelhor, 1979; Groth, 1979; Landis, 1956), possibly because they perceive the experiences to be less traumatic (Finkelhor, 1979); (b) there is a double standard toward nudity in that society is more concerned about males exposing themselves to females as opposed to male children; (c) the dual nature of the taboo broken (homosexual as well as adult–child sexual activity) may increase the secrecy surrounding the event and decrease the likelihood that it will be reported (Raybin, 1969); and (d) males may not report painful experiences as frequently as females, especially as they mature and are increasingly expected to be strong.

In any case, Swift's (1977) point is well taken that a closer examination of male victims is imperative as this group is at high risk for committing sexual offenses later in life (Groth, 1979; Tyler, 1983). This phenomenon of the intergenerational transmission of sexual abuse is a familiar theme in the literature. If further research corroborates the hypothesis that sexually victimized boys grow up to be sexual abusers, programs directed to the early identification and treatment of victimized boys would, hopefully, result in the prevention of sexual offenses by this population in later life.

Child sexual abuse does not appear to be related to social class, although reliable data are lacking (Rosenfeld, 1977). The Child Sexual Abuse Project in Santa Clara, California, involving 400 suburban families, demonstrated that incest cuts across all socioeconomic groups (Giaretto, 1976a). However, a disproportionate number of the fathers in court cases are from the lower classes (Spencer, 1978), and one large retrospective study of college students showed that lower-income girls were 2–3 times as likely to be abused than girls from average income families (Finkelhor, 1979). Finkelhor's (1984) review of reported cases suggests that victimized boys are more likely than girls to come from single-parent, financially impoverished homes where physical abuse is also present.

Research attempting a comprehensive demographic assessment related to child sexual abuse is sorely needed. Our understanding about the pervasiveness of the problem is limited by the extent to which information published on child sexual abuse represents selected, small, and proportionally nonrepresentative segments of the total population of child abuse victims (Finkelhor & Hotaling, 1984; Kroth, 1979). This lack of research information includes knowledge about the psychological consequences to victims. The aforementioned surveys, estimates, and reports deal only with the acts of abuse, and to a lesser extent the psychological impact they have on the victims (i.e., Finkelhor, 1979; Fromuth, 1986).

PSYCHOLOGICAL EFFECTS

A review of the literature on the psychological effects of sexual abuse on victims finds most reports based on clinical impressions, retrospective surveys and anecdotal accounts. A host of methodological difficulties is evident in these reports, from which most conclusions about the psychological and behavioral effects of sexual abuse have been drawn. Sexual abuse is inconsistently defined across studies, making a comparison of findings difficult. Available information on the long-term effects of sexual abuse is retrospective as opposed to longitudinal and typically represents victims who seek help for problems. There is limited information about victims who may have either not been affected by abuse, benefited from it, or coped with any difficulties successfully on their own. Recently, there have been a few relatively well-designed studies appearing, including a number of large retrospective studies of college students (e.g., Finkelhor, 1979; Fromuth, 1986) and a representative sample of adults drawn from San Francisco (Russell, 1984). Only two studies have examined children or adolescents shortly after the abuse was identified and employed a comparison group (McNeill & Brassard, 1984; Reisinger, 1981). Few studies have employed objective measures, let alone psychometrically sound measures relying mainly on clinical impressions or judgment. Male victims have been largely ignored.

The early studies looking at psychological effects on female child victims (Bender & Grugett, 1952; Rassmussen, 1934) concluded that the victims sustained no lasting effects. Again, these studies had serious methodological problems. For example, Rasmussen defined impairment as the victims being unable to live outside an institution, and Bender and Grugett used psychosis as one criterion. If one expands these rather severe criteria, different conclusions may be reached. The retrospective studies of college students (Finkelhor, 1979; Fromuth, 1985; Gagnon, 1965; Landis, 1956) indicate that only a small percentage of persons who were sexually abused as children could be considered to have severely impaired adult lives (such as a prison or mental hospital experience). However, one half to one third of the victims reported some long-term ill effects of the sexual offense on their emotional development.

- It has been suggested by many writers, based on their clinical experience, that when intrafamilial sexual abuse occurs it is a symptom of general dysfunction within the family (Finkelhor, 1979; Giaretto, 1976a; Kaufman et al., 1954; Rosenfeld, 1977). They also hypothesize that this dysfunctional pattern, rather than the sexual abuse per se, is the major cause of victims' later adjustment difficulties.

There is some empirical data to support this process hypothesis. Johnston (1979) reported that many of the same negative symptoms seen in her population were there before the incest occurred. Herman and Hirschman (1977) reported that severity of complaints in their population of adult women abused as children was more related to the degree of family disorganization and deprivation in their histories than to the acts of incest. Fromuth (1986), in her retrospective study of college students, discovered that the significant relationships found between incidents of childhood sexual abuse and subjects' self-reporting of psychological adjustment were attributable to the family background of the victim. Finally, Reisinger (1981), in a comparison study of the psychopathological differences between matched groups of latency-aged incest victims, incest victims' siblings, outpatient clients and normal school children, obtained results which suggested that family environment and not incest per se seemed to account for differences between the groups.

The clinical literature provides evidence that sexual abuse, and its correlates, may have devastating effects on a child's psychological development. Studies that look at clinical populations report high correlations between child sexual abuse and negative behaviors that indicate psychological difficulties. Odyssey Institute in New York City surveyed 118 female drug abusers and found that 44% of the women experienced incest as children. Sixty-four percent of the offenders were parents or other family members of that generation. Siverson, a family therapist who has treated 500 cases of adolescent drug addiction, found that 70% were involved in some form of family sexual abuse (Benward & Denson-Gerber, 1973). James and Meyerding (1977) interviewed 200 prostitutes in Seattle and found that 22% of the women had been incest victims. In another study of adolescent prostitutes in the Minneapolis area, 75% were victims of incest. In a survey of runaways, sexual abuse was listed as one of three primary reasons why children chose to leave home (Benward & Densen-Gerber, 1973).

The literature suggests several hypotheses as to what aspect of a childhood sexual encounter actually accounts for resultant psychological harm. Summit and Kryso (1978), based on their clinical experiences, postulated that psychological harm occurs not so much as a result of the sexual experience itself or from the act of adult exploitation but from the perception by the child that the sexual acts are socially inappropriate and that the trust and security in the relationship has been exploited. They further state that psychological harm does not correlate with the forcefulness or the perversity of the encounter but with the quality of the environmental response (e.g., parents, social agencies). On the other hand, Finkelhor's (1979) survey indicates that traumatic results are correlated with the amount of force used, increased age difference between the victim and the perpetrator, and a father–daughter relationship.

A recent review of extant studies (Browne & Finkelhor, 1986) tentatively supports Finkelhor's findings, adding the presence of genital contact as an additional factor that appears to contribute to trauma for the victim. The climate of the emotional response did receive some support in that negative parental response was related to greater behavioral disturbances in the victims.

Intrafamilial Child Sexual Abuse

Research on child sexual abuse has been driven by two separate bodies of theory. One form of work has been developed by scholars working with sex offenders (primarily pedophiles; see Otey & Ryan, 1985) and the other by scholars interested in incest victims and their families (Giaretto, 1981). Social learning theory has powerfully influenced the first group, while family systems theory has largely guided the latter (Finkelhor, 1984).

Family systems researchers have concentrated almost exclusively on father–daughter incest, which the theory explains best. Father–daughter incest is relatively rare (with a prevalence rate of 1–4.5%), although a serious form of abuse. Sexual maltreatment perpetrated by an extended family member, acquaintances, and strangers has been largely ignored by these researchers and clinicians.

In nuclear families experiencing father–daughter incest two patterns have been observed. The pattern that has received the most clinical notation is the endogenous or enmeshed family, originally described by Weinburg in his classic clinical study of 203 incestuous families (Rosenfeld, 1977). These family members give one another very little nurturance and support while exhibiting extreme dependency and inability to form relationships outside the home. The family is characterized by a mother who often came from an abusive family herself and experienced deficient mother–daughter relationships (Giaretto, 1976b; Kaufman et al., 1954; Spencer, 1978). The typical father is described as introverted (DeVine, 1980), shy, ineffectual, and having a history of difficulty in social relationships (Gagnon, 1965; Herman & Hirschman, 1981). Events leading to incest usually include breakdowns in the husband–wife and the mother–child relationships. The mother emotionally and physically withdraws from the family, usually turning over her child care and household duties to the daughter. A father–daughter coalition forms. Deprived of a partner, his sexuality perhaps in question, the father may be willing to sexualize this coalition. Unprotected by her mother and lacking a history of warm supportive family relationships, the daughter is in a highly vulnerable position and incest is likely to occur (Finkelhor, 1979; Giaretto, 1976b; Kaufman et al., 1954).

The second pattern is characterized as the multiproblem family. Family life is a series of crises with immaturity and acting-out behaviors predominating (Gottlieb, 1980; Rosenfeld, 1977). The father is seen as imperious and domineering. The mother is immature and dependent, filling the role of a child in the family rather than an adult (Sgroi, 1983; Summit & Kryso, 1978).

A possible third pattern concerns abuse occurring in a stepfamily. Stepfathers appear to abuse stepdaughters at much higher rates (17% vs. 2% biological fathers) and at more serious levels of violation (i.e., forced penile vaginal penetration, anal intercourse) than biological fathers (Russell, 1984). Finkelhor (1979) reported similar high rates in his survey (1979) as did the National Incidence Study (National Center on Child Abuse and Neglect, 1981a). Several explanations for the comparatively high rates of stepfather abuse, including the inhibiting effects of the incest taboo, have been put forth. Additional explanations concerning the higher rates of sexual abuse in stepfather–daughter relationships are the absence of early bonding that commonly occurs between biological fathers and their children when the fathers engage in caregiving activities, the feelings of competition between mother and daughter when the mother remarries and pays less attention to the daughter, and competition between the daughter and the mother for the stepfather's attention (Finkelhor, 1984; Russell, 1984). Pierce and Pierce (1985), in their study of 205 substantiated cases, found that males were also victimized more often by a stepfather than by a natural father and they were victimized significantly more often by stepfathers than females (23% vs. 8%), when the study controlled for the presence of the perpetrator in the home. In this study the natural father was significantly more likely to be the perpetrator in cases involving females (41%) than in cases involving males (20%). The incest taboo and the early bonding hypothesis offer explanations for higher rates of stepfather abuse and would apply in the case of male victims, but these explanations cannot account for the higher percentage of male over female victims in the Pierce and Pierce study. In addition, Dolan (1984) has suggested that stepfamilies may experience greater dysfunctional family dynamics (i.e., power imbalances, weak parental coalitions) which makes sexual abuse of both sexes more likely. She sees the sexually abusive stepfamily as similar to the multiproblem family mentioned above.

Sroufe and his colleagues have studied the "incestuous" family from another, previously neglected, perspective—the seductive mother–son relationship and its consequences for mother–daughter relationships within the same family (Sroufe et al., 1985; Sroufe & Ward, 1980). Eighteen mothers were reliably identified as engaging in seductive behavior (i.e., squeezing the buttocks, full-lipped kisses) with their 2-year-old sons when assessed as part of a larger prospective study of high-risk mothers and their children. Forty-four percent of the seductive mothers reported a history of incest, while only 8% of the control mothers reported such a history. The researchers examined (a) 18 mother–first-born son dyads where seductive behavior was identified at age 2, (b) 17 cases where a sibling was available with either the first- or second-born child exposed to seductive behavior from the mother at the 2-year-old assessment, and (c) 6 cases of seductive behavior identified at age 2 where a mother–older sister dyad was available. All dyads were compared with matched controls to discern the consequences of the seductive mother–son behavior for mother–daughter relationships.

Sroufe and colleagues found that seductiveness was a stable pattern of behavior and it was part of a coherent pattern of family relationships. Seductive mothers engaged in high rates of "nonresponsive intimacy" (i.e., physical behaviors with sensual or sexual attributes that interfered with the child's completion of assigned tasks) and "generational boundary dissolution" (i.e., mothers engaging in role reversal, treating the child as a contemporary) with their first-born sons, were derisive and hostile to their daughters, and were not seductive with other male or female children in the family. Two of the boys with seductive mothers were referred later for sexually inappropriate behavior at school and one was found to have been engaged in mother–son incest for several years (Sroufe et al., 1985).

This fascinating research confirms several nonobvious hypotheses drawn from family system theory and offers intriguing insights as to how incest may be transmitted intergenerationally. The authors propose that the mothers are reconstructing in their own nuclear families a relationship pattern that they know from their own histories. They state that ". . . a stable pattern of seductive behavior will only derive from a history of parentification (spousification), unmet emotional needs, and maternal unavailability (e.g., Boszormenyi-Nagy & Spark, 1973). Such women know only distance (inaccessibility) between mothers and daughters and have feelings of self-depreciation. Thus, their hostility toward their daughters, which takes its special form due to the entire constellation of past family relations, is understandable" (Sroufe et al., 1985, p. 319). Unfortunately, fathers in this sample were unavailable for study.

Effects on Female Victims of Child Sexual Abuse

Some authors (Sloane & Karpinsky, 1942; Summit & Kryso, 1978) have suggested that incest is least harmful psychologically for younger children, because of their naivete, lack of cognitive development, and ignorance of social stigma surrounding the event, with the risks increasing as the subject approaches adolescence. Giaretto (1976b) disagreed, asserting that this is merely the time bomb effect with the event producing most notable acting-out behavior during adolescence, independent of the age at which the incest occurred. In their review of the literature Browne and Finkelhor (1986), however, concluded that the six studies examined found no consistent relationship between age of onset and trauma. They left it an open question as to whether the lack of finding was due to the quality of the studies or the true absence of an effect for age of onset. Only one of the studies reviewed studied children (ages birth–18) shortly after the abuse was identified (Tufts, 1984) and this study did not have a comparison group. The other five studies were retrospective accounts by adults or evaluations of adults in treatment. Thus, it seems unlikely that the question regarding the relationship between psychological effects and the age of onset has been adequately addressed.

Further research looking at the psychological effects of sexual abuse on children must take into account the child's developmental level. Adverse psychological sequelae will be demonstrated in different ways depending on the child's level of psychosocial maturation. The typical ways an infant has of reacting to stress and emotional trauma are obviously different from that of a school-aged child or adolescent.

School-aged children react to stressful events in their lives in terms of aberrant social competencies, behavioral problems, or academic difficulties (Achenbach & Edelbrock, 1981; Achenbach, 1982). Adolescents typically react to negative life events with more severe and obvious acting-out or withdrawn behavior evident in the school, family, or other social situations (Quay & Werry, 1979). Instruments used to describe and compare children must adequately tap the psychological and behavioral manifestations of specific developmental levels and possess adequate psychometric properties.

Despite methodological difficulties, there is some agreement in the clinical and empirical literature as to some common impacts on victims. These commonly reported effects focus primarily on the symptoms and reactions of preadolescent, adolescent, and adult women who were sexually abused as children. A brief review of the findings of selected studies is presented below.

Effects on the Preadolescent Victim. One study of preadolescent victims (Reisinger, 1981) compared four groups of girls between the ages of 6 and 12 (these groups consisted of 15 incest victims, incest victims' siblings, outpatient clients and normal school children) for possible psychopathological differences as measured by the Personality Inventory for Children, the Children's Sentence Completion Test, the Draw-a-Family Test, and the Thematic Apperception Test. The incest victims were significantly more pathological when compared to normal controls but indistinguishable from the outpatient group and their siblings. A wide variety of symptoms were noted which included unmet dependency needs, insecurity, dysfunctional families, and disturbance in family roles. The similarity between the victims and siblings suggest that family factors, and not the incest per se, are responsible for the pathological functioning of the victims.

McNeill and Brassard (1984) compared 20 elementary school-aged incest victims (ages 6–11; 7 years, 8 months was the mean age) with 20 control children matched for grade, socioeconomic status, family size, family structure, birth order, race, and classroom type. The girls were compared on standardized instruments measuring school achievement (Stanford Achievement Test), IQ (Peabody Picture Vocabulary Test – Revised), social competency and behavior problems using both parent (Child Behavior Checklist, Achenbach & Edelbrock, 1981) and teacher ratings (Walker Problem Behavior Identification Checklist, Walker, 1976). The incest group performed significantly more poorly on the combined and individual measures of school achievement, social competency and behavior problems, yet no IQ differences were found. Three quarters of the victims (15) performed in the deviant range on at

least one of the measures as compared to two of the controls. The profile of the elementary-school-age incest victim which emerged was that of a girl who is achieving below expectations, is having difficulties with peer relations, and is presenting acting-out, hyperactive, depressive, and aggressive behaviors at home and school.

Two other studies examined children's reactions shortly after the victimization or its identification but did not use comparison groups. The Division of Child Psychiatry at the Tufts New England Medical Center gathered data on families involved in a treatment program specifically designed for such families (Tufts, 1984). Children ranged in age from infancy to 18 years and were divided into three age groups: preschool, latency, and adolescent. Children were assessed for overt behavior, somatization, self-esteem, and internalized emotional states. The preschool group evidenced "clinically significant pathology" in 17% of the cases in that they were more disturbed compared to a normal population but were less disturbed compared to a psychiatric population. The latency group looked much worse than the preschool group with 40% of this group scoring in the most disturbed range. With a few exceptions the adolescent group looked normal except on a neuroticism scale. In addition to the absence of a control group, the Tufts study employed less than ideal measures. The Louisville Behavior Checklist has weak validity data (Gordon, 1985) and the Piers–Harris Self Concept Scale was normed over 20 years ago on a small town in Pennsylvania, making its norms questionable when applied to a contemporary New England urban sample (Jeske, 1985).

Friedrich, Urguiza, and Beilke (1986) used the Achenbach Child Behavior Checklist with their sample of 61 sexually abused girls maltreated within the 24 months prior to the study. Having been referred by a sexual assault center, these children were seen in the outpatient department for evaluation. Forty-six percent of the sample had scores in the clinical range of the Internalizing Scale (e.g., depression, fearful, withdrawn behavior) and 39% had significantly elevated scores on the Externalizing Scale (e.g., acting-out behaviors). Latency-aged children exhibited externalizing behaviors similar to those reported in the McNeill and Brassard (1984) study, while the children 5 years of age and under tended to exhibit internalizing behaviors.

In summary, the research on sexually abused preadolescent girls suggests significant adjustment problems in a number of important psychological and behavioral domains when compared with matched controls or the standardization samples of norm-referenced tests. The reviewed research consistently demonstrates that 40–70% of the victims studied exhibited significant adjustment problems in one or more domains of psychological and behavioral functioning.

Effects on Adolescent Victims. A review of the literature produced four clinical reports of the effect of incest on adolescent victims. Three of these reports were based on clinical impressions and symptom presentation (Jorne, 1979; Knittle & Tuana, 1980; MacVicar, 1979) and the fourth report used projective techniques (Kaufman, Peck, & Tagiuri, 1954). All four studies reported presenting symptoms such as learning difficulties, sexual promiscuity and somatic complaints. In addition, Knittle and Tuana (1980) described a number of clinical symptoms based upon the 48 families of adolescent victims they treated. The symptoms included the victims' isolation and alienation from peers, distrust of adults, guilt, shame, anger turned inward (depression, suicide attempts), unmet dependency needs, and a helpless victim mentality.

The study that presents the most complete data of the reviewed literature is that of Kaufman et al. (1954). They offer demographic information and results using projective techniques. Depression and guilt were universal clinical findings in the 11 girls who ranged in age from 10 to 17 years. These girls were referred from a variety of sources, but all had been involved in incestuous relationships with a father or father substitute for more than 1 year. The authors report no difference in the level of psychopathology of the victims as a function of involvement with a father or father substitute. The range of presenting symptoms were comparable with those of the other studies. Clinical impressions derived from the Rorschach, the Thematic Apperception Test (TAT) and the Goodenough Draw-a-Man Test revealed trends of depressive anxiety, confusion over sexual identity, fears of sexuality, oral deprivation, and oral sadism. In addition, the girls uniformly saw the mother figures in the TAT as cruel, unjust, and depriving.

Women in Treatment as Adults. Four studies using comparison groups examined women who were sexually abused as children, and who were currently in treatment as adults. The two studies using comparison groups were done with women who were incest victims in childhood. Herman and Hirschman (1981) compared 40 adult women who had incestuous relationships (defined as any physical contact with their father that had to be kept secret) with 20 women whose fathers had been seductive but not overtly incestuous. All the subjects were outpatients in psychotherapy. The groups were roughly matched for age, social class, race, and religious background. Seductive behavior on the part of fathers was defined as behaviors that did not include physical contact and a requirement for secrecy but were clearly sexually motivated. These behaviors included peeping, exhibitionism, leaving pornographic materials for the daughter to find, sharing confidences of sexual exploits, or demanding detailed descriptions of the daughters' real or imagined sexual activities. Women who had experienced overt incest had a significantly higher rate of running away, attempted suicide, and pregnancy during adolescence than the comparison group. This study also suggested a relationship between incestuous families and wife beating.

In the second study, Meiselman (1980) compared the MMPI records of 16 female psychotherapy patients who gave histories of incest with those of 16 nonincest-reporting patients matched for age, education, ethnic group, and referred by the same therapist. The mean profiles for the groups were very similar. There was no significant difference between the groups on any of the scales. However, a prediction that incest-history patients would report more problems in the sexual area than the controls was confirmed. The overall pattern of results suggested that, while the report of incest may not be specifically linked with any diagnostic category, it was associated with the report of various kinds of sexual problems.

Harrison and Lumry (1984) examined 62 adult women drawn from a sample of 191 patients consecutively admitted to a dual-disorder program (coexisting substance use and psychiatric disorder) in a large metropolitan hospital. Twenty-nine percent of the female sample had been sexually victimized in childhood (defined as age 17 and under). With one exception, the offenders were relatives of the victims. Twelve of the 18 perpetrators were parents (10 fathers, 1 stepfather, and 1 adoptive mother) and the remainder were brothers and uncles. Of the rest of the sample, 21% reported sexual victimization as an adult. Child victims were compared with the adult victims and the nonabuse controls.

Family dysfunction appeared to play a major role in the lives of the child victims, even when compared with adult victims. The child victims had parental alcoholism in 67% of the cases as opposed to 46% of adult victims. The dual-disorder program drew such high rates of psychiatric and psychosocial dysfunction that it was impossible to distinguish the victims from non-victims by diagnostic category or level of functioning. Child victims were significantly younger, less likely to have married, and more likely to have made multiple attempts at suicide. Five of the child victims as compared with none of the adult victims had made two or more suicide attempts, and 10 of the child victims as compared with two of the nonvictims had a history of self-mutilation. The three groups were similar in their lack of social skills and resources and in their general level of isolation from stable support systems.

Finally, Tsai, Feldman-Summers, and Edgars (1979) compared child sexual abuse victims seeking therapy with two control groups—a sexually abused group not seeking therapy that considered themselves well adjusted, and a nonabused matched control group. They gave their 90 subjects the Minnesota Multiphasic Personality Inventory and asked them to report on their current adjustment and psychosexual functioning. The clinic abused group had fewer orgasms, were less satisfied sexually, and less satisfied in their relationships with men as compared to the other two groups, which did not differ from one another. The MMPI profiles suggested that the clinic abused group had a history of poor family relationships, poor self-concept, and difficulties with sexual involvement and with their choice of male partners.

In summary, the reviewed research suggests that female victims in treatment as adults seem to evidence problems with sexual adjustment and heterosexual relationships and were at greater risk for suicide and sexual acting out in adolescence than comparison groups composed of nonabused women in treatment or women who were victimized but report good adjustment. However, the incidence of child sexual abuse does not seem to be associated with the occurrence of specific diagnostic entities in adult life.

Retrospective Surveys of Adult Female Victims. Five retrospective surveys of female college students examining the psychological effects of childhood sexual victimization are reported in the literature (Briere & Runtz, 1985; Finkelhor, 1979; Fromuth, 1986; Sedley & Brooks, 1984; Seidner & Calhoun, 1984). The studies address several common adjustment difficulties, but the findings are not consistent. A number of these studies have reported sexual problems in victims. Significantly lower sexual self-esteem was found by one investigator (Finkelhor, 1979) but not by another investigator replicating the Finkelhor study (Fromuth, 1986). Another study, using a matched control group, found that victims were higher on a self-acceptance scale and reported experiencing a greater number of sexual activities and having a higher level of interest and investment in sexual activities than controls. In regard to reported victim depression, the findings were similarly contradictory. Sedley and Brooks (1984) reported that victims evidenced significantly greater symptoms of depression (65% vs. 43%) and anxiety (63% to 41%) than controls and that the symptoms were more likely to result in contacting a doctor or in being hospitalized (18% vs. 4%). Fromuth (1986) found no relationship between scores on the Beck Depression Inventory, or scores obtained on the depression and anxiety scales of the SCL-90, and a history of child sexual abuse. However, she did find a significant relationship between a history of child sexual abuse and scores on the Phobic Anxiety Scale. Briere and Runtz (1985) also used the SCL-90 and found that victims had significantly more depressive symptoms than controls.

The study of Sedley and Brooks (1984) was the only study to examine self-destructive thoughts and actions. They found that significantly more victims reported thoughts of wanting to hurt themselves (39% vs. 16% controls) and having actually attempted suicide (16% vs. 6%) than controls. Finally, Seidner and Calhoun (1984) reported that victims scored significantly lower on measures of social maturity and integrity, were more likely to transgress cultural morals and had less internalized values than controls.

In summary, based upon the retrospective studies of adult females, there are long-term psychological effects as a result of child sexual abuse. Typically, victims do not meet the requirements of specific diagnostic categories; however, both clinical and nonclinical samples tend to report more sexual adjustment problems, difficulties with heterosexual relationships, and suicidal thoughts or actions. Increased rates of depression and/or anxiety may co-occur with a history of victimization, but the occurrences of these symptoms seems to depend upon the availability of environmental support (i.e., parental).

Effects on Male Victims of Sexual Abuse

The incest literature has mainly concentrated on victimization of females. Retrospective studies indicate that there is a significantly underreported population of male victims as well (Finkelhor, 1979; Swift, 1977). Case studies of incestuous families report that a high percentage of male perpetrators were child victims of sexual abuse (Tyler, 1983). Recently, research has begun to offer support for the observation drawn from these clinical reports. When compared with nonoffender controls researchers have found 5 (Langevin, Handy, Hook, Day, & Russon, 1983) to 10 times (Pelto, 1981) as many childhood victimization experiences in the backgrounds of incest offenders. Groth and Burgess (1979) compared a group of 106 child molesters with 64 police officers and found that 32% of the molesters had been sexually traumatized in childhood as opposed to only 3% of the police officers. Ongoing studies of sex offenders report that the majority of offenders were sexually abused or traumatized as children (Longo & Groth, 1983; Prendergast, 1979). Groth and Longo (cited in Freeman-Longo, 1985) found that 80% of their convicted offenders had such a history as compared with 29% of the drug abusers in their study. Freeman-Longo (1985) offered his clinical observation that the frequency of sexual victimization is a major factor in differentiating victims who later victimize others and victims who do not. Thus, while the reported research has methodological flaws, the obvious result of the sexual abuse of male children is that they are at high risk for becoming perpetrators of sexual abuse in adulthood.

The literature presents eight interesting case studies of father–son incest in which family intervention and psychological diagnosis of the father was attempted (Dixon, Arnold, & Calestro, 1978; Langsley, Schwartz, & Laubain, 1968; Raybin, 1969). One theoretical issue presented by these studies was the relative influence of homosexual behavior and family interaction patterns in influencing male child sexual abuse. The conclusions from these eight case studies are that family dynamics are an important variable contributing to the overt abuse. In some of the families, the abuse was only homosexual; in other families both male and female children were abused. The family dynamics appeared similar to those found in father–daughter incest, including a poor marital relationship, an overburdened or inadequate mother who had abdicated her sexual role, and the mother's silent collusion with the family "secret." Moreover, these dynamics included a father with a poor sexual adjustment, a history of poor judgment, and problems with impulse control. Examining the mother–son relationship, Sroufe's excellent empirical studies also implicate family interaction patterns in the development of incestuous relationships (Sroufe et al., 1985; Sroufe & Ward, 1980).

The only report of the psychological effects of male child sexual abuse is found in Dixon et al. (1978). Homicidal and/or suicidal ideation was present in four of the six identified patients. Three of the patients had a history of self-destructiveness in some form, ranging from suicidal gestures and self-mutilation to reckless use of drugs and multiple accidents.

Sexual Abuse by a Stranger

Most studies indicate that only a small percentage of child sexual abuse occurs between strangers (Finkelhor, 1979; Groth, 1979; Russell, 1983). The literature presents no empirical studies of the effects of this type of abuse. Case reports and clinical impressions suggest that children who are sexually abused by strangers suffer fewer enduring consequences than children who are sexually abused by family members. This difference may be partially attributable to the child's sense of betrayal and/or psychological entrapment with family members.

However, there is general agreement that stranger rape may precipitate immediate traumatic effects. A number of authors have focused specifically on the effects of rape on the victim and the rape trauma syndrome in children (Burgess & Holstrom, 1974; Schultz, 1973). They describe this syndrome as consisting of an acute phase in which disorganization may be either quite apparent or be masked by an apparent calm. It is followed by a long-term reorganization phase that may last many months. Typical signs of anxiety may appear during this phase including somatic symptoms, nightmares, and phobias. The reaction of the family is seen as very important either in facilitating or retarding the child's mastery of the traumatic event.

MacVicar (1979) reports clinical symptoms and treatment of seven victims who had a single forcible encounter with a stranger. She states that the two most important factors determining the severity of the disturbance were the age of the girl and the presence or absence of previous neurotic difficulties. There also may be developmental differences among victims in adjustment to these experiences. MacVicar found that the four adolescent girls in her sample were more able to assimilate and master the trauma than the two latency-aged victims.

Child Pornography

In 1977, there were at least 264 different magazines produced in America each month that depicted sexual acts among children or between children and adults. This figure does not include the vast numbers of films or other media materials available (Densen-Gerber, 1980).

Child pornography, the visual reproduction of the sexual abuse of a child, has become big business. It is estimated to generate a half-billion to a billion dollars in profits a year. In recent years the public has become alarmingly aware of this industry and there have been attempts to limit its influence. In 1978, the Protection of Children Against Sexual Exploitation Act was enacted to halt the production and dissemination of pornographic material involving youngsters. In 1982, the United States Supreme Court held that the dissemination of pornography using children is illegal regardless of whether the material is judged legally obscene.

Law enforcement officials estimate that as many as 1 million youngsters, ranging in age from infancy to 16, are sexually molested and then filmed or photographed (*Ladies Home Journal*, 1983). Children become involved in child pornography in many ways. Commercial operators have been known to pick up youngsters who are runaways, to pose as a friend of the family, or to direct child care facilities. Clinical experience suggests that incest victims and neglected children are easy targets for the porn operator.

Until recently, the professional literature reported only one case of a child who was evaluated and treated after the breakup of a child pornography ring (Schoettle, 1980a, 1980b). The

child was initially anxious and depressed. Projective testing revealed themes of helplessness, depression, victimization, and a denial or pulling away from sexual concerns. The child's anger was not directed at the offenders but at her mother for failure to protect her.

More recently, Ann Burgess of Boston City Hospital and her colleagues have extensively studied children involved in pornographic exploitation (Burgess, 1984; *Ladies Home Journal*, 1983). Many of the youngsters withdraw, avoiding all social contact. She believes that the secrecy demanded by the pornographers leaves children feeling that they are society's outsiders and increases the chances they will turn to antisocial behavior.

Child Prostitution

Densen-Gerber (1980) defines child prostitution as the use of, or participation by, children under the age of majority in sexual acts for reward or financial gain with adults or other minors when no force is present. It has been estimated that there are more than one-half million children in the United States who are actively involved in prostitution. Our knowledge of developmental psychology suggests that many children cannot completely comprehend what he or she is consenting to or evaluate the personal consequences. Older adolescents may well comprehend the immediate sexual actions but are grossly unable to comprehend the longer-term psychological effects upon their growth.

The popular media has described the degrading lifestyle of these children and the large numbers of runaways involved (Cline, 1977; Radar, 1982), but no research studies of the psychological effects of this form of abuse could be found. Given the enormous recent growth in the child pornography as well as child prostitution industry, these forms of child sexual exploitation merit professional concern and research, as well as child advocacy on a national and international level.

THEORETICAL EXPLANATIONS

Independent of theory development in child maltreatment, researchers working with sex offenders (usually clinical or forensic psychologists by training) had been building theories (influenced predominantly by social learning theory) to explain the development of sexually deviant behavior, including child molestation (e.g., Becker & Abel, 1985). Clinicians/researchers working with incest victims and their families began drawing from family systems theory (e.g., Giaretto, 1981). Offender-based research looked at the offender in isolation, ignoring family variables, and victim researchers focused almost exclusively on the father–daughter dyad, ignoring abuse perpetrated by extended family members and acquaintances (Finkelhor, 1984).

Examining both literatures, Finkelhor (1984) developed a powerful four-factor model that ties the psychological and sociological literature as well as offender-driven and victim-driven research together in a coherent and testable framework that does not distinguish between intra- and extrafamilial abuse. He proposes that all factors relating to sexual abuse could be grouped into four essential preconditions that must be met in order for sexual abuse to occur:

Motivation

First, a potential offender needs to have some desire to abuse a child. Components of this motivation theory include what Finkelhor terms emotional congruence (sexual contact with a child meets an important emotional need), sexual arousal (the child could supply sexual gratification for that person), and blockage (other sources of sexual gratification appear unavailable or seem less satisfying). The three components are not preconditions themselves in that all are not required for motivation to sexually abuse a child, although all may be present in any given situation. Finkelhor, from his review of the literature, offers explanations at the individual and at the socio-cultural level for how each of the four factors and their subcomponents might develop. For instance, in regard to the emotional congruence component of the motivation precondition, he offers such individual explanations as (a) an arrested emotional development, (b) a need to feel powerful and controlling, and (c) a reenactment of a childhood trauma as a means of ameliorating the residual hurt. A socio-cultural explanation offered is the masculine need to be dominant in sexual relationships.

Overcoming Internal Inhibitors

In order to abuse, a perpetrator not only must be motivated but must also overcome internal inhibitions that block acting on the motivation. Most members of society have such inhibitions which may vary in intensity. These inhibitions may be very strong (e.g., they are strongly attracted to children but have even stronger internal controls) or relatively weak (e.g., they are only mildly inhibited but not strongly attracted to children). Individual reasons for disinhibition include alcohol, impulse disorders, or a family incest history. Possible socio-cultural explanations for why some individuals are able to overcome internal inhibitions include social toleration for deviance committed when drunk or social toleration of sexual interest in children.

Factors Predisposing to Overcoming External Inhibitors

While the first two factors dispose a perpetrator to child sexual abuse, they do not account for who is chosen for a victim or why abuse occurs in any given situation. This third precondition addresses forces in the external environment, outside of the perpetrator and the victim, that inhibit or disinhibit the perpetrator. The research and clinical literature indicates that mothers play a central role in protecting children from abuse. A mother's incapacitation or absence has been repeatedly associated with increased rates of abuse. Other external deterrents include the child's involvement with neighbors, teachers and friends, and the family's openness to public scrutiny. The lack of an opportunity for the offender and child to be alone together is an effective external inhibitor. Other socio-cultural explanations for why some offenders are able to overcome external inhibitions suggested by Finkelhor include barriers to women's equality, erosion of social networks, and an ideology honoring the sanctity of family life.

Overcoming the Resistance of the Child

Children are able to avoid abuse or resist it and thus they play a large role in determining whether they are abused. Individual factors identified through research as influencing the likelihood of being abused include a history of emotional insecurity or deprivation, a lack of knowledge about sexual abuse, a situation of unusual trust between child and offender (e.g., the offender is a parent), and the use of coercion. Children may

avoid abuse by overt refusal, by immediately telling a responsive adult of overtures made to them,
or by giving the impression that they would do
these things if approached. Any event that makes
a child feel emotionally vulnerable increases the
chances that the child will be more open to the
overtures of an offender and if he or she is
abused, these acts make it less likely that he or
she will have someone upon whom they can
depend. However, if the offender uses force the
child's vulnerability may not play any role in
determining whether or not abuse occurs. Socio-
cultural explanations suggested by Finkelhor as
predisposing offenders to overcome the child's
resistance are the paucity of sex education for
children in this country and the social powerlessness of children.

In Finkelhor's model, all four preconditions are
essential if abuse is to occur and be understood.
There are a number of advantages of this model,
including its comprehensiveness in addressing
both intra- and extrafamilial abuse, the fact that
it places the blame for the abuse on the offender
and not on the victim, the family dynamics, or
the mother; that it includes both individual (psychological) and environmental/ecological (sociological) explanations for the development of
preconditions; and that it suggests a methodology for evaluating and intervening with offenders, victims, and their families.

Finally, successful theoretical explanation of
child sexual abuse must also account for the disproportionate numbers of male offenders;
Finkelhor (1979) provides an interesting beginning in this direction. He suggests several factors
which may contribute to the greater incidence of
male sexual abuse perpetrators, including that of
women's greater responsibility for and greater
closeness to children may inhibit inappropriate
sexual behavior; that men are socialized to see
sexual gratification as an independent act, in
contrast with women's emphasis on a mutually
shared experience, and thus men more readily
perceive another person as an object; and that
men are often socialized to seek out partners of
inferior status while women often choose older
and larger partners. The present review of the
literature consistently suggests that the rates of
sexually abusive male perpetrators is significantly higher than female perpetrators; although
there are some tentative explanations offered
for this phenomenon these explanations do not
seem sufficiently comprehensive. Research drawn
from animal studies, anthropology, and socio-

biology may add to our understanding of this
phenomenon.

INTERVENTIONS

At this point it seems clear that child sexual
abuse is clearly a form of psychological maltreatment. The research documents that the occurrence of sexual abuse is associated with
emotional distress and behavioral disturbances
on the part of victims. This, then, raises the question of what can be done to intervene on behalf
of victims or potential victims.

Prevention

Prevention may be the most widely touted and
least practiced intervention available to mental
health and medical professionals. Fortunately, a
number of effective preventive programs have
been developed for both intra- and extrafamilial
sexual abuse (see Conte, 1984, for a review, and
National Committee for the Prevention of Child
Abuse, 1985, for a list of resources). Approaches
focus on providing information to parents, on
teaching children to identify problem situations
and protect themselves, and on providing more
intensive help for families at risk for sexual
abuse.

Brassard, Tyler, and Kehle (1983) describe in
detail school programs designed to prevent
intrafamilial sexual abuse. Highlighted are prevention efforts that focus on the provision to both
parents and children of factual information on
sexual abuse, appropriate and inappropriate
touch, the respective role responsibilities of parents and children, and a sex education approach
that stresses the values of nonexploitation and
discrimination in the choice of whether to engage
in sexual behavior and the choice of partners.

Most programs, however, focus their prevention efforts exclusively on children, tailoring the
program to a particular age group. While programs vary widely in presentation format and
duration, almost all include a group presentation, with a common set of concepts: the child
has a right to control access to his own body; the
difference between appropriate and inappropriate touch; secrets; the importance of trusting
one's feelings; how to say no when inappropriately touched; and how to identify people who
can help (Conte, Rosen, Saperstein, & Shermack, 1985). Several of the programs have used
some form of evaluation, usually a pretest–post-

test interview or questionnaire, that demonstrated increased knowledge of prevention concepts following the intervention (Plummer, 1984; Ray, 1984; You're in Charge, 1982). Others have used comparison groups and have found a significant increase in knowledge of children in treatment as compared to the control group (Conte et al., 1985; Downer, 1984).

While all of the reported programs seem to demonstrate some increase in knowledge as a result of the prevention presentations, the lasting benefits of such programs have been questioned (Conte, 1984). Knowledge of prevention concepts does not necessarily translate into effective prevention skills (e.g., escape, reporting to a concerned adult). Group presentations do not result in increased knowledge in all children (Conte et al., 1985), and some presentation formats may actually mislead children. For example, Conte (1984) reports that a group of children viewing a filmstrip on Penelope Mouse, sexually abused by her uncle, told their teacher after the presentation that they thought only mice were sexually abused. Formats may also increase fearfulness, or be so short-lived in their effects as to make the utility of one-shot presentations questionable (Plummer, 1984). In summary, the prevention programs and their evaluators have effectively stimulated research on the effectiveness of prevention programs and highlighted methodological issues that need to be addressed (Conte, 1984).

Analogue approaches using single-subject designs offer a solution to some of the difficulties with group presentations and their evaluation. A behavioral program designed to teach preschool children to resist typical lures offered by potential kidnappers or child molesters was demonstrated to be effective after a week of daily training (Poche, Brouwer, & Swearingen, 1981). Training was completely maintained for one of the two children tested on a 3-month follow-up and partially maintained by the second child. The authors recommended a 2–3-month "booster" session for maintenance of training. The extreme vulnerability of preschool children to all types of sexual abuse makes this particular program attractive not only for protection from strangers but as a means of preventing further abuse when intrafamilial abuse is suspected or known. Conte (1984) has raised ethical questions about the effects of adult lures that do not result in abuse. Will the experiment result in a desensitization of the children to adult strangers

approaching them on the playground? It is a good question and it illustrates the complexity of conducting prevention programs and research.

Crisis nurseries are a support service which offer temporary shelter for abused children as well as a place for parents in crisis to leave their children until the crisis abates (usually within several days). Other services such as parenting classes, family therapy, and marital or individual therapy are sometimes offered to help parents prevent the occurrence or reoccurrence of intrafamilial child abuse (Tyler, 1978). An empirical evaluation of these nurseries has not been done. Although the program's rationale appears sound and the community response is quite positive, evaluation of these programs is needed.

Treatment

In issues related to treatment of child sexual abuse, law and practice have focused almost exclusively on the punishment and rehabilitation of the offender (Kroth, 1979; Tyler & Brassard, 1984). Recently, comprehensive treatment programs involving the entire family have been developed specifically for intrafamilial sexual abuse (Gottlieb, 1980; Kroth, 1979; Sgroi, 1983). For pedophiles (adults with sexual attraction exclusively toward underage children) who molest unfamiliar children, incarceration, and occasionally aversion therapy, remains the primary treatment modality (Kroth, 1979; Poche, Brouwer, & Swearingen, 1981). While treatment effectiveness (defined here as recidivism) is moderate for this latter group, experts in the area are pessimistic about treatment success (Costell, 1980; Groth, 1979). This has led to an increased interest in adolescent sex offenders—a group which clinicians feel is more likely to respond positively to treatment (see Otey & Ryan, 1985).

Of the comprehensive treatment programs only two to date have published evaluation results. The Child Sexual Abuse Treatment Program (CSATP) in Santa Clara County, California, is the best known and the first to report its findings (Giaretto, 1981; Kroth, 1979). This multimodal, family-oriented therapeutic package consists of treatment by a variety of professionals and student volunteers as well as a self-help component. No recidivism of father–daughter incest was reported for 34 families completing the program during the six-month evaluation (Kroth, 1979). In addition, on a number of behavioral and academic measures victims showed moderate improvement. The cross-sectional evaluation of program effectiveness examined families at the beginning, middle, and end of therapy. The poor matching of comparison groups, the asking of fathers and not victims if abuse had reoccurred, in addition to the use of a relatively weak evaluation paradigm, limits the confidence one can have in the results. However, given the apparent short-term success of CSATP, a longitudinal follow-up of program participants and a replication of this model in other settings are hoped for.

The second program to report treatment results was Connecticut's Sexual Trauma Treatment Program (STTP). In the STTP model, each family member or participant was assigned a therapist. The collective therapists utilized a variety of interventions such as art therapy and family therapy in their work with the abusive family (Sgori, 1983). One of the strengths of this model is the detail with which the interventions are described, and thus are replicable, by future researchers. Improvement was shown in approximately 50% of the problems addressed in treatment over a 2-year period. In contrast to the enthusiastic reports from the Santa Clara group, Sgori stresses the tremendous difficulty of effecting positive change within this population. The low level of participation in the program on the part of offending fathers may account in part for their lower success rate.

CONCLUSIONS AND DIRECTIONS

Child sexual abuse is a form of psychological abuse. The empirical studies, although fraught with methodological difficulties, indicate that for many children sexual abuse has long-term negative psychological and behavioral effects. The etiological factors determining these longer-term effects seem to be a combination of at least four important factors: the actual immediate psychological and physical impact upon the child; the established patterns of intervention among the immediate family members; the therapeutic qualities of the immediate environmental response to the acts of sexual abuse; and finally, the idiosyncratic manner in which the child assimilates, accommodates, and comes to understand the meaning and implications of these abusive acts in his or her cognitive system.

Finkelhor (1984) has proposed a promising four-factor model that attempts to explain intra- and extrafamilial abuse, integrates psychological

and sociological research, places appropriate responsibility on the offender, and focuses intervention and research efforts. While several prevention programs have been demonstrated to be effective, results from evaluations of comprehensive treatment programs for incestuous families have been mixed.

Sound empirical research and efforts to validate Finkelhor's model are sorely needed in this area. Suggested research focuses include (a) direct observation of incest-family interaction similar to the study done by Burgess and Conger (1978) with physically abusive, neglectful, and normal families; (b) longitudinal studies of populations at risk for sexual abuse in conjunction with direct observation methods such as the work being done in the University of Minnesota's Mother–Child Project (Egeland & Sroufe, 1981); (c) intensive examination of sexually abused children who appear invulnerable to the negative effects of child sexual abuse; and (d) examination of the optimal psychosexual development and gender-identity formation.

On a policy level several approaches are desirable, such as (a) the national collection of sexual abuse statistics, commonly defined and reported across states; (b) effective prevention programs for children should be implemented and evaluated across the country in the schools; and (c) treatment model development and evaluation along the lines of the Santa Clara and Connecticut programs and the adolescent sex offender program as described by Otey and Ryan (1983); these should be continued if families, victims and offenders are to be understood and helped and child sexual abuse prevented.

REFERENCES

Abel, G. G., Mittelman, M. S., & Becker, J. V. (1985). Sex offenders: Results of assessment and recommendations for treatment. In M. H. Ben-Aron, S. J. Hucker, and S. J. Webster (Eds.), *Clinical criminology* (pp. 191–205). Toronto, Canada: M & M Graphics.

Achenbach, T. M. (1982). *Developmental psychopathology* (2nd ed.). New York: Wiley.

Achenbach, T. M., & Edelbrock, C. S. (1981). Behavioral problems and competencies reported by parents of normal and disturbed children aged 4 through 16. *Monographs of the Society for Research in Child Development*, 46(Serial No. 188).

Becker, J. V., & Abel, G. G. (1985). Methodological and ethical issues in evaluating and treating adolescent sexual offenders. In E. M. Otey and G. D. Ryan (Eds.), *Adolescent sex offenders: Issues in research and treatment.* Rockville, MD: United States Department of Health and Human Services DHHS Publication No. (ADM)85-1396.

Bender, D., & Blau, A. (1937). The reaction of children to sexual relations with adults. *American Journal of Orthopsychiatry, 7,* 500-518.

Bender, L., & Grugett, A. (1952). A follow-up study of children who had atypical sexual experience. *American Journal of Orthopsychiatry, 2,* 825-837.

Benward, J., & Densen-Gerber, J. (1973). Incest as a causative factor in antisocial behavior: An exploratory study. *Contemporary Drug Problems, 4,* 322-340.

Boszormenyi-Nagy, I., & Spark, G. (1973). *Invisible loyalties: Reciprocity in intergenerational family therapy.* New York: Harper & Row.

Brant, R. S. T., & Tisza, V. B. (1977). The sexually misused child. *American Journal of Orthopsychiatry, 4*(1), 80-90.

Brassard, M. R., Tyler, A. H., & Kehle, T. J. (1983). School programs to prevent child sexual abuse. *Child Abuse and Neglect, 7,* 241-245.

Briere, J., & Runtz, M. (1985, August). *Symptomology associated with prior sexual abuse in a nonclinical sample.* Paper presented at the annual meeting of the American Psychological Association, Los Angeles, CA.

Browne, A., & Finkelhor, D. (1986). Impact of child sexual abuse: A review of the research. *Psychological Bulletin, 99,* 66-77.

Burgess, A. W., & Holmstrom, L. L. (1974). Crisis and counseling requests of rape victims. *Nursing Research, 23*(3), 196-202.

Burgess, A. W. (Ed.). (1984). *Child pornography and sex rings.* Lexington, MA: Lexington Books, D. C. Heath and Co.

Burgess, R. L., & Conger, R. D. (1978). Family interaction in abusive, neglectful, and normal families. *Child Development, 49,* 1163-1173.

Cline, F. (1977, January 18). A haven for the sexually exploited. *New York Times,* p. 28.

Conte, J. R. (1984, August). *Research on the prevention of sexual abuse of children.* Paper presented at the Second National Conference for Family Violence Researchers, Durham, NH.

Conte, J. R., Rosen, C., Saperstein, L., & Shermack, R. (1985). An evaluation of a program to prevent the sexual victimization of young children. *Child Abuse and Neglect, 9,* 319-328.

Cooper, I., & Cormier, B. M. (1982). Intergenerational transmission of incest. *Canadian Journal of Psychiatry, 27*(3), 231-235.

Costell, R. M. (1980). The nature and treatment of male sex offenders. In B. B. Jones, L. L. Jenstrom, & K. MacFarlane (Eds.), *Sexual abuse of children: Selected readings* (pp. 29-30). Washing-

ton, DC: DHHS Publications No. (OHDS) 78-30161.

Densen-Gerber, J. (1980). Child prostitution and child pornography. In B. B. Jones, L. L. Jenstrom, & K. MacFarlane (Eds.), *Sexual abuse of children: Selected readings* (pp. 77-81). Washington, DC: DHHS Publication No. (OHDS) 78-30161.

DeVine, R. (1980). Incest: A review of the literature. In B. B. Jones, L. L. Jenstrom, & K. MacFarlane (Eds.), *Sexual abuse of children: Selected readings* (pp. 11-15). Washington, DC: DHHS Publication No. (OHDS) 78-30161.

Dixon, K. N., Arnold, L. E., & Calestro, K. (1978). Father–son incest: Underreported psychiatric problem? *American Journal of Psychiatry, 135*(7), 835-838.

Doek, J. E. (1981). Sexual abuse of children: An examination of European criminal law. In P. Mrazek & C. H. Kempe (Eds.), *Sexually abused children and their families* (pp. 75-84). New York: Pergamon Press.

Dolan, K. J. (1984, August). *The role of stepfamilies in severity of reported cases of child sexual abuse.* Paper presented at the Second National Family Violence Conference at the University of New Hampshire, Durham, NH.

Downer, A. (1984). *Evaluation of talking about touching.* Available from A. Downer, Committee for Children, PO Box 15190, Seattle, WA 98115.

Egeland, B., & Sroufe, L. A. (1981). Attachment and early maltreatment. *Child Development, 52,* 44-52.

Finkelhor, D. (1979). *Sexually victimized children.* New York: The Free Press.

Finkelhor, D. (1984). *Child sexual abuse: New theory and research.* New York: Free Press.

Finkelhor, D., & Hotaling, G. T. (1984). Sexual abuse in the National Incidence Study of Child Abuse and Neglect. *Child Abuse and Neglect, 8,* 23-28.

Fraser, B. G. (1981). Sexual child abuse: The legislation and the law in the United States. In P. Mrazek & C. H. Kempe (Eds.), *Sexually abused children and their families* (pp. 55-73). New York: Pergamon Press.

Freeman-Longo, R. E. (1985). The adolescent sexual offender: Background and research prospectives. In E. M. Otey and G. D. Ryan (Eds.), *Adolescent sex offenders: Issues in research and treatment* (pp. 130-146). Rockville, MD: U.S. Department of Health and Human Services/DHHS Publication No. (ADM) 85-1396.

Friedrich, W. N., Urguiza, A. J., & Beilke, R. (1986). Behavioral problems in sexually abused young children. *Journal of Pediatric Psychology, 11,* 47-57.

Fromuth, M. E. (1986). The relationship of childhood sexual abuse with later psychological and sexual adjustment in a sample of college women. *Child Abuse and Neglect, 10,* 5–15.

Gagnon, J. (1965). Female child victims of sex offenses. *Social Problems, 13,* 176–192.

Gelles, R. (1975). The social construction of child abuse. *American Journal of Orthopsychiatry, 45,* 363–371.

Gelles, R. (1982). Problems in defining and labeling child abuse. In R. H. Starr, Jr. (Ed.), *Child abuse prediction: Policy implications.* Cambridge, MA: Ballinger.

Giaretto, H. (1976a). Humanistic treatment of father–daughter incest. In R. Helfer & C. H. Kempe (Eds.), *Child abuse and neglect.* Cambridge, MA: Ballinger Publications.

Giaretto, H. (1976b). The treatment of father–daughter incest. *Children Today, 4,* 34–35.

Giaretto, H. G. (1981). A comprehensive child sexual abuse treatment program. In P. B. Mrazek & C. H. Kempe (Eds.), *Sexually abused children and their families* (pp. 179–198). New York: Pergamon Press.

Gordon, B. N. (1985). Review of Louisville Behavior Checklist. In J. V. Mitchell, Jr. (Ed.), *The ninth mental measurements yearbook* (pp. 634–635). Lincoln, NE: Buros Institute of Mental Measurements, University of Nebraska–Lincoln.

Gottlieb, B. (1980). Incest: Therapeutic intervention in a unique form of sexual abuse. In K. G. Warner (Ed.), *Rage and sexual assault: Management and intervention.* Germantown, MD: Aspen Publications.

Groth, N. A. (1979). *Men who rape.* New York: Plenum Press.

Groth, N. A., & Burgess, A. W. (1979). Sexual trauma in the life histories of rapists and child molesters. *Victimology, 4,* 10–16.

Harrison, P. A., & Lumry, A. E. (1984, August). *Female sexual abuse victims: Perspectives on family dysfunction, substance abuse and psychiatric disorders.* Paper presented at the Second National Conference for Family Violence Researchers, University of New Hampshire, Durham, NH.

Herman, J., & Hirschman, L. (1977). Families at risk for father–daughter incest. *Signs: Journal of Women in Culture and Society, 2,* 735–756.

Herman, J., & Hirschman, L. (1981). Families at risk for father–daughter incest. *American Journal of Psychiatry, 138,* 967–970.

James, J., & Meyerding, J. (1977). Early sexual experiences as a factor in prostitution. *Archives of Sexual Behavior, 7,* 31–42.

Jeske, R. J. (1985). Review of Piers–Harris Children's Self-Concept Scale. In J. V. Mitchell, Jr. (Ed.), *The ninth mental measurements yearbook* (pp. 960–961). Lincoln, NE: Buros Institute of Mental Measurements, University of Nebraska–Lincoln.

Johnston, M. S. (1979). The sexually mistreated

child: Diagnostic evaluation. *Child Abuse and Neglect, 3,* 943–951.

Jorne, P. S. (1979). Treating sexually abused children. *Child Abuse and Neglect, 3,* 235–290.

Kaufman, I., Peck, A., & Tagiuri, C. (1954). The family constellation and overt incestuous relations between father and daughter. *American Journal of Orthopsychiatry, 24,* 266–279.

Kercher, G. A., & McShane, M. (1984). The prevalence of child sexual abuse victimization in an adult sample of Texas residents. *Child Abuse and Neglect, 8,* 495–501.

Kinsey, A. C. et al. (1953). *Sexual behavior in the human female.* Philadelphia: Saunders.

Knittle, B. J., & Tuana, S. J. (1980). Group therapy as primary treatment for adolescent victims of intrafamilial sexual abuse. *Clinical Social Work Journal, 8*(4), 236–242.

Kroth, J. A. (1979). *Child sexual abuse: Analysis of a family therapy approach.* Springfield, IL: Charles C Thomas.

Ladies Home Journal (1983, April). Innocence for sale. Author.

Landis, J. T. (1956). Experiences of 500 children with adult sexual deviation. *Psychiatric Quarterly, 30,* 91–109.

Langevin, R., Handy, L., Hook, H., Day, D., & Russon, A. (1983). Are incestuous fathers pedophilic and aggressive? In R. Langevin (Ed.), *Erotic preference, gender identity and aggression.* NY: Erlbaum Associates.

Langsley, D. G., Schwartz, M. N., & Laubain, R. H. (1968). Father–son incest. *Comprehensive Psychiatry, 9*(3), 218–226.

Longo, R. E., & Groth, N. A. (1983). Juvenile sexual offenses in the histories of adult rapists and child molesters. *International Journal of Offender Therapy and Comparative Criminology, 27,* 150–155.

MacVicar, K. (1979). Psychotherapeutic issues in the treatment of sexually abused girls. *Journal of Child Psychiatry, 2,* 342–353.

Manarino, A. P., & Cohen, J. A. (1986). A clinical–demographic study of sexually abused children. *Child Abuse and Neglect, 10,* 17–23.

McNeill, L., & Brassard, M. R. (1984, September). *The behavioral correlates of father–daughter incest with elementary school aged girls.* Paper presented at the Fifth International Congress on Child Abuse and Neglect, Montreal, Canada.

Meiselman, K. (1980). Personality characteristics of incest history, psychotherapy patients: A research note. *Archives of Sexual Behavior, 9,* 195–197.

Mrazek, P. B., & Mrazek, D. A. (1981). The effects of child sexual abuse: Methodological considerations. In P. B. Mrazek & C. H. Kempe (Eds.), *Sexually abused children and their families.* New York: Pergamon Press.

National Center on Child Abuse and Neglect.

(1981a). *Study findings: National study of the incidence and severity of child abuse and neglect.* Washington, DC: DHHS Publication No. (OHDS) 81-30325.

National Center on Child Abuse and Neglect. (1981b). *Study methodology: National study of the incidence and severity of child abuse and neglect.* Washington, DC: OHDS.

National Committee for Prevention of Child Abuse (1985). *Child sexual abuse prevention resources.* Chicago, IL: Author (332 S. Michigan Ave. Suite 1250, Chicago, IL 60604-4357).

Navarre, E. L. (1983). *Sexually abused children, prevention, protection and care.* Indianapolis: Indiana University School of Social Work.

Otey, E. M., & Ryan, G. D. (Eds.). (1985). *Adolescent sex offenders: Issues in research and treatment.* Rockville, MD: United States Department of Health and Human Services DHHS Publication No. (ADM) 85-1396.

Pelto, V. (1981). *Male incest offenders and non-offenders: A comparison of early sexual history.* Dissertation, United States International University. Ann Arbor, MI: University Microfilms.

Pierce, R., & Pierce, L. H. (1985). The sexually abused child: A comparison of male and female victims. *Child Abuse and Neglect, 9,* 191-199.

Plummer, C. (1984, April). *Research on prevention: What school programs teach children.* Paper presented at the Third National Conference on Sexual Victimization of Children, Washington, DC.

Poche, C., Brouwer, R., & Swearingen, M. (1981). Teaching self-protection to young children. *Journal of Applied Behavior Analysis, 14,* 169-176.

Prendergast, W. E. (1979, October). The sex offender: How to spot him before it's too late. *Sexology.*

Quay, H. C., & Werry, J. S. (1979). *Psychopathological disorders of childhood* (2nd ed.). New York: Wiley.

Radar, D. (1982, September 5). Child on the run: A deepening American tragedy. *Parade,* pp. 4-7.

Rasmussen, A. (1934). Die bedeutung sexueller attentate auf kinder unter 14 jahren fur die entwicklung von geisteskrankheiten und charakteranomalien. *Acta Psychiatrie et Neurologie, 9,* 351.

Ray, J. (1984). *Evaluation of the child sexual abuse prevention program.* Unpublished manuscript available from the author at Rape Crisis Network, N1226 Howard Street, Spokane, WA 98201.

Raybin, J. B. (1969). Homosexual incest. *The Journal of Nervous and Mental Disease, 148(2),* 105-109.

Reisinger, M. C. (1981). *Psychological test profiles of latency aged female incest victims: A comparative study.* Unpublished doctoral dissertation, Brigham Young University.

Rosenfeld, A. (1977). Sexual misuse and the family. *Victimology: An International Journal, 2,* 226-235.

Russell, D. E. H. (1983). The incidence and prevalence of intrafamilial and extrafamilial sexual abuse of female children. *Child Abuse and Neglect, 7,* 133-146.

Russell, D. E. H. (1984). The prevalence and seriousness of incestuous abuse: Stepfathers vs. biological fathers. *Child Abuse and Neglect, 8,* 15-22.

Schoettle, U. C. (1980a). Treatment of the child pornography patient. *American Journal of Psychiatry, 137(9),* 1109-1110.

Schoettle, U. C. (1980b). Child exploitation, a study of child pornography. *Journal of the American Academy of Child Psychiatry, 19,* 289-299.

Schultz, L. G. (1973). The child sex victim: Social, psychological and legal perspectives. *Child Welfare, 11(3),* 147-156.

Sedley, M. A., & Brooks, B. (1984). Factors associated with a history of childhood sexual experience in a nonclinical female population. *Journal of the American Academy of Child Psychiatry, 23,* 215-218.

Seidner, A., & Calhoun, K. S. (1984, August). *Childhood sexual abuse: Factors related to differential adult adjustment.* Paper presented at the Second National Conference for Family Violence Researchers, University of New Hampshire, Durham, NH.

Sgroi, S. M. (1983). *Handbook of clinical intervention in child sexual abuse.* Lexington: D. C. Heath and Co.

Sloane, P., & Karpinsky, E. (1942). Effects of incest on participants. *American Journal of Orthopsychiatry, 12,* 666-673.

Spencer, J. (1978). Father–daughter incest: A clinical view from the corrections field. *Child Welfare, 57(9),* 518-528.

Sroufe, L. A., Jacobvitz, D., Mangelsdorf, S., DeAngelo, E., & Ward, M. J. (1985). Generational boundary dissolution between mothers and their preschool children. *Child Development, 56,* 317-325.

Sroufe, L. A., & Ward, M. J. (1980). Seductive behavior of mothers of toddlers: Occurrence, correlates and family origins. *Child Development, 51,* 1222-1229.

Summit, R., & Kryso, J. (1978). Sexual abuse of children. *American Journal of Orthopsychiatry, 48(2),* 237-251.

Swift, C. (1977). Sexual victimization of children: An urban mental health center survey. *Victimology, 2(2),* 322-327.

Tsai, M., Feldman-Summer, S. S., & Edgars, M. (1979). Childhood molestation: Variables related to differential impacts on psychosexual functioning in adult women. *Journal of Abnormal Psychology, 88,* 407–417.

Tufts' New England Medical Center, Division of Child Psychiatry (1984). *Sexually exploited children: Service and research project.* Final report for the Office of Juvenile Justice and Delinquency Prevention. Washington, DC: U.S. Department of Justice.

Tyler, A. H. (1978). *Conceptualization and development of a model crisis nursery.* Unpublished masters thesis, University of Utah.

Tyler, A. H. (1983). *A comparison of child-abusing and nonabusing fathers on measures of: Marital adjustment, life-stress, and social support.* Unpub-lished doctoral dissertation, University of Utah.

Tyler, A. H., & Brassard, M. R. (1984). Abuse in the investigation and treatment of intrafamilial child sex abuse. *Child Abuse and Neglect, 8,* 47–53.

Walker, H. M. (1976). *Walker problem behavior identification checklist.* Los Angeles, CA: Western Psychological Services.

Walters, D. R. (1975). *Physical and sexual abuse of children: Causes and treatment.* Bloomington: Indiana University Press.

You're in Charge, Inc. (1982). An instructional program available from You're in Charge, Inc. 1618 Yale, Salt Lake City, Utah.

6

Substance Abuse

Michael J. Cohn

One day Susie was found walking through the halls of her school. Students would ask her where she was going and she would stare blankly into space muttering silently to herself. Finally, the school counselor saw her out walking the halls during class time and tried to talk to her. Susie became enraged and uncontrolled. It was later discovered that Susie was suffering from drug-induced psychosis, which may have been the result of PCP use. Susie's parents indicated they had no idea she was taking drugs.

Pete went to a party on a Saturday night in the small midwestern city where he lived. The next day he found himself in jail. The police officer told him that after the party, Pete had been driving his car and had run into a man who was jogging on the side of the road. Pete had swerved all over the road prior to hitting the man. The man was in serious condition in the local hospital. Pete had no memory of the occurrence, as he had been drinking heavily the night before and had struck the man in an alcohol-induced state known as a blackout.

Jim is 12 years old. He came into a local hospital emergency room after having made a suicidal gesture, attempting to stab himself with a Boy Scout knife. The social worker who interviewed him asked him why he had done such a thing. Jim could only state that he was tired of living and saw no hope. Jim's parents accompanied him to the hospital. It was discovered by the social worker that Jim's father was an

actively drinking alcoholic. The social worker asked him if he tried to commit suicide because of his father's drinking. Jim said that his father was mean to him and to his mother and that he could no longer stand being in the house with all of the angriness, which is why he tried to stab himself.

BACKGROUND

Although the three cases just described are composites of actual cases and do not necessarily reflect specific incidents, they illustrate the emotional trauma that young people experience as a result of their own use of drugs or alcohol or the use of alcohol or drugs in the lives of people close to them.

As Peterson (1978) and Ling and del Prado (1978) note, use of drugs throughout the world in order to achieve a state of mood alteration has occurred for centuries. Most cultures restricted the use of drugs for such purposes to certain groups within the culture. The groups included *adult* members of the culture who achieved the right to use such chemicals due to age, success, or initiation rites, or all three. Frequently, the role of substances included enhancing one's ability to experience the spiritual component of life. Usually, individuals who participated in these activities did so in a somewhat controlled environment where they were monitored by other members of the group in case assistance was needed.

Today, young people throughout the world use mocd-altering substances probably more than ever before in the world's history. Greater accessibility to substances that provide more potent effects, under virtually any circumstances, poses a significant threat to the psychological health and safety of young people worldwide. A new culture has developed over the last two decades which endorses recreational use of substances. This new youth culture created the phenomenon of substance use we experience today, regrettably with frequent tragic effects for the users, their families, communities, and societies. Peterson (1978) and Ling and del Prado (1978) note that international efforts addressing the issue of youth substance use and abuse are summarized by the General Assembly of the United Nations in establishing the United Nations Fund for Drug Abuse Control. This fund helps interested governments or organizations meet objectives that include:

1. Limiting the supply of illegal drugs by stopping uncontrolled production and manufacturing;
2. Providing capabilities, administrative and technical, to existing agencies concerned with the elimination of illicit trafficking of substances;
3. Developing education and special international campaigns designed to prevent substance abuse;
4. Developing methods to treat, rehabilitate, and socially integrate substance-dependent persons by providing facilities; and
5. Conducting extensive research on substance abuse and its control.

Although the United Nations Division of Narcotic Drugs is active in training officers for enforcement of illicit drug trafficking, it recognizes that the most long-lasting intervention in addressing substance use and abuse is reducing the demand for substances, especially illicit substances. This chapter includes an overview of issues related to the psychological consequences of substance use. A large portion of the chapter will be directed to exploring efforts to address demand reduction.

DEFINITION

For purposes of definition, substance use refers to the use of mood-altering chemicals to achieve a specific mood-altering effect. Substance abuse refers to the use of mood-altering chemicals to achieve a specific mood-altering effect, but where control over the use of these substances is lost. Addiction refers to an individual's use of substances in a manner that interferes with the individual's ability to perform in one or more major areas of life.

These definitions account for the individual who uses the substance infrequently, but still suffers negative consequences as a result of such use. For example, a 16-year-old who drinks to celebrate his birthday, and then drives his friends to a movie and suffers an accident en route would be an example of substance abuse. An example of substance use might be the young person who feels the need to drink in order to calm down or attain a state of greater calm than currently experienced. "Addiction" refers to the young user of marijuana who uses marijuana at least once each day, whose grades suffer, whose performance in school suffers, and whose ability to relate effectively with family members suffers as well.

Although the definitions listed above describe the addictive process, it is important to delineate the definition of psychological maltreatment through the use of drugs or alcohol by a young person or those around him. The following definition for psychological maltreatment is suggested (Hart, Germain, & Brassard, 1983):

> Psychological maltreatment occurs in association with substance abuse by the virtue of a system of cultural/societal and familial characteristics that contribute to and maintain a child's self-destructive behavior through the child's use of mood-altering chemicals or exhibition of maladaptive behaviors as a result of being raised in a family with chemically-dependent parents or siblings. Delayed or distorted development and negative consequences may occur in family relationships, peer relationships, and vocational and educational dimensions of the child's life as well as in development of more general age-appropriate behaviors and levels of maturity. Factors contributing to psychological maltreatment include, but are not limited to: Societal denial of the severity of chemical abuse; media's encouragement of chemical abuse through equating it with adulthood; failure to confront media encouragement for chemical use; failure to promote self-discipline and delay of gratification strengths for youth; failure to prepare children for critical thinking and choice-making in regard to chemical use; and failure to provide stigma-free assistance to the chemical abusers. (p. 7)

It is important to note also that there are several psychological manifestations of the illness of chemical dependency or chemical abuse. The first form is *denial*. The psychological defense of denial becomes exaggerated through one's use of chemicals. Denial is a part of the illness of abuse or addiction and is a predictable component of the progression of the illness. In order to justify one's continued use of drugs or alcohol, a person will believe that he or she can control his or her use. This is readily seen from an example such as the following:

> A group of nursing students from a local midwestern university came to Fairbanks Hospital for a training session. The nursing students were asked how many of them smoked tobacco cigarettes. One of the nursing students indicated that she was involved with smoking and she was asked to justify her reasons for her use. She had smoked a pack of cigarettes or more a day for several years. Her response was that she could "stop anytime she wanted to."

This is an example of denial, when people believe that they, in fact, can control something which has become uncontrollable.

Another psychological manifestation of chemical abuse is *rationalization*. A nursing student in the same group was asked how she justified her use. She indicated that she needed to smoke cigarettes "because of the pressure of nursing school and its demands" upon her. Such making of excuses allows people to justify their continued use of drugs, which in fact are creating the psychological manifestations in order to perpetuate the abuse of the substances. Drug use appears to exaggerate common defense mechanisms used by an individual to maintain certain behavior. In a very real sense, drug use creates a barrier to objective self-evaluation.

A third manifestation is that of *minimizing*. Another nursing student was asked how she justified her continued use. She indicated that "her use was a habit." It was explained to this nursing student that a habit is a ritual designed to make one's life easier, such as lacing one's shoes in the morning after getting up without thinking about it. In actuality, the nursing student did not have a habit, but instead had an addiction and would likely suffer withdrawal symptoms if she attempted to stop smoking the cigarettes. It is necessary to call the addiction

what it is, and not downplay the seriousness of the situation.

A fourth psychological manifestation of the illness is *blaming*. To distract others from the real issue of the use of substances, a young person or an adult is likely to blame others for the problem, doing everything possible rather than focusing on the real issue behind the use or abuse of the substances. For example, parents will blame the school for the child's problems, feeling that the school, having identified the student as using drugs, is harassing them rather than looking for the real reasons why their child has been misbehaving.

It is important to note that individuals living in an environment where there is an individual abusing or addicted to chemicals will likely suffer from the same psychological manifestations as the individual using the substances. Therefore, their functioning may become impaired psychologically as well, and they may manifest some of the same feelings of denial or justification for the patient's continued use. For example, a parent may feel that "all the other kids are drinking; I want my son to be a part of what other children are doing so that he is accepted." This may be one rationalization that a parent may give in order to justify the child's use, not recognizing that this "enables" the child to continue his or her use, which inevitably will create more problems for the child and the family.

In terms of our definition of psychological maltreatment it is important to recognize that psychological maltreatment in terms of substance abuse or addiction may be acts of omission as well as commission. Ignoring the fact that a child may be abusing alcohol several times a week, despite the encounters with law enforcement agencies or school authorities, may in fact be an issue of neglect. The parents are not providing the child with the care that they need to overcome this very serious and potentially deadly problem.

The American Medical Association (1977) identified alcoholism as a disease in 1956, because there was evidence of an identifiable progressive syndrome that impaired a number of systems of the body and mind. It is important, therefore, to examine chemical abuse and addiction as a progressive illness much like diabetes or cancer; one that can be treated more successfully in its early stages than when it is allowed to reach stages where it is more difficult to reverse. It should be noted, also, that there is no cure for addiction. Addiction results in an altered life-style and is much like diabetes. A person can learn to live a happy, healthy lifestyle through treatment but will never be able to return to the use of chemicals if they are to maintain a recovering orientation.

It is also important to note that abuse of drugs by a young person may result in lifelong problems. Observers at Fairbanks Hospital have noted developmental delays or developmental arrests in children who are admitted to the hospital. Young people who began their drug use at age 12, for example, at age 16 still appear to be functioning emotionally and academically as a 12-year-old. The question arises, are drug-induced learning disabilities present? To assist in researching this question, a teacher at Fairbanks Hospital has received a grant to conduct such a study. Certainly, many young people exhibit erratic behavior, which may fit the criteria for behavior or emotional disturbance categories under P.L. 94-142. Depression, and in particular suicide, are very common side effects of drug/alcohol abuse (Swanson & Cohn, 1985).

Recognizing all of these factors obligates schools and/or other community agencies that are responsible for the socialization of children to be alert for signs of substance abuse and addiction, to intervene appropriately, and to insist that a child receive treatment at the earliest possible moment. Without such responsible actions, these agencies could be legitimately cited for neglect. It is also important to note that, according to Indianapolis Police Department data, 60% of all child abuse cases occur while an individual is living in a household where there is a drinking or using adult. Such data suggest that physical acts may be committed which result in physical or emotional scars to children even though children may not be using the drug themselves. This means that children are vulnerable not only through their own use of drugs or alcohol, but are vulnerable to maltreatment through others' consumption.

It is also important to recognize that the greater society of the United States, through advertising and other mechanisms for promoting the use of drugs or alcohol, essentially condones the abuse of substances. This gives a significant double message to a child who is attempting to learn how to function in that particular society. The distinctions for use in terms of age are no longer clear. As a result, society's abuse of drugs and alcohol may be condoned. Perhaps society itself is providing a psychological suggestion to young people that use of substances is an acceptable and appropriate way of behaving when, in fact, there are many health risks (e.g., drinking and driving) that young people are inviting through involvement with such chemicals.

DEMOGRAPHIC CHARACTERISTICS

Substance use and abuse dramatically affects the lives of United States citizens. The billions of dollars lost to the U.S. economy alone comes close to accounting for 25% of the national deficit. This affects the inflationary spiral and has an indirect influence on global economics. Additional human costs in terms of death due to overdose, accidental death (as exemplified in the staggering loss of life on U.S. highways), and personal injury in terms of substance-induced illnesses such as lung cancer, are incalculable. The great tragedy is that the majority of these problems are preventable (Manatt, 1983).

American Statistics

An excellent study regarding trends of student substance use in America from 1975 to 1980 was conducted by the National Institute on Drug Abuse (NIDA) in Washington, DC (Johnston, Bachman, & O'Malley, 1981). This study primarily examined substance use by high school seniors during those 5 years. Specifically, the substances used, as well as the prevalence and frequency of their use, were examined in detail.

According to Johnston et al. (1981), one of the best indicators of potential substance abuse is frequency of use. Those young people who use substances on a daily basis are more vulnerable to abusing the substances and are more likely to suffer the negative consequences of substance use. Substance abuse is defined in the NIDA study as use of the substance on 20 or more occasions in the preceding 30 days. The one exception to this rule is cigarettes, where students were explicitly asked about the use of one or more cigarettes per day. As of 1980, a slight decrease in daily use has been seen in two categories. The use of marijuana and cigarettes has declined 1.2% and 4.1%, respectively. This means that approximately 9% of high school seniors graduating in 1980 used marijuana on a daily basis and 21% of high school seniors used cigarettes on a daily basis. These decreases are significant since awareness of health risks and peer disapproval seem to be accounting for the decline. It is hoped by some observers that this does mark the fact that a peak in use of cigarettes and marijuana has been reached by young people and that we are starting to see a decline. Other observers, rather than seeing an overall decline in substance abuse, feel that young people are simply changing their choice of substances.

Figure 6.1 shows the daily prevalence in a number of substance categories including inhalants, stimulants, sedatives, and barbiturates. Use of all these substances has increased. In fact, some observers feel there is a substantial increase in stimulant use which may be replacing other types of illicit substance use. One might find in terms of daily use in the average class of 30 high school seniors, 3 daily users of marijuana, 2 daily alcohol users, 6 daily cigarette smokers, and frequent users of stimulants, barbiturates, and other substances. One disturbing trend has been a gradual, yet steady, increase in the numbers of young people who use illicit substances other than marijuana. Use of stimulants and cocaine seems to account for this recent change.

One of the disturbing findings of the Johnston et al. (1981) study is that use seems to be approximately the same throughout all regions of the United States, with the Northeast having a slightly larger percentage of use by young people, and the South having the lowest percentage of young people using illicit substances. Illicit substance use by young people in the United States is a pervasive, comprehensive problem as documented by this particular study.

Another significant problem observed by people studying substance use by youth in the United States is the trend to use substances at younger and younger ages. Marijuana use dramatically increased among young people from the 6th through the 12th grades during the period from 1975 to 1980. This dramatic increase in marijuana use influences the data in terms of demonstrating that illicit substance use in general has increased (see Figure 6.2).

PSYCHOLOGICAL EFFECTS

In a number of Western cultures, many children begin substance use in primary grades (Peterson, 1978). By the time these young people reach the age of 9 or 10, many children have been exposed to or are involved in substance use. Substance use can result not only in damage to an individual, but also in tremendous disruptions in the

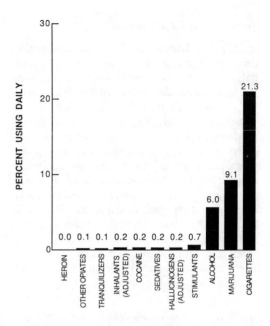

Figure 6.1. Thirty-day prevalence of daily use, 11 types of drugs, class of 1980. (From Johnston et al., 1981.)

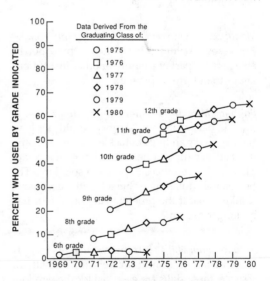

Figure 6.2. Use of any illicit drug: Trends in lifetime prevalence for earlier grade levels. (From Johnston et al., 1981.)

community, enormous costs for treatment of an individual, and a great deal of stress within family interactions (Cohn, Blix, Boyd, Denton, Essex, McNaught, Owens, & Warren, 1981).

Theoretical Explanations

In order to address the issue of demand reduction (in other words, to reduce the desire of individuals to use substances for recreational purposes) it is necessary to determine what characteristics individuals might have that would lead them to substance use. According to Glenn and Warner (undated), a number of social changes have occurred over the last 50 years that have given young people in the United States fewer opportunities to learn the basic social skills of self-discipline, judgment, and personal responsibility from responsible adult role models. Glenn and Warner (p. 4) identify a number of characteristics of individuals that contribute to their becoming "high risk" for problems such as substance use. These individuals have inadequacies in one or more of the following categories.

Identification with Viable Role Models. Deficiencies in this area make an individual vulnerable because he or she does not see him- or herself as a person whose attitudes, values, and behaviors allow him or her to be successful in his or her environment.

Identification with and Responsibility for "Family" Processes. A vulnerable person would not be able to feel a part of a family or other institutions larger than him- or herself.

Faith in "Miracle" Solutions to Problems. A vulnerable person in this category would not have the necessary abilities to tackle the problem and does not see him- or herself as being able to apply personal resources to problem solutions. The person may dull him- or herself with substances, thinking that if the problem cannot be felt, it is no longer present.

Intrapersonal Skills. Intrapersonal skills include one's ability to communicate with oneself. In essence, these skills are essential for the development of skills such as self-discipline, self-control, or self-evaluation. Impulse control or delayed gratification abilities are limited with this kind of individual.

Interpersonal Skills. Interpersonal skills allow a person to communicate and form relationships with other people in his or her environment. Interpersonal skills are essential in order to be able to listen and understand, to be able to communicate one's desires in an assertive manner, and so on. A vulnerable person in this category may be dishonest with others and have difficulty giving or receiving assistance from other people.

Systemic Skills. A vulnerable person in this category may be unable to adapt to limits within a particular situation. This is essential in order to be able to act responsibly or to react adaptively. A person in this category is likely to act in an irresponsible manner, refusing to accept the consequences of behavior and blaming others for his or her problems. This person probably perceives him- or herself as a victim and feels helpless in many situations.

Judgment Skills. Judgment skills are essential in order to understand relationships. A vulnerable person in this category is unable to differentiate appropriate from inappropriate behavior and is likely, therefore, to engage in a number of self-destructive activities.

It is essential that competencies be developed in each of these areas in order for a person to be able to successfully function in most, if not all, societies throughout the world. Aggressive attempts at demand reduction must result in developing judgment skills, developing problem-solving abilities, strengthening identification with family processes, strengthening identification with viable role models, identifying successful role models, and developing skills in intrapersonal and interpersonal relationships. If these fundamental needs in social skills are developed, an individual has less need to turn to substance use and abuse as an alternative to problem solving.

From a Maslovian point of view, one might say that effective social skills in relationships correlate especially with security and self-esteem needs. If children successfully develop social skills, they feel more secure and competent, resulting in enhanced levels of self-esteem. Such enhanced skills may help make them less vulnerable to the seven acts of psychological maltreatment (i.e., rejecting, degrading, terrorizing, isolating, corrupting, exploiting, and emotional unresponsiveness) discussed elsewhere in this book. Furthermore, such a child is more likely to ask for help, tolerating less of such victimizing behaviors.

INTERVENTION

Demand Reduction and Prevention

Problems associated with youth drug use have grown to such a proportion it is clear that enforcement and treatment approaches are at best stop-gap remedial steps that have an impact on only a small part of the problem. Strong emphasis needs to be placed on educational–preventive efforts that have the potential for impact on large numbers of young people throughout the world by preventing their involvement in the use of substances such as alcohol, tobacco, marijuana, and other illicit substances.

Essentially, five approaches to prevention exist as identified by the National Institute on Drug Abuse. The first approach is "giving information." This approach is based on the assumption that if people are given the facts about such things as substances, they will be able to make a decision not to use substances that may be harmful to them. Regrettably, this approach has not been found effective and in fact has been argued in some quarters to contribute to more substance use as the result of providing young people with information about substances themselves. Giving information may excite the interest of young people who are developmentally at a time of life in which their curiosity is at a peak. Also, unfortunately, the basic approach to prevention in United States schools today is simply giving information. Schaps, DiBartolo, Palley, and Churgin (1978) studied 127 prevention programs in a grant from the United States National Institute on Drug Abuse and found that the most effective programs have a broader social base and address the earlier-identified seven categories of high-risk individuals.

The second model for prevention is the psychosocial approach. This approach addresses a number of competency areas discussed by Glenn and Warner (undated). Programs have been developed that address such issues as resisting peer pressure and promoting positive self-esteem, both of which address intrapersonal and interpersonal skills, problem-solving skills, and, in some cases, combine this approach with giving drug facts (Knowles, Bodman, & Palley, 1979).

A third approach provides alternative activities for young people in an effort to meet social needs and to develop strong interpersonal skills. A number of alternative approaches have also been addressed that provide young people with an opportunity to identify with viable role models and develop an identification with family or community processes.

The fourth approach is the community or school climate approach. It suggests that conditions inherent in the environment contribute to the dissatisfaction and alienation of young people from their communities, schools, homes, or other environments. To promote a climate that most suitably involves young people and reduces the amount of alienation they experience, the environment must be assessed and activities developed that focus on problem areas. A number of successful school and community climate-change programs have been developed throughout the country (Manatt, 1979).

A fifth approach to prevention is the networking model. This model suggests that no single agency (i.e., home, school, industry, government) alone contributes to the problems that young people have with substance abuse. Every responsible community agency must make a response to the substance abuse problem if it is truly to be reduced or eliminated. Since substance abuse is such a pervasive phenomenon among young people in the world today, and especially in the United States, all resources must be brought to bear on young people's need to use substances (Cohn et al., 1981).

Schaps et al. (1978), in their study of 127 prevention programs in the United States, found that programs that address the psychosocial approach and the alternative activities approach, while additionally giving information about substances to young people, have been most effective. Programs that address alternative activities alone have also been effective and in some cases psychosocial programs alone have been found to be effective in preventing young people from using substances and promoting competencies previously described. Generally, prevention programs or programs addressing the issue of demand reduction have lacked comprehensiveness. Some have been found to be successful in a number of cases, but need to be implemented in a more systematic fashion (starting at kindergarten or earlier and continuing throughout the senior year of high school) in order to have the maximum impact possible.

Community Action

Over the last several years many communities around the country have organized to address the issue of youth substance abuse. A number of these communities have been spurred on by the efforts initiated by members of an organization known as PRIDE (Parents Resource Institute for Drug Education) at Georgia State University. The founders of this organization have in some cases been exposed to youth substance abuse as a result of having children engaged in such activities. Others have lent their professional expertise in helping the lay public throughout the United States address this very significant and destructive problem. The PRIDE office, along with other community organizational groups such as the National Federation of Parents for Drug Free Youth, Families in Action, and Organization of Parents Against Drugs, have organized to aggressively address the issue of youth substance abuse and use. Many of the organizations began as a result of a child becoming dependent on a substance and parents attempting unsuccessfully to seek services (Cohn et al., 1981; Manatt, 1979).

During the early 1970s, most attention was paid to people who had progressed to the addictive or abusive stage of drug abuse, suffering overdoses or other crises. In the 1980s, organizations are oriented more towards prevention. Many consider it unnecessary for young people to use substances of any kind on a regular, recreational basis. One of the focal points for efforts to address youth substance use has been the educational community's recognition that young people spend a good deal of their day in school. Sometimes the schools have borne the brunt of the blame for youth substance-use problems as many children exchange substances or are exposed to substances in the school environment. Generally, communities, schools, and parents have realized that substance use among people is an epidemic problem and recognize that cooperative efforts are necessary to see that the problem is reduced (Cohn et al., 1981).

Generally, community groups are formed in one of three ways: (a) community members themselves have seen the need for intervention, often as a result of a drug raid in the community; (b) parents have painfully formed a parent support group once their own child's involvement has been discovered; and (c) the school has realized that a problem of in-school substance use has occurred and the community has been solicited for assistance (Cohn et al., 1981). Each of these three methods of community action has worked in various communities, depending on the make-up of the community, but the most successful groups have focused on the issue of how to assist

adolescents in reaching adulthood substance-free. Each group has found it necessary and important to include leaders from all areas of the community, including parents, school representatives, and community leaders.

In the most successful community action groups, it has been found that the group must work within the community in a nonblaming fashion. Some programs have been particularly noteworthy. In one community, parents themselves have been trained as leaders to train other parents in substance education so that the parents are well aware of what is occurring among young people today. Many other communities have used this approach successfully. Another community has developed a parent program on how to help adolescents resist peer pressure. Many of the communities have organized parent awareness programs, educating parents by the use of films such as *For Parents Only: What You Need to Know about Marijuana* (Kelly, 1980), as a focal point for discussion. Other communities have trained panel members to make presentations about the various aspects of youth substance use; many of the groups recognize that the problem of substance use is primarily a symptom as well as a problem in and of itself. It is a symptom of disruption within society and within the family system and many of the groups have organized programs that focus on strengthening families as a way to prevent youth behavior problems. Other communities have organized family activity days to promote family involvement, recognizing that one of the best buffers for prevention of substance use and other behavior problems is involvement of young people in their community, and preferably with other members of their families.

Alternative activities have been shown to reduce alienation and to help young people feel they can make a significant contribution to their community, family, or school (Schaps et al., 1978). When young people feel their needs are being met in such a positive way (e.g., needs for attention, respect, being valued) they are less vulnerable and are less likely to become involved in self- or other destructive activities.

Currently there are approximately 350,000 people in the National Federation of Parents organization and hundreds of parents' action groups around the United States. Other countries are examining or are becoming involved in this movement as well, as seen in the presence of several international representatives at the PRIDE convention in April, 1982, in Atlanta. Many of these organizations have been able to attract funding from community-based industries. Industry recognizes the valuable contribution that such organizations make as many young people are coming to their industries in entry-level positions, bringing substance use and dependencies with them. Industries are interested in supporting community groups that have something to offer in terms of addressing the substance use problem. It may be that this kind of grass-roots effort will ultimately lead to awareness and more creative programs to prevent young people from getting involved in substance use, which will have a significant impact on demand for substances. Such organizations, in fact, may have more potential than any other approach (Cohn et al., 1981).

Enforcement

One cannot address the issue of substance use and abuse without addressing the issue of enforcement. Law enforcement agencies including police, the military, the judiciary, and other agencies have been frustrated for years in the United States and other countries by dealers in illicit substances. It seems that when one of the substances is controlled, another group of popularized substances appears. Police have been provided training and education in order to address the issue of youth substance use. Many times, however, because of the enormous amounts of money involved, those who are caught are often able to post bail and leave the country, thus escaping prosecution.

In terms of the issue of demand reduction, new steps seem to be taken in many communities around the country. Efforts to break the connection in selling illegal drugs have generally affected only a minor amount of the total trafficking in illicit substances. Adopting another strategy, a number of communities have focused on demand reduction, and not only on chemical or substance distributions, but also on those people who use illicit substances, again addressing the issue of demand reduction. The attitude of many law enforcement people is that they want to make it well known that the use of substances in their jurisdiction will not be tolerated (Cohn et al., 1981).

In some communities, special hot lines have been set up so that an anonymous telephone caller can leave information about substances being distributed among young people. Law enforcement officials then follow up on the information. In some cases, prosecutors and police have taken aggressive steps to promote demand reduction and prevention activities. For example, in Marion County, Indiana, the prosecutor's office in conjunction with a local drugstore chain and a local advertising agency planned a 10-week public service announcement campaign entitled "Drugs: It Takes Guts to Say No," aired on television and radio September 8–17, 1981. Billboards, bus cards, electric signs, and newspapers also carried the slogan. Representatives from the same prosecutor's office have consulted with schools and corporations in the Indianapolis area and other parts of the state promoting the concept of demand reduction. An important point that needs to be addressed in law enforcement is that even if illegal drugs or substances were eliminated completely from the scene, the consumption of alcohol, and over-the-counter substances, prescription substance abuse, and inhalant abuse would still be significant problems among young people because of the accessibility, inexpensive nature, and legality of these substances. As a result, more and more law enforcement officials are becoming aware that it is necessary to emphasize changing the attitude of the consumer as well as intervening in the supply of substances (Cohn et al. 1981).

CONCLUSIONS AND DIRECTIONS

It is clear that substance use and abuse is a significant problem among youth in the United States and generally throughout the world. Programs focusing on demand reduction are scattered and lack comprehensiveness in most cases. Treatment services are frequently not available in sufficient quantities to meet the demand for services. There are probably enough professionals who are trained to work with adolescents experiencing substance use and abuse problems, if these professionals could be sufficiently organized. Alcohol abuse seems to be increasing among young people in the United States at present. The picture, however, is not totally gloomy. Concrete action can be taken to remedy the situation we are currently facing. Organization, motivation, and dedication are ingredients necessary to confront the problems of substance use and abuse among our youth. Many communities are beginning to organize, because they are motivated by the tragedies they have encountered. They are dedicated to the ultimate goal of reducing and possibly eliminating substance abuse from their communities and their children.

Research Issues

A number of research issues need to be addressed, especially in the area of demand reduction. Programs that have been developed to focus on this problem often lack comprehensiveness in terms of age of the target child. Evaluations are often poor. Frequently they address only one measure of effectiveness of the program such as self-concept development. Prospective or follow-up studies need to be conducted in order to determine long-term effects of program interventions. Prospective studies may help address this issue by comparing young people who use and abuse substances with those who do not to determine what contributes to involvement in substance use and abuse.

In developing a comprehensive program, it is necessary to take a number of steps focusing on demand reduction. The following considerations identified by Cohn et al. (1981, p. 17) should be made.

1. Require college-level training of all education majors in the areas of prevention and/or substance education.
2. Encourage implementation of substance prevention strategies in programs, kindergarten through 12th grades, emphasizing safety issues and operating within the current health curriculum.
3. Encourage a total community response to the problem, emphasizing the need to develop meaningful programs as alternatives to substance use and abuse.
4. Provide training to all school administrators and school improvement strategies that contribute to reductions in disruptive behaviors.
5. Publish up-to-date substance education resource manuals for educators to utilize within their classes.
6. Continue to provide in-service training to professionals in the areas of prevention.
7. Utilize media campaigns to stimulate interest in and awareness of the problem and provide a forum for solutions.

Treatment

1. Establish a network of inpatient facilities specifically designed to treat the chemically dependent adolescent. At present many ado-

lescents who are in need of services have to travel long distances from their families to receive specialized inpatient treatment.
2. Expand outpatient services to facilitate an adolescent's treatment and follow-up support.
3. Increase community and professional awareness in the prevention, identification, and family approach to treatment of the substance-using adolescent.

Community Action

1. Develop a nationwide association with an executive director capable of coordinating the following activities: (a) training for newly organized community groups, (b) communication among all of the United States' community groups, (c) a national newsletter, and (d) a national consulting service.
2. Utilize existing resources of the National Institute on Drug Abuse and United Nations more effectively.
3. Increase communication and utilize other national or international resources more effectively.
4. Improve communication among law enforcement agencies, community social service agencies, and parent groups who plan and execute substance abuse awareness programs.
5. Encourage the development of programs oriented towards intervening with first offenders as an alternative to expulsion from school or incarceration. Such programs should be conducted cooperatively with law enforcement, school, and mental health agencies.
6. Develop programs to educate medical service providers regarding youth substance abuse. Discuss screening, treatment, and referral procedures.
7. Encourage the development of school–police–community programs that provide substance education for youth and encourage cooperation between the three agencies.

REFERENCES

American Medical Association. (1977). *Manual on alcoholism.* Chicago: Author.

Cohn, M. J. (Chairman), Blix, S., Boyd, E. E., Denton, M., Essex, W., McNaught, S. W., Owens, A., & Warren, S. (1981). *Substance abuse subcommittee report, Indiana White House conference on children and youth.* Indianapolis, IN: Unpublished report.

Glenn, H. S., & Warner, J. W. (undated). *The developmental approach to preventing problem dependencies.* Cincinnati: Reprinted by North Hospital.

Hart, S. N., Germain, R., & Brassard, M. R., (1983). *Proceedings summary for the international conference.* Available from Stuart Hart, Office for the Study of the Psychological Rights of the Child, Indiana University–Purdue University in Indianapolis, 902 West New York Street, PO Box 647, Indianapolis, IN 46223.

Johnston, L. D., Bachman, J. G., & O'Malley, P. M. (1981). Highlights from student drug use in America, 1975–1980. Rockville, MD: National Institute on Drug Abuse.

Kelly, M. C. (1980). *For parents only: What you should know about marijuana* [Film]. Rockville, MD: National Institute on Drug Abuse.

Knowles, C. D., Bodman, K. T., & Palley, C. S. (1979). *Teaching tools for primary prevention: A guide to classroom curricula.* Rockville, MD: National Institute on Drug Abuse.

Ling, G. M., & del Prado, J. G. (1978). International challenge of drug abuse: Perspective from the United Nations. In Peterson, R. C. (Ed.), *The international challenge of drug abuse.* Rockville, MD: National Institute on Drug Abuse.

Manatt, M. (1979). *Parents, peers and pot.* Rockville, MD: National Institute on Drug Abuse.

Manatt, M. (1983). *Parents, peers and pot, part II.* Rockville, MD: National Institute on Drug Abuse.

Peterson, R. C. (Ed.) (1978). *The international challenge of drug abuse.* Rockville, MD: National Institute on Drug Abuse.

Schaps, E., DiBartolo, R., Palley, C. S., & Churgin, S. (1978). *Primary prevention evaluation research: A review of 127 program evaluations.* Walnut Creek, CA: Pacific Institute for Research and Evaluation.

Swanson, G. B., & Cohn, M. (1985, November). Drugs and teenage suicide: What you should know. *Listen,* pp. 11–14.

7

Emotional Neglect and Stimulus Deprivation

Jacqueline A. Schakel

Matthew was born with an underdeveloped esophagus which caused him to be unable to take milk from his mother in the normal way. Doctors instructed Matthew's parents in a procedure to feed him using a tube to his stomach, and his mother fed him meticulously. Afraid of Matthew's "delicacy" and fearful of her assumed inadequacy as a mother to this handicapped child, Matthew's mother cared for his physical needs but did not cuddle or play with him. At age 15 months, Matthew was lethargic, withdrawn, and motorically retarded. He did not smile and had not begun to talk. When placed in the medical center and given normal attention, Matthew showed remarkable gains. (Case study adapted from Gardner, 1972)

Jennifer was the youngest child born to a mother whose older five children had already left home and whose husband only occasionally dropped by to pay a visit. After caring for Jennifer at home for 5 years, Jennifer's mother got a job working the night shift at a job she didn't like, but which paid enough money to pay rent and buy food. She began to think of Jennifer as just another burden preventing her from getting ahead. Depressed and convinced that life had passed her by, Jennifer's mother did little more than provide food and clothing for Jennifer. She frequently did not bother to get Jennifer up in time for school. Jennifer began wetting the bed at home, later showing aggressive behavior at school, and, finally, becoming extremely

withdrawn. Jennifer's mother did not respond to requests for a conference from the teacher. At age 10, Jennifer attempted suicide.

BACKGROUND

Few people would deny the pernicious effects on children of a lack of parental stimulation and emotional support. Affective and social deprivation, parental detachment or indifference, and parental failure to understand and meet the emotional needs of children are all conditions that can create and foster relationships that are potentially harmful to the psychological development and welfare of children. As with other forms of child abuse and neglect, however, it has been difficult to study the prevalence and effects of emotional neglect. Not only is there the ubiquitous problem of agreeing on a definition of the construct, but psychologists, medical personnel, social workers, and the legal profession each have their own characteristic ways of viewing the problem, intervening, and looking at prevention.

Emotional neglect has been recognized as a serious problem for many years, but it has been studied very rarely. Gardner (1972) pointed out that it has long been known that infants will not thrive if caretakers are hostile to them or even merely indifferent. He related the story of Frederick II, ruler of Sicily in the 13th century, who had infants reared by silent and minimally available caretakers in order to see what language would develop naturally in these children. Unfortunately, this misguided experiment resulted in the deaths of many of the infants before they reached their first birthday. The effects of "maternal deprivation" were later more systematically studied by looking at institutionalized children (Bowlby, 1951; Burlingham & Freud, 1944; Goldfarb, 1945; Spitz, 1945). These authors found children reared in institutions to be delayed in almost all areas of development, and their problems were attributed not to a lack of adequate physical care, but to the unavailability of a consistent caretaker (Green, 1980).

Studies conducted several years later on noninstitutionalized children showed that similar problems could be found among children in intact homes (Coleman & Provence, 1957; Prugh & Harlow, 1962); thus researchers reported that it was not a *lack* of mothering but insufficient or distorted maternal care that led to the problems observed.

During the 1960s and 1970s the medical literature increasingly reported case studies of these children using the phrase "failure to thrive" to describe their condition (e.g., Bullard, Glaser, Heagerty, & Pivchik, 1967; Elmer, 1960; Evans, Reinhard, & Succop, 1972; Leonard, Rhymes, & Solnit, 1966). The phenomenon, diagnosed from medical signs, including serious growth failure despite adequate nutrition, was traced to a lack of maternal emotional care of the infant.

While the discovery of failure-to-thrive syndrome brought the medical profession face-to-face with the consequences of emotional neglect, the psychology profession continued its long-standing involvement with the question of the effects of unresponsive parenting. Although the term *emotional neglect* did not come into wide usage until recently, psychologists had long stressed the importance of meeting children's emotional needs (e.g., Erikson, 1950; Maslow, 1968) and had long suspected that some forms of emotional disturbance were attributable to inadequate emotional care (Eisenberg, 1957; Horney, 1937; Kanner, 1943).

There has been a recent surge of interest in emotional neglect by the social work and legal professions due to national, state, and local efforts to combat child abuse and neglect. In 1981, results of a national survey in the United States of 26 counties in 10 states gave an estimate of the actual incidence of six major categories of maltreatment (Office of Human Development Services, 1981). Estimates, including children not reported to child protective services in addition to those who were, showed that, conservatively, 1 child per 1,000 can be classified as seriously emotionally neglected. Obviously, emotional neglect is a problem that deserves attention.

DEFINITIONAL CONSIDERATIONS

Part of the reason for the lack of research on emotional neglect has been the problem in defining it. When forms of child maltreatment are categorized, four types are usually identified: physical abuse, emotional abuse, physical neglect, and emotional neglect. Some authors add sexual abuse as a separate fifth category. It is clear, however, that these categories overlap. It is difficult to imagine a physically or sexually abusive relationship which is not also emotionally neglectful in some sense. One can also readily assume that a child who is physically neglected might also be neglected in other ways, and severe emotional neglect may blur into emotional abuse (Bourne, 1979).

In addition to the problem of separating the effects of types of maltreatment, there is also the problem that emotional neglect is defined differently by different professionals and lay people. Giovannoni, Conklin, and Iiyama (1978) have pointed out that "neglect" is a term that is part of at least four different vocabularies—legal, medical, social work, and lay. Psychological and sociological might also be added; and these definitions may vary depending on whether one is a researcher or a practitioner. Obviously, the definition chosen in any particular case will influence research, practice, and policy formulation.

Definitions vary from the global to the specific. Some (e.g., Gil, 1979) have proposed a broad definition of abuse (including emotional neglect) in which society is implicated as a main cause. Most definitions, however, emphasize the role of the parents in emotional neglect. The National Center on Child Abuse and Neglect (1978) has defined it as "failure to provide the psychological nurturance necessary for a child's psychological growth and development." Dean (1979) defined emotional neglect, in contrast to "psychological nurturance," as

> (An) act of omission, frequently the result of parental ignorance or indifference. As a result, the child is not given positive emotional support and stimulation. Parents may give adequate physical care to their child but leave him or her alone in a crib

for long periods of time, seldom cuddle or talk to the child, or fail to give him or her encouragement and recognition. (p. 19)

These definitions clearly put the responsibility on the caretaker. Some legal definitions require that for reporting purposes the neglect must be intentional; that is, given notice of harm to their child, caretakers still do not change their behavior.

It has been questioned, however, whether actions can be considered neglectful regardless of their impact or harm to the child (Giovannoni et al., 1978). Some definitions, particularly those in use by the legal profession, emphasize the need to identify overt signs of psychological harm (Flannery, 1979; Wald, 1976) such as diagnosable anxiety, depression, withdrawal, or aggressive behavior. This tightening of the definition of emotional neglect for legal purposes naturally has the effect of reducing the number of cases that are viewed by authorities as clear-cut emotional neglect.

One must also discuss the definition of emotional neglect from a medical perspective, as infants suffering from emotional neglect have received much attention from physicians under the diagnosis of "failure-to-thrive syndrome." This syndrome has also been described as maternal deprivation syndrome (Patton & Gardner, 1962), deprivation dwarfism (Gardner, 1972), psychosocial dwarfism, and emotional deprivation syndrome (MacCarthy, 1979). Based on medical signs, this definition is more specific than most social work or psychological definitions, but it encompasses just one portion of the children who suffer from an emotionally neglectful relationship—those who react to deprivation so severely that they are affected physically.

No discussion of definitions of emotional neglect should fail to treat the idea of cultural relativity. With the possible exception of the medical definition of nonorganic failure to thrive, each definition of emotional neglect is subject to cultural interpretations. What constitutes emotional neglect in one culture may be normal child-rearing practice in another, as there is, of course, no universal standard for child rearing. Korbin (1980) gives the example of the practices in the West of isolating children in their own rooms at night, making children wait for meals, and allowing children to "cry themselves out." These would be perceived as constituting emotional neglect in some cultures. As our understanding

of child abuse and neglect is based almost entirely on studies that have been done in the United States and other parts of the Western world, it is important that ethnocentrism be avoided in defining and dealing with such problems. Yet it is also important that child maltreatment not be overlooked in an attempt to be culturally sensitive (Korbin, 1980; Whiting, 1976).

Thus it appears that although attempts to find a specific universal definition of emotional neglect may be futile, agreement can occur on the components of a definition. The inattention of caregivers to children's emotional needs must be present along with the effect of harm to the child. In the studies that will be reviewed in this paper, a variety of definitions have been used. The reader should keep this in mind as the results of these studies are considered.

ANTECEDENTS

Parent Characteristics

Most of the early studies of emotional neglect focused on identifying the characteristics of the parents (almost always the mother) that were believed to cause them to be neglectful to their children. In these early studies, emphasis was on personality characteristics. Barbero, Morris, and Redford (1963) found mothers of failure-to-thrive infants to be depressed and helpless, suffering from low self-esteem and environmental stress. Fischoff (1973) identified them as having severe personality disorders, while Elmer (1960) and Leonard, Rhymes, and Solnit (1966) identified alcoholism as a contributor. Galdston (1968), taking a psychoanalytic perspective, differentiated two types of neglecting parents. The first type uses "projection" as a primary defense mechanism. They regard their child as the embodiment of their own undesirable characteristics and distance themselves. The second type of parent uses denial as a primary defense mechanism. The parents fail to see the child as their own, lack empathy, and thus are unable to care for the child emotionally.

Evans, Reinhard, and Succop (1972) studied 45 families with failure-to-thrive infants and identified three groups of mothers. One group of mothers were those who were extremely depressed because of a recent loss of parent or spouse. This group was the only one given a good prognosis. The second group were mothers who were also depressed but chronically so. These mothers lived under very deprived living conditions. The third group contained mothers who were angry and hostile and perceived their children as "bad." In this third group, abuse and neglect were both present.

Fathers were seldom mentioned in the literature on emotional neglect except as bystanders. For example, MacCarthy (1979) described them this way: "Fathers often show concern . . . but seem unable to prevent the damage . . . perhaps because of insufficient contact or because of their own too great dependency on the mother."

Parent–Environment Interaction

Other researchers on the topic of neglect have looked more at the social and environmental factors that they believe contribute to the neglectful relationship. Their research has focused mostly on lower-class families, and in these studies physical and emotional neglect are often both present. Pavenstadt (1967) described parents who tended to recreate the patterns of deprivation that they had experienced as children. These parents failed to achieve a feeling of competency as parents, were unable to provide adult role models for their children, and let their own needs take precedence over those of their children. They did not provide emotional stimulation and had little verbal communication with their children.

Polansky and his colleagues (Polansky, Chalmers, Buttenwieser, & Williams, 1981; Polansky, DeSaix, Wing, & Patton, 1968) studied families in rural communities in Appalachia and in lower-class urban communities in Philadelphia. They identified what they call the "apathy–futility" syndrome in neglecting mothers. These mothers were incompetent, passive, apathetic, unresponsive and had what Polansky describes as "an uncanny skill in bringing to consciousness the same feelings of futility in others" (pp. 40–41). They attributed this syndrome chiefly to a reaction to living in a poor and stressful environment.

A report by Jacobs and Kent for the World Health Organization (1976) pointed out the many parent–environment profiles that can lead to emotional neglect. They classified these many patterns into three categories: (a) deficient "mother-crafting" skills, (b) social origins, and (c) psychological origins. The parents falling into the first category were poorly informed, often young, lacking support systems, and sometimes mentally retarded. "Social origins" encompassed the group described earlier by Polansky and colleagues. "Psychological origins" encompassed parents with character disorders, acute situational stress reactions, and sometimes psychoses, as described in the early research on parent characteristics. Thus it can be seen that there is more than one specific pattern which will result in emotional neglect.

Most of these lists of characteristics are based solely on clinical case studies. When researchers have attempted to use control groups, they have found that some of the same characteristics also define nonneglecting parents and situations. Giovannoni and Billingsley (1970) compared impoverished groups of neglecting and adequate mothers and found that the neglecting mothers had more children, frequently lacked a husband, and were experiencing greater stress. No other differences were identified. Thus the search for characteristics that differentiate "the emotionally neglecting parent" has not been particularly fruitful. Obviously there are a variety of personality types, social conditions, and other factors that may contribute to the neglectful relationship.

Parent–Child Interaction

Conceptualizing emotional neglect and failure to thrive in terms of parental or environmental factors alone encourages the view of the infant or child as a passive victim of the parent's distorted or insufficient caretaking. This view is at odds with recent risk research on the infancy period, which has pointed out that a child brings a "differential vulnerability" to the relationship. The impact of the child's qualities on his or her later development, on the mother's response, and on the quality of the mother–child interaction are all important to understanding emotional neglect. For example, dissonant interactions between a mother who is restrained and inhibited and an infant who is highly active may lead to problems that might be classified as emotional neglect.

Only a few researchers recently have attempted to consider these factors. Gordon and Jameson (1979), deciding that failure-to-thrive syndrome was due to difficulties in the mother–child interaction, compared a group of failure-to-thrive infants and their mothers to a control group of infant hospital inpatients and their mothers.

They used the Ainsworth strange situation to assess mother–infant attachment. Six of the 12 failure-to-thrive pairs showed an insecure attachment; only 2 of the 12 control pairs did.

In a comprehensive group of studies on the development of abusive and neglectful relationships, Egeland and his colleagues (Egeland & Brunnquell, 1979; Egeland & Sroufe, 1981; Egeland, Breitenbucher, & Rosenberg, 1980) adopted an at-risk approach. They wanted to find out why some parents abuse and neglect their children, while others displaying the same characteristics and under the same stress do not. Their research, because of its at-risk and longitudinal design, allowed them to more accurately distinguish causes from consequences of maltreatment. A variety of parental, child, environmental, and interactional measures were taken on a group of 267 mothers considered at risk for abuse, neglect, and other forms of maltreatment. Starting in the last trimester of pregnancy, the families were observed and tested at regularly scheduled intervals. From the total sample, a subsample of mothers who abused, neglected, or in some way mistreated their infants ($n=26$) was identified and compared with another subsample of mothers who provided adequate care. The mothers in each group were chosen on the basis of rating scales designed by the authors. Of the 26 cases, physical abuse was noted in 5, failure to thrive in 4 (medically diagnosed), neglect and abuse in 3, and severe neglect in 14.

This study "represents a first attempt to differentiate good from inadequate mothers on the basis of data collected before any specific abuse or neglect has occurred." The study results showed that measures based primarily on assessment of infant characteristics were least effective in prediction when used alone. Mother personality variables contributed minimally. What *did* contribute from the mother measures were the data indicating the mothers' understanding of the psychological complexity of the children and the mother–child relationship. By far the most useful predictors were the measures of the mother–child pair behaviors—the observations done during feeding at 3 and 6 months of age and play at 6 months of age. They concluded that "variables taken from an interactive situation where a mother's response is influenced by the baby's preceding behavior are the most useful in discriminating good from inadequate mothers" (Egeland & Brunnquell, 1979, p. 232).

CONSEQUENCES

The consequences of the emotionally neglectful relationship appear to be as varied as the patterns of parent, child, and environmental characteristics that lead to emotional neglect. It is clear, however, that the consequences can be quite severe. A report by the Office of Human Development Services (1981) showed that, of the six major categories of maltreatment they identified, emotional neglect had the highest proportion (74%) of demonstrably serious impairments such as attempted suicides, drug overdose, and severe medical problems. Only a few studies of the consequences of emotional neglect are available, but they have also stressed their seriousness. The Egeland studies cited earlier studied the effects of "psychological unavailability." Of the four forms of maltreatment that they identified (physical abuse, verbal abuse, psychological unavailability, and physical neglect) they found psychological unavailability to be the most "severely malignant and pervasive." While children in this kind of relationship were found to be robust at 3 months of age, they were functioning poorly at 6 months. There were no securely attached infants in this group at 18 months of age. At 24 months these infants displayed frequent whining, frustration, and negative affect. They showed the largest decline in scores on the Bayley Scales from 9 months to 24 months of any maltreatment group. As Egeland and his colleagues continue to study these children into their school years, more information will be gathered on the pervasive effects of emotional neglect for the home and school environments.

The only other follow-up studies of emotionally neglected children have been studies of medically diagnosed failure-to-thrive infants. MacCarthy (1979) reported that these infants, if placed in a hospital or with foster parents, become cheerful and active. Eventually, however, they are likely to begin to seek attention and they will become "shallowly affectionate." Later, unpleasant traits such as spitefulenss or selfishness appear. Stealing is reported to be common among such children. Polansky and his colleagues (Polansky et al., 1981) have concluded, based on case studies, that around age 11 or 12 "a fairly high proportion of these withdrawn and pitiable youngsters undergo a reorganization of defenses. Their anxious emptiness becomes hidden behind a shield of brittle, hostile defiance; in other words, they 'turn mean'." These observations, however, are not based on clear research evidence.

The only study reporting actual follow-up data on a group of failure-to-thrive youngsters was that by Hufton and Oates (1977). They reported that by age 6 most of the children had behavioral and educational difficulties. Ten of the 21 children studied were rated as abnormal on the basis of a teacher questionnaire. Mothers reported high incidences of lying, temper tantrums, speech problems, enuresis, and hyperactivity. Two thirds of the children were 1–2 years behind in academic subjects in school.

INTERVENTIONS

Good research is the first step toward making informed decisions about intervening in cases of emotional neglect. Obviously, research will need to continue in order for us to gain an understanding of the complexities. In the meantime, however, it is important to intervene in cases where there is hope for change. As emotionally neglecting parents are unlikely to self-report, it is often up to school personnel, medical personnel, and other agencies to find the children who are being emotionally neglected.

Problems in Identification and Reporting

Emotional neglect can persist unidentified for a long time. Professionals are generally unwilling to identify and report emotional neglect formally because of the difficulty in meeting legal guidelines. To report or not is a decision to be made in each individual case, and it depends on the reporting laws of a given location. To intervene is a decision that must be made in each case of emotional neglect. Although some lay people believe that the helping professions should not intervene in families where emotional neglect is occurring (cf. Boehm, 1964), some form of intervention will have to occur either at home or at school.

There are those who have discouraged the reporting of emotional and other forms of neglect because they believe there is systematic bias that targets only poor and minority families. But there is no evidence that permitting the reporting of neglect has aggravated class disparities (Bourne

& Newberger, 1979). Whether reported or not, emotional neglect is found in all social classes and can be seen also in "those children of the well-to-do who spend their lives with a succession of different nursemaids and in a series of boarding schools and camps" (Kempe & Kempe, 1978).

In identifying and intervening in cases of emotional neglect, decisions must be made as to how much money and time and what kinds of resources are worth allocating. In countries and states with scarcer resources, the boundaries of what constitutes emotional neglect (officially) may be narrowed. The Office of Human Development Services (1981) study shows that of all known cases of emotional neglect, only 20% are reported to child protection services. In other instances it may be up to the professionals in schools and other agencies to identify and serve children outside the bounds of the formal reporting and intervention system.

Identifying the Emotionally Neglected Child

There are many signs that point to the *possibility* of emotional neglect. Practitioners must keep the research in mind when identifying emotional neglect, however, and realize that a child showing any or all of these characteristics may or may not be emotionally neglected.

Identifying the Failure-to-Thrive Infant. This is usually the purview of the medical profession as they are the people who have contact with children at such a young age. Failure-to-thrive infants have been characterized as showing minimal smiling and vocalization, lack of cuddliness, and an absence of stranger fear (Leonard et al., 1966). They have shown feeding difficulties, vomiting and diarrhea (Bullard, Glaser, Heagarty, & Pivchik, 1967) and sometimes have circulatory problems (cold hands and feet even in summer) (MacCarthy, 1979). Past the age of 2, children who have suffered from emotional neglect have been shown often to be of short stature and developmentally delayed in motor and language skills. These children often have an expression of dejection, apathy, indifference and/or submission (MacCarthy, 1979). They may be unable to play either alone or with others, may lack normal aggression, and may show what seems to be a lack of attachment to their mothers.

Other characteristics such as avoidance of eye contact, extremes of spasticity or decreased muscle tone, and abnormal sleep patterns have been noted (Barbero, 1982; Wolff & Money, 1973).

Identifying the Emotionally Neglected Older Child. As has been discussed, some children not identified as failure to thrive in infancy may be identified later as emotionally neglected. For these children, school and other agency personnel will probably be the first to notice and attempt to deal with the problem. Emotional neglect is rarely manifested in physical signs, although the child may show speech disorders and lags in physical development. More often it is observed through behavioral indicators. The Region X Child Abuse and Neglect Center (1980) describes several possible behavior manifestations that may be observed by educators. They include habit disorders (sucking, biting, rocking, enuresis, eating disorders), conduct disorders (withdrawal, destructiveness, cruelty, stealing), neurotic traits (sleep disorders, inhibition of play), psychoneurotic reactions (hysteria, obsession, compulsion, phobias, hypochondria), behavior extremes (overcompliance, passivity, aggression), overly adaptive behaviors which are either inappropriately adult or infantile, lags in emotional or intellectual development and attempted suicide. Other indicators including clinging, demanding attention, possessiveness, acting out, low self-esteem, distrust, listlessness, and language delays have also been mentioned (Bavolek & Comstock, 1980).

It seems clear that the emotionally neglected child will react according to his or her own characteristics and the situation. Any form of emotional disturbance or behavior disorder might be in part a result of emotional neglect, but not all emotionally disturbed children are emotionally neglected. In most cases parental behavior can help distinguish whether emotional neglect has occurred.

Observations of the family situation will help determine if children's behavior is a result of emotional neglect. Polansky, Hally, and Polansky (1977) developed an instrument called the Childhood Level of Living Scale which measures physical care as well as cognitive and emotional nurturance. They recommended that research be done to determine if such an instrument could help predict those children who are likely to be severely damaged by neglect. Others recommend careful observation of parent–child interactions.

Intervention

Once a child and family are identified, interventions may vary widely. There is very little research on the adequacy and effects of various forms of intervention in cases of emotional neglect. Treatment may focus on the child, the parent, or the environment. Interventions which focus on the parent (mother, in particular) have been the most common. Traditionally, psychotherapy with the mother has been considered necessary. Its advocates believe that only by helping the mother understand her feelings toward her child will her behavior change. But even these advocates have come to believe that therapy with the mother must be supplemented with other types of intervention.

Intervention in the case of failure-to-thrive syndrome has usually consisted of providing help and support for the mother during the hospitalization of her child. It is believed that once the infant begins to thrive it is possible to break the cycle of maternal insufficiency and frustration. But Evans et al. (1972), Leonard et al. (1966), and Fischoff (1973) have all cautioned that mothers may resist this kind of intervention. It has been suggested that the parents' feelings of guilt may be mobilized by the infant's improvement while in the hospital. Thus, Green (1980) believes it is important not to terminate the intervention with a mother upon the child's discharge. Kempe and Kempe (1978) have also stressed that treatment of a mother must take into consideration her own need for nurturance in addition to teaching her the responsibilities of mothering.

Reports on the effectiveness of interventions with failure-to-thrive infants and their parents vary. Ayoub, Pfeifer, and Leichtman (1980) reported an intervention with 100 failure-to-thrive infants and their mothers, half from lower-SES families and half from middle- and upper-SES families. This intervention focused on "reshaping the mother–infant attachment" and included 4–14 days of hospitalization, plus follow-up home services. Education and counseling were provided to the mothers and a stimulation program was provided for the children with parental involvement. Results showed positive changes in mother–child interaction and positive changes in infants (fewer incidences of crying, irritability, and vomiting) in 55 of the dyads. In 25 dyads there was little change, while in 20 dyads mothers continued to show a complete inability to interact effectively with their infants. Thus, an intervention focusing on changing the pattern of interaction does show promise in some cases.

Interventions with older children have taken many forms. Some authors such as Kempe and Kempe (1978) recommend individual play therapy and, in some extreme cases, a therapeutic play school. Because emotionally neglected children have both emotional and cognitive difficulties, they may require psychoeducational assistance in school. All can benefit from a supportive relationship with a kind and predictable adult. Although some authors have advocated placement with a mother substitute, current consensus seems to be to attempt to keep the child at home with his or her natural parents and provide support in and out of the home.

Very little data is available on the effectiveness of programs for families where emotional neglect occurs. Bavolek and colleagues (Bavolek & Comstock, 1980; Bavolek & Dellinger–Bavolek, 1980) have reported on a "Nurturing Program for Parents and Children" in which they worked on parents' developmental expectations, skills in empathy, and awareness of children's needs. The program involved parents and children, and included $2\frac{1}{2}$ hours of meetings, once per week for 15 weeks. They reported significant improvements in parents' expectations, empathy, and self-awareness; in family interactions (cohesion, independence, and communication); and in children's self-esteem and awareness of others' needs. Much more information is needed on the effectiveness of this type of intervention.

Prevention

Green (1980) suggested that prevention of emotional neglect is likely, ultimately, to require broad economic and social reform. It will be necessary to examine how well societies prepare their members for infant and child care. In societies where parents are socially isolated and are not given help in understanding child development, the incidence of child neglect will be higher (Korbin, 1980). Classes for expectant mothers and fathers should be made available in all hospitals and, wherever possible, should continue after the birth of the child. Such things as education of adolescents for parenthood, courses in life skills and coping techniques, and help in the form of

day care, homemaker services, and home helpers for at-risk families have been suggested as preventive measures. Economic considerations and government support or lack of support for the "nonbasics" in social services and education will, no doubt, determine whether such preventive measures are given priority.

Research will need to continue so that identifying "at-risk" families will become more accurate. Green (1980) suggested that current pencil-and-paper techniques have not achieved validity and reliability for screening. He suggests clinical interviews and observations for identifying at-risk situations, and the research by Egeland and colleagues cited earlier supports this. During pregnancy, it is possible to assess such things as feelings about the pregnancy and the prospects about keeping the baby, expectations and understanding of child development and the mother–child relationship, and outside support that the mother is receiving. Some postpartum risk signals may include delay in naming the baby, poor tolerance of crying, difficulty in handling the baby, intolerance of messiness, and perceptions of the baby as an adult. Unwanted pregnancies, alcoholism, high stress, lack of coping skills, single parenthood, and unhappy marriages all may contribute, but alone are not necessarily indications that a child will be neglected. Cultural factors should also be considered in pinpointing the high-risk situation. For example, in some cultures twins are less valued than single births and thus may be at risk for emotional neglect (Korbin, 1980).

CONCLUSIONS AND DIRECTIONS

Despite problems with definitions, varying ideas on when and how to report and intervene, and a scarcity of research data on etiology and effectiveness of treatment, a review of the literature on emotional neglect allows us to draw some conclusions about the problem. We can see that the crucial ingredients in a neglecting relationship include a high-risk parent, a vulnerable infant, and a stressful environment. We can also conclude that although emotional neglect can occur with other forms of abuse and neglect, it may also occur with good physical care and inflict just as much or more damage. Obviously the effects of emotional neglect are serious and pervasive. Whether legislators need to become more involved in the arena of emotional neglect is arguable and ultimately will be decided by what each society considers to be important. Clearly, though, people in the helping professions need to be sensitive to the problem and make informed decisions about intervention. The link between research results and practical applications, as always, will be a most important one.

REFERENCES

Ayoub, C., Pfeifer, D., & Leichtman, L. (1980). Treatment of infants with nonorganic failure to thrive. In *Selected readings on child neglect*, OHDS 80-30253). Washington, DC: Office of Human Development Services.

Barbero, G. J. (1982). Failure to thrive. In M. H. Klaus, T. Leger, & M. A. Trause (Eds.), *Maternal attachment and mothering disorders.* Skillman, NJ: Johnson & Johnson.

Barbero, G. J., Morris, M. G., & Redford, M. T. (1963). Malidentification of mother–baby–father relationships expressed in infant failure to thrive. *Child Welfare, 42,* 13–18.

Bavolek, S. J., & Comstock, C. M. (1980). *Nurturing program for parents and children.* Eau Claire: University of Wisconsin.

Bavolek, S. J., & Dellinger–Bavolek, J. (1980). *Identifying and reporting child abuse and neglect.* Eau Claire: University of Wisconsin.

Boehm, B. (1964). The community and the social agency define neglect. *Child Welfare, 43,* 453–464.

Bourne, R. (1979). Child abuse and neglect: An overview. In R. Bourne & E. H. Newberger (Eds.), *Critical perspectives on child abuse.* Lexington, MA: D. C. Heath & Company.

Bourne, R., & Newberger, E. H. (1979). "Family autonomy" or "coercive intervention"? Ambiguity and conflict in the proposed standards for child abuse and neglect. In R. Bourne & E. H. Newberger (Eds.), *Critical perspectives on child abuse.* Lexington, MA: D. C. Heath & Company.

Bowlby, J. (1951). Maternal care and mental health. *Bulletin of the World Health Organization, 31,* 355–533.

Bullard, D. M., Glaser, H. H., Heagerty, M. C., & Pivchik, E. C. (1967). Failure to thrive in the "neglected child." *American Journal of Orthopsychiatry, 37,* 680–690.

Burlingham, D., & Freud, A. (1944). *Infants without families.* London: Allen & Unwin.

Coleman, R., & Provence, S. A. (1957). Developmental retardation (hospitalism) in infants living in families. *Pediatrics, 19,* 285–292.

Dean, D. (1979). Emotional abuse of children. *Children Today, 8,* 18–20.

Egeland, B., Breitenbucher, M., & Rosenberg, D. (1980). Prospective study of the significance of life stress in the etiology of child abuse. *Journal of Consulting and Clinical Psychology, 48,* 195–205.

Egeland, B., & Brunnquell, D. (1979). An at-risk approach to the study of child abuse: Some preliminary findings. *Journal of the American Academy of Child Psychiatry, 18,* 219–235.

Egeland, B., & Sroufe, L. A. (1981). Developmental sequelae of maltreatment in infancy. In R. Rizley & D. Cicchetti (Eds.), *New directions for child development: Developmental prespectives in child maltreatment.* San Francisco: Jossey–Bass.

Eisenberg, L. (1957). The fathers of autistic children. *American Journal of Orthopsychiatry, 27,* 715–724.

Elmer, E. (1960). Failure to thrive: Role of the mother. *Pediatrics, 25,* 717–725.

Erikson, E. H. (1950). *Childhood and society.* New York: W. W. Norton & Co.

Evans, S. L., Reinhard, J. B., & Succop, R. A. (1972). Failure to thrive: A study of 45 children and their families. *Journal of the American Academy of Child Psychiatry, 11,* 440–457.

Fischoff, J. (1973). Failure to thrive and maternal deprivation. In M. H. Klaus & A. A. Fenaroff (Eds.), *Care of the high risk neonate.* Philadelphia: Saunders.

Flannery, E. J. (1979). Synopsis: Standards relating to abuse and neglect. In R. Bourne & E. H. Newburger (Eds.), *Critical perspectives on child abuse.* Lexington, MA: D. C. Heath & Company.

Galdston, R. (1968). Dysfunctions of parenting: The battered child, the neglected child, the exploited child. In J. G. Howells (Ed.), *Modern perspectives of international child psychiatry.* Edinburgh: Oliver & Boyd.

Gardner, L. I. (1972). Deprivation dwarfism. *Scientific American, 227,* 76–82.

Gil, D. G. (1979). Unraveling child abuse. In R. Bourne & E. H. Newberger (Eds.), *Critical perspectives on child abuse.* Lexington, MA: D. C. Heath & Company.

Giovannoni, J. M., & Billingsley, A. (1970). Child neglect among the poor: A study of parental adequacy in families of three ethnic groups. *Child Welfare, 49,* 196–204.

Giovannoni, J. M., Conklin, J., & Iiyama, P. (1978). *Child abuse and neglect: An examination from the perspective of child development knowledge.* San Francisco: R & E Research Associates, Inc.

Goldfarb, W. (1945). Psychological privation in infancy and subsequent adjustment. *American Journal of Orthopsychiatry, 102,* 247–255.

Gordon, A. H., & Jameson, J. C. (1979). Infant-mother attachment in patients with nonorganic failure to thrive syndrome. *Journal of Child Psychiatry, 18,* 251–259.

Green, A. H. (1980). *Child maltreatment: A handbook for mental health and child care professionals.* New York: Jason Aronson.

Horney, K. (1937). *The neurotic personality of our time.* New York: W. W. Norton & Co.

Hufton, I. W., & Oates, R. K. (1977). Nonorganic failure to thrive: A long term follow-up. *Pediatrics, 59,* 73–77.

Jacobs, R. A., & Kent, J. (1976). *Psychosocial profile of parents of failure to thrive infants.* Geneva: World Health Organization.

Kanner, L. (1943). Autistic disturbances of affective contact. *Nervous Child, 3,* 217–250.

Kempe, R. S., & Kempe, C. H. (1978). *Child abuse.* London: Open Books.

Korbin, J. E. (1980). The cultural context of child abuse and neglect. *Child Abuse & Neglect, 4,* 3–13.

Leonard, M., Rhymes, J., & Solnit, A. (1966). Failure to thrive in infants: A family problem. *American Journal of Diseases of Children, 111,* 600–612.

MacCarthy, D. (1979). Recognition of signs of emotional deprivation: A form of child abuse. *Child Abuse and Neglect, 3,* 423–428.

Maslow, A. H. (1968). *Toward a psychology of being.* Princeton: Van Nostrand.

National Center on Child Abuse and Neglect (1978). *Interdisciplinary glossary on child abuse and neglect.* Washington, DC: U.S. Department of Health, Education, and Welfare.

Office of Human Development Services (1981). *Results of a national study of the incidence and severity of child abuse and neglect.* (DHHS Pub. OHDS 81-30325). Washington, DC: U.S. Department of Health and Human Services.

Patton, R. G., & Gardner, L. I. (1962). Influence of family environment on growth: The syndrome of "maternal deprivation." *Pediatrics, 30,* 957–962.

Pavenstadt, E. (Ed.) (1967). *The drifters — Children of disorganized lower class families.* Boston: Little Brown.

Polansky, N. A., Chalmers, M. A., Buttenwieser, E., & Williams, D. P. (1981). *Damaged parents: An anatomy of child neglect.* Chicago: University of Chicago Press.

Polansky, N. A., DeSaix, C., Wing, M., & Patton, J. D. (1968, October). Child neglect in a rural community. *Social Casework,* 467–474.

Polansky, N. A., Hally, C., & Polansky, N. F. (1977). *Profile of neglect: A survey of the state of knowledge.* (OHDS 77-02004, pp. 3–7). Washington, DC: U.S. Department of Health, Education & Welfare.

Prugh, D. G., & Harlow, R. G. (1962). "Masked deprivation" in infants and young children. In *Deprivation of maternal care: A reassessment of its effects.* Geneva: World Health Organization.

Region X Child Abuse and Neglect Resource Center (1980). *The educator's role in the prevention and treatment of child abuse and neglect.* Seattle: Author.

Spitz, R. A. (1945). Hospitalism: An inquiry into the genesis of psychiatric conditions of early childhood. *Psychoanalytic Study of the Child, 1,* 53–74.

Wald, M. S. (1976). State intervention on behalf of "neglected" children: Standards for removal of children from their homes, monitoring the status of children in foster care, and termination of parental rights. *Stanford Law Review, 28,* 628–706.

Whiting, L. (1976). Defining emotional neglect. *Children Today, 5*(1), 2–4.

Wolff, G., & Money, J. (1973). Relationship between sleep and growth in patients with reversible somatotropin deficiency (psychosocial dwarfism). *Psychiatric Medicine, 3,* 18–27.

8

Psychologically Unavailable Caregiving

Byron Egeland and Martha Farrell Erickson

CASE STUDIES: PSYCHOLOGICAL UNAVAILABILITY

Melanie

During the early years of Melanie's life, home visitors consistently described interaction between Melanie and her mother as mechanical and functional, with no sense of warmth or joy. Although Melanie's mother always saw that Melanie was well fed, clean, and neatly dressed, she admitted that she hated having to care for Melanie when she was a baby and felt overwhelmed with the responsibility. She received no help or emotional support from Melanie's father, who could not understand why yelling "shut up" did not stop the baby's crying. When Melanie was 7 months old, her mother placed her in a group foster home, but Melanie's paternal grandmother removed her and insisted that Melanie's mother take her home.

During a home visit when Melanie was 2 years old, her mother seemed detached and disinterested in the child. When asked how she dealt with her toddler's need for attention, the mother stated flatly, "I try to keep her away from me. I ignore her. I treat her like an adult so she'll hurry up and be one." The mother's unresponsiveness and its impact on Melanie was apparent in a laboratory problem-solving situation designed to assess how the mother–child pair were coping with the

2-year-old's emerging autonomy. Melanie's mother provided no cues to help Melanie solve the difficult problems and gave no feedback when Melanie attempted the tasks on her own. The mother ignored Melanie's initial polite requests for help, which soon escalated to whining and crying. Ten minutes into the session Melanie was screaming and hitting the plexiglass box through which she could see, but not reach, a special treat. Her mother sat silently in the corner, seemingly oblivious to her child's frustration. Likewise, in a series of teaching tasks when Melanie was 42 months old, her mother failed to provide appropriate instruction or support and Melanie consequently became agitated, tearful, and finally aggressive toward her mother. Over the next 2 years, Melanie became increasingly noncompliant and aggressive at home, engaging her mother in frequent, intense power struggles—apparently the only way to elicit any response from her mother.

The long-term consequences of this pattern of emotional neglect are striking. When Melanie was 5 years old, her preschool teachers described her as "desperately dependent." She attempted nothing without being encouraged or persuaded, and she reacted to the smallest challenge by crying and clinging to the nearest adult. In social situations with peers she often stood outside the group sucking her thumb and twisting her hair. When she did engage in activities with peers she frequently became involved in fights and soon threw herself on the floor and cried. She clearly had not developed the competence and self-esteem necessary to cope with the demands of the preschool environment.

Eric

Eric's mother rarely interacted with him except to discipline him. When he cried during early infancy his mother "showed him who's boss" by locking him in his room. Later when he began to crawl and explore, his mother confined him to a playpen during his waking hours. When Eric was 2 years old, his mother was observed to spank him frequently, to never provide positive reinforcement, and on one occasion, to lock him in the bathroom, threatening to turn out all the lights if he continued to cry. In laboratory situations at both 24 and 42 months, Eric's mother issued occasional harsh, impatient commands, but otherwise sat with her arms folded and ignored Eric. At 24 months Eric's response was to cry and tug persistently on his mother's leg in a futile attempt to get her help. But by 42 months, Eric glared at his mother, quietly and defiantly refusing to follow her orders.

When interviewed about her ideas regarding child behavior and child-rearing, Eric's mother answered, "Don't know" to almost every question. (The only exception was the question, "What would you change about your life?" to which she replied that she certainly would not have children again.) She seemed to have no knowledge of, or interest in, what was important for her child's healthy development.

Not surprisingly, Eric has presented serious behavior problems both in and out of the home. At age 4, he attended nursery school for only a few weeks. His aggressive, noncompliant behavior "created chaos" and led to the teacher's request that he not return until his behavior changed. By the time he reached kindergarten age Eric was "on the streets," according to home visitors, coming and going whenever and wherever he pleased. His mother made few attempts to manage his reckless, defiant behavior. On one occasion when he stood on the dining room table as if to jump off, his mother told him, "Go ahead and jump. I hope you break your neck."

The house was full of objects which Eric had damaged, either deliberately or accidentally, during his rambunctious antics. In kindergarten, Eric was observed to hit, pinch, and scratch his classmates whenever the teacher was not looking. His teacher described him as "hardened and tough—a child whom nothing can touch" and said that "no one can develop a trusting relationship with that child."

Studies of the effects of child abuse and neglect have revealed a diversity of negative outcomes for the young victims. Some abused children have been described as withdrawn, passive, apathetic and unresponsive, while others have been described as aggressive, hostile, and oppositional (e.g., Martin & Beezeley, 1977; Kempe & Kempe, 1978). While the range of intellectual abilities varies widely among abused and neglected children, a disproportionately large number of these children fall below average on measures of intelligence (Sandgrund, Gaines, & Green, 1974; Martin, Beezeley, Conway, & Kempe, 1974). A problem with many studies of abuse is that abusive families often are multiproblem families, with homes characterized by chaos, disruption, and general deprivation. Thus, the effects of abuse often are confounded with the effects of these broader environmental influences. In a study which systematically controlled for socioeconomic status, Elmer (1977) found a large number of problems among both abused and nonabused children, and concluded that the consequences of abuse were "less potent for the child's development than class membership" (p. 110). Furthermore, research typically has focused on overt, easily identified forms of abuse. Thus, studies have overlooked more subtle, but equally pernicious, types of maltreatment, particularly the failure of caregivers to provide the sensitive, responsive caregiving necessary to facilitate healthy social/emotional development of young children.

In this chapter, we discuss findings from a prospective, longitudinal investigation of early development. These data (a) provide substantial documentation of negative effects of abuse, apart from the consequences of poverty and other environmental influences; and (b) provide striking evidence of the severe effects of insensitive, unresponsive parenting—what we have termed psychological unavailability of the caregiver. We also consider the implications of these findings for early intervention.

MINNESOTA MOTHER–CHILD INTERACTION PROJECT

The Minnesota Mother–Child Project is a prospective, longitudinal study designed to study the development of a sample of high-risk children. As part of this investigation, we have studied the various factors that influence the quality of care the child receives, particularly the causes of abuse and neglect, and we have examined the effects of various forms of maltreatment on the development of the child from birth through preschool. A sample of 267 mothers was selected from primiparous pregnant women considered to be at risk for later caretaking problems. Risk factors included low socioeconomic status, age ($\overline{X}$ = 20.5, range = 12–34), lack of support (62% single at time of baby's birth), chaotic living conditions and large amounts of life stress. The mothers all were receiving prenatal care through public assistance at the Maternal and Infant Care Clinic, Minneapolis Health Department. The base rate for reported abuse and neglect in this public health clinic population is 1–2%, considerably higher than for the state in general. Detailed and comprehensive data have been collected on the child, mother, and life situations, and observations of the mother and child were done at regularly scheduled intervals. Data collection began with assessment of maternal personality and attitude during the 36th week of pregnancy and has included observation of the neonate, interviews with the mother every 6 months, detailed assessment of the child, observation of mother–child interaction in a variety of natural and laboratory situations, and observations of the children in preschool and day-care settings. Currently the children are 6–7 years of age, and information is being gathered on their adjustment to school.

This research is guided by developmental/organizational theory (Sroufe, 1979). From this perspective, development is described as a series of issues, a sequence of adaptations. Each phase of development is characterized by issues of particular importance, and these issues present special challenges to the individual's ability to integrate behavior in adaptive ways. Individual differences arise with respect to the quality of adaptation to these challenges. Each level of development involves new elements of behavior that represent the integration and differentiation of former accomplishments. Thus, successful adaptation (healthy resolution of an issue) is influenced by the way earlier issues were resolved, and the quality of adaptation to a current issue lays the groundwork for adaptation to subsequent issues.

We are interested particularly in the social and emotional development of these high-risk children, so in our research we have chosen tasks which allow us to assess how the child is negotiating each stage of development, and we define social and emotional competence in terms of healthy resolution of salient issues at any given stage. For example, in the first year of life, a major issue is to establish a sense of trust and security. This is accomplished by forming a secure relationship (attachment) with the caregiver (the mother in the case of our subjects). Thus, at 12 and 18 months of age we have assessed the quality of the mother–child attachment, with the competent child being defined as one who demonstrates a secure attachment. At 2 years of age, a major issue is the child's emerging autonomy, so we have assessed the child in a problem-solving task with the mother, looking at competence in terms of the child's autonomous efforts at problem solving. When the children were $3\frac{1}{2}$ years of age, we were interested in the child's socialization, particularly in the development of self-control and self-esteem. So we observed the child in two situations (one with the mother, one without) and assessed such things as the child's self-esteem, persistence, enthusiasm, and frustration tolerance in dealing with a variety of tasks. And in the preschool, when the children were 4–5 years of age, we assessed the child's social and emotional competence as demonstrated in positive interaction with peers, acceptance of adult guidance, and a confident, assertive approach to classroom activities. This developmental/organizational approach to the assessment of social/emotional competence is unique in at least two ways. First, this approach dictates that we look not at individual behaviors, but rather at patterns of behavior, how the child organizes his/her behavior around these salient developmental issues. Second, this approach allows that behaviors have different meanings at different ages. For example, noncompliance in a 2-year-old might be viewed as a normal part of the child's struggle for autonomy, whereas that same degree of noncompliance might be cause for concern in a 4-year-old child who would have been expected to settle into a more accepting, compliant pattern of interaction with adults.

DIFFERENT PATTERNS OF MALTREATMENT AND THEIR EFFECTS ON THE DEVELOPMENT OF CHILDREN

While the Mother–Child Project has examined the entire qualitative range of caregiving, the relatively high incidence of maltreatment among this high-risk sample has allowed us to focus on the consequences of maltreatment, addressing the question of whether specific patterns of maltreatment result in specific developmental outcomes (Egeland & Sroufe, 1981a; Egeland & Sroufe, 1981b; Egeland, Sroufe, & Erickson, 1983). From among the original sample of 267 mothers, four maltreatment groups were identified: physically abusive ($N = 24$), hostile/verbally abusive ($N = 19$), neglectful ($N = 24$), and psychologically unavailable ($N = 19$). Also, from the original high-risk sample we selected a control group of nonmaltreated children ($N = 85$), allowing us to distinguish the consequences of maltreatment from those of poverty and other risk factors. Mothers in the physically abusive group presented behaviors ranging from frequent, intense spanking in disciplining their children to unprovoked angry outbursts resulting in serious injuries, including extensive bruises, cuts, and cigarette burns. Mothers in the hostile/verbally abusive group chronically found fault with their children, criticizing them in a harsh manner. Whereas many physically abusive mothers were not constantly hostile or rejecting (but rather prone to violent, unprovoked outbursts), the mothers in the verbal-abuse group engaged in constant degrading and harassment of their children. Mothers in the neglect group were irresponsible or incompetent in managing day-to-day child-care activities. They failed to provide for the necessary health or physical care of their children and did little to protect them from possible dangers in the home. While these mothers sometimes expressed interest in their children's well-being, they lacked the skills, knowledge, or understanding to provide consistent and adequate care. Mothers in the psychologically unavailable group were unresponsive to their children and, in many cases, passively rejecting of them. These mothers appeared to be detached and uninvolved with their children, interacting with them only when it was necessary. They did not display any pleasure in interacting with their child, nor did they respond positively toward the child's attempts to elicit

interaction. They usually provided for the physical needs of the child and were not physically abusive or overtly rejecting of the child. The psychologically unavailable mothers were poor at comforting their children at a time of distress, and they did not share in the positive experiences of the children. In general, they were withdrawn, displayed flat affect, and seemed depressed. There was no indication that these mothers derived any pleasure or satisfaction from their relationships with their children.

Mothers in all maltreatment groups were identified on the basis of information obtained from observations of mother and infant in the home 7 and 10 days postpartum and when the infant was 3, 6, and 12 months of age. During each of these visits, a child-care rating scale (Egeland & Deinard, 1975) was completed and the mother was asked questions regarding her caretaking skills, feelings toward the infant, disciplinary practices, and so on. In addition, observational data and other information were collected systematically when each mother visited the Maternal and Infant Care Clinic and when mothers visited our laboratory with their infants at ages 9, 12, 18, and 24 months. The validity of our staff's identification of maltreating mothers was supported by additional information. All mothers in the physical-abuse group have been under the care of child protection or have been referred to child protection by someone outside of the project. Mothers in the neglect group are or have been under the care of a public health nurse or child protection. Independent raters' observations of mothers and infants at 12 and 18 months in a situation requiring that the mother set limits for her child and at 24 months in a problem-solving task supported the identification of mothers in the hostile/verbal abuse group and in the psychologically unavailable group. If there was some question whether a mother was maltreating her child or if the maltreatment was borderline, the case was not included in either the control group or in any of the maltreatment groups.

To determine the effects of maltreatment, each maltreatment group was compared to the control group on a number of child-outcome variables assessed from the time the children were 3 months of age through the preschool years. Since physical abuse often accompanies the other forms of maltreatment, each of the maltreatment groups was subdivided into "with physical abuse" and "without physical abuse." Thus, for example, the psychologically unavailable group which also contains subjects who were physically abused was compared to the control group, and, in a separate set of analyses, the psychologically unavailable without the physical abuse group was compared to the control group. This procedure allowed us to separate the effects of physical abuse from the consequences of other forms of maltreatment. Outcome measures included observations of mother and infant in feeding and play situations at 3 and 6 months, in the Ainsworth Strange Situation to assess the quality of attachment at 12 and 18 months, in a tool-use problem-solving task at 24 months, and in a series of teaching tasks at 42 months. The children also were observed alone in a barrier box task at 42 months of age and in their preschool or day-care setting when they were approximately $4\frac{1}{2}$–5 years of age. The Bayley Scales of Infant Development were administered to the infants at 9 and 24 months. Longitudinal assessment allowed the cumulative effects of maltreatment to be traced. Following is a brief summary of the findings which have been reported in detail in earlier publications (cf. Egeland & Sroufe, 1981b; Egeland et al., 1983).

Our findings demonstrate that outcomes for children from each maltreatment group were severe and varied. In many areas of social and emotional competence, the maltreated children were functioning much more poorly than were their age-mates from similar backgrounds who did not have a history of abuse. A large proportion of children who were physically abused were anxiously attached at 18 months of age. At 24 months, when observed in a problem-solving task with their mothers, these children were angry, noncompliant, and lacking enthusiasm for the task. At 42 months in a problem-solving task alone, these children were hyperactive and distractible, presented a considerable amount of negative affect, and demonstrated poor self-control and low self-esteem. They were less creative in their approaches to the problem-solving task than were nonmaltreated children. In a series of teaching tasks with their mothers, these 42-month-old children lacked enthusiasm and persistence, were noncompliant, negativistic, and showed little affection for their mothers. They were reliant on their mothers, but avoided the mother except when seeking help. In preschool, these physically abused children were noncompliant and expressed a great deal of negative emotion. Children whose mothers were

hostile, rejecting, and verbally abusive looked much the same as the children in the physical abuse group. In general, these children were angry and noncompliant.

Among neglected children—those children whose mothers, either through incompetence or indifference, failed to meet their child's basic health and physical needs—there also was a high proportion of anxiously attached children at 18 months of age. At 24 months these neglected children had poor coping skills in the problem-solving task. At 42 months in the problem-solving task alone these children were low in self-esteem, showed poor impulse control, and lacked flexibility and creativity in their approaches to the problem. They were highly distractible and withdrew frequently from the task. This group of children appeared quite unhappy, presenting the least positive and the most negative affect of all groups. In the teaching tasks with their mothers, these children lacked persistence and enthusiasm and were avoidant of their mothers. Also, in the preschool, these children were highly dependent on their teachers for nurturance and support. The neglected children lacked impulse control and generally did not have the skills necessary to cope with the various situations in the preschool environment.

While the consequences for children in all maltreatment groups were serious, the results among children whose mothers were psychologically unavailable were most dramatic. Psychological unavailability resulted in a marked decline in competence from infancy through the preschool years. While at 3 months the infants in the psychologically unavailable group (without physical abuse) actually were more robust than infants in the control group, by 6 months there were no significant differences between the groups. Neither were there differences between the groups on the Bayley Scales of Infant Development given at 9 months. Differences in the proportion of infants in the attachment groups for the control and psychologically unavailable groups approached significance at 12 months and were highly significant at 18 months. At 12 months, 43% of the infants in the psychologically unavailable group (without physical abuse) were classified as anxious avoidant. By 18 months, 86% of these children were classified as anxious avoidant, and surprisingly there were *no* securely attached infants in that group. These results indicate that a mother who is emotionally unavailable is likely to have an infant with a specific attachment pattern, anxious avoidant. (The importance of these findings will be discussed later in this paper.) At 24 months in the problem-solving tasks with their mothers, the children whose mothers were psychologically unavailable looked angry, extremely frustrated, noncompliant and displayed a great deal of negative affect. A striking finding for these children whose mothers were psychologically unavailable was the marked decline in their performance on the Bayley Scales of Infant Development (Bayley, 1969) between 9 and 24 months. Whereas at 9 months the average mental score for the psychologically unavailable group was approximately 118, by 24 months the mean developmental quotient of this group was approximately 87.

At 42 months in a problem-solving task alone children whose mothers were psychologically unavailable lacked creativity in their approach to the problem. In the teaching tasks with their mothers these children were less persistent and enthusiastic than were children in the control group. They were noncompliant, negativistic, avoidant of their mothers, and expressed little affection toward their mothers. In preschool these children were rated by observers as being noncompliant, expressing a great deal of negative emotion, lacking impulse control, and highly dependent on preschool teachers for help and support. Teachers' ratings on the Preschool Behaviors Questionnaire (Behar & Stringfield, 1974) and the Behavior Problem Scale (Erickson & Egeland, 1981) revealed highly significant differences between control group children and children whose mothers were psychologically unavailable. These maltreated children presented many behavior problems in the preschool and, most notably, they displayed a number of behaviors considered potent indicators of psychopathology (e.g., nervous signs, self-abusive behavior). In general, these children demonstrated poor adjustment both in situations with their mothers and in interaction with teachers and peers in the preschool environment.

In sum, children in all maltreatment groups functioned poorly from infancy through the preschool years. A wide range of maladaptive behaviors was represented in each maltreatment group. The psychologically unavailable pattern was particularly devastating to the child's development. The sharp decline in the intellectual functioning of these children, their attachment disturbances and subsequent lack of social/emotional competence in a variety of situations is cause for great concern. The consequences of this form of maltreatment are particularly disturbing when considered in light of the fact that this is probably the least likely pattern of maltreatment to be detected. These findings must lead us to a careful reexamination of our society's definition of child abuse and a consideration of means for early identification and intervention to help prevent the cumulative, malignant effects of this form of maltreatment.

ISSUES REGARDING THE DEFINITIONS OF ABUSE

Criteria for the identification of abuse must be based on a careful consideration of the effects of the parents' behavior on the child's development. As we have just pointed out, our research clearly indicates that emotional unresponsiveness is devastating to young children. We contend that this pattern of parenting must be a major component in any definition of abuse and neglect.

Our research results lead us to emphasize two other points regarding definitions of abuse. First, our close observation of mother–child interaction in a variety of situations has revealed that maltreatment is far more prevalent than incidence figures usually suggest. By getting to know the families, starting before the birth of their first child, we observed and became aware of abuse, neglect, and other forms of maltreatment which were not obvious to the various social agencies that interacted with the family on a more superficial basis. Many of the physically abused children in our sample did not receive broken bones or other obvious physical signs. However, the chronic physical punishment and abuse resulted in highly negative developmental outcomes for the child. It should be noted that all families maltreating their children were referred to the proper agency for evaluation and treatment.

Second, our research findings demonstrate that abuse should not be viewed only as an isolated incident, but as an environment. In the case of physical abuse, it often is assumed that the actual abuse occurs in an otherwise normal home. However, we have found that in addition to overt abuse and neglect, the homes of many of these children are characterized by chaos, disruption, and disorganization. Drug and alcohol abuse are common, the mothers often are physically abused, and, in general, the homes provide a very aversive environment for raising the children. For the maltreated children, the home environment fails to meet the needs of the child in many different areas and for many of these children, the chaos and disruption have a very negative and cumulative effect on the child's development.

For the majority of these children in our maltreatment groups the maltreatment started at or even before birth in that the general caretaking environment was inadequate. For example, in examining the etiology of maltreatment in our study, we found that maltreating mothers were not prepared for the birth of their babies (e.g., they had neither made plans for where the baby would sleep nor had they obtained equipment for caring for the baby) and their expectations about raising babies were not realistic. Maltreated children tended to have lower birth weights than nonmaltreated children (despite similar gestational age), suggesting the possibility of poor nutrition during pregnancy among maltreating mothers (Egeland & Brunnquell, 1979). By following our families longitudinally we have observed that for the majority of maltreating families the abuse or neglect is chronic and, despite efforts by various social agencies, the caretaking environment does not improve. The effects of maltreatment, particularly in the case of children whose mothers are psychologically unavailable, are cumulative.

CHILD–CAREGIVER ATTACHMENT AND ITS IMPORTANCE FOR SUBSEQUENT DEVELOPMENT

A careful examination of attachment theory and research is essential to our consideration of early identification and intervention with children who are victims of maltreatment in the form of psychologically unavailable parenting. Previous research has demonstrated the significance of emotional responsiveness in fostering a secure attachment between child and caregiver. And a large body of literature, both theoretical and empirical, has addressed the importance of early attachment for the child's subsequent development.

Attachment theory has its roots in psychoanalytic work, which emphasizes the importance of early experience for a person's later development, and in ethological/evolutionary theory, which proposes that all infants are biologically disposed to form intimate relationships, relationships which are essential for survival. In human infants this close infant–caregiver relationship serves a physically protective function, but also paves the way for subsequent emotional and social development. By attachment we do not mean a bond formed immediately after birth, but rather a relationship that develops over the first year of the infant's life, following repeated interaction between the infant and caregiver. Attachment is well established only after the infant has developed the ability to discriminate among individuals and to recognize that an object, the caregiver in this case, exists even when it is not in sight, developments normally accomplished by the second half of the first year of life. By 6 months of age the infant typically begins taking the initiative in seeking contact with the caregiver, smiling more for the caregiver than for others, protesting when they are separated, and often showing some stranger anxiety. By 12 months of age attachment usually is well established. With perhaps some very rare exceptions, every infant forms an attachment, but there are individual differences in the quality of that attachment. Attachment may be secure or anxious. Secure attachment is facilitated by the caregiver's sensitivity, responsiveness, and predictability in meeting the infant's needs.

The attachment relationship is manifest through attachment behaviors: physical contact, eye contact, affective sharing, the infant's seeking proximity to the caregiver. The hallmark of attachment is proximity-seeking, and when the infant is distressed, he or she is easily comforted by the caretaker. However, attachment also is manifest through the child's ability to use the caregiver as a secure base from which to explore. In the caregiver's presence, the child is able to explore his or her environment in a confident fashion, and if frightened, can return to the caregiver for comfort and reassurance. Thus, a securely attached child will exhibit a balance of attachment behaviors and exploration. Secure attachment promotes proximity-seeking, it enables the child to be comforted by the caregiver when distressed, and it also facilitates exploration, essential to healthy development of the child.

As we pointed out in Egeland, Sroufe, & Erickson (1983) through this early primary relationship, or attachment, the infant forms representational models of others and self. Such models, it is suggested, are carried forward through life and strongly influence the ways in which the child relates to others, approaches the environment, and resolves critical issues in later stages of development. A person who has formed a healthy, secure attachment with a responsive caregiver "is likely to possess a representational model of attachment figure(s) as being available, responsive, and helpful and a complementary model of himself [sic] as at least a potentially lovable and valuable person" (Bowlby, 1980, p. 242). The securely attached child, with positive expectations of self and others, is more likely to "approach the world with confidence and, when faced with potentially alarming situations, is likely to tackle them effectively or to seek help in doing so" (Bowlby, 1973, p. 208). And he or she is more likely to enter into other loving, trusting relationships.

In contrast, infants whose needs have not been met consistently, whose attachment behavior was responded to inadequately or inappropriately, come to expect that care is not available or dependable. These children view the world as "comfortless and unpredictable; and they respond either by shrinking from it or doing battle with it" (Bowlby, 1973, p. 208). These children with insecure attachments are less prepared to cope with later adverse experiences, and they often tend to behave in ways which bring about more adverse experiences (Bowlby, 1982).

The Ainsworth Strange Situation Procedure (Ainsworth, Blehar, Waters, & Wall, 1978) has facilitated the accumulation of extensive empirical evidence in support of these theoretical propositions. The Strange Situation is a 20-minute videotaped procedure consisting of eight episodes in which the infant is observed in an unfamiliar room filled with toys, with an unfamiliar adult female in the room, with the mother both present and absent. Infants are classified into three major groups, primarily on the basis of their behavior during the reunion episodes following separation from the mother. The largest group consists of the securely attached infants who greet their mother positively, actively seek proximity or interaction with the mother, accept comfort from the mother if distressed, and display few, if any, negative behaviors toward her. These infants typically explore and play during the preseparation episodes, evidence that the mother provides security in the unfamiliar environment. Infants who exhibit substantial negative behavior toward the mother during the reunion episode are classified as anxiously attached. Infants are classified as anxious/avoidant when they avoid the mother by

turning away, looking away, ignoring her. These anxious/avoidant infants show little or no preference for their mother over the stranger. The second group of anxiously attached infants are called anxious/resistant since they show angry resistance to their mothers upon reunion. They often exhibit a high level of distress during separation or even when the mother is present. Upon reunion the anxious/resistant infants often appear ambivalent, actively seeking proximity with the mother, yet angrily pushing her away. They are extremely difficult to comfort.

Using the Ainsworth procedure, a number of researchers have found quality of attachment relates to later competence. Securely attached infants were found to be more cooperative at 22 months with mother and another adult (Main, 1973), more enthusiastic, persistent, actively positive, and compliant in problem-solving at age 2 (Matas, Arend, & Sroufe, 1978), more socially competent with peers at age $3\frac{1}{2}$ (Waters, Wippman, & Sroufe, 1979), and more ego-resilient at age 5 (Arend, Gove, & Sroufe, 1979). While those studies used middle-class families, in our own study of lower-socioeconomic-class mothers who are socially and emotionally at risk, secure attachment also has been found to predict later competent functioning. Securely attached infants have been reported to be more sociable as toddlers (Pastor, 1981), more compliant at age 2 with their mothers and at $4\frac{1}{2}$ years with preschool teachers (Erickson & Crichton, 1981; Erickson, Farber, & Egeland, 1982), have better self-control in the preschool (Egeland, 1983), and be less dependent on preschool teachers (Sroufe, Fox, & Van Pancake, 1983). Our recent examination of the relationship between quality of attachment and behavior problems in preschool yielded striking evidence of the importance of attachment for later competent functioning. Among 27 children identified by both teachers and observers as having behavior problems in preschool (acting out, withdrawn, and attention problems) only 7 had been securely attached at 12 and 18 months of age. In contrast, among 21 children who clearly were functioning well in the preschool, 15 had been classified as having secure attachments at 12 and 18 months. While both anxious/resistant and anxious/avoidant children were functioning more poorly in preschool than were children who had been securely attached as infants, anxious/avoidant children differed most strikingly from the secure infants. Children in the anxious/resistant group were judged by observers to have poorer social skills and to be less confident and assertive than were children who had been securely attached as infants.

Children who had been classified as anxious/avoidant in infancy were observed to be highly dependent on preschool teachers, noncompliant, and poorly skilled in social interaction with peers. Teachers described them as hostile, impulsive, giving up easily, and withdrawn. In general, these children presented a picture of extensive and varied behavior problems in preschool (Egeland et al., 1983).

These behaviors represent the maladaptation we would predict for a child with an attachment figure who is emotionally unresponsive. Previous research has demonstrated that the primary determinants of secure attachment with the mother are maternal sensitivity, responsiveness, and cooperation (Ainsworth et al., 1978). Mothers of securely attached infants are psychologically accessible, sensitively responding to their infant's cues and signals without interfering with ongoing infant behavior. They encourage a reciprocal, "give-and-take" interaction with their infant. In contrast, mothers of anxiously attached infants lack this sensitivity and cooperation. Mothers of anxious/avoidant infants in particular are rejecting and avoid physical contact with their infants. They are not responsive to the needs of the child, particularly when the child is crying and upset. (As noted earlier, 86% of the children in our study whose mothers were in our psychologically unavailable maltreatment group were classified as anxious/avoidant in the Strange Situation procedure at 18 months.)

IMPLICATIONS FOR INTERVENTION

We believe there are strong indicators even before the baby's birth that a mother is unlikely to provide the sensitive, responsive care necessary for the infant's optimal development. As noted earlier, maltreating mothers in our study did not make basic preparations for their babies' births. Furthermore, even in the hospital immediately after the babies' births, these mothers showed less interest in their babies (as judged by nurses) than did mothers who subsequently provided adequate care. Prenatal assessment indicated that these mothers did not know what to expect of their babies in terms of behavior and development milestones, and, very importantly,

they lacked understanding of the psychological complexity of their child and their relationship with their child. They did not understand that the infant is an autonomous being, yet is highly dependent on the caretaker. They did not recognize that the infant is capable of a reciprocal relationship, yet has needs that are separate from those of the mother. This lack of understanding manifests itself in the mother's failure to recognize her ambivalent feelings which of necessity accompany childcare. They would view the infant and caring for the infant as a total-positive or total-negative experience without being able to separate out both the positive and negative. Finally, mothers lacking in understanding tend to interpret the child's behavior in terms of their own needs and feelings rather than in terms of the reality of the situation. For example, in discussing the oppositional behavior of 2-year-old children, certain mothers would say that this behavior is due to the fact that they are poor mothers or because the child is a "bad child." They did not understand that this behavior is a normal part of the toddler period of development.

We propose a program of preventive intervention with these high-risk mothers beginning during the last trimester of pregnancy. This would be a multipronged intervention focusing on several aspects of caregiving. The major goal would be to help the mother understand her child's behavior. For example, a mother might attribute an infant's protest over separation as "trying to manipulate her" or because the child is "spoiled." We would try to help the mothers understand that protest over separation, the negativism of the 2-year-old, and so on, are normal behaviors which reflect the developmental issues at that particular age.

A second major and highly related goal would be to help these mothers be better perspective-takers, learning to be sensitive to what the infant is experiencing and thus to respond more appropriately to the infant's cues and signals. To accomplish these goals we would work with the mothers around concrete childcare tasks, such as feeding, dressing and play. This would allow the intervener to model sensitive and responsive care and the use of age-appropriate play materials designed to stimulate cognitive growth and exploration. (These play materials also could be made available for the mothers to check out for use at home with their infants temporarily.) We would videotape the mothers and their children in these various interaction situations and then watch the videotape, discussing with the mother what the baby was experiencing in that situation, how the mother's behavior was influencing the baby, and what signals the baby was giving the mother about his or her needs and feelings at the time. We also would bring together mothers with infants of similar ages. This would allow the mothers to see what other infants of approximately the same age are doing, helping the mother to develop more realistic expectations for her baby. Group activities with other mothers and their infants also might provide some peer support to the mothers.

In preparing to intervene with high-risk mothers and their children, we must ask what might underlie a mother's inability to provide sensitive and responsive care for her child. It would seem that for many of these mothers their own unmet emotional needs are seriously interfering with their ability to respond to the needs of their children. A number of research studies have shown that maltreating mothers often are experiencing unusual amounts of social and economic stress (Alvy, 1975; Garbarino, 1976). Also, many abusing parents were themselves abused and neglected (Steele & Pollock, 1968). While among our own subjects both maltreating and non-abusing mothers were experiencing considerable amounts of life stress, a far greater proportion of the abusing mothers were single at the time of the baby's birth, and these abusing mothers reported far less support from the alleged father of the baby and from their own families than did mothers who were providing adequate care for their children (Egeland & Sroufe, 1981b). Any intervention attempt must include efforts to meet the mother's own emotional needs and to help the mother recognize how her needs influence the way she perceives her infant and her relationship with her infant. We would propose to begin in pregnancy to provide support and encouragement to the mother. This probably would best be accomplished by beginning with concrete help with real-life problems.

Clearly we are not suggesting traditional psychological services for these mothers, but rather an extensive and intensive outreach program which would continue during the first years of the infant's life. The effectiveness of such intervention would be evaluated longitudinally using the kinds of developmentally oriented assessments we have described earlier. We would hope that these interventions would facilitate the development of a secure mother–infant attachment relationship in the first year of life and pave the way for healthy resolution of subsequent developmental issues.

REFERENCES

Ainsworth, M. D. S., Blehar, M., Waters, E., & Wall, S. (1978). *Patterns of attachment.* Hillsdale, NJ: Lawrence Erlbaum Associates.

Alvy, K. T. (1975). Preventing child abuse. *American Psychologist, 30,* 921–928.

Arend, R., Gove, F., & Sroufe, L. A. (1979). Continuity of individual adaptation from infancy to kindergarten: A predictive study of ego-resiliency and curiosity in preschoolers. *Child Development, 50,* 950–959.

Bayley, N. (1969). *The Bayley scales of infant development.* New York: The Psychological Corp.

Behar, L., & Stringfield, S. (1974). A behavior rating scale for the preschool child. *Developmental Psychology, 10*(5), 601–610.

Bowlby, J. (1973). *Attachment and loss, Vol. II: Separation: Anxiety and anger.* London: Hogarth.

Bowlby, J. (1980). *Attachment and loss, Vol. III: Loss, sadness and depression.* New York: Basic Books.

Bowlby, J. (1982). Attachment and loss: Retrospect and prospect. *American Journal of Orthopsychiatry, 52*(4), 664–678.

Egeland, B. (1983). Comments on Kopp, Krakow, and Vaughn's chapter. In M. Perlmutter (Ed.), *The Minnesota symposia on child psychology* (Vol. 16, pp. 129–185). Hillsdale, NJ: Lawrence Erlbaum.

Egeland, B., & Brunnquell, D. (1979). An at-risk approach to the study of child abuse: Some preliminary findings. *Journal of the American Academy of Child Psychiatry, 18,* 219–235.

Egeland, B., & Deinard, A. (1975). *Child care rating scale.* Unpublished text, University of Minnesota, Minneapolis, MN.

Egeland, B., & Sroufe, L. A. (1981a). Attachment and early maltreatment. *Child Development, 52,* 44–52.

Egeland, B., & Sroufe, L. A. (1981b). Developmental sequelae of maltreatment in infancy. In R. Rizley and D. Cicchetti (Eds.), *New directions for child development: Developmental perspectives in child maltreatment.* San Francisco, CA: Jossey Bass.

Egeland, B., Sroufe, L. A., & Erickson, M. (1983). The developmental consequence of different patterns of maltreatment. *Child Abuse and Neglect, 1,* 459–469.

Elmer, E. (1977). *Fragile families, troubled children.* Pittsburgh: University of Pittsburgh Press.

Erickson, M. F., & Crichton, L. (1981). Antecedents of compliance in two-year-olds from a high-risk sample. Paper presented at the biennial meeting of the Society for Research in Child Development, Boston, MA, April 1981.

Erickson, M., & Egeland, B. (1981). *Behavior problem checklist technical manual.* Unpublished manuscript, University of Minnesota.

Erickson, M. F., Farber, E. A., & Egeland, B. (1982). Antecedents and concomitants of compliance in high-risk preschool children. Paper presented at the annual meeting of the American Psychological Association, Washington, DC, August 1982.

Garbarino, J. (1976). A preliminary study of some ecological correlates of child abuse. *Child Development, 47,* 178–185.

Kempe, R., & Kempe, C. H. (1978). *Child abuse.* London: Fontana/Open Books.

Main, M. (1973). *Exploration, play and level of cognitive functioning as related to child–mother attachment.* Unpublished doctoral dissertation, Johns Hopkins University.

Martin, H. P., & Beezeley, P. (1977). Behavioral observations of abused children. *Developmental Medicine and Child Neurology, 19,* 373–387.

Martin, H. P., Beezeley, P., Conway, E. F., & Kempe, C. H. (1974). The development of abused children. *Advances in Pediatrics, 21,* 25–73.

Matas, L., Arend, R., & Sroufe, L. A. (1978).

Continuity of adaptation in the second year: The relationship between quality of attachment and later competence. *Child Development, 49,* 547–556.

Pastor, D. L. (1981). The quality of mother–infant attachment and its relationship to toddler's initial sociability with peers. *Developmental Psychology, 17*(3), 326–335.

Sandgrund, A., Gaines, R. W., & Green, A. H. (1974). Child abuse and mental retardation: A problem of cause and effect. *American Journal of Mental Deficiency, 79,* 327–330.

Sroufe, L. A. (1979). The coherence of individual development: Early care, attachment, and subsequent developmental issues. *American Psychologist, 34,* 834–841.

Sroufe, L. A., Fox, N., & Van Pancake, V. (1983). Attachment and dependency in developmental perspective. *Child Development, 54,* 1615–1627.

Steele, B. F., & Pollock, C. B. (1968). A psychiatric study of parents who abuse infants and small children. In R. E. Helfer and C. H. Kempe (Eds.), *The battered child.* Chicago, IL: University of Chicago Press.

Waters, E., Wippman, J., & Sroufe, L. A. (1979). Attachment, positive affect and competence in the peer group: Two studies in construct validation. *Child Development, 50,* 821–829.

9

Influence by Negative and Limiting Models

Cathy F. Telzrow

Todd is a 9-year-old youth who lives in an urban setting. His parents both work outside the home, and he is on his own a good bit of the time. He frequently watches television after school, and enjoys programs about policemen and street crime. His father is a brusque, outspoken man given to shouting and abusive language. On frequent occasions, he loudly belittles Todd's mother when meals are not on time or the food is not to his liking. Todd's mother may be described as a meek, weary woman, although she spanks Todd and his two siblings often when they are late coming home or get in trouble in school.

Todd has become friends with a somewhat older boy in the neighborhood who has talked to Todd about his activities with a youth gang. Todd has heard that the gang has been involved in a number of minor offenses in the neighborhood, including some vandalism. The boy tells Todd they have a plan to get quite a lot of money, and challenges Todd to pass the initiation to become a member of the gang so he can "get rich" too. The initiation requires Todd to steal some merchandise from a neighborhood store operated by an elderly couple. Todd reasons that stealing the merchandise should be easy, given the feebleness of the couple, and feels grown up and powerful at the thought of having money of his own and being a part of the gang.

Glenda is an attractive young woman, age 22. She has just graduated from college and is starting a new job as a teacher in a small school district. She is a bright, ambitious woman who has been accepted into graduate school and plans to pursue a doctorate in educational administration. Her career goal is to become a school superintendent.

For a course she is taking, Glenda is required to interview several school administrators, and she makes an appointment to talk with her superintendent, Mr. Ferguson. Mr. Ferguson greets Glenda cordially, and seems flattered that Glenda wishes to interview him about his superintendency. At the conclusion of the structured interview, Glenda shares her career goal with Mr. Ferguson. He scoffs openly. "You—a pretty woman like you—why, what on earth would you do with an advanced degree?" Mr. Ferguson asked derisively.

Glenda blushed, and felt herself stammer as she responded, "Why, I aspire to the highest degree in my field, just as you have."

"But you're a *woman*," Mr. Ferguson replied, incredulously. "You don't *have* to work—you'll have a husband to support you, and children—I'm sure you plan to have children, and you know how harmful it is for children when mothers work. And do you really think a school board would ever have respect for—much less hire—a woman superintendent?"

Glenda felt her face grow hot, and her eyes sting with tears. She left Mr. Ferguson's office quickly, saying very little. On her drive home, his words replayed endlessly in her mind. She saw herself in competition for a superintendent's job and losing to a male candidate. Her fantasies advanced to a confrontational meeting with angry school board members, and Glenda saw herself dissolve in tears, as she had with Mr. Ferguson that afternoon. "Maybe he's right," she thought, as she parked her car. On the way into her apartment, Glenda discarded the notes from her interview with Mr. Ferguson in the waste can on the curb. "Guess I won't need these," she thought.

BACKGROUND AND THEORY

Human beings learn from observing the behavior of others. While many factors have been shown to influence to what degree and under what circumstances such incidental learning will occur, it is believed to be of critical import to the development of socialization, as well as other important aspects of interpersonal skills. This chapter will describe the dynamics of social learning, and will review in particular the influence of negative and limiting models on children's development. In the first portion of the chapter, the theoretical constructs of social learning theory will be presented together with major empirical evidence for the validity of this theory of behavior acquisition. Subsequent sections will focus on specific negative or limiting models of relevance for aggressive behavior, sex-role stereotyping, ethnic stereotyping, consumerism, and portrayal of handicapped persons.

Review of Social Learning Theory

As Albert Bandura (1962) pointed out over two decades ago, human beings can acquire complex behaviors merely from observing the actions of others. Were all human learning dependent upon a system of reinforcement contingencies such as that proposed by strict behaviorism (Skinner, 1971), the acquisition of new patterns of behavior would progress at a snail's pace (Bandura, 1974b), and the kinds of learning which appear to rely most extensively upon observation and imitation might not occur at all (Bandura, 1969, 1974a, 1977; Slobin, 1968). The ability of human beings to learn via observation is indicative of their superior intellectual capacity, which permits them to store information symbolically, as well as the human propensity to create self-regulatory influences (Bandura,

1974b). Bandura (1969) asserts that social learning represents the primary means of transmitting acquired behavior, and indicates that any behavior resulting from direct experience can be learned via observation.

Attentional Processes. An interactive network of four components is central to the concept of social learning theory, as described by Bandura (1969, 1974a, 1977). The first component is attentional processes, and Bandura (1969) asserts that in order for modeled events to be a source for learning, adequate attentional processes are necessary. Attentional processes are subject to two major types of influence: those associated with the modeled event, and those which are qualities of the observer. Examples of factors in the modeled event which may cause it to have increased salience for the observer include the existence of high-status models (Bandura, 1977), the sex of the model (Bandura, 1965; Bandura, Ross, & Ross, 1963; Raskin & Israel, 1981), and whether or not the model exhibits control over resources (Bandura et al., 1963). The rate and complexity of stimuli in the modeled event have been reported to be important factors in behavior acquisition (Bandura, 1965), and there is evidence that certain types of models (e.g., televised models) are intrinsically reinforcing for most observers (Bandura, Grusec, & Menlove, 1966). Examples of observer qualities which may affect the degree to which a given modeled event will be learned include arousal level (Bandura & Rosenthal, 1966; Schachter & Singer, 1962; Walters & Amoroso, 1967), as well as such traits as dependency (Cohen, 1971; Ross, 1966); need for social approval (Lipton, 1971; Marlowe, Beecher, Cook, & Doob, 1964); and preexperience (Roberts & Wurtele, 1981). Bandura (1965) suggests that the observer's anticipation of the positive or negative consequences of imitating a modeled event may be reflected in increased attention.

Retention Processes. The second component in the social learning theory model relates to those processes concerned with memory and recall. Unless modeled events are interpreted and internalized, they have been shown to decay quickly and to leave little lasting impression. Thus *symbolic coding* is a necessary prerequisite for imitative behavior (Bandura, 1969, 1977). Symbolic coding, which generally occurs via either imaginal or verbal processes (Bandura, 1974a; Gerst,

1971) represents the system by which the modeled event is encoded and represented in memory. Individual differences may exist in the type of symbolic coding preferred (Bandura, 1977). For example, verbal mediation has been demonstrated to be an especially salient means of symbolic encoding for some children (Bandura et al., 1966).

Once the modeled event is represented in memory, additional cognitive processes are involved in maintaining the event and incorporating this into the individual's behavioral repertoire. Such factors as cognitive organization and symbolic and motor rehearsal are believed to be critical to the retention of the modeled event over time (Anderson & Bower, 1973; Bandura, 1969, 1977). The human capacity for cognitive structuring, such that the modeled event is restructured and organized, results in uniquely high-level types of learning (Anderson & Bower, 1973). Practicing the behavior, first symbolically, either by describing verbally or actively visualizing the activity and subsequently by overt actions, has been demonstrated to produce the highest levels of observational learning (Jeffrey, 1976).

Motor Production Processes. The degree to which the observer possesses the physical prerequisites for performing the observed event is an important factor in determining whether or not the modeled event will in fact be imitated. Bandura (1965) demonstrated, for example, that young preschool children modeled a significantly greater number of motor responses than accompanying verbalizations, possibly due to their relative facility for performing such tasks. Similarly, imitation by most of us of the precise behavior of professional tennis players may not be possible because of limitations in our motor processes.

Other important aspects of the motor production process include the observer's sensitivity to his or her own approximations of the modeled event, as well as the accuracy of the feedback from such imitative attempts. The bidirectional relationship between external variables, such as the modeled event and positive and negative reinforcement, and internal variables, such as the individual's own physical characteristics, is apparent during this stage of the social learning process. Compromise between what the individual observes and what he or she is able to perform results in what Bandura (1969) calls an

"amalgam" of modeled event and observer characteristics.

Motivational Processes. The final component in Bandura's social learning theory relates to the motivational system of the observer. This system incorporates both internal and external motivational schema. While Bandura (1969, 1974b, 1977) does not reject the important role played by external contingencies, he asserts that internal motivation is critical in determining whether or not a given modeled event will be reproduced by the observer.

Numerous studies have demonstrated the manner in which external reinforcers can influence the degree to which modeled events are imitated. Walters and Parke (1964) suggest that vicarious reinforcement of models' deviant behavior is an important mechanism for maintaining social control. Reinforcement of both models (Bandura, 1969; Parke & Walters, 1967) and observers (Kanereff & Lanzetta, 1960) have been demonstrated to be of relevance in social learning. The value of external reinforcement in shaping the social learning of autistic-like children has been demonstrated by Baer, Peterson, and Sherman (1967) and Lovaas (1967).

While reinforcement of models or observers has been shown to be of importance in social learning, it is not entirely dependent upon external contingencies (Bandura, 1974b). Bandura (1965) distinguishes between learning and performance, and emphasizes that although a given behavior may have been acquired (i.e., learned), it may not be performed because of inhibitory effects. Of relevance in this context are the frequently cited sex differences in display of physical aggression. Several experts (Goodenough, 1931; Sears, 1951) have reported that males exhibit significantly more physical aggression than females. However, Bandura (1965) has demonstrated that by manipulating positive incentives, females can be induced to display similar levels of aggression. The evidence for sex differences in exhibition of physical aggression, therefore, may be related to performance differences, rather than male–female differences in learning.

Of critical importance to Bandura's theory of social learning is the interactive system of internal and external motivators. Behavior is modified, according to social learning theory, by internal responses, such as cognitive factors, as well as environmental conditions (Anderson & Bower, 1973; Bandura, 1974b). Furthermore, the potential influence of external and internal factors is bidirectional, such that an individual's cognitive restructuring can alter behavior, thus modifying external contingencies. Examples of the interactive relationship of internal and external motivational processes are best illustrated by Bandura's (1969, 1974b) concepts of *inhibition* and *disinhibition*. Inhibition describes the process by which individuals refrain from performing a modeled event because of proscriptions against it. Children may inhibit swearing, for example, because of cognitive devaluing of such behavior. Disinhibition is the process by which previous inhibitions are altered. Thus a child's exposure to high-status models who are reinforced for swearing may lead to the cognitive restructuring of the inhibition against swearing.

Social learning theory literature describes three primary sources of modeled behavior: the family, the peer group, and symbolic models, such as television or other media. In the sections which follow, negative and limiting models originating from all three systems will be discussed. However, because of the increasingly important role of such symbolic models as television, cinema, and other popular media in the lives of young people (Bandura, 1971), special attention will be given to the influence of symbolic models.

DEFINITION

Negative and limiting models are discussed in this chapter within the larger context of psychological maltreatment, such as that which accompanies physical and sexual abuse; negative and limiting models represent a more subtle, yet in some ways more insidious, influence on the lives of children. Because of the widespread and institutionalized nature of negative and limiting models in the popular media, for example, the potentially harmful influences of these portrayals may be unrecognized.

As described here, negative and limiting models may be live (e.g., a parent or peer) or symbolic (e.g., television, popular songs) models. Negative and limiting models depict undesirable behavior (e.g., physical aggression, sexual promiscuity) or stereotypic or misrepresented portrayals of groups of individuals, especially minorities. Such modeled behavior results in an alteration of the viewers' perceptions of self or others, resulting in an impediment to optimal achievement or an increase in undesirable behavior.

VIOLENT AND AGGRESSIVE MODELS

Bandura (1976) indicates that there are three major sources of violent and aggressive models in American society: the family, the subculture, and symbolic models, especially television. Evidence for the negative effects of aggressive family models on young children comes from such classic work as that done by Glueck and Glueck (1950), who reported high levels of parental aggression in the families of delinquent boys. Patterson (1976) indicates that by as young as 3 or 4 years of age, children in families where coercive interaction patterns are practiced have acquired a high number of coercive behaviors. McCord, McCord, and Zola (1959) reported that sons of criminals tended to be more likely to exhibit criminal behavior, especially if their fathers were cruel and neglecting. Bandura and Walters (1959) indicated that in middle-class families where children exhibited aggressive behavior, parents modeled and reinforced combative attitudes and behaviors, even though their overt behavior was not punitive.

The studies just cited emphasize the relationship between aggressive parental models and the development of such behavior in children. Also of significance in American society today is the underexposure of children to positive adult models in the family. Bronfenbrenner (1980) describes several important changes in the pattern of socialization of children, including a dramatic increase in the number of working mothers, a reduction in the number of adults, other than parents, in the home, and a growing number of single-parent (especially father-absent) homes. Bronfenbrenner (1980) concludes that such forces have contributed to a substantial reduction in the amount of contact between parent and child and, by inference, a relative lessening of the parent's role in the care and development of children. Kagan (1980) also has expressed concern that the role of the American family has decreased in practical importance in socialization of children, and cautions that other institutions have not emerged to replace the family's role. Guidubaldi (1980) echoes these sentiments, and suggests that the increased exposure of children to other models, in light of the decreased interaction with adult models, may be associated with increases in juvenile crime, violence, and substance abuse, as well as poorer academic achievement.

The role of the peer group in providing increasingly salient social models during childhood and adolescence has been noted (Bandura, 1976; Floyd & South, 1973; Hartup, 1970). Several investigators have examined the influence of the peer group on the development of violent and aggressive behavior in children (Hartup & Lougee, 1975). Short (1968) reported that in aggressive subcultures status may be gained through physical prowess, such as street fighting. Hicks (1965) reported that preschool boys exhibited more immediate aggressive behavior following observation of a peer model, as opposed to an adult model. Siman (1973) indicates that adult and peer behavioral expectations are more similar than dissimilar, and that the strong influence of peer models in the development of antisocial behavior is restricted to deviant subcultures. The influence of peer models on the development of aggressive behavior in children appears to be closely tied to disinhibitory effects (Hartup & Lougee, 1975). Bandura (1974a, 1974b) describes the important role of self-exonerating devices in the acquisition and display of deviant behavior, and demonstrated the effects that collective responsibility and victim dehumanization can have on the display of aggression (Bandura, Underwood, & Fromson, 1975). Since peer groups may constitute vehicles for the cultivation of such conditions, increased aggressive behavior may be exhibited within these contexts.

Although the potential for exposure to violent adult and peer models, resulting in the display of increased aggressive behavior in children, has been demonstrated by these studies, perhaps of greater significance is the increasingly important role of media violence in socialization of children (Bronfenbrenner, 1980; Guidubaldi, 1980). The very accessibility of television by children causes it to be a profoundly powerful influence. Nearly 98% of homes in the United States have at least one television set (Culkin, 1977), and that set is likely to be turned on for approximately 6 hours per day (Comstock & Rubinstein, 1971; Liebert, 1975). During the period when children watch television, approximately eight violent episodes per hour occur (Comstock & Rubinstein, 1971). Also of significance is the finding that parents tend not to monitor their children's TV viewing,

and in fact, may release control of the TV channel knob to the children in the family (Rubinstein, Comstock, & Murray, 1971).

The effect of television violence on aggressive behavior of children has been studied extensively. Numerous studies have reported that such negative models are associated with the expression of violence in children and that such effects are immediate (Ellis & Sekyra, 1972) as well as lasting (Eron, Huesman, Lefkowitz, & Walder, 1972, 1974). Liebert and Baron (1972) reported that viewing aggressive content from actual television programs led to increased length of aggressive attacks against a victim, as well as more aggressive behavior during free play. Their results were demonstrated for both boys and girls in two age groups (5–6 years and 8–9 years). Of special significance is the finding that television may expose youngsters to novel forms of violence, which they appear to internalize and display on subsequent occasions. One somber example of this phenomenon is a report that following the release of *The Deer Hunter*, no fewer than 29 suicides occurred in a manner identical to the Russian roulette scenario depicted in that film (Mann, 1982). Similarly, the outbreak of airline hijackings during 1969–1970 (Bandura, 1976) and the more recent rash of drug tampering following the well-publicized Tylenol scare are sobering examples of the powerful influence of the media on social behavior.

There is convincing evidence that exposure to violent and aggressive models has lasting, as well as immediate, effects. In their 10-year longitudinal study of the effects of grade 3 viewing of TV violence on 19-year-olds' display of aggressive behavior, Eron et al. (1972, 1974) reported a lasting influence of such viewing habits for 211 boys from their original study. While concerns about the methodology employed by Eron et al. have been reported (Becker, 1972; Howitt, 1972; Kaplan, 1972; Kay, 1972), the authors contend that strong evidence supports their conclusions of a causal relationship between early viewing of TV violence and the expression of aggressive behavior as young adults (Huesman, Eron, Lefkowitz, & Walder, 1973). In fact, Eron et al. (1974) indicate that ". . . one of the best predictors of how aggressive a boy will be at age 19 is the violence of television programs he prefers at age eight" (p. 420). Of import are the authors' findings that such results were not demonstrated for females and that in fact, a diet of TV violence may lead to a decrease in exhibition of aggression for girls (Eron et al., 1974).

A 5-year follow-up study of 732 New York City residents demonstrated significant correlations between TV content violence scores and children's aggression (McCarthy, Langher, Gersten, Eisenberg, & Orzcek, 1975). In this study, mothers were interviewed regarding hours per weekday spent in TV viewing and the names of the four preferred television shows. Programs were categorized into one of five types, and each program was assigned a violence score based on the pooled ratings of three judges. In addition to information about children's TV viewing habits, interviewers obtained data from mothers regarding behavior problems. These descriptions served as the basis for a rating along a psychological impairment continuum performed by two psychiatrists. Degree of aggressiveness was judged by the youngster's display of behaviors indicative of three factors: conflict with parents, fighting, and delinquency. Both type and amount of TV viewing were found to be significantly related to aggressive behavior.

Some research exists which suggests that heavy viewing of TV violence may be associated with desensitization to the negative effects of such content. For such children, increased amounts of TV violence must occur in order to provoke a negative response. Drabman and Thomas (1976) reported that exposure to filmed violence may act as a buffer against reaction to real-life aggression. In their study, experimental children viewed a violent filmed segment, and then were asked to watch a room of children on a videotape screen and to seek adult assistance if necessary. The level of aggressive behavior reached before experimental children sought adult assistance was significantly greater than that observed in a population of control children who had not first viewed the violent TV segment. The authors speculate that increased diets of violent television for children may hamper their ability to judge real-life violence appropriately (Drabman & Thomas, 1975).

While the evidence appears to support a social-learning viewpoint, such that observation of violent models will result in increased expression of aggressive behavior, some studies report a decrease in aggressive behavior following television violence. Perhaps most notable among these studies of the "cathartic effect" of media violence are those conducted by Feshbach and his colleagues (Feshbach, 1961; Feshbach & Singer, 1977). In these studies, adolescent and preadolescent boys were demonstrated to show a reduction in aggressive behavior following a diet of television violence, a finding which the authors attribute to a cathartic effect, such that the boys could release aggressions vicariously through the media. Manning & Taylor (1975) suggest that the failure of experimenters to separate hostile from aggressive behavior may have resulted in conflicting findings in studies of television violence. Their results demonstrated that instigation was associated with both increased hostility and aggression, but that viewing filmed violence was associated with a reduction in hostility, suggesting that such violent content may produce a cathartic effect for this emotion.

Clearly, many variables affect the degree to which violent television models will influence children's behavior. One such variable is the self-esteem of the individual. Baran (1974) hypothesized that low-self-esteem children, who are thought to represent more field-dependent individuals, may be most vulnerable to the influences of negative models presented on television. His study of the interactive effects of self-esteem, sex, and stimuli demonstrated that while low-esteem males and females demonstrated more imitation overall, high self-esteem subjects modeled more aggression while low-self-esteem children acquired significantly more prosocial behavior.

Socioeconomic status also has been shown to be an important variable in determining the degree to which negative and limiting models will influence children's behavior. McCarthy et al. (1975) reported that children from families with one or more indicators of lower socioeconomic status (e.g., low rent, receiving public assistance, from a single-parent family, or lower levels of maternal education) were likely to be heavy TV viewers. Such results confirm findings reported by Medrich (1979) that heavy TV viewing is one characteristic associated with multiple-problem families. He indicates that children from heavy-viewing families are likely to have less parental control over their viewing habits, to be permitted to stay up later, and to do less well in school. The relationship between educational level of mother and degree of TV watching was demonstrated clearly in Medrich's (1979) study. He reported that nearly 50% of families in which the mother had not graduated from high school were characterized as constant television households, in contrast to only 19% of families where the mother had a college degree.

TV viewers may be influenced both by the motives of the aggressor (Berkowitz & Alioto, 1974) and by the consequences he or she receives (Bandura, 1965). The ability of children to perceive and act upon such information may be an age-related phenomenon, according to a study reported by Collins, Berndt, and Hess (1974). They found that young children (kindergartners) tended to recall only aggressive content of a viewed television segment, and to omit information about motives of the aggressor or consequences which occurred. In contrast, older children (fifth and eighth graders) tended to supply more of these details when asked to recount viewed TV segments. Collins et al. (1974) also reported that recall of consequences appears to occur at a younger age than recall of motives, suggesting that consequences to the aggressor will have greater salience for younger TV viewers, and that their comprehension of motives will be limited.

Still another important variable in the question of TV's influence on children concerns parental involvement in the child–TV exchange. Even positive television messages, such as those associated with Sesame Street and other educational programs, can be enhanced when parents either participate in the viewing or discuss the content with their children (Bogatz & Ball, 1971; Chu & Schramm, 1975). Monitoring children's television viewing may represent one means by which parents can influence the potentially harmful effects of the medium. While there is considerable evidence to indicate that parents do not control children's viewing (Guidubaldi, 1980; Rubinstein et al., 1971), Heald (1980) reports that parents who were provided guidance in TV program selection demonstrated significantly more control over their children's TV viewing.

A less immediate but perhaps more far-reaching issue of parental control over children's television relates to adult support for the development of effective children's programming. Even conscientious parents who wish to monitor children's TV may be frustrated by the lack of good alternatives to the violent, stereotyped offerings. Yet despite the bulk of evidence associating television violence with both immediate and longitudinal displays of aggressive behavior in children, government agencies have been slow to recommend sanctions. In a review of the 1971 report of the Surgeon General's Scientific Advisory Committee on Television and Social Behavior, Goranson (1975) describes the perplexing disregard for the evidence displayed in that report. The committee instead focused upon methodological flaws of the accumulated evidence and side-stepped the existing data by underscoring the difficulties inherent in interpretation of such research. Goranson (1975) discusses one potential explanation for the behavior of the Committee—biased selection procedures for committee members which may have occurred as a result of TV networks' vetoing the participation of some distinguished researchers viewed to be likely to take a stance against TV violence. Even when regulation does occur, the results may be less than hoped for. For example, in a recent comparison of cartoons which did, and did not, meet the National Association of Broadcasters' Code for Violence, Cramer & Mechem (1982) reported that while entertainment value had decreased, violence had not. As a response to this problem, Raspberry (1980) calls for a compromise between antitelevision activists, such as Action for Children's Television (ACT), and those who steadfastly resist all efforts to modify current programming. The reality, Raspberry reminds us, is that good children's shows cannot exist without sponsors, but that reliable sponsors may steer clear of children's programming because of the potential for controversy.

SEX-ROLE STEREOTYPES

The representation of male and female sex-role behavior via symbolic modeling represents an important mechanism for the transmittal of beliefs about sex-appropriate behavior (Liebert, 1975). This section will review briefly the ways in which male and female behaviors are portrayed in the media and will discuss the implications of such modeling for children.

Several aspects of the portrayal of male and female models on television and in periodicals have been studied. These include achievement levels, styles of interpersonal interaction, and physical appearance. Manes and Melnyk (1974) reported that television distorts the expression of social skills of high female achievers, depicting only lowest-achieving females (aspiring actresses, maids) as successful in relationships with men. In contrast, women cast in the highest achieving roles (doctors, lawyers, successful artists, and businesswomen) were portrayed as either unmarried or unsuccessfully married. In a second study comparing male and female workers, Manes and Melnyk (1974) found that females were 10 times more likely to be portrayed as either unmarried or unsuccessfully married than the males in their study.

In addition to perpetuating stereotypes regarding female achievement (i.e., women who are successful in careers cannot be simultaneously successful in personal interactions), television also has been demonstrated to sustain other stereotypes about females. Downs and Gowan (1980) investigated prime-time television programs to determine the relative contributions of males and females in roles associated with administration of reinforcement and punishment. They report that the 41 programs analyzed contained more males in general, and that the males tended to display greater control of both rewards and punishment, indicating higher levels of power and status. Men were viewed as positive or negative models with approximately equal probability, suggesting that television males may model negative behaviors, particularly for young male viewers (Downs & Gowan, 1980). In contrast, females were demonstrated to give fewer total responses, but approximately two thirds of the responses given were categorized as positive. The authors suggest that the salience of female television characters for young female viewers may be increased by their comparatively limited appearance. In addition, since two out of three of the behaviors modeled by female TV characters were shown to be positive, female characters may represent a more positive model for young girls.

In a study of television dramas, Hodges, Brandt, and Kline (1981) reported significant male–female differences among the violent programs studied. The authors indicate that statements in such programs are twice as likely to be made by males than by females, and that females are twice as likely to make statements reflecting "pawn" rather than "origin" behavior. An analysis focusing on soap operas showed no significant sex differences in the number of statements made, but revealed that both male and female statements were more likely to be indicative of "pawn-like" behavior. The authors (Hodges et al., 1981) conclude that the depiction of women in television dramas is consistent with stereotypic portrayals of females as guilt-ridden and

anxious, but helpless to act responsibly and with purpose.

Two studies of magazine advertisements during the decade of the 1960s (Sexton & Haberman, 1974; Venkatesan & Losco, 1975) reported little change in the ways in which women were portrayed during this period, even though this decade was synonymous with an era of women's rights and equality issues. Venkatesan and Losco (1975) sampled magazines from three major categories: general (e.g., *Reader's Digest*), women's (e.g., *Cosmopolitan*), and men's (e.g., *Argosy*). They reported that women were portrayed as sex objects to a lesser degree in the latter part of the decade studied, although most changes were associated with advertisements in women's magazines. According to the authors, nearly 25% of all magazine advertisements including females depict them as dependent upon men.

The Sexton and Haberman (1974) analysis included 1,827 advertisements from five popular magazines— *Good Housekeeping, Look, Newsweek, Sports Illustrated*, and *TV Guide*. Their conclusions were that women tended to be portrayed in social situations to a much greater degree than business or impersonal settings. Over 30% of the ads for cigarettes, beverages, automobile, and airline travel portrayed women as "obviously alluring" as recently as the early 1970s. When women were featured in work settings, their roles were judged to be traditional.

Mamay and Simpson (1981) analyzed three roles commonly used to portray females in 306 television commercials: maternal, aesthetic, and housekeeping. Fifty-nine percent of the commercials analyzed included females in one of these roles. While the majority of these reflected maternal roles, the proportion of aesthetic commercials more than doubled from the morning to the evening hours, perhaps as a reflection of audience and sponsor shifts. Similarly, the number of commercials featuring females in housekeeping roles fell from 28% in the afternoon to 10% in the evening hours. Of specific interest is the authors' analysis of the portrayal of children in television commercials. Mamay and Simpson (1981) report that children are depicted as "self-centered consumers" who do not work or contribute in a meaningful way to the family unit.

Scheibe (1979) analyzed over 6,000 TV advertisements aired during the mid-1970s. In comparing her findings with earlier studies, she reports that female roles have broadened. Fewer women were depicted in domestic roles, and both males and females were seen in higher-level occupations. Scheibe (1979) notes that the role expansion observed for females did not hold true for men, who were not depicted in the home or in nontraditional roles outside the home. She notes that the portrayal of men in stereotyped roles is demonstrated in two major ways: either men are product demonstrators, in which they provide some authoritative information regarding a product, or they are depicted as helpless and submissive to women as product users. Scheibe's (1979) analysis of children's roles on television commercials demonstrated significant sex stereotyping, with toys being clearly differentiated as male or female. Scheibe does note that sponsors appear to be sensitive to the need for expansion in the traditional roles in which men and women have been cast.

In a study of televised toy commercials, Feldstein and Feldstein (1982) reported approximately twice the number of boys as girls during two separate periods. Furthermore, girls were more likely to be portrayed in passive rather than active roles in the commercials in which they did appear. The preponderance of male children in television advertisements for toys is significant, since evidence exists that televised models can influence sex stereotyping of toys. Cobb, Stevens–Long, and Goldstein (1982) exposed 36 preschool children (18 each male and female) to videotaped segments of male and female Muppets delivering traditional sex stereotypes for neutral toys. Following the videotape, subjects were found to play with stereotyped toys to a significantly greater degree. The rejection of opposite-sex-stereotyped toys was especially strong for males, as has been demonstrated in earlier studies (Raskin & Israel, 1981). The authors (Cobb et al., 1982) conclude that "'neutral' toys can be effectively stereotyped by television fantasy figures" (p. 1079).

Perpetuation of sex stereotypes in toy sales does not appear to be limited to television advertisements. Studies have shown that such traditional toy selections are modeled by department store sales personnel as well. Ungar (1982) reported that sales clerks in toy departments gave significantly more stereotyped than neutral responses, regardless of retail setting or age. Traditional recommendations occurred most often when given to a male consumer seeking suggestions for a male child.

While these studies suggest that sex-role stereotypes exist in both live and symbolic modeling conditions, is there evidence that such limiting models affect children's learning? In a study of the relationship between television viewing and perceptions of sex-role stereotypes, McGhee and Frueh (1980) reported that boys and girls in grades 1, 3, 5 and 7 classified as heavy TV viewers (25 or more hours per week) had more stereotyped perceptions of males and females than their lighter-viewing peers. The authors also reported that the perception of male sex-role stereotypes is maintained across all grade levels for heavy-viewing children, although there is a diminution of such stereotypic thinking for children who do not partake of such a heavy TV diet.

In an interesting study of the suggestibility of young children to media sex roles which run counter to stereotyped portrayals, Drabman, Robertson, Patterson, Jarvie, Hammer, and Cordua (1981) reported that the perceptions of even preschool-aged children are impervious to such influence. Children who viewed a videotaped scene of a visit to a doctor's office, in which the sex of the doctor and nurse were opposite to the traditional roles, maintained their stereotyped images of such occupational roles, and changed their memory of the videotape to match such perceptions. The authors suggest that sex-role stereotypes appear to be established before children enter first grade, and that incidental learning, such as that which appears on television, may not be an effective means of altering such stereotypes.

CONSUMERISM

Advertising represents a major influence on the lives of consumers. It has been estimated that the average child views approximately 20,000 television advertisements per year (Rossiter, 1979). Furthermore, there is evidence that children represent an important consumer group. Szybillo, Sosanic, and Tenenbein (1977), for example, reported that 80% of all families questioned about restaurant choices indicated that children participated in the restaurant selection. Caron and Ward (1975) found that one quarter of children's requests to Santa Claus were for items advertised on television. A group of 400 children, ages 2–10 years, were demonstrated to identify with accuracy approximately 75% of products displayed on television commercials (Burr & Burr, 1977). Furthermore, the authors reported that use of an "I saw it on TV" plea to exhort parents to purchase products was one of the two approaches which most often resulted in item purchase.

In a study involving 80 children, ages 6–9 years, Rust and Watkins (1975) reported that physical action is extremely salient in children's television commercials. Message monologues, in contrast, as well as oblique or abstract messages, do not maintain the attention of young viewers. Such findings suggest that television commercials which feature concrete, action-oriented fare may be more likely to be attended to as a prerequisite for modeled behavior.

Laurie (1975) also emphasized the importance of visual appeal to young children, and reported that jingles requiring complex linguistic processing may not be optimal for child consumers. Nevertheless, the young viewers require some degree of realism, and may reject commercials which are too extreme or exaggerated.

Rossiter (1979) reported that children's understanding of television commercials is closely related to age, and that heavy viewing within a given developmental period is not associated with greater commercial understanding. Children's affective reactions to TV advertisements are reported to become less favorable over time. However, heavy viewers seem to maintain favorable attitudes about television commercials longer. The behavioral effects of viewing TV advertisements are not age related; child requests to parents to purchase items seen on TV remain consistent across the ages studied, and heavy TV viewing was associated with more requests of parents.

One specific realm of consumerism of relevance to children and youth is the image of drug and alcohol use as portrayed in the media. With use of such substances increasing in record numbers (Bourgeois & Barnes, 1979), the exposure of young people to this specific type of advertising is of critical import. Smart and Krakowski (1973) surveyed 13 of 15 magazines with the widest Canadian circulation, including such common periodicals as *Reader's Digest*, *TV Guide*, *Time*, *Family Circle*, and *Redbook*. They identified 80 references to drugs and alcohol in the 400 issues surveyed. Their analysis demonstrated that the magazine coverage focused on adolescent and teenage use, while largely ignoring adult use of such substances. Furthermore, the vast majority of the features concerned marijuana, heroin, or multiple drugs, to the exclusion of alcohol and

tobacco. The authors concluded that magazines represent a perpetuation of stereotypes rather than an effective vehicle for social change.

Smart and Krakowski's (1973) survey of television advertising about drugs indicated that advertisements supporting drug use outnumbered antidrug messages at a rate of approximately 30 to 1. Drug advertisements were most prevalent during prime-time hours, representing approximately 75% of the number of commercials shown during this period, although only 4% of the total number of commercials. Types of drugs demonstrated in the Smart and Krakowski (1973) survey included beer (37.6%), headache (22.4%) and stomachache remedies (11.9%), and tobacco (9.8%).

What effects does advertising for drugs and alcohol have on the behavior of consumers? Donohue (1975) reported that black children surveyed perceived that taking a pill or some other medication is the best course of action when not feeling well. Bourgeois and Barnes (1979) indicate that consumption of beer was positively related to advertising in print media, but that broadcast media were associated with a reduction in consumption. Christiansen, Goldman, and Inn (1982) demonstrated that alcohol-related expectancies, such as those conveyed by parents, peers, and the media, are well-established by age 12, in absence of direct experience with alcohol.

As with other aspects of television programming, the family background of children is an important variable in determining the effects of TV advertising. Reid, Bearden, and Teel (1980) reported that socioeconomic status is an important variable in the degree to which children learn from TV advertisements for cereal. Similarly, Giudicatti and Stening (1980) reported that socioeconomic status was a significant factor in the degree to which 6–12-year-old children comprehended content of advertisements, were aware of the sponsor and the sponsor's intent to sell, and had the ability to discriminate between the commercial message and the specific product. These authors also demonstrated that age is another important source of variance in determining what impact commercial messages will have on children. The authors concluded that the relative disadvantage that children of low socioeconomic status have when interpreting commercials accurately is compounded by the greater amount of television viewing they do (Giudicatti & Stening, 1980; Medrich, 1979).

Unfortunately, although parents have been demonstrated to possess the potential for mitigating some of the negative effects of TV commercials, the evidence is that they rarely capitalize on such opportunities (Robertson, 1979).

PORTRAYAL OF MINORITIES

Since the Civil Rights Act of 1964, there have been increased awareness and sensitivity about the portrayal of ethnic minorities in the media. Currently, nearly two decades following that affirmation of equality, there is evidence that ethnic stereotypes continue to be perpetuated.

Experts suggest that information about various groups (e.g., ethnic minorities) is obtained from television vis-á-vis three sources (Donagher, Poulos, Liebert, & Davidson, 1975). The first of these refers to appearance or recognition, which is generally assessed by the frequency with which individuals associated with various groups appear. Numerous studies suggest that the appearance of ethnic minorities on television is proportionately low. A recent study of 1,145 characters on children's television programs reported that only 3.7% were black, 3.1% were Hispanic, and 0.8% were Asian. Only one of the 1,145 characters—Tonto—was Native American (Barcus, 1983). Similarly, Gerbner and Gross (1976) indicate that 75% of all leading characters on prime-time television are white, middle- or upper-class males. It appears that on the basis of frequency alone, the heavy TV viewer is in danger of distorting the ethnic representation of the United States.

The second source of information about ethnic minorities is the formal role status portrayed by group members (Donagher et al., 1975). Role status is defined both by occupational and social factors. DeFleur and DeFleur (1967) have reported that children obtain more information about jobs and professions from television than from personal experience within the family or community. Such findings suggest that the occupational roles in which ethnic minorities are cast represent a potentially powerful influence on young children's perceptions about minorities. The evidence suggests that while white males are disproportionately portrayed as professionals (Donagher et al., 1975; Gerbner & Gross, 1976), that black males tend to be cast as servants, entertainers, or, more recently, in law enforce-

ment roles (Clark, 1972; Colle, 1968; Roberts, 1970–71).

Character portrayals represent the third basis for information about ethnic minorities from the television medium. In a study involving 300 school-aged children, Greenberg (1972) reported that 40% of the group had established concepts about the way blacks look, talk, and dress from network entertainment. Once again, the bulk of evidence suggests that ethnic stereotypes may be perpetuated by ethnic portrayals on television. Black television characters have been shown to display comical behaviors which provoke ridicule, or as careful, law-abiding citizens (Clark, 1972; Roberts, 1970–71). While there is evidence that recently blacks have been cast in roles depicting them as "good people"—working hard, obeying laws, doing the "right thing," and making amends when things go wrong (Liebert, 1975)—the level of competence exhibited by black TV characters is depicted as less than that of whites (Waters, 1977). Donagher et al. (1975) report that male and female black TV characters represent somewhat distinct populations. Black males are portrayed as altruistic and law abiding, though nonassertive, which once again perpetuates a stereotype of a passive, somewhat incompetent individual. Black females, as described in the Donaher et al. (1975) analysis, delayed gratification and attempted to resolve conflict through explanation or negotiation. While these roles are somewhat more positive than in earlier television portrayals (Barcus, 1983), they do not represent black individuals as assertive, competent, purposeful individuals.

PORTRAYAL OF
HANDICAPPED PERSONS

The portrayal of handicapped and disabled persons in the media can have critical influence over perpetuating or dispelling prejudice associated with such conditions. What limited information is available indicates, unfortunately, that the images portrayed in the media do not represent handicapped or disabled persons realistically.

Donaldson (1981) analyzed 85 half-hour prime-time television segments to determine the visibility of handicapped persons during these heavy-viewing periods. She reported that fewer than 1% of the total TV characters were portrayed as handicapped persons, compared to

15–20% of the general population reported to be handicapped. Of special interest is Donaldson's (1981) finding that the vast majority of handicapped roles on television were feature characters, while few if any appeared in incidental or minor roles. More importantly, Donaldson (1981) noted that many of the segments featuring handicapped or disabled persons portrayed these roles as negative, such as social deviants or problems for society. She concludes that such portrayals of handicapped persons on television may sustain the kinds of stereotypes held by the general public.

The important role the media play in sustaining or altering views about the handicapped has been emphasized by numerous experts. Nelson (1978) indicates that stigmas arise from images which are not personalized, and that education of both individuals and groups can be critical in changing these stereotypes. He emphasizes, as does Donaldson (1981), that the portrayal of handicapped persons in the media tends to be distorted, such that disabled individuals are either not included or are central characters. Such individuals seldom are seen in routine scenes with the handicap being incidental to other activities; nor are they seen in commercials (Nelson, 1978).

Among the sources of prejudice against handicapped persons are social customs and norms that place a high status on physical attractiveness, including youth, wholeness, and bodily perfection (Gellman, 1959). The television medium appears to perpetuate this set of values, which seriously limits the portrayal of handicapped persons in meaningful roles (Gellman, 1959; Vash, 1981). While attempts to encourage less stereotyped portrayals of handicapped persons have been recommended (English, 1971), results thus far have been discouraging (Roessler & Bolton, 1978).

The critical importance of changing limiting models of handicapped persons to these individuals' self-esteem is emphasized by Reynolds (1980), who indicates that fulfillment of the objectives underscored by P.L. 94-142 is not possible without simultaneous fulfillment of social objectives. Unfortunately the portrayal of handicapped persons in textbooks, a source of modeling with which school children have most direct access, also falls woefully short of what might be hoped for. Ochoa and Shuster (1980) reviewed seven social studies textbook series, and found that most were devoid of adequate

references to handicapped or disabled persons. In fact, two of the most commonly used social studies texts contained no specific content relating to this population.

A survey of 74 children's books reviewed by the Council on Inter-racial Books for Children (1982) reported similar results. The total number of children's books which included portrayals of handicapped persons was only slightly greater than the Council's previous survey 5 years earlier. In addition, the Council reports that the kinds of roles in which handicapped persons are cast often represent them as "pitiable or pathetic, laughable, nonsexual, incapable of full participation in society, burdens to others, objects of violence, their own worst enemies or superhumans capable of miracles" (p. 9).

The portrayal of mental illness in the media may be among the more distorted of all disabilities. Wahl (1976) indicates that television portrays mental health professionals such as psychologists as omnipotent and prone to use confrontational therapies which produce immediate, dramatic results. Furthermore, mental disturbance is inaccurately represented in numerous ways: schizophrenia and split personality are equated, conversion hysteria is purported to be commonplace, and psychopaths are routinely homicidal. Perhaps the most deleterious of the myths perpetuated by television is the image that mental illness is equated with danger to others.

CONCLUSIONS AND DIRECTIONS

The research cited in this chapter suggests that negative and limiting models represent a potentially powerful force in the lives of children as they interact with adults, peers, and subcultures and are exposed to such media as television, magazines, and even textbooks. Studies indicate that the popular media are replete with models who are characterized by aggressiveness, nonproductivity, or drug use. Furthermore, the manner in which male and female sex roles, ethnic minorities, and the handicapped are portrayed continues to perpetuate stereotyped images of these groups. The degree to which negative and limiting models will influence the social development of children is dependent upon numerous variables, including both child characteristics and qualities of the modeled event. Given the potentially critical influence of these negative and limiting models in shaping the attitudes of young people, psychologists and other human service personnel are well advised to become cognizant of the nature and extent of such models and to incorporate social learning theory principles in the design of intervention systems.

Changing or mitigating the influence of negative and limiting models on the lives of young people necessitates a reversal of the trends described here. The important potential of adult models, other than parents, would be recognized and fostered within organized institutions such as schools, churches, and youth groups in order to maximize positive adult influences. Recognizing the reality of peer modeling can serve as the basis for the development of organized positive peer influences, such as has occurred through athletic programs and youth clubs. Television, radio, and other media could be compelled, when giving exposure to such undesirable behaviors as drug use, aggression, sexual promiscuity, or suicide, to include the presentation of more positive behavioral alternatives. In addition, such presentations could be accompanied by appropriate adult debriefing which permits young people opportunities to integrate information into a broader identity rather than to adapt such behaviors without evaluation. The discussion groups organized by churches and community groups following the TV broadcasts about the nuclear holocaust provide such a model. Finally, media presentation of groups of individuals would emphasize options and alternatives rather than narrow, stereotyped portrayals. In each instance, the objective is to replace the negative and restrictive nature of models to which young people are exposed with broader, more positive alternatives.

REFERENCES

Anderson, J. R., & Bower, G. H. (1973). *Human associative memory.* Washington, DC: V. H. Winston & Sons.

Baer, D. M., Peterson, R. F., & Sherman, J. A. (1967). The development of imitation by reinforcing behavioral similarity to a model. *Journal of the Experimental Analysis of Behavior, 10,* 405–416.

Bandura, A. (1962). Social learning through imitation. In M. R. Jones (Ed.), *Nebraska symposium on motivation: 1962.* Lincoln: University of Nebraska Press.

Bandura, A. (1965). Influence of models' rein-forcement contingencies on the acquisition of imitative responses. *Journal of Personality and Social Psychology, 1,* 589–595.

Bandura, A. (1969). *Principles of behavior modification.* New York: Holt, Rinehart and Winston.

Bandura, A. (Ed.) (1971). *Psychological modeling.* Chicago: Aldine–Atherton.

Bandura, A. (1974a). Analysis of modeling processes. In A. Bandura (Ed.), *Psychological modeling: Conflicting theories.* New York: Lieber–Atherton.

Bandura, A. (1974b). Behavior theory and the models of man. *American Psychologist, 29(12),* 859–869.

Bandura, A. (1976). Social learning analysis of aggression. In E. Ribes–Inesta & A. Bandura (Eds.), *Analysis of delinquency and aggression.* Hillsdale, NJ: Lawrence Erlbaum Associates.

Bandura, A. (1977). *Social learning theory.* Englewood Cliffs, NJ: Prentice–Hall.

Bandura, A., Grusec, J. E., & Menlove, F. L. (1966). Observational learning as a function of symbolization and incentive set. *Child Development, 37,* 499–506.

Bandura, A., & Rosenthal, T. L. (1966). Vicarious classical conditioning as a function of arousal level. *Journal of Personality and Social Psychology, 3,* 54–62.

Bandura, A., Ross, D., & Ross, S. A. (1963). A comparative test of the status envy, social power, and secondary reinforcement theories of identifactory learning. *Journal of Abnormal and Social Psychology, 67,* 527–534.

Bandura, A., Underwood, B., & Fromson, M. E. (1975). Disinhibition of aggression through diffusion of responsibility and dehumanization of victims. *Journal of Research in Personality, 9,* 253–269.

Bandura, A., & Walters, R. H. (1959). *Adolescent aggression.* New York: Ronald Press.

Baran, S. J. (1974). Prosocial and antisocial television content and modeling by high and low self-esteem children. *Journal of Broadcasting, 18(4),* 481–495.

Barcus, F. E. (1983). *Portrayal of minorities.* Newtonville, MA: Action for Children's Television.

Becker, G. (1972). Causal analysis in R-R studies: Television violence and aggression. *American Psychologist, 27(10),* 967–968.

Berkowitz, L., & Alioto, J. (1973). The meaning of an observed event as a determinant of its aggressive consequences. *Journal of Personality and Social Psychology, 28,* 206–217.

Bogatz, G. A., & Ball, S. (1971). *The second year of Sesame Street: A continuing evaluation.* Princeton, NJ: Educational Testing Service.

Bourgeois, J., & Barnes, J. G. (1979). Does advertising increase alcohol consumption? *Journal of Advertising Research, 19(4),* 19–29.

Bronfenbrenner, U. (1980). Ecology of childhood. *School Psychology Review, 9*(4), 294–297.

Burr, P. L., & Burr, R. M. (1977). Parental responses to child marketing. *Journal of Advertising Research, 17*(6), 17–20.

Caron, A., & Ward, S. (1975). Gift decisions by kids and parents. *Journal of Advertising Research, 15*(4), 15–20.

Christiansen, B. A., Goldman, M. S., & Inn, A. (1982). Development of alcohol-related expectancies in adolescents: Separating pharmacological from social-learning influences. *Journal of Consulting and Clinical Psychology, 50*(3), 336–344.

Chu, G. C., & Schramm, W. (1975). *Learning from television: What the research says.* Washington, DC: National Society of Professionals in Tele-communications.

Clark, C. (1972). Race, identification, and television violence. In G. A. Comstock, E. A. Rubinstein, & J. P. Murray (Eds.), *Television and social behavior. Vol. V: Further explorations.* Washington, DC: U.S. Government Printing Office.

Cobb, N. J., Stevens–Long, J., & Goldstein, S. (1982). The influence of televised models on toy preference in children. *Sex Roles, 8*(10), 1075–1080.

Cohen, H. (1971). Imitative behavior in high and low dependent preschool children as a function of nurturance and nurturance withdrawal. *Dissertation Abstracts International, 31,* 6871.

Colle, R. D. (1968). Negro image in the mass media: A case study in social change. *Journalism Quarterly, 45*(1), 55–60.

Collins, W. A., Berndt, R. J., & Hess, V. L. (1974). Observational learning of motives and consequences for television aggression: A developmental study. *Child Development, 45,* 799–802.

Comstock, G. A., & Rubinstein, E. A. (Eds.) (1971). *Television and social behavior, Vol. 1: Media content and control.* Rockville, MD: U.S. Dept. of HEW.

Council on Inter-racial Books for Children (1982). Disabled persons said to be poorly portrayed in children's books. *Education of the Handicapped, 8*(22), 9.

Culkin, J. (1977, October). The new literacy: From the alphabet to television. *Media & Methods,* 64–67; 78–81.

Cramer, P., & Mecham, M. B. (1982). Violence in children's animated television. *Journal of Applied Developmental Psychology, 3*(1), 23–39.

DeFleur, M. L., & DeFleur, L. (1967). The relative contribution of television as a learning source for children's occupation knowledge. *American Sociological Review, 32,* 777–789.

Donagher, P. C., Poulos, R. W., Liebert, R. M., & Davidson, E. S. (1975). Race, sex and social example: An analysis of character portrayals on inter-racial television entertainment. *Psychological Reports, 37,* 1023–1034.

Donaldson, J. (1981). The visibility and image of handicapped people on television. *Exceptional Children, 46*(6), 413–416.

Donohue, T. R. (1975). Effect of commercials on black children. *Journal of Advertising Research, 15*(6), 41–47.

Downs, A. C., & Gowan, D. C. (1980). Sex differences in reinforcement and punishment on prime-time television. *Sex Roles, 6,* 683–694.

Drabman, R. S., Robertson, S. J., Patterson, J. N., Jarvie, G. J., Hammer, D., & Cordua, G. (1981). Children's perception of media-portrayed sex roles. *Sex Roles, 7*(4), 379–389.

Drabman, R. S., & Thomas, M. H. (1975). The effects of television on children and adolescents: Does TV violence breed indifference? *Journal of Communications, 25,* 86–89.

Drabman, R. S., & Thomas, M. H. (1976). Does watching violence on television cause apathy? *Pediatrics, 57*(3), 329–331.

Ellis, G. T., & Sekyra, F. (1972). The effect of aggressive cartoons on the behavior of first-grade children. *Journal of Psychology, 81,* 37–43.

English, R. W. (1971). Combating stigma towards physically disabled persons. *Rehabilitation Research and Practice Review, 2,* 19–27.

Eron, L. D., Huesmann, L. R., Lefkowitz, M. M., & Walder, L. O. (1972). Does television violence cause aggression? *American Psychologist, 27*(4), 253–263.

Eron, L. D., Huesmann, L. R., Lefkowitz, M. M., & Walder, L. O. (1974). How learning conditions in early childhood—including mass media—relate to aggression in late adolescence. *American Journal of Orthopsychiatry, 44*(3), 412–423.

Feldstein, J. J., & Feldstein, S. (1982). Sex differences on televised toy commercials. *Sex Roles, 8*(6), 581.

Feshbach, S. (1961). The stimulating versus cathartic effects of vicarious aggressive activity. *Journal of Abnormal and Social Psychology, 63,* 381–385.

Feshbach, S., & Singer, R. D. (1977). *Television and aggression.* San Francisco: Jossey-Bass.

Floyd, H. H., Jr., & South, D. R. (1973). Dilemma of youth: The choice of parents or peers as a frame of reference for behavior. *School Psychology Digest, 2*(2), 23–27.

Gellman, W. (1959). Roots of prejudice against the handicapped. *Journal of Rehabilitation, 25,* 4–6.

Gerbner, G., & Gross, L. (1976, April). The scary

world of TV's heavy viewer. *Psychology Today,* 41–45; 89.

Gerst, M. D. (1971). Symbolic coding processes in observational learning. *Journal of Personality and Social Psychology, 19,* 7–17.

Giudicatti, V., & Stening, B. W. (1980). Socioeconomic background and children's cognitive abilities in relation to television advertisements. *The Journal of Psychology, 106,* 153–155.

Glueck, S., & Glueck, E. (1950). *Unraveling juvenile delinquency.* Cambridge, MA: Harvard University Press.

Goodenough, F. L. (1931). *Anger in young children.* Minneapolis: University of Minnesota Press.

Goranson, R. E. (1975). The impact of TV violence. *Contemporary Psychology, 20*(4), 291–293.

Greenberg, B. S. (1972). Children's reactions to TV blacks. *Journalism Quarterly, 49,* 5–14.

Guidubaldi, J. (1980). The status report extended: Further elaborations on the American family. *School Psychology Review, 9*(4), 374–379.

Hartup, W. W. (1970). Peer interaction and social organization. In P. H. Mussen (Ed.), *Carmichael's manual of child psychology* (Vol. II). New York: John Wiley & Sons.

Hartup, W. W., & Lougee, M. D. (1975). Peers as models. *School Psychology Digest, 4*(1), 11–22.

Heald, G. R. (1980). Television viewing guides and parental recommendations. *Journalism Quarterly, 57*(1), 141–144.

Hicks, D. J. (1965). Imitation and retention of film-mediated aggressive peer and adult models. *Journal of Personality and Social Psychology, 2*(1), 97–100.

Hodges, K. K., Brandt, D. A., & Kline, J. (1981). Competence, guilt, and victimization: Sex differences in attribution of causality in television dramas. *Sex Roles, 7,* 537–546.

Howitt, D. (1972). Television and aggression: A counterargument. *American Psychologist, 27*(10), 969–970.

Huesmann, L. R., Eron, L. D., Lefkowitz, M. M., & Walder, L. O. (1973). Television violence and aggression: The causal effect remains. *American Psychologist, 28*(2), 617–620.

Jeffrey, R. W. (1976). The influence of symbolic and motor rehearsal in observational learning. *Journal of Research in Personality, 10,* 116–127.

Kagan, J. (1980). The influences of the family. *School Psychology Review, 9*(4), 298–311.

Kanereff, V. T., & Lanzetta, J. T. (1960). Effects of task definition and probability of reinforcement upon the acquisition and extinction of imitative responses. *Journal of Experimental Psychology, 60,* 340–348.

Kaplan, R. M. (1972). On television as a cause of aggression. *American Psychologist, 27*(10), 968–969.

Kay, H. (1972). Weaknesses in the television-causes–aggression analysis by Eron et al. *American Psychologist, 27*(10), 970–973.

Laurie, L. (1975). Measuring commercial impact. *Journal of Advertising Research, 15*(4), 23–25.

Liebert, R. M. (1975). Modeling and the media. *School Psychology Digest, 4*(1), 22–29.

Liebert, R. M., & Baron, R. A. (1972). Some immediate effects of televised violence on children's behavior. *Developmental Psychology, 6*(3), 469–475.

Lipton, M. B. (1971). Individual differences in the imitation of models. *Dissertation Abstracts International, 31,* 5624.

Lovaas, O. I. (1967). A behavior therapy approach to the treatment of childhood schizophrenia. In J. P. Hill (Ed.), *Minnesota symposia on child psychology* (Vol. I). Minneapolis: University of Minnesota Press.

Mamay, P. D., & Simpson, R. L. (1981). Three female roles in television commercials. *Sex Roles, 7*(12), 1223–1232.

Manes, A. L., & Melnyk, P. (1974). Televised models of female achievement. *Journal of Applied Social Psychology, 4*(4), 365–374.

Mann, J. (1982). What is TV doing to America? *U.S. News & World Report, 93*(5), 27–30.

Manning, S. A., & Taylor, D. A. (1975). Effects of viewed violence and aggression: Stimulation and catharsis. *Journal of Personality and Social Psychology, 31*(1), 180–188.

Marlowe, D., Beecher, R. S., Cook, J. B., & Doob, A. N. (1964). The approval motive, vicarious reinforcement and verbal conditioning. *Perceptual and Motor Skills, 19*(2), 523–530.

McCarthy, E. D., Langher, T. S., Gersten, J. C., Eisenberg, J. G., & Orzceck, L. (1975). The effects of television on children and adolescents—violence and behavior disorders. *Journal of Communication, 25,* 71–85.

McCord, W., McCord, J., & Zola, I. K. (1959). *Origins of crime: A new evaluation of the Cambridge–Somerville youth study.* New York: Columbia University Press.

McGhee, Paul E., & Frueh, T. (1980). Television viewing and the learning of sex-role stereotypes. *Sex Roles, 6,* 179–188.

Medrich, E. A. (1979). Constant television: A background to daily life. *Journal of Communication, 29*(3), 171–176.

Nelson, B. (1978). *Creating community acceptance for handicapped people.* Springfield, IL: Charles C Thomas.

Ochoa, A. S., & Shuster, S. K. (1980). *Social studies in the mainstreamed classroom, K–6.* Boulder,

CO: Social Science Education Consortium, Inc.

Parke, R. D., & Walters, R. H. (1967). Some factors influencing the efficacy of punishment training for inducing response inhibition. *Monographs of the Society for Research in Child Development*, 32(1, Serial No. 109).

Patterson, G. R. (1976). The aggressive child: Victim and architect of a coercive system. In E. Mash, L. Hamerlynck, & L. Handy (Eds.), *Behavior modification and families*. New York: Brunner/Mazell.

Raskin, P., & Israel, A. C. (1981). Sex-role imitation in children: Effects of sex of child, sex of model, and sex-role appropriateness of modeled behavior. *Sex Roles*, 7(11), 1067-1077.

Raspberry, W. (1980). Scaring kids' shows off TV. *Young Children*, 36, 11-12.

Reid, L. N., Bearden, W. O., & Teel, J. E. (1980). Family income, TV viewing and children's cereal ratings. *Journalism Quarterly*, 57(2), 327-330.

Reynolds, M. C. (1980). Introduction: The changing social environment. In M. C. Reynolds (Ed.), *Social environment of the schools*. Reston, VA: Council for Exceptional Children.

Roberts, C. (1970-71). The portrayal of blacks on network television. *Journal of Broadcasting*, 15, 45-53.

Roberts, M. C., & Wurtele, S. K. (1981). Effects on different types of pre-experience on imitation in children. *The Journal of Psychology*, 115, 289-290.

Robertson, T. S. (1979). Parental mediation of television advertising effects. *Journal of Communication*, 21, 12-25.

Roessler, R., & Bolton, B. (1978). *Psychosocial adjustment to disability*. Baltimore: University Park Press.

Ross, D. (1966). Relationship between dependency, intentional learning, and incidental learning in preschool children. *Journal of Personality and Social Psychology*, 4, 374-381.

Rossiter, J. R. (1979). Does TV advertising affect children? *Journal of Advertising Research*, 19(1), 49-53.

Rubinstein, E. A., Comstock, G. A., & Murray, J. P. (Eds.) (1971). *Television and social behavior, Vol. IV. Television in day-to-day life: Patterns of use*. Rockville, MD: U.S. Dept. of HEW.

Rust, L., & Watkins, T. A. (1975). Children's commercials: Creative development. *Journal of Advertising Research*, 15(5), 21-26.

Schachter, S., & Singer, J. (1962). Cognitive, social, and physiological determinants of emotional state. *Psychological Review*, 69(5), 379-399.

Scheibe, C. (1979). Sex roles in TV commercials. *Journal of Advertising Research*, 19(1), 23-27.

Sears, P. S. (1951). Doll play aggression in normal young children: Influence of sex, age, sibling status, father's absence. *Psychological Monographs*, 65(6, whole No. 323).

Sexton, D. E., & Haberman, P. (1974). Women in magazine advertisements. *Journal of Advertising Research*, 14(4), 41-46.

Short, J. F., Jr. (Ed.) (1968). *Gang delinquency and delinquent subcultures*. New York: Harper & Row.

Siman, M. L. (1973). Peer group influence during adolescence. *School Psychology Digest*, 2(2), 19-23.

Skinner, B. F. (1971). *Beyond freedom and dignity*. New York: Knopf.

Slobin, D. I. (1968). Imitation and grammatical development in children. In N. S. Endler, L. R. Boulter, & H. Osser (Eds.), *Contemporary issues in developmental psychology*. New York: Holt, Rinehart, & Winston.

Smart, R. G., & Krakowski, M. (1973). The nature and frequency of drugs content in magazines and on television. *Journal of Alcohol and Drug Education*, 18(3), 16-23.

Szybillo, G. J., Sosanic, A. K., & Tenenbein, A. (1977). Should children be seen but not heard? *Journal of Advertising Research*, 17(6), 7-12.

Ungar, S. B. (1982). The sex-typing of adult and child behavior in toy sales. *Sex Roles*, 8(3), 251.

Vash, C. L. (1981). *The psychology of disability*. New York: Springer.

Venkatesan, M., & Losco, J. (1975). Women in magazine ads: 1959-71. *Journal of Advertising Research*, 15(5), 49-54.

Wahl, O. (1976). Six TV myths about mental illness. *TV Guide*, March 13, 4-8.

Walters, R. H., & Amoraso, D. M. (1967). Cognitive and emotional determinants of the occurrence of imitative behavior. *British Journal of Social and Clinical Psychology*, 6(3), 174-185.

Walters, R. H., & Parke, R. D. (1964). Influence of response consequences to a social model on resistance to deviation. *Journal of Experimental Child Psychology*, 1, 269-280.

Waters, H. F. (1977). What TV does to kids. *Newsweek*, February 21, 63-70.

10

Psychological Abuse from Prejudice and Cultural Bias

Daniel J. Reschly and Susan Graham-Clay

Prejudice and cultural bias are among the most intractable, pervasive, and damaging of all the kinds of psychological abuse of children. Virtually every society in every era, from the earliest recorded history to the present, has been affected by these maladies in one way or another. The current era is different only in the scope, the many variations, and the potentially disastrous consequences of prejudice and cultural bias. Prejudice and cultural bias are a part of the other potentially disastrous human problems of the current era (e.g., population explosion, nuclear annihilation, and abject poverty). Each of these problems, serious in their own right, are confounded and exacerbated by prejudice and bias (Ehrlich & Feldman, 1977).

This chapter is meant to cover an enormous amount of information in a very general way. We attempted to formulate a broad framework within which facts, concepts, and theories can be organized and, most importantly, interventions be identified and evaluated. We therefore organized the paper around basic concepts, theory and research, developmental patterns, and interventions.

BASIC CONCEPTS

Definitions

Prejudice and cultural bias have been defined in different, but parallel, ways. Allport (1954) de-fined prejudice as follows: "Ethnic prejudice is an antipathy based on a faulty and inflexible generalization. It may be felt or expressed. It may be directed toward a group as a whole, or toward an individual because he [sic] is a member of that group" (p. 10). A similar definition was provided by Jones (1972), who described prejudice as ". . . a negative attitude toward a person or group based upon a social comparison process in which the individual's own group is taken as the positive point of reference" (p. 3). Jones noted that the behavioral manifestation of prejudice is discrimination. Cultural bias is a more inclusive and pervasive phenomenon in which an entire culture, its institutions and its people, are regarded as inferior.

Prejudice is regarded as an attitude, and cultural bias is assumed to rest on prejudicial attitudes. The conventional view is that attitudes have three components—cognitive, affective, and behavioral (Rosenfield & Stephan, 1981). The three components of attitudes may be learned at different developmental stages and may be inconsistent (e.g., feelings may differ from beliefs). However, inconsistency in attitudes, called dissonance, is uncomfortable, particularly if the individual is confronted with, and cannot escape from, the dissonance (Festinger, 1957). In such instances the individual makes changes in one or more of the attitude components in order to achieve consistency, and thereby reduce dissonance.

Object

The object of prejudice or cultural bias varies widely, from physical differences that are immediately apparent to subtle differences in beliefs or customs that only become apparent through knowing the individual or through reacting to some group marker. The differences among people in color or sex are among the most obvious and most widely exploited through prejudice and bias. Differences in religious customs or ethnicity often are less visible, but are, nonetheless, the basis for intense prejudice and discrimination in some instances. The white–nonwhite color distinctions in the United States and elsewhere are examples of the former (Barbarin, Good, Pharr, & Siskind, 1981), while the differences among peoples in Northern Ireland (Catholic vs. Protestant) and in the Middle East among Muslim sects (Sunni vs. Shi'ite) are examples of the latter. Visible differences clearly are not required, and occasionally the objects of prejudice and bias are forced to make themselves visible through some marker (e.g., the German Nazi requirement that Jews wear the Star of David).

Degrees of Severity

Both prejudice and cultural bias may be imposed upon a people in varying degrees of severity. Prejudice may vary from very subtle, unconscious preferences or dislikes to overt, violent actions. Kovel's 1970 work, discussed by Jones (1972), distinguished between aversive and dominative racism. Aversive racism occurs when an individual believes his or her group is superior, and is vaguely aware or even unaware of this belief, but does nothing overtly. In contrast, dominative racism involves conscious discriminative intent and overt action where possible. Because aversive racism is so subtle, often vaguely perceived or even unconscious, it may be even more difficult to overcome.

Cultural bias also reflects varying degrees of severity, from vague preferences to the extreme of genocide. Historical concepts such as "white man's burden" or "manifest destiny" are examples of culturally biased views which were used to sanction a wide range of policies leading to the subjugation of native peoples. Numerous forms of cultural bias exist today and, like prejudice, many of these forms are subtle and unconscious, but insidious. The cultural heritage of many people has been denied, ignored, or deni-

grated in the United States, often from either a "melting pot" or "white man's burden" assumption about culture. The far extreme of cultural bias is genocide, a systematic effort to destroy an entire group of people.

Level of Analysis or Scope

Prejudice and cultural bias appear at and may be analyzed from different levels and scopes. There is no doubt that prejudice and bias exist at the international (United Nations Report, 1979), national, state and community (Barbarin et al., 1981) levels. Moreover, the scope of prejudice and bias may vary from individuals, to societal institutions, and finally, to the entire culture (Jones, 1972). A figure from Jones (1972) (Figure 10.1) illustrates these different levels and scopes of prejudice and bias. In practical situations, the different levels and scopes of prejudice/bias usually are related, and interventions need to be targeted accordingly.

Effects on Children

The effects of prejudice and cultural bias on children are multiple and severe. These effects have

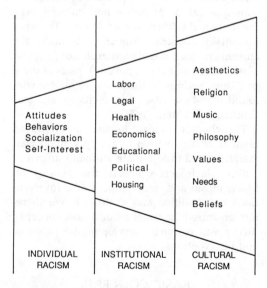

Figure 10.1. Model for the analysis of prejudice/bias. (From *Prejudice and Racism* (p. 115) by J.M. Jones, 1972, Reading, MA: Addison-Wesley. Copyright 1972 by Newbery Awards Records, Inc. Reprinted with permission of Random House.)

been documented in numerous formal studies, in the great literature of many eras, and in our own informal observations. The effects of prejudice/bias can and often do include all the important dimensions of human development, from prenatal nutrition to nursing care for the elderly; from the likelihood of being the product of "wanted" pregnancy to the likelihood of being evaluated as a unique person rather than according to perverse stereotypes; and from the quality of preschool health care to the probability of being the victim of violent crime. These are but a few of the many direct and indirect effects of prejudice and cultural bias.

There is another set of effects of prejudice and cultural bias which are, in our judgment, less well established and usually less severe. For many decades the prejudiced or bigoted person has been believed to suffer severe consequences from being prejudiced. Ehrlich and Feldman's (1977) quotation of the 19th century English scientist, Thomas Huxley, is representative of this view: ". . . no human being can arbitrarily dominate over another without grievous damage to his own nature . . . no slavery can be abolished without a double emancipation, and the master will benefit by freedom more than the freed-man" (p. 46). Similar, though less comprehensive, assertions have been made by scholars who emphasize prejudice as the reflection of unhealthy personality dynamics.

Although we certainly do not believe prejudice improves mental health (our views are quite to the contrary), we doubt the nature and degree of the negative consequences suffered by most prejudiced persons. Katz (1976a) reported slight relationships of mental health and prejudice for representative samples of persons. The very rare extreme prejudice that becomes an obsession and is expressed in extreme, irrational ways like random violence involves, without any doubt, a deranged mind, or mob psychology (also deranged in our view). However, the typical kind and degree of prejudice has relatively few mental health consequences for the individual child. From the point of view of the "just world," that seems unfair.

However, prejudice and bigotry on the part of children certainly are disadvantages, especially in the diverse society and world in which we live. We could cite many disadvantages associated with prejudice and cultural bias, from the impoverished perspective on human culture and diversity to maladaptive and ineffective

reactions in cross-cultural, social, political, and economic relationships.

THEORY AND RESEARCH

Theory and research on prejudice and cultural bias have been pursued vigorously in the past two or three decades. Social psychology and sociology have been the major disciplines involved with attempts to explain bias and prejudice. We now have a rich fund of information on these topics, but the theory and research to date do not adequately account for the pervasiveness and strength of prejudice and bias.

It is perhaps important to note at the outset that theory and research, like all other human endeavors, occur within a cultural milieu. The context provided by the cultural milieu influences scientific efforts to formulate and test hypotheses and to explain various phenomena. Science is never totally objective in the sense of being free of cultural influences. The choice of what to study, how to formulate hypotheses, and how to explain results are crucial decisions in any scientific enterprise. Each of these decisions is influenced by cultural milieu, often in ways that are so subtle that the individual scientist is unaware of the influences. The study of these influences, called the sociology of knowledge, has provided insight into the interaction of science and culture (Chesler, 1976). None of us, scientists included, is completely objective. We all are products of a cultural milieu. The interaction of science and culture is particularly important in attempts to understand the theory and research on prejudice and cultural bias.

Theory

There are many theories attempting to explain the phenomena of prejudice and cultural bias (Jones, 1972). Like many other topics in the social sciences, each of the theories explains some, but not all, of the important aspects of the phenomena (Chesler, 1976). These theories vary in several dimensions. One of the most important dimensions is the relative emphasis on the individual versus the entire society. Theories which stress the underlying psychodynamic causes of prejudice (e.g., authoritarian personality—Adorno, Frenkel–Brunswick, Levinson, & Sanford, 1950) are quite different from those which stress societal ideology or economic system exploitation. These theoretical differences have obvious implications for how research on prejudice/bias is designed and, perhaps most importantly, have clear implications for the design of intervention efforts.

It is important to note that prejudice and cultural bias are both individual and group phenomena. Change strategies must, therefore, be directed at individuals, at groups, and at the entire society. Excessive emphasis on either (i.e., on the bigoted individual or the racist or sexist society) can lead to perceptions of helplessness (e.g., "What can I do to change an economic system that has existed for centuries?" or, "What difference does it make if I only influence my own kids, or the few people with whom I come into contact?"). The thesis of this chapter is that workable solutions must focus on both the individual and the society, and that social change can only come about through efforts at all levels, individual and group. Finally, as we shall note in our interventions section, attitude and behavior change is most effective when various levels of prejudice and bias are addressed.

Social Science Research

Social science research has been a major influence on social policy concerning prejudice and cultural bias. Today there exists a rich literature on several critical issues such as how prejudice is learned, developmental factors, and interventions to eliminate prejudice. Much remains to be learned about these issues, but much useful information is available now. This information has positively influenced court decisions and legislation which created legal prohibitions to prejudice and bias.

In a number of analyses, the 1954 Supreme Court decision in *Brown v. Board of Education* has been seen as a triumph of social science research (Rosenfield & Stephan, 1981). The Brown decision extensively quoted and cited social science research on the effects of segregation. The conclusion—separate but equal is inherently unequal—was based in large part on an amicus curiae brief submitted by 32 scientists. In this brief, the deleterious effects of segregation on self-esteem and social achievement were stressed. The Brown decision, followed by numerous court cases on federal civil rights, was perhaps the single most important civil rights event in the 20th century (Hirschhorn, 1976).

Social science research on prejudice has progressed at a steady pace over the decades since the Brown decision. A great deal of refinement in methodology has occurred, and many of the early findings cited by the Supreme Court in 1954 have been revised or made more conditional. Good examples of this refinement appear in Katz (1976a) with regard to acquisition of racial attitudes, and in Rosenfield and Stephan (1981) concerning the effects of desegregation. The findings of contemporary research on these issues are perhaps disappointing in that desegregation and interracial contact do not automatically improve attitudes and school achievement. In retrospect, those expectations were probably naive and unrealistic. However, the kind of contact that yields positive results and the characteristics of effective desegregation are better known now than ever before. One is reminded of "two steps forward and one backward," an old cliche, which, nonetheless, fits these developments.

Not all is well, nor uniformly positive in the realm of social science research on prejudice and cultural bias. Social science research has been used as the basis for negative stereotypes about minority groups and to support biased social policies (Kamin, 1974). The nature–nurture issue, especially the assertion of a hereditary basis for group differences on ability tests, is probably the most notorious of the uses of social science research to either justify prejudice or to limit social policies designed to overcome prejudice and bias. Jensen's (1969) conclusion that compensatory education had failed may have been a major influence on social policy restrictions on the expansion of compensatory education. Although Jensen was very careful to state his conclusions tentatively in light of the limitations in the available evidence, others with seemingly impressive scientific credentials were not so cautious. The prime example is Shockley (1971), a Nobel Prize laureate (in physics) who has advocated rather direct interpretations of race influences on the superficial basis of skin color. Shockley's (1971) statement, "nature has color-coded groups of individuals . . ." (p. 375) is, in our judgment, a racist statement which, because it appeared in a well-respected, rigorously refereed social science journal, is all the more objectionable. Some of the statements by minority psychologists about ability testing over the past decade, which on superficial analysis appear intemperate and irrational, are understandable in the context of Shockley's allegations about color coding (Reschly, 1981). However, the overwhelming majority of psychologists who use ability tests do not agree with the hereditary differences hypothesis. Banning these tests would, in our view, do little toward refuting the hereditary differences view, but would, in all likelihood, increase the subjectivity in educational classification/placement decisions.

Another problem with social science research in this area is overgeneralization, especially from studies contrasting minority samples with white samples. Moynihan's (1967) report on the deterioration of black families is a clear case of overgeneralization, both in the report and in subsequent reactions to the report (Chesler, 1976). Moynihan reported several indices indicating the breakdown of black families. Black families were higher (i.e., in less favorable positions) on these indices compared to white families. However, the differences typically were of the magnitude of 25% for black families versus 10% for white families. Unfortunately, these kind of results often were understood to mean "most, if not all," for black families, and "few, or none" for white families. Obviously, these interpretations were incorrect.

Henderson (1981) provides an insightful discussion of the problems in making generalizations about minority persons from social science research. Here the caveats concerning generalizations to individuals from group data are of paramount importance. A little knowledge can, indeed, be dangerous. Studies of minorities are needed and, as we have noted, this research can be very useful. However, results from these studies also can be the basis for stereotypes (e.g., the matriarchal nature of black families) which create inaccurate and unfair expectations concerning black children.

In balance, social science research and theory have been far more positive than negative in advancing the cause of minorities. It is absolutely crucial that these research results and theories be subjected to careful scrutiny, especially regarding the *representativeness* of the results. The most important use of the social sciences is in the design, implementation, and evaluation of interventions designed to prevent or eliminate prejudice and cultural bias, topics which we address in the final section of this paper.

DEVELOPMENT AND LEARNING

It is a truism to observe that prejudice is learned. That very essential fact leads to the consideration of developmental factors and learning mechanisms (i.e., when and how prejudice is learned).

Developmental Factors

The acquisition of racial attitudes has been investigated now for many years. Some of the early evidence (Clark & Clark, 1947) apparently was a decisive influence on the Brown desegregation decision. There are a number of methodological issues in this research, not the least of which are the questionable practices of measuring attitudes with preschool and early school-age children, and assuming that attitude indices mean the same at younger and older ages.

Despite these problems, different measures of children's racial attitudes are fairly consistent (Rosenfield & Stephan, 1981), and there is fairly broad agreement on the general features of racial attitude formation. Racial awareness is established fairly early, by age 3 or 4 according to most accounts (Goodman, 1964; Katz, 1976a). Full integration of the essential three components of racial attitudes is believed to be achieved by ages 8–10, or about fourth grade. By grade 4, many children have acquired the stereotypes associated with minority groups (Rosenfield & Stephan, 1981).

This developmental evidence has clear implications. If prejudice is to be prevented, interventions must begin fairly early and continue throughout the developmental years. We cannot wait until individuals are mature, can "think for themselves," and thereby make up their own minds. The early learning, particularly the affective component, may not be readily accessible to conscious thought, easily analyzed, or easily modified. Furthermore, because racial attitude components are probably learned at different ages and, perhaps, by different mechanisms, intervention efforts must also focus on different aspects (e.g., cognitive, affective, and behavioral) and use different learning mechanisms (e.g., information, simulations, etc.).

Learning Mechanisms

Jones' (1972) assertion that racial prejudice is learned in the environmental norm within which the individual is socialized directs our attention to the entire social milieu. It is doubtful that specific experiences, isolated events, or single learning mechanisms (principles) account for the development of racial attitudes.

Katz (1976a) suggested that racial attitudes are acquired in complex, multifaceted ways. She analyzed five mechanisms which have been suggested as particularly important: (a) direct instruction from parents and others; (b) reinforcement for prejudice by adults and peers; (c) child-rearing practices that are harsh and rigid, leading to authoritarian personality traits; (d) cognitive factors, particularly as outcomes of personality trends; and (e) perceptual factors, particularly the associations developed with the distinctive cues that define the group. Katz noted that some evidence supports each of these mechanisms, but none are sufficient alone to account for the degree and pervasiveness of prejudice.

In contrast to the formal mechanisms in the previous analysis, Jones (1972) suggested the rather simple, straightforward mechanisms of (a) straight transmission from parent, other adult, or peer to the child; (b) observation of situations and behaviors where minority persons appear in a negative role; and (c) subtle, often unconscious associations of minority persons with negative situations. These mechanisms are particularly useful to our analysis because they imply careful examination of the overt and covert depictions of minority persons throughout the culture. Moreover, the enormous influence of modeling and social learning theory (Bandura, 1969) can be applied to learning, maintenance, and revision of racial attitudes.

> You can be part of the problem
> You can be part of the solution
> But you are one or the other
> There is no neutral or middle ground

The above, with our slight modifications, is from Eldridge Cleaver as quoted by Jones (1972, p. 178). From this perspective, we all have a choice, to be part of the problem or to contribute to the solution. To be neutral and to do nothing is to *tolerate* prejudice and cultural bias.

There is much that needs to be done at all levels, on an individual, person-to-person basis at one extreme to an international, nation-to-nation level at the other. The problems of prejudice and cultural bias are so large, and there are so many levels, that it is tempting to nearly all of us to be passive, to feel helpless, and to do nothing. Again, we emphasize, there is much to be done and everyone is needed in this battle. The first prerequisite, the most important tool, is individual commitment.

Government: National and International Relations

Prejudice and cultural bias are world-wide problems. There are very few societies, especially those with large, diverse populations, who escape entirely from these problems. Moreover, prejudice between national populations is far too common. Concerted international efforts have generally been organized only in the context of the most blatant racist policies, and then, the usual mechanism has been the relatively ineffective device of economic boycotts (United Nations Report, 1979). Nonetheless, these sanctions call attention to the problems and serve notice that the rest of the world does not condone blatantly racist policies. As individuals, we can support the sanctions through exercising our political rights and making similar efforts through the other institutions within which we participate (e.g., legal, religious, economic, and educational). These are small, but important, steps to take.

At the national government level we can support policies which attempt to ensure equal rights for minorities, and support those persons who advocate vigorous enforcement of those policies. In recent years candidates for some political offices have differed significantly on these issues.

Societal Institutions

Prejudice and cultural bias have been obvious in many of our institutions throughout our history. It has only been in recent decades that the most obvious forms of prejudice have been eliminated. The prejudice that exists in many of our institutions today is less obvious, more controversial, and more resistant to change.

Thorough discussion of the prejudice and bias that exists today in our institutions is beyond the scope of this paper. (For further treatment of this topic, see chapter 11 by Jones and Jones in this volume.) Prejudice and bias do exist in key institutions—legal (e.g., unequal treatment from law enforcement personnel), education (e.g., unequal emphasis on different cultural heritages), economic (e.g., unequal employment opportunity), and religious. More examples could be cited, and each of these institutions could be analyzed in far greater depth (see Barbarin, 1981; Katz, 1976b for relevant discussions). A very important and controversial related issue is the mechanism or procedure whereby we reform our present institutions. Another way to frame the discussion is to contrast the different notions of equal opportunity: equal treatment versus equal results.

Criteria for Institutional Racism. In a number of recent publications in scholarly journals or books, institutional racism has been defined simply as unequal results (Barbarin, 1981; Fiman, 1981; Jones, 1972; Jones & Wilderson, 1976). Thus, an institution may be regarded as racist even if there is no intent or process which is racist either by design or effect. For example, any disproportionality in educational classification and placement might be regarded as discriminatory. This notion of equal results has been advocated recently for a variety of social, legal, educational, and economic institutions, where, in practice, equal results amounts to imposition of quotas and rather reverse discrimination.

The equal-results notion of fairness is highly controversial, and likely to remain so for some time (Lerner, 1981). The major problem is that it requires *unequal treatment* of persons according to their race, ethnicity, sex, and so on. Unequal treatment on these bases is pretty much parallel to the definitions of prejudice and bias we cited earlier. We do not wish to dwell on this controversy, only to note its existence and our discomfort with the notion of quotas or reverse discrimination.

Equal treatment is the alternative notion of fairness as well as a widely cited and agreed upon criterion for examining institutions for prejudice and cultural bias. Equal treatment is firmly supported (in opinion surveys) by the general public (Lerner, 1981) and is deeply embedded in court and legislative action (Hirschhorn, 1976). At a minimum, societal institutions have a clear legal mandate to treat minority and majority clients equally.

Equal Treatment. We have far to go in the realm of equal treatment. Systematic bias in how clients/participants/citizens are treated still exists as a formidable barrier to equal opportunity for minorities. Equal and representative treatment is essential, from the characteristics of the heroines (and heroes) in the school books our children read to the advertising in the mass media. Equal treatment and fair portrayal of minorities in our institutions and cultural symbols is essential. Equal treatment, though more

prevalent than a few decades ago, is still an ideal to which we aspire. Our efforts as individuals and in groups are needed to ensure equal treatment for all persons.

School Desegregation. One of the most carefully studied interventions with a social institution is the effects of school desegregation (Rosenfield & Stephan, 1981). School desegregation in the United States has occurred under widely differing conditions, over a period of many years, and with varying degrees of community support. Not surprising, then, is the fact that the school desegregation effects on prejudice and cultural bias are far from uniform or consistent (Rosenfield & Stephan, 1981). Interracial contact alone does not produce more positive attitudes and less discrimination, a finding reported many years ago by Allport (1954). The overall effects of school desegregation for the entire society are not now known, and will not be known for many years. We think those overall effects, especially when contrasted to the pre-1954 Brown decision situation, will ultimately be seen as very positive, for all children and for the entire society. Furthermore, the factors related to successful desegregation with positive outcomes for all students are better known (Rosenfield & Stephan, 1981) and could be more widely implemented. The link between what we know and what is implemented regarding more positive intergroup change depends on individuals, acting singly and in concert. It is the issue of individual change to which we now turn our attention.

Individual Change

It is inconceivable to us that either societal institutions or individuals could change alone without corresponding changes in the other. Institutions and individuals are intertwined and inseparable, at least in a pluralistic, democratic society. A variety of methods have been proposed and studied to foster individual change.

Prevention. Prevention is the ultimate objective of interventions designed to reduce prejudice and cultural bias. We assume, on good logic and evidence, that prejudice is not innate. Evidence cited earlier indicated the rather early acquisition of racial awareness. However, racial awareness does not imply negative attitudes. Awareness alone probably means nothing about the attitude, only that a racial attitude could be formed.

Preventive efforts need to be targeted to the ages where intergroup attitudes are formed, by age 3 or so to about age 10. As noted earlier, racial attitudes often are well established by the fourth grade (ages 9 or 10). Parents are probably the single most important influence on children's intergroup attitudes. The acquisition of positive intergroup attitudes would ideally occur naturally through children living with diverse persons in an environment where there is intergroup equality, positive interaction, and mutual respect. When those characteristics are not attained, the next most important preventive interventions are formal and informal means to teach the essential equality and humanity of all persons. This can be done in a variety of ways, from parental direct instruction, reinforcement, and modeling, to systematic use of mass media (e.g., children's books and games, television, etc.), to presenting positive examples of intergroup interaction.

Attitude Change. Prevention is not likely to be entirely successful in the foreseeable future. The problem of changing prejudicial attitudes is, therefore, an important part of reducing prejudice and cultural bias. There is a fairly rich literature in social psychology on attitude change. As noted earlier, attitudes are believed to have three components—cognitive (beliefs), affective, and behavioral tendencies. The literature is replete with reports of instances where behavior stayed the same despite changes in beliefs or feelings. People saying they have changed or changes on attitude questionnaires do not necessarily produce behavioral changes. However, behavioral changes are very unlikely as long as the beliefs and feelings are prejudicial. Therefore, changes in components of attitudes are always worthwhile.

There is ample evidence of changes in at least some of the components of intergroup attitudes with children (Katz, 1976c) and with adults (Sedlecek & Brooks, 1981). Perhaps the most fundamental step in producing attitude change is creation of dissonance, or inconsistency in components of attitudes. Presentation of fair and accurate information is often an essential first step in the process of changing attitudes. This is a particularly important step because information can be transmitted through mass media to which nearly *all* preschoolers are exposed, and

in the public school curriculum which, again, influences nearly all children. If information is inconsistent with other components of the attitude, there is at least the possibility that other experiences, particularly intergroup interaction, will produce additional changes. The kind of interaction or contact that is effective in changing attitudes has been studied extensively in recent years.

Contact/Interaction Effects. Allport (1954) suggested certain criteria that determined whether intergroup contact positively changed attitudes. His criteria were as follows: (a) equal status; (b) pursuit of common goals; (c) sanctions and support by authorities and institutions (e.g., by law or by custom); and (d) perception of common interests and common humanity. Rosenfield and Stephan (1981) report evidence from desegregation studies which generally confirm these basic criteria. Contact certainly is desirable in efforts to achieve a more just society, but the kind of contact also seems to be crucial. Contact alone, especially in the context of inequality, is probably *not* very useful.

CONCLUSIONS

Prejudice and cultural bias are among the most serious and difficult problems in our world. All other problems are confounded to varying degrees by this very fundamental concern. Although there is much to be learned about these phenomena, there is a great deal of useful information that we can apply. The critical intervening variable is *us*, and people like us. We need to be committed, on behalf of all people, but especially children, to a fair and just society. There is much we can do when we decide to become part of the solution.

REFERENCES

Adorno, T. W., Frenkel–Brunswik, E., Levinson, D. J., & Sanford, R. N. (1950). *The authoritarian personality.* New York: Harper.

Allport, G. W. (1954). *The nature of prejudice.* Reading, MA: Addison–Wesley.

Bandura, A. (1969). *Principles of behavior modification.* New York: Holt, Rinehart, & Winston.

Barbarin, O. A. (1981). Community competence: An individual systems model of institutional racism. In O. A. Barbarin, P. R. Good, O. M. Pharr, & J. A. Siskind (Eds.), *Institutional racism and community competence.* Rockville,

MD: U.S. Department of Health and Human Services, National Institute of Mental Health.

Barbarin, O. A., Good, P. R., Pharr, O. M., & Siskind, J. A. (Eds.) (1981). *Institutional racism and community competence*. Rockville, MD: U.S. Department of Health and Human Services, National Institute of Mental Health.

Chesler, M. A. (1976). Contemporary sociological theories of racism. In P. A. Katz (Ed.), *Towards the elimination of racism*. New York: Pergamon.

Clark, K. B., & Clark, M. (1947). Racial identification and preference in Negro children. In T. M. Newcomb & E. L. Hartley (Eds.), *Readings in social psychology*. New York: Holt.

Ehrlich, P. R., & Feldman, S. S. (1977). *The race bomb: Skin color, prejudice, and intelligence*. New York: Quadrangle/The New York Times Book Co.

Festinger, L. (1957). *Theory of cognitive dissonance*. Evanston, IL: Row, Peterson & Co.

Fiman, B. C. (1981). The difference indicator: Quantitative index of institutional racism. In O. A. Barbarin, P. R. Good, O. M. Pharr, & J. A. Siskind (Eds.), *Institutional racism and community competence*. Rockville, MD: U.S. Department of Health and Human Services, National Institute of Mental Health.

Goodman, M. E. (1964). *Race awareness in young children* (2nd ed.). New York: Crowell-Collier.

Henderson, R. W. (1981). Nonbiased assessment: Sociocultural considerations. In T. O. Oakland (Ed.), *Nonbiased assessment*. Minneapolis, MN: University of Minnesota, National School Psychology Inservice Training Network.

Hirschhorn, E. (1976). Federal legal remedies for racial discrimination. In P. A. Katz (Ed.), *Towards the elimination of racism*. New York: Pergamon.

Jensen, A. R. (1969). How much can we boost IQ and scholastic achievement? *Harvard Educational Review, 39*, 1–123.

Jones, J. M. (1972). *Prejudice and racism*. Reading, MA: Addison-Wesley.

Jones, R. L., & Wilderson, F. (1976). Mainstreaming and the minority child: An overview of issues and a perspective. In R. L. Jones (Ed.), *Mainstreaming and the minority child*. Reston, VA: Council for Exceptional Children.

Kamin, L. J. (1974). *The science and politics of IQ*. New York: Halstead Press.

Katz, P. A. (1976a). The acquisition of racial attitudes in children. In P. A. Katz (Ed.), *Towards the elimination of racism*. New York: Pergamon.

Katz, P. A. (1976b). *Towards the elimination of racism*. New York: Pergamon.

Katz, P. A. (1976c). Attitude change in children: Can the twig be straightened? In P. A. Katz (Ed.), *Towards the elimination of racism*. New York: Pergamon.

Lerner, B. (1981). Equal opportunity versus equal results: Monsters, rightful causes, and perverse effects. In W. B. Schrader (Ed.), *Admissions testing and the public interest: New directions for testing and measurement, Number 9*. San Francisco: Jossey-Bass.

Moynihan, D. P. (1967). *The Negro family: The case for national action*. Washington, DC: U.S. Department of Labor.

Reschly, D. (1981). Psychological testing in educational classification and placement. *American Psychologist, 36*, 1094–1102.

Rosenfield, D., & Stephan, W. G. (1981). Intergroup relations among children. In S. S. Brehm, S. M. Kassin, & F. X. Gibbons (Eds.), *Developmental social psychology*. New York: Oxford University Press.

Sedlecek, W. E., & Brooks, G. C., Jr. (1981). Eliminating racism in educational settings. In O. A. Barbarin, P. R. Good, O. M. Pharr, & J. A. Siskind (Eds.), *Institutional racism and community competence*. Rockville, MD: U.S. Department of Health and Human Services, National Institute of Mental Health.

Shockley, W. (1971). Models, mathematics, and the moral obligation to diagnose the origin of Negro IQ deficits. *Review of Educational Research, 41*, 369–377.

United Nations (1979). *UN report of the world conference to combat racism and racial discrimination (1979)*. New York: United Nations.

11

Racism as Psychological Maltreatment

Reginald L. Jones and James M. Jones

BACKGROUND

It is profound in its simplicity; children are our future. Profound though that concept may be, adults still have the notion that the important business of society concerns adult activities, such as buying and selling, artistic creation, waging war, provocative displays of militaristic integrity, political campaigning, economic decision making, legislative maneuvering, and so on. The games adults play define, for better or worse, adult American society. Do we prepare our children to play these same games? How do we prepare them? Adults do not have the same roles or status in the grown-up world. How does one's place in the lineup or status influence how one prepares children for adult life?

The simple observation we would like to make is this: The adult world dictates the roles, relations, and goals to which we can aspire. The parameters of fortune and circumstance dictate the prospects, while the functions of imagination and practical planning circumscribe socialization choices. Our future—our children—has little to say until it may be too late. Those born of favorable circumstance may not suffer as a result. Those born of less positive ones may suffer a lifetime frustrated in opportunity. Simply put, some children are abused by virtue of the parents they have, the environment in which they are raised, and the society that prescribes, knowingly or not, a limited range of opportunities while widely purveying the myth of bound-

less opportunity and unmitigated fairness for all.

For many, abuse began centuries ago. Racism in the United States is old. As citizens we speak of affirmative action and equal opportunity. Our leaders argue with, we believe, real conviction, that fairness and equality are the only principles ultimately upon which a great nation such as this can rest. Fairness can be instituted as policy, but practice lags behind. It lags because we as a people have a past, a past in which fairness and equality simply did not apply to all our citizens. This past follows us and makes a mockery of the righteous pronouncements of today. Our children suffer and often do not know why. We hate ourselves until we sense the scam, then hate the perpetrators. But it is all "cruel and unusual punishment," especially for a child who not only does not know what is going on, nor why, but also had no choice along the way.

DEFINITIONS

Cultural Bias

The notion of cultural bias is intimately connected to the concept of cultural racism. The basic premise is that human beings are identified with and belong to human groups that share territory, language, song, and tradition. These commonalities can roughly be called culture. Culture is a determinant of behavior as it defines the context for competence, that which will perpetuate the species (or more narrowly, the human group). The circumstances to which a group's adaptation must conform will vary with different aspects of the environment, including physical (temperate climate vs. arid or tropical), agrarian versus industrial, and other features. Those adaptations may also include other human groups, whose presence may be a major factor in the socialization of young people for competence within that environment.

Moving quickly to the context of the United States, when the competence socialization requirements of a human group are at variance with the standards of competence for a politically and economically more powerful group with whom it must share a system, it is a certainty that the former will suffer cultural bias. This form of bias can be called *reactionary* bias. That is, the bias is built into the situation because reaction to the realities of disadvantage and oppression support socialization practices that in the long run disadvantage the reacting group in the "open market." There is a second form of cultural bias we call *evolutionary* bias. This refers to the fact that different human groups evolve from a set of cultural/ecological circumstances which have merit in the total scheme of the human condition. However, when such cultural parameters unfold, they are undervalued by a dominant society, and the members of the group who possess them are correspondingly undervalued. For example, in this society, literate/ abstract reasoning and writing are dominant values, and the possession of skills that follow from oral traditions leading to a variety of interpersonal and social competencies are relatively undervalued. In graduate psychological training programs, minority students are often praised for their "clinical sensitivities," and in some ways damned because they do not grasp the abstractions of research and writing as easily.

Cultural Bias and Prejudice in Child Abuse and Neglect

Patterson and Thompson (1980) propose a definition of emotional neglect which emphasizes that societal, as well as parental, shortcomings can result in the emotional neglect of children. Their definition sets the stage for the melding of prejudice and racism with psychological mal-

treatment or emotional abuse which is at the core of this chapter. Our thesis:

> A variety of institutional practices, rooted in cultural bias and prejudice, conspire to abuse and neglect Third World children.*

Specifically:

- There is emotional abuse when Third World peoples and their cultures are represented in narrow, stereotyped ways in children's literature and textbooks.
- Emotional abuse is a consequence when stereotyped, narrow, and superficial treatment of Third World people and their cultures are presented on television.
- Emotional abuse is at issue when teachers and other school personnel respond to Third World children in stereotyped ways, subject them to verbal abuse, and engage in a variety of practices which show disrespect for Third World cultures, lifestyles, languages, and cognitive styles.

Psychological Effects and Demographic Characteristics

A model from our notion of culture bias that fits the general structure of child abuse and neglect is presented in Figure 11.1. In our conception, abuse can be conceived as (a) excessive negative experience (the most commonly held view)— these are acts of commission—and/or (b) a deficiency of positive experience—acts of omission. Reactionary bias refers to the former and evolutionary bias the latter. Viewed in historical perspective, we note that oppression through slavery, which maintained barriers that insured disproportionate poverty and psychic trauma are examples of excessive negative experiences. Reactionary bias reflects the not-so-subtle consequence of that abusive experience, as families suffering such abuse had to prepare (socialize) their children for what they understood to be the reality they would face. As a result, parents often discouraged high expectations, and reined in curiosity lest a child wander into alien territory and suffer additional negative consequences, thus saddling the child with the consequences of the adult's experiences. These parental behav-

*We use the term *Third World* to refer to children of color—Asians, blacks, Native American, Spanish surname—in lieu of the term minority, which we view as pejorative.

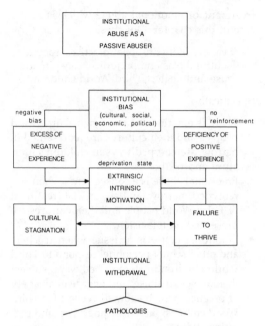

Figure 11.1. Institutional bias and child abuse/ neglect: A model.

iors disadvantaged a child in competition with others.

Adapting to this reality could cause a child to fail at the evaluative tasks that establish his or her "competence." As a result, children are characterized as being weak in ego strength, failing in curiosity, lacking in internal control, and so on (to the degree that these can be adequately diagnosed—there is much room for doubt here). The children are blamed and are the objects of labels of deficiency that persist until they drop out of competition with others.

We have scarcely begun to look into the evolution of black and other Third World cultures. It will suffice to state that with the possible exception of Asian cultures, psychological analysis has not uncovered a single trait or variable that is presumed to characterize Third World individuals that would be widely acknowledged as a positive characteristic for anyone. The deficit model defines maltreatment as the deficiency of positive experience. The deficiency emanates, for the most part, from the ethnocentrism of white America, which fails to evaluate anything that is not of a Western European, advanced industrial genre in a positive light. This reflects a failure of decentering (to borrow a Piagetian concept for this cultural analysis) which

simply makes it impossible to imagine that black people could possess anything valuable other than muscles for running and jumping and flair for "soul." Thus children from Third World cultures face a paucity of positive experiences in the broader context. Seeking out such experiences causes one to retreat from the broader context and stay within a limited arena where one's behavior receives reinforcement.

Putting the two forms of bias together, we perceive a conspiracy of sorts. The reactionary bias produces behaviors that are noncompetitive in the general scheme of things. The evolutionary bias insures that one's instinctive intelligence will be of minimal utility in the broader societal context, often driving Third World children deeper into a cultural homogeneity where real bias takes further hold. Excessive negative experience feeds into paucity of positive experience, which further predisposes a child to reactionary bias. So, for this innocent child, a history of racial and cultural relations and evolution combine with specific circumstances of his or her birth to provide certain socialization experiences that widen the gap between what this society promises and what the child can reasonably expect to obtain.

In extreme cases, children lose a lot early and fail to survive adolescence. In worse cases, children may survive adolescence and face profound failure and frustration born of insidious and pernicious racism and cultural bias. This "perpetrator-less" crime is among the worst this society commits against its own citizens.

Institutional Abuse

Excess Negative Experiences. It is our belief that many institutional arrangements and practices are the loci of the emotional abuse of Third World children. In the present section we focus upon the schools as representative of institutional abuse simply because children spend so much time in them. Any litany of abusive or potentially abusive school-related practices affecting Third World children (as well as all children) would most certainly include exclusion from school (Children's Defense Fund, 1974), placing excessive and unnecessary pressure on the child to perform (Plank, 1975), corporal punishment by school personnel (Cable, 1975; Duncan, 1973), inappropriate medical diagnostic labeling by teachers (Brown, 1977), and exposure to seriously maladjusted teachers (Amiel, 1972). These are important elements of the abuse picture and deserve full study in their own right. In the present section, however, we limit our discussion to the subtle abuse of Third World children that is a consequence of interactions between teachers/adults and Third World children.

A study by Coates (1972) of white adult behavior toward black and white children was revealing in the subtle bias exhibited. Male and female white adults used verbal statements to train 9-year-old black or white male children on a discrimination problem. Bogus information was given to the adults. The dependent variable was the adults' statements to the children. A Sex × Race of child interaction was found. Males were more negative with black children than with white children, whereas there was a nonsignificant difference between the two races for females. In trait-rating sessions following the training session, both males and females rated black children more negatively than white children (e.g., the black children were evaluated as being more shy, unattractive, unsociable, colorless, unenthusiastic, unpleasant, immature, dull, unfriendly, cold, and unreliable).

A study by Rubovits and Maehr (1973) is widely cited. In this experiment 66 white female teachers in training, admittedly inexperienced, were given a lesson plan to teach four pupils. The pupils were assigned bogus IQs on a random basis, all of whom in fact had similar IQs and were randomly selected from the 7th and 8th grades. One black pupil and one white pupil were given IQs in the gifted range (IQs 130–135), and one black pupil and one white pupil were given IQs in the average range (IQs 98–120). The teacher was given a seating chart with the student's name and IQ, indicating whether the student had been selected from the school's gifted program or from the regular track. In addition to being assigned students on basis of the chart, the teachers were also asked to read the label and IQ so as to use this information to be better able to deal with the student. An observer, who did not know whether students were labeled gifted or not, recorded teacher interaction.

The results were amazing, but from the perspective of hindsight, perhaps should not have been too surprising. The white students received far more total attention than black students; fewer statements were requested of blacks; more statements of blacks than of whites were ignored; black students were praised less and criticized more; more statements were requested of gifted than of nongifted students; and gifted students were criticized more than were nongifted students, even though there was little difference made in the spontaneous comments by the groups (thus they were not called on more because they volunteered less). The significant difference in criticism was accounted for by the presence of black students in the gifted group. They received the majority of all the criticism. Nongifted black students received more attention than gifted black students. Overall, the following pattern emerged: A white gifted student received a great deal of attention and was called on frequently, encouraged and praised. For blacks, giftedness was associated with less positive treatment, little attention, and little praise. Finally, in follow-up interviews and questionnaires, the gifted white student was chosen most frequently as the most liked student, the brightest student, and the certain leader of the class. The black gifted student was usually identified as the least liked in the group. A majority of the teachers said he or she was unfriendly toward them. A number of teachers in describing the black gifted student used such terms as *angry* and *militant*. A few teachers even said they were afraid of the student. An amazing analysis based on a phony IQ score!

Subjects in the Coates (1972) study were actually below average with respect to their progress in school and their performance on achievement tests. Moreover, subjects in the Coates study were told that the experimental tasks were known to be of moderate difficulty for the child subjects. In the Coates study, therefore, it was not expected that the children would do well at the outset. Children in Rubovits and Maehr's (1973) study, on the other hand, were represented as either of average or gifted status. It was to be expected, then, that good performance would characterize the gifted students, whether black or white. How surprising then it was to find that gifted black children were interacted with and judged more negatively than were black or white children labeled average, or white children labeled gifted. The inescapable conclusion is that in interactions with white adults, black children are subjected to more negative verbal experiences than their white peers and, moreover, being labeled gifted does nothing to mitigate these negative experiences for black children;

indeed, being so labeled appears to exacerbate them.

Other studies support our thesis. For example, Jackson and Cosca (1974) found significant disparities in the treatment of Mexican Americans (vs. Anglo-Americans) in terms of teacher use of praise, acceptance or use of students' ideas, teacher questioning, teacher's giving of positive feedback, all noncriticizing teacher talk, and all student speaking. In all instances, Mexican-American students were recipients of the more negative interactions. In a similar study Gay (1975) found that black students did not participate as often as white students in class discussions, and that white students participated in more academic and substantive ways and received more encouragement and praise from teachers, while blacks participated more in procedural and behavioral or discipline interactions. Hillman and Davenport (1978) found that blacks received a greater proportion of product questions, gave no response to more questions, received more criticism from teachers for their behaviors, had more self-initiated questions or relevant comments, were the recipients of greater teacher nonacceptance of a student question or response, and received more teacher feedback to a student question or response. These findings are at odds with results presented by Rubovits and Maehr (1973) and by Gay (1975), which showed that white students received far more attention from teachers than black students, as well as with the data presented by Jackson & Cosca (1974), which indicated that white students received greater teacher attention than did Mexican-American children in the same classroom. Minor differences in findings are probably due to teacher status (experienced vs. preservice teachers); experimental mode (laboratory, e.g., Rubovits and Maehr, 1973, or naturalistic, e.g., Gay, 1975; Hillman & Davenport, 1978; Jackson & Cosca, 1974); geographical location (Georgia, Texas, Michigan, etc.); classroom racial composition (i.e., predominantly black, predominantly Mexican American, predominantly white); and probably other variables. Setting aside these possible explanations for minor differences in findings among the studies, it is important to emphasize that with but a single exception (i.e., Byalick & Bersoff, 1974, who found teachers to positively reinforce opposite-race children more) a clear result is common to all investigations: Third World children are the recipients of far more negative teacher comments and classroom experiences than are white children, a finding which provides strong support for our contention that Third World children often are emotionally abused in classrooms.

Deficiency of Positive Experiences. While there are clear examples of excess negative experiences as enumerated above, we believe that deficiencies in positive experience are the more pervasive and pernicious. In focusing upon deficiencies in positive experiences, it is our contention that such deficiencies are to be found in the daily lives of Third World children and not solely in isolated and occasional encounters with racist individuals as some would have us believe. Consequently, a deficiency of positive experience in the lives of Third World children deserves careful scrutiny. In this section of the chapter, therefore, we identify and discuss two areas we believe to be especially representative of deficient positive experiences in the lives of Third World children—the portrayal of Third World lifestyles and cultures on commercial television, and the representation of Third World history, culture, and lifestyles in textbooks and children's fiction. Reflection on the following statistics will reveal the reasons for our concern.

Let us first consider television. The 1970 U.S. Census estimated that 96% of all American households have a television set; studies in which children and adolescents are present have reported that 98–99% of such households have television sets (cited in Iiyama & Kitano, 1982). Comstock, Chaffee, Katzman, McCombs, and Roberts (1978) indicated that children ages 2–11 view television on an average of 27.6 hours per week and teenagers (ages 12–17) view television an average of 21.9 hours per week. One study (Greenberg & Atkin, 1982) found that poor black children (9–10 years old) watched television 7 hours per weekday, as contrasted with 6 hours per weekday for poor white children and 4 hours per weekday for "better off children."

With respect to textbooks, during the first 18 years of life the average child reads more than 30,000 textbook pages. Moreover, the Council on Interracial Books for Children (1977) estimates that 75% of a student's schoolwork and 90% of the homework focus on textbooks. Books and television then represent significant parts of daily lives of children, and are in special need of scrutiny as passive abusers of children. In our view, the abuse represented by television and books should be considered as "passive" since we rarely find these days—due to a variety of controls and guidelines—clear evidence of racist content in books and television programming. Thus we are not surprised that Broderick (1973), following her analysis of the image of blacks in children's fiction as revealed in the evaluation of 64 books, concluded that most of the books she evaluated could be classified as condescendingly racist or traditionally liberal, do-gooder books. Few books were categorized as outright racist even though many included racist incidents.

Television and Third World Peoples. In this section we review the portrayal of Third World peoples on commercial television, with special attention to the consequences of such portrayal for the socialization (and possible abuse) of Third World children. Before embarking upon our analysis, we acknowledge three points at the outset. The first is that while media portrayal of low-SES and Third World groups is far from adequate, the same can be said for its portrayal of the middle and upper classes; it is probably the case that commercial television is not truly representative of any segment of American life as it has, correctly, never claimed to be. Second, we acknowledge Greenberg and Atkin's (1982) view that the equation of racist program content and negative effects on viewers is far too simple a construction of the problem since, "The characteristics that youth bring to television combine with the attributes of the television content to produce varying type of exposure, interpretation and consequences" (p. 234). Third, we are well aware that the major purpose of commercial television is to entertain. Without quarreling with this purpose, our concern is that pernicious outcomes for Third World children are a consequence of television's entertainment objectives.

The widely held view among social scientists, including the present writers, is that the media, both print and nonprint, influence the social and attitudinal development of children. In keeping with our earlier-stated thesis that emotional abuse is a consequence when stereotyped, narrow, and superficial treatments of Third World cultures are presented in the media, we present data from several studies to support our contention. Consider, first, Berry's (1980) informal analysis of television content vis-a-vis its representation of Third World cultures and life-

styles. Among home and family factors Berry observed these representations on television programs: (a) frequent disruptions by violence and aggressive behavior between parents and siblings, (b) female-dominated households whether or not a male is present, and (c) frequent friction between males and females. Among race and nationality factors his observations included (a) Latino and Hispanic males preoccupied with "macho" image, (b) limited interest in education on the part of parents and children, (c) personal and social values that seem to deviate from the norm, (d) lack of cognitive skills to solve personal and related problems, and (e) the "minority" male as powerless and wanting to be dependent on others. Among community factors, Berry observed (a) crime-ridden and disorganized communities, (b) dirty and unkempt communities, and (c) community people who are unbothered by living in poor housing and with crime. Berry's final category was career and occupational factors, for which he cited these representations: (a) unemployment as the fault of the lower-class person who does not value work, (b) lower career aspirations on the part of males and females, (c) work which does not contribute much to society, and (d) stereotyped jobs held by males and females.

Empirical studies both support and refute Berry's (1980) subjective impressions. With respect to the representation of blacks and whites on television, a study by Greenberg and Atkin (1982) was revealing. The investigators drew a sample of 101 white characters from television shows having significant numbers of black characters. This approach is unique in that analyses were undertaken to determine if blacks were at least similar to those whites appearing on the same show with them, since they provide the most accessible comparative reference for young viewers in terms of potential role models. Among Greenberg and Atkin's findings were that two thirds of the blacks and three fourths of the whites were males. The black characters, more typically found in family settings, were somewhat more likely than white characters to be women. Next, the sample of black characters is strikingly younger than the white sample, with two thirds of the blacks in their 20s or younger compared to less than one half of the white sample in these age groups. Elderly and middle-aged blacks were scarcely represented. Regarding occupations, Greenberg and Atkin found that one third of the television blacks versus one half of the whites have an identifiable job; whites are more likely to be professionals and managers. With respect to programming context, nearly one half the blacks were cast in situation comedies and an additional one fifth in Saturday cartoons, more than double the rate for white characters. No significant black–white differences were found in giving, seeking or receiving advice, information, or orders. The topics of conversation were similar, although whites were found to be more likely to talk about business and about crime.

Other studies were similarly revealing. Northcott, Seggar, and Hinton (1975) found that blacks on television were relegated to more minor roles and in less prestigious occupations, but were portrayed as equally competent, industrious, and physically attractive as whites. Hinton, Seggar, Northcott, and Fontes (1974), in their analysis of television program content, found blacks to be more moral and kind, whereas whites were more dominant in relationships. And finally, a content analysis of commentary by all-white announcers of professional football games showed a bias against black players (Rainville & McCormick, 1977). These researchers transcribed comments about 33 pairs of black and white players matched by position and accomplishment. The results revealed that white players received more favorable references to physical ability, mental ability, and achievement off the field and were more likely to be the recipients of commentator praise and sympathy. Moreover, whites were described as more aggressive and blacks as recipients of the aggression.

By 1969, one half of all television dramas included a black performer (Dominick & Greenberg, 1970). Since that time approximately 6–9% of all characters in television shows have been black. Other minorities are represented with much less frequency and Greenberg and Atkin (1982) speculate that "the absence of portrayals of other minorities could contribute to a weak self-concept among their young people" (p. 217). And while nonblack Third World peoples have not been entirely absent from the nonprint media, distorted and stereotyped images of them have persisted through the years. Iiyama and Kitano (1982) call attention to the many stereotypes of Asian Americans in movies and television and summarize their conclusion by asserting that Asians gain power in the white world only

through their mastery of mysterious Eastern knowledge of drugs and diabolical tortures, such as Fu Manchu villains attempting to conquer the world, and Asians can gain acceptance by becoming passive, dependent, and Americanized. Furthermore, Asian characters have been unduly stereotyped and are more likely to be seen as priests and martial arts experts (*Kung Fu*), pimps, assassins, and mobsters (*Hawaii Five-O*), loyal supporters of police officers, coroners, or captains (*Police Story, Hawaii Five-O, Quincy, Star Trek*), coolies, cooks, laundrymen, or gardeners (*Bonanza, McHale's Navy*), and nurses or doctors' receptionists (*MASH, The Brian Keith Show*).

Native Americans also are victims of media stereotyping. Morris (1982) notes, for example, that "while most American Indian cultures revere cooperation, sharing, the wisdom that comes with old age, and living in balance with nature . . . television programming instills the opposing white values of competition, materialism, youthfulness, and progress at the expense of nature" (p. 198). Generally, the visual image is that of a Plains Indian even though there are hundreds of tribes, each with their own language, religion, and other distinguishing aspects. Native American women, when present at all, are relegated to lesser roles in which they are generally depicted as quiet, passive, dull, and hard working. Respect and independence, which characterize many Native American women, or Navajo or Mohawk women who hold considerable power in their matrilineal societies, are virtually never portrayed (Morris, 1982). With respect to Native American males, one survey (U.S. Commission on Civil Rights, 1977) noted that only six distinct occupational roles were assigned: Chief, guide, adventurer, hunter, ranch foreman, and deputy sheriff. These nonprofessional roles certainly present a limited set of potential models for the developing Native American child and do nothing to foster broad understanding among non-Native American children. Images of Hispanics transmitted by television are no more positive than those for Asians, blacks, and Native Americans. Greenberg and Baptista–Fernandez (1979) analyzed commercial television for their content and characterization of Hispanics and found that the majority of Hispanic characters in commercial television from 1975 to 1978 could be characterized as law breakers, law enforcers, and comic characters.

There are many reasons for concern about images presented on television vis-a-vis Third World children. A first reason is that Third World children are more likely to accept television images as true. In a Race × Class confounded study (which, therefore, must be interpreted with caution), for example, low-socioeconomic-status Mexican-American children were more likely than middle-class white subjects to report that they believed the message of television cartoon characters who endorsed a certain pre-sweetened cereal (Atkin, 1980). In a study of identification with television characters, blacks and whites were found to identify equally with white television characters, but black children were three times as likely to identify with black characters as white children were. When one notes that the characters identified with were the individuals such as Freddy Washington, J. J. Evans, George Jefferson, Louise Jefferson, Florida Evans, and so on, who can hardly be viewed as representative of persons we wish to serve as models for black children, there is cause for concern.

In a related vein, black children more than white children were likely to report that (a) black men and women on television were comparable to those in real life, (b) that blacks on television talk like blacks in real life, (c) that jobs held on television by black men and women are like those they hold in real life, and (d) that black mothers, fathers, wives, husbands, police officers, doctors, and secretaries seen on television behave like they do in real life. Moreover, significantly larger numbers of blacks versus white youths report that they learned most of what they know about the jobs men and women have, how men and women make decisions and solve problems, how black people dress, talk, and behave, and how parents interact with one another and with teenagers from television. To the extent that the images presented and characters portrayed are limited, stereotyped, pejorative, and show a lack of respect for Third World cultures, we must conclude that the Third World child is being abused by exposure to such content. Indeed, Patterson and Thompson (1980) believe:

> Any lack of respect . . . will distort the child's sense of his [sic] own internal reality and hence his [sic] sense of self-esteem and self-confidence with respect to what he [sic] can expect from others; or else it

will distort his [sic] views of external reality and hence his [sic] capacity to cope with the real world. Such a lack would constitute neglect (abuse) in the full sense. (p. 63)

PORTRAYAL OF THIRD WORLD PEOPLES IN CHILDREN'S TEXTBOOKS AND STORYBOOKS

As prelude to a consideration of racism in children's literature, Banfield (1980) suggests that we should proceed on at least four premises. First, we must realize that literature and textbooks reflect the values of a society and serve to perpetuate and reinforce these values, and, second, that every intellectual discipline (e.g., the social sciences, philosophy) is pressed into service to provide the theoretical and "scientific support for these values." Third, Banfield observes that educational institutions play a critical role in the reinforcement and perpetuation of these values, first by socialization of teachers and students so that they internalize and accept these values and, second, by the cultivation and development of scholars who will continue to present theoretical arguments in support of these values in increasingly sophisticated ways. Finally, every possible form of communications media is utilized to guarantee the widest possible dissemination of those ideas considered valuable and desirable by society.

Stereotypes of Afro-Americans can be traced back to Western encounters with Africans (Jordan, 1968) and were well developed in the early 1800s in the pre–Civil War period. The ideology, developed in part to justify the plantation system of slavery, was well entrenched in the southern states and was based on three racist myths: (a) the black was by intellect and temperament naturally suited to be a slave of the white, (b) slavery was the natural lot of the African and so ordained by the Creator, and (c) rigid discipline and control were necessary and beneficial to the African barbarian (Banfield, 1980). Not surprisingly, these myths found their way into the literature of the period and in various forms in textbooks every since. Indeed, as Banfield (1980) notes, "It becomes readily apparent that evidence of racism in literature and textbooks, far from being eliminated as time passes and the society becomes more enlightened, consistently reappears in successive historical periods in increasingly subtle and sophisticated forms—making it even more difficult to detect, and, therefore, all the more insidious and dangerous" (p. 14).

It should not be too surprising, then, to find that the Third World child, even in 1985, encounters textbooks with dominating perspectives that the United States is a white country, and that the prime architects of U.S. life and history have been white males. And while Third World people and their contributions are being increasingly included in textbooks, the treatment is rarely from the perspective of Third World people. Consider, for example, this statement which appears in an American history textbook: "To live in the South was to live in daily fear of slave violence." Such a statement is clearly written from a white perspective. The sentence could have just as easily been written, "To live in the South was to live in the daily hope of a successful rebellion against slave owners" (The Council on Interracial Books for children, 1977), a black perspective.

Textbooks also are Eurocentric. More recent textbooks now give black reactions to slavery, but there still is scant attention given to life in African countries. Students, therefore, are given no sense of who African Americans were before they were forcibly brought to America. Nor are they given insights into the rich sets of values, beliefs, and skills they brought with them. Too often the student reader is left with the view that black Americans lack a cultural heritage.

The methods by which Third World peoples have been included in textbooks have also been subjected to scrutiny. Three major forms have been identified: inclusion as greats, as contributors, and as protestors. In the Great Man approach, history is recounted through the activities of a relatively few statesmen, soldiers, merchants, and so forth, virtually all of whom are white and male. Recent textbooks include selected Third World individuals and women as "Greats," but selection for inclusion is, of course, subjective. Who is included and who is not can have much to say to the young reader. Older textbooks, for example, routinely preferred Booker T. Washington's moderation to W. E. B. Du Bois' antiestablishment views. The nonviolent approach of Martin Luther King has often been preferred to the more militant style of Malcolm X, or the approaches of Nat Turner as compared to Denmark Vesey, who led slave

revolts (Council on Interracial Books for Children, 1977).

Third World people are often included by listing their contributions. Thus, Native Americans gave us corn, Afro-Americans gave us jazz, and so on. These contributions are, for the most part, treated as tangential to the main flow of history. The fact that Third World peoples often were not beneficiaries of their contributions is not emphasized. For example, while history textbooks will now acknowledge that thousands of blacks bore arms during World Wars I and II, they continue to ignore or lightly treat discrimination in the armed forces and the racism to which the black veterans returned. We are increasingly witnessing a shift in attention from the world the slaveholders made (Genovese, 1972) to slavery from the perspective of the slave (Blasingame, 1972), although much of the revisionist thinking has yet to be fully integrated into textbooks used in public schools.

Newer textbooks focus on the liberation movements of the 1960s and 1970s but they rarely place the movements in a historical context that show them as part of a continuum of protest. Thus, protesters, like contributors and greats, are selectively identified. The fact that the United States was born out of violent revolution is well established, yet most textbooks still imply that only legal protest is legitimate. The progress that has been achieved through active and passive resistance—violent as well as nonviolent tactics and by legal as well as extralegal methods—has not been given the attention it deserves.

The Council on Interracial Books for Children (1977) addressed the problem of omission as a racist pattern characteristic of children's books. Many books have no, or limited, Third World characters when we have every reason to expect that they would be represented, especially when the story is set in an urban area. In commenting on such voids, the Council (1977) notes "this is the racism of total omission; Third Worlders are invisible or next to invisible, when in fact they are there. Such unjustifiable omission tends to support ethnocentricity in the white reader . . ." (p. 10). Many books, of course, have mixed characters, and a more limited number have primarily Third World characters. In such books, the Council notes, in general, the existence of racism in the characters' lives is not acknowledged. The impression is created that racism does not exist and that problems experienced by the characters are purely personal. A racist act may be presented but the author neglects to comment on it, leaving the young reader with the impression that it was correct. A Third World character may be shown as bitter and too distrustful of whites, but the origins of the feelings are never explained, possibly leaving the young reader with the impression that the characters' grievances are without cause. The Council concludes with these observations:

> By ignoring the reality of racism and its economic origins, such books are deceitful and do nothing to prepare children of any color for the society around them. In the Third World child they encourage confusion and self-hatred [a reasonable, but undocumented, assertion] and, in the white child, they encourage chauvinism and a distortion of reality. Such books reflect an unwillingness to face the truth about U.S. society and about the responsibility of whites, who hold power and who are accountable for racism. At most, racism becomes an unpleasant, minor aberration, rather than a central pivot of this society which affects everyone living it. (p. 11)

Bias in children's fiction has also been studied. For example, Smith (1979) investigated bias in books for preschool children that are designed to portray black children. The study's primary focus was on the treatment of male and female parent figures in books written to portray black children in relationship to their families. Smith's sample of books, all published between 1960 and 1975—and which were identified by 9 teachers and 2 librarians as those most frequently read by, read to, and borrowed for children—consisted of 30 books in which only black children and families were characterized and 30 books in which only white children were characterized. Content analysis led Smith to these conclusions:

1. Black mothers and white fathers work outside the house. Most white mothers do not work (a phenomenon that is now changing and may or may not be reflected in more recent children's story books), and black fathers are often unemployed.
2. White parents tend to show more liking for their children. They spend more time with them, play with them, take them on more outings, help them with their activities, and are generally more affectionate toward them.
3. Black parents shout, spank, and otherwise reprimand their children more often.
4. Black parents are less affectionate to one another.

Our point should be clear: presentation of such erroneous and pejorative views as presented in Smith's analysis can be said to constitute emotional abuse.

Prize-winning storybooks written for children are especially disturbing. Ostensibly, these books represent the best of children's literature as judged by librarians and literary critics, and hence are to be highly recommended as vehicles for communicating the ideas about racial equality, justice, and cultural differences we all long to see in children's books. Yet, a close analysis of many of the prize-winning books reveals serious flaws in them; some of the books do nothing to support the cause of eliminating bias in children's literature. *The Slave Dancer*, for example, won the 1973 Newbery Prize, the most coveted award in children's book publishing, but in review articles aptly titled "*The Slave Dancer* is an Insult to Black Children" (Mathis, 1977) and "Racism and Distortions Pervade *The Slave Dancer*" (Tate, 1977), *The Slave Dancer*'s author, Paula Fox, is taken to task for a variety of stereotypes about blacks and Africans which the book perpetuates. The book is also criticized for its historical inaccuracies.

Biographical works receiving the Newbery Prize have also received critical scrutiny (McCann, 1972) and have similarly been judged to include many racial insensitivities. We are led to the conclusion, then, that even in children's work judged to possess the highest literary merit, many evidences of racism are to be found. The possible emotional abuse to Third World children as a result of exposure to such literature need hardly be belabored.

In recent years, an increasing number of books for children have attempted to deal directly with the problem of racism, but the perspective is almost all white oriented. As The Council on Interracial Books for Children notes (1977), the theme in many of the books is that Third World people (and blacks in particular) are defective until they prove themselves worthy of white approval. The Council notes this can be accomplished by working oneself up the ladder through personal individual virtue, as many immigrant groups have done. The Council was unequivocal in its rejection of such an approach and wrote, "The whole formula is fraudulent, and to foist it on children is truly abusive. . . ." The Council goes on to assert that racism will never be eliminated by denial of its existence, or by individual solutions instead of social solutions. The problem will not go away by saying that underneath we are all the same.

INTERVENTIONS

Problems of bias and racism in books for Third World children will probably always exist, but we are confident that the numbers of such books can be significantly reduced if authors would follow guidelines for the evaluation of instructional materials developed by the California State Board of Education (1974). The Board wrote:

> In order to project the cultural diversity of our society, instill in each child a sense of pride in his or her heritage, eradicate the seeds of prejudice, and encourage the individual development of each child, instructional materials, which portraying people (or animals having identifiable human attributes), shall include a fair representation of majority and minority group characters portrayed in a wide variety of occupational and behavioral roles, and present the contributions of ethnic and cultural groups, thereby reinforcing the self-esteem and potential of all people and helping the members of minority groups to find their rightful place in our society.

> 1. Descriptions, depictions, or labels which tend to demean, stereotype, or be patronizing toward minority groups [sic] must not appear.

> 2. When diverse ethnic or cultural groups are portrayed, such portrayal must not depict differences in customs or lifestyles as undesirable and must not reflect an adverse value judgment of such differences.

> 3. Instructional materials that generally or incidentally reflect contemporary American society, regardless of the subject area, must contain references to, or illustrations of, a fair proportion of diverse ethnic groups.

> 4. Mentally active, creative, and problem-solving roles, and success and failure in those roles, should be divided in fair proportion between majority and minority group characters. (It is necessary to look to the consequences of activities undertaken by majority and minority group characters presented in the material. Positive or negative results, success or failure, can flow from the undertaking of any tasks, and it is not suggested that all characters succeed at all times. A pattern of success or failure, however, should not emerge as correlated with the race, ethnicity, or cultural background of the character.)

> 5. The portrayal of minority characters in roles to which they have been traditionally restricted by society should be balanced by the presentation of nontraditional activities for characters of that race.

> 6. Minority persons should be depicted in the same range of socioeconomic settings as are persons of the majority group.

> 7. Depiction of diverse ethnic and cultural groups should not be limited to the root culture, but rather expanded to include such groups within the mainstream of American life.

> 8. If professional or executive roles, or vocations, trades, or other gainful occupations are portrayed, majority and minority groups should be presented therein in fair proportion. (Although no specific number of percentage for each statutorily noted minority group is specified, "tokenism" for any minority group is as unacceptable in instructional materials as it is in the real world of employment.)

> 9. Whenever developments in history or current events, or achievements in art, science, or any other field are presented, the contributions of minority peoples, and particularly the identification of prominent minority persons, should be included and discussed when historically accurate.

> 10. Imbalance or inequality of any kind, when presented for historical accuracy, should, in the student edition of the instructional materials, be interpreted in the light of contemporary standards and circumstances.

In order to portray accurately the cultural and racial diversity and the male and female roles in our society, instructional materials must encourage students to understand not only the historical roles and contributions of women and Third World peoples, but also the forces which shaped those roles and contributions and how and why the contemporary roles and contributions of women and minorities are different.

CONCLUSIONS

It should be obvious to the informed reader that the racism child-abuse picture has many faces. The most well-developed area is that which draws relationships among poverty, low socio-economic status, race, and abuse—the essential notion being that frustrations of low economic status and life in hostile environments lead to frustrations which lead to the abuse of children. This territory has been explored by others (Belsky, 1978) and, therefore, has not received attention in this chapter. But other areas could have been developed as well. For example, an interesting but unstudied topic is the relationship between emotional and physical abuse of children and Third World parent views that extraordinary means of discipline are necessary in order to prepare their children for existence in a racist and hostile society. Those who wrestle with definitions of abuse have called our attention to the fact that the line between abuse and excessive corporal punishment is often a thin one. Could it be, for example, that in their zeal to prepare children for existence in a hostile environment, that some parents have crossed the line—from punishment to abuse?

Because their effects on children have been persuasive but, unfortunately, have received too little attention within the context of child abuse, we have focused our attention in this chapter on the media, children's textbooks and storybooks, and teachers as abusers of Third World children. The literature cited reveals that problems of racism-related abuse have been well documented but solutions and intervention strategies have lagged behind. Our strong view is that it is now time to attend to the racism-related abuse of children, with special emphasis upon intervention strategies.

REFERENCES

Amiel, S. (1972). Child abuse in schools. *Northwest Medicine, 71,* 808.

Atkin, C. K. (1980). Effects of television advertising on children. In E. Palmer & A. Dorr (Eds.), *Children and the faces of television.* New York: Academic Press.

Banfield, B. (1980). Racism in children's books: An Afro-American perspective. In R. Presswerk (Ed.), *The slant of the pen—Racism in children's books.* Geneva: World Council of Churches.

Belsky, J. (1978). Three models of child abuse: A critical review. *Child Abuse and Neglect, 2,* 37–49.

Berry, G. L. (1980). Children, television, and social class roles: The medium as an unplanned social curriculum. In E. L. Palmer & A. Dorr (Eds.), *Children and the faces of television.* New York: Academic Press.

Blasingame, J. W. (1972). *The slave community.* New York: Oxford University Press.

Broderick, D. M. (1983). *Image of the black in children's fiction.* New York: R. R. Bowker.

Brown, G. W. (1977). School: Child advocate or adversary. *Clinical Pediatrics, 16,* 439–446.

Byalick, R., & Bersoff, D. N. (1974). Reinforcement practices of black and white teachers in integrated classrooms. *Journal of Educational Psychology, 66,* 473–480.

Cable, M. (1975). The federal child. In M. Cable (Ed.), *The little darlings: A history of childrearing in America.* New York: Charles Scribner's Sons.

California State Board of Education. (1974). *Guidelines for evaluation of instructional materials.* Sacramento: State Board of Education.

Children's Defense Fund. (1974). *Children out of school in America.* Cambridge, MA: Author.

Coates, B. (1972). White adult behavior toward black and white children. *Child Development, 43,* 143–154.

Comstock, G., Chaffee, S., Katzman, N., McCombs, M., & Roberts, D. (1978). *Television and human behavior.* New York: Columbia University Press.

Council on Interracial Books for Children. (1977). *Guidelines for selecting bias-free textbooks and storybooks.* New York: Author.

Dominick, J., & Greenberg, B. (1970). Three seasons of blacks on television. *Journal of Advertising Research, 10,* 21–27.

Duncan, C. (1973). They beat children don't they? *Journal of Clinical Child Psychology, 2,* 13–14.

Fox, P. (1973). *The slave dancer.* Scarsdale, NY: Bradbury Press.

Gay, G. (1975). Teacher's achievement expectations of and classroom interactions with ethnically different students. *Contemporary Education, 48,* 166–172.

Genovese, E. D. (1972). *Roll, Jordan, roll. The world the slaves made.* New York: Vintage Books.

Greenberg, B. S., & Atkin, C. K. (1982). Learning about minorities from television: A research agenda. In G. L. Berry & C. Mitchell–Kernan (Eds.), *Television and the socialization of the minority child.* New York: Academic Press.

Greenberg, B., & Baptista–Fernandez, P. (1979). *Hispanic Americans: The new minority on television.* East Lansing: Michigan State University, Department of Communication.

Hillman, S. B., & Davenport, G. G. (1978). Teacher–student interactions in desegregated schools. *Journal of Educational Psychology, 70,* 545–553.

Hinton, J., Seggar, J., Northcott, H., & Fontes, B. (1974). Tokenism and improving imagery of blacks in TV drama and comedy: 1973. *Journal of Broadcasting, 18,* 423–432.

Iiyama, P., & Kitano, H. L. (1982). Asian Americans and mental health. In G. L. Berry & C. Mitchell–Kernan (Eds.), *Television and the socialization of the minority child.* New York: Academic Press.

Jackson, G., & Cosca, C. (1974). The inequality of educational opportunity in the Southwest: An observational study of ethnically mixed classrooms. *American Educational Research Journal, 11,* 219–229.

Jordan, W. D. (1968). *White over black.* Baltimore: Penguin Books.

McCann, D. (1972). Racism in prize-winning biographical works. In D. McCann & G. Woodard (Eds.), *The black American in books for children: Readings in racism.* Metuchen, NJ: The Scarecrow Press.

Mathis, S. B. (1977). *The Slave Dancer* is an insult to black people. In D. McCann & G. Woodard (Eds.), *Cultural conformity in books for children.* Metuchen, NJ: The Scarecrow Press.

Morris, J. S. (1982). Television portrayal and the socialization of the American Indian child. In G. L. Berry & C. Mitchell–Kernan (Eds.), *Television and the socialization of the minority child.* New York: Academic Press.

Northcott, H., Seggar, J., & Hinton, J. (1975). Trends in TV portrayal of blacks and women. *Journalism Quarterly, 52,* 741–744.

Patterson, P. G. R., & Thompson, M. G. G. (1980). Emotional child abuse and neglect: An exercise in definition. In R. Volpe, M. Breton, & J. Mitton (Eds.), *The maltreatment of the school-aged child.* Lexington, MA: Lexington Books.

Plank, E. L. (1975). Violations of children's rights in the classroom. *Childhood Education, 52,* 73–75.

Rainville, R., & McCormick, E. (1977). Extent of covert racial prejudice in pro-football announcers' speech. *Journalism Quarterly, 54,* 20–26.

Rubovits, P. C., & Maehr, M. L. (1973). Pygmalion in black and white. *Journal of Personality and Social Psychology, 25,* 210–218.

Tate, B. (1977). Racism and distortions pervade *The Slave Dancer.* In D. McCann & G. Woodard (Eds.), *Cultural conformity in books for children.* Metuchen, NJ: The Scarecrow Press.

U.S. Commission on Civil Rights (1977). *Window dressing on the set.* Women and minorities in television. Washington, DC: U.S. Government Printing Office.

12

Maltreatment as a Function of the Structure of Social Systems

David G. Gil

INTRODUCTION

This essay explores the institutional context of human abuse of which "psychological abuse" is but one inseparable dimension. A basic premise of this exploration is that different manifestations of human abuse (i.e., verbal, physical, and psychological) as well as different contexts of abuse (i.e., interpersonal, domestic, institutional, and societal) cannot be understood apart from one another, but only as internally related functions of social, economic, and political dynamics rooted in particular societal structures and corresponding value systems and ideologies.

Whatever its form and context, human abuse seems to be a direct or indirect outcome of socially evolved and enforced inequalities in the organization of work and the exchange of work products, and in the resulting statuses, rights, and relations of individuals, age groups, sexes, classes, races, peoples, and so on, for socially structured inequalities, irrespective of substance and form, are never the product of free and voluntary choices. Rather, they are always rooted in coercive processes and relations, and once established coercively within or between social groups, they require continuous coercive measures (i.e., institutional violence) for their reproduction and maintenance. Such ongoing coercive measures are usually intrinsic aspects of socialization into established, inegalitarian social orders and corresponding ideologies which interpret and justify the inequalities. Socialization into inegalitarian social orders is usually reinforced by elaborate systems of conformity-inducing rewards and sanctions and is always backed up by internal and external security apparatuses of physical coercion—the police and military forces of the state in inegalitarian societies.

An important corollary of the foregoing observation is that the presence in a society of coercive measures or institutional violence, to maintain socially structured inequalities, tends to result in counterforce or "reactive violence" by oppressed, exploited, frustrated, and alienated individuals and groups. This creates a vicious circle or chain reaction of abuse from which humankind has, so far, failed to extricate itself, largely because of resistance, by economically privileged and politically dominant groups, to the transcendence of socially structured inequalities.

DEFINITIONAL ISSUES

As the meanings of such key concepts as "institutions," "abuse," and "violence" tend to vary in scholarly and popular discourse, I will begin by clarifying my understanding of these concepts.

Social Institutions

The concept of "social institutions" refers to a universally observable tendency in human societies, namely the temporary stability of patterns of actions, interactions, and thought of a society's mode of existence and subdomains of its way of life, such as the economic domain, the family or kinship domain, the socialization or child-rearing and education domain, the political or social control domain, the religious or ideological domain. As a caveat, it should be noted that none of these institutional domains exist as separate, independent functions. Rather, they overlap and interact continuously and the combined interaction effects of all the institutional domains result in the regulation or patterning (institutionalization) of human behavior, relations, and thought processes in given societies.

The institutionalization of behavior, relations, and thoughts evolved gradually through history as humans in different groups and locations, in pursuit of survival, interacted with their natural environments and with one another within and across generations. Since the human species, as a result of evolution, lacks genetically transmitted specific modes of existence, humans all over the globe developed and institutionalized different modes of existence fitting different natural and social conditions. Socially constructed cultures thus assumed functions analogous to genetic programs for survival of other species. While human behavior, relations, and thoughts tend thus to be shaped by social institutions as they exist at any moment of history, these institutions, in turn, are the products of earlier and current human actions, interactions, and thoughts, and are continuously being reproduced, as well as transformed, by contemporary human behavior and thought. Humans collectively, whether they cooperate or compete in their efforts to survive, are thus masters or architects, as well as objects or servants, of their social institutions, and of entire institutional orders into which the institutions combine.

The institutional domains noted above are abstractions or summations of different sets of concrete human activities oriented toward survival and societal continuity. At a more concrete level, one can identify within these abstract institutional domains specific agencies which carry out the functions of the domains. Thus, farms, factories, mines, and stores are concrete agencies of the economic domain; schools, day care centers, foster homes, and child care facilities are concrete agencies of the socialization domain; executive bureaucracies, legislatures, and courts are concrete agencies of the political domain; and churches, libraries, and communi-

cation media are agencies of the religious and ideological domain.

The language of the social sciences lacks precision and often fails to distinguish between the abstract level of social institutions and the concrete level of specific agencies of institutional domains. Thus, the term *institution* is used also to refer to specific agencies of institutional domains, as when child care facilities are called children's institutions, and banks financial institutions. This ambiguous use of language does, however, reveal important internal relations between concrete agencies and corresponding abstract social institutions. These relations are that the behavior and mentality of people within concrete institutional agencies are shaped and limited by the dynamics of the corresponding institutional domains. Thus, the policies and practices of schools and child care facilities tend to reflect the dynamics of the socialization domain, while the policies and practices of banks and business firms tend to reflect the dynamics of the economic domain. Hence, when an entire institutional order and its domains involve abusive tendencies, these tendencies will invariably permeate the policies and practices of its concrete institutional agencies.

Abuse or Violence

The concept of violence refers to human-originated relations, processes, and conditions which obstruct both the free and spontaneous unfolding of innate physical, intellectual, and emotional potential of humans and the drive toward growth, development, and self-actualization, by interfering with the fulfillment of peoples' inherent biological, psychological, and social needs.

Implicit in this view of abuse or violence is the assumption that humans, like seeds, have a tendency toward spontaneous growth and development. Seeds will grow into healthy, mature plants only when embedded in nutritious soil, and when nurtured by rain and sunshine. Analogously, human development will be inhibited, or violated, unless humans live in natural and social environments compatible with their developmental needs. One further assumption underlying this conception of abuse or violence is that humans are not compelled by nature to relate to other humans in violent, domineering, exploiting, and oppressive ways, though they have the capacity to do so. Yet, the capacity to relate to others nonviolently, cooperatively, supportively, and lovingly is also present. Which of these capacities will emerge as the dominant tendency in a group of people depends on the institutional order and ideology they have evolved for themselves throughout their history (Benedict, 1970; Turnbull, 1972).

Erich Fromm, the noted social scientist and psychoanalyst who studied the sources and dynamics of violence in Europe during the 1930s, reached similar conclusions to those suggested here:

> It would seem that the amount of destructiveness to be found in individuals is proportionate to the amount to which expansiveness of life is curtailed. By this we do not refer to individual frustrations of this or that instinctive desire but to the thwarting of the whole of life, the blockage of spontaneity of the growth and expression of man's [sic] sensuous, emotional, and intellectual capacities. . . . The more the drive toward life is thwarted, the stronger is the drive toward destruction; the more life is realized, the less is the strength of destructiveness. Destructiveness is the outcome of unlived life. (Fromm, 1941, pp. 183–184)

Violence, according to Fromm, is not a primary human tendency but a reaction to a prior blocking of spontaneous, constructive life energy.

Abusive acts, relations, and conditions may occur among individuals and also between individuals, social institutions and their agencies, and entire societies. An individual may violate another's integrity physically and/or psychologically by creating and maintaining conditions which deprive, injure, exploit, and oppress. Similarly, agencies of social institutions such as schools, child care facilities, and welfare services, as well as business corporations, may, through their policies and practices, disregard the developmental needs of people they serve, and may thus subject them to conditions that violate their development. Finally, entire societies may, through their values, policies, and laws, evolve and sanction structured inequalities such as poverty, discrimination by class, race, sex, or age, unemployment, and inflation, which all inevitably violate the development of many individuals and groups.

Human abuse resulting from societal conditions is referred to here as "institutional violence." Institutional violence, whenever it is present in a society, is inherent in established social patterns and legitimized practices. Personal violence, on the other hand, involves acts which usually conflict with prevailing social norms and laws. Personal and institutional violence cannot, however, be understood apart from one another. Rather, they interact with and reinforce one another. They are merely different symptoms of the same underlying social realities, values, mentality, institutions, and dynamics.

Personal violence, as suggested in Fromm's conclusion, is one way in which people react to stresses and frustrations caused by the institutional violence they encounter in everyday life. Personal violence appears to be fed by developmental energy which is transformed into destructive behaviors when blocked by institutional violence. Institutional violence is, therefore, the source or cause of personal violence which, in turn, may lead to chain reactions as successive victims become agents of further violence.

INSTITUTIONAL ABUSE IN THE UNITED STATES AND ITS PSYCHOLOGICAL EFFECTS

Based on the foregoing analysis of the concepts of social institutions and abuse or violence, we can now examine whether institutional abuse is an intrinsic aspect of the social order of the United States and of the policies and practices of the concrete agencies of our institutional order, including socialization and child care facilities. The scope of human abuse in any society corresponds to the extent to which the intrinsic needs of its members are frustrated, and their development is inhibited as a result of the normal workings of the society's institutions. This analysis begins, therefore, by identifying intrinsic developmental and existential human needs, and then examines whether these needs can now be fulfilled in our society.

Human Needs

Many students of human development consider fulfillment of the following related needs essential to healthy development:

1. Regular access to life-sustaining and enhancing goods and services.
2. Meaningful social relations, and a sense of belonging to a community involving mutual

respect, acceptance, affirmation, care, and love.

3. Meaningful and creative participation in accordance with one's innate capacities and stage of development in productive processes of one's community and society.

4. A sense of security, derived from continuous fulfillment of needs for life-sustaining and enhancing goods and services, meaningful relations, and meaningful participation in socially valued productive processes.

5. Becoming all that one is capable of becoming, or, in Maslow's terms, self-actualization through creative, productive work (Dewey, 1935; Fromm, 1955; Maslow, 1970).

The extent to which these basic needs are capable of being realized rather than frustrated in a society depends on the structures, dynamics, and values of its institutional order, or, more specifically, the manner in which means of production are controlled, used, developed, and conserved; work and production are organized; goods and services are exchanged and distributed; and social, civil, and political rights are distributed. Accordingly, an analysis of institutional violence in the United States involves a review of the workings of these fundamental social processes (Gil, 1973, 1981).

Resource Management

In the United States, a minority of the people, either individually or as corporations, own and control most means of production, exchange, and distribution, including land and other natural resources, factories, banks, commercial and service establishments, transportation and communications, and knowledge and technology. The majority of the people, on the other hand, do not own and/or control sufficient resources to survive by working with what they control. Hence, the majority depend for survival on selling their labor, knowledge, and/or skills at the discretion and in the interest of the minority who own or control productive resources. The propertyless differ among themselves by origin, race, history, and culture; by sex and age; and by education, skills, and attitudes. These differences tend to divide them as they compete for employment and income, goods and services, and rights.

Owners and managers use the resources they control to produce goods and services for sale to realize profits. Profits are largely reinvested to expand control over means of production and markets. The competitive drive toward accumulation of capital and control over resources and markets is an important factor shaping the logic of everyday life and affecting the consciousness, behavior, and mutual relations of people. The quality and quantity of products, the extent to which production corresponds to actual needs of the population, the quality of the labor process, and the effects of production on people, communities, the environment, and the conservation of resources—all these considerations are less important in shaping production decisions than criteria of profitability and concentration of capital (Baran & Sweezy, 1966; Hunt & Sherman, 1981).

Organization of Work and Production

The organization of work and production in the United States reflects the division of the population in terms of control over means of production. The propertied classes rely on the labor of propertyless workers who, in turn, depend on employment by individual and corporate owners. In general, the higher the ratio of employment-seeking workers to available jobs, the lower the average level of wages, and the higher the average rate of profits. Owners tend, therefore, to favor an oversupply of workers relative to jobs, which forces workers to compete for scarce jobs.

The competition for jobs results not only in personal rivalries, but also in intergroup conflicts and discrimination by race, sex, and age. Competition results not only from job scarcities but also from the drive for advancement in pyramidal, bureaucratic organizations, and corresponding wage and prestige systems. Hierarchical structures, in turn, seem necessary to supervise and control workers who are not prepared for self-direction, and who usually lack incentives to maximize productivity, since the fruits of their labor do not belong to them. This competition for jobs and for advancement to more desirable positions tends to reduce opportunities for meaningful human relations in workplaces and throughout society, since individuals who are forced to compete for the same scarce positions and opportunities are unlikely to develop close, caring, and meaningful relationships. It also tends to inhibit the development of solidarity among workers and unemployed individuals, and it gives rise to loneliness, frustration, and alienation, which, in turn, may lead to depression, alcoholism, drug addiction, domestic violence, crime, and suicide (U.S. Congress, 1976).

Unemployment, which seems a regular feature of capitalist economies, has many destructive consequences. It holds down the general level of wages, depresses the self-image of unemployed workers, and induces insecurity among employed workers who may lose their jobs at the discretion of employers. The emotions of unemployed workers usually affect the milieu of their families, who suffer emotionally along with their economic deprivation. Furthermore, unemployment has consequences beyond the households directly involved, since reduced household incomes are reflected in the economic realities of communities and society.

While unemployment dehumanizes its victims, employment under prevailing conditions can be a mixed blessing as it usually does not provide opportunities to actualize one's potential. Workers are usually considered and treated as means to the ends of employers. They are not perceived as whole and unique individuals, but as functions or components of production processes—"hired hands." When one is treated as a replaceable attachment to a machine, one's self-image suffers and one's development as a whole person with multifaceted capacities is stunted.

As a result of employers' efforts to increase efficiency, productivity, and profits, the tasks of most workers have been reduced to simple routines, each a step in complex production processes of which workers are kept ignorant. Consequently, workers are no longer competent and knowledgeable masters of production in their fields, but are, in the revealing jargon of economists, "factors of production." Apart from their earlier separation from the material means of production, workers have, since the industrial revolution, been separated from the nonmaterial means, the knowledge component of production. This, the ultimate stage of expropriation, deprives workers of their human essence—their sense of integrity and autonomy—and thus completes their transformation into easily marketable and replaceable commodities (Braverman, 1974; U.S. Department of Health, Education, and Welfare, 1972; Pope John Paul II, 1982).

Socialization

The transformation of most work into routines requiring little or no initiative, creativity, and intellectual effort, and of workers into uncritical performers of routine tasks within authoritarian work settings, has inevitably affected child rearing, socialization, and formal education. These interrelated processes, in any society, prepare the young to fit into established patterns of adult life and to take their place in the prevailing division of labor.

The established patterns of life and work in the United States today require mainly conforming and apathetic workers. Such workers are produced through prevailing modes of life and human relations in homes, schools, churches, and neighborhoods. These destructive consequences of current patterns of child rearing, socialization, and formal education do not result from conscious, intentional practices on the part of parents, teachers, and educational authorities. Rather, they automatically result from growing up in homes, schools, and neighborhoods segregated both by social class and race and by attitudes, expectations, and aspirations. Consequently, though not intentionally so designed, the patterns of child rearing, socialization, and formal education in the contemporary United States result in massive and differential underdevelopment of the rich potential of most children and youth (Bowles & Gintis, 1976; Gil, 1979).

Most individuals in the United States are not expected, nor do they have opportunities, to use their innate capacities in the normal course of employment. Therefore, many individuals either fail to fully develop their capacities or allow developed capacities to atrophy from lack of use. The result is a society in which most people function below their potential. This underdevelopment progressively reduces the capacity of culturally and developmentally damaged generations to nurture those following them.

Moreover, ongoing efforts to enhance efficiency and productivity through further refinements in the subdivision of labor will intensify psychological conditions and processes which result inevitably in developmental deficits. This trend will be reversed only when people are expected and have the opportunity to integrate their intellectual, physical, and emotional capacities in their work and in other domains of everyday life, when they will no longer be factors but rather masters of production and of their own existence.

Irrationality and Waste

A further feature of aggregate production in the United States is irrationality. While production tends to be planned, rational, and efficient in terms of profit considerations of individual firms, aggregate production is unplanned, irrational, inefficient, and wasteful in terms of the real needs of the population, the survival and development of communities and regions, and the conservation of resources and the environment. This internal contradiction of capitalist production occurs because individual businesses and the economy as a whole are not oriented toward actual needs of all people. Rather, the focus is on "effective demand" as reflected in purchasing decisions and on maximizing profits. The needs of people who lack adequate purchasing power are, therefore, neither considered nor met under prevailing patterns of production and distribution.

Moreover, the absence of planning geared to the needs of all people and to the long-range needs of communities and society results not only in severe underproduction in terms of people's needs, but in wasteful overproduction of unnecessary goods and services. People with surplus purchasing power are induced to buy these products by means of technically sophisticated, yet mindless, advertising. Further aspects of irrationality and waste in capitalist production are frequent, arbitrary changes of models and fashions, and planned obsolescence of many products. The massive waste in production is a major, objective source of inflation, intrinsic to capitalist dynamics. Inflation, generated by waste, in turn stimulates subjective, social, and psychological tendencies which reinforce the inflationary process.

Lack of economic planning geared to the needs of all people and communities, along with waste-generated inflationary practices, leads inevitably to periodic economic crises to which individual firms respond by cutting back production and by laying off employees. From a big-business perspective, such crises balance and regulate the economy in the absence of planning. From the perspective of individuals, households, small enterprises, and communities, these crises usually mean disaster.

Distribution of Goods and Services, and of Social, Civil, and Political Rights

In the United States, goods and services are available mainly through markets. Purchasing power in the form of money or credit is, therefore, necessary to secure goods and services. The quantity and quality of available goods and services which people can obtain depends mainly on their wealth and their incomes from wealth, work, and government grants and subsidies. The distribution of wealth and income in the United States has always been characterized by major inequalities among individuals, households, age groups, sexes, ethnic groups, and social classes. Poverty, defined as income insufficient to secure an acknowledged, minimally adequate standard of living, is built into the fabric of our society in that large segments of the population own little or no income-producing wealth, nor are they assured access to gainful employment.

Propertyless people of all ages who have never secured employment or who have lost their jobs are usually doomed to poverty. Whatever purchasing power they command derives from government transfer payments or from extralegal practices (i.e., crime). Transfer payments to poor people tend to be very low. These payments usually do not raise income levels to the U.S. Government's poverty index, a measure derived from a short-term, emergency food budget, and which corresponds to less than two thirds of the "low-level budget" for urban households as determined by the U.S. Bureau of Labor Statistics. During recent years, over 30,000,000 individuals were living in households with incomes at or below the official poverty level, despite government assistance. Another 40,000,000 were "near poor" according to a 1980 report of the National Advisory Council on Economic Opportunity (see Shabecoff, 1980). "Near poverty" corresponds to 125% of the official poverty index. The incidence of poverty and near poverty is disproportionately higher among children, youth, aged persons, women (especially in single-parent families), racial minorities, and Native American tribes.

Individuals who have never secured employment, who have lost their jobs, or who have retired from work are not the only persons who exist in or near poverty. Many regularly employed workers live in or near poverty since the legal minimum wage does not assure incomes above the poverty line. Furthermore, the prevailing wage structure leaves about one third of the entire population in or near poverty.

In theory, every citizen of the United States is entitled to equal civil and political rights. In reality, however, these rights are distributed unequally, as they are subtly associated with material wealth and income, and with race, sex, age, occupation, education, and social class. The economically powerful, especially white males, tend to acquire disproportionally large shares of social prestige and political influence. Public authorities often treat the well-to-do more politely and more favorably than poor people, especially when the latter are members of racial minorities. Even in courts of law and in the correctional system, wealthy and prestigious individuals and corporations are often able to secure preferential treatment with the help of expensive lawyers.

Access to the communication media to promote views on public issues also tends to be easier for economically powerful and socially prominent individuals and groups. Since political influence and power depend to no small extent on access to established media, or on economic resources to create alternative media, those who lack ample economic resources usually also lack opportunities to acquire political influence.

Ideology

Central to any social ideology are positions on the following related value continua: equality/inequality; affirmation of community and individuality/selfishness; cooperation/competition; and liberty/domination. Our dominant ideology is oriented toward the right poles of these value continua, although many would deny this. We proclaim that "all men are created equal," but we seem to live by the premise that individuals, groups, classes, and peoples are intrinsically unequal in worth and are consequently entitled to unequal shares of resources, goods, and services, and to unequal social, civil, and political rights. We affirm the sanctity of all life, commend "community spirit," and condemn selfishness in our religious and philosophical traditions, but we do not seem to value the lives and individuality of others. We easily disregard community concerns and interests, and we seem to accept selfishness as a guiding principle of everyday life and human relations. We teach children in homes and schools to share and cooperate, but nearly all domains of adult existence are permeated by acquisitiveness and competitiveness. We are enthusiastic advocates of liberty and "human rights" as abstract principles, but we do not hesitate to dominate and exploit other individuals, classes, races, and peoples, and to use them as means to our needs.

Realization of Fundamental Human Needs

Having reviewed the prevailing patterns of basic social processes and their corresponding ideological tendencies, it is now possible to examine whether fundamental human needs can be realized, and innate human capacities can unfold freely, within the established social order of the United States. Such an examination serves as an "acid test" of institutional violence in any society.

The fundamental, interrelated needs we are concerned with here are needs for (a) basic material goods and services, (b) meaningful human relations conducive to the emergence of a positive sense of identity, (c) meaningful and creative participation in socially valued productive processes, (d) a sense of security, and (e) self-actualization.

Basic Material Goods and Services. Analysis of our institutional and ideological context revealed that large segments of the population now lack access to an adequate level of basic goods and services because they do not own and control sufficient means of production, and because they do not possess unconditional rights to gainful employment and adequate income. The debilitating, dehumanizing, and alienating consequences of unemployment and poverty frustrate the realization of the material needs of millions of individuals and households, and therefore inhibit their healthy development.

Meaningful Human Relations. Next, the analysis revealed many obstacles to meaningful, mutually caring human relations which are conducive to the development of a positive sense of identity, in places of work, and in other public settings as well as in people's homes. These obstacles derive largely from pervasive, structurally induced competition for employment, promotions, preferred positions, conditions, and opportunities.

Meaningful human relations are usually not possible among individuals who are unequal in prestige, status, and power, and who evaluate, use, and control one another as means in the pursuit of selfish ends. Meaningful relations are unlikely to develop when households function as separate economic units, each trying to survive as well as possible in a noncooperative way of life. Finally, meaningful relations are often undermined in the private domain when people's developmental energy is blocked in the public domain, and when they react to the frustrations of everyday life through interpersonal violence in intimate relations.

Meaningful and Creative Participation in Socially Valued Productive Processes. This is beyond the expectations of most people when (a) employment is not assured; (b) most available jobs are designed as fragmented meaningless routines, to be performed in alienating, oppressive, and exploiting conditions; and (c) child care, socialization, and formal schooling result inevitably in massive underdevelopment of innate human capacities.

A Sense of Security. This tends to emerge when people's needs for goods and services, for meaningful human relations, and for meaningful participation in society's productive endeavors can be realized regularly. Because these needs were shown to be unrealizable in the context of prevailing societal dynamics and values, few individuals can be expected to develop a genuine sense of security and, indeed, many suffer a nagging sense of insecurity.

Self-actualization. Self-actualization is usually not possible for people whose material, relational, developmental, and security needs are unrealizable. Given the factors articulated above, it is clear that few individuals can be expected to realize their need for self-actualization.

The foregoing analysis suggests that life in the United States now involves widespread frustration of people's intrinsic needs. When individuals live under such conditions, their innate capacities do not usually unfold freely and fully and their development is consequently stunted. Accordingly, our society and its established institutional order appears to be a development-inhibiting or people-abusing social environment. This fact is often acknowledged with respect to people living in poor and low-income homes. Paradoxically, this is also true, though in differ-

ent ways, for people living in middle-income and affluent homes. Material adequacy and affluence do not by themselves lead directly to the realization of relational, developmental, security, and self-actualization needs, as they cannot insulate individuals from the dehumanizing effects of inegalitarian, selfish, competitive, exploitative, and antagonistic patterns of everyday life.

Institutional Violence and the U.S. Legal System

Throughout history, the ultimate sources blocking spontaneous unfolding of human potential have been those social, economic, legal, and political structures which result in inequalities in status, power, and rights. All social formations—from patriarchy and slavery through feudalism, capitalism, imperialism, and totalitarianism—which involve such inequalities as a basis for domination and exploitation are, therefore, intrinsically violent. They violate the individual development of their members and bring forth violent reactions from oppressed individuals and groups.

Like all social systems involving structural inequalities, capitalism originated in, and is sustained by, overt and covert forces. Its major inequalities, as shown in the foregoing analysis of the social order of the United States, are the division of the population into property-controlling minorities and propertyless majorities, as well as related divisions by income, occupation, education, residence, sex, age, race, origin, and so on.

Human societies were not always divided into propertied and propertyless classes. Whenever and wherever this division evolved, it was established not voluntarily, but through coercive processes. Only then did it become institutionalized as "law and order," rationalized and justified through religion, philosophy, legal theory, and ideology, and transmitted and stabilized through processes of socialization and social control. The maintenance of this human-created division continues to depend upon subtle forms of coercion and, not infrequently, on overt violence.

In a formal sense, the United States is a political, but not an economic, democracy. Throughout our history we have secured important civil and political rights and liberties, though they are not always observed in practice. Many observers suggest, however, that our political system, like all capitalist states, is in fact a subtle dictatorship of propertied minorities over majorities who would not consent voluntarily to exist under conditions of oppression, exploitation, deprivation, and poverty, unless the minorities were able to maintain and defend the established order through ideological hegemony, socialization, and, as a last resort, through "legitimate" force and coercion by the military, the police, and various secret services (Milibrand, 1969).

The fact that people in the United States periodically elect legislators and executives does not mean that they can choose freely between the established capitalist system and an egalitarian alternative system. People now decide only who will govern the established order, not whether to maintain or to change that order. The latter issue is beyond our present political agenda. Groups which intend to place this choice on the political agenda encounter fierce resistance and repression. Moreover, election campaigns are costly, and candidates lacking personal wealth who challenge the interests of propertied classes are unlikely to secure the necessary financial support to campaign for political office. Also, wealthy advertisers, to a large extent, control the communications media. Political groups opposed to capitalism therefore face severe obstacles to the dissemination of their ideas through the media.

The Constitution of the United States and our legal system are important tools towards preserving and reproducing the established, inegalitarian–abusive social order and its skewed distribution of power and wealth. Property rights are guaranteed by the Constitution while no comparable guarantees exist for the fulfillment of people's material, relational, developmental, security, and self-actualization needs. Our frequently articulated human rights to development and individuality are not assured through law and the Constitution, and are certainly not implemented in practice. Under prevailing conditions, for large segments of the population, these rights are nothing but abstractions—a fiction and a myth.

The philosophy of equality and liberty that permeates the Declaration of Independence did not shape the Constitution. Rather, our Constitution accepts and protects inequalities of wealth and of wealth-related rights—the major sources of institutional violence in our society. Symbolic of this shift in philosophy is a provision of the Constitution wherein slavery is acknowledged implicitly, and the value of "other persons" is set as three-fifths of "free persons." Though this

dehumanizing and blatantly violent provision is no longer in force, and though a Bill of Rights and other important amendments were added, the Constitution continues to uphold inequalities of wealth and associated social and political inequalities, and does not guarantee the fulfillment of people's developmental needs. Hence, that Constitution, and the legal system derived from it, maintains institutional violence, whether or not the framers intended these results.

PSYCHOLOGICAL ABUSE IN AGENCIES AND SETTINGS OF SOCIALIZATION

Given the inegalitarian structures, values, and dynamics of the prevailing way of life in the United States and the related intensity of human abuse, psychological and other forms of abuse may be expected to pervade agencies and settings of socialization. Abuse is likely to be more prevalent and intense in settings serving children from socially and economically disadvantaged groups than in settings serving children from privileged groups.

In accordance with the general conception of human abuse developed for this study, abuse in socialization settings is a function of socially maintained conditions in these settings which tend to inhibit optimum physical, intellectual, social, and emotional maturation. Such conditions are incompatible with the unfolding of children's innate, rich capacities, and the emergence of a positive sense of identity, competence, belonging, and security, and instead may cause children to develop a poor self-image and a sense of inadequacy, hopelessness, mistrust, and powerlessness. Such outcomes tend to occur when the "social purpose" of socialization settings is to promote conformity and adaptation to prevailing, inegalitarian social and economic realities rather than free and full development of innate talents and capacities. When the social purpose is not even "average functioning" but merely social control and custodial care, as is the case in many settings for neglected, dependent, and delinquent children, then the intensity of abuse is more severe, and the outcome for children is, at best, marginal.

It follows that the key variable of socialization settings, which determines the extent of abuse they inflict upon children, is the social purpose or the social expectations which permeate their material and nonmaterial milieu, their brick and mortar, their architecture, the mentality of their personnel, and their policies and practices (Gil, 1974). When that purpose and these expectations are optimum human development, and when the resources, policies, and practices of a setting match that purpose, then the level of abuse is near zero and children will tend to develop in accordance with their capacities. Conversely, when the purpose and expectations, and corresponding resources, policies, and practices, are not geared toward full human development but toward a more realistic goal reflective of a way of life involving human abuse, then the setting will be more-or-less abusive towards the children in its care, and one should not be surprised when many children fail to actualize their innate potential.

When these criteria are applied to socialization settings across the United States, one finds that only a small portion of these settings are actually oriented toward optimum development of children. These settings serve mainly children of privileged classes who are being prepared for leading roles in economic, political, professional, scientific, and cultural domains. Among these settings are elite boarding schools and colleges and public schools in high-income residential areas. However, even in these settings, psychological and other forms of abuse are not negligible, for these settings tend to be highly competitive, and they tend to define success in narrow, materialistic terms. They also subtly promote ideological and behavioral conformity, and their tolerance for individuality is frequently limited. There are thus development-inhibiting tendencies operating in the milieu of these elite settings, which means that even children of privileged groups may not escape the consequences of institutional abuse.

The social purpose and expectations of the main body of schools in the United States, the schools which serve the children of the middle and working classes, which means the vast majority of our children, are shaped largely by the realities of the established organization of work and production. In other words, these schools are preparatory settings for the prevailing work system. Their social purpose is, therefore, to mold the minds and bodies of children so that they will adjust without too much conflict to the uncertain, constantly changing demands of the "marketplace." Since that market has only limited demand for the vast creative potential innate to every generation of children, schools tend to waste and suppress much of that

potential. When parents, professionals, and the public blame schools for what seem to be "poor academic results," their complaints should be directed at the social system behind the schools, for schools are not independent agencies, and are not free to disregard the societal context which shapes their reality and the social purpose implicit in that reality. In terms of that reality and purpose, the schooling system is actually highly successful. Its intrinsic mission is to serve as a transmission belt to feed successive generations of children into a dehumanizing marketplace. This mission is now carried out through large doses of abuse via the combined effects of the structures, values, and dynamics of existing mass settings of socialization (Gil, 1979).

When we finally inquire into the social purpose and expectations of schools and agencies which serve children of marginal population groups, of poor people, of irregular and migrant workers, and of recipients of public assistance, we are forced to conclude that that purpose is to prepare the next generation of socially marginal people, or in the apt terms of a keen observer of these settings, "processing for unfitness" (Liazos, 1970). While the abusive practices of mainstream schools and socialization settings promote at least a fit between graduates and market demands, the abusive practices of facilities serving poor children and those children labeled "neglected, dependent, delinquent," and so forth result in unfitness instead. As graduates of these settings, many of these severely abused individuals will exist at the bottom of our socially and economically stratified society, and, in turn, will produce the "surplus" people of subsequent generations. As long as a society requires marginal strata of surplus people for its particular mode of existence, the dynamics of stratified socialization invariably reproduce such an underclass. The intensely abusive dynamics which permeate schools and facilities serving children in the United States are concrete tools for the reproduction of this underclass.

INTERVENTIONS: OVERCOMING AND REDUCING INSTITUTIONAL ABUSE

Analysis of the sources and dynamics of human abuse in the institutional order and dominant ideology of the United States suggests that overcoming abuse and violence, whatever their forms and settings, requires political rather than merely professional interventions. The transformation of our society into a nonviolent one requires redesigning and reconstructing our social, economic, political, and cultural institutions in accordance with egalitarian, cooperative, and genuinely democratic values. In such a transformed society, everyone would be considered equal in worth, in spite of individual differences, and all would be entitled to participate in production and to satisfy their needs out of society's collectively created wealth. Domination and exploitation in human relations, on local and global levels, would be eliminated, and the globe's natural resources would be protected and considered the shared life base of humankind.

Such revolutionary transformations seem necessary to assume survival of the human species and prevent mutual destruction of fiercely competing peoples. Yet, these transformations will not be accomplished through brief, cataclysmic events, but through extended political processes involving social movements working for changes in consciousness, practice, and human relations, and committed to comprehensive liberation on a global scale.

While these long-range political goals will have to be pursued energetically in order to create a way of life conducive to human development for all, the following significant social reforms can and should be put on the political agenda right now, in order to reduce the scope of human abuse and suffering as quickly as possible.

First, an unconditional, legal right should be established for all individuals to participate in meaningful ways in socially necessary production, irrespective of fluctuations in the aggregate scope of production. Workers should be entitled to wages compatible with a decent standard of living as measured by the Bureau of Labor Statistics. To assure an unconditional right to work, Congress would have to adjust the legal length of the work day or work week to assure a continuous match between the number of available workers and the actual number of work positions in public and private enterprises. And, to assure adequate wages, Congress would have to adjust and link the minimum wage level to the actual costs of a decent standard of living (Gil, 1983).

A further necessary policy, linked to the right to work, involves a redefinition of the concept of work. The concept would be expanded to include child care by parents, and care of sick and handicapped individuals by relatives. Once these socially necessary functions are considered part of our national product (GNP), people performing them—mothers, fathers, and other related individuals—would be entitled to decent wages and would not be forced to seek other work or subsist on public welfare. Their wages would be paid out of general revenues analogous to the wages of all individuals performing public service functions. This policy is not meant to force parents to care for their children, but to provide an opportunity and a choice to do so whenever they prefer child care work to other options.

Next, legislation should establish an unconditional income guarantee at levels compatible with an adequate standard of living. This income guarantee would be for individuals who are unable to benefit from the right to work because of age, illness, or handicapping conditions. To round out this set of policy reforms aimed at reducing institutional abuse, a universal, comprehensive health maintenance system, focused on prevention and cure, should be established by law and maintained through general revenues. Such a system should also provide family planning services and abortions.

A fair, loophole-free progressive tax on income and wealth is needed to implement the foregoing set of policies. Such a tax system should allow a tax-free basic income at the level of an adequate standard of living. Earned or unearned income above that level and wealth should be subject to a progressive tax. Special-interest loopholes should be eliminated and regressive sales taxes and the regressive social security system should be phased out as the proposed tax reforms are implemented. It should be noted that the functions of social security would be superseded by the work and income guarantees and by the health maintenance system.

The policies sketched here are feasible, though not easily attainable, within the prevailing social, economic, and political order. They do not require changes in the U.S. Constitution. They merely require appropriate acts of Congress. As demonstrated by countries like Sweden, policies similar to those proposed can work within the context of capitalist, political democracies. While privileged classes in the United States are likely to resist such policies vehemently, progressive forces committed to a humanistic, nonabusive society should nevertheless pursue these reforms energetically in the political arena.

It is important to note here that the policies proposed above as steps toward the reduction of institutional human abuse do not involve real costs to the national economy but merely a significant redistribution of claims to the goods and services produced in our economy. Hence, the political argument which will certainly be raised, that we cannot afford these policies since they are too costly, is simply not valid. Not only do these policies cost nothing in aggregate economic terms, but they are also likely to generate, over time, considerable benefits in economic, social, and psychological terms. Their only costs are political, since the tax reforms on which these policies depend involve challenges to vested interests of privileged classes.

To conclude this sketch of strategies for overcoming and reducing institutional abuse, the assumptions underlying this exploration should be recalled. The basic assumption is that coercively established and maintained inequalities within and among social groups are constant sources of institutional and personal abuse and violence. This suggests that elimination of socially maintained inequalities should lead toward the elimination of violent and abusive acts and conditions, and reductions of inequalities should result in corresponding reductions of violence and abuse. The proposed policy reforms—the right to work and to decent wages, the expanded definition of work and the corresponding entitlement to decent wages for parents caring for children and relatives caring for sick and handicapped individuals, the income guarantee for nonworkers, the universal health maintenance system, and the comprehensive tax reforms—all would result in significant reductions of inequalities of social statuses and rights. These policy shifts would completely eliminate the current underclass of marginal and surplus people and with it would disappear the most abusive socialization facilities identified in this study. Furthermore, since the proposed policies would over time cause major changes in the organization and quality of work and in working conditions, mainstream schools which prepare children for the world of work will inevitably undergo significant modifications and will become less wasteful of human capacities, and hence less abusive in their impact on children.

It follows that just as violence breeds further violence through chain reactions, reductions of coercively created and maintained social inequalities should initiate reverse chain reactions, resulting in a gradual reduction of institutional abuse throughout society. Should we eventually

generate sufficient political commitment and courage to overcome all social inequalities from our way of life, there is little doubt but that institutional abuse would decline even further, and would ultimately vanish altogether.

REFERENCES

Baran, P. A., & Sweezy, P. (1966). *Monopoly capital*. New York: Monthly Review Press.

Benedict, R. (1970, June). Synergy: Patterns of the good culture. *Psychology Today, 4*, 53–55, 74–77.

Bowles, S., & Gintis, H. (1976). *Schooling in capitalist America*. New York: Basic Books.

Braverman, H. (1974). *Labor and monopoly capital*. New York: Monthly Review Press.

Dewey, J. (1935). *Liberalism and social action*. New York: G. P. Putnam's Sons.

Fromm, E. (1941). *Escape from freedom*. New York: Rinehart and Co.

Fromm, E. (1955). *The sane society*. Greenwich, CT: Fawcett.

Gil, D. G. (1973, 1981). *Unravelling social policy* (3rd ed.). Cambridge: Schenkman.

Gil, D. G. (1974). Institution for children. In A. L. Schoor (Ed.), *Children and decent people*. New York: Basic Books.

Gil, D. G. (1979). The hidden success of schooling in the United States. *The Humanist*, November–December, *39*(6), 32–37.

Gil, D. G. (1983). Rethinking strategies against unemployment (rev. version of "100 × 8 = 114.3 × 7"). *Socialist Forum, 4*, 112–113.

Hunt, E. K., & Sherman, H. J. (1981). *Economics*. New York: Harper and Row.

Liazos, A. (1970). *Processing for unfitness*. Unpublished doctoral dissertation, Brandeis University.

Maslow, A. H. (1970). *Motivation and personality*. New York: Harper and Row.

Milibrand, R. (1969). *The state in capitalist society*. New York: Basic Books.

Pope John Paul II (1982). *On human work—Laborem exercens*. Boston: Daughters of St. Paul.

Shaberoff, P. (1980, October 19). Attacks on social spending called a threat to the poor. *The New York Times*, p. 24.

Turnbull, C. M. (1972). *The mountain people*. New York: Simon and Schuster.

U.S. Congress. (1976). *Study for Joint Economic Committee, estimating social costs of national economic policy*. Washington, DC: U.S. Government Printing Office.

U.S. Department of Health, Education, and Welfare. (1972). *Work in America*. Cambridge, MA: MIT Press.

13

Living in Dangerous Environments

Ofra Ayalon with Elizabeth Van Tassel

After midnight on May 15, 1974, three armed Palestinian terrorists raided an apartment in a small Israeli border town. They killed the father, his pregnant wife, and a 4-year-old boy. The surviving 5-year-old daughter almost bled to death from her gunshot wounds. Many years later, she still could not get over the disturbing memory of the man with the gun who had a broad smile on his face as he was shooting the "fire into her belly."

A few hundred yards away a group of over 100 teenagers from a nearby town were camping in a school building. Within minutes they were taken hostage by the same armed terrorists, who held the youths at gunpoint, shot their legs, used them as sandbags in the windows, thwarted their attempts to help and nourish wounded friends, and threatened to kill them. Before the terrorists were killed by the military rescue force, they had executed 22 youngsters and wounded 56. Five years later, catastrophic expectations still haunted a girl who had survived. "Night after night I imagine hearing the announcer on the radio saying: a survivor of the Ma'alot massacre was saved again from yet another terrorist attack. . . ."

A month prior to the Ma'alot massacre, three terrorists crossed the Lebanese border into an Israeli town. They ransacked every apartment in two adjacent buildings, shooting everybody in sight. Eighteen residents (eight women, eight children, and two men) were killed that morning. On the top floor, the military rescuers found a blood-stained 8-year-old girl hiding in the closet, her dead puppy clasped tightly in her arms. On the floor, dead, were her mother, sister, and two brothers. "I tried to stop their blood with my hands," she gasped, "but mother told me to hide, lest they will find out that I was not dead and come back. . . ."

On April 8, 1980, three armed terrorists invaded a children's home in a kibbutz. They tied up the only adult, a babysitter for two of the infants, killed another 1-year-old, and held the babies and toddlers at gunpoint for the rest of the night. At some point they asked for and received a fresh supply of milk, which they never fed to the children. By morning the perpetrators were lying dead on the floor, as the rescuers freed the panicked children. Upon reunion with their parents, the main complaint of the 3-year-olds concerned their despair that their parents had been unable to come to their relief. Their world of security and trust had been shattered.

Dror (1973) defines terrorist activities as acts imposing enormous terror on random populations by insane groups acting outside the law. Terrorists use murder, physical assault, and threat. They abuse their victims to extort some gain from a third party, such as a target state, or to attract the attention of the mass media (Hacker, 1976; Jenkins, 1982). Terrorists frequently strike societies that place a high value on individual human lives, and they often choose particularly treasured groups, such as children, as their victims (Ayalon & Soskis, 1986).

The targeted victims are trapped, because they cannot predict the assault nor strike back. The inability to foresee such events or to prevent them makes terrorism a constant threat that increases victims' vulnerability and anxiety. Terrorization, like militant acts, engenders extreme stress in victims through direct threats. Stress is perpetuated by (a) threats to one's own life; (b) threats of injury, pain, and disability; (c) threats to kin (being hurt themselves or separated from them); and (d) threats to one's values and self-image (Lazarus, 1966).

In a terrorist attack, such as hostage taking, two more factors combine to escalate the stress: the uncertainty (Rachman, 1978) and the total helplessness of the victim (Seligman, 1975). In the hostage situation, the ability of the victim to deny images of their death is reduced abruptly (Ochberg & Soskis, 1982).

Such persecutions demand from victims behavioral as well as emotional responses that are not available in most individuals' or groups' repertoires of reactions. They are followed by short- and long-term posttraumatic stress disorders and personality changes (American Psychiatric Association, 1980).

FACTORS INFLUENCING THE MANNER OF COPING WITH TERRORISM

The concept of coping has lost its meaning due to imprecise word usage, lumping together both adequate and inadequate stress reactions. However, the success of any coping reaction must be judged primarily by its results, namely its contribution to the survivor's well-being during the four critical phases of stress: the warning phase, the actual occurrence, the immediate recovery, and the long-range phase of adaptation.

Coping is a survival formula. As such, it is a process including any behavior that proves effective in canceling or reducing the physical or the psychological threat and that also leads to management of self and others in gaining control over the situation. The nature of coping lies in its flexibility to change with the changing circumstances and with the duration of each phase.

Lazarus (1976) has provided a classification of adult stress reactions, dividing them into five categories, which convey action, underlying emotions, and defensive aims:

- flight in fear, the aim of which is the elimination of threat;

- fight in anger, which is geared to attacking the stressor or its representatives;
- immobility in panic, which takes the form of paralysis of thought and action, designed to avoid anxiety, often resulting from conflicting drives;
- resourcefulness, which through an active search for alternatives is sometimes successful in converting the threat into a challenge for change, growth, and achievement; and
- intrapersonal palliative strategies, which are employed to moderate distress when action fails. These are mental acts that reduce the threat not in reality but in the mind of the individual.

The degree of adaptivity of any stress reaction is assessed according to the immediate circumstances and to its effectiveness over time. Coping reactions that prove adaptive at one phase may have deleterious after-effects. In some of the cases flight turned out to be the most appropriate reaction for saving the lives of the fugitives. But for many, flight, which terminated one stress, created a new one—the stress of long-lasting and unrelieved guilt for having abandoned their fellows and having been saved at their expense. Another example of this "boomerang" effect is evident in the shame and self-rejection experienced by some survivors who had initiated contact and conversation with their captors. They later consider this behavior as repellent and humiliating, in the light of retrospective knowledge of the terrorists' murderous acts.

The choice of stress reaction is partly determined by personal and ecological factors, directly influenced by situational characteristics. While adaptive coping is nourished by intellectual resources and ego strength, its effects may be curbed by lack of social support, previous adverse experience, emotional disturbance, guilt feelings, high anxiety, and a sense of being dwarfed by authority (Wolfenstein, 1957).

PATTERNS OF SURVIVAL IN VICTIMIZED CHILDREN AND ADOLESCENTS

A previous study (Ayalon, 1983) on the effects of terrorist attacks on Israeli children explored the social ecology that contributed to the children's vulnerability and resilience. During the years 1974–1980, 14 terrorist raids involving the capture and killing of hostages were launched against Israeli civilian targets. Scrutinizing the immediate and the long-term community responses, it was found that responses varied along the dimensions of pretraumatic levels of organization, cohesiveness, self-reliance, and sense of purpose. Adaptive responses occurred in communities that were small, homogeneous, well established, autonomous, and self-reliant (e.g., kibbutzim). Adaptive community responses did not occur in communities overburdened with stresses of acculturation, alienation, economic difficulties, and political inferiority. In these communities (usually towns of new immigrants), the immediate effects of the terrorist attacks were much more severe. These communities also paid a much greater toll in loss of life (Ayalon, 1982).

The children involved in these 14 face-to-face assaults ranged in age from 5 months to 16 years. They were taken hostage, were brutalized, witnessed the murder of their parents, siblings and schoolmates, were injured, and a great many were killed while held captive.

Data on survivors' reactions and rehabilitation were drawn from a longitudinal follow-up study, using clinical case material, observations, interventions, surveys, psychosocial questionnaires, drawings, and interviews. The data were collected at three crucial phases of the children's predicament: the onset of the crisis, the rehabilitation in the wake of the crisis (usually after a military rescue operation), and 5–8 years later.

Immediate Response to the Onset of the Terrorist Attack

Fight. Fighting back is scarce in reported terrorist attacks (Schrieber, 1978). Fantasies of fighting were reported by a few adolescent hostages who planned a "suicide rescue operation" and managed to snatch a knife from a captor's bag. It is impossible to predict the adaptability of such plans, as they were nipped in the bud by the bewildered resistance of the rest of the group.

Flight. Flying from captors at the onset of attack was feasible in many cases, but was practiced by only a few. One 8-year-old girl overcame her initial confusion and paralysis and managed to escape her slaughtered mother's and siblings' fate by hiding in a closet. A 16-year-old girl hid from her captors in the bathroom, then found shelter under a corpse during the rescue raid,

and finally threw herself from a second-floor window, in spite of having been wounded. Seventeen students escaped from the terrorists by jumping out of the windows, following their fleeing teachers. The same happened in another attacked town; a 15-year-old boy jumped from a third-floor window, followed by his 14-year-old brother, and then by more children and adults. The decision to escape also was charged with a conflict between a life-preserving tendency and a sense of responsibility toward others. Some hostages refrained from fleeing because they felt responsible for younger siblings.

In all the above-mentioned cases, the children were on their own, the responsible adults being either missing or dead. Interviews after a couple of years with the same children revealed a mixture of a sense of self-reliance with shame and guilt over having been spared the hardship of their classmates, but less guilt was apparent than that admitted by those children who escaped totally unharmed after the rescue operation.

Paralysis and Panic. Among the overt manifestations of panic were screaming, crying, and trembling fits, running around aimlessly, loss of bladder control, and fainting. The word "panic" was used repeatedly in the interviews to convey "unbearable horror." Freezing was described by survivors as a temporary loss of voluntary mobility of limbs or tongue, accompanied by total numbing of thoughts and feeling. For example, a 5-year-old girl in Ma'alot who had witnessed the slaughter of her family and was severely wounded, described herself later as been "turned to stone," unable to move or feel any pain. One 8-year-old girl said she felt "stunned and unable to take even one step toward my dying mother and sister lying there on the floor crying for help." The shock and paralysis took quite a time to wear off.

Palliative Modes of Coping. When all avenues of escape were closed and the stress was prolonged over a period of time, other patterns of managing stress arose. Omens and portents, along with magical, superstitious thinking, served as mechanisms to "restore some order and logic to the children's disrupted world-image" (Terr, 1979).

As almost no support was available from peers and very scant information from the outside, captives withdrew into fantasies and memories of childhood, parents, and friends back home. These served to distract their attention from the present misery and to provide the badly lacking warmth of trusted figures.

Support and solace were sought in appealing to God's help and saying prayers, which were in tune with these children's religious upbringing. There were individual differences in the conviction with which religious rituals were followed and relied upon. One girl, who found a prayer book in her pocket, urged others to pray. "Two girls refused to say their prayers and now they are among the dead," she concluded.

Parental dictums and warnings were elicited in half-delusional states. One girl claimed to have heard her father's voice in her dream, instructing her to say thanksgiving to the Lord for saving her. She was convinced that this was an omen that predicted her rescue. Another teenager attributed her good luck to paternal instructions: "My father had told me always to sit in a corner when there is trouble. So I did, never moved from the wall." Some youngsters felt that they were being punished for some sins, particularly for disobeying their parents by going on that trip. Desperate attempts at repentance took the form of confessions and asking for absolution, bargaining and taking vows to reform, promises for contribution to charity and for complete obedience to God and parents. Pleas for divine support were common under threat of death.

Resourcefulness. As stress lingered on, new patterns of active coping emerged, characterized by role taking and altruistic behavior. Some activities took much courage—serving as sandbags at the windows, shielding others from bullets, or even planning a suicidal rescue attempt. One girl, age 17, who in particular seemed to have tried to gain more control than most, committed risky endeavors by shielding the terrorists against bullets from the outside while they were negotiating and by jolting the muzzle of one of their guns away from an outside negotiator. On other occasions she attempted to establish contact with the rescue forces.

Only a few individuals summoned enough energy to be active—caring for the wounded and comforting and nurturing the others. The activities seemingly served to distract them from the overwhelming fears as well as benefiting the others.

The benefit of activity under stress is paramount (Gal & Lazarus, 1975). Those who mus-ter the energy to be active gain a sense of purpose, or at least succeed in distracting their thoughts from their ill fate. In spite of its obvious advantages, it seems that only a few people spontaneously initiate activity under extreme stress of this kind (see also Jacobson, 1973).

Contact with Captors. Deciphering the captors' facial expressions became vital to victims. Eyes and mouth became salient features for predicting potential dangers. The Ma'alot hostages were subjected to the effects of their captors' gazes: "I was overwhelmed by his terrible eyes, which looked through me, reducing me to nothing. I felt his looks could kill," or else, "I could not believe he would do me any harm after I had looked into his eyes." But prediction failed for one 5-year-old survivor who watched an armed stranger smiling at her face while firing his bullets into her belly.

When the terrorists seemed less tense, a couple of hostages ventured to talk to them. One girl approached them boldly, challenging their murderous intentions as contradictory to their religion. Engaging in conversation with those "in utter control" seemed to have helped the girl to regain some feeling of security, especially since she was indulging in the illusion of "talking them out of it." Later she suffered self-deprecatory guilt feelings for "contaminating myself by contact with the murderers of my mates." No conversion signs of positive feelings toward captors were obvious or even conceivable in the situation where victims endured humiliation and abuse (cf. Fields, 1980).

Secondary Victimization

Secondary victimization is a complex phenomenon in which social stigma adheres to the survivors. This phenomenon contains the seed for prolonged or permanent personality injury that will affect the survivor's future. Evidence of secondary victimization were revealed in our follow-up interviews conducted 1–8 years after the terrorist attack. There was a need of the survivor for an enormous amount of compassion and nurturance to compensate for crushed feelings of trust and self-esteem, sometimes complicated by contradictory needs to express pent-up rage and to regain mastery and independence. These needs become harder to satisfy when coupled with secondary injury such as rejection and scapegoating on the part of the community (Symonds, 1980).

Hostility in different guises was experienced by the surviving hostages on their returning home and going back to school. The school authorities' demands for discipline and conformity to norms and regulations bluntly overlooked the special physical and emotional needs of the children. The students, who found concentration an impossible chore, were accused of taking advantage of the situation. On the whole, they were urged to "forget it all and come back to normal" as soon as possible. Peers in school responded with a mixture of curiosity and rejection: "They looked at us as if we were pariahs," complained one of the girls.

Jealousy toward any possible prerogative also was prevalent in the outside circle and among the survivors themselves. Suspicions and accusations were hurled at them and extended to their families as well, accentuating the social isolation. Animosity of the bereaved families toward survivors took pathological forms. For example, a bereaved family whose daughter had been killed cursed and threw stones at a cousin who came back alive from the ordeal. This behavior, which persisted for 2 years, stopped only when this cousin's brother was killed in a military action.

Discrimination, real or imagined, against those who were physically abused aggravated the feelings of ongoing victimization: "I wish they knew how it feels to be captured by terrorists, then maybe they would stop ridiculing and bullying me over my amputated arm," said one 23-year-old male survivor. "They only keep me in my job out of pity."

Social pressures to exhibit the signs of mourning have been exerted on those who tried to shake off their grief: "Whenever I laughed aloud they criticized me," said one of the girls. One 13-year-old complained about his teachers' ignoring his newly acquired fears: "They shouldn't have put me on guard duty at the school gate so soon after what happened. I was shaking with fear." "Children call us names, they think that we are bragging whenever we try to talk about what happened" said a 14-year-old. She continued, "They call us 'chickens' when we show signs of fear. Had they been there. . . ."

Recuperation

Acute symptoms of traumatic neurosis were observed in the children during the first few months. These coincided with Lindemann's

(1944) profile of prolonged traumatic reaction: shock, bewilderment, partial loss of temporal and spatial orientation, preoccupation with catastrophic ideas and images, prolonged grief, crying spells and lability of moods, loss of appetite, and sleep disturbances. The threshold for tolerating noises, darkness, and unexpected movements was temporarily lowered. Some survivors expressed a pronounced self-consciousness, a special mark that sets them apart from other people. This period of immediate recuperation was marked by a compulsive need for repetitive recounting of the experience, as the survivors tried to master anxieties they could not cope with at the time by reliving the event in fantasy. Not heeded and treated, these symptoms may develop into a lasting acute neurosis (Horowitz, 1976; Janis, 1971).

Long-Term Effects on Personality, Identity, and Lifestyle

For most children a normal level of adjustment to age-specific tasks was observed. Children resumed schooling. Adolescents, having finished high school, were drafted into the army if their physical health permitted. Eventually some married and became parents and useful productive people. For a small number of survivors, their plight turned into a lever for special endeavors, such as excellence in military operations and high academic and professional achievements. None drifted into delinquency or became psychotic. Two cases of attempted suicide were reported. But an in-depth follow-up study, which is still ongoing, lends some preliminary findings which scratch beneath this surface. They reveal psychological residuals of the trauma: confusion over identity, lasting anxieties, depressive inclinations, survivor guilt, and tendencies toward social and religious extremes.

One major transformation of self-image noted among the interviewees was an emergence of a "survivor's identity." Whether the new identity was adopted or denied, it became the scale and measure of all ensuing experiences. The most extreme manifestation was provided by a young man who began to sign correspondence using a self-administered title: "Survivor of Ma'alot." Others presented themselves in much the same way in new social contexts. The event and publicity have bestowed a certain halo with which there was a reluctance to part. At the other extreme we found young people who resented being reminded of the events and by no means would agree to be considered a "survivor."

The passing of time has not reduced the impact of the experience. Recurring events of a similar nature in other parts of the country evoked a strong sense of identification with the victims and renewed traumatization. But even without such reminders, a catastrophic expectation of recurrence of the disaster lingers on.

The experience imprinted upon a number of survivors led them to a conviction of having been "chosen for life" by supernatural forces. This has been reinforced by their "good luck" in having survived the ordeal. They have a feeling of immunity, of being protected. For others, the very same experience has been registered as a proof of being guilty and condemned, and consequently of being eligible for further persecution.

"Survivor guilt" was partly attenuated by having been moderately wounded. The injury provided secondary gains and an "atonement to God." Having paid a toll, some children assumed that they would be exempt from further harm.

Other characteristics found among the survivors centered on relations with others. Here, too, dichotomization was found between an attitude of resentment, bordering on paranoid suspicion of others, or an attitude of altruism or self-sacrifice. The first is probably a part of the syndrome of unspent aggressiveness projected on others. The second attitude seems to activate a need for reversing the image of "victim" into the image of the "rescuer," conveying a sense of mastery and control. There is more than a hint of ritualist "appeasement of the Gods" ingrained in these behaviors.

INTERVENTION AND PREVENTION

The arena which seems at first glance to be most appropriate for conducting stress-prevention intervention with children, prior to or following a traumatic event, is the school. The school is a good choice since it encompasses vital peer-group interaction opportunities and the presence of qualified adults.

A large-scale preventive program was developed in the University of Haifa School of Education. The program, called Community Oriented Preparation for Emergency—COPE (Ayalon, 1978, 1979a), is a series of structured, open-ended suggestions for coping activities to develop skills "to grapple effectively with unexpected and temporarily insoluble problems" (Caplan, 1979). In accordance with Caplan's mode of primary, secondary, and tertiary intervention, COPE provides training in (a) generic skills for operating effectively under stress, (b) developing self-trust and tolerance for distress, (c) finding new solutions when the old ones have failed, and (d) developing and employing specific skills required by the situation.

It is proposed that a crucial determinant of the children's ability to cope with stress is the ability to ventilate "unspent emotions," either by talking, drawing, or reenacting the stressful situation. The techniques offered by COPE are varied, flexible, and amenable to change by the program leader. Extensive use is made of ambiguous pictures and photographs, stimuli for role playing and for expressive writing. Carefully chosen short stories and poems are used for the same purpose (Ayalon, 1979b). Several simulation games were specially devised and conveniently packaged into the program. On the whole, the child's language of play and fantasy, creative as well as communicative expressions, are carefully employed to help nurture and strengthen the children's ability to cope with unforeseen stress, and to handle previous grievances. Children are encouraged to work through their feelings using a variety of modes of expression. The focus of training is not only the ventilation of emotion and the development of cognitive problem-solving skills, but also the prompting of a number of specific behavioral skills, such as relaxation and downgrading reactions to fearful stimuli.

Activity is regarded as a most adaptive and appropriate behavior under stress. The COPE program provides opportunities for children to develop an active attitude toward stress, either as a direct attempt at reducing the stressor or using activity as a palliative device for the period of possible confinement.

The COPE model was first implemented during an intensive crisis intervention after a terrorist raid on a community. Two men and two small girls were killed, while the whole neighborhood was caught in gunfire. Psychological services of the school system identified 54 children as the "near-miss high-risk" population. These children manifested acute anxiety states, frightening fantasies, and fear of the dark, of noises, and of the beach (the scene of the crime). Haunted by images of the murdered girls, these children could not concentrate and displayed crying spells, headaches, stomachaches, sleeplessness, and clinging to parents.

A crisis intervention was designed for all these children (8–14 years old), grouped according to age. Each group was conducted by a member of the crisis team for 5 consecutive days, 4 hours each day, within the school setting (Ben-Eli & Sella, 1980).

The intervention consisted of ventilation of affect and working through feelings, facilitated by the use of paint, clay, puppets, creative writing, and dialogue. Relaxation and desensitization were also employed. Guidance was given to the children's parents. The recuperation followed a sequence of stages:

1. *Initial ventilation.* The chaotic expressions of bewilderment and fear, through finger paints, were accompanied by sighs and weeping.

2. *Abreaction.* Rehearsals of the traumatic events, both by narration and role playing, took place as children were beginning to regain control. Some chose to act the roles of the victims while others agreed to be the terrorists, letting themselves be "captured" and "killed."

3. *Channeling of aggression.* Anger and violent emotions discharged through scenarios of vengeance and retaliation against the aggressors. First signs of relief were noticed during a mimicked execution of puppet terrorists. (Worried teachers, who could not tolerate the upsurge of aggression for fear of creating "hate" attitudes in their students, were later much relieved to find out that the angry feelings did not linger long.)

4. *Extinction of phobic reactions.* The extinction of fear reactions to the beach was carried out with the parents' help. Much support and encouragement were needed until the prestress level of confidence was retrieved. One 14-year-old stated: "My father took me to the shore. I saw the terrorists' boat, the rocks on which they smashed the head of the little girl. I regret having seen the boat, it haunts me in my dreams. But I am not afraid of the sea any longer." In addition, gradual exposure to noise has been conducted during relaxation (i.e., desensitization). But the use of imagery has led only to partial relief.

5. *Cognitive reappraisal of the experience.* Road maps and clay models of the scene were created by the children, accompanied by detailed reconstruction of the sequence of events. Participants focused on their recollections, trying to evaluate each reaction in the light of retrospective knowledge: those who hid, others who fled, the girl who stopped to pick up another fleeing little girl, the little one who summoned enough courage to push back her captor and to flee for her life. The children were especially perturbed by what happened to one family, where a mother smothered her little baby trying to hush her crying while the terrorists killed her husband and other daughter. By reappraising this situation, the children reached an understanding that enabled them to make a condolence visit to this bereaved young woman, having come to terms with their ambivalent feelings towards her act.

6. *Acceptance and reconciliation.* At this stage, expression has become more structured. Children regained their writing skills and used them in their struggle to gain mastery over their stormy reflections. They became engaged in a "poetic dialogue," writing poems to each other. Later they published these poems in a memorial format. Drawing changed into illustrative portrayals of the scenery and of the victims. Erecting a memorial signified the beginning of acceptance of the loss.

7. *Mapping alternatives.* Provided with all the information about the event, participants engaged in suggestions for future encounters with threat and danger. The feelings that had been expressed in earlier phases were now channeled into a problem-solving mode designed to consider what could be done differently in future stressful events. By focusing both on working through their feelings of the past trauma and the present and future eventualities, the children slowly "came to terms" with the stress of being near-miss victims.

During this period families were counseled in how to respond to their children. The parents were encouraged to share their own feelings with their children and to work together through the difficult period of recuperation. The reactions subsided gradually and the children resumed their daily activities. The follow-up surveys, at 2 months and at 8 months later, found no persistence of symptoms in any of the children, with a few exceptions for which treatment was resumed. As the survey included a sample of the entire child population of the town, an interesting phenomenon became obvious: The impact of trauma on the children changed depending upon the actual physical distance from the scene of the event. The further the children lived from the site of the attack, the less they were affected (with the exception of a few vulnerable children, who had previously gone through a personal crisis that had been reactivated by the attack).

At a time when social scientists and policy makers argue about preferred strategies to curb world terrorism, we have chosen to shed some light on the fate of the victims. We have tried to understand what determines the behavior of a person who has become a pawn in a gory game not of his or her making. Can such behavior be predicted? Can it be channeled to assist the victims to regain control over their threatened lives? Assessments of psychological damage have been used to determine the amount of compensation due (Eitinger, 1964; Lifton, 1967; Niederland, 1968) and to initiate suitable treatment methods (Fields, 1977; Frankl, 1970; Fraser, 1973; Klein, 1968; Kliman, 1973). We suggest that such assessment be used to study *the potential prevention of the psychic trauma of victimization*. Stress-prevention programs are in their preliminary stages of development and should be researched, modified, and consolidated. As far as we know, no systematic evaluation of such programs has been undertaken with children. Both the challenges and needs are great. The present clinical description of our programs will hopefully stimulate such research.

DEFINITIONS AND BACKGROUND RESEARCH

Few circumstances place a child at greater risk for psychological maltreatment than exposure to dangerous environments. Dangerous environments are defined as conditions which threaten the physical and/or psychological being of the child as well as the child's primary caretakers (Burzynski, 1983). Children in these environments are helpless to alter the dangerous conditions or to escape the threat. Most prominent among these conditions is war. The London Institute for the Study of Conflict has 200 current wars registered in its files. These are only politically defined wars and do not include environmental hazards such as civil strife, terrorists, and racial persecution (P. Janke, personal communication, 1981). Thus, many children in the world are growing up under conditions which are deleterious to both their physical and psychological health.

Children and War

Much of our current knowledge of children's reactions to the severe stressors of war is based on clinical observations made during and after World War II. Grubrich-Simitis (1981) stated that the insight into the psychological trauma suffered by the survivors of war was slow to develop and in fact initially met with resistance. The syndromes of refugee neurosis and repatriation neurosis, among the first labels given to the adult survivors, implied that the trauma suffered by the survivors was comparable to common adjustment problems resulting from environmental change (p. 417). Friedman (1949) was among the first to accurately identify what is now known as posttraumatic stress disorder among the concentration camp survivors he observed during their reimprisonment in Cyprus on their way to Palestine. The syndrome he described included severe psychosomatic and depressive reactions, sexual dysfunctions, flatness of affect, and what would later become known as survivor guilt (Grubrich-Simitis, 1981). He noted that adolescent prisoners showed a marked retardation in their psychosexual development, including regression to infantile dependency, intensification of narcissism, and a revival of early castration anxieties provoked by the perpetual threat of death (Grubich-Simitis, 1981).

Observations of children made in England and in Czechoslovakia, many in the Terezin concentration camp, indicated, however, that children seemed to display fewer psychologically traumatic symptoms than did adults during and after the war (Freud & Burlingham, 1943; Freud & Dann, 1951; Langmeier & Matejcek, 1975). It was noted that among the children who suffered the most severe stresses, many were able to adapt reasonably well in a comparatively short time, although effects such as increased sensitivity and vulnerability to minor environmental change remained (Langmeier & Matejcek, 1975). Critical factors related to adjustment centered on the nature of the trauma, the age of the victim, predisposing personality factors, and most importantly the child's emotional relationship with his family prior to and during the war (Freud & Burlingham, 1943; Langmeier & Matejcek, 1975). Freud and Burlingham (1943), however, cautioned about long-term effects.

> It is a common misunderstanding of the child's nature which leads people to suppose that children will be saddened by the sight of destruction and aggression. . . . Instead of turning away from them in instinctive horror, as people seem to expect, the child may turn towards them with primitive excitement. The real danger is not that the child, caught up all innocently in the whirlpool of the war, will be shocked into illness. The danger lies in the fact that the destruction raging in the outer world may meet the very real aggressiveness which rages in the inside of the child. At the age when education should start to deal with these impulses confirmation should not be given from the outside world that the same impulses are uppermost in other people. Children will play joyfully on bombed sites and around bomb craters, they will play with blasted bits of furniture and throw bricks from crumbled walls at each other. But it becomes impossible to educate them toward a repression and of a reaction against destruction while they are doing so. . . . It must be very difficult for them to accomplish this task of fighting their own death wishes when, at the same time, people are killed around them. Children have to be safeguarded against the primitive horrors of the war, not because horrors and atrocities are so strange to them, but because we want them . . . to overcome and estrange themselves from the primitive and atrocious wishes of their own infantile nature (pp. 21–24).

Recent investigations of children in Ireland, the Middle East, and Israel seem to confirm this notion of resilience and adjustment in children under the stress of war (Fraser, 1973; Heskin, 1980; Kristal, 1978; Lyons, 1971; Milgram & Milgram, 1976; Rofe & Lewin, 1982; Zak, 1982; Ziv, Kruglanski, & Shulman, 1974; Ziv & Israel, 1973); others, however, have not (cf. Fields, 1977). In general, these investigations are few in number and are limited in comparability due to a number of design and methodological problems among the Israeli studies; for example, the use of single assessments (usually of anxiety) as the dependent measure (Garmezy, 1983). Furthermore, the time frame in these studies has been grossly inconsistent: most have taken place in a relatively short time after the impact phase. Studies that would assess the long-term sequelae of war on children controlling for the nature and length of the child's predicament, involvement, and background conditions which may ameliorate or exacerbate the stress reaction simply have not been completed.

Children's Reactions to Specific Acts of Trauma

A small but more systematic body of knowledge has developed around children's reactions to specific acts of trauma. In adults these reactions are defined as posttraumatic stress disorder if they include the following diagnostic criteria: (a) the existence of recognized stressors that evoke significant symptoms of distress in almost anyone; (b) one of the following: recurrent and intrusive recollections of events, recurrent dreams or events, or sudden acting or feeling as if the traumatic event were reoccurring because of an association with an environmental or ideational stimulus; (c) numbing of responses, as displayed by diminished interest in one or more significant activities, feelings of detachment or estrangement or constricted affect; (d) at least two of the following symptoms: hyperalertness and exaggerated startle responses, sleep disturbances, survivor guilt, memory impairment or trouble concentrating, avoidance of activities that arouse recollections of traumatic events, and intensification of symptoms by exposure to events that symbolize or resemble the traumatic event (American Psychiatric Association, 1980, p. 238). In children, a somewhat different constellation of symptoms seems to occur.

Studies on children's reactions to specific but severe trauma, most notably Terr's studies on the kidnapping of the children of Chowchilla (1979, 1981, 1983) and Pynoos and Eth's investigation of children who have witnessed a parent's murder (Eth & Pynoos, 1984) suggested the following additional features: Children display no stress-induced amnesia about the experience and no true flashbacks; they engage in compulsive repetitions such as repeated dreams, posttraumatic play, and unconscious reenactments of acts similar to the traumatic event. Little elaboration or defense appears in the play. Instead of relieving anxiety, play creates more. Play and reenactments do not appear to offer children ways to remove the loss of trust and ways to reassure self that such events will not happen again. Longstanding repeated reenactments take the form of personality changes (Terr, 1979).

There are significant cognitive–perceptual changes, such as (a) distortions of visual or auditory perceptions; (b) durational distortions; (c) time condensations and distortions; (d) omens retrospectively discovered; (e) a sense of prediction or clairvoyance; and (f) a foreshortened sense of the future. Finally, there is the collapse of early developmental accomplishments, specifically the disruption of basic trust and the loss of a sense of autonomy.

Pynoos and Eth (1984) have noted age-related differences not found by Terr (1979). Preschoolers initially appeared withdrawn, subdued, or mute. They reacted with anxious attachment behavior but displayed a short period of sadness due to their limited ability to sustain a dysphoric mood. They were extremely vulnerable to anxiety, as exhibited in self-stimulatory actions, and they commonly engaged in reenactments and posttraumatic play.

School-aged children showed a greater diversity and inconsistency in behavior. They reported somatic complaints as well as poor impulse control and the lost of trust in adult restraint. A decline in school performance was noted. The reactions of adolescents began to resemble the adult posttraumatic disorders.

Coping strategies used by the preadolescent to limit anxiety included (a) denial in fantasy, which lessened the pain by imaginary reversal of outcomes; (b) inhibition of spontaneous thoughts, which worked to avoid reminders of the events; (c) fixations to trauma, usually exhibited as a journalistic recounting of the events and which represented failed attempts at mastery (similar to Terr's description of posttraumatic play); and (d) fantasies of future harm, which may supplant memories of initial events and result in a constriction of memory and activities.

Pynoos and Eth (1984) reported being impressed with children's immediate effort to reverse their helplessness through cognitive reappraisals or mental plans that alter the precipitating events, undo the violent act, reverse the consequence, or gain safe retaliation. Because of

their limited cognitive skills, preschool children do not appear to imagine alternative actions that they might have taken to alter the outcome, and, therefore, were the most helpless. Prompt attention to and discussion of the trauma offers immediate relief for most children and may lessen initial fear and prolonged anxiety (Ayalon, 1983; Terr, 1979). Preschoolers, however, may require time before they are able to verbalize or reenact the episode (Pynoos & Eth, 1984). Engagement in compulsive play and reenactments should be stopped either by interpretation or command (Terr, 1979).

As our knowledge of how children cope and adjust to specific acts of trauma begins to develop, so too does our awareness of other environments, perhaps less dangerous than that of war, that place children under long and continued stress with which they cannot successfully cope. Rutter (1981) has called attention to the psychological problems that tend to occur frequently among children living in cities; Moore (1974) to the effects on the child of multiple, unpredictable, and conflicting caretaking environments; and Eiduson (1983) to the effects of growing up in a nontraditional family lifestyle.

Finally, the stress of living in a world of conflict and fear affects children's coping. In addition to war and strife, there are fears related to pollution, unemployment, economic depression, hunger, and the great possibility of nuclear accidents. Although lacking perhaps in personal intensity, these fears add to the existing stressors of childhood and increase the risk of psychological numbness and immobility, as illustrated by the comments of children after the Three Mile Island nuclear accident:

> I don't look forward to the future. . . . We're all "antsie" these days. . . . There's too much tension, too much hassle. . . . I hope there'll be a lot less unhappiness. . . . Most people will be more caring but not until we have a terrible upheaval. . . . Will people ever be more caring? There is so much tension now from the uncertainty in the world. . . . Maybe if there were no threats of war and a lot of other things, people would have friendlier interactions. . . . America is going down the drain, people just don't get along. . . . I'm outraged that leaders can consider the world's population expendable. . . . Yet what can we do? (Schwebel & Schwebel, 1981, p. 269).

DANGEROUS ENVIRONMENTS AND PSYCHOLOGICAL MALTREATMENT

The numbness and immobility expressed by these children appear to have spread to researchers as well. There can be no doubt that dangerous environments place children at risk for all seven acts of psychological maltreatment described in chapter 1 of this volume. The neglect of research in this area, especially in comparison to the many investigations of adults, appears to constitute an eighth act of maltreatment, defined by Lifton as "selective professional numbing"—a detachment that develops in researchers in order to investigate painful subjects, among the most painful of whom are young victims (Totten & Totten, 1984). Lifton sums up the problems of research in this area succinctly.

I was absolutely amazed to find that 15 years after this tragic turning point in human history, nobody had studied it. . . . I've often thought of that as one of my major discoveries, the absence of a study. You see, I've observed that it's easy to study trivial issues—but really threatening, highly significant problems are usually too hot for scholars to address. . . . There are two reasons for this I think. One is that they're disturbing and frightening. And another reason is that investigators don't like to have their assumptions questioned. . . . For me, working in Hiroshima meant examining and re-examining and recreating a whole body of ideas about death, death symbolism, and the symbols of the continuity of life (Totten & Totten, 1984, pp. 81–82).

REFERENCES

American Psychiatric Association. (1980). *Diagnostic and statistical manual of mental disorders* (3rd ed.). Washington, DC: American Psychiatric Association.

Ayalon, O. (1978). *Rescue! A teachers guide for coping with emergencies*, Issum. Com. University of Haifa (Hebrew).

Ayalon, O. (1979a). Community oriented preparation for emergency: C.O.P.E. *Death Education, 3,* 227–245.

Ayalon, O. (1979b). Is death a proper subject for the classroom? *International Journal of Social Psychiatry, 25,* 252–258.

Ayalon, O. (1982). Children as hostages. *The Practitioner, 226,* 1773–1781.

Ayalon, O. (1983). Coping with terrorism: The Israeli Case. In D. Meichenbaum and M. Jaremko, (Eds.), *Stress reduction and prevention* (pp. 293–340). New York: Plenum.

Ayalon, O., & Soskis, D. (1986). Survivors of terrorist victimization: A follow-up study. In N. Milgram (Ed.), *Stress and Coping in Time of War: Generalizations from the Israeli Experience.* New York: Brunner/Mazel.

Ben-Eli, Z., & Sella, M. (1980). Terrorists in Nahariya. *Journal of Psychology and Counseling in Education, 13* (Hebrew).

Burzynski, P. (1983, August). *Psychological effects of living in dangerous environments.* Paper presented at International Conference on the Psychological Abuse of Children and Youth, Indianapolis, IN.

Caplan, G. (1979). *Mastery of stress: Psychological aspects.* Paper presented at International Congress of Psychosomatic Medicine, Jerusalem.

Dror, Y. (1973). *Crazy states.* Israel Ministry of Defence Publication (Hebrew).

Eiduson, B. T. (1983). Conflict and stress in non-traditional families: Impact on children. *American Journal of Orthopsychiatry, 53,* 426–435.

Eitinger, L. (1964). *Concentration camp survivors in Norway and Israel.* Oslo: Universitetsforlaget.

Eth, S., & Pynoos, R. (1984). Developmental perspectives on psychic trauma in childhood. In C. R. Figley (Ed.), *Trauma and its wake.* New York: Brunner–Mazel.

Fields, R. (1977). *Society under siege.* Philadelphia: Temple University Press.

Fields, R. (1980). Victims of terrorism: The effects of prolonged stress. *Evaluation and Change,* pp. 76–83.

Frankl, V. (1970). *Man's search for meaning.* New York: Touchstone.

Fraser, M. (1973). *Children in conflict.* New York: Basic Books.

Freud, A., & Burlingham, D. (1943). *War and children.* New York: Foster Parents' Plan for War Children, Inc.

Freud, A., & Dann, S. (1951). An experiment in group upbringing. *Psychoanalytic Study of the Child, 6,* 127–168.

Friedman, P. (1949). Some aspects of concentration camp psychology. *American Journal of Psychiatry, 105,* 601–606.

Gal, R., & Lazarus, R. (1975). The role of activity in anticipating and confronting stressful situations. *The Journal of Human Stress,* pp. 4–20.

Garmezy, N. (1983). Stresses of childhood. In M. Garmezy & M. Rutter (Eds.), *Stress coping &*

development in children (pp. 43–84). New York: McGraw-Hill.

Grubrich-Simitis, I. (1981). Psychoanalytic investigations of the effects of concentration camp experiences on survivors and their children. *Psychoanalytic Study of the Child, 36,* 415–450.

Hacker, R. H. (1976). *Crusaders, criminals, crazies: Terrorism in our time.* New York: Norton.

Heskin, K. (1980). *Northern Ireland: A psychological analysis.* New York: Columbia University Press.

Horowitz, M. (1976). *Stress response syndromes.* New York: Jason Aronson.

Jacobson, S. (1973). Individual & group responses to confinement in a skyjacked plane. *American Journal of Orthopsychiatry, 43*(3), 459–469.

Jenkins, B. M. (1982, March). *Talking to terrorists.* The Rand Paper Series, Santa Monica, CA: Rand Corporation.

Klein, H. (1968). Problems in psychotherapeutic treatment of Israeli survivors of Holocaust. In H. Krystal (Ed.), *Massive psychic trauma.* New York: International Universities Press.

Kliman, A. (1973, September). *The Cronin Flood Projects.* Subcommittee on Disaster Relief of the Community & Public Works, U.S. Senate.

Kristal, L. (1978). Bruxism: An anxiety response to mental stress. In C. D. Spielberger & I. G. Sarason (Eds.), *Stress and anxiety* (Vol. 5, pp. 45–59). New York: Wiley.

Langmeier, J., & Matejcek, Z. (1975). *Psychological deprivation in childhood.* New York: Halsted Press.

Lazarus, R. (1966). *Psychological stress and the coping process.* New York: McGraw-Hill.

Lazarus, R. (1976). *Patterns of adjustment.* New York: McGraw-Hill.

Lifton, R. (1967). The human meaning of disaster. *Psychiatry, 39,* 1–18.

Lindemann, E. (1944). Symptomatology and management of acute grief. *American Journal of Psychiatry, 101,* 141–148.

Lyons, H. A. (1971). Psychiatric sequalae of the Belfast Riots. *British Journal of Psychiatry, 118,* 265–273.

Milgram, R., & Milgram, N. (1976). The effect of the Yom Kippur War on anxiety levels in Israeli children. *Journal of Psychology, 94,* 107–113.

Moore, J. G. (1974). Yo Yo children. *Nursing Times, 70*(49), 188–189.

Niederland, W. (1968). The psychiatric evaluation of emotional disorders in survivors of Nazi persecution. In H. Krystal (Ed.), *Massive psychic trauma.* New York: International Universities Press.

Ochberg, F., & Soskis, D. (Eds.). (1982). *Victims of terrorism.* Westview Special Studies in National and International Terrorism, Colorado.

Pynoos, R. S., & Eth, S. (1984). The child as witness to homicide. *Journal of Social Issues, 40,* 81–108.

Rachman, S. (1978). *Fear and courage.* London: Pergamon Press.

Rofe, Y., & Lewin, I. (1982). The effect of war environment on dreams and sleep habits. In C. D. Spielberger, I. G. Sarason, & N. A. Milgram (Eds.), *Stress and anxiety* (Vol. 8, pp. 67–79). Washington, DC: Hemisphere.

Rutter, M. (1981). The city and the child. *American Journal of Orthopsychiatry, 51,* 610–625.

Schrieber, J. (1978). *The ultimate weapon.* New York: William Morrow & Co.

Schwebel, M., & Schwebel, B. (1981). Children's reactions to the threat of nuclear plant accidents. *American Journal of Orthopsychiatry, 51,* 260–270.

Seligman, M. (1975). *Helplessness: On depression, development and death.* San Francisco: W. H. Freeman & Co.

Spielberger, C. D., Sarason, I. G., & Milgram, N. A. (Eds.). (1982). *Stress and anxiety* (Vol. 8). Washington, DC: Hemisphere.

Symonds, M. (1980). The "second injury" to victims of violent crimes. *Evaluation and Change,* pp. 36–38.

Terr, L. (1979). Children of Chowchilla: A study of psychic trauma. *Psychoanalytic Study of the Child, 34,* 552–623.

Terr, L. (1981). Psychic trauma in children. *American Journal of Psychiatry, 138,* 14–19.

Terr, L. (1983). Chowchilla revisited: The effects of psychic trauma for years after a school bus kidnapping. *American Journal of Psychiatry, 140,* 1543–1550.

Totten, S., & Totten, M. W. (1984). *Facing the danger.* Trumansburg, NY: The Crossing Press.

Wolfenstein, M. (1957). *Disaster.* Glencoe, IL: Free Press.

Zak, J. (1982). Stability and change of personality traits: Possible effects of the Yom Kippur War on Israeli youth. In C. D. Spielberger, I. G. Sarason, & N. A. Milgram (Eds.), *Stress and anxiety* (Vol. 8, pp. 93–96). Washington, DC: Hemisphere.

Ziv, A., & Israel, R. (1973). Effects of bombardment on the manifest anxiety level of children living in Kibbutzim. *Journal of Consulting and Clinical Psychology, 40,* 287–291.

Ziv, A., & Kruglanski, A., & Schulman, S. (1974). Children's psychological reactions to wartime stress. *Journal of Personality and Social Psychology, 30,* 24–30.

PART 3
INTERDISCIPLINARY PERSPECTIVES

14

Emotional Abuse and the Law

Janet Corson and Howard Davidson

Emotional abuse is a difficult concept to define for many disciplines, but most of all for the area of law. In this chapter, it is hoped that the reader will get an understanding of how cases of emotional maltreatment of children are dealt with by the legal system.

A brief history of federal legislation dealing with child abuse has been included, as well as a more extensive section on how individual states treat the concept of emotional abuse or mental injury in their statutes. Discussion of how this problem has been handled within the courts and by child protective service agencies is also included.

Even though there is very little reported case law in the area of emotional abuse, a few significant cases have been presented. These should be helpful to those who work within the legal process on behalf of abused and neglected children. Suggestions are also given for training and information sharing that should be available for these individuals.

Finally, a section dealing with a framework for developing relevant state legislation and agency policies has been included. Since no model laws or policies exist on this topic at the present, it is hoped that this section will provide assistance to those individuals or organizations who are interested in legislative and regulatory reform in this area.

Our laws, agency policies, and judicial processes have a long way to go before cases of emotional abuse will be easily accepted and appropriately handled. The authors believe that much more can be done within the legal system

to protect children from suffering serious injury caused by emotional maltreatment. Through the more effective dissemination of information, the consciousness of lawmakers, the judiciary, and practicing attorneys can be enhanced and raised. This should help provide a more favorable forum for appropriate state intervention in emotional abuse cases.

THE CHILD ABUSE PREVENTION AND TREATMENT ACT

On January 31, 1974, federal legislation known as the Child Abuse Prevention and Treatment Act was signed into law as Public Law 93-247. The following discussion includes a synopsis of the legislative history of this bill (see History of Child Abuse Prevention and Treatment Act: Public Law 93-247, 1978). This law is significant because it is the first and only federal law to recognize the concept of "mental injury" or emotional abuse.

The passage of Public Law 93-247 began the first coordinated federal effort to deal with the area of child abuse and neglect. Up to that point, federal funds for state and local child protection efforts were available primarily through the child welfare services program under the Social Security Act. However, in 1973 only 1% of the funds received by the entire child welfare program had been directed toward the problem of child abuse. This small allocation of funds reflected the lack of national awareness of the problem of child abuse, which was soon to change. With the introduction of the new legislation in 1973, hearings were conducted in four major cities to hear testimony regarding this issue. Because of the overwhelming bipartisan support it received, the bill was quickly signed into law the following year. The Child Abuse Prevention and Treatment Act provided for

(1) the establishment of a National Center on Child Abuse and Neglect within the Department of Health, Education and Welfare; (2) mandated programs for the collection and dissemination of information, including the incidence of child abuse and neglect; (3) a source of funding for basic research in the area of child abuse and neglect; (4) a source of funding for service delivery, resource, and innovative demonstration projects designed to prevent and/or treat child abuse and neglect; (5) an advisory board to assist the Secretary of Health, Education, and Welfare in seeking to coordinate federal programs; and (6) encouragement to states by way of grants for the payment of expenses involved in developing, strengthening, and carrying out child abuse and neglect prevention and treatment programs. (History of Child Abuse Prevention and Treatment Act: Public Law 93-247, 1978, p. 572)

In Section 3 of the Act, the term "child abuse and neglect" was defined as

the physical or mental injury, sexual abuse, negligent treatment, or maltreatment of a child under the age of eighteen by a person who is responsible for the child's welfare under circumstances which indicate that the child's health or welfare is harmed or threatened thereby as determined in accordance with regulations prescribed by the Secretary. (42 U.S.C. s5102, 1983)

This definition and other sections of the Act have been amended by Public Law 95-266 in 1978, and by Public Law 98-457 in 1984. However, these amendments are not discussed here because they did not affect the requisite response to "mental injury" under the Act. The above definition of child abuse was not considered a "model law" for the states to routinely follow. Rather, it served as a general guideline to the states as to what they must include in their own definitions of abuse and neglect if they wished to receive funding under the Act.

The idea of including mental injury as a category of child maltreatment provoked comment and created problems from the time of its first proposal. In a "Dissenting View" contained in a congressional report written before the bill was passed, Representative Earl Landgrebe commented on the problems associated with including a term like *mental injury*. He warned that it was too difficult to define, with the probable result being a different definition in each of the 50 states. He also stated that it would be impossible to provide "clear-cut evidence" to support a claim of mental injury. There would be no "objective and definable" evidence as there was in cases of physical abuse. And finally he thought the bill gave too much leeway to the Secretary of Health, Education and Welfare to define the term *mental injury* and thus "completely eliminated the rights of parents" relative to state agencies empowered by the Act (Landgrebe, 1974, p. 2772).

Representative Landgrebe has been proven correct in his assumption that mental injury would be a difficult term for the states to define. In the first year (1974) that state grants were made available under this Act, only three states qualified for federal funding under the Act out of a possible 57 states and U.S. territories. One of the two largest stumbling blocks was "the requirement for comprehensive definition of child abuse and neglect (especially as it relates to reporting instances of known or suspected 'mental injury') . . ." (History of Child Abuse Prevention and Treatment Act: Public Law 93-247, 1978, p. 575). By 1977, the number of eligible states had increased to 40, and today there are only 5 states and one U.S. territory that are not eligible to receive a share of the federal funding made possible by the Act. Clearly, this federal legislation has had a significant impact on the states including "mental injury" under their definitions of child abuse and neglect.

DEFINING MENTAL INJURY

Defining mental injury within the law has always been a difficult task. While the Child Abuse Prevention and Treatment Act provided a guideline for state statutes with its definition of child abuse and neglect, it did not define mental injury. The majority of states have followed suit in that they did not define mental injury or any comparable term used in their statutes.

However, there are seven states which do define mental injury in their statutes (see Category 3 in the appendix of this chapter, on State Statutes). A typical example of the definition used by these states is that of Nevada: "a substantial injury to the intellectual or psychological capacity of a child as evidenced by an observable and substantial impairment of his ability to function within his normal range of performance or behavior" (Nev. Rev. Stat. s200.5011(2), 1983).

Where a definition of mental injury or emotional abuse is not included in the law, it is left to the child protective service agencies of that state to determine how they will identify and act upon the mental injury of a child. Since these agencies have the responsibility of investigating all child maltreatment reports and presenting them when appropriate to the court system, the absence of a precise statutory definition requires them to provide clear guidelines to their caseworkers on the investigation and response to this type of case.

Two states which have made special efforts through their state child welfare agencies to do this are Virginia and Mississippi. In both states the child welfare agency leadership consulted with a variety of professionals involved in the area of child abuse and neglect to come up with workable definitions and guidelines which are now included in their state agency manuals. Because of their thoroughness, these definitions and guidelines are discussed in detail. Although they are not offered as models, they may be useful examples for other states that are grappling with the problem of defining emotional abuse. Since the definitions and guidelines used by the two states are so similar, they have been combined and summarized for purposes of this discussion.

Mental abuse was defined by the two states as "acts or threatening statements made and/or allowed which result in mental injury or harm to the child. Mental refers to emotional, intellectual or psychological functioning" (Virginia Department of Social Services, hereafter referred to as Virginia, 1985, p. 6b, and Mississippi Department of Public Welfare Definitions of Child Abuse and Neglect with Guidelines, hereafter referred to as Mississippi, 1984, p. 7). The guidelines of these states stipulate that there must be a connection between the parent's or caretaker's behavior and the child's mental problems for mental abuse to have occurred. It is necessary that this behavior either cause the mental difficulty or perpetuate it in some way. Also, it is noted that these caretaker behaviors may be obvious or subtle, explicit, stated, or implied (Mississippi, 1984; Virginia, 1985).

In order to facilitate identification of mental abuse, examples of abusive behaviors by the caretaker are given, as well as examples of the child's behavior. These examples are *not* all-inclusive. Caretaker behavior or threat of behavior is described as "rejecting, intimidating, humiliating, ridiculing, chaotic, bizarre, violent, hostile, or excessively guilt-producing" (Virginia, 1985, p. 6c; Mississippi, 1984, p. 7). Mississippi also includes as separate items "acts of exploitation, scapegoating of one child in a family, and custody struggles where children become pawns between parents and witness their parents belittling, harassing or blaming each other" (Mississippi, 1984, p. 8).

The children's behaviors listed by the guidelines are to be considered as possible evidence of mental difficulties only after organic causes have been ruled out. They include, but are not limited to, "excessive need for sucking, feeding and sleeping problems, unrealistic fears, enuresis, stuttering, lethargy, depression, runaway behavior, stubborn or defiant activity, poor school performance, poor peer relationships, extensive denial, suicide threats, property destruction, and violent behavior towards others" (Mississippi, 1984, p. 8; Virginia, 1985, p. 6c).

Mental neglect is defined as "failure, on a periodic or continuing basis, regardless of cause, to provide adequate nurture to meet the child's mental needs which results in a substantial impairment of intellectual, psychological or emotional well-being and functioning of the child" (Mississippi, 1984, p. 5). Virginia adds "The parent allows, or does not prevent the infliction of mental harm or injury to the child" (Virginia, 1985, p. 6c).

Again, both states stipulate that there must be a *direct relationship* between the caretaker's failure to provide appropriate nurture and the child's difficulty. Caretaker behaviors that are indicative of mental neglect include, but are not limited to, "overprotection, ignoring, indifference, rigidity, apathy, a chaotic lifestyle, and other behaviors related to the caretaker's own mental problems" (Virginia, 1985, p. 6d; Mississippi, 1984, p. 5). On the part of the child, behaviors which may indicate mental neglect include, but are not limited to, "feeding and sleeping problems, rocking, enuresis, excessive masturbation, excessive fears, age-inappropriate fears, inability to form trusting and mutual relationships, apathy, depression, low self-esteem, self-denial, suicidal behavior, impaired memory, difficulty in concentrating, mental confusion and disorientation, psychological 'numbing,' pseudo-maturity, poor school performance, intense symbiotic relationships, functional or social retardation, and functional/organic disorders, such as failure to thrive syndrome and psychosocial dwarfism" (Mississippi, 1984, p. 5; Virginia, 1985, p. 6d).

Both states define "nurture" to include "parental behaviors such as intimacy, affection, structure, consistency, communication, responsiveness, acceptance, encouragement and spontaneity" (Virginia, 1985, p. 6d; Mississippi, 1984, p. 5). Virginia cautions that "intimacy does not include sexual behaviors" (Virginia, 1985, p. 6d). While neither Virginia nor Mississippi has kept any statistics on how the above guidelines have affected the handling of mental abuse and neglect cases by their caseworkers, supervisors from their child protective services units were willing to make some general observations about the effects of the guidelines.

Melzana Fuller, Program Manager, Child Protective Services, Social Services, Mississippi Department of Public Welfare, commented that since the inclusion of the new guidelines in her state agency's manual, she has not noticed any significant increase in the number of mental abuse and/or neglect cases being reported by the caseworkers. She felt this was probably due to the fact that the concept of mental abuse and/or neglect was still an ambiguous one for most caseworkers. On the positive side, it was noted that the guidelines did provide for some consistency in Mississippi's state-administered welfare system. All Mississippi counties now process these types of cases when presented, whereas previously, there were some that refused to do so (M. Fuller, personal communication, September 9, 1983).

A state welfare supervisor for the Virginia State Department of Social Services stated that the guidelines have helped to clarify the concept of mental abuse and neglect for many Virginia caseworkers by providing examples of behaviors associated with such maltreatment. Unfortunately, caseworkers often identify one of these behaviors and assume it is enough to establish a case of mental abuse or neglect. For example, parents or children will admit that one spouse physically abuses the other spouse and it is then assumed that the children are being mentally abused. In these situations caseworkers are failing to apply the Virginia definitions of mental

abuse and neglect, which require that in addition to the existence of abusive or neglectful parental behaviors, the child must demonstrate significant mental difficulty that is *attributable* to the parents' behavior. Without this crucial link a case of mental abuse or neglect does not exist in the state of Virginia (J. Tondrowski, personal communication, September 12, 1985).

CATEGORIZATION OF STATE STATUTES

In this section the state statutes defining child abuse and/or neglect have been examined in order to discern which states included emotional abuse and/or neglect in their laws and to compare how they had done so.

The National Clearinghouse on Child Abuse and Neglect Information maintains a computerized database which contains extracts from all state laws on child abuse and neglect. That portion of the statute referring to some form of emotional abuse and/or neglect was found through a search within their files using the terms *emotional*, *mental* and *psychological* during the spring of 1985.

Classically, the terms *abuse* and *neglect* have two different meanings. Abuse implies an active role on the part of someone. In order to abuse another, someone has to do something. Abuse infers commission, while neglect infers an omission. Many states define abuse and neglect together, making no distinction in their statutes. The distinction also is moot for the courts. Whether the child has been abused through verbal accusations and name calling or has been emotionally injured because of someone's failure to act, the potential actions which can be taken by the court to protect the child remain the same (see Appendix, pp. 199–201).

1. *States which include some reference to the infliction of mental injury in their neglect and/or abuse definitions.* By far, the most commonly used term denoting emotional abuse is mental injury. Many states include the infliction of an injury, whether mental, emotional, or physical, in their definitions of abuse and/or neglect. A representative statute of this group is that of Virginia:

> "Abused or neglected child" shall mean any child whose parents or other person responsible for his care: Creates or inflicts, threatens to create or inflict, or allows to be created or inflicted upon such child

a . . . mental injury by other than accidental means, or creates a substantial risk of . . . impairment of mental functions; . . . (Va. Code 16.1-228 (A)(1), Supp. 1984)

Other states using a similar definition for abuse and/or neglect are Arkansas, District of Columbia, Kansas, Louisiana, Missouri, New Mexico, Pennsylvania and West Virginia. (See the Appendix, pp. 199–201, for specific citations.)

2. *States which define abuse and/or neglect as harm or threatened harm to child's health or welfare and include mental injury or a comparable phrase as one possible cause of such harm.* The state of Oklahoma's statute defining abuse and neglect is representative of this group:

"Abuse and neglect," as used herein, means harm or threatened harm to a child's health or welfare by a person responsible for the child's health or welfare. Harm or threatened harm to a child's health or welfare can occur through: Non-accidental . . . mental injury . . . or negligent treatment or maltreatment. . . . (Okla. Stat. Ann. tit. 21, s845, 1983)

Other states using a similar definition for abuse and/or neglect are Alabama, California, Florida, Hawaii, Kentucky, Maine, Michigan, Montana, North Dakota and Utah.

3. *States which define the term mental injury.* Legislators have had a difficult time defining the term *emotional abuse*. With physical abuse, the child has suffered an observable physical injury. A few states list the types of physical injury they consider serious enough to constitute abuse, such as lacerations, bone fractures, and burns while generally cautioning that the list is not comprehensive. Most states, however, do not list types of physical injury, possibly considering it unnecessary. "Mental injury" is also left undefined by most states that include the term. This creates an obvious difficulty, as mental injury is not as apparent as a physical injury and therefore is much harder to prove. In response to this, some states which use the term in their statutes do define it. In most cases, the state has included the "infliction of mental injury" in its definition of abuse and/or neglect or in its definition of harm or threatened harm to the welfare of a child.

A good example of the most commonly used definition for mental injury can be found in Nevada's Definition of Abuse and Neglect: "'Mental injury' means a substantial injury to the intellectual or psychological capacity of a child as evidenced by an observable and substantial impairment of his ability to function within his normal range or performance or behavior," (Nev. Rev. Stat. s200.5011(2), 1983). Other states with similar definitions are Idaho, Rhode Island, South Carolina, South Dakota, Vermont, and Wyoming. Rhode Island goes further in its definition and gives examples (again, not all-inclusive) of "diminished psychological functioning" as related to "failure to thrive; ability to think or reason; control of aggressive or self-destructive impulses; acting-out or misbehavior, including incorrigibility, ungovernability, or habitual truancy . . ." (R.I. Gen. Laws 40-11-2(3), Supp. 1984).

Wyoming and South Dakota caution that the child's "impairment in his ability to function within a normal range of performance and behavior" must be judged "with due regard to his culture" (Wyo. Stat. s14-3-202(a) (ii)(A) (1977) and S.D. Codified Laws 26-8-6(7), Supp. 1984). These states specifically allow for the cultural differences that exist in the behaviors of their people.

4. *States that define emotional abuse and/or neglect by specifically describing the child's condition or behavior.* The state statutes included in this category are those of Arizona, New Hampshire, and Wisconsin. While these states defined mental injury in a similar manner, there was no one statute that was representative of the wording used. It should be noted that all three statutes are defining abuse and not neglect.

Arizona and Wisconsin list behaviors such as "severe anxiety, depression, withdrawal or untoward aggressive behavior" as evidence of serious emotional damage (Ariz. Rev. Stat. s8-201(2), Supp. 1984 and Wisc. Stat. Ann. s48.981(cm), West Supp. 1984–85). Arizona includes the stipulation that the emotional damage must be diagnosed as such by a medical doctor or psychologist. In Wisconsin, the parent or legal custodian must have failed to obtain appropriate treatment for the child before the child is considered abused.

In contrast to Arizona's requirement of medical diagnosis, New Hampshire defines an abused child as "any child who has . . . (d) been psychologically injured so that said child exhibits symptoms of emotional problems generally recognized to result from consistent mistreatment or neglect . . ." (N.H. Rev. Stat. Ann. s169-C 3II(d), Supp. 1983).

5. *States that permit intervention for impairment of emotional health only when it has been caused by physical injury or inadequate physical care.* These states recognize a child's emotional health or well-being as being separate from her/his physical health, but only mention the infliction of "physical injury" when defining child abuse. The idea of a "mental injury" is not included. A representative statute of this group is New York's definition of abuse:

> "Abused child" means a child less than eighteen years of age whose parent or other person legally responsible for his care . . . (i) inflicts or allows to be inflicted upon such child physical injury by other than accidental means which causes or creates a substantial risk of . . . or protracted impairment of . . . emotional health. . . . (N.Y. Fam. Ct. Act s1012(e) (i), McKinney, 1983; N.Y. Soc. Serv. law s371(4-B), McKinney 1983)

Other states with similar language are Delaware and Illinois.

Delaware and New York define a "neglected child" as a child "whose physical, mental, or emotional condition or well being has been impaired or is in imminent danger of becoming impaired due to the failure of the parent or guardian to exercise a minimum degree of care or reasonable care" (Del. Code tit. 11 s1102(b), 1979; N.Y. Fam. Ct. Act s1012(f) (i), McKinney, 1983). Looking at the wording of these two statutes, it is implied that a child's emotional health will only be in danger from physical injury or from the failure of a parent to give minimum care. It precludes the notion that there are actions not of a direct physical nature which can be abusive.

A New York court was faced with this situation in the case of *In re Shane T.* (1982). The judge ruled that the verbal assaults inflicted by the father resulted in physical injury to his son in the form of stomach pains. Thus, the boy was adjudicated "abused" because the requirement of "infliction of physical injury" had been satisfied by the judge's creative interpretation of the statute's wording (see the section on court cases in this chapter for a more thorough discussion of this case). It seems the inclusion of the term "mental injury" in the definition of abuse would preclude the necessity for such maneuvering.

6. *States that use the terms "mental," "psychological," and "emotional" only when defining neglect.* For the states in this category, their only reference to "mental injury," "emotional health," or a comparable term occurs in their definition of neglect. As discussed earlier, neglect implies a more passive role on the part of the parents or guardians. They are guilty of an omission, rather than of an overt act which is usually associated with abuse. However, a few states do include overt acts or an act by parents or the guardian as part of their definition of neglect. In general, though, the definitions in this section are of a more passive nature than those used to describe abuse.

Rather than providing a definition for a "neglected child," Georgia defines a "deprived child" as "a child who (A) Is without . . . care or control necessary for his . . . mental or emotional health . . ." (Ga. Code Ann. s15-11-2(8) (A), 1981).

Maryland's definition of neglect describes the failure of the parents to act:

> "Neglected child" means a child who has suffered or is suffering significant . . . mental harm or injury from (1) the absence of his parents, guardian or custodian, or (2) the failure of the child's parents, guardian or custodian to give proper care and attention to the child and the child's problems. . . ." (Md. Fam. Law Code Ann. s5-701(g), 1984)

Minnesota's statute is also of a passive nature: "'Neglect' means failure by a person responsible for a child's care . . . to protect a child from conditions or actions which imminently and seriously endanger the child's . . . mental health when reasonably able to do so . . ." (Minn. Stat. Ann. s626.556(2) (c), Supp. 1985).

Ohio's definition has a section that refers specifically to the child's mental condition: "'Neglected child' includes any child: . . . (D) whose parents, guardian, or custodian neglects or refuses to provide the special care made necessary by his mental condition" (Ohio Rev. Code Ann. s2151.03(D), Page 1976).

Tennessee has a broader definition of neglect which also includes abuse: "'Dependent and neglected child' means a child . . . (G) Who is suffering from or has sustained a . . . mental condition caused by brutality, abuse or neglect" (Tenn. Code Ann. s37-102 (10)(G), Supp. 1984).

7. *States that refer to "endangering" the mental condition of the child.* There are four states in this category: Indiana, Nebraska, New Jersey, and Washington. Nebraska's definition of abuse and

neglect is representative of this category: "Abuse or neglect shall mean knowingly, intentionally, or negligently causing or permitting a minor child . . . to be (a) placed in a situation that may endanger his . . . mental health . . ." (Neb. Rev. Stat. s28-710(3), Supp. 1984).

While Indiana and Washington have similar definitions, they are titled differently. Indiana's definition is for a "child in need of services" and Washington's is for a "dependent child."

New Jersey does not use the term *endanger* in its statute, but the words used have a similar meaning. Its law defines an abused or neglected child as "a child whose . . . mental or emotional condition has been impaired or is in imminent danger of becoming impaired as the result of the failure of his parent or guardian . . . to exercise a minimum degree of care" (N.J. Stat. Ann. 9:6-821(C)(4), Supp. 1984). Many states used a similar definition when defining the term "neglect" by itself.

8. *States with unusual usage of the terms "mental," "emotional," "psychological," or other comparable terms.* Some states included here used the above terms in their child abuse and neglect laws, but did so in an uncommon manner. Thus, their statute did not readily fit into any of the other categories. Also included in this category are states that used a phrase or a term not found in other statutes. These states may appear in another category, too, especially since a few states used one or more of the terms in several of their laws related to child abuse and neglect.

Connecticut, as part of its definition of abuse, includes a child who "(c) is in a condition which is the result of maltreatment such as, but not limited to . . . emotional maltreatment . . ." (Conn. Gen. Stat. Ann. s46b-120(C), Supp. 1985).

Iowa defines a "child in need of assistance" as an unmarried child "f. Who is in need of treatment to cure or alleviate serious mental illness or disorder, or emotional damage . . . and whose parent, guardian, or custodian is unwilling or unable to provide such treatment" (Iowa Code Ann. s232.2(5)(f), West Supp. 1983).

Mississippi's definition of abuse states: "In addition to physical injury, abuse encompasses a situation in which a child's mental health has been adversely affected in some substantial way as determined by examination by competent health professionals" (Miss. Code Ann. s43-23-3(i), 1981).

North Carolina's definition of abuse states:

"(1) Abused juvenile. Any juvenile less than 18 years of age whose parent or other person responsible for his care: . . . (d) Creates or allows to be created serious emotional damage to the juvenile and refuses to permit, provide or participate in treatment . . ." (N.C. Gen. Stat. s7A-517(1)(d), 1981).

North Dakota was the only state to use the term "traumatic abuse." Its statute defines abuse as follows: "'Abused child' means an individual under the age of eighteen years who is suffering from serious physical harm or traumatic abuse caused by other than accidental means by a person responsible for the child's health or welfare" (N.D. Century Code s50-25.1-02(2) Supp. 1983).

In 1985, the Oregon legislature enacted into law a bill which included the term "mental injury" in Oregon's statutes for the first time. It included in the definition of abuse "(b) any mental injury to a child, which shall include only observable and substantial impairment of the child's mental or psychological ability to function caused by cruelty to the child, with due regard to the culture of the child" (1985 Or. Laws, ch. 723, p. 1607). While this law stipulates that the mental injury be caused by cruelty to the child, it does not require that the "cruelty" be inflicted by the parent or the guardian for the child to be considered "abused," nor does it define the term *cruelty*. Most likely it will be left to the Oregon child protective services to provide the guidelines for implementation of this new statute.

Texas and Massachusetts are two states which make no attempt to define abuse in their laws but which include either the term *mental* or *emotional* in their reporting laws. The one for Texas states: "Any person having cause to believe that a child's . . . mental health or welfare has been adversely affected by abuse or neglect shall report in accordance with Section 34.02 of this code" (Tex. Fam. Code Ann. s34.01, Vernon's 1975). Massachusetts has a similarly stated reporting law. The main difference is that it refers to a "child . . . suffering serious . . . emotional injury resulting from abuse inflicted upon him . . ." (Mass. Gen. laws Ann. 119 s51A, Supp. 1984).

9. *States whose child abuse and neglect laws do not include the use of terms "mental," "psychological," "emotional," or other comparable terms.* Two states fell into this category: Alaska and Colorado. However, Colorado's statute has been ruled to include the concept of emotional abuse by the

Colorado Supreme Court. In *In re D.A.K.* (1979), the court stated that it presumed that the General Assembly meant to include emotional abuse as well as physical abuse in its definition of abuse. (See page 201 for Update on Alaska's statute.)

In comparing the above categories of statutes, there seem to be varying degrees of specificity afforded the area of emotional abuse or mental injury. The laws range in specificity from those which do not include the terms *mental, emotional,* or *psychological* to those which not only define *mental injury,* but specifically describe the child's condition or behavior. The majority of statutes fall between these two extremes. Thus, it would appear that most state legislatures think it necessary to include the concept of emotional abuse or mental injury in their child abuse laws, but have done so in a cursory manner, leaving the job of providing definitions and identifying specific behaviors to their child protective agencies.

THE NEED FOR LEGISLATION, CHILD PROTECTIVE AGENCY, AND JUDICIAL GUIDANCE

The successful adjudication of an emotional abuse and/or neglect case involves at least five separate factors: (a) the precise language of the state law; (b) the child protective service agency regulations, guidelines and other policies; (c) the personal attitudes and training of the agency caseworkers; (d) the opinions and competency of the attorneys representing the caseworkers; and (e) the attitudes and knowledge of the judges deciding such cases.

Without appropriate legislation, the hands of the judges are usually tied. As noted in the Appendix of this chapter, almost all of the states make some reference in their laws to emotional abuse and/or neglect or mental injury. These should usually be a sufficient basis for agency intervention or the filing of a court petition alleging emotional abuse and/or neglect. However, the clearer the intent of the legislature as expressed by the statute, the easier it will be for a caseworker or a judge to interpret the law. Consequently, a state which specifically includes the concept of mental injury, and even defines it in its statute, will make the intervention process much clearer. If a statute is causing problems for caseworkers or judges, legislators should be educated as to why that statute needs to be more specific; that is, how the present statute is un-

duly complicating the process and either leading to inappropriate intervention or no intervention at all when it is necessary to protect a child from serious harm. Exemplary laws from other states should be shown to the legislators. If possible, statistics comparing the number of mental injury cases reported and confirmed in the home state with those in surrounding states could be used. Most importantly, they need to understand the devastating effects of emotional abuse and/or neglect and the need, in some cases, for government intervention. Since most laws are minimally adequate for state intervention purposes but limited in their specificity, the responsibility of providing guidelines and working definitions falls to the child protective service agencies. It is the agency caseworkers who must investigate cases and collect evidence. Clear guidelines and definitions make their job easier. Dean (1979), in her article on emotional abuse, has several suggestions for agencies and caseworkers who are presenting emotional abuse cases to the court system:

> Contact the Juvenile Court and establish agreement on definitions and guidelines for court referrals; document the abuse and its negative impact on the child; use expert witnesses such as psychologists and psychiatrists; determine what other interventions have been attempted and what results were achieved. (p. 18)

Examples of comprehensive definitions and guidelines are included in this chapter in the section on "Defining Mental Injury." This type of definition and guideline will highlight the need for adequate documentation in order to successfully intervene in an emotional abuse case. The assistance of mental health experts will usually be required. Often, it is the only way to establish the harmful nature of the child's behavior and the underlying problems causing the behavior, or the link between the parent's behavior and the child's condition.

Even though attorneys usually are responsible for presenting cases in court, most of the evidence must be collected by the caseworker. However, the attorney should have knowledge of what types of evidence are admissible under state law and should guide the caseworker to collect this type of information. The attorney for the agency should also be aware of any reported or unreported cases in which children have been adjudicated emotionally abused.

The same type of information should also be available to juvenile or family court judges. They need to be educated as to the long-term effects of emotional abuse and/or neglect, and how debilitating it can be. They also need to have demonstrated to them that emotional abuse can be proven just as physical abuse is proven. Case law on the subject should be presented to them, especially from their own state or district. Finally, they must realize that court intervention for emotional maltreatment is sometimes needed in order to help many families whose children have been seriously harmed. Without it, some parents are unwilling to accept the services offered to them and to their child.

Obviously, the more knowledgeable the participants in the agency and judicial processes are about emotional abuse, the better the chances for successful handling of these cases. Acquiring the right kind of evidence is crucial at the point of initial investigation and at the points of considering forcible intervention, the extension of outside placement, the continuation of treatment, or the termination of parental rights. By following the above suggestions, a state or county should be well on its way to better protecting children from severe harm caused by emotional abuse or neglect.

Selected Court Cases

Ideally, in order to compare the relative usefulness to the judiciary of the state statutes on emotional maltreatment, one would have to do a survey of trial court cases to determine how many decisions were based solely or largely upon the presence of emotional abuse and/or neglect. Since these decisions are not generally available, such a comparison was not possible. The written case decisions discussed below were found through the database of the National Clearinghouse on Child Abuse and Neglect Information, the BNA *Family Law Reporter* (a looseleaf reporting service found in many law libraries), the Mississippi Child Protective Services unit, and in an article by Dean (1979).

Oregon, prior to 1985, did not use the terms *mental, psychological,* or *emotional* in its statutes. This omission was noted by the Oregon Supreme Court and was the basis for its decision in *Burnette v. Wahl* (1978). The plaintiffs in this case were five minors who instituted actions, through their guardian, for psychological and emotional injuries caused by the alleged failure of their mothers to perform their parental duties. The Supreme Court of Oregon upheld the dismissal of the case. It stated that psychological and emotional injuries have been found only in cases where such injuries result from physical acts inflicted upon minors and that there were no cases supporting recovery of damages resulting solely from failure to support or to provide nurturance to minors. The court also noted that the legislature had not undertaken to create a legal basis for court action due to emotional injuries, even though it had enacted statutes to provide for the proper care and nurturing of minors.

It should be noted that this was a civil damage suit, and it was therefore probably considered differently than would a case which was attempting to terminate parental rights because of emotional abuse or injuries. That is, a court might be more liberal in its interpretation of a statute where the purpose was to protect a child from harm, rather than to award him money for the transgressions of his parent.

Colorado also falls into the category of states whose child abuse and/or neglect laws do not specifically address emotional, mental, or psychological maltreatment in their laws. In *In re D.A.K.* (1979), the Supreme Court of Colorado affirmed a trial court's determination that a minor was a deprived and dependent child due to emotional abuse and lack of parental care. The court held that "emotional abuse may leave scars more permanent and damaging to a child's personality than bodily bruises from a physical beating." Further, the court noted that even though the state statute did not define the term *abuse,* it presumed that the General Assembly meant to include emotional abuse as well as physical abuse.

At the time of *In re B.A.M.* (1980), the South Dakota Supreme Court affirmed a lower court's decision to terminate the father's parental rights based on his incarceration for the murder of the child's mother. The court spoke of the trauma and emotional detachment from her father that the child had experienced as a result of seeing and hearing some of the events surrounding the murder and having the house set on fire by the father after the murder. It was felt that returning the child to the father would cause severe emotional problems in the child. The court's main basis for terminating parental rights in this case was abandonment, since the father was in prison and could not properly provide the child with a stable home environment. However, not all prisoners' parental rights are terminated. The added consideration of the emotional harm the father had caused the child, as well as his volatile temperament and indiscretions in the child's presence, were the factors that convinced the court that termination was in the best interest of the child. This case is a good example of how emotional harm or abuse can be a major consideration rather than the sole basis for the termination of parental rights.

In *Kimsey v. Kimsey* (1981), the Supreme Court of Nebraska upheld a termination of parental rights by a lower court. The Nebraska Supreme Court relied on a physician's testimony that the child's severe mental illness was caused by lack of permanency. The child's condition had been diagnosed as childhood schizophrenia induced by numerous placements. Expert testimony is often crucial in these types of cases, especially when the statute requires the establishment of a causal relationship between the parents' behavior and the child's emotional state.

In *New Jersey Division of Youth and Family Services v. C.M.* (1981), a county court found the children to be abused and neglected because of the causal relationship between the mother's inability to care for and nurture the children (she suffered from chronic schizophrenia) and the children's mental and emotional disabilities. She had also refused offers of assistance from social services and was not assuring that her children attended school on a regular basis, even though they needed special education. Thus, the court determined their emotional health to be at risk by reason of the actions and inactions of the mother.

This case is representative of many neglect cases, in that the children are removed from the parents' custody because of what the parents fail to do. Even though the court mentions the acts of the mother, it appears that her failure to accept psychiatric treatment, to keep her children in school and to provide a decent home environment was mainly responsible for the removal of her children, rather than anything she did.

Four relevant cases come from the State of New York. The first case, *In re Evelyn Q.* (1979), dealt with a petition to extend placement of the child with the Department of Social Services. The court granted the petition because a preponderance of the evidence, including testimony of psychologists and of the child, indicated that the child could become emotionally abused or neglected if returned to the mother.

New York is a state that narrowly defines "abuse" as the infliction of physical injury, yet that did not deter the court from basing its decision on the possibility of emotional abuse. Since there was no physical injury in this case, it appears here that the court felt it necessary to look to the definition of a neglected child under New York's Family Court Act to support its position. This law states that a "neglected child" means a child "(i) whose physical, mental, or emotional condition has been impaired or is in imminent danger of becoming impaired as a result of the failure of his parent . . . to exercise a minimum degree of care . . ." (N.Y. Fam. Ct. Act s1012(f), McKinney, 1975).

The next case, *In re Leif Z.* (1980), concerned a boy who was emotionally abused by his stepmother. The family court stated that the boy had been subjected to an "unabated course of cruelty and emotional torment" and, therefore, the evidence was sufficient to support a finding that the child was a neglected child under section 1012(f) of the New York Family Court Act (the same section that is cited in the preceding case). Because there is no mention of physical abuse in this case, it seems that the court was again forced by the absence of an alternative to look to the neglect laws for support of its decision.

The case of *In re Shane T.* (1982) differs from the two cases discussed above in that it relies on the definition of abuse found in the New York Family Court Act. As stated above, that provision stipulates that the child must have suffered the infliction of a physical injury in order to be designated an "abused child." The family court was cognizant of this requirement and discussed it at length. The father of the minor in this case had continually called his son, aged 14, a "fag," "faggot," and "queer" and told him he should have been a girl over the course of several years. This torment resulted in the boy experiencing stomach pains and receiving therapy. In its discussion, the court concluded that while the statute includes the infliction of a physical injury, it does not specify that the injury be inflicted by force. "Rather, to constitute abuse, mere words are sufficient provided that their effect on the child falls within the language of the statute." The court, therefore, found the boy to be an abused child, the father to have abused his son, and the mother to have abused her son since she did not "act meaningfully to protect the boy."

In a more recent case, *In re Keith R.* (1984), a 5-year-old boy was diagnosed by two psychiatrists as "an extremely disturbed child whose preoccupation with sexual matters is so intense as to suggest very strongly that he has been exposed to unusual and explicit sexual conduct" (p. 256). The court ruled that the specific allegations of sexual abuse had not been established. However, the court agreed to consider evidence as relevant to the issue of whether the mother could be held responsible for her son's emotional condition under the neglect provision of the state Family Court Act. The Family Court Act stipulates that in cases of neglect based on impairment of the child's emotional condition, there must be a demonstration that the impairment was "clearly unattributable to the willingness or inability of the respondent to exercise a minimum degree of care toward the child" (N.Y. Fam. Ct. Act s1012(h); McKinney, 1975). Based on this provision, proof of the child's emotional condition (which was established by expert testimony) and the applicability of the concept of *res ipsa loquitur** to a case of this kind, the Court decided that the mother could be considered responsible for the boy's emotional condition, since she was the primary caretaker during the time the child exhibited the "exceedingly troubled behavior." Also, there was "direct testimony that the mother was gay and allowed the child to witness her in bed with her girlfriend" (*In re Keith R.*, 1984, 258 Ftnt. 3). Consequently, the Court made a finding of neglect.

Obviously, the review of four cases is insufficient to assess how the New York family courts are interpreting and applying the child abuse and neglect laws of that state. However, it does appear that if a child in that state is in danger of being emotionally abused, is being or has been emotionally abused, or has suffered a physical disorder or injury because of emotional abuse, the judges seem to be willing and able to use the statutes to protect such children.

A 1984 case decided in a youth court of Mis-

Res ipsa loquitur in the context of child abuse is defined as "proof of injuries sustained by a child or of the condition of a child of such a nature as would ordinarily not be sustained or exist except by reason of the acts or omissions of the parent . . . shall be prima facie evidence of child abuse or neglect . . ." (N.Y. Fam. Court Act. s1046(a)(ii), McKinney 1975).

sissippi, (M. Fuller, personal communication, April, 1985), involved M., a 9-year-old boy from his mother's first marriage, who lived with his natural mother, a stepfather and two younger female siblings. His treatment in the home differed greatly from that of his siblings because he was perceived to be displaying "acting-out behaviors like those of his natural father." He was forced to sit in the car for hours while his family went shopping in the mall or visited friends, was not allowed to play with his sisters, was compelled to stay in his room and not socialize with the family, was not allowed to talk at mealtime, was refused meals if his chores were not done properly, was sent to school without a lunch or lunch money, and was ordered to stand in the middle of a room for an extended period of time for punishment.

Based on the substantiation of these facts and the report of a clinical psychologist that the boy was the victim of emotional abuse, the court adjudicated him to be an emotionally neglected and/or abused child under the law. However, the court found that there was no *intentional* abuse or neglect on the part of the mother and the stepfather. This was probably due to three factors: (a) the parents sincerely thought what they were doing was in M's best interests; (b) they accepted the welfare department's suggestions of counseling for the parents and the child; and (c) they agreed to placement of the child in foster care.

In an article for *Children Today*, Dean (1979), a supervisor in the San Diego County Probation Department, described five cases which resulted in judgments of emotional abuse by the San Diego County Juvenile Court. These cases had one or more of the following characteristics: "(1) An act that in itself is sufficient to establish abuse; (2) Differential treatment of one child in the family; and (3) A reduction in the child's functioning that can be linked to abusive treatment" (Dean, 1979, p. 19).

Three cases, Patty, Mark, and Sandra, demonstrated the characteristic of "emotional abuse resulting from an act sufficient in itself to establish abuse" (Dean, 1979, p. 19). One child, Patty, was forced to wear signs labeling her misbehavior ("I am a liar" or "I hit my little sister") wherever she went. Mark, an adolescent, had to wear only a diaper and stand in the front yard as punishment for his misbehavior. Both suffered public humiliation that the court considered a violation of their "right to reasonable and just discipline in the privacy of the home" (p. 19) and it therefore found them, to be emotionally abused. Sandra's parents shaved her head after she returned home late one night. Even though it was a one-time occurrence, the Court deemed her punishment "inappropriate, resulting in obviously long-term effects and continuing mental suffering" (p. 19).

Cindy was a child who was treated differently than her siblings and suffered because of it. Her parents viewed her as a difficult child who required rigid discipline. Because of this she was not allowed to eat with the family, wore cast-off clothing, had more household tasks, and was not allowed to participate in afterschool activities. Consequently, her self-esteem was low and she perceived herself as deserving such treatment. Since this treatment was observable and tangible, it was legally established that Cindy was an emotionally abused child.

Paul was an example of a child whose reduced functioning was due to emotional abuse. Paul was an adopted child who did not live up to his parents' expectations. They found several things disappointing about him: his physical appearance, his performance in school, and his inability to compete athletically. His parents' disappointment was obvious to him. At age 12 he was placed in a military school and returned home only for holidays. His reduced functioning was demonstrated by his poor performance in school after an incidence of parental rejection and by his lower test scores at ages 12 and 14 than at age 7 in spite of a good IQ. He was referred to court when he ran away at age 16. Dean notes that after "documenting specific instances when emotional abuse had occurred and showing a chronic pattern of reduced functioning, Paul was accepted by the court as an emotionally abused minor" (p. 20).

After reading through the above cases, one may wonder if the precise language of a law is that important, since most courts are usually able to maneuver around the statutory wording to effect the desired result of protecting the child. However, in the opinion of the authors, precise, clear statutory language is important. State legislatures, through the statutes they enact, can make it clear to child protective service agencies and to the courts that emotional abuse or neglect can in some circumstances be a serious threat to the health and welfare of children.

Guidance for the Drafting of Legislation

Emotional maltreatment has been one of the most frequently discussed topics by legal commentators who have urged reform of child abuse and neglect laws. Some scholars have urged precise statutory language on emotional abuse and neglect so as to assure that state intervention will be appropriately used in such cases. Others have supported broader laws so as not to limit the protections children can be afforded by the courts. However, it is a fact that in most judicial proceedings where emotional harm is alleged, there is a fusing of such claims with contentions of physical, medical, or educational neglect, as well as a common fact pattern involving physical or sexual abuse or severe parental mental illness or alcohol or drug abuse. Rarely have child protective service agencies petitioned courts *merely* because children were lacking adequate parental affection, parents were "psychologically unavailable," or children were simply alleged to be unloved and unwanted, resulting in their lack of self-esteem.

Professor Michael Wald, in a seminal article on the appropriate legal grounds for state intervention with "neglected" children (Wald, 1975), has suggested that it is essential that such intervention be premised solely on damage done to the child, rather than on parental shortcomings. Wald asserts that without existing measurable damage to the child it is extremely difficult both to predict the likelihood of future adverse impact on the child of the parental neglect, as well as the adverse impact of the intervention itself (which Wald was one of the first legal scholars to demonstrate). Permissible intervention, he has submitted, should not be based on harm allegedly "caused" by parental conduct, since experts find it extremely difficult to assess whether given parental behaviors have caused a specific detrimental impact on a child. Wald's greatest contribution to this issue has been his early leadership within the legal community of those who avow that governmental interference with the parent–child relationship may itself be emotionally devastating to the child.

The position of authorities like Wald, who call for statutory grounds for intervention due to emotional maltreatment to be very specific and narrow, has been reflected in three separate sets of written model acts or standards for state child abuse and neglect laws. One proposal, which emerged from a U.S. Justice Department commission, would permit legal intervention only where the child's health (i.e., mental or physical) has been seriously impaired and the parents fail to provide or cooperate with treatment (U.S. Department of Justice, 1980). Legislative guidelines issued by the U.S. Department of Health and Human Services take a different, albeit limited, approach. They would require proof that the parent was responsible for an impairment of the child's intellectual or psychological capacity (i.e., they either inflicted it or allowed it to be inflicted). That impairment would have to be both *observable* and *substantial* and be related to the child's ability to function within his or her normal range of performance and behavior (U.S. Department of Health and Human Services, 1983).

The American Bar Association's Commission on Juvenile Justice Standards, which issued a volume on child abuse and neglect, stated in its final standards that court involvement due to parental mistreatment of children (called here "coercive intervention") should be permitted for emotional mistreatment only when a child was *already* "suffering serious emotional damage" (a requirement in both the Justice Department and HHS models), but it went further to *describe* how the damage was to be measured ("by severe anxiety, depression, or withdrawal, or untoward aggressive behavior toward self or others"). Finally, it concurred with the Justice Department approach in that it further required that forcible intervention be allowed only where "the child's parents are not willing to provide treatment" for the damaged child (American Bar Association Juvenile Justice Standards Project, 1980, Standard 2.1c).

In summary, one area where all these disparate models connect is in the need for proof that there has been *actual* measurable damage done to the child. Mere concern for what "might happen" as a consequence of emotional maltreatment in the distant or foreseeable future is not enough. It should be stated, however, that there is no similar agreement in cases of physical abuse, since many experts believe that intervention in those cases should not be put off merely because a child has not yet suffered a serious injury.

In 1976 a conference of 120 professionals who work with neglected children resulted in a consensus statement on emotional maltreatment that court intervention was appropriate only when

the child *was suffering* "handicapping stress . . . manifested in patterns of inappropriate behavior" and (like the ABA and Justice Department standards) the child's parents failed "to recognize the need for or accept help or change" (Whiting, 1976, p. 4). How to set concrete legislative standards for measuring such actual damage is a supreme challenge. One commentator (Gesmonde, 1972) suggests that the law should concretely detail *specific* parental and child behavior indicative of emotional neglect.

The authors' analysis of present state legislation related to judicial intervention due to "mental" or "emotional" injury of children has disclosed that most states have very vague and general statutory language related to psychological maltreatment. Where there is some degree of precision in the law's language, the statutes generally follow the above standards; they call for actual proof of harm to the child, often substantial, serious, significant, or protracted. The states with more precise language on this topic are split as to whether there must be a showing that the parents "inflicted" the injury or merely "allowed" it to occur (the HHS model), or that the parents simply failed to provide the necessary care for the child's mental and emotional health (the ABA/Justice Department model). Indeed, the Wald view (reflected in his coauthorship of the ABA standards) can itself be contrasted with another legal author's position that courts *should* be forced to find a causal relationship between parental conduct and its adverse impact on the child (Stoetzer, 1975).

There is a counterargument for broader statutory language that neither requires a showing of actual severe harm to the child nor requires that a parent caused the harm or refused to help remediate it. That argument suggests that if our child protective service agencies and courts are to effectively render aid to maltreated children, then they must have the broadest possible authority to do so, subject only to the constitutional requirements which provide due process and equal protection under the law. However, no state laws today go as far as the Child Welfare League of America's 1973 *Standards for Child Protective Services*, which recommended intervention when children are simply "denied normal experiences of being loved, wanted, secure, and worthy." Yet, most laws generally do not require the proof of *actual damage* to the child which diverse legal scholars have agreed should be incorporated in the law, but rather permit child protective service and court involvement against the wishes of a parent merely where there is some *risk* of harm or where the child is lacking some vaguely defined "proper care" considered as necessary for him or her.

One other thing that state laws generally do not do is to distinguish between emotional "neglect" (defined by one author as the unavailability of parents which results in a change of behavior of a once "normal" developing child) and emotional "abuse" (defined by the same author as the active parental rejection of a child through constant criticism, disapproval, disrespect, and denial of worth of children; ten Bensel, 1984). The state laws also rarely make an effort to define what emotional harm *is*. Finally, they also are deficient in that they, almost without exception, fail to specify the types of expert testimony that might be helpful to the courts or child protective service agencies in either measuring actual emotional injury to the child, gauging the likelihood and extent of possible future injury, or determining whether and how parental actions or inactions have caused or contributed to the child's problems. One criticism of overly broad state intervention laws is that inadequately trained investigative case workers can make unilateral decisions that children have been mentally injured, or are likely to be injured, and that judges will rely on those opinions. In response, one state child protective service agency has a policy that in order to support an allegation of mental injury "a medical professional such as a physician, psychiatrist, psychiatric social worker, or psychiatric counselor must be the source of diagnosis" (Illinois Department of Children and Family Services, 1982, Appendix B (17)).

Given our knowledge of what legal, child welfare, and psychiatric authorities have written concerning this topic, as well as our access to relevant state legislation and suggested national guidelines for such legislation, it is possible for us to provide a general template for legislative and regulatory policy reform in this area. Without specific legislative, agency, and judicial guidance, many cases may be brought unnecessarily before the courts, while other children will be denied the attention and protection that their cases warrant. What we propose is clearly applicable not only to language used in the laws themselves, but also to the child protective service (CPS) agency policies and protocols that govern how child maltreatment reports will be

investigated and further acted upon. This point is important because, according to data compiled by the American Humane Association, substantiated cases of emotional maltreatment frequently result in CPS system supervision (over 80% of reported cases in 1981 and over 66% in 1982), and they lead to long-term service involvement by CPS more often than any other type of reported maltreatment (The American Humane Association, 1984).

First of all, we would generally concur with those authorities who suggest that intervention in emotional maltreatment cases be predicated upon the establishment of actual injury to the child. We would further agree that this injury should be both substantial and likely to pose serious protracted difficulties for the child unless it is treated, with parental cooperation, and/or the parent(s) agree to change their behavior which allowed (or caused) this harm to occur. The only possible exception to these rules might be with cases exhibiting *gross* deviations from the normal range of parental conduct where, even though the child has not yet suffered an "injury," (a) harm can be *reliably predicted,* or (b) it is shown by *clear and convincing* evidence that the child will suffer severe behavioral disturbance if the conduct is allowed to continue. Examples of situations where evidence of potential physical or psychological endangerment might appropriately be the basis for forcible state intervention include leaving an infant unattended in the house for long periods of time; tying or chaining a child to the bed (or locking a child in the closet) for extended durations or on repeated occasions; or certain bizarre and violent acts, such as where a parent chops the head of a child's doll off with a knife and says, "It's the doll or you!"

Second, we would urge that "injury" be defined as precisely as possible, despite the fact that no law can specifically cover every possible type of harm. It is simply not in the best interests of either the child or the parents to bring a case to court under a vague and general statute, as is now typical. A further requisite element should be that these injuries have some demonstrable impact on the child's level of behavioral or cognitive functioning. Relevant effects should be both physical and nonphysical. Laws which restrict intervention in mental injury cases only to situations where there are accompanying life-threatening physical effects are, in our view, too restrictive.

It is critical that the mandatory-reporting laws, child welfare system enabling legislation, and juvenile court jurisdiction statutes be *consistent* in covering these issues. The child protective service agency's investigative guidelines/procedures/protocols should help the case worker focus on behaviors of the child and conduct of the parents that *may* be indicative of severe emotional maltreatment. Certainly, any pervasively bizarre or exaggerated behavior or statements of the child should be cause for the worker to secure a comprehensive mental health evaluation for the child. Likewise, where the worker has information which suggests that the child has been the victim of repetitious parental terrorizing, rejection, severe isolation, sexual exploitation, unconscionable missocialization, or morally corrupting and degrading acts, a complete professional evaluation is certainly called for.

Where the child is diagnosed as suffering from a serious mental injury, but the parents agree to participate in an available and professionally recommended corrective/therapeutic program, child protective system intervention should only be *voluntary*, and no court action should be initiated. We strongly urge that legislation and agency regulations make mental health services for the family in a suspected emotional maltreatment case available without the necessity of court involvement. Under Public Law 96-272, the federal Adoption Assistance and Child Welfare Act of 1980, agencies are encouraged to make "reasonable efforts" to prevent child maltreatment victims from being unnecessarily removed from their homes. Placement of emotionally maltreated children is far more likely when there is judicial system intervention, and such children are especially vulnerable to severe psychological harm caused by their forcible removal from their family home.

Finally, the applicable laws and policies which govern the response to emotional maltreatment of children should require that CPS agencies and courts document mental injuries through expert diagnoses (and testimony where required) of medical doctors, psychiatrists, and psychologists. Court rules should encourage judges to seek out the advice of psychosocial experts when emotional abuse or neglect is at issue. Given the complexities of these matters, more stringent standards might involve requiring two or more properly licensed or certified mental health professionals to provide written evaluations and be available for in-court testimony.

APPENDIX: STATE STATUTES

1. *States that include some reference to the infliction of mental injury in their neglect and/or abuse definitions.*

Arkansas – Definition of Abuse: Reporting Law, Ark. Stat. Ann. §42-807(b) (Supp. 1983);

District of Columbia – Definition of Abuse: Court Code, D.C. Code Ann. 16-2301(23) (1981);

Kansas – Definition of Abuse and Neglect: Reporting Law, Kan. Stat. Ann. §38-1502(b) (Supp. 1984);

Louisiana – Definition of Abuse: Reporting Law, La. Rev. Stat. §14:403(B)(3) (Supp. 1985);

Missouri – Definition of Abuse: Reporting Law, Mo. Rev. Stat. §210.110(1) (Supp. 1984);

New Mexico – Definition of Abuse: Court Code, N.M. Stats. §32-1-3(M) (1981);

Pennsylvania – Definition of Abuse: Reporting Law, Pa. Stat. Ann. tit. 11 §2203 (Supp. 1984);

Virginia – Definition of Abuse: Court Code and Reporting Law, Va. Code §16.1-228(A)(1) (Supp. 1984) and Va. Code §63.1-248.2(A) (Supp. 1984);

West Virginia – Definition of Abuse: Welfare Code, W.Va. Code §49-1-3(a)(1) (Supp. 1984).

2. *States that define abuse and/or neglect as harm or threatened harm to a child's health or welfare, and include mental injury or a comparable phrase as one possible cause of such harm.*

Alabama – Definition of Abuse: Reporting Law, Ala. Code §26-14-1(1) (Supp. 1984);

California – Definition of Abuse: Welfare Code, Cal. Welf. & Inst. Code §18951(e)(4) (West 1980);

Florida – Definition of Abuse and Neglect: Reporting Law, Fla. Stat. Ann. §415.503(1)(3) (Supp. 1983 and 1984 Fla. Sess. Law Ch. 84-226 S6 West);

Hawaii – Definition of Abuse and Neglect: Reporting Law, Hawaii Rev. Stat. §350-1(1) (Supp. 1983);

Kentucky – Definition of Abuse and Neglect: Reporting Law, Ky. Rev. Stat. §199.011(6) (Rep. Vol. 1982);

Maine – Definition of Abuse and Neglect: Reporting Law, Me. Rev. Stat. tit. 22, §4002-(1) (Supp. 1984-1985);

Michigan – Definition of Abuse: Reporting Law, Mich. Comp. Laws. Ann. §722.622(c) (Supp. 1984–1985);

Montana – Definition of Abuse and Neglect: Reporting Law, Mont. Rev. Codes Ann. §41-3-102(2)(3) (1983);

North Dakota – Definition of Harm: Reporting Law, N. D. Century Code §50-25.1-02(4) (Supp. 1983);

Oklahoma – Definition of Abuse and Neglect: Reporting Law, Okla. Stat. Ann. tit. 21 §845 (1983);

Utah – Definition of Abuse and Neglect: Reporting Law, Utah Code Ann. §78-3b-2(1),(2) (1982 Interim Supp.).

3. *States that define the term "mental injury."*

Idaho – Definition of Mental Injury: Court Code and Reporting Law, Idaho Code Ann. 16-1602(m) (Supp. 1984);

Nevada – Definition of Abuse and Neglect: Reporting Law, Nev. Rev. Stat. §200.5011(2) (1983);

Rhode Island – Definition of Abuse and Neglect: Reporting Law, R.I. Gen. Laws §40-11-2(3) (Supp. 1984);

South Carolina – Definition of Abuse and Neglect: Reporting Law, S.C. Code Ch. 7, §20-7-490(G) (1985);

South Dakota – Definition of Neglected or Dependent Child: Court Code, S.D. Codified Laws 26-8-6(7) (Supp. 1984);

Vermont – Definition of Abuse and Neglect: Reporting Law, Ver. Stat. Ann. tit. 33 §682(7) (Supp. 1985);

Wyoming – Definition of Abuse: Reporting Law, Wyo. Stat. §14-3-202(a) (ii) (A) (1977).

4. *Other states that define emotional abuse and/or neglect by specifically describing the child's condition or behavior.*

Arizona – Definition of Abuse: Reporting Law & Court Code, Ariz. Rev. Stat. §8-546(A)(2) (Supp. 1984), and Ariz. Rev. Stat. §8-201(2) (Supp. 1984);

New Hampshire – Definition of Abuse: Reporting Law, N.H. Rev. Stat. Ann. §169-C 3 II(d) (Supp. 1983);

Wisconsin – Definition of Emotional Damage: Reporting Law, Wisc. Stat. Ann. §48.981(cm) (West Supp. 1984–85).

5. *States that permit intervention for impairment of emotional health only when it has been caused by physical injury or inadequate physical care.*

New York – Definition of Abuse: Court Code, N.Y. Fam. Ct. Act §1012(e)(i) (McKinney 1983) and Welfare Code, N.Y. Soc. Serv. Law §371(4-b) (McKinney 1983);

Delaware – Definition of Abuse: Reporting Law, Del. Code tit. 16-§902 (1983);

Illinois – Definition of Abuse: Court Code, Ill. Ann. Stat. ch. 37, §702-4(2) (Smith-Hurd Supp. 1985) and Reporting Law, Ill. Ann. Stat. ch. 23, §2053 (Smith-Hurd Supp. 1985).

6. *States that use the terms "mental," "psychological," and "emotional" only when defining neglect.*

Georgia – Definition of a Deprived Child: Court Code, Ga. Code Ann. §15-11-2(8)(A) (1981);

Maryland – Definition of Neglect: Md. Fam. Law Code Ann. §5-701(g) (1984);

Minnesota – Definition of Neglect: Reporting Law, Minn. Stat. Ann. §626.556(2),(c) (Supp. 1985);

Ohio – Definition of Neglect: Court Code, Ohio Rev. Code Ann. §2151.03(D) (Page 1976);

Tennessee – Definition of Neglect: Court Code, Tenn. Code Ann. §37-102(10)(G) (Supp. 1984).

7. *States that refer to "endangering" the mental condition of the child.*

Indiana – Definition of child in need of services: Court Code, Ind. Code Ann. §31-6-4-3(a)(2) (Burns Supp. 1984);

Nebraska – Definition of Abuse and Neglect: Reporting Law, Neb. Rev. Stat. §28-710(3) (Supp. 1984);

New Jersey – Definition of Abuse and Neglect: Court Code, N.J. Stat. Ann. 9:6-8.21(c),(4) (Supp. 1984);

Washington – Definition of Dependent Child: Court Code, Wash. Rev. Code Ann. §13.34.030(2)(c) (Supp. 1985).

8. *States with unusual usage of the terms "mental," "emotional," "psychological," or other comparable terms.*

Connecticut – Definition of Abuse: Court Code, Conn. Gen. Stat. Ann. §46b-120(c) (Supp. 1985);

Iowa—Definition of Child in Need of Assistance: Court Code, Iowa Code Ann. §232.2(5)(f) (West Supp. 1983);

Massachusetts—Reporting Law: Mass. Gen. Laws Ann. 119 §51A (Supp. 1984);

Mississippi—Definition of Abuse: Court Code, Miss. Code Ann. §43-23-3(i) (1981);

North Carolina—Definition of Abuse: Court Code, N.C. Gen. Stat. §7A-517(1)(d) (1981);

North Dakota—Definition of Abuse: Court Code, N.D. Century Code §50-25.1-02(2) (Supp. 1983);

Oregon—Reporting Law: 1985 Or. Laws Ch. 723, 1607 (1985); to be codified as Or. Rev. Stat. 418.740(1)(b);

Texas—Reporting Law: Tex. Fam. Code Ann. §34.01 (Vernon's 1975).

9. *States whose child abuse and neglect laws did not include the use of terms "mental," "psychological," "emotional," or other comparable terms.*

Alaska—Alaska Stat. §47.17.070(1) (1984);

Colorado—Colo. Rev. Stat. 19.10-103(1) (1978 & Supp. 1983).

Update on Alaska's Statute: In 1985, Alaska amended one of its statutes regarding child protection to include the terms *mental* and *emotional*. Published in 1986, it reads: "a) A court may enjoin or limit a person from contact with the child if the Attorney General establishes by a preponderance of the evidence that the person . . . 3) . . . has engaged in conduct that constitutes a clear and present danger to the mental, emotional or physical welfare of a child." (Alaska Stat. §47.17.069(a)(3), Supp. 1986)

REFERENCES

American Bar Association Juvenile Justice Standards Project/Institute of Judicial Administration (not officially approved by the ABA). (1980). *Standard relating to abuse and neglect* (standard 2.1c). Cambridge, MA: Ballinger.

American Humane Association. (1984). *Trends in child abuse and neglect: A national perspective.* Denver, CO: Author.

Ariz. Rev. Stat. §8-201(2) (Supp. 1984).

Burnette v. Wahl, 284 Or. 705, 588 P.2d 1105 (1978).

Child Abuse and Neglect Defined, The Child Abuse Prevention and Treatment Act of 1974, 42 U.S.C. §5102 (1983).

Child Welfare League of America. (1973). *Standards for child protective services.* Author.

Conn. Gen. Stat. Ann. 46b-120(c) (Supp. 1985).

Dean, D. (1979). Emotional abuse of children. *Children Today, 8,* 18–20+.

Del. Code Tit. II §1102(b) (1979).

Ga. Code Ann. §15-11-2(8)(A) (1981).

Gesmonde, J. (1972). Emotional neglect in Connecticut. *Connecticut Law Review, 5,* 100–116.

History of Child Abuse Prevention and Treatment Act: Public Law 93-247. (1978). *U.S. Code of Congressional and Administrative News, 3,* 572–579.

Illinois Department of Children and Family Services. (1982). *Child abuse and neglect investigation decisions handbook* (Appendix B (17). Springfield, IL: Author.

In re B.A.M., 290 N.W. 2d 498 (S.D. 1980).

In re D.A.K., 596 P.2d 747 (1979).

In re Evelyn Q., 4200 N.Y.S. 2d 468 (Fam. Ct., 1979).

In re Keith R., 474 N.Y.S. 2d 254 (Fam. Ct., Richmond Co., 1984).

In re Leif Z., 431 N.Y.S. 2d 290 (Fam. Ct., 1980).

In re Shane T., 115 Misc. 2d 161, 453 N.Y.S. 2d 590 (Fam. Ct., Richmond Co., 1982).

Iowa Code Ann. §232.2(5)(f) (West Supp. 1983).

Kimsey v. Kimsey, 302 N.W. 2d 707 (Neb., 1981).

Landgrebe, E. (1974). Dissenting views on S. 1191. *U.S. Code of Congressional and Administrative News, 2,* 2771–2772.

Mass. Gen. Laws Ann. 119 §51A (Supp. 1984).

Md. Code Ann. FL5-701(g) (1984).

Minn. Stat. Ann. §626.566(2)(c) (Supp. 1985).

Miss. Code Ann. §43-23-3(i) and §43-21-105(m) (1981).

Mississippi Department of Public Welfare Definitions of Child Abuse and Neglect with Guidelines, 1984, pp. 5–8.

N.C. Gen. Stat. §7A-517(1)(d) (1981).

N.D. Century Code §50-25.1-02(2) & (4) (Supp. 1983).

Neb. Rev. Stat. §28-710(3) (Supp. 1984).

Nev. Rev. Stat. §200.5011(2) (1983).

New Jersey Division of Youth and Family Services v. C. M., 436 A.2d 1158 (N.J. Juv. and Dom. Rel. Ct., 1981).

N.H. Rev. Stat. Ann. §169-C 3 II(d) (Supp. 1983).

N.J. Stat. Ann. 9:6-8.21(C)(4) (Supp. 1984).

N.Y. Fam. Ct. Act. §1012(h) (McKinney, 1975).

N.Y. Fam. Ct. Act. §1012(e)(f)(h) (McKinney, 1983).

N.Y. Soc. Serv. Law §371(4-B) (McKinney, 1983).

Ohio Rev. Code Ann. §2151.03(D) (Page, 1976).

Okla. Stat. Ann. Tit. 21, §845 (1983).

1985 Oregon Laws, Ch. 723, 1607; to be codified as Or. Rev. Stat. 418.740(1)(b).

Public Law 96-272, 42 U.S.C. §420-427, §470-477, 1986.

R. I. Gen. Laws 40-11-2(3) (Supp. 1984).

S. D. Codified Laws 26-8-6(7) (Supp. 1984).

Stoetzer, J. B. (1975). The juvenile court and emotional neglect of children. *University of Michigan Journal of Law Reform, 8,* 351–374.

ten Bensel, R. W. (1984). Child abuse and neglect. *Juvenile and Family Court Journal, 35*(4), 23–31.

Tenn. Code Ann. §37-1-202(10)(G) (1984).

Tex. Fam. Code Ann. §34.01 (Vernon's 1975).

U.S. Department of Health and Human Services, National Center on Child Abuse and Neglect. (1983). *Child protection: A guide for state legislation;* Section 4(i). Washington, DC: Author.

U.S. Department of Justice, Office of Juvenile Justice and Delinquency Prevention. (1980).

Standards for the administration of juvenile justice, report of the National Advisory Committee for juvenile justice and delinquency prevention (standard 3.113e). Washington, DC: Author.

Va. Code 16.1-228(A)(1) (Supp. 1984).

Virginia Department of Social Services, Protective Services, 1985, Vol. VII, Sec. III, Chap. A, pp. 6b, 6d.

Wald, M. (1975). State intervention on behalf of "neglected" children: A search for realistic standards. *Stanford Law Review, 27,* 985–1040.

Whiting, L. (1976). Defining emotional neglect— A community workshop looks at neglected children. *Children Today, 5,* 2–5.

Wisc. Stat. Ann. §49-981(cm) (West Supp. 1984–85).

Wyo. Stat. §14-3-202(a)(ii)(a) (1977).

15

Legislative Approaches to Psychological Maltreatment: A Social Policy Analysis

Gary B. Melton and Ross A. Thompson

The concept of psychological maltreatment touches on fundamental values of a society concerning the needs and rights of children. When formalized in legal statutes, this concept assumes added importance and meaning as a statement of social policy concerning the limits of parental authority and the conditions which mandate state intervention into family life. For this reason, legal definitions of psychological maltreatment are potentially controversial and merit considerable caution, in view of the diversity of values which exist in our pluralistic society concerning what practices constitute "appropriate" parenting behaviors. Unlike concepts of maltreatment which are used for theoretical, research, or treatment purposes, legal concepts of psychological maltreatment have profound implications for the relationship between children, family, and the state, the integrity of family life, and our society's tolerance of diverse childrearing goals and practices.

In this chapter, we discuss some of the considerations which enter into applying the concept of psychological maltreatment to the formulation of social policy for children and families. We begin with an overview of basic principles of social policy analysis and their relevance to the concept of child maltreatment, and suggest that a multilevel analysis of the usefulness of a psychological maltreatment construct is needed. Next we discuss some of the important considerations entailed in defining psychological maltreatment for the purpose of legislative initiatives; we emphasize the necessity of a stringent, limited definition for legal purposes. We arrive at this conclusion because of our recognition that knowledge about psychological maltreatment is limited, and that it is essential to minimize the risk of unwarranted and potentially harmful intervention into family life on the basis of possibly invalid criteria. Finally, with these factors in mind, we return to a multilevel analysis to consider how the concept of psychological maltreatment should be considered at the societal, institutional, and individual levels of policy application.

In effect, we are proposing that a more careful analysis be undertaken of the concept of psychological maltreatment than has been common in policy on child abuse and neglect. The child protection system has really evolved only in the past two decades with the "discovery" of battered-child syndrome, sexual abuse, and so forth. With each discovery has come a wave of new legislation, conceived more in the desire to "do something" than to meet carefully crafted policy objectives. As we have argued elsewhere (Melton, in press), policy on child maltreatment has been based primarily on a priori concepts of childhood and family life rather than empirical analysis of the phenomenon. In the end, though, we are convinced that child welfare is

203

more likely to be enhanced by a rational than a visceral response to the admittedly and deservedly emotion-laden concept of psychological maltreatment.

SOCIAL POLICY AND THE CONCEPT OF CHILD MALTREATMENT

Broadly speaking, there are two ways of analyzing the merit of proposals for statutory reform. First, one may assess the degree to which the proposal is consistent with fundamental values of the society. According to some legal philosophers (e.g., Dworkin, 1975, 1977, 1982; Fuller, 1964), the law is inextricably intertwined with moral precepts. In this "natural" approach to the law, unjust law is really not law. Law can be found in the social contract under which people live. To a large extent, the American political and legal systems are based on such a principle; human rights are conceptualized as "inalienable." In such a view, enacted statutes serve only to provide a moral guidepost concerning norms in the natural social order (cf. Pound, 1959, p. 130). Formally, these concepts are institutionalized in the American legal system in the deference shown to the Constitution, especially the Bill of Rights and the 14th Amendment. The Supreme Court has held that rights which are embedded in the Constitution, whether expressly or implicitly, are "fundamental" (*San Antonio Independent School District v. Rodriguez*, 1973). To be valid, any intrusion by the state into these fundamental rights must be motivated by a sufficiently weighty rationale to withstand "strict scrutiny." That is, there must be a compelling state interest underlying the action, the action must be closely related to the interest, and it must be the least intrusive means of meeting the state's interest.

Of course, not all policy decisions involve moral and legal imperatives. If a proposal passes constitutional muster and is ethically benign, there still is a question of whether it is wise. Indeed, utilitarians and their jurisprudential descendents, the legal realists (e.g., Llewellyn, 1962), begin with the question of the pragmatism of a legal rule or its application. In any case, this second format for considering the merit of a proposed law is what has come to be termed *policy analysis*, "the application of reason, evidence, and a valuative framework to public decisions" (MacRae & Haskins, 1981, p. 2). In most instances, policy analysis relies heavily on economic decision-making models; that is, policy analysts generally attempt to apply a rational calculus to policymaking. The expected value of each alternative on variables considered by the society to be important is compared, and the alternative which has the greatest social utility (or the least disutility) is selected.

Child Maltreatment and Fundamental Rights

Both ways of evaluating potential legislation are relevant to suggestions for expanded criteria for abuse and neglect. First, from the standpoint of fundamental values, it is widely recognized that the state has a compelling interest in preventing serious harm to its minor citizens; parents are not "free . . . to make martyrs of their children" (*Prince v. Massachusetts*, 1944, p. 170). The state's interest is as basic as self-preservation: "A democratic society rests, for its continuance, upon the healthy, well-rounded growth of young people into full maturity as citizens, with all that implies" (*Prince v. Massachusetts*, 1944, p. 168). Moreover, the state may have a moral duty to ensure the well-being of dependent minors. Although the *parens patriae* power (i.e., the state's power to protect dependent citizens) initially arose from the sovereign's pecuniary interests,* it has evolved into a much broader power (see *In re Gault*, 1967, pp. 16–17) grounded in the moral duty to provide minors with the primary goods owed all persons. Primary goods are those "things which it is supposed a rational man wants whatever else he wants," including "rights and liberties, opportunities and powers, income and wealth" (Rawls, 1971, p. 92). Primary goods are morally important because they enable choices. Applying the Rawlsian analysis to children, Brown (1982) has suggested that, at a minimum, "[p]rimary goods for children will surely include education, sound bodies, and an emotional makeup of sufficient stability to render choice and action possible, both as children and, later, as adults" (p. 214).

It is undeniable that the state's *parens patriae* power is expansive, as currently interpreted. In

---

*The *parens patriae* power arose from the sovereign's interest in protecting the wealth of incompetent persons. There are no taxes on a squandered estate!

its application, for example, children are made to attend school, are prohibited from working, and so forth. On the other hand, it is widely recognized that family privacy is also a fundamental right (see, e.g., *Roe v. Wade*, 1973, pp. 152–153, and cases cited therein). This interest applies even *after* a judgment of abuse or neglect. In requiring a moderately stringent standard of proof (i.e., "clear and convincing evidence") in order to establish that the standard for termination of parental rights has been met,* the Supreme Court concluded that "[t]he fundamental liberty interest of natural parents in the care, custody, and management of their child does not evaporate simply because they have not been model parents or have lost temporary custody of their child to the State. Even when blood relationships are strained, parents retain a vital interest in preventing the irretrievable destruction of their family life" (*Santosky v. Kramer*, 1982, p. 753).

Some argue that the fundamental value placed on family privacy is inimical to the welfare of children; these scholars would place greater emphasis on state interests (see, e.g., Feshbach & Feshbach, 1976, 1978; Garbarino, 1977; Garbarino, Gaboury, Long, Grandjean, & Asp, 1982). Such "child savers" tend to perceive children as highly vulnerable and to vest the state with a duty to ensure children's well-being. In their value system, family privacy (i.e., parental autonomy) works more to shield abusive conduct from public scrutiny than to protect the integrity of the family as a socializing institution.

Others, arguing for increased control by children over their own fate, claim that the interests of parents and children are seldom the same (see, e.g., Melton, 1982). In the view of such "kiddie libbers," children possess their own interests in autonomy and privacy (Melton, 1983b). Although less concerned with protection than empowerment of children and recognition of their personhood, these scholars also tend to deemphasize family privacy because of its untoward effects on children's individual privacy.

Nonetheless, it is difficult to dispute the analysis of the Supreme Court that, absent a finding of parental unfitness, "the child and his parents share a vital interest in preventing erroneous ter-

mination of their natural relationship" (*Santosky v. Kramer*, 1982, p. 760). The family is the cornerstone of Western social organization and the primary structure for nurturance and protection of the child. In view of the fact that the state is ill-prepared to assume this role, the utmost care must be taken to avoid erroneous or unnecessary intrusions into the family.

At a minimum, the state must make explicit the criteria for intervention into family life. Although indeterminate standards for invoking state jurisdiction over families persist in many states (Mnookin, 1975), justice demands the elimination of vague criteria whenever possible. As a general rule, vague standards for limitations on parental liberty and family privacy are constitutionally impermissible because they fail to give fair warning of legally prohibited conduct and they open the door to unbridled, arbitrary exercise of judicial discretion. Concerns about vagueness are especially warranted in the family law context (see, e.g., *Algaser v. District Court of Polk County, Iowa*, 1975), because there is rarely social consensus about what constitutes "inadequate" or "unfit" parental behavior. In the absence of clear criteria, judges are unable to rely on precedent for their decisions. Instead, they must make a subjective judgment, usually with little basis other than their own hunches and values about the factors important to the healthy socialization of children. With no clear legal rule and no clear social and moral norm, there is substantial risk that, contrary to the most basic principles of distributive justice, similar cases will be treated differently under law.

In short, it is clear that any attempt to expand abuse/neglect jurisdiction into psychological maltreatment will intrude upon family interests which are both constitutionally protected and fundamental to the American social order. To justify such an intrusion, there must first be evidence of a compelling state interest; that is, there must be a demonstration that the well-being of children and, ultimately, the state is seriously harmed by such failure to regulate parental practices. Moreover, there must be a demonstration that state intervention is closely related to the compelling interest of the state and is no more intrusive than necessary to meet that interest. These are clearly stringent criteria, and they must be seriously addressed by those who propose to extend the state's mandate and to intervene in cases of "psychological maltreatment."

---

*Falk (1983) has argued that the logical conclusion of the Supreme Court's analysis should have been establishment of a still more stringent standard of proof (i.e., beyond a reasonable doubt).

Child Maltreatment and Utilitarian Policy Analysis

Even if these thresholds are passed, we are still left with the second evaluative framework, namely the utilitarian calculus of the policy analyst. Do the social benefits of the expansion of state jurisdiction over psychologically abusive parental practices sufficiently outweigh its risks to families to warrant new legislation? Unfortunately, this analysis of social utilities may be largely a problem of determining the policy alternative which is least harmful to children, families, and the society, rather than most optimal. Although there are significant problems with the criteria which Goldstein, Freud, and Solnit (1973, 1979) would use for such state intervention (cf. Katkin, Bullington, & Levine, 1974; Melton, 1978; Wald, 1980), their suggested substitution of the term *least detrimental alternative* for the traditional standard of the *best interests* of the child may be a useful reminder of the limits of the state's ability to meet children's developmental needs. With the overwhelming evidence for the failures of foster care systems in most states (see, e.g., Bush & Gordon, 1978; Mnookin, 1973), there is a question of whether the state can even guarantee protection from harm, much less healthy socialization, to the children whom it takes into its care. In addition, our approach to treating abusive families is woefully inadequate. In even the best demonstration projects, for example, the abuse recidivism rate is disturbingly high (see, for reviews, Melton, 1984; Rosenberg & Hunt, 1984; Sudia, 1981). When professionals often cannot eliminate even the grossest forms of physical violence against children, there is good reason to wonder about the likely success of interventions designed to change more subtle forms of "maltreatment." More importantly, state intervention in itself may foster family dysfunction and impair healthy development in subtler forms of maltreatment by criminalizing family conflict. In short, the state may be ineffective in protecting maltreated children whether it removes them from the home, intervenes within the home, or exercises benign neglect. In this context, proposals for expanding jurisdiction over psychological maltreatment raise the question of whether the state's action, or failing to act, presents the greatest risk of harm.

This rather depressing question is really a series of questions relating to the target of state intervention. Whether the type of proposed policy analysis is a comparison of the fit between proposed legislation and fundamental values or a utilitarian balancing of benefits and risks, the calculus is likely to be different at various levels of the society. For example, as we describe below, legislation on psychological maltreatment raises different issues when it is applied to families than when it is applied to schools. Similarly, although not directly germane to the discussion of this chapter, a consensual definition of psychological maltreatment may be very useful for furthering research on the phenomenon even if it has little utility—or even substantial disutility—as a concept in law (cf. Aber & Zigler, 1981).

At a minimum, therefore, it is useful to consider the question of the merits of the concept of psychological maltreatment at three levels: societal, institutional, and individual. These levels are roughly analogous in ecological theory to macrosystem, exosystem, and microsystem (cf. Bronfenbrenner, 1979; Garbarino, 1982); that is, one might first analyze the usefulness of the concept of psychological maltreatment as the basis for planning policy at a societal level. Will the concept of psychological maltreatment assist in the formulation of a national child and family policy, a policy which is still currently unsystematic in this country (cf. Kamerman & Kahn, 1978; Keniston, 1977; National Academy of Sciences, 1976)? Second, one might consider whether the concept of psychological maltreatment would be useful in shaping legislative policy governing the operation of the various institutional settings of which children are a part (e.g., schools, group homes, day care centers). Finally, the utility of the concept of psychological maltreatment should be considered at the level at which abuse/ neglect adjudication is most commonly applied: the individual family.

When a multilevel analysis is undertaken, it becomes clear that there is not yet a persuasive case for adopting psychological maltreatment as a basis for legal regulation at societal and individual/familial levels. However, the concept may have social utility for legislation at the institutional level. Before describing the various calculations entailed in such a multilevel analysis, however, it is useful to establish some foundation concerning policy-relevant aspects of the concept of psychological maltreatment; that is, regardless of the level of social application, to consider what kinds of considerations enter into the use of the concept of psychological maltreatment for legal policy.

In the following section, we outline some of the important factors entailed in defining this concept for the purpose of legislative initiatives, and thus draw attention to the ways in which such legal definitions of maltreatment can (and should) differ from those which may be used for research or treatment purposes. These considerations include (a) the requirement of definitions which can be reliably applied on a case-by-case basis, (b) a developmental and child-oriented approach to defining psychological maltreatment, and (c) the formulation of guidelines which take into account the extent of our understanding of the origins, consequences, and treatment of psychological maltreatment of children.

ISSUES IN FORMULATING POLICY ON PSYCHOLOGICAL MALTREATMENT

Reliable Guidelines

Guidelines which are used for policy-making purposes should be as constrained and specific as possible to permit reliable assessments of alleged maltreatment on a case-by-case basis. As already noted, vague definitions raise questions of unconstitutionality and injustice due to unbridled judicial discretion. Moreover, from a policy-analytic perspective, they raise the possibility of harmful side effects resulting from either reaching beyond, or not as far as, policy makers intended. Thus, criteria of psychological maltreatment which include terms like "exploiting," "isolating," and "missocializing" appear to raise such difficulties. Can a parent who requires offspring to help with domestic or farm chores expect to be accused of exploiting the child? Should a judge interpret "missocialization" to include inculcating unusual religious beliefs in a child (or fostering no religious commitments at all)? Does it pertain to whether parents encourage strong, traditional gender identities in their children, or foster the development of non-traditional values (compare Morin & Schultz, 1978, with Rosen, Rekers, & Bentler, 1978)? Is a parent who seeks to limit contacts with neighborhood children who, she believes, perhaps erroneously, to be bad influences guilty of isolating her child? The answers to these questions are

not at all obvious given such broad value-laden concepts, and this ambiguity heightens the probability of essentially arbitrary legal decision making. Such definitional vagueness also complicates the tasks of law enforcement and social services agencies, potentially resulting in an overextension of their limited resources and a diversion of attention from more pressing concerns.

Obviously, cultural and subcultural values affect how individuals define the limits of parental authority, and thus it behooves policy makers and the social scientists who advise them to acknowledge and account for the influence of such biases in developing legal policies which apply to a heterogeneous society. Cultural and subcultural diversity in child-rearing goals is an obvious case in point. Less obvious are the effects of cultural or class values on the design and interpretation of research concerning the effects of parenting practices. For example, students of infant–mother attachment in America have identified patterns of "secure" and "insecure" infant behavior which seem to be related to the quality of caregiving, including such extremes as abusive, neglectful, and "psychologically unavailable" maternal care (Egeland & Sroufe, 1981). Although this American research is convincing, cross-cultural research has shown that the same patterns of "insecure" infant behavior are much more common in countries like West Germany, Japan, and Israel, and are viewed by researchers in these countries as resulting from cultural child-rearing norms and infant temperament rather than aberrant care (see Lamb, Thompson, Gardner, & Charnov, 1985, for a review). Thus the interpretation of infant "insecurity" and its origins sometimes depends on the context in which it is observed and the perspective of the investigator. The same is likely to be true of other research in this area. In short, when definitions of child abuse are broadened to encompass the concept of "psychological maltreatment" there is much greater latitude for definitions to be based on parochial values.

Of course, advocates for children are justifiably concerned with protecting the neglected offspring of parents who are absent, grossly disinterested or otherwise "psychologically unavailable." The issue is not whether some children suffer from such experiences in ways which offend the community and adversely affect the

children themselves. At issue, rather, is whether
the concept of "psychologically unavailable" parenting specifically and explicitly identifies such
cases and no others. It is certainly easy to see
how a community or social worker, armed with
such a broad guideline, could insist on intervention into families in which parents are very busy
but not neglectful. It is the danger of unwarranted intervention which reliable guidelines
should help to mitigate.

It should be noted that some researchers have
begun to develop more specific, behaviorally
based inventories which have promise for defining child abuse more precisely and reliably,
including psychological maltreatment. For example, Giovannoni and Becerra (1979) have developed a 92-item checklist of specific incidents and
conditions associated with maltreatment based
on the records of 949 cases from the protective
service systems of four California counties. The
items are grouped under ten classifications (i.e.,
physical injuries, nutritional state, supervision
and protection, hygiene/cleanliness/protection
from the elements, medical and health care,
drug and alcohol use, moral and legal issues,
sexual abuse, school problems, and emotional/
psychological maltreatment), and most offer
more specific, circumscribed criteria than are
commonly found in the literature (although
probably still too broad to serve as sound bases
for legislation). Such an approach may be useful not only for developing more reliable definitions of psychological maltreatment, but also for
helping to distinguish the effects of different
kinds of maltreatment more objectively in future
research (see Schneider-Rosen, Braunwald, Carlson, & Cicchetti, 1985, for an example of application of Giovannoni & Becerra's guidelines).

Developmental Focus
on the Child

Giovannoni and Becerra's (1979) inventory focuses on child characteristics and behavior rather
than parental practices. In contrast, many definitions of child maltreatment focus almost exclusively on the adult's behavior and/or the quality
of living conditions, with less attention to their
effects on the child. There are several reasons to
believe that an emphasis on child outcomes as
they result from parental practices—rather than
on parental behavior per se—will lead to more
reliable and valid statutory definitions of child
maltreatment (Wald, 1975, 1976, 1982).

First, it is very difficult to predict with reasonable certainty the effects of specific parental
practices on a particular child (e.g., Maccoby &
Martin, 1983; Sameroff & Seifer, 1983). Developmental psychologists have long recognized that
the interactions between a child's characteristics
(e.g., temperament, gender) and parental and
social influences are complex; different children
are likely to react in much different ways to the
same parental practices (Lerner, 1982). Second,
even with respect to chronic, long-term stresses
such as those associated with child maltreatment, researchers are increasingly recognizing
that children are not affected in the same way—
sometimes not affected at all—by stressful circumstances. For example, Garmezy's research
(Garmezy, 1983; Garmezy & Tellegen, 1984) on
"stress-resistant" children vividly describes how
some children maintain healthy psychological
functioning in the face of extremely difficult living conditions, partly as a result of the strengths
they derive from other life circumstances. These
circumstances, which have been called "protective" factors by Rutter (1979, 1983), may include
support from someone in the child's broader
social network (e.g., a teacher at school), the assistance of another, nonabusive family member,
or characteristics of the child (including sex and
personality characteristics). Taken together, they
indicate that the prediction of how a child may
be affected by stressful conditions is a difficult,
complex task. Third, as the array of protective
factors identified by these researchers indicates,
one must also look beyond the home environment to understand the effects of maltreatment
on the child. Because child maltreatment is the
product of a multiplicity of factors, including
those from the broader social ecology (Belsky,
1980; Parke & Collmer, 1975), the effects of maltreatment on the child are likely to vary depending on the availability of other supports in the
child's world.

For these reasons, therefore, parental conduct
is, by itself, a poor predictor of the child's psychological or emotional experience in the family;
while some children may be significantly and
adversely affected by the adult's maltreatment,
others may exhibit greater resiliency even in the
face of very difficult circumstances. For the latter group, the potential benefits of intervention
into the family may be substantially outweighed
by its risks to the child. Coercive legal intervention may, in fact, undermine some of the
supports which exist for the child's healthy func-

tioning. Thus by focusing on parental practices per se, the risks of inappropriate and harmful state intervention are likely to be increased. Alternatively, by defining psychological maltreatment in terms of how the child is affected by parental actions, legal policy is more appropriately focused on the adequacy of the child's functioning. Indeed, it is arguable that the state has no compelling interest in intervention, absent demonstrable harm to the child.

An emphasis on the child also centers policy-making attention on the child as the target of any intervention strategy, and thus not only the justification for intervening in the family but also the efficacy of treatment can be appraised in child-centered ways. For example, the success of any intervention (e.g, supportive services to the family, foster care placement, etc.) can be better evaluated in terms of improvement in the child's condition, rather than a change in parental behavior. This is important given the evidence, discussed earlier, that these interventions may, in fact, have adverse consequences for the child.

Partly for these reasons, therefore, the Juvenile Justice Standards Project (1977) would mandate intervention based on evidence of the child's "emotional damage, evidenced by severe anxiety, depression, or withdrawal or untoward aggressive behavior or hostility toward others" (p.55) and parental unwillingness to provide necessary treatment. Such a definition emphasizes how the child is affected by alleged parental maltreatment, with an added caveat concerning the adult's willingness to secure treatment independently of coercive intervention.

Of course, the child, the concern of policy makers, is a developing organism, and this seriously complicates efforts to develop child-centered guidelines for defining psychological maltreatment. In other words, guidelines must be framed using different criteria for children of different ages, since the expression of many psychological processes varies significantly with the developmental level of the child. To illustrate this, Aber and Zigler (1981) have documented how three of the criteria of emotional damage cited above from the Juvenile Justice Standards Project (withdrawal, aggression, and depression) are manifested in significantly different ways at different ages. For example, there are important changes from infancy through adolescence in the causes and types of aggressive behavior manifested by children and their understanding

of aggression in themselves and others (Feshbach, 1970; Piaget, 1932). This makes the concept of "untoward aggressive behavior or hostility" meaningful only when defined in age-appropriate ways. Similarly, recent advances in the treatment of depression in young children have occurred only with the recognition that children sometimes do not present a symptom picture like that of adults (Philips, 1979). Taken together, these considerations mandate definitions of psychological maltreatment which are not only child-centered but also adopt a developmental orientation.

The developmental orientation also has implications for our earlier consideration of the effects of specific parenting practices on children; that is, different children may be affected in various ways by the adult's behavior because they are of different ages. Thus, children may be especially vulnerable to particular kinds of maltreatment at certain periods of development (Aber & Zigler, 1981). For example, rejection or isolation may be more traumatizing at early ages when attachments to caregivers are of primary importance, but have much less impact on adolescents who have extrafamilial sources of social support. On the other hand, other forms of maltreatment (e.g., sexual abuse) may have a greater impact at later ages. Moreover, there may be profound immediate harm with much less long-term developmental effect (cf. Wallerstein, 1984, on age-related long-term effects of divorce), raising further issues concerning the time frame within which child outcomes are assessed.

Formulation of the criteria for psychological maltreatment thus entails exceedingly complex considerations involving the age of the child and the interaction of parental practices with child characteristics in determining child outcomes. As we note below, establishing definitions along these lines threatens to tax our very limited understanding of the effects of certain forms of psychological maltreatment on children.

The Application of Research Knowledge

Although researchers have begun to study systematically the origins and sequelae of physical maltreatment (e.g., Elmer, 1977; Martin, 1976), there is almost no comparable research on psychological maltreatment. More specifically, we have little or no information concerning three issues of central importance to attempts to define psychological maltreatment for the purpose of legislative initiatives.

First, we know little concerning the incidence and etiology of specific forms of psychological maltreatment when viewed independently of other kinds of abuse. The issue of etiology is especially important in helping to clarify the complex origins of the conditions resulting in child maltreatment, and thus becomes crucial when broader definitions of maltreatment are proposed. For example, if certain forms of psychological maltreatment have their origins in broader social and economic conditions (e.g., a child is left alone for long periods because her working mother cannot afford a babysitter), then attempts to define and address these problems must take into account these broader systemic factors as well as the specific family in question. Similarly, it is now well documented that children typically suffer during and after the divorce of their parents (Hetherington, 1979). Obviously the parents' behavior is volitional and harmful to the child, but could it be fairly termed abusive?

Thus the complex etiology of certain forms of maltreatment—and our limited understanding of these origins—imposes constraints on the ability to formulate definitions of psychological maltreatment which are appropriate for legal policy. In addition, as the examples described above illustrate, information concerning the etiology of specific forms of psychological maltreatment help to define the limits of effective legal intervention, by identifying those conditions which are essentially outside the state's power to remedy without incurring greater harm to the child. Even though children suffer as a result of divorce, for example, few would argue that parental conflict should be a basis for invocation of abuse/neglect jurisdiction. Thus information concerning the origins of pscyhological maltreatment is necessary to define the conditions warranting legal intervention and the interventions which are likely to be helpful. Absent such information, defining this phenomenon for legislative purposes has a shaky foundation.

Second, we have little information concerning the sequelae of specific forms of psychological maltreatment by parents, as already noted. In particular, existing research provides little basis for (a) distinguishing the long-term effects of abusive parental practices from short-term or more transient effects, (b) distinguishing the unique effects of different forms of psychologi-

cal maltreatment from the effects of physical or sexual abuse or of marked neglect with which they are often linked, and (c) distinguishing the sequelae of psychological maltreatment from the influence of confounding variables, such as social class (see Toro, 1982). Clearly, such information would help in assessing how significantly children are affected by different forms of psychological maltreatment when viewed independently of other correlates. Such information is important both in justifying legal intervention into the family and in balancing the risks of such intervention against the benefits which may be derived by the child.

Third, we have little specific information about how psychological maltreatment can best be treated in families who have been identified by the legal system. At present, for example, we cannot easily distinguish children who should be removed from the home from those who should remain with the family for supportive assistance. Most importantly, we do not know how to protect children from the emotionally harmful consequences of the state's intervention, even if it entails providing assistance to the child within the family. Another issue complicating our limited understanding of treatment issues concerns parental cooperation: is any kind of within-family strategy likely to succeed if the parent is resistant to treatment? If not, how should the risks of removing the child (see Mnookin, 1973) be weighed against the risks of leaving the child in an abusive family environment? These kinds of considerations are central to efforts to develop legal definitions of psychological maltreatment because coercive interventions are themselves psychologically intrusive, and thus policymakers face the risk of the intervention being worse than the problem itself when legal concepts of abuse are broadened to include emotional or psychological maltreatment.

Clearly, our lack of information concerning the etiology, sequelae, and treatment of psychological maltreatment provides an agenda for much-needed research into this phenomenon. But from the standpoint of formulating legal policy, this gap in knowledge limits the ability to broaden existing guidelines concerning child abuse and neglect. Expansion heightens the risk of unwarranted intervention into the home based on potentially invalid criteria. Indeed, some have argued that, given how little we know about the origins and outcomes of various forms of emotional maltreatment, this concept should not be used at all in judicial decision making concerning intervention in families. For example, Goldstein, Freud, and Solnit (1979) have argued that "even if 'emotional neglect' could be precisely defined, recognition of how little we know about the 'right' treatment, and how little consensus there is about treatments, should caution against using the power of the state to intervene" (p. 77). While they offer perhaps too strong an argument in this regard, it is nevertheless clear that legislative initiatives concerning child maltreatment must take into account the limited research knowledge which exists concerning the origins, consequences, and treatment of psychological abuse of children.

Given the foregoing considerations, it is arguable that the kind of limited definition of psychological maltreatment which would be appropriate for legal policy may not, in fact, identify a unique population of families for treatment. That is, the kinds of psychological maltreatment which could justify intervention (based on existing knowledge) may occur largely in families in which physical abuse, physical neglect, or both also take place. Indeed, it is possible that acceptable levels of reliable identification of psychological maltreatment will occur only when there is also physical maltreatment. If either proposition is true, the concept of psychological maltreatment will serve no useful purpose in legal decision making, at least at an individual level.

The difficulties inherent in adequately and validly distinguishing psychological forms of maltreatment from other forms are well illustrated in a recent study of the circumstances associated with various forms of child maltreatment (Herrenkohl, Herrenkohl, & Egolf, 1983). Case records of all families charged with child abuse over a 10-year period ($N = 328$) in a two-county area of northeastern Pennsylvania were examined to identify the characteristics surrounding incidents of child maltreatment. Herrenkohl and his colleagues gathered information concerning child behavior, parenting behavior, and problems and conflicts experienced by adults within the family. Although only one family was cited for emotional abuse, there were 188 reported incidents of "emotional cruelty," and thus the circumstances associated with this form of psychological maltreatment could be compared with those associated with either physical abuse or neglect. The authors reported that only 5 out of 31 circumstances assessed—

four of them related to adult problems or conflict—significantly distinguished incidents of emotional cruelty from mild and nonabusive parent disciplinary incidents. Moreover, only three circumstances (adult illness, fighting, or the departure of the head of the family) were uniquely associated with emotional cruelty. None of these variables would themselves justify legal intervention, and in no case was more than 2.1% of the variance associated with emotional cruelty explained by any of these circumstances. Thus, even though Herrenkohl and associates focused on a wide range of family-related circumstances, there was nevertheless little useful information by which incidents of emotional cruelty could be differentiated from other kinds of parent–child interaction (either abusive or nonabusive) with any confidence.

Although this conclusion is certainly not encouraging to those who are concerned with children who are emotionally maltreated within the family, it illustrates the caution which must be inherent in defining a broad concept like "psychological maltreatment" for the purpose of legislative initiatives. Until future research provides the information necessary for delineating the specific characteristics associated with incidents of psychological maltreatment, their outcomes for children, and the most useful intervention strategies for assisting afflicted children, policy makers are wisely hesitant to develop legal guidelines which significantly expand the concept of abuse into this area. The alternative is to heighten the risk of intervention in an unwarranted and potentially harmful fashion on the basis of possibly invalid criteria.*

A MULTILEVEL ANALYSIS

Given these guidelines concerning how the concept of psychological maltreatment should be used in legislative initiatives, it is now possible to return to the kind of multilevel analysis we earlier proposed—that is, how useful is the concept of psychological maltreatment when viewed

*Conclusions similar to our own were reached by several commentators on a resolution on psychological abuse introduced in the American Psychological Association's Council of Representatives. See the statements of the Division of Clinical Psychology (Routh, 1984), the Division of Child, Youth, and Family Services (Rosenberg, 1984), and the American Psychology-Law Society (Weithorn, 1984).

from the perspective of the individual child and family, the child in a social institution, and the child in society at large?

Individual

As we conclude above, the concept of psychological maltreatment is most problematic at the level of the individual family, because it is at that level that such legal regulation has the most potential for harm. As we have already discussed, there is a strong legal presumption against state intervention in the family. At present, there simply is not sufficient evidence for the reliability and validity of assessments of psychological maltreatment and of effective (or even benign) interventions resulting from such assessments. Even the characteristics of the population at issue, and whether they differ from those currently subject to child protective jurisdiction, are not clear. Furthermore, as we have indicated, the concept of psychological maltreatment has not been sufficiently well-defined to permit reliable, child-oriented definitions which are suitable for legal policy. For these reasons, we doubt that the concept of psychological maltreatment, as it presently exists, provides a useful basis for legal intervention at the level of the individual family.

Institutional

Because the harm of misapplication at the institutional level is substantially less than at the individual level, there may be some utility in applying the concept of psychological maltreatment to the regulation of providers of services to children. To put the point into terms familiar to psychologists, the greater danger in intervention in families, given the fundamental value placed on family privacy, is a Type I error—intervention in the absence of a clear basis. On the other hand, the greater danger in regulation of state-funded or state-sanctioned children's services is a Type II error—failure to act when some basis for intervention exists.

The general duty of the state to safeguard the welfare of children escalates when it directly assumes the role of parent (e.g., when children are placed in state hospitals) and when it acts *in loco parentis* for brief periods of time (e.g., when children attend public schools). At a minimum, the state owes persons in its care protection from harm (*New York State Association for Retarded Chil-*

dren, Inc. v. Rockefeller, 1973). Due process demands that, when the state institutionalizes persons, it minimizes intrusions upon freedom from bodily restraint, it provides safe conditions, and it provides the habilation necessary to maintain freedom and safety (*Youngberg v. Romeo,* 1982). It is arguable that the limited right to these provisions found in *Youngberg* includes a right to freedom from deterioration of developmental skills (*Youngberg v. Romeo,* 1982, concurring opinion of H. Blackmun, joined by W. J. Brennan and S. D. O'Connor; see also Halpern, 1976). In short, whereas fundamental rights are implicated when there *is* an intrusion into family life, they are also involved when there is *not* regulation of institutions. Thus, the presumptions with which a policy analysis begins differ at these two social levels.

In addition, from a cost–benefit perspective, false positives are less significant concerns in institutional regulation. Although gratuitous allegations may result in an unwarranted diminution of services to children and an unjust sullying of professional relationships, the child–institution relationship is presumably less fragile and basic than the child–parent relationship. Hence, there is probably less objective risk from state intrusion into the affairs of institutions.

At the same time, there is special risk of psychological harm in the everyday lives of children in many of the settings which serve them. The pernicious psychosocial effects of "total institutions" are well documented in the sociology of deviance (see, e.g., Goffman, 1961; McEwen, 1980). Many residential facilities undeniably fit such a category; even the public schools are sufficiently closed, coercive institutions that they often bear the risk of protecting debilitating social environments from public scrutiny and regulation (but compare *Ingraham v. Wright,* 1977, with Bersoff & Prasse, 1978, and Melton, 1980–81). Thus, there is special reason for legal scrutiny of the institutions serving children.

In short, concerns about reliability and validity of definition of maltreatment and potential efficacy of intervention are of less concern in the oversight of institutions than in attempts by the state to regulate family life, because the dangers deriving from inappropriate intervention are reduced. That is not, of course, to say that such concerns are irrelevant to policies about the regulation of institutions. However, the concept of psychological maltreatment may be more useful in identifying institutional practices which are potentially harmful to children and should be barred or regulated.

A Tenth Circuit case, *Milonas v. Williams* (1982), illustrates some of the demeaning practices which should be prohibited. In *Milonas*, officials at a residential school were found to censor "negative thinking" in correspondence and even to administer polygraphs to detect such thoughts as part of a behavioral regimen. There was also "undue punishment, if not outright brutality" (p. 940), including overuse of isolation. Although the practices involved were generally not physically abusive, few would argue that the state should permit such treatment of children, most of whom were placed in the school under state auspices and with state funds. The highly confrontational group therapies and other controversial treatments (e.g., degradation ceremonies when runaways are returned) used in some residential programs for juvenile delinquents and substance abusers also warrant special scrutiny because of their psychologically destructive potential.* In short, although the concept of invasion of privacy—including censorship of mail, sanctions for thinking the "wrong" thoughts, and intense public confrontation—may be too broad and controversial to attain sufficient reliability to be used in the regulation of family life, such a concept is probably useful as a basis for regulation of institutions. More generally, if reasonable care is taken in formulating its definition, the construct of psychological maltreatment may offer a helpful framework for regulating institutional behavior.

Societal

Finally, at the societal level, psychological maltreatment seems to be a concept which is too broad to provide any guidance for shaping legislative policy. At best, the use of the concept will not inform policy; at worst, it will create additional problems. It is naive to believe that significant progress will be made on legislative (or administrative) solutions to problems of nuclear armament, racism, sexism, terrorism, inequality,

*Strong confrontation might be especially harmful when the juvenile's misbehavior is a depressive equivalent (see Chiles, Miller, & Cox, 1980). In such an instance, emotionally charged confrontation might damage already fragile self-esteem.

and so forth by relabeling these broad social problems in terms of the psychological abuse of children. This conclusion is not to deny the significance of many social problems which are not usually defined as "children's issues" (e.g., crime) for the psychological well-being of children and youth (Foundation for Child Development, 1977; Melton, 1983a). The point, though, is that describing racism, for example, as psychological maltreatment does little, if anything, to assist in our understanding of policy alternatives which might combat this reprehensible phenomenon.

Indeed, it would be unsurprising to find that such psychologizing would actually inhibit effective policy formulation. The implication of such approaches is that societal problems are really symptomatic of a sort of "battering nation syndrome." By adopting such a perspective, there is the risk of diverting attention from necessary political and economic reforms, or from more constructive policy alternatives. Besides, the real issue is not the prevention of psychological abuse; it is instead the promotion of healthy socialization. Rather than to focus collective energy on ferreting out the psychological harm to children inherent in certain social phenomena, it would probably be more productive to consider what sorts of environments for children *should* be fostered. In other words, assuming a value of respect for children as persons and a goal of promoting the acquisition of traits and skills consistent with full participation in a democratic society, what policies should be followed? Even this positive approach is controversial. It implies significant reordering of national priorities (Keniston, 1977; National Academy of Sciences, 1976) and reconceptualization of the nature and status of children (Melton, 1983a, 1983b, 1984).

The application of the concept of psychological maltreatment at a societal level also raises a question of who should be held responsible for such abuse. For example, would a legitimate legislative approach be to invoke the jurisdiction of the family court if parents consciously or unconsciously instill bigotry in their children? Elevating a term which has become associated with intervention in the family to the level of broader social problems seems to invite such illogical attacks on societal ills through intervention and regulation of microlevel institutions such as the family.

CONCLUSION; A QUESTION OF PARADIGMS

In view of the requirements of social policy analysis and the demands they impose on the concept of psychological maltreatment for the purpose of legislative initiatives, we view this concept as having greater value for the regulation of social institutions than for intervention into families or for addressing broader social problems. However, we also think it important to reconsider the broader issue of whether a focus on the issue of psychological maltreatment is wise as a matter of policy generally. Perhaps resources would be better spent in examination of ways in which children and families can be empowered (cf. Rappaport, 1977; Ryan, 1971). Attention to the regulation and treatment of individual families may miss the key point of ways to enhance the well-being of children and families. The implicit illness model may, in fact, divert attention from root causes of distress in families and the low status of children. Especially given the limits of therapeutic technology, there needs to be a reconsideration of the purposes and means of state action. It may well be that an emphasis on child *protection* ultimately is an ineffective starting point; rather, the *promotion* of child welfare may be a better framework for policy.

REFERENCES

Aber, J. L., & Zigler, E. (1981). Developmental considerations in the definition of child maltreatment. In R. Rizley & D. Cicchetti (Eds.), *Developmental perspectives on child maltreatment* (pp. 1–29). San Francisco: Jossey–Bass.

Algaser v. District Court of Polk County, Iowa, 406 F. Supp. 10 (S.D. Iowa 1975), *affd*, 545 F.2d 1137 (8th Circ. 1976).

Belsky, J. (1980). Child maltreatment: An ecological integration. *American Psychologist, 35*, 320–335.

Bersoff, D. N., & Prasse, D. (1978). Applied psychology and judicial decision making: Corporal punishment as a case in point. *Professional Psychology, 9*, 400–411.

Bronfenbrenner, U. (1979). *The ecology of human development: Experiments by nature and design.* Cambridge, MA: Harvard University Press.

Brown, P. G. (1982). Human independence and proxy consent. In W. Gaylin & R. Macklin (Eds.), *Who speaks for the child?: The problems of proxy consent* (pp. 209–222). New York: Plenum.

Bush, M., & Gordon, A. C. (1978). Client choice and bureaucratic accountability: Possibilities for responsiveness in a social welfare bureaucracy. *Journal of Social Issues, 34*(2), 22–43.

Chiles, J. A., Miller, M. L., & Cox, G. B. (1980). Depression in an adolescent delinquent population. *Archives of General Psychiatry, 37*, 1179–1184.

Dworkin, R. (1975). Hard cases. *Harvard Law Review, 88*, 1057–1109.

Dworkin, R. (1977). *Taking rights seriously.* Cambridge, MA: Harvard University Press.

Dworkin, R. (1982). "Natural" law revisited. *University of Florida Law Review, 34*, 469–524.

Egeland, B., & Sroufe, A. (1981). Developmental sequelae of maltreatment in infancy. In R. Rizley & D. Cicchetti (Eds.), *Developmental perspectives on child maltreatment* (pp. 77–92). San Francisco: Jossey–Bass.

Elmer, E. (1977). *Fragile families, troubled children.* Pittsburgh: University of Pittsburgh Press.

Falk, P. (1983). Why not beyond a reasonable doubt?: *Santosky v. Kramer. Nebraska Law Review. 62*, 602–620.

Feshbach, N. D., & Feshbach, S. (1976). Punishment: Parent rites versus children's rights. In G. P. Koocher (Ed.), *Children's rights and the mental health professions* (pp. 149–170). New York: Wiley.

Feshbach, S. (1970). Aggression. In P. H. Mussen (Ed.), *Carmichael's manual of child psychology* (Vol. 2, 3rd ed., pp. 159–259). New York: Wiley.

Feshbach, S., & Feshbach, N. D. (1978). Child advocacy and family privacy. *Journal of Social Issues, 34*(2), 114–121.

Foundation for Child Development. (1977). *National survey of children.* Unpublished manuscript.

Fuller, L. (1964). *The morality of law.* New Haven: Yale University Press.

Garbarino, J. (1977). The price of privacy in the social dynamics of child abuse. *Child Welfare, 56*, 565–575.

Garbarino, J. (1982). *Children and families in the social environment.* New York: Aldine.

Garbarino, J., Gaboury, M. T., Long, F., Grandjean, P., & Asp, E. (1982). Who owns the children? An ecological perspective on public policy affecting children. In G. B. Melton (Ed.), *Legal policies affecting child and youth services* (pp. 43–63). New York: Haworth.

Garmezy, N. (1983). Stressors of childhood. In N. Garmezy & M. Rutter (Eds.), *Stress, coping, and development in children* (pp. 43–84). New York: McGraw-Hill.

Garmezy, N., & Tellegen, A. (1984). Studies of stress-resistant children: Methods, variables, and preliminary findings. In F. Morrison, C.

Lord, & D. Keating (Eds.), *Advances in applied development psychology* (Vol. 1). New York: Academic Press.

Giovannoni, J. M., & Becerra, R. M. (1979). *Defining child abuse.* New York: Free Press.

Goffman, E. (1961). *Asylums.* New York: Doubleday.

Goldstein, J., Freud, A., & Solnit, A. J. (1973). *Beyond the best interests of the child.* New York: Free Press.

Goldstein, J., Freud, A., & Solnit, A. J. (1979). *Before the best interests of the child.* New York: Free Press.

Halpern, C. R. (1976). The right to habilitation: Litigation as a strategy for social change. In S. Golann & W. J. Fremouw (Eds.), *The right to treatment for mental patients* (pp. 73–98). New York: Irvington.

Herrenkohl, R. C., Herrenkohl, E. C., & Egolf, B. P. (1983). Circumstances surrounding the occurrence of child maltreatment. *Journal of Clinical and Consulting Psychology, 51,* 424–431.

Hetherington, E. M. (1979). Divorce: A child's perspective. *American Psychologist, 34,* 851–858.

In re Gault, 387 U.S. 1 (1967).

Ingraham v. Wright, 403 U.S. 651 (1977).

Juvenile Justice Standards Project. (1977). *Standards relating to abuse and neglect* (tentative draft). Cambridge, MA: Ballinger.

Kamerman, S. B., & Kahn, A. J. (Eds.). (1978). *Family policy: Government and families in 14 countries.* New York: Columbia University Press.

Katkin, D., Bullington, B., & Levine, M. (1974). Above and beyond the best interests of the child: An inquiry into the relationship between law and social action. *Law and Society Review, 8,* 669–687.

Keniston, K. (1977). *All our children: The American family under pressure.* New York: Harcourt Brace Jovanovich.

Lamb, M. E., Thompson, R. A., Gardner, W. P., & Charnov, E. L. (1985). *Infant–mother attachment: The origins and developmental significance of individual differences in strange situation behavior.* Hillsdale, NJ: Erlbaum.

Lerner, R. M. (1982). Children as producers of their own environment. *Developmental Review, 2,* 342–370.

Llewellyn, K. N. (1962). *Jurisprudence: Realism in theory and practice.* Chicago: University of Chicago Press.

Maccoby, E. E., & Martin, J. A. (1983). Socialization in the context of the family: Parent–child interaction. In P. H. Mussen (Ed.), *Handbook of child psychology. Vol. 4: Socialization, personality, and social development* (E. M. Hetherington, Vol. Ed., 4th ed., pp. 1–101). New York: Wiley.

MacRae, D., Jr., & Haskins, R. (1981). Models for policy analysis. In R. Haskins & J. J. Gallagher (Eds.), *Models for social policy: An introduction.* Norwood, NJ: Ablex.

Martin, H. P. (Ed.). (1976). *The abused child.* Cambridge, MA: Ballinger.

McEwen, C. A. (1980). Continuities in the study of total and nontotal institutions. *Annual Review of Sociology, 6,* 143–185.

Melton, G. B. (1978). The psychologist's role in juvenile and family law. *Journal of Clinical Child Psychology, 7,* 189–192.

Melton, G. B. (1980–1981). Legal policy and child development research: A selective review. *Child and Youth Services, 3*(3/4), 1, 13–20.

Melton, G. B. (1982). Children's rights: Where are the children? *American Journal of Orthopsychiatry, 52,* 530–538.

Melton, G. B. (1983a). *Child advocacy: Psychological issues and interventions.* New York: Plenum.

Melton, G. B. (1983b). Toward "personhood" for adolescents: Autonomy and privacy as values in public policy. *American Psychologist, 38,* 99–103.

Melton, G. B. (1984). Developmental psychology and the law: The state of the art. *Journal of Family Law, 22,* 445–482.

Melton, G. B. (in press). The child in child welfare. In J. Gilgun, Z. Eisikovits, & I. Schwartz (Eds.), *Rethinking child welfare: International perspectives.*

Milonas v. Williams, 691 F.2d 931 (10th Cir. 1982).

Mnookin, R. H. (1973). Foster care: In whose best interest? *Harvard Educational Review, 43,* 599–638.

Mnookin, R. H. (1975). Child custody adjudication: Judicial functions in the face of indeterminancy. *Law and Contemporary Problems, 39,* 226–293.

Morin, S. F., & Schultz, S. J. (1978). The gay movement and the rights of children. *Journal of Social Issues, 34*(2), 137–148.

National Academy of Sciences. (1976). *Toward a national policy for children and families.* Washington, DC: Author.

New York State Association for Retarded Children, Inc. v. Rockefeller, 357 F. Supp. 752 (E.D.N.Y. 1973), *enforced sub nom.* New York State Association for Retarded Children, Inc. v. Carey, 393 F. Supp. 715 (E.D.N.Y. 1975) *and* 409 F. Supp. 606 (E.D.N.Y. 1976), *aff'd,* 596 F.2d 27 (2d Cir. 1979, *enforced,* 492 F. Supp. 1099 (E.D.N.Y. 1980).

Parke, R. D., & Collmer, C. W. (1975). Child abuse: An interdisciplinary analysis. In E. M. Hetherington (Ed.), *Review of child development research* (Vol. 5, pp. 509–590). Chicago: University of Chicago Press.

Philips, I. (1979). Childhood depression: Interpersonal interactions and depressive phenomena. *American Journal of Psychiatry, 136,* 511–515.

Piaget, J. (1932). *The moral judgment of the child.* London: Kegan Paul.

Pound, R. (1959). *Jurisprudence* (Vol. 2). St. Paul, MN: West.

Prince v. Massachusetts, 321 U.S. 158 (1944).

Rappaport, J. (1977). *Community psychology: Values, research, and action.* New York: Holt, Rinehart & Winston.

Rawls, J. (1971). *A theory of justice.* Cambridge, MA: Harvard University Press.

Roe v. Wade, 410 U.S. 113 (1973).

Rosen, A. C., Rekers, G. A., & Bentler, P. M. (1978). Ethical issues in the treatment of children. *Journal of Social Issues, 34*(2), 122–136.

Rosenberg, M. S. (1984, September 15). Unpublished memorandum to M. Brewster Smith on behalf of Division 37, American Psychological Association.

Rosenberg, M. S., & Hunt, R. D. (1984). Child maltreatment: Legal and mental health issues. In N. D. Reppucci, L. A. Weithorn, E. P. Mulvey, & J. Monahan (Eds.), *Children, mental health, and the law* (pp. 79–101). Beverly Hills, CA: Sage.

Routh, D. K. (1984, July 18). Unpublished memorandum to M. Brewster Smith on behalf of Division 12, American Psychological Association.

Rutter, M. (1979). Protective factors in children's responses to stress and disadvantage. In M. W. Kent & J. E. Rolf (Eds.), *Primary prevention of psychopathology: Social competence in children* (Vol. 3, pp. 49–74). Hanover, NH: University Press of New England.

Rutter, M. (1983). Stress, coping, and development: Some issues and some questions. In N. Garmezy & M. Rutter (Eds.), *Stress, coping, and development in children* (pp. 1–41). New York: McGraw-Hill.

Ryan, W. (1971). *Blaming the victim.* New York: Vintage.

Sameroff, A. J., & Seifer, R. (1983). Familial risk and child competence. *Child Development, 54,* 1254–1268.

San Antonio Independent School District v. Rodriguez, 411 U.S. 1 (1973).

Santosky v. Kramer, 455 U.S. 745 (1982).

Schneider-Rosen, K., Braunwald, K. G., Carlson, V., & Cicchetti, D. (1985). Current perspectives in attachment theory: Illustration from the study of maltreated infants. In I. Bretherton & E. Waters (Eds.), *Growing points in attachment theory and research. Monographs of the Society for Research in Child Development.* Serial No. 209, *50,* Nos. 1–2.

Sudia, C. E. (1981). What services do abusive and neglecting families need? In L. H. Pelton (Ed.), *The social context of child abuse and neglect* (pp. 268–290). New York: Human Sciences Press.

Toro, P. A. (1982). Developmental effects of child abuse: A review. *Child Abuse and Neglect, 6,* 423–431.

Wald, M. (1975). State intervention on behalf of "neglected" children: A search for realistic standards. *Stanford Law Review, 27,* 985–1040.

Wald, M. (1976). State intervention on behalf of "neglected" children: Standards for removal of children from their homes, monitoring the status of children in foster care, and termination of parental rights. *Stanford Law Review, 28,* 623–706.

Wald, M. (1980). Thinking about public policy toward abuse and neglect of children: A review of *Before the best interests of the child. Michigan Law Review, 78,* 645–693.

Wald, M. (1982). State intervention on behalf of endangered children: A proposed legal response. *Child Abuse and Neglect, 6,* 3–45.

Wallerstein, J. S. (1984). Children of divorce: Preliminary report of a ten-year follow-up of young children. *American Journal of Orthopsychiatry, 54,* 444–458.

Weithorn, L. A. (1984, May 11). Unpublished memorandum to M. Brewster Smith on behalf of Division 41, American Psychological Association.

Youngberg v. Romeo, 457 U.S. 309 (1982).

16

Psychological Maltreatment in Education and Schooling

Stuart N. Hart, Marla R. Brassard, and Robert B. Germain

A high-school student steps from a school bus into the snow and dies. The investigation of his death reveals no physical pathology. It appears as if he just stopped living. A review of his life history establishes that he felt unloved, rejected, ignored, put down, and incompetent throughout a large portion of his life due to the actions of those around him at home and at school. School personnel conclude that these experiences led to his death, that he was simply "erased" as a human being little by little, until he ceased to exist, and became a "cypher." One of the boy's teachers is affected powerfully by the tragedy. He pledges that he will never again pay so little attention to a student who shows symptoms of a great need for someone to care.

This is an outline of the plot of *Cypher in the Snow* (Brigham Young University, 1974), a true story made into a film. The film depicts psychological maltreatment in both school and home, maltreatment which could have been reduced in occurrence and impact through action by school personnel. The film has been in demand among educators all across the country, possibly because they recognize that it depicts a teaching responsibility that deserves high priority, but is generally neglected.

Psychological maltreatment (e.g., mental cruelty/injury, emotional abuse, and neglect) is a problem of major proportions which occurs under a wide variety of conditions and which is believed to be destructive to the development of children. It is expressed through negative human interaction and insufficient human interaction where it is needed. Schooling involves human interaction. It requires more of the growing-up time of young people than any other waking activity during the developmental period, with the possible exception of television viewing. Attempts to understand and eliminate psychological maltreatment must focus not only on the home and neighborhood but also on the school and schooling. The school is the only institution in our society (and most others) through which virtually all young people pass. The manner in which they pass provides opportunities for close and relatively objective observation by professionals who are capable of identifying symptoms of maltreatment which require intervention. The school experience also provides opportunities for those within the school to maltreat children.

Educators and education have been encouraged to assume major responsibilities for identifying, reporting, and reducing child abuse and neglect (Broadhurst, 1978; Drews, 1972; Garbarino, 1979; Gil, 1969; Jones & Fox, 1979; Levin, 1983; Martin, 1973; Tower, 1984). The point has been made strongly, and occasionally with dramatic emphasis, by the titles of some of the articles addressing this topic: "The growing horror of child abuse and the undeniable role of the schools in putting an end to it" (Martin, 1973, p. 51), and "No turning back: The school and child maltreatment" (Bolton, 1983, p. 25). We consider such emphasis well directed. We intend in this chapter to clarify the manner in which these proposed responsibilities and associated practices have been and should be focused on psychological maltreatment, and the manner in which schools as institutions and their employees maltreat children.

This chapter will contain three major sections. The first will deal with the responsibilities of school systems to identify, report, correct, and prevent psychological maltreatment which originates outside of the school environment. The second will deal with psychological maltreatment which is perpetrated through the institutional structures, processes, and personnel of schooling. The third section will deal with recommendations for goals, practices, and training to enable schools and their personnel to deal with psychological maltreatment responsibly.

This chapter is organized around a particular set of theoretical and conceptual models. We adhere to a transactional model (Kadushin & Martin, 1981) of psychological maltreatment which recognizes the occurrence of transactions within and across the various levels of human ecological systems (Bronfenbrenner, 1979; Garbarino, 1977a; Garbarino & Vondra, 1983; Valentine, Freeman, Acuff, & Andreas, 1985). In addition, we assume that psychological maltreatment is an attack on basic motivational or needs systems (Maslow, 1970; Glasser, 1965) and that human beings are best understood from developmental and holistic perspectives (Erickson & Egeland, in press; Montagu, 1970; Pelletier, 1977). See chapter 1 of this volume for a more detailed review of these models.

PSYCHOLOGICAL MALTREATMENT ORIGINATING OUTSIDE OF SCHOOL

Rationale and Focus for Involvement in Child Maltreatment

When relationships between child maltreatment and schooling are given attention, consideration is generally limited to maltreatment which occurs outside school environments and which might be identified, reported, reduced, or prevented through the actions of school personnel. Coverage by authoritative sources, both earlier (Drews, 1972) and more recently (Broadhurst,

1984; Tower, 1984), have dealt with child maltreatment in this manner. Particular attention will be given in this section to books by Broadhurst (1984) and Tower (1984) because they represent organizations with major responsibilities and commitments in this area. Broadhurst's (1984) work, *The Educator's Role in the Prevention and Treatment of Child Abuse and Neglect*, was written for and published by the U.S. Department of Health and Human Services, while Tower's (1984) work, *Child Abuse and Neglect: A Teacher's Handbook for Detection, Reporting, and Classroom Management*, was written for and published by the National Education Association.

Educators have been considered to be potentially valuable sources of help in dealing with child maltreatment because they have repeated contacts with children which allow them to acquire developmental and behavioral norms from first-hand experience. These norms allow teachers to make informal judgments about the degree to which a child's physical or behavioral characteristics differ significantly from those of age-mates or from the child's own previously displayed characteristics (Bolton, 1983; Broadhurst, 1984; Fairorth, 1982; Fossum & Sorenson, 1980). If estimates of the incidence level of child maltreatment among school-age children are accurate (that they represent 50% of all abused and neglected children; Broadhurst, 1984) educators would appear to have ample opportunity for involvement.

Educators are mandated by law in most states to report suspected child maltreatment (Levin, 1983). They have been encouraged to become involved in preventing and identifying child maltreatment by a wide variety of authors and by the Education Commission of the States (Jones & Fox, 1979), the National Center on Child Abuse and Neglect (Broadhurst, 1984), the National Education Association (1982), and the National Parents and Teachers Association (1985).

Teachers have been singled out for their potential to be effective sources of identification (Fairorth, 1982), reduction (Education Commission of the States, 1976), and prevention of child maltreatment (Bolton, 1983). Characteristics believed to be intrinsic to the very nature of the role of "teacher" are consistent with these expectations. As examples: teachers are believed to be deeply committed to children at a personal level (Broadhurst, 1984) and to be concerned with the "whole child" (American Humane Association, 1971); and their efforts to produce learning are likely to be reduced by the impact of child maltreatment on their students (Broadhurst, 1984).

Types and Sources of Maltreatment Given Attention

Historically, major emphasis has been given to physical abuse and neglect perpetrated by parents and other adult caretakers in the home. Drews' research on practices within the schools for dealing with child maltreatment asked respondents to ". . . describe in detail a recent case of physical abuse . . ." (1972, p. 117), and she emphasized that schools frequently allow a maltreated child to ". . . return to his home day after day only to be the victim of continued abuse" (1972, p. 115). Even very recent publications that give important attention to psychological maltreatment have found it difficult to resist implying that psychological maltreatment is relegated to somewhat lesser importance than other forms of maltreatment. When Broadhurst (1984, p. 2) described estimates of the extent of child abuse and neglect she specifically identified physical and sexual maltreatment as the categories covering incidence rates. Broadhurst (1984), Fairorth (1982), and Tower (1984), in their recent writings on the responsibilities of education/educators in dealing with child maltreatment, focus almost exclusively on maltreatment perpetrated in the home. Broadhurst represents this emphasis as she states, ". . . child abuse and neglect usually occur in the privacy of the home . . ." (1984, p. 2).

The pervading presence of psychological maltreatment has been recognized in descriptions of the impact of all forms of child abuse and neglect. This recognition is usually expressed in descriptions of the influences of child maltreatment on psychological and behavioral characteristics of the child. The items listed as behavioral and psychological symptoms/sequelae of physical maltreatment and of sexual abuse rival and in some cases surpass in quantity those of a physical nature (Broadhurst, 1984; Tower, 1984). However, it is rare indeed for an author to specifically state that psychological maltreatment is a part of all forms of child maltreatment. Exceptions exist. Broadhurst includes in her opening comments on emotional maltreatment the following statements: "Emotionally maltreated children are not always physically abused. But physically abused children are almost always emotionally maltreated as well" (1984, p. 19).

Direct attention has, however, been focused on psychological maltreatment and the responsibilities for educators and education. Drews (1972, p. 121) indicated that responses to her survey of school districts found, "An overwhelming number felt that emotional abuse and neglect were seen much more frequently than was physical abuse," and that respondents, ". . . were concerned that the former is often much more harmful to the child." Leavitt (1981) identified psychological maltreatment as ". . . probably the area in which teachers and other school professionals can make the greatest contribution in a direct manner" (p. 270). When it is given direct and specific attention, it is often recognized to be very difficult to deal with because so little is known about it (Leavitt, 1981) and because it is so hard to detect, prove, or report (Tower, 1984).

Psychological maltreatment is usually presented to educators under the heading of "emotional abuse" (Tower, 1984) or "emotional maltreatment" (Broadhurst, 1984). The definitions in such contexts tend to emphasize verbal abuse, rejection, unequal treatment, and inadequate affection or concern for the child. Broadhurst's list ". . . includes blaming, belittling or rejecting a child; constantly treating siblings unequally; and persistent lack of concern by the caretaker for the child's welfare" (1984, p. 19), and Towers identifies ". . . belittling, rejecting, and in general not providing a positive, loving emotional atmosphere in which a child can grow" (1984, p. 29). The composite of symptoms of psychologically maltreated individuals covers a wide range of behavioral and personal–social adjustment disorders (e.g., bizarre and extreme behavior, habit and conduct disorders, self- and other destructive behaviors, withdrawal, sleep and waste elimination problems, antisocial and delinquent behavior, eating disorders, psychosomatic disorders). It is obvious, as Broadhurst indicates, "The behavior of emotionally maltreated and emotionally disturbed children is similar" (1984, p. 19). This issue will be raised later, in the section on recommendations.

Parents who emotionally maltreat have been described as having unrealistically high expectations for their children and being prone to verbally criticize their children when these expectations are not met. Tower offers suggestions which are specific to helping the child who is psychologically maltreated. They include providing attention, encouraging the child to express her/himself, informing the parents of the child's needs, and facilitating access to counseling to help the parents with their problems (1984). In a later section of her book, she identified the two paramount needs (basic psychological needs) of all maltreated children as improvement of self-concept and the experience of success through doing something correctly.

A number of authors have concluded that psychological maltreatment is very difficult to deal with and that difficulties appear to be related to a lack of definition and standards of evidence. Tower states, "This is perhaps the most difficult area to detect or prove and certainly difficult to report. Social service agencies are so overwhelmed with physical and sexual injuries that the less concrete report of emotional abuse may be screened out" (1984, p. 29). The situation had changed very little from that analyzed by ten Bensel and Berdie in 1976, when they noted the difficulties existing in regard to identifying emotional abuse and neglect.

Roles and Responsibilities Identified for Educators

Very little in the way of specific roles, responsibilities, or strategies for educational systems and personnel has been developed or suggested in regard to psychological maltreatment. The recommendations made for child maltreatment more generally conceived are evidently assumed to apply for the several different categories of maltreatment. They give primary importance to identifying and reporting child abuse and neglect (Broadhurst, 1978, 1984; Drews, 1972; Garbarino, 1979; Tower, 1984). In fact, it has been noted that when involved, "The educator's legal role in cases of child abuse is generally limited to identification" (Fairorth, 1982, p. 65).

Generally, it is made clear that educators are required to report suspected cases of maltreatment and that they should not acquiesce to school system pressure to remain silent. In addition, it has been strongly recommended that school personnel should not use the threat of reporting as leverage to get perpetrators to change or attempt to handle a case on their own in lieu of reporting (Drews, 1972). The literature is full of descriptions of the characteristics of maltreated children, intended to help in their identification. Reference to state statutes and local policy in determining actions to be taken within the school system and in relationships with protective service is suggested to ensure that the type of maltreatment and procedures being followed are within guidelines given for developing and handling reports (Broadhurst, 1984; Tower, 1984).

Tower's (1984) coverage of areas of responsibility and involvement for educators, written under the auspices of the National Education Association, may be considered of particular relevance to educators. She gives consideration to some topics not generally given attention (e.g., preparation for court appearances). Her suggestions for helping the child in the classroom are directed toward enhancing self-image, enabling classmates to understand the maltreated child, stimulating other reports of maltreatment, educating children in regard to abuse and neglect, and helping the foster child adjust.

Broadhurst (1984) provides advice for the handling of interviews with the child and his or her parents which should reduce the likelihood of exacerbating tensions and maltreatment. The advice is sensitive to the psychological conditions associated with maltreatment (e.g., anger, need for privacy and confidentiality, avoidance of unnecessary prying).

Suggestions for the prevention of child maltreatment have been offered. Suggestions emphasize the following points: parent education for adults, counseling programs for parents to reduce stress and develop competencies, financial support for child needs, friendly visits to homes for assessment and support, education of children to recognize and resist maltreatment, teacher–student relationships to assist in identifying dangerous conditions in the home, parenting and family-life education for school-age children, preparation for building social support systems, and the use of the school as a center for family services (Broadhurst, 1984; Fairorth, 1982; Garbarino, 1979; Tower, 1984). Garbarino (1979) extends his focus beyond the one-to-one and family interaction levels. He suggests that prevention must incorporate planning and action at higher levels of the human ecological system, community and society, to reduce support for violence and produce a cultural ideology of childhood which removes children from the category of property and establishes commitments to their rights and healthy development. For example, he recommends that schools act as family support centers and that they become involved in community-wide action to secure basic rights for children (Garbarino, 1979).

When the focus on roles and responsibilities

of educators is specific to psychological maltreatment, it usually deals with identification through recognition of (a) maltreating behaviors/conditions directed at the child and (b) symptoms presented by the child (Tower, 1984, pp. 29–30; Broadhurst, 1984, pp. 18–19). Occasionally, attention has been given to recognizing and understanding antecedents present in the characteristics of perpetrators, to helping procedures, and to difficulties inherent in dealing with psychological maltreatment (Tower, 1984). The maltreating behaviors/conditions presented are generally based on rather narrow conceptualizations of mental cruelty or emotional abuse and neglect. They deal with one-to-one human interaction. The lists presented by Broadhurst (1984) and Tower (1984) in their books are representative.

Increased attention is beginning to be focused on psychological maltreatment and the responsibilities of schools and their personnel. Germain, Brassard, and Hart (1985) have recently described the roles of school professionals in dealing with psychological maltreatment, with special emphasis on school psychologists, and Garbarino, Guttman, & Seeley (1986) have produced a book to guide professional practice which is focused on psychological maltreatment.

Effectiveness of Education and Educators

The level of participation and effectiveness of educators in dealing with child maltreatment has been generally disappointing. Early recognition of this came from Drews, who stated, "for the older child who is physically abused, his school may be his only recourse. And yet it is this very source of help that so often lets him flounder and return to his home day after day only to be the victim of continued abuse" (1972, p. 115). In 1983, 11 years after Drews' analysis, Levin found that "Recent literature indicates that school personnel generally seriously underreport and often mishandle suspected child abuse and neglect because of failure to recognize the signs of abuse and failure to report suspected abuse to the proper authorities" (Levin, 1983, p. 15).

Evidence of this condition is found in the reports of the American Humane Association, which provide national statistics regarding sources of reports of child maltreatment. In the years 1981, 1982, and 1983 schools reported approximately 13% of the cases (American Humane Association, 1983, 1984, 1985, 1986). This is clearly below what might be expected on the basis of the relatively high incidence level of child maltreatment believed to exist for school-age children. In 1983, 12.2% of the "emotional maltreatment" cases for which information was available were reported by school personnel, in comparison to the 45.6% reported by nonprofessionals (American Humane Association, 1985). These low reporting rates may be due to the lack of school system preparedness and of guidance for school personnel. Early investigation of these conditions by Drews (1972) found that 49% of school system central office administrators reported the existence of a standard operating procedure, and that only 24% of building administrators and personnel agreed. Her conclusion was that it is "pointless" for high-level administrators to be aware of a policy which is not known to front-line personnel working with students. In a later article by Brenton (1977, p. 52) the executive director of the National Committee for Prevention of Child Abuse is quoted as stating that a majority of school districts have no set policies or procedures. While improvements may have been made, this hindrance to educator effectiveness continues to deserve attention. The Education Commission of the States found 20% of large school districts and 36% of small school districts without policies in 1978 (Jones & Fox, 1979). A more recent review (Levin, 1983) complained about the same problem.

Other reporting problems include school administrators who set a negative tone and sometimes obstruct reporting (Garbarino, 1979; Broadhurst, 1984); school personnel who are reluctant to interfere in family privacy (Garbarino, 1979; Broadhurst, 1984), feeling that parents have the right to treat and discipline their children as they wish (Levin, 1983; Broadhurst, 1984); frustration with inadequate case handling (Drews, 1972); unclear definitions of child abuse and neglect (Garbarino, 1979); lack of confidence (Volpe, 1981), competence, and preparation (O'Block, Billimoria, & Behan, 1981; Volpe, 1981; Zgliczynski & Rodolfa, 1980) to deal with child abuse and neglect issues; and poor responses or a lack of follow-through from community agencies (Broadhurst, 1984; Jones & Fox, 1979). Civil court cases are being won against those who fail to report child maltreatment (Besharov, 1978). This fact alone argues for improvements in the handling of cases by school personnel.

A number of authors have called for preservice training as a means of increasing teacher effectiveness in dealing with child maltreatment. Zgliczynski and Rodolfa (1980) surveyed 494 nationally accredited teacher education programs for inclusion of preservice programs on child abuse and neglect. They found that, while 55% of the respondents (40% of the total) provided some information to their students, only 7% presented comprehensive preparation. Bartlett's (1982) survey of early childhood education and elementary education preservice programs found instruction being offered in approximately three fifths of the programs responding, and in those only on a limited basis (e.g., not required, small amount of time given to subject, mostly theoretical in nature). Bartlett found primary emphasis placed on introducing the topic and clarifying teacher responsibilities. Thus, while preservice training might be a viable solution, reports do not verify its successful implementation.

In-service training has also been cited as potentially productive in increasing reporting by school-based professionals (Broadhurst, 1975). However, Jones and Fox (1979) found the results of the nationwide assessment of school policies and practices regarding child abuse and neglect conducted by the Education Commission of the States (1976, 1979) to reveal that a majority of small school districts and a substantial minority of large school districts were without programs. The lack of existing or adequate school policy has been a historical reality of the response of school systems to the child abuse and neglect problem (Brenton, 1977; Broadhurst, 1984; Drews, 1972; Jones & Fox, 1979; Levin, 1983). We agree with the contention that educators are not prepared to recognize or deal with child maltreatment.

Education has committed itself at the national level to help reduce child maltreatment. However, it seems unlikely that this commitment will be sufficiently implemented within local school communities without (a) the support of effective pre- and in-service training for educators, (b) local educational leadership, and (c) standardized policies and procedures in the local school community.

Recommendations, and in some cases models, have been provided for each of these areas. Recommendations for preservice training usually emphasize offering information to clarify identification and reporting, including child maltreatment topics in a required class, and giving sufficient time and opportunities for field work (Bartlett, 1982). Zgliczynski and Rodolfa (1980) suggest a module they have developed and offered in a required educational psychology class. It includes 6 hours of lecture and discussion which would include basic information on abuse, identification of an abused child, skills training for listening to and communicating with a child, reporting laws, and guidance in identifying and reporting suspected cases. In-service training programs and models such as "Project Prevention" described by Broadhurst (1975) and the "Toronto Model" described by McClare (1983) provide direction, tested through project application, for the development of policies, guidelines, and training of staff. The recent publications authored by Broadhurst (1984) and Tower (1984), in combination, provide extensive guidance for the development of the curriculum for in-service training. A particularly good model for the development of comprehensive approaches to dealing with child abuse is evolving as a part of the work of the Council on Child Abuse of Tacoma, Washington (contact Maryls Olsen, 708 S. G. Street, PO Box 1357, Tacoma, WA 98401). The Council's programs, which give particular emphasis to sexual abuse, include preservice and in-service training for educators, parent and child education, and prevention and case-handling segments. These programs have been offered in collaboration with universities, public school systems, and community service units. This model is reported to have been requested for consideration in all 50 states and in some foreign countries (Marlys Olsen, personal communication, September 11, 1985).

The materials reviewed provide very little in the way of guidance for dealing with psychological maltreatment beyond identifying the symptoms of victims and giving some attention to the acts of such maltreatment and the characteristics of perpetrators. The more general guidance provided on child maltreatment applies to psychological maltreatment but is not sufficiently specific to its difficulties and complexities.

The relatively poor record of action by school personnel in suspected cases of child maltreatment remains, in spite of the recommendations for improvement which have been given. In part this appears to be due to a lack of application of these suggestions. A survey was conducted in 1985 by the Office for the Study of the Psychological Rights of the Child to determine the manner in which nationally honored college/university schools of education and selected public school systems are preparing educators to deal with child abuse and neglect. The higher education institutions surveyed by telephone and/or in writing were those identified as being in the top 10 according to the opinions of professors throughout the country (*How Professors Rated Faculty in 19 Fields*, 1983). The school systems surveyed were selected from those which have published materials on child maltreatment and those which had been recommended in publications or by higher-education personnel as having established programs. None of the college/university programs of teacher education indicated that they mandate training. The majority of the public school systems offer programs on an occasional, irregular basis.

It is apparent that educators are presently inadequately prepared and supported in dealing with child maltreatment. Psychological maltreatment is given relatively little attention in work being done in the schools, especially when it occurs apart from other forms of child abuse and neglect. Recommendations for improving these conditions will be presented in the third section of this chapter.

PSYCHOLOGICAL MALTREATMENT IN SCHOOLING

Rationale

Though child abuse and neglect have generally been conceptualized and dealt with by educators as though they occurred outside the school, increasing attention has been given to the potential for and occurrence of maltreatment in schools. There is evidence to indicate that maltreatment of children, perpetrated by an educator, may continue for years while being ignored by school personnel aware of its existence (Niederpruem, 1986). Garbarino has commented that when a broad definition of maltreatment is used, ". . . that sees violence against children as intrinsically abusive and refusal to provide service as inherently neglectful, many schools are directly culpable for maltreatment" (1979, p. 199). The position that schooling and educators are directly culpable for maltreatment, and particularly psychological maltreatment, in a variety of forms producing highly destructive consequences has been echoed and expanded by others (Campbell-Smith, 1983; Gottlieb & Gottlieb, 1971; Hart, 1985; Hyman, 1983, 1985; Krug-

man & Krugman, 1984; Lynch, 1984; Paulson, 1983).

It is clearly appropriate to focus attention on psychological maltreatment associated with school and schooling. Educators are surrogate parents who have the responsibility for guiding and facilitating the healthy personal and social development of young people for 13 years during the developmental period. While the responsibilities of the school are numerous, some are particularly pertinent to the issues of concern here. Garbarino indicates, "Schools have a legal, moral, and historical mandate to ensure that each and every child has a direct and enduring relationship with adults or groups of adults that have an interest in the child's welfare" (1979, p. 203). Lynch (1984) has identified the conditions of impressionability and vulnerability of students to the treatment and influences of adults *in loco parentis* to require prohibition of certain actions/behaviors by educators. In comments focused on sexual maltreatment, but applicable to all forms of child maltreatment, he states:

> The relationship between pupil and teacher is recognized by law to be a very special one. No other relationship between minors and adults outside the family is clothed with so many mutual obligations in common law, including the *in loco parentis* paradigm. Teaching historically is accorded special status, socially as well as legally because of the recognition that an adult has something special and important to give a student, which requires an extensive relationship of dependence of the student upon the adult. (Lynch, 1984, p. 11)

Educators and peers involved in the schooling process are part of an important human ecological system of day-to-day direct interaction, a system which in all probability has strong influence on the psychological development and functioning of its young members. It thereby deserves careful analysis (Bronfenbrenner, 1979). Research has suggested that school experiences may make substantial differences in the quality of a child's life (Rutter, 1979).

We know very little about psychological maltreatment as expressed in educational environments. Its nature, antecedents, and consequences are just beginning to be explored. We are still in the first phases of clarifying psychological maltreatment as it exists outside of educational environments. This section is an attempt to apply the knowledge and perspectives so far developed regarding psychological maltreatment, along with what is known about other forms of maltreatment existing within school settings. What follows is somewhat speculative in nature and offered primarily for heuristic value.

Organizational Concepts

In considering conditions associated with schooling which might be interpreted as embodying psychological maltreatment, the seven acts identified in chapter 1 of this volume (Hart, Germain, & Brassard) will be applied. Those acts are rejecting, degrading, terrorizing, isolating, corrupting, exploiting, and denying emotional responsiveness. A very similar set of acts, with the omission of "exploiting," incorporation of "degrading" within "rejecting," and labeling of "denying emotional responsiveness" as "ignoring," are set forth as the major dimensions of psychological maltreatment by Garbarino, Guttman, and Seeley (1986) in their recent book for practitioners dealing with this topic.

The acts of psychological maltreatment, in our opinion, derive their destructive power through their ability to frustrate and distort the fulfillment of basic psychological needs. An explanation of this position is presented in chapter 1. The "deficiency" needs as described by Maslow (1968, 1970) are most clearly relevant. Those needs include physiological needs, safety needs, belongingness and love needs, and esteem needs. Maslow (1968, 1970) has indicated that a failure to meet these needs leads the individual to develop a wide variety of maladaptive and destructive patterns of living. Biehler and Snowman (1982) have detailed the importance of taking these needs into consideration in educating children, the manner in which individuals are essentially dependent on assistance from others in meeting their deficiency needs, and the negative effects on student behavior and development which result from a lack of needs satisfaction. Experts writing about child maltreatment as it relates to the responsibilities of educators tend to view the negative impact of maltreatment or prescriptive elements for helping maltreated children in a manner consistent with Maslow's theory (Krugman & Krugman, 1984; Peterson & Roscoe, 1983; Tower, 1984). Focusing on "positive self-esteem" in a manner which has it subsuming many of the basic psychological needs of concern here, Krugman and Krugman say it ". . . is the essence of the child's identity, and it

rises and falls in relation to the behavior of those interacting with the child" (1984, p. 286).

We consider certain conditions of schooling to impact somewhat directly and negatively through blocking, distorting, or reducing fulfillment of "deficiency" needs and of attempts to pursue self-actualization (a general label for "growth" needs). These conditions include the following: discipline/control through fear and intimidation (particularly attacks on physiological and safety needs); low quantity and quality of human interaction (attacks on belongingness and love needs); limited opportunities/encouragement to develop competency and self-worth (attacks on esteem needs); encouragement to be/remain dependent (attacks on esteem and self-actualization needs); denial of opportunities for healthy risk taking (attacks on esteem and self-actualization needs).

"Deficiency" needs are met primarily through relationships between people (Maslow, 1968, 1970). In these relationships, the people involved may represent themselves, groups of individuals in close association, or a variety of organizations and institutions. Therefore, it is important to incorporate organizing concepts similar to those of the human ecological system mentioned earlier in chapter one. Campbell-Smith (1983), Hyman (1985), Paulson (1983), and Plank (1978) have each suggested that maltreatment comes in forms originating from, or channeled through, somewhat different levels of the human ecological system. Collectively, they could be organized within a societal/institutional level, a common educational practices level, and a specific teacher–student(s) interaction level. The child-influencing characteristics of all three of these levels are probably derived from combinations of factors existing in and across all levels of the human ecological system, and each level may have direct impact on the child through the "microsystem" of interaction experienced as day-to-day reality. However, the most directly related origins of these conditions/actions are primarily in the macrosystems, exosystems, and microsystems, respectively. For example, the low expectations set for mathematics performance for a female child by a classroom teacher would be consistent with and influenced by institutionalized societal attitudes (macrosystem); the very limited opportunity to make choices to risk involvement in adventurous field experiences offered to students by a classroom teacher is often a matter of school board policy (exosystem); and the use of physical pain as a method of discipline applied to a child might be a result of the modeling of such methods experienced by that teacher as a child in his or her classrooms or family (microsystem).

The Nature of Psychological Maltreatment in Schooling

At least five conditions of school life appear to embody psychological maltreatment. They are described below with examples given where available and appropriate.

Discipline and Control through Fear and Intimidation. Much concern has been focused on the negative impact and ineffectiveness of punitive disciplinary practices used in the schools. Stones (1984), in his review of the psychological factors in punishment, defines punishment as the subjecting of human beings to painful stimuli, physical or mental, which generate negative emotional states in the learner. Punishment "broadly defined" in this manner would include not only corporal punishment, but also "Teacher disapproval, rejection, reproof, rejection of work, continuous experience of failure . . ." (Stones, 1984, p. 3). Stones earlier (1979) had indicated that since the clinical use of punishment had been found to be problematic, referring to the works of Hunt and Matarazzo (1973) and Solomon (1964), its use in classrooms rests on even more uncertain ground. Findings in regard to punishment suggest that educators are generally unaware of the relatively high frequency of their use of punishment in comparison to encouraging/praising behaviors (see White, 1975, for rates of teacher approval and disapproval). Stones notes that punishment is used both to maintain order and to communicate failure to learn. Under either condition he concludes that it will depress student learning, increase ill mental health, and cause future behavioral problems through the tension, fear, resentment, hostility, and disappointment it produces. According to Stones, the level of punishment applied and accepted is influenced by "attitudes and practices in society at large" (Stones, 1984, p. 2).

Hyman and his colleagues (1983, personal communication, 1986; Hyman & Wise, 1979; Hyman & D'Alessandro, 1984) have explored in detail the nature of corporal punishment in the schools (over 1 million official reports a year in their opinion) and its psychological correlates.

They have judged corporal punishment to be inherently psychologically destructive by teaching aggressive behavior, lowering educational achievement, being applied differentially according to race, sex, and socioeconomic class, and by producing psychological denigration and humiliation. Hyman is certainly not alone in his criticisms of this form of discipline (see Clarizio, 1977; Dubanoski, Inaba, & Gerkewicz, 1983). The British Psychological Society (Stones, 1984), the American Psychological Association (1975), the National Education Association (1972), the National Committee for Prevention of Child Abuse (1982), and the National Association of School Psychologists (1986) have each taken official positions against the use of corporal punishment in the schools

Verbal abuse, unfair criticisms, and put-downs by parents and teachers have been identified as forms of psychological maltreatment. In Brown's opinion, "kids who are the victims of persistent put-downs don't walk around with bruises on their arms and legs, but often they're damaged just as much as if they'd been physically assaulted" (Brown, 1979, p. 12). He also indicates that repeatedly telling a person she or he is "bad," or "clumsy," or cannot do anything right can destroy the child's self-image. Research on teacher approval/disapproval indicates that it has powerful effects on student attitudes and behavior. Krugman and Krugman (1984) indicate that "Verbal abuse is one of the most common types of child abuse and can easily be unrecognized but inflict much damage to a child's self-esteem" (p. 285). Their investigations of psychological maltreatment in a classroom found verbal abuse ". . . was one of the most characteristic behaviors . . ." (p. 285) of the teacher and that it ". . . led to a dramatic lowering of self-esteem in 13 of the 17 children" (p. 285).

It is apparent that punishment, or coercive discipline, is channeled through the three levels of the human ecological system mentioned above: the societal/institutional level, common educational/classroom practices level, and specific teacher–student(s) interaction level. It has been recognized that such practices not only produce negative effects on the individuals at whom they are directed, but also set up a chain of reactions that are destructive to future generations. Stones (1984) and Hyman (1983) have indicated that the observation and experiencing of such discipline, with particular attention being given to violence in the form of corporal punishment, further institutionalize it. Marion (1982) indicates that child abuse is linked to societal acceptance of coercive discipline. Gil (1970) has documented the high degree of approval society gives to violence through physical punishment.

The recent works of Hyman (1985) and Krugman and Krugman (1984) focus clearly and powerfully on psychological maltreatment at the teacher–student(s) interaction level. In the cases they describe, they carried out evaluations of children thought to have been maltreated by their teachers. They provide evidence indicating that psychological maltreatment in the form of punitive discipline and control procedures which intimidate and stimulate fear are capable of producing psychological trauma in child victims.

In the case of third and fourth graders investigated by Krugman and Krugman, psychologically abusive teacher behaviors included (a) expressing verbal put-downs, harassment; (b) labeling ("stupid," "dummy"); inconsistent, erratic behavior; (c) screaming at children until they cried; (d) making inappropriate threats to try to control the classroom; (e) allowing some children to harass and belittle others; (f) setting unrealistic academic goals for age/grade level; (g) use of homework as punishment; (h) using fear-inducing techniques (e.g., tying string to a child's chair and pulling it out from under him); (i) throwing homework at children; and (j) using physical punishments (pinching, slapping, shaking, and pulling ears) (1984, p. 285).

Seventeen of the 27 students in the class exhibited symptoms of emotional trauma which were not a part of their previous histories. Those symptoms included excessive worry about school performance, change from positive to negative self-perception, change to negative perceptions of school, verbalized fear that the teacher would hurt the children, excessive crying about school, headaches, stomachaches, decreased functioning in social situations outside of school, nightmares and other sleep disturbances, school avoidance and refusal, and withdrawn behaviors and depression (Krugman & Krugman, 1984, pp. 284–285). Evidence indicated that such conditions had existed within this teacher's classes for 5 years with no action taken. School administrators were reluctant to act, even when confronted with the evidence produced. In part, Krugman and Krugman suggest this is because the children were so eager to please – in order not to antagonize the teachers' unpredictable and

erratic personality and incur his wrath and verbal abuse – that at times, to an outside observer, the classroom seemed to be unusually quiet and compliant (1984, p. 285). This was evidently considered as proof by school administrators that the teacher was doing a good job. Krugman and Krugman noted that while the symptoms in this case strongly resemble those associated with "school avoidance/phobia," probably because in both situations reactions to uncontrollable anxiety are being expressed, that this is clearly not the same syndrome since, unlike "school avoidance/phobia cases," when specific teacher contact was removed the symptoms for most of the children ceased.

Hyman (1985) investigated and analyzed the conditions associated with psychological maltreatment of children in a first-grade class. The teacher in this case tied students to their seats, taped their mouths shut, overly limited opportunities to use toilet facilities unless students were willing to suffer penalties, verbally denigrated children, and threatened them to keep them from informing their parents of their experiences. The child victims were found to exhibit stress-related symptoms including: vomiting, nausea, headaches, stomachaches, nightmares, earaches, fear of the dark, thumb sucking, crying, enuresis, encopresis, eyelash pulling, hair pulling, insomnia, excessive dependency, hyperactive/anxious behavior, fear of strangers, withdrawn behavior, and avoidance of school and school-related activities (Hyman, 1985).

Hyman's analysis of this, and other somewhat similar cases which he describes, led him to conclude that ". . . there is a clear case to be made for a posttraumatic stress disorder caused by educators' verbal and physical abuse of children" (1985, p. 15). He views physical and psychological maltreatment, in agreement with Navarre in this volume, as two sides of the same coin. While he estimates that this form of psychological maltreatment is not as widespread as institutional/societal and routine physical/psychological abuse perpetrated through schooling, its psychological effects are so destructive that it deserves specific attention within the diagnostic standards of the helping professions. He suggests it be considered for inclusion within the *Diagnostic and Statistical Manual of Mental Disorders, Third Edition* (American Psychiatric Association, 1980) as a category which might be labeled "educator-induced posttraumatic stress syndrome."

If consideration is given to the probable impact of such methods of discipline, it is likely that they would fall under the acts of psychological maltreatment labeled "terrorizing" (e.g., threatening to inflict physical pain), "degrading" (e.g., publicly humiliating a student), and "rejecting" (e.g., condoning harassment of a student by other students). These tend to be acts of commission rather than acts of omission, and as such, represent maltreatment in the form of abuse. Peers as well as adults terrorize, degrade, and reject one another in educational environments. Peer maltreatment should be addressed under the general categories of psychological maltreatment. However, this will have to be dealt with in a later work.

Low Quantity and Quality of Human Interaction. Evidence exists which indicates the importance of having a social support network that incorporates frequent, dependable, and caring interactions with others to enable one to be psychologically healthy. Egeland and associates (Egeland & Erickson, 1983) have established this need as essential for the healthy development of young children. Henricksen (1982) has identified its importance in producing psychologically well-adjusted adolescents, and Feuerstein and Hoffman (1982) have emphasized its critical importance as a psychological right and necessity in learning.

Schools, however, do not generally provide for such relationships. Complaints in this regard have focused on a number of conditions existing within school systems, including depersonalized environments (Laury & Meerloo, 1967); lock-step practices which greatly limit oral communication (Plank, 1978); and tracking systems which overly limit relationships, expectations, and positive self-image (Gottlieb & Gottlieb, 1971). Goodlad (1983) found, in studying the conditions in over 1,000 schools, that 7 minutes per day is the average amount of time given by teachers to person-to-person interactions with students. This might not be quite so bad if it were not for the evidence that students experience little in the way of supportive human interaction with adults in their homes (Bronfenbrenner, 1979; Henricksen, 1982).

In analyzing the potential for malpractice suits to be brought against educators for psychological maltreatment, Lynch (1984) describes research which indicates that the use of "differential verbal stimuli" is a powerful tool in the hands of teachers for shaping pupil behavior and self-

concept (see Good & Grouws, 1977). He cites the work of Good and Brophy (1973), which indicates that, in communicating with their classes, teachers tend not to expect or wait for responses from students they have categorized as slow or poor. While recognizing that cause-and-effect relationships have not yet been sufficiently established, Lynch concludes that withholding communication is devastating to students and that it represents a form of psychological maltreatment which may eventually be established as grounds for malpractice action.

These conditions tend to place young people more and more under the influence of peers. It has been shown that disproportionate influence by siblings may limit the intellectual development of those of later birth order in a family (Zajonc, 1976). It may very well be that the relatively high level of influence by peers, as compared to adults, on young people in school similarly limits development. The increases being experienced and predicted for use of institutionalized child care, downward extensions (student age) in formal schooling, and use of electronic learning supports in education suggest that more decreases in social support will be experienced in the future. Available research evidence (Gordon, 1983; Weaver, Negri, & Wallace, 1980) identifies advantages in academic development through "home schooling" (Holt, 1983; Moore & Moore, 1984). This involves the educating of children at home by their parents or parent surrogates, who are likely to be involved in substantially more direct interactions with their students than would be the case for classroom teachers (Moore & Moore, 1984). Many supports appear to exist which justify concern about insufficiencies in the quantity and quality of involvement with adults experienced by children in traditional schooling and for the need to counteract trends in this direction.

The low levels of cognitive, affective, and psychomotor interaction between educators and students appear to be examples of acts of "rejecting" (e.g., responding differentially to high- and low-ability students), "isolating" (e.g. overly limiting opportunities to communicate) and "denying emotional responsiveness" (e.g., maintaining depersonalizing environments). Because they are for the most part acts of omission, these would be forms of psychological neglect. Support for these conditions is channeled through the various ecological levels: the macrosystem (e.g., generally low value given to time- and energy-consuming relationships between adults and children); exosystem (e.g., high ratios of students to teachers set by administrators/school boards); and microsystem (e.g., individual classrooms organized along industrial assembly-line models).

Limited Opportunities To Develop Competencies, To Be Worthwhile, and To Be a Contributor. Educational systems have been criticized for abusing children through neglect. Campbell-Smith (1983) indicates that schools have neglected their responsibilities to help students achieve confidence and social competence, concern for others, the ability to deal with uncertainty and complexity, and the ability to apply practical experience in making judgments leading to action. Among the practices or failings of schools viewed as limiting the development of competencies and a sense of self-worth are (a) inadequate appreciation and planning for developmental readiness and developmental needs; (b) inappropriate developmental goals; (c) overemphasis on theoretical and academic topics and inadequate curricula; and (d) lack of individualization for special needs and insensitivity to individual differences, as expressed in the emphasis on norm-referenced measurement, teaching in lock-step manner, and caste-like tracking systems (Brown, 1977; Gold, 1978; Plank, 1975; Lynch, 1984).

Traditional schooling encourages and displays deference to those with natural and well-developed language and quantitative facility in comparison to other talents/strengths. Such strong respect is given to language strengths that vocabulary tests nearly stand on their own as intelligence tests in our society, where such tests are validated in part by the degree to which they correlate with educational achievement. Heavy emphasis on language strengths frequently results in those with relative strength in non-language areas being less valued by others and eventually themselves. Researchers (Austin, 1975) involved in the project to revise the Wechsler Intelligence Scale for Children (Wechsler, 1974), which provides global measures of verbal and nonverbal functioning, recognized that school goals and curricula give little reinforcement to individuals whose relative strengths lie in non-verbal areas. In his recent book on multiple intelligences, Gardner (1983) has recognized the need for expanded school curricula which would appreciate and stimulate the development of a much wider range of abilities.

In addition to its narrow focus on verbal intelligence, traditional schooling tends to emphasize relatively low levels of intellectual activity, thereby limiting' development of competency and preparedness for life's challenges. An extensive review of studies of classroom recitation by Gall (1970) indicated that teachers overwhelmingly, in up to 80% of their questioning, emphasize acquisition of facts and knowledge rather than ability to interpret, synthesize, evaluate, or apply. Rowe (1974) found that teachers tend to allow too little time for their students to answer questions orally, and by doing so limit the quality of their responses. Glasser (1969) has complained strongly and eloquently about the mindless manner in which educators pursue curricula regardless of the readiness of their students for it or the meaningfulness of its content. He has also complained about the manner in which students are failed "for their own good" and learn, thereby, to become failures. A more subtle form of forcing students to experience chronic failure exists in the common practice of requiring poor readers to acquire the majority of their information through reading and to spend a major portion of their school day pursuing reading, their area of greatest weakness. In reviewing research into the effects of failure (Nicholls, 1979; Weiner, 1979), Biehler and Snowman conclude that "Because low achieving students attribute failure to low ability, future failure is seen as more likely than future success" (1982, p. 382).

There are other factors which limit the development of competencies. Sexual and racial bias reduce opportunities and encouragement for development (see Reschly & Graham-Clay, chapter 10 in this volume). Expressions of such bias have been strong enough at times to justify dismissal of teachers (Lynch, 1984). Students are perpetually in the process of moving toward becoming contributors rather than actually being contributors (Henricksen, 1982). Teaching which is tuned to norm-referenced measurement continues to be emphasized, instead of procedures which move students more clearly toward the development of identifiable competencies which would be embodied in criterion-referenced measurement. Mastery-learning procedures require more than the educational establishment is willing to give. The list goes on and on.

These conditions might be considered to fall under acts of "degrading" and "corrupting." They degrade children by treating them as though they are incapable of the higher thought processes required for reasoning, critical thinking, and judgment necessary to deal effectively with decision making on complex issues. They degrade them by treating them, not as individuals, but as items in a set of common units to be taught through the assembly-line models of industry, and in so doing, they corrupt them in their perspectives on the value of human life and individuality. The emphasis on verbal intelligence in our society, on norm-referenced evaluation in our schools, and on the types of questioning used by teachers in their classrooms are indications of the influences of macrosystem, exosystem, and microsystem levels of the human ecology, respectively.

Encouragement To Be/Remain Dependent. Though many of our educational systems include within their goals for students the development of self-reliance and responsible independence, there is little to indicate that curricula and educational techniques are aimed at such development. Students are generally not given the responsibility to make decisions about issues that are of much consequence.

The "Eight Year Study" of progressive education (wherein students participated in determining content, methods and programs to be pursued) provided ample evidence of the ability of students to be successful when given more than the usual amount of responsibility for decision making (Aiken, 1942). Its influence on present-day practices is difficult to identify. Henricksen (1982) concluded from his research on the youth culture of Sweden that modern-day students are at the mercy of manipulation by modern marketing practices, partly due to the lack of encouragement they experience to become responsible decision makers. Melton's review of the competencies of children, their opportunities, and their desires to have choice-making rights, leads him to indicate that they ". . . often have the cognitive capacity to exercise rights and perhaps function as 'mature minors' at least in a limited way earlier than they frequently are thought to be able" (1983, p. 41). The continuing neglect of the importance of educating young people toward becoming critical thinkers, capable of responsible independence, is exemplified by the lack of consideration given these issues in the recent wave of educational reform reports (National Commission on Excellence in Education, 1983; National Science Board Commission on Precollege Education in Mathematics, Science and Technology, 1983). It could be argued that the high level of teenage automobile accidents, substance abuse, and pregnancy out of marriage are results of the limited manner in which young people experience guided, developmentally appropriate opportunities to make choices about substantive issues.

These conditions might be considered to be produced through acts of "corrupting" (e.g., producing vulnerability to marketing manipulation) and "degrading" (e.g., expecting a low level of personal responsibility). The relevance of the major ecological levels, macrosystem, exosystem, and microsystem, is apparent in the influences of society, educational systems, and educators which limit decision making on the part of young people.

Denial of Opportunities for Healthy Risk Taking. Many of the points made previously apply to this area. The emphasis in schooling placed on memorization of facts, on convergent thinking, on remaining relatively dependent on adults throughout one's school career, and on being controlled through fear of punishment all would tend to direct and encourage students toward playing it safe, thereby avoiding adventure and challenges. Maslow's (1968) basic needs theory indicates that this overemphasis on safety will substantially inhibit growth.

It has been noted that conditions which reduce healthy risk taking are universal in our society regardless of the populations served (Goodlad, 1969; Gottlieb & Gottlieb, 1971). It has also been noted that educators communicate, make assignments, organize their classrooms, and schedule activities in ways which match their expectations for students (Lynch, 1984), and which, thereby, influence behavior and self-concepts toward prescribed and limiting roles (microsystem level).

The lack of challenge and adventure associated with schooling in the Western world (macrosystem level) has been described by Gibbons (1974) as giving students little opportunity to confront their anxieties, explore their inner resources, or come to terms with the world and the future it holds for them. Carl Rogers (1961) has made it clear that he believes the manner in which educators generally direct the learning experiences of students promotes learning of no real consequence (exosystem and microsystem levels). Part of what is needed, according to

Rogers, is for individuals to drop their defensiveness, to pursue their uncertainties, and to seek self-discovery in areas that would significantly affect behavior. These recommendations are in direct conflict with the strong emphasis on safety needs presently applied in schooling.

These conditions might be considered to be expressions of "terrorizing" (e.g., controlling through fear of punishment), "corrupting" (e.g., reinforcing disproportionate valuing of safety in contrast to risk or challenge), and "degrading" (e.g., displaying low expectation levels for students). They are both abusive and neglectful.

General Considerations. Much of the material reviewed in this section is speculative. The development of operational definitions of the acts of maltreatment, along with research to clarify its forms, impact, and mediators, will be necessary as prerequisites to determine the degree to which the conditions described in this section are manifestations of psychological maltreatment. The body of knowledge for other types of child abuse and neglect is not very much advanced beyond that for psychological maltreatment. The value of the present knowledge base for a broad conception of child maltreatment has been strongly questioned because of the poor quality of research which has been characteristic of child abuse and neglect investigations (Goldbloom, 1984). Even so, this should not keep people from attempts to remedy what are generally believed to be destructive conditions.

In attempting to remedy conditions of schooling which are assumed to be psychologically destructive, the cautions raised by Melton and Thompson in this volume regarding legal and policy issues should be considered. Legal intervention would be inappropriate, and probably ineffective, in dealing with most cases of psychological maltreatment which are expressions of general societal/institutional or common educational practices. Analysis of such conditions by representatives of the school and community could be pursued in a manner which would test their congruence with community values, expert opinion, and research findings on child development and education. Findings and conclusions from school and community action of this type might give direction to mediation or modification of these conditions for the purposes of prevention or reduction of maltreatment.

Psychological maltreatment at the specific teacher–student interaction level, which represents a genuine threat to healthy adjustment, might justify intervention of a variety of types. Prevention might be promoted through preservice and in-service training for educators and through clear statements and commitments on human rights, best practices, and ethical behavior by school systems and professional associations. Specific cases within a school system might warrant the application of procedures for lodging complaints regarding unethical behavior, informal and formal school system investigatory and corrective procedures, and, in some instances, criminal prosecution.

RECOMMENDATIONS FOR REDUCING PSYCHOLOGICAL MALTREATMENT THROUGH SCHOOLING

Schools have been recognized as agencies with great potential for identifying and reducing child maltreatment (Brassard, Tyler, & Kehle, 1983; Broadhurst, 1984). Programs have been suggested and developed to enable schools to be more effective in this regard (McClare, 1983; Brassard et al., 1983; Volpe, 1981).

For schools to become more effective in dealing with psychological maltreatment, they will have to consciously focus attention on this issue area and on the developing body of associated knowledge. This will probably require the formation of study committees; processes by which critical issues will be identified and debated; the development of a broad base of support among educators, parents, and students to deal with those issues/problems considered most important and most susceptible to influence by responsible action; application of the specialist knowledge and skills of school psychologists, counselors, and social workers; and then the development, execution, and follow-up of plans for prevention and correction. In other words, a lot of hard work, sustained over a long period of time, will be necessary.

This section of this chapter provides suggestions to enable school systems to reduce psychological maltreatment of young people which occurs in and outside of schooling environments. The content of this section is organized to fall within six subsections: (a) basic points of view to be applied in planning for school programs; (b) roles and responsibilities for schools; (c) schooling conditions prerequisite for constructive action; (d) school–community relationships; (e) preparation for school roles and responsibilities; and (f) directions for research.

Recommendations

Psychological maltreatment should be recognized as a pervasive condition of human interaction which is present in virtually all settings and levels of the human ecology, and certainly both in and outside of school environments. In a world where the conditions of child rearing are providing less dependable, frequent, and intense relationships with and monitoring by adults, the schools may very well be the institutions with the greatest potential for insuring that the basic psychological needs of children are met. Schools, or educational systems, are the only institutions through which virtually all members of the child population pass. The very nature of their purposes, emphasizing the learning and development of children, and of their relationships with children *in loco parentis*, argue for their preeminence in protecting children and assuring realization of their potentials.

The major areas given attention in child abuse and neglect research are sociological/environmental factors, the role of the child, and psychological personality characteristics of the maltreating parent (Smith, 1984). In developing plans for reducing the psychological maltreatment of young people which occurs in and outside of school environments, these areas should be emphasized. Their characteristics have been detailed in other chapters of this book. Consideration of these three areas is likely to be accomplished in a somewhat systematic manner if models of the human ecological system are applied (Valentine, Freeman, Acuff, & Andreas, 1985). The role of the child should be analyzed in a manner respecting the dynamic system which is the individual, including psychological needs, interactions between physical and psychological dimensions, and interactions between the child and other levels of the human ecology. Outside of school, the family, neighborhood, peers, and community characteristics should be given emphasis. Within school, the influences of societal/institutional themes, common educational practices, and specific teacher–student(s) interactions should be given attention.

Particular attention should be given to the actions of adults or peers, in or outside of school environments, which fall under the categories of rejecting, degrading, terrorizing, isolating, corrupting, or denying of emotional responsiveness. These acts are the ones presently given the most support by research (Egeland & Erickson, 1983; Hyman, 1985; Krugman & Krugman, 1984; Rohner & Rohner, 1980) and by expert opinion (Garbarino & Vondra, chapter 2 in this volume; Hart, Germain, & Brassard, chapter 1 of this volume; Hart, Germain, & Brassard, 1983).

In the school environment, as suggested in this chapter, these acts are expressed through conditions which discipline and control through fear and intimidation; overly limit the quantity and quality of human interaction; overly limit opportunities/encouragement to develop competency and self-worth; encourage children to be dependent beyond their needs; and deny opportunities for healthy risk taking. The intensity, frequency, and duration of these acts/conditions, interacting with the personal–social resources and perspectives children bring to the experience, will determine the degree to which destructive consequences will accrue. There are presently no standards for determining the weight to be given to these dimensions of maltreatment, other than that which is implied by presently available child-development knowledge.

In conceptualizing the nature of the impact of psychological maltreatment on children, emphasis should be given to the manner in which such maltreatment appears to produce deviant behavior which is maladaptive. The works of Krugman and Krugman (1984), Hyman (1985), and Hart (1985) argue that psychological maltreatment produces emotional or behavioral problems which place the child's behavior outside the range of that which is usual for age-peers and which, by its nature, produces personal and social maladjustment.

As previously noted, Hyman (1985) has identified a cluster of symptoms caused by stress occurring in the schools. A series of studies began after he conducted a clinical evaluation of a 17-year-old girl who had been severely paddled by an educator. The symptoms were much like those observed in adults suffering from posttraumatic stress disorder. However, there were some differences, especially the absence of vivid flashbacks. Clinical evaluations of 20 more cases revealed similar symptoms expressed by child victims, and additionally, symptoms expressed by the parents of child victims including anxiety, depression, and intense rage directed at the school. A retrospective study of over 50 families with children who had been abused in school supported initial clinical impressions (Clarke, 1986). Hyman (personal communication, 1986) is presently conducting a study to establish baseline data as to the nature and extent of physical and psychological abuse in the schools. Preliminary data appear to indicate that the core of the problem is the psychological aftereffect of both types of abuse. As a result, Hyman has proposed a diagnostic subcategory called "educator-induced posttraumatic stress disorder" the symptoms of which include sleep disturbances, avoidance of school, fear reactions to people who resemble the perpetrator, lack of interest in activities previously enjoyed, withdrawal or acting out (the latter being much more frequent), deteriorating school work, and the development of a variety of tics and mannerisms. The mothers of the victims often suffer depression and anxiety which sometimes reach clinical proportions when there is no resolution. The fathers tend to react with rage and have in some cases attacked the offending educator.

Other efforts intended specifically to relate emotional consequences to psychological maltreatment experiences have also been initiated. For example, work is presently underway to produce DSM III syndrome category standards to cover reactions to child sexual abuse (Corwin, 1985). This trend is quite compatible with the manner in which child maltreatment researchers and authors have identified child-expressed symptoms of all forms of maltreatment, and particularly of psychological maltreatment, to parallel symptoms of emotional/behavioral disorders. For school personnel, the dimensions and standards of Public Law 94-142 (1975), the Education for All Handicapped Children Act, delineating its "serious emotionally disturbed" category should be helpful in identifying children who may be experiencing psychological maltreatment (see Appendix B). These dimensions, behaviorally and school-learning oriented, are probably more appropriate to the responsibilities of education systems, and certainly better understood by school personnel. This is not to say that all children exhibiting serious emotional/behavioral disorders have experienced psychological maltreatment. It should be recognized, however, that the present state of knowledge suggests that such disorders are the result of physiological and/or experiential conditions. To the degree that they are the result of experience, that experience has embodied psy-

chological maltreatment whether intentional or unintentional, from single or multiple sources.

Because of the many complications and complexities associated with the meanings, standards and procedures to be applied to psychological maltreatment, it is recommended that a school committee or task force be formed within or across schools, which will act as a resource unit and in an advisory capacity. The responsibilities of such a committee/task force could range from helping school and community representatives to formulate and activate policy to providing advisory, case-study, and liaison services regarding specific cases. It should include mental health and child-development specialists such as school psychologists, counselors, and social workers, as well as representatives of the teaching and administrative staff. Such a committee/task force probably should be given the responsibility of dealing with all child-maltreatment cases, regardless of the nature of the maltreatment, and could additionally be a resource to the school and parents in other special areas of concern regarding child learning and adjustment (e.g., advancement or retention in placement, matching students to teachers, and project opportunities). If a broad range of responsibilities were set for this unit, it would justify giving it a title with positive and comprehensive connotations, such as "child development committee."

Roles and Responsibilities of Schools

The responsibilities identified for school personnel in regard to child maltreatment in general also apply to psychological maltreatment. In this section school personnel responsibilities for identification, reporting, and the correction and prevention of psychological maltreatment will be described. Under each major role category, the emphases we judge to be particularly important and logically supported by the positions and conditions presented in this chapter will be identified.

Identification. The seven acts of psychological maltreatment described in this chapter, and the particular forms of these acts given specific reference in the statute and regulations of one's state of residence, provide some direction for identifying psychological maltreatment. Symptoms of serious emotional/behavioral disorders may be expressions of the impact of psychological maltreatment on a child. Where such conditions exist, an investigation of contributing and mediating factors should be made.

The identification procedures for psychological maltreatment should be consistent with those provided by the National Center on Child Abuse and Neglect specific to educators (Broadhurst, 1984). The behavioral characteristics Broadhurst identifies as indicators of emotional maltreatment (1984), along with the academic and behavioral clues she relates more generally to maltreatment (1984), are easily subsumed under the major dimensions of the "serious emotional handicaps" as presented in P.L. 94-142 (1975). Because of the complexities associated with psychological maltreatment, it is recommended that the identifications of psychological maltreatment be made through consultation with school-based mental health specialists (e.g., school psychologist, social worker, or counselor). The consultation should focus on determination of the manner in which evidence is to be obtained (e.g., interview, observation, standardized assessment, review of developmental history), the nature of communication to be pursued with suspected perpetrators, and alternatives for reporting to be applied.

Reporting. Where psychological maltreatment appears to exist, on the basis of acts and consequences, it should be reported to local officials as prescribed by state law. Whether the maltreatment under consideration exists in or outside the school environments, it must be reported. If it exists in the school environment, appropriate school officials/committees should be informed so that they may begin a process of correction and prevention, including investigation of the degree to which the maltreatment experience is being shared by other students in the class, program, or relationship where it exists (Krugman & Krugman, 1984). In most states, community child-protective service units do not accept or process reports of child maltreatment by school personnel. Where such conditions are considered to be sufficiently severe, a criminal offense may be dealt with as a legal matter (Janet Corson, personal communication, November 23, 1985). School personnel should be informed regarding the manner in which their state and community would deal with out-of-home maltreatment and, specifically, that which occurs in the schools. If maltreatment exists outside of the schools, appropriate school officials/committees

should be alerted to prepare to work with community services assigned to the case with the ultimate purposes of correction and prevention.

In general, it is recommended that all cases of psychological maltreatment, and, in fact, all cases of child maltreatment be channeled through a "child-development committee" such as suggested in a previous section. This committee can be formulated to (a) systematically follow appropriate investigation and reporting procedures, (b) provide necessary feedback to the identifying teacher and other school authorities, and (c) work cooperatively with school and community resources in attempts to correct and prevent maltreatment. School committees and multiple disciplinary teams such as this have been recommended by others (Broadhurst, 1978; ten Bensel & Berdie, 1976; Tower, 1984) for application in child maltreatment work within the schools. They do not, however, relieve the staff member who originally identified the maltreatment of the responsibility to insure that the maltreatment is reported.

Correction and Prevention. Child-development experts have provided much advice regarding the developmental characteristics of children and conditions and techniques for supporting healthy development (Hetherington & Parke, 1979). There is no evidence to suggest that this advice is being applied in a systematic, comprehensive, or dependable fashion in school systems. Though the psychological maltreatment cause-and-effect relationships are presently unclear, what is known provides direction for the planning of correction and prevention strategies which will be compatible with child-development knowledge and present or developing trends in schooling. The recommendations in this subsection represent our recommendations for integrating these factors.

For the purposes of both correction and prevention, a school or school system committee of the type previously identified should be in effect to guide goal setting, planning, and action phases for the school system's efforts.

In regard to correction of cases of established psychological maltreatment, the following directions are suggested: An investigation of the stresses and resources present in the major dimensions of the child's ecological systems of influence should be conducted. This would include a psychological evaluation of the child, as well as an analysis of the child's family, neighborhood, school, and community social systems conducted in cooperation with the applicable school or community child-protective committees or systems. The evaluations and analyses should give primary consideration to the present levels of psychological need fulfillment. The characteristics of the child and other factors likely to impede or facilitate progress toward healthy psychological development and functioning should also be investigated. The standards of P.L. 94-142 (1975) which delineate the major dimensions and criteria for a determination of serious emotional handicaps may be particularly helpful if trends toward or the establishment of behavioral/emotional disorders are accepted as possible symptoms of psychological maltreatment. It is not recommended that maltreated children be automatically categorized as handicapped, although some may be, but rather that the model for school system evaluations of those suspected of being handicapped should be applicable.

The results of the evaluations and analyses should be translated into an individual educational plan (IEP) as suggested by Wishon (1979) and Peterson & Roscoe (1983) and as required for handicapped children (Public Law 94-142, 1975). Child protective service and legal action on cases of psychological maltreatment are unlikely to provide major or continuing assistance (Corson & Davidson, chapter 14 in this volume; Thomas, 1984). For this reason, the prescriptions and services provided by other community resources, including the schools, properly coordinated, offer the greatest potential for improving conditions for the victim and perpetrators of maltreatment.

A wide range of prescriptive elements might be included in the program to help a child and those around him to reduce maltreatment and encourage healthy development. Included among these would be: individual and group (family) counseling; stress-management training; establishment of social support networks; specific competency training; provision of a mentor to guide toward improved functioning; monitoring by a friendly visitor to the home or classroom; respite for or separation of those individuals involved in the maltreatment. In some cases perpetrator characteristics will dictate that the child, or children, be separated from the perpetrator, whether the perpetrator functions in or outside of school. In such cases, decisions will have to be made to determine whether the per-

petrator's role (as parent or teacher) in working with children should come to an end, be suspended until sufficient improvement occurs, or continue under conditions of careful monitoring and prescription application.

Progress toward improvement should be monitored by one or more representatives of the school system or school community (e.g., teacher, administrator, school psychologist, omsbudsman, PTA representative). Reduction in the acts of maltreatment and the symptoms of maladjustive deviance, along with enhanced functioning specific to the goals of therapeutic procedures, would provide evidence of progress. Evidence of improvement or the lack of it would be used to guide the development of modifications in the IEP.

The above suggestions deserve consideration for cases in which psychological maltreatment occurs in the absence of or in combination with other forms of maltreatment.

In regard to the prevention of psychological maltreatment, the following directions are suggested: The major goals of prevention would be directed toward insuring the healthy psychological development of young people. In terms of the concepts and constructs emphasized in this chapter, this would mean the fulfilling of basic psychological needs as conceptualized by Maslow (1970) and Glasser (1965). The schools are capable of providing, at a variety of points within and across the systems of human ecology, many supports and services which would increase the likelihood of achieving healthy psychological development and reduce the likelihood of psychological maltreatment, for present and future generations of students. Most of the suggestions to be made in this section are consistent with what most people would want for their own children. They are not new ideas. In a way, the list is a compendium of the good things which should happen to children, and would be dictated by common sense as well as knowledge of conditions likely to optimize child development. At the risk of sounding like Isaiah predicting what the world will be like with the coming of the Messiah, we make the following recommendations.

At the individual child level, efforts should be made to insure that each child feels safe, cared about, of worth, increasingly competent, and increasingly responsible for his or her choices. If these conditions are given primary importance, the child will be less likely to be subjected to maltreatment and more likely to be able to survive successfully any maltreatment which is experienced. In a sense, this means providing a program fitted to the developmental needs and readiness of each student which emphasizes these aspects of development. Specific attention would be given to helping the child understand and assert the rights of children to fair treatment; to apply family, school, and community resources when under threat of violation of these rights; to analyze critically the factors present in psychologically unhealthy situations and the alternatives for modifying those conditions; to prepare to act to change or avoid destructive conditions; and to manage one's own reactions to stress. In addition, each child would be helped to appreciate and respect others; to be sympathetic and empathic in regard to the experience of others; to understand and be able to apply child-development and parenting knowledge; and to personally direct the fulfillment of his or her psychological needs from a holistic orientation integrating physical, psychological, and where personally selected, spiritual dimensions.

At the school level, personnel and material resources would be organized and applied to achieve the goals for individuals as identified above. Schools would emphasize their "liberating" potentials rather than their "censoring" potentials (Campbell-Smith, 1983). Violence, coercion, and other punitive practices would be eliminated. Psychological needs fulfillment would be given priority over, but in a highly complementary manner with, more usual academic and nonacademic curricula. Specific attention would be given to the development of realistically high levels of self-esteem, mutual respect, and social responsibility. The programs for children would be individualized and set to insure an optimum combination of success and challenge. Long-term, dependable relationships of high intensity and frequency would be established between children and adults in schools, possibly through developing something in the way of in-school families which should be sustained across school years. A wide range of potentials should be given value and support for development. Preparation for family life and parenting should be given high priority, required as a regular part of the curriculum throughout the secondary school years for all students, and offered on a regular basis to parents and school personnel. Stress management training should be offered to parents and pro-

vided to all school staff and to all students, at all ages and levels as developmentally appropriate.

The early years of education for children should provide low teacher-to-student ratios, while basic skills, personal and social confidence, and competence are being established. The later years of schooling should place teachers increasingly in the role of resources to students directing their own learning. Students should be helped to become critical thinkers and choosers in areas of entertainment (e.g., television, movies, music) and consumerism. The schools should become community centers and resource centers during days and evenings to offer family members opportunities for safe pursuit of social relationships, continuing education, and vocational and leisure competencies. Varied and extensive involvement of parents, families, and school staffs should be emphasized.

It is worth noting that concern regarding psychological health and maltreatment issues, though not always put in those terms, has stimulated the development of some promising programs and concepts which are consistent with the recommendations which have been presented. Some of these deserve consideration for general application. In Harbor Springs, Michigan, the senior high school has become the town's senior citizen center, thereby increasing intergenerational relations to the benefit of all involved (*Across the Age Gap: Elders Enrich a Michigan High School*, 1981). Corporal punishment has been banned by the Board of Education of the Los Angeles, California, schools and by increasing numbers of other school communities. Schooling of children by their parents, sometimes in cooperation with the public school, is being pursued all across the country. Teacher-pupil ratios are being reduced dramatically in the primary grades in Indiana as a part of Project Prime Time (Smith, 1985). Nationally, programs for the gifted and talented are giving attention to performing arts, graphic arts, leadership, and many other valuable characteristics in addition to academic and intellectual strengths. In some school systems, the school is becoming a base for extended-family-like conditions as school doors are kept open beyond traditional school hours for vocational, hobby, and other special interest pursuits and to offer a protected and healthy environment for latchkey children. "Project Prevention: To Be Born and Grow Well," a highly regarded school-based educational program to prevent mental retardation, appears to hold genuine promise for being translated to focus on prevention of psychological maltreatment (Litch, 1980). These are but a few examples of promising directions presently underway.

Programs and materials intended to prevent child maltreatment are being produced and marketed by commercial (e.g., McGraw-Hill, Marvel Comics), professional (e.g., National Education Association), and advocacy organizations (e.g., Girl Scouts of America, National Committee for Prevention of Child Abuse, American Humane Association). They cover a wide variety of topics, including helping children recognize and deal with inappropriate behavior (particularly sexual behavior) of adults directed toward them (Marvel Comics, 1984); teaching children to appreciate and assert their rights in dealing with adults (*Strong Kids, Safe Kids*, 1984); protecting oneself when left without adult supervision, for those euphemistically labeled latchkey or "self-care" children (*Safe and Sound at Home Alone*, 1983). Clearly these topics deal with psychological issues. Information regarding the wide range of programs and materials available regarding child maltreatment may be acquired by addressing requests to the National Center on Child Abuse and Neglect, the National Committee for Prevention of Child Abuse, and the American Humane Association. The Office for the Study of the Psychological Rights of the Child may be able to provide information regarding resources specific to psychological maltreatment. See Appendix E for contact information for these agencies.

Programs intended to assist in the prevention and handling of child maltreatment should be evaluated by objective sources to determine their focuses on maltreatment, victims, and perpetrators, and their effectiveness and appropriateness as teaching tools. Examples of such evaluations exist (Hart, Kinder, Mrazek, & Brassard, 1985).

Overreactions to child maltreatment channeled through media and some child-protection programs may be producing abusive conditions by terrorizing children (Spock, 1986). Consideration should be given to this possibility in the evaluation of specific prevention programs.

Schooling Conditions Prerequisite for Constructive Action

If school systems and their personnel are to be expected to provide the necessary resources to fulfill responsibilities to protect children and correct and prevent maltreatment, certain conditions must exist. Within the schools there must be a commitment to the rights of children; an awareness of the precursors and correlates of maltreatment; an understanding of child development and competency in applying constructive techniques for influencing it; and policies, procedures, and accountability to reduce psychological maltreatment and pursue healthy psychological development.

For the most part, these conditions do not exist. The nature of childhood, the rights of children, and the place of children in society should be given serious and critical consideration at national, state, regional, and local levels. Political, religious, philosophical, psychological, medical, and educational groups should embark on a cooperative search for common ground which will set direction for goals, policies, procedures, and the allocation of resources. The schools need not wait for these other groups; they should begin now, as local and state entities, to establish positions on these issues. Direction for this effort will be found in the work of Melton (1983) devoted to child advocacy, Hart (1982) on children's psychological rights, Feshbach & Feshbach (1978) on children's rights in general, and Baumrind (1978) on relationships between parents' rights and children's rights as well as protection rights and choice rights.

As indicated in a previous section, pre- and inservice programs to produce awareness and preparedness among educators to deal with child maltreatment have been insufficient in scope, frequency, quality of presentation, and impact on school practices. It is apparent that such preparation is needed, should be required at pre- and in-service levels, and should incorporate follow-up programs to review and expand previous training. A first step would be the acknowledgment of this need at public school and higher education levels, with specific individuals or committees assigned the responsibility to insure the development and offering of such programs. Some of the dimensions which should be incorporated in such programs are identified in a later section.

The following conditions should be established within school environments to reduce psychological maltreatment: (a) commitment and preparedness by school staff to apply positive, nonpunitive disciplinary techniques; (b) encouragement, preparation, and reinforcement for team teaching and the involvement of parents and other adults as classroom resources and aides; (c) development and application of curricula to systematically pursue competencies which will produce critical thinkers and responsible autonomy; (d) selection of administrators who are capable of providing child advocacy and educational leadership; (e) selection and preparation processes for educators which will result in psychologically healthy teachers being placed in classrooms; (f) establishment of organizational structures which insure frequent one-on-one and small-group interactions between adults and students to produce opportunities for modeling, mediating, and interpersonal communication; and (g) frequent, dependable assistance from school mental health specialists. Many of these suggestions have been made by others (Campbell-Smith, 1983; Gottlieb & Gottlieb, 1971; Plank, 1975; ten Bensel & Berdie, 1976).

Authoritative sources (Broadhurst, 1984; Tower, 1984) have recommended that schools have clear, reliable, and effective policies to insure that child maltreatment will be responsibly dealt with. The major recommendations have generally focused on identification and reporting. They are applicable to maltreatment which is psychological in nature. Tower (1984) has provided a list of elements to be given consideration in the establishment of policies.

School–Community Relationships

Responsible management of psychological maltreatment requires that definitions and standards be developed which represent the convergence of expert and lay community opinion (Garbarino & Gilliam, 1980; Garbarino, Guttman, & Seeley, 1986; Hart, Germain, & Brassard, 1983; Hart, Gelardo, & Brassard, 1986). The effective management of correction and prevention through schooling, as dealt with in this chapter, requires a program of goals, procedures, and supports which are held in common and are mutually supported across school, family, and community agency structures, and which embody frequent interactions between these structures. This argues for the schools to be accessible, and in fact to actively solicit family and community involvement in schooling and to reach out to families and communities to participate more fully in the aspects of their lives which influence the development of children. The "child-development committee" structure recommended earlier in this chapter could logically assume, or be assigned, responsibility for developing plans and supervising their implementation in efforts to achieve the interactions desired by and most appropriate to a specific school community. Certainly, a beginning in this direction could be achieved through placing representatives of the community's child protective service team on the school's child-development committee and vice versa, or by the establishment of an advisory committee on child maltreatment problems within the schools which would have representatives of the families of school-age children and of the community's child protective service team as members. A detailed and tested program for the management of child abuse cases in the schools, labeled "The Toronto Model" (McClare, 1983), deals specifically with many of the suggestions made here and by Tower (1984).

Preparation of Educators for Roles and Responsibilities

Teacher selection, preservice training, and in-service training all require attention in the preparation of educators to deal with child maltreatment. While the specific content of programs in these areas would need to incorporate the relevant aspects of psychological maltreatment as described within this chapter, the more general recommendations made by others in these areas are appropriate.

Teachers should be selected and trained in a manner which will decrease the likelihood that they will personally display the characteristics of those who maltreat children and that they will, instead, exhibit the characteristics of healthy psychological functioning. Therefore, some consideration should be given to assessment in training programs and hiring practices to determine the extent to which important positive or negative characteristics are present. The purposes of assessment might be to identify those to be screened out of a set of applicants, those to be selected and reinforced in their plans to teach, or those to be given special training to reduce or enhance characteristics exhibited. The characteristics of those who maltreat have been identified by others (Smith, 1984; Wolfe, 1985). The characteristics of individuals who are psychologically healthy have also been identified (Maslow, 1968, 1970; Rogers, 1961, 1964, 1983).

Campbell-Smith has made specific suggestions regarding the criteria for teacher selection which should be applied if maltreatment in the schools is to be reduced; they include understanding, empathy, tolerance, emotional maturity, flexibility, and personal integrity (1983, p. 333).

As a result of her review of school practices, Drews (1972) strongly emphasized the need for special training programs for teachers to enable them to deal responsibly with child maltreatment. This recommendation has been made by many others during recent years. In regard to preservice training, Bartlett has indicated that the following conditions should exist: teachers should be sensitized to their responsibilities regarding child maltreatment; training should include emphasis on identification and characteristics of maltreated children and on appropriate procedures to follow when a case is suspected; instruction specific to child maltreatment should occur in the required program of teacher training; the number of hours of instruction should exceed 5.5 hours, which was the average found to exist in early childhood and elementary school teacher preparation; and methodology should be compatible with the characteristics of the instructor and the student population (1982). Zgliczynski and Rodolfa (1980) have developed and tested a 6-hour instructional module which displays promise for covering these areas, with the addition of emphasis on communication skills to be applied in working with the maltreated child.

In-service training programs to prepare educators have been developed and applied (Broadhurst, 1978; Broadhurst & Howard, 1975; Volpe, 1981; McClare, 1983). The programs incorporate several days of workshops, are usually offered to the full range of school personnel, and apply curricula covering topics such as characteristics of maltreated children, identification and reporting procedures (local and state), and follow-up procedures. Some programs, "Project Protection" being an example (Broadhurst & Howard, 1975), deal with the psychodynamics of maltreating families, procedures for working with children and families, and prevention of maltreatment.

In the judgment of the authors, Broadhurst (1984) and Tower (1984) outline and detail the issues deserving consideration by educators in a manner providing sufficient structure for the development of effective preservice and in-service training programs for educators.

Research Needed to Provide Direction

Recommendations for dealing with the major research issues of psychological maltreatment have been presented by Rosenberg and Germain, chapter 17 in this volume. Research specific to schooling should focus on (a) the pre- and in-service training necessary for educators to understand, identify, and deal with psychological maltreatment; (b) the effectiveness of promising programs for identifying maltreated children and helping victims and perpetrators through school–community services; (c) procedures for assessing the likelihood that teacher candidates and teachers will psychologically maltreat students (e.g., mental health, problem-solving, and stress-reducing behaviors); (d) the nature of and degree to which psychological maltreatment acts have been committed in classrooms as judged by teacher and student populations; and (e) the psychological maltreatment precursors of serious emotional/behavioral problems in students.

A FINAL COMMENT

In closing this chapter it is important to recognize that those who maltreat others generally do not set out consciously to do them harm. This is believed to be true of parents as well as others, including educators. It is also probable that those who maltreat in ways that have substantial or lasting negative impact on young people are in the minority. This, however, should not relieve those who care about the welfare of others, children in particular, from attempting to clarify related conditions and to prevent and correct conditions which appear to foster maltreatment.

REFERENCES

Across the age gap: Elders enrich a Michigan high school. (1981, March). *Life Magazine, 4*(3), 123–128.

Aiken, W. M. (1942). *The story of the eight-year study.* Vol. 1 in Commission on the Relation of School and College of the Progressive Education Association (Ed.), *Adventure in American education series.* New York: Harper and Bros.

American Humane Association. (1971). *Guidelines for schools to help protect neglected and abused children.* Denver, CO: Author.

American Humane Association. (1983). *Annual*

report, 1981: Highlights of official child neglect and abuse reporting. Denver, CO: Author.

American Humane Association. (1984). *Highlights of official neglect and abuse reporting, 1982.* Denver, CO: Author.

American Humane Association. (1985). *Highlights of official neglect and child abuse reporting, 1983.* Denver, CO: Author.

American Humane Association (1986). *Highlights of official neglect and child abuse reporting, 1984.* Denver, CO: Author.

American Psychiatric Association. (1980). *Diagnostic and statistical manual of mental disorders* (3rd ed.). Washington, DC: Author.

American Psychological Association. (1975). Psychologists oppose use of corporal punishment in schools. *News.* Washington, DC: Author.

Austin, J. (1975). *The new WISC-R: Research and implications for use.* Presentation at the meeting of the Indiana Psychological Association, Indianapolis.

Bartlett, P. M. (1982). *An investigation of child abuse/neglect: Instruction offered in early childhood education preservice programs.* Palo Alto: R & E Research Associates.

Baumrind, D. (1978). Reciprocal rights and responsibilities in parent–child relations. *Journal of Social Issues, 34*(2), 179–196.

Besharov, D. J. (1978). The legal aspects of reporting known and suspected child abuse and neglect. *Villanova Law Review, 23,* 458.

Biehler, R., & Snowman, F. (1982). *Psychology applied to teaching.* Boston: Houghton Mifflin.

Bolton, F. G., Jr. (1983). No turning back: The school and child maltreatment. *Educational Leadership, 40,* 25–26.

Brassard, M. R., Tyler, A., & Kehle, T. J. (1983). School programs to prevent intrafamilial child sexual abuse. *Child Abuse and Neglect, 7,* 241–245.

Brenton, M. (1977). What can be done about child abuse? *Today's Education, 66,* 51–53.

Brigham Young University. (1974). *Cypher in the snow.* Provo, UT: Author.

Broadhurst, D. D. (1975). Project Protection in Maryland: A school program to combat child abuse. *The Education Digest, 61*(2), 20–23.

Broadhurst, D. D. (1978). What schools are doing about child abuse and neglect. *Children Today, 7,* 22–36.

Broadhurst, D. D. (1984). *The educator's role in the prevention and treatment of child abuse and neglect.* Washington, DC: National Center on Child Abuse and Neglect, U.S. Department of Health and Human Services.

Broadhurst, D. D., & Howard, M. C. (1975). More about Project Protection. *Childhood Education, 52*(2), 67–69.

Bronfenbrenner, U. (1979). *The ecology of human development: Experiments by nature and design.* Cambridge: Harvard University Press.

Brown, G. W. (1977). School: Child advocate or adversary? *Clinical Pediatrics, 16*(5), 439–446.

Brown, T. (1979, Winter). Putting down kids. *Journal of Canadian Society for Prevention of Cruelty to Children, 2,* 11–13.

Campbell-Smith, M. (1983). The school: Liberator or censurer? *Child Abuse and Neglect, 7,* 329–337.

Clarizio, H. (1977). A case against the use of corporal punishment by teachers. In D. Hamachek (Ed.), *Human dynamics in psychology and education: Selected readings.* Boston: Allyn and Bacon.

Clarke, J. (1986). *A retrospective study of severe corporal punishment in the schools.* Unpublished doctoral dissertation, Temple University, Philadelphia.

Corwin, D. (1985). *The sexually abused child disorder.* Paper presented to the National Summit Conference on Diagnosing Child Sexual Abuse, Los Angeles.

Drews, K. (1972). The child and his school. In C. H. Kempe & R. E. Helfer (Eds.), *Helping the battered child and his family* (pp. 115–123). Philadelphia: J. D. Lippincott.

Dubanoski, R. A., Inaba, M., & Gerkewicz, K. (1983). Corporal punishment in schools: Myths, problems and alternatives. *Child Abuse and Neglect, 7,* 271–278.

Education Commission of the States. (1976). *Education policies and practices regarding child abuse and neglect and recommendations for policy development* (ECS report No. 85). Denver: Author.

Education Commission of the States. (1979). *Education policies and practices regarding child abuse and neglect: 1978* (ECS report No. 109). Denver: Author.

Egeland, B., & Erickson, M. F. (1983). *Psychologically unavailable caregiving: The effects on development of young children and the implications for intervention.* Paper presented at the International Conference on Psychological Abuse of Children and Youth, Indianapolis, Indiana University.

Erickson, M., & Egeland, B. (In press). A developmental view of the psychological consequences of maltreatment. *School Psychology Review.*

Fairorth, J. W. (1982). *Child abuse and the school.* Palo Alto: R & E Research Associates.

Feshbach, N. D., & Feshbach, S. (1978). Toward an historical, social and developmental perspective on children's rights. *Journal of Social Issues, 34*(2), 1–7.

Feuerstein, R., & Hoffman, M. B. (1982). Intergenerational conflict of rights: Cultural imposition and self-realization. *Viewpoints in Teaching and Learning, 58*(1), 44–63.

Fossum, L., & Sorenson, L. (1980). The schools see it first: Child abuse/neglect. *Phi Delta Kappan, 62,* 274.

Gall, M. D. (1970). The use of questions in teaching. *Review of Educational Research, 40,* 707–721.

Garbarino, J. (1977a). The price of privacy in the social dynamics of child abuse. *Child Welfare, 56* (9), 565–575.

Garbarino, J. (1977b). The human ecology of child maltreatment. *Journal of Marriage and the Family, 39,* 721–736.

Garbarino, J. (1979). The role of the school in the human ecology of child maltreatment. *School Review, 87*(2), 190–213.

Garbarino, J., & Gilliam, G. (1980). *Understanding abusive families.* Lexington, MA: Lexington Books.

Garbarino, J., & Vondra, J. (1983). *Psychological maltreatment of children and youth.* Paper presented at the International Conference on Psychological Abuse of Children and Youth, Indianapolis, Indiana University.

Garbarino, J., Guttman, E., & Seeley, J. (1986). *The psychologically battered child: Strategies for identification, assessment and intervention.* San Francisco: Jossey–Bass.

Gardner, H. (1983). *Frames of mind.* New York: Basic Books.

Germain, R., Brassard, M., & Hart, S. (1985). Crisis intervention for maltreated children. *School Psychology Review, 14*(3), 291–299.

Gibbons, M. (1974). Searching for the right passage from childhood and school. *Phi Delta Kappan, 55,* 596–602.

Gil, D. (1969). What schools can do about child abuse. *American Education, 5*(4), 2–5.

Gil, D. (1970). *Violence against children.* Cambridge, MA: Harvard University Press.

Glasser, W. (1965). *Reality therapy.* New York: Harper & Row.

Glasser, W. (1969). *Schools without failure.* New York: Harper and Row.

Gold, H. (1978, Spring). Children's rights and child abuse. *Day Care and Early Education,* pp. 25–27.

Goldbloom, R. (1984). *Where do we go from here?* Presentation to the Fifth International Congress on Child Abuse and Neglect, Montreal, Canada.

Good, T. L., & Brophy, J. E. (1973). *Looking in classrooms.* New York: Harper & Row.

Good, T. L., & Grouws, D. (1977). Teaching effects: A process–product study in 4th grade mathematics classrooms. *Journal of Teacher Education, 28,* 49.

Goodlad, J. I. (1969). Schools vs. education. *Saturday Review, 52*(16), 60.

Goodlad, J. I. (1983). A study of schooling: Some findings and hypotheses. *Phi Delta Kappan, 64*(7), 465–470.

Gordon, E. (1983). Home tutoring programs gain respectability. *Phi Delta Kappan, 64*(7), 398–399.

Gottlieb, B. H., & Gottlieb, L. J. (1971). An expanded role for the school social worker. *Social Work, 16*(4), 12–21.

Hart, S. (1982). The history of children's psychological rights. *Viewpoints in Teaching and Learning, 158*(1), 1–15.

Hart, S. (1985). *Psychological maltreatment and schooling.* Paper presented to the Annual Convention of the American Educational Research Association, Chicago.

Hart, S., Gelardo, M., & Brassard, M. (1986). Psychological maltreatment. In J. Jacobsen (Ed.), *The psychiatric sequelae of child abuse.* Springfield: Charles C Thomas.

Hart, S., Germain, B., & Brassard, M. (Eds.). (1983). *Proceedings Summary of the International Conference on Psychological Abuse of Children and Youth.* Indiana University: Office for the Study of the Psychological Rights of the Child.

Hart, S., Kinder, R., Mrazek, P., & Brassard, M. (1985). Videotape review: Child sexual abuse: What your children should know. *School Psychology Review, 14*(2), 385–390.

Henricksen, B. (1982). *Your money or your life.* Aberdeen University Press.

Hetherington, E. M., & Parke, R. D. (1979). *Child psychology: A developmental perspective.* New York: McGraw-Hill.

Holt, J. (1983). Schools and home schoolers: A fruitful partnership. *Phi Delta Kappan, 63,* 391–394.

How professors rated faculty in 19 fields. (1983, January 15). *Chronicle of Higher Education,* 6.

Hunt, W. A., & Matarazzo, J. D. (1973). Three years later: Recent developments in the experimental modification of smoking. *Journal of Abnormal Psychology, 81,* 107–114.

Hyman, I. (1983). *Psychological correlates of corporal punishment and physical abuse.* Paper presented at the International Conference on Psychological Abuse of Children and Youth, Indianapolis, Indiana University.

Hyman, I. A. (1985). *Psychological abuse in the schools: A school psychologist's perspective.* Paper presented to the annual convention of the American Psychological Association, Los Angeles.

Hyman, I. A., & D'Alessandro, J. (1984, September). Good, old-fashioned discipline: The politics of punitiveness. *Phi Delta Kappan, 66*(1) 39–45.

Hyman, I., & Wise, J. (Eds.). (1979). *Corporal punishment in American education.* Philadelphia: Temple University Press.

Jones, C. D., & Fox, M. S. (1979). American educational systems and child abuse and neglect. *Child Abuse and Neglect, 3,* 179–184.

Kadushin, A., & Martin, J. A. (1981). *Child abuse: An event.* New York: Columbia University Press.

Krugman, R. D., & Krugman, M. K. (1984). Emotional abuse in the classroom: The pediatrician's role in diagnosis and treatment. *American Journal of Diseases of Children, 138,* 284–286.

Laury, G. V., & Meerloo, J. A. M. (1967). Mental cruelty and child abuse. *Psychiatric Quarterly, 41*(2), 203–254.

Leavitt, J. E. (1981). Helping abused and neglected children. *Childhood Education, 57*(5), 267–270.

Levin, P. (1983). Teacher's perceptions, attitudes and reporting of child abuse/neglect. *Child Welfare, 62*(1), 14–19.

Litch, S. (1980). Project prevention: To be born and grow well. In *Towards the prevention of mental retardation in the next generation* (Vols. I and II). Washington, DC: U.S. Department of Health and Human Services.

Lynch, P. D. (1984). *Psychological abuse of children: Implications for malpractice and dismissals of teachers.* Paper presented at the annual convention of the American Educational Research Association, New Orleans.

Marion, M. (1982). Primary prevention of child abuse: The role of the family life educator. *Family Relations, 31,* 575–582.

Martin, D. L. (1973). The growing horrors of child abuse and the undeniable role of the schools in putting an end to it. *The American School Board Journal, 160*(11), 51–53.

Marvel Comics. (1984). *Spider-man and power pak* (Vol. 1, No. 1). New York: Marvel Comics Group.

Maslow, A. (1968). *Toward a psychology of being.* New York: Van Nostrand Reinhold.

Maslow, A. (1970). *A theory of human motivation.* New York: Harper & Row.

McClare, G. (1983). The management of child abuse and neglect cases in schools: The Toronto model. *Child Abuse and Neglect, 7,* 83–89.

Melton, G. (1983). *Child advocacy: Psychological issues and interventions.* New York: Plenum.

Montagu, A. (1970). A scientist looks at love. *Phi Delta Kappan, 51*(9), 463–467.

Moore, R., & Moore, D. (1984). *Home style teaching.* Waco, Texas: Word Book.

National Association of School Psychologists. (1986). *Position on corporal punishment.* Washington, DC: Author.

National Commission on Excellence in Education. (1983). *A nation at risk.* Washington, DC: U.S. Government Printing Office.

National Committee for Prevention of Child Abuse. (1982). *NCPA policy statement on corporal punishment in schools and custodial settings.* Chicago: Author.

National Education Association. (1972). *Report of the Task Force on Corporal Punishment.* Washington, DC: Author.

National Education Association. (1982). *NEA resolution B-35: Child abuse.* Washington, DC: Author.

National Parent Teachers Association. (1985). *National PTA takes action.* Chicago: Author.

National Science Board Commission on Precollege Education in Mathematics, Science and Technology. (1983). *Educating Americans for the 21st century.* Washington, DC: National Science Board–National Science Foundation.

Neiderpruem, K. (1986, March 14). Ex-teacher sentenced for child abuse. *Indianapolis Star,* p. 21.

Nicholls, J. G. (1979). Quality and inequality in intellectual development: The role of motivation in education. *American Psychologist, 34,* 1071–1084.

O'Block, F. R., Billmoria, A., & Behan, M. (1981). National survey of involvement of school psychologists with child abuse. *School Psychology Review, 10,* 62–64.

Paulson, J. S. (1983). Covert and overt forms of maltreatment in preschools. *Child Abuse and Neglect, 7,* 45–54.

Pelletier, K. R. (1977). *Mind as healer, mind as slayer.* New York: Dell.

Peterson, K. L., & Roscoe, B. (1983). Neglected children: Suggestions for early childhood educators. *Childhood Education, 64*(7), 2–5.

Plank, E. L. (1975). Violations of children's rights in the classroom. *Childhood Education, 52*(2), 73–75.

Public Law 94-142. (1975). *The education for all handicapped children act.*

Rogers, C. (1961). *Personal thoughts on teaching and learning.* Boston: Houghton Mifflin.

Rogers, C. (1964). *On becoming a person: A therapist's view of psychotherapy.* Boston: Houghton Mifflin.

Rogers, C. (1983). *Freedom to learn—for the 80's.* Columbus, OH: Charles Merrill.

Rohner, R. P., & Rohner, E. C. (1980). Antecedents and consequences of parental rejection: A theory of emotional abuse. *Child Abuse and Neglect, 4,* 189–198.

Rowe, M. B. (1974). Wait-time and rewards as instructional variables, their influence on language, logic, and fate control, Part I: One-wait-time. *Journal of Research in Science Teaching, 11,* 81–94.

Rutter, M. (1979). Protective factors in children's responses to stress and disadvantage. In M. W. Kent & J. E. Rolf (Eds.), *Primary prevention of psychopathology, Vol. 3: Social competence in children* (pp. 49–74). Hanover, NH: University Press of New England.

Safe and sound at home alone. (1983). New York: Girl Scouts USA.

Smith, B. C. (1985, September 30). Primetime. *Indianapolis Star.* Indianapolis.

Smith, S. (1984). Significant research findings in the etiology of child abuse. *Social Casework: The Journal of Contemporary Social Work, 65(6),* 337–346.

Solomon, R. L. (1964). Punishment. *American Psychologist, 19,* 239–253.

Spock, B. (1986, April 14). Fingerprinting a no-no? *Indianapolis Star,* p. 36.

Stones, E. (1979). *Psychopedagogy.* New York: Methuen.

Stones, E. (1984). Psychological factors in punishment. *Schools and Teaching, 1(4),* 1–5.

Strong kids, safe kids. (1984). [Film or videocassette.] Hollywood: Parmount Pictures.

ten Bensel, R. W., & Berdie, J. (1976). The neglect and abuse of children and youth: The scope of the problem and the school's role. *The Journal of School Health, 8,* 453–461.

Thomas, P. (1984). *Developments to the legal concept of emotional abuse.* Presentation to the Fifth International Congress on Child Abuse and Neglect, Montreal, Canada.

Tower, C. C. (1984). *Child abuse and neglect: A teacher's handbook for detection, reporting, and classroom management.* Washington, DC: National Education Association.

Valentine, D. P., Freeman, M. L., Acuff, S., & Andreas, T. (1985). Abuse and neglect: Identifying and helping school children at risk. *School Social Work Journal, 9(2),* 83–99.

Volpe, R. (1981). The development and evaluation of a training program for school-based professionals dealing with child abuse. *Child Abuse and Neglect, 5,* 103–110.

Weaver, R. A., Negri, A., & Wallace, B. (1980). Home tutorials vs. the public schools in Los Angeles. *Phi Delta Kappan, 62(4),* 254.

Wechsler, D. (1974). *Wechsler intelligence scale for children — revised.* New York: Psychological Corporation.

Weiner, B. (1979). A theory of motivation for some classroom experiences. *Journal of Educational Psychology, 71,* 3–25.

White, M. A. (1975). Natural rates of teacher approval and disapproval in the classroom. *Journal of Applied Behavior Analysis, 8,* 367–372.

Wishon, P. H. (1979). *School aged victims of sexual abuse: Implications for educators.* Paper presented at the Conference of the National Association for the Education of Young Children, New York.

Wolfe, D. A. (1985). Child-abusive parents: An empirical review and analysis. *Psychological Bulletin, 97(3),* 462–482.

Zajonc, R. B. (1976). Family configuration and intelligence. *Science, 192,* 227–236.

Zgliczynski, S., & Rodolfa, E. (1980). The teacher's responsibility to the abused child. *Journal of Teacher Education, 50,* 41–44.

17

Psychological Maltreatment: Theory, Research, and Ethical Issues in Psychology

Mindy S. Rosenberg and Robert B. Germain

Researchers have approached the study of child maltreatment from a number of different theoretical perspectives that span multiple levels of analysis (cf. Parke & Collmer, 1975). The majority of theories, however, have focused primarily on child physical abuse and more recently on child sexual assault (e.g., Finkelhor, 1984; Finkelhor & Browne, 1985), with relatively less theoretical and empirical work pursued in the area of child neglect (Polansky, Chalmers, Buttenwieser, & Williams, 1981, is an exception). Psychological maltreatment, on the other hand, is a veritable newcomer to the research community. While the phenomenon of psychological maltreatment is certainly familiar and its occurrence can be recognized clinically both alone and in conjunction with other maltreatment forms, the empirical literature on the topic is in the process of evolving.

The purpose of this chapter is to discuss the potential contributions of psychology to the study of psychological maltreatment. The chapter is divided into two major sections. The first section is focused on research issues, including a description of the ecological and developmental approaches that guide research on psychological maltreatment, followed by two research applications of these theoretical perspectives. Next, we address the question of psychology's unique contributions to the empirical study of psychological maltreatment. The second major section addresses specific ethical dilemmas that arise when conducting research with maltreated children and their families.

THEORETICAL PERSPECTIVES

What theoretical perspectives would be useful in guiding research on psychological maltreatment? Two perspectives appear particularly relevant for our purposes: the ecological and developmental approaches, which were introduced briefly in Hart, Germain, & Brassard (chapter one of this volume).

Research and the Ecological Approach

Before the emergence of an ecological approach, the research base in child maltreatment consisted of several discrepant, unitary models to explain etiology, including models emphasizing psychiatric, sociological, and social-situational factors (cf. Parke & Collmer, 1975). Because the theoretical assumptions that underlie the definition of a social problem like child maltreatment have inherent approaches to its solution (Caplan & Nelson, 1973), the particular model adopted has implications beyond mere academic debate. The ecological perspective, conceptualized originally by Bronfenbrenner (1979), elaborated and applied to child maltreatment by Garbarino

(1977), provides an integrated conceptual system to understand the complexities associated with maltreatment. In this sense, the ecological perspective offers both researchers and practitioners a broad conceptual framework to guide research design and intervention efforts.

Belsky (1980) summarizes the ecological perspective of child maltreatment as follows:

> While abusing parents enter the . . . family with developmental histories that may predispose them to treat children in an abusive or neglectful manner, stress-promoting forces within the immediate family . . . and beyond it . . . increase the likelihood that parent–child conflict will occur. The fact that a parent's response to such conflict and stress takes the form of child maltreatment is seen to be a consequence both of the parent's own experience as a child . . . and of the values and childrearing practices that characterize the society or subculture in which the individual, family, and community are embedded. (p. 330)

Thus, the ecological perspective directs researchers and practitioners to interrelated variables from different ecological levels, rather than focusing on single or multiple correlates of child maltreatment within one level. Implicit in this perspective is the idea that the etiology of child maltreatment is multiply determined, as is its solution. Child maltreatment, in general, is conceived as a maladaptive response between family and child to an environment that does not provide the resources and supports necessary to offset the stress and maltreating behavior. According to Garbarino (1979), the basic premise of an ecological analysis is to "identify situations in which the conditions of life conspire to compound rather than counteract the deficiencies and vulnerabilities of parents" (pp. 5–6).

Consider an example of a child who has been identified as both physically and psychologically maltreated. In adopting an ecological perspective, we would look not only at individual-level characteristics, such as parental personality attributes and childrearing history or the child's temperament and presence of a disability, but we would also look at interaction patterns that characterize the parent–child relationship, such as those that result from a mismatch in temperamental styles. The impact of familial-level factors would be important, such as the psychological effects on children of witnessing violent marital interactions or growing up in a family

with inappropriately close or distant boundaries. Family isolation from informal and formal support systems in the face of unmanageable stress and parental unemployment are examples of potentially relevant community-level variables. Finally, societal factors include the sanctioning of physical punishment and psychological threat to control children's behavior. By considering variable interrelationships within and across multiple levels in our research, we will be closer to understanding the complexity of child maltreatment in general, and psychological maltreatment specifically.

At present, the limited scope of research on psychological maltreatment leaves some very basic questions unanswered. For example, when we discuss the etiology of psychological maltreatment, we often find ourselves resorting to a similar variable constellation as the one we use in describing physical abuse. However, it is unclear from the current research base which etiological variables may overlap in causing psychological versus other maltreatment forms, and which variables may be unique to psychological maltreatment. Furthermore, from an ecological perspective, it is necessary to ask whether certain variables (or variable combinations) at particular levels of analysis have more weight than others in contributing to the phenomenon.

Research and Developmental Approach

What would it mean to adopt a developmental approach in research on psychological maltreatment? The most basic step, of course, is to acknowledge the child as an evolving organism progressing through the various stages of cognitive, social, and emotional development (Kessen, 1965). It follows that the child's experience of different parenting practices will vary as a function of the child's developmental status. For example, Spitz's (1945) classic work on the impact of socioemotional deprivation of very young children reared in orphanages illustrates the importance of the caregiver–infant attachment relationship for the child's cognitive and socioemotional development. However, the psychological impact of a similar level of parental emotional deprivation may not be as devastating to an older child, and may or may not result in different forms of emotional damage. Here it is also important to consider the child's developing relationship to other systems, such as school, peer, and community, and the ability of these systems to influence and compensate potentially for negative parenting practices. School-aged children with access to a peer group, a coach, or a teacher can take advantage of multiple sources of support and feedback, in contrast to an infant or toddler, whose emotional sustenance is drawn primarily from its parents.

One of the major research issues in the areas of psychological maltreatment is the need to acknowledge developmental processes in the operational definition of the phenomenon. On a general level, there has been considerable attention given to the myriad of problems involved in defining what is meant by psychological maltreatment (e.g., Giovannoni & Becerra, 1979; Lourie & Stephano, 1978). Recently, the attempts at definition increasingly include references to developmental considerations (see Garbarino & Vondra, chapter 2; Hart, Germain, & Brassard, chapter 1; and Melton & Thompson, chapter 15 in this volume).

Garbarino, Guttman, & Seeley (1986) have gone beyond discussion of developmental issues, to the point of specifying parental behaviors thought to constitute psychological maltreatment across the stages of infancy to adolescence. For example, their general definition of "rejecting" (which is one of five parental maltreating behaviors) involves ". . . behaviors that communicate or constitute abandonment, defining the child as not a part of the family, refusal to touch or show affection to the child, or refusal to acknowledge the child's accomplishments." Next, they go on to define what is meant by "rejecting" at four developmental periods:

> In infancy, the critical aspect of rejecting is the parent's "refusal" to accept the child's primary attachment; e.g., abandonment, discouraging infant attachment. In early childhood, the critical aspect of rejecting is actively excluding the child from family activities; e.g., not taking the child on family outings, refusing the child's affiliative gestures, placing the child away from the family. [For school age] the critical aspect . . . is consistently communicating a negative definition of self to the child; e.g., frequent belittling, scapegoating the child as part of a family system. In adolescence, the critical aspect of rejection is parental refusal to acknowledge the changing social roles expected of the child; i.e., toward more autonomy and self-determination; e.g., verbal humiliation and excessive criticism, expelling the child from the family. (p. 22)

Certainly, the problem of defining psychological maltreatment in a developmental context is a difficult research issue that will require the integration of knowledge in such areas as child development and family systems theory.

RESEARCH APPLICATIONS

Throughout this volume, numerous research ideas have been suggested to increase our knowledge about psychological maltreatment. Virtually all contributors have addressed the multitude of problems inherent in defining psychological maltreatment, whether it be from a psychological, educational, or legal perspective. Clearly, construct operationalization and validation represents the first step in the research process. Currently, there at least two theoretical proposals to operationalize psychological maltreatment that incorporate an ecological and developmental approach (see Garbarino, Guttman, & Seeley, 1986; Hart, Germain, & Brassard, chapter 1, this volume). The next step, of course, is to determine the definition's empirical validity in a sample of children and families already identified as "psychologically maltreating" by protective services and in various other comparison groups (e.g., physically abusive, neglectful, and non-maltreating families).

Since the empirical study of psychological maltreatment is relatively new, the research possibilities appear endless. In this section, we will offer two very different examples of research areas where the ecological and developmental approaches are important in problem conceptualization. These areas are mediating variables and child outcome and the ecological context of service delivery.

Mediating Factors and Child Outcome

Children who have been maltreated by their parents do not necessarily evidence psychopathological outcomes (Kaufman & Zigler, 1986). Some children who have experienced psychological and other forms of maltreatment grow up to engage in meaningful intimate relationships, become loving parents, and lead productive work lives. However, what is interesting about the previous two statements is that we probably know this information more from our personal experience (e.g., being friends with someone who has described her/his relationship with parents as emotionally abusive or neglectful yet leads a successful life, or having a similar experience oneself) than from the current empirical literature. Because the sequelae of child maltreatment do not always include psychological dysfunction, one of the interesting research questions becomes, "Which individual, family, and environmental factors are operative in shielding some children from the deleterious effects expected from growing up in a maltreating home?"

A number of researchers are beginning to address the issue of mediating variables and risk factors as a way to explain why some children appear to function well and others do less well in the face of aversive circumstances. Rutter (1979) originally coined the idea of protective factors, which are defined as "those attributes of persons, environments, situations, and events that appear to temper predictions of psychopathology based on an individual's at-risk status. Protective factors provide resistance to risk and foster outcomes marked by patterns of adaptation and competence" (Garmezy, 1983, p. 73). In contrast, vulnerability factors tend to increase the effects of stressors and contribute to children's risk for psychological dysfunction (Rutter, 1983).

Are there variables that influence children's response to adversity by protecting or making them more vulnerable? Several studies provide a relatively consistent answer. Rutter and colleagues (Rutter, Cox, Tupling, Berger, & Yule, 1975; Rutter, Yule, Quinton, Rowlands, Yule, & Berger, 1975) identified six familial vulnerability factors associated with a child's risk for psychiatric disorder: marital discord, low socioeconomic status, large family size with overcrowding, paternal criminality, maternal psychiatric disorder, and admission of the child into the care of local authorities. The authors also identified a constellation of factors that protected children from psychiatric risk: positive personality dispositions (e.g., socially responsive; positive mood), gender (girls were less vulnerable than boys), parental warmth, and a supportive school environment that reinforced children's coping efforts. Other research on protective factors, including studies of poor, competent black children in urban ghettos (described in Garmezy, 1981) and a longitudinal investigation of Hawaiian children born into poor, unstable families with parental men-

tal health problems (Werner, Bierman, & French, 1971; Werner & Smith, 1977, 1982) find a similar constellation of factors: positive personality attributes; family cohesion, warmth, and rule setting; and support figures in the environment. In the Project Competence studies of children at risk for psychopathology based on maternal diagnosis of serious mental health disorders or child behavioral dysfunction (Garmezy, 1981; Garmezy, Masten, & Tellegen, 1984), IQ also functioned as a protective factor.

The specific protective and vulnerability factors operating in situations of psychological maltreatment have yet to be identified. We do not know, for example, whether the same protective factors reported above will compensate for the negative effects of psychological abuse and neglect or whether different factors may emerge.

Certainly, one potential vulnerability factor to investigate is the type and extent of other maltreatment experienced (e.g., physical abuse, sexual abuse) and witnessed (e.g., interparental violence) by the child, and the age at which these experiences occur. Elementary-school-aged children who have witnessed extreme physical violence between their parents have been found to exhibit both internalizing (e.g., depressive symptomatology) and externalizing problems (e.g., aggressive and delinquent behaviors), and difficulties providing appropriate solutions to problems involving interpersonal conflict (Goodman & Rosenberg, in press; Rosenberg, 1984). Although the children in the latter sample were not abused physically, psychologists have speculated that children who witness constant verbal degradation (e.g., name calling, threats) and violence (e.g., beatings, use of weapons) perpetrated by their fathers against their mothers, often accompanied by threats not to interfere, are being maltreated psychologically (e.g., Walker & Edwall, in press).

The research task of investigating the effects of protective and vulnerability factors in situations of psychological maltreatment should be done in the context of an ecological and developmental perspective. What would this entail? First, both protective and vulnerability factors can be identified easily at multiple levels, including individual, parent–child, family, and environmental factors (see Cicchetti & Rizley, 1981). Second, careful conceptualization should be given to the ways in which the child's developmental characteristics (e.g., chronological age, cognitive stage, level of emotional maturity) interact with other systems characteristics (e.g., stage of family life-cycle development, organization of peer network) in the prediction of child outcome. The main research questions that emerge from such an analysis are (a) what combination of protective factors at which level(s) is necessary to offset the particular vulnerabilities at other level(s), and (b) how would these particular combinations vary according to the developmental needs of the child and family?

Ecological Context of Service Delivery

Psychologists who apply an ecological approach to the study of psychological maltreatment are faced with the task of analyzing the radiating effects of the phenomenon across multiple system levels. From this perspective, it becomes just as important to study the social systems' reactions in dealing with the phenomenon of psychological maltreatment as it is to study individual children's reactions. Why would psychologists be interested in this type of question? One reason is that the ways in which social systems (i.e., child protective services, juvenile courts) accommodate to the psychological maltreatment label may have important implications for the provision of child and family services. The following example of a policy change in the juvenile justice system illustrates this point.

In 1974, the Juvenile Justice Delinquency Prevention Act mandated that status offenders (juveniles whose "crimes" would not be labeled as such if they were over 18 years of age, e.g., truancy, promiscuity) were no longer to be detained in institutions housing delinquent youth, and made funds available for community-based services. In a comprehensive study of federal, state, and community response to this policy change, one of the interesting points noted was the creative ways in which community agencies adapted to this change and the resulting effects on service delivery (Zatz & Handler, 1982). In some states, it was easier to obtain services if the child was labeled a status offender (i.e., CHINS: children in need of supervision; PINS: persons in need of supervision; MINS: minors in need of supervision) than if he or she were labeled delinquent. In other states, the opposite was true. Consequently, many a creative social worker was able to reframe a youth's offenses to fit the specific funding categories for that state. Other states had less flexible policies that sometimes prevented youth from receiving services.

What are the implications concerning psychological maltreatment? Primarily speculations, at this point. One potential implication of broadening the legal definition of child maltreatment to include psychological forms might involve changes in reporting and subsequent service availability at the community level. Many of us have had the experience of reporting a family suspected of maltreatment, only to find out later that the family was unable to obtain services. At present, there is a shortage of quality services for the treatment of families with documented physical abuse and neglect as well as for the treatment of emotional problems in general. Scarce resources and large caseloads often force social workers to focus on the most severe forms of maltreatment, to the neglect of many families and children needing attention. Would the inclusion of psychological maltreatment as a reportable offense (as it already is in some states) increase reports to such an extent that it would be impossible to follow through with services? On the other hand, could the overload in reports then be used to demonstrate need for additional funding? If the intent behind identification of psychologically maltreated children and their families is to provide service, then social service workers could reframe their clients' behavior to match whichever psychological labels are receiving service funds at the time. Data gathered on these types of questions may help in the development of improved service delivery policies, which would ultimately affect children and families.

Psychology's Role in the Study of Psychological Maltreatment

What are psychology's unique contributions to increasing our understanding of the psychological maltreatment of children and youth? As a science, psychology is concerned most generally with the study and prediction of human behavior. As an applied discipline, psychology is involved in the design, implementation, and evaluation of intervention strategies, both to prevent the onset of psychological disorder and to ameliorate the effects of disorder once detected. Given these basic goals, the following areas represent examples of psychology's contributions to the study of psychological maltreatment:

Description of the Impact of Psychological Maltreatment. By virtue of its focus on the individual's emotional processes, psychology is in an excellent position to provide an account of the victim's subjective experience of psychological maltreatment. Such an account would be helpful in beginning to understand the meaning of the perpetrator's acts toward the victim and the resulting short- and long-term effects. It would also provide researchers with clues as to which salient variables warrant further study.

Relationship of Multiple Interest Areas Within Psychology. Several interest areas within psychology can contribute unique theoretical perspectives on the topic of psychological maltreatment. Areas with immediate relevance include clinical, community, and developmental psychology. Each of these areas has its own approach to studying behavior, and will consider different variables to be important in its analysis of psychological maltreatment. For example, the study of clinical psychology, which emphasizes the etiology and treatment of individual, couple, and family dysfunction, can provide similar information for the specific problem of psychological maltreatment. In contrast, community psychology is concerned with the study of social settings and their interface with individuals, with prevention rather than cure, and focuses on strengths rather than pathology (Rappaport, 1977). It would be natural for community psychologists to conceptualize psychological maltreatment along the lines of an ecological approach, but they would be more likely to intervene with populations of maltreated people (or those at risk for maltreatment) than with individuals, and their intervention strategies would differ from clinical psychology as well (Rosenberg & Reppucci, 1985). Finally, developmental psychologists would be concerned primarily with the effects of psychological maltreatment on the child's developmental status. Researchers who are knowledgeable about and can integrate these different areas in psychology have the potential to contribute a broader conceptualization of psychological maltreatment that more closely approximates the phenomenon's complexity.

Relationship of Psychology to Law. Recently, there has been an explosion of interest in research issues involved in the interface between psychology and law (e.g., Reppucci, Weithorn,

Mulvey, & Monahan, 1984). In the case of psychological maltreatment, there are multiple avenues for fruitful research and practice, including such topics as child custody disputes, children's memory for psychologically maltreating acts and their credibility as witnesses, and the balance between child, parent, and state rights. Certainly, the ability to make progress on the problem of psychological maltreatment requires the collaboration of psychology and law.

ETHICAL ISSUES

The ethical issues that confront researchers who study children from maltreating families are numerous and complex. Children, in general, constitute a special population of human subjects whose vulnerability and cognitive limitations require careful consideration. Young children are often unable to determine adequately what is in their best interest regarding participation in a proposed study. The dimension of maltreatment complicates the situation further when participation in research may contribute to additional child victimization. In considering the unique ethical issues involved in child maltreatment research, it is important to note the distinction between "ethical dilemmas," which arise in situations where there is more than one ethical solution, and ethical problems that are resolved out of the researcher's convenience or self-interest (Beauchamps & Childress, 1983; Weithorn, in press). In this section, we will explore several ethical dilemmas facing researchers who wish to study maltreated children and their families, including the areas of informed consent, confidentiality, and the physical and psychological safety of participants. We raise the following ethical dilemmas in the context of child maltreatment in general, and refer to specific ethical concerns regarding psychological maltreatment where relevant.

Informed Consent

Ethical guidelines for conducting research with human participants have been established by the federal government (Department of Health, Education, and Welfare, 1978; Department of Health and Human Services, 1981) and professional organizations (e.g., American Psychiatric Association, 1979; American Psychological Association, 1982). These guidelines direct researchers to develop specific plans in addressing the issue of informed consent. Included in these guidelines are the following elements: (a) an explanation of the procedures to be followed, including the identification of those participants who are in the experimental group; (b) a description of the discomforts and risks that may arise as a result of the research procedures; (c) a description of expected benefits; (d) an offer to answer questions about the procedures; and (e) an obligation to respect the participant's freedom to discontinue an activity and/or withdraw from the study at any given time. These elements can be categorized into three general domains: information, voluntariness, and competency (Meisel, Roth, & Lidz, 1977). Ethical dilemmas arise in each of these domains when studying maltreated children.

Information. In the first domain of informed consent, sufficient information is provided to help participants choose whether they wish to become involved in the study. Here, the issues of incomplete disclosure and deception provoke the most debate. The primary question facing maltreatment investigators is whether to disclose to participants that the research involves child maltreatment; that is, individuals in the experimental group(s) were chosen because they maltreat or are at risk for maltreating their children, and those in the comparison group(s) were chosen because they do not. A completely open disclosure to the experimental group may risk parental refusal to participate, response distortion, unintended consequences of labeling, and/or cause additional psychological trauma (cf. Kinard, 1985; Weithorn, in press). In addition, the stigma associated with the maltreatment label may affect not only the individuals involved but also the settings in which the study is conducted (e.g., schools). For these reasons, some investigators claim (and we agree) that the negative effects of full disclosure could outweigh the positive intent (Hart, personal communication, 1986; Kinard, 1985).

Additional information about potential discomforts or hazards as a result of research participation must also be described. In cases of child maltreatment, there may be instances where the types of questions asked of parents and children may elicit uncomfortable feelings, but the collection of the information is nonetheless essential. For example, one of us (MSR) is interested in the psychological effects of witnessing interparental violence on children's socioemotional development. In the process of studying this problem, it is necessary to gather data from the parent (typically the mother) about the type and frequency of marital violence witnessed by their child (e.g., shoving, beating), and whether the child has experienced various forms of maltreatment (e.g., physical abuse and neglect, sexual abuse). It is an understatement to say that gathering this type of information requires clinical sensitivity, since the mothers often feel guilty, embarrassed, and/or responsible for what has happened to their child. Many investigators run into the same situation when they attempt to take a careful history of the types of maltreatment experienced by children in their samples. Similarly, the potential for children to become upset by specific questions or activities must be acknowledged in the consent form, as well as a plan for dealing with the child's painful feelings and ending on a happy note.

Voluntariness. The second domain of informed consent is concerned with providing individuals with the assurance of freedom to participate in research without coercion or inappropriate persuasion (Meisel et al., 1977). Ethical questions arise when research and service provision overlap in the same setting (e.g., social service agencies, hospitals, shelters for victims of domestic violence) and staff members do not specify clearly that individuals can receive services independent of participating in research. Moreover, clients may consider some institutions (e.g., hospitals and social service agencies) or situations (e.g., court-ordered therapy) inherently coercive, so that the concept of voluntariness becomes fuzzy. For example, in cases of substantiated maltreatment, parents or guardians are already involved in a coercive process with the threat of losing their children. Consequently, they may feel obligated to participate in research, and fear retribution if they do not cooperate. Here, a clear distinction must be drawn between the parents' or guardian's right to receive services that are not contingent on research participation. Likewise, in some institutions where individuals receive low- or no-cost services, they may feel that they have to participate in a particular study in exchange for receiving such services.

Competency. The third aspect of informed consent involves the issue of competency. When children are involved in research, special attention is given to the question of whether they can understand the procedures and purpose of the research, and whether they can indicate a preference to participate (National Commission, 1977). Federal regulations require permission from the parent or guardian and assent from the child before data can be collected (Department of Health and Human Services, 1983). "Assent" is defined as the child's agreement to participate in research and is distinguished from "consent," which implies a more abstract appreciation of the implications involved in participation. In reviewing current research on children's competencies to assent and consent, Weithorn (1983, 1984) concludes that in general, school-age children are capable of providing assent, while adolescents are capable of providing consent.

One ethical concern that arises in working with maltreated children is the potential for increased familial conflict if disparity exists between family members' willingness to be involved in research. As Kinard (1985) notes, situations in which children refuse to participate may exacerbate already strained parent–child relationships. Furthermore, in families where there is wife battering, both mother and child may risk increased physical and psychological maltreatment if they wish to participate in research and the perpetrator does not.

Confidentiality

Perhaps one of the thorniest problems facing child maltreatment researchers involves the conflicting issues of confidentiality versus the legal mandate to report suspected maltreatment. Researchers often struggle over whether they need to convey to participants their professional responsibility to report suspected maltreatment, and if so, in what way. Institutional Review Boards (IRBs) vary in this regard. Some IRBs argue that investigators need to include a specific statement in the consent form noting that confidentiality will be maintained except when state law does not protect such confidentiality, such as in cases of homicide, suicide, or child abuse and neglect. Other IRBs suggest that it is permissible to leave off the latter part of the statement that refers specifically to child mal-

treatment. In still other cases, IRBs will go along with the argument of not needing to put anything in the consent form that should be known by the responsible person. Clearly, there is some variation in this matter.

One of the ways in which researchers handle this problem is to obtain participants from a variety of agencies that are known to work with maltreatment cases (e.g., protective services, public health departments). In this way, researchers can feel buffered from the immediate responsibility to report suspected maltreatment, since these cases have either been reported or agency personnel are aware of the maltreatment risk. Researchers who use community samples as comparison groups will need to plan for what they will do in situations where maltreatment is suspected.

Physical and Psychological Safety

The study of maltreating families presents unique ethical concerns about family members' physical and psychological safety as a result of their research participation. Specifically, the issue is whether research procedures (e.g., interviews, questionnaires, interactional tasks) can increase the risk of additional physical and/or psychological maltreatment in families where maltreatment is a potential or identified problem (Back, 1984). Safety concerns are raised not only by grant reviewers and university institutional review boards, but also by subject referral sources such as social service agencies and therapists. For example, therapists often conduct an initial screening of their clients to determine who may be inappropriate for participation in the study, and one of the clinical judgment variables frequently used is the potential for further maltreatment as a result of research participation.

Straus (1981) makes several important comments regarding subject safety, particularly in the realm of family violence. Generally, he argues that researchers should consider the following risk criterion in developing their procedures: subjects' risks for participating in research should not be greater than the ordinary risks of daily life. Based on this criterion, Straus (1981) maintains that standard interview procedures and observational methods present a "normal risk" to family members rather than provoking additional maltreatment. He further asserts that it is most important to observe the patterns of interaction that might eventually lead to maltreatment rather than the maltreatment per se.

Although standard methodological procedures may appear to present a "normal risk," it is conceivable that safety problems may arise in spite of precautions taken to minimize risk. For example, during the course of a subject interview, it may be discovered that a child's idiosyncratic method of coping with an abusive parent may in fact exacerbate the maltreatment. Does the interviewer empathically listen, or does he or she attempt to intervene by helping the child develop more adaptive coping strategies? Likewise, a child may participate in a study with a nonoffending parent. Does the researcher need to assess what impact participation will have on the child if he or she goes home and discusses the interview with the offending parent? Or how do researchers protect children from the potential of further maltreatment when parents leave a family interaction task with unresolved conflict and anger? Clearly, these examples illustrate the necessity for investigators to add safeguard measures onto their procedures to protect children and families from the unintended negative consequences of research.

In summary, researchers who study psychological and other forms of child maltreatment are often faced with a number of complex ethical decisions where there may be more than one ethically defensible solution. In these situations, investigators need to identify various alternatives and the consequences of following a particular plan. The continuation of research on child maltreatment is vitally necessary despite the inherent difficulties in applying scientific and ethical standards to this population. When one considers the implications of not conducting such research (Rosenthal & Rosnow, 1984), the benefits far outweigh the problems.

CONCLUSION

In this chapter, we have explored the contributions that psychology could offer to the study of psychological maltreatment. We have examined two theoretical perspectives and the ways in which their application can reflect the conceptual complexities of psychological maltreatment. We have also addressed examples of ethical dilemmas that face investigators who conduct research with maltreated children and their families. Clearly, the complexity of the problem will be both a theoretical and practical challenge to psychology.

REFERENCES

American Psychiatric Association. (1979). Model law on confidentiality of health and social service records. *American Journal of Psychiatry, 130,* 739.

American Psychological Association. (1982). *Ethical principles in the conduct of research with human participants.* Washington, DC: Author.

Back, S. M. (1984, August). *Ethical issues in family violence research.* Paper presented at the Second National Family Violence Research Conference, Durham, NH.

Beauchamps, T. L., & Childress, J. F. (1983). *Principles of biomedical ethics.* New York: Oxford University Press.

Belsky, J. (1980). Child maltreatment: An ecological integration. *American Psychologist, 35,* 320–335.

Bronfenbrenner, U. (1979). *The ecology of human development: Experiments by nature and design.* Cambridge, MA: Harvard University Press.

Caplan, G., & Nelson, S. (1973). On being useful: The nature and consequences of psychological research on social problems. *American Psychologist, 28,* 199–211.

Cicchetti, D., & Rizley, R. (1981). Developmental perspectives on the etiology, intergenerational transmission, and sequelae of child maltreatment. *New Directions for Child Development, 11,* 33–55.

Department of Health, Education, and Welfare. (1978). 45 CRF Section 46.116.

Department of Health and Human Services. (1981). Final regulations amending basic HHS policy for the protection of human research subjects. *Federal Register,* January 26, Part X, 8365–8392.

Department of Health and Human Services. (1983). Additional protections for children involved as subjects in research. *Federal Register, 48,* 9814–9820.

Finkelhor, D. (1984). *Child sexual abuse: New theory and research.* New York: The Free Press.

Finkelhor, D., & Browne, A. (1985). The traumatic impact of child sexual abuse: A conceptualization. *American Journal of Orthopsychiatry, 55,* 530–541.

Garbarino, J. (1977). The human ecology of child maltreatment. *Journal of Marriage and the Family, 39,* 721–736.

Garbarino, J. (1979). An ecological approach to

child maltreatment. In L. Pelton (Ed.), *The social context of child abuse and neglect.* New York: Human Sciences Press.

Garbarino, J., Guttman, E., & Seeley, J. (1986). *Dealing with psychological maltreatment: A handbook for practitioners.* San Francisco, CA: Jossey-Bass.

Garmezy, N. (1981). Children under stress: Perspectives on antecedents and correlates of vulnerability and resistance to psychopathology. In A. I. Rubin, J. Aronoff, A. M. Barclay, & R. A. Zucker (Eds.), *Further explorations in personality.* New York: Wiley Interscience.

Garmezy, N. (1983). Stressors of childhood. In N. Garmezy & M. Rutter (Eds.), *Stress, coping, and development in children.* New York: McGraw-Hill.

Garmezy, N., Masten, A. S., & Tellegen, A. (1984). The study of stress and competence in children: A building block for developmental psychopathology. *Child Development, 55,* 97–111.

Giovannoni, J. M., & Becerra, R. M. (1979). *Defining child abuse.* New York: Free Press.

Goodman, G. S., & Rosenberg, M. S. (in press). The child witness to family violence. In D. J. Sonkin (Ed.), *Domestic violence on trial: Psychological and legal dimensions of family violence.* New York: Springer.

Kaufman, J., & Zigler, E. (1986). Do abused children become abusive parents? Manuscript submitted for publication.

Kessen, W. (1965). *The child.* New York: Wiley & Sons.

Kinard, E. M. (1985). Ethical issues in research with abused children. *Child Abuse and Neglect, 9,* 301–311.

Lourie, I., & Stephano, L. (1978). On defining emotional abuse. *Proceedings of the Second Annual National Conference on Child Abuse and Neglect.* Washington, DC: Government Printing Office.

Meisel, A., Roth, L. H., & Lidz, C. W. (1977). Toward a model of the legal doctrine of informed consent. *American Journal of Psychiatry, 134,* 285–289.

National Commission for the Protection of Human Subjects of Biomedical and Behavioral Research. (1977). *Report and recommendations on research involving children.* (DHEW Publication No. OS 77-0004). Washington, DC: U.S. Government Printing Office.

Parke, R., & Collmer, C. (1975). Child abuse: An interdisciplinary review. In E. M. Hetherington (Ed.), *Review of child development research* (Vol. 5, pp. 509–590). Chicago: University of Chicago Press.

Polansky, N., Chalmers, M. A., Buttenwieser, E., & Williams, D. P. (1981). *Damaged parents: An anatomy of child neglect.* Chicago: University of Chicago Press.

Rappaport, J. (1977). *Community psychology: Values, research and action.* New York: Holt, Rinehart & Winston.

Reppucci, N. D., Weithorn, L. A., Mulvey, E. P., & Monahan, J. (Eds.). (1984). *Children, mental health, and law.* Beverly Hills, CA: Sage.

Rosenberg, M. S. (1984). *The impact of witnessing interparental violence on children's behavior, perceived competence, and social problem solving abilities.* Unpublished doctoral dissertation, University of Virginia.

Rosenberg, M. S., & Reppucci, N. D. (1985). Primary prevention of child abuse. *Journal of Consulting and Clinical Psychology, 53,* 576–585.

Rosenthal, R., & Rosnow, R. L. (1984). Applying Hamlet's question to the ethical conduct of research: A conceptual addendum. *American Psychologist, 39,* 561–563.

Rutter, M. (1979). Protective factors in children's response to stress and disadvantage. In M. W. Kent & J. E. Rolf (Eds.), *Primary prevention of psychopathology: Social competence in children* (Vol. 3). Hanover, NH: University Press of New England.

Rutter, M. (1983). Stress, coping, and development: Some issues and some questions. In N. Garmezy & M. Rutter (Eds.), *Stress, coping, and development in children.* New York: McGraw-Hill.

Rutter, M., Cox, A., Tupling, C., Gerger, M., & Yule, W. (1975). Attainment and adjustment in two geographic areas: I. The prevalence of psychiatric disorder. *British Journal of Psychiatry, 126,* 493–509.

Rutter, M., Yule, B., Quinton, D., Rowlands, O., Yule, W., & Berger, M. (1975). Attainment and adjustment in two geographic areas: III. Some factors accounting for area differences. *British Journal of Psychiatry, 126,* 520–533.

Spitz, R. A. (1945). Hospitalism: An inquiry into the genesis of psychiatric conditions in early childhood. In A. Freud et al. (Eds.), *The psychoanalytic study of the child* (Vol. 1). New York: International Universities Press.

Straus, M. A. (1981). Protecting human subjects in observational research: The case of family violence. In E. E. Filsinger & R. A. Lewis (Eds.), *Assessing marriage: New behavioral approaches.* Beverly Hills, CA: Sage.

Walker, L. E. A., & Edwall, G. E. (in press). Domestic violence and determination of visitation and custody in divorce. In D. J. Sonkin (Ed.), *Domestic violence on trial: Psychological and legal dimensions of family violence.* New York: Springer.

Weithorn, L. A. (1983). Involving children in decisions affecting their own welfare. In G. B.

Melton, G. P. Koocher, & M. J. Saks (Eds.), *Children's competence to consent* (pp. 235–260). New York: Plenum.

Weithorn, L. A. (1984). Children's capacities in legal contexts. In N. D. Reppucci, L. A. Weithorn, E. P. Mulvey, & J. Monahan (Eds.), *Children, mental health, and law* (pp. 25–55). Beverly Hills, CA: Sage.

Weithorn, L. A. (in press). Informed consent for prevention research involving children: Legal and ethical issues. In the National Institute of Mental Health (Ed.), *Preventing mental disorders: A research perspective*. Washington, DC: NIMH Press.

Werner, E. E., Bierman, J. M., & French, F. E. (1971). *The children of Kauai: A longitudinal study from the prenatal period to age ten*. Honolulu: University of Hawaii Press.

Werner, E. E., & Smith, R. S. (1977). *Kauai's children come of age*. Honolulu: University of Hawaii Press.

Werner, E. E., & Smith, R. S. (1982). *Vulnerable but invincible: A study of resilient children*. New York: McGraw-Hill.

Zatz, J., & Handler, J. (1982). *Neither angels nor thieves: Deinstitutionalization of youth in the juvenile justice system*. Washington, DC: The National Academy of Sciences Press.

18

Psychological Maltreatment: Integration and Summary

Stuart N. Hart and Marla R. Brassard

IMPORTANCE OF PSYCHOLOGICAL MALTREATMENT

Is psychological maltreatment important enough to justify using limited child welfare resources to understand and combat it? This is an important question in light of Gil's (1970) comment that compared with poverty, racial discrimination, and inadequate provisions for medical care and education, child abuse does not constitute a major social problem. Egeland and Erickson (chapter 8 of this volume) note that abusive families are often multiproblem families with homes characterized by disruption, chaos, and deprivation, which confound the effects of abuse with broader environmental influences. Their research has powerfully demonstrated the specific and detrimental effects of all forms of maltreatment, but most particularly psychological maltreatment in the form of psychological unavailability. The devastating effects of psychological maltreatment on social and emotional functioning go well beyond the general effects of an adverse environment.

Hart, Germain and Brassard's review of the literature (chapter 1) leads them to conclude that direct and severe forms of psychological maltreatment frequently result in severe emotional and behavior problems in child victims. Many of the authors in this volume agree that mal-

adaptive deviance is an outcome of psychological maltreatment. Psychological maltreatment in its various forms is seen as the cause of learning and behavior disorders in children, as well as long-lasting psychological distress in adults. Psychological maltreatment interacts with and exacerbates the effects of poverty and inadequate provision of medical care and education. It acts independently in a destructive manner when physical and economic needs are being met.

An additional question could be raised. Why should we study child maltreatment and not human maltreatment in general? We would answer that there is evidence that maltreatment in the developmental period has longer lasting and more detrimental effects on the victim than maltreatment at later stages of the life cycle. In addition, children are the state's responsibility as well as its future. Finally, the study of psychological maltreatment and its effects provides an excellent opportunity to expand our knowledge of factors which optimize and impede normal development.

In this concluding chapter, an attempt is made to integrate and summarize major issues and themes considered throughout this volume. The presentation is organized in three sections: points of agreement, controversial issues, and recommendations.

POINTS OF AGREEMENT

Lack of Definition and Standards Is the Greatest Obstacle to Research and Intervention

The absence of an operational definition of psychological maltreatment and its subcomponents is the single greatest obstacle to research, legal intervention, and the development of social policy regarding psychological maltreatment. All of our authors agree on this point. In addition, most of our authors recognize the need to produce a range of definitions. It is generally agreed that narrow definitions should be produced for legal intervention and that broad definitions will be necessary to address subtle, insidious effects of less obvious forms of abuse (e.g., cultural bias and prejudice, the influence of negative and limiting models in the media).

Other definition and standards issues exist. The majority of those issues are controversial in nature and, therefore, will be dealt with in the second section of this chapter. However, many of the points of agreement that follow should assist in resolving definition and standards issues.

Psychological Maltreatment Is Complex, Multidimensional, and Violent in Nature

A Wide Variety of Manifestations of Maltreatment Exist. The authors make several important points about the various manifestations of psychological maltreatment. First, in regard to classifying psychological maltreatment, Garbarino and Vondra (chapter 2) suggest that there are two separate, overlapping forms. One is directed at the victim (e.g., physical, mental cruelty) and the other is an indirect form, such as abuse, occurring as a by-product of behavior that has another subject entirely as its target (e.g., witnessing severe marital discord in one's parents).

A second point is that in any abusive situation there are likely to be two consequences to the victim. The first is the direct psychological effect resulting from the maltreatment, such as feelings of fear, denigration, and rejection. The second is the learning of destructive interaction patterns as modeled by the abusive adult.

Third, physical and psychological reactions to abuse cannot be easily separated from one another. Navarre (chapter 3) clearly states, "As we learn more about the mind, the body, the social environment and their interaction, it becomes more and more clear that physical, psychological, and social survival are different facets of the same struggle. Severe risk to any of the three may bring about similar consequences for the individual" (pp. 16–17). Schakel (chapter 7) makes a similar point when discussing emotional neglect. She believes that insufficient or distorted maternal nurturance may result in developmental delays and death, even when physical care has been meticulous. The physical and the psychological are inseparably intertwined. Failure to thrive and psychosocial dwarfism are examples of physical threats to the life of a child that are the direct result of severe forms of maternal deprivation.

Finally, as Egeland and Erickson contend, abuse is not considered to be an isolated incident, but an environment. Abuse does not occur in otherwise normal homes—the homes of the maltreating families in their high-risk sample were characterized by chaos, disruption, and disorganization. Drug abuse, alcohol abuse, and wife-beating occurred commonly in these families. And for many of these children, the environment provided a low threshold for abuse prior to birth because the mothers were not prepared for the birth, their expectations in regard to parenting were unrealistic, and they probably had poor prenatal nutrition and care (inferred from low birthweights).

Maltreatment is Placed on a Continuum of Care. Navarre suggests that we define maltreatment acts as being on the severe, negative end of a continuum of caretaker behaviors. These behaviors are identified as aversive on the basis of the probability of their resulting in psychological and physical harm to the victim.

Violence and Coercion Are at the Core of Maltreatment. Gil (chapter 12) states that child abuse is "reactive violence from the oppressed," and that negative human behaviors become dominant when expansiveness of life is curtailed. Gil believes that institutional and personal violence result from frustrations and stresses created by socially sanctioned inequalities. Gil's thoughts are echoed to some extent by other authors. Hart, Brassard, and Germain (chapter 16) discuss institutional abuse perpetrated by schools through their common practices and procedures; for example, use of discipline and control which create fear and intimidation, limited opportunities to develop competency and self-worth in school settings, and encouragement to remain dependent on school routine and personnel. Hyman's comments about corporal punishment in the schools are similar. He describes physical punishment as racist, sexist, and classist, and demonstrates that its excessive use is empirically associated with juvenile delinquency and adult commission of violent crimes. Hyman believes that it co-occurs with emotional concomitants of denigration and humiliation, and that there is no support for its use as a parenting or pedagogical tool.

Finally, Jones and Jones (chapter 11) identify slavery as a violent means of oppression. They attribute much racism to feelings and patterns of behavior derived from that history, and find such patterns apparent today in the way blacks are still oppressed in more subtle ways. They identify two forms of bias that operate to make blacks less competitive and less valued in the market place: first, blacks are socialized in their own culture, which reinforces competencies less valued by the politically and economically dominant white culture and second, they have evolved characteristics which are not valued by the dominant culture. Thus, black Americans are disadvantaged environmentally, in terms of socialization provided by an oppressed subculture, and genetically in terms of past selection forces, selection at odds with what the dominant culture values in our current society.

The Subjective Meaning Ascribed to Maltreatment by Victims Should be Incorporated in Definitions. Garbarino and Vondra (chapter 2) encourage attention to the subjective reality of the child as a primary concern of researchers and clinicians. Navarre (chapter 3) suggests that the degree of abuse, and thus the degree of harm experienced, may be related to the subjective meaning that a particular action or pattern of interactions has for a victim. And Rosenberg and Germain (chapter 17) consider describing the impact of psychological maltreatment on victims as the first of three areas where psychology can make a unique contribution to empirical and clinical work in the area.

The Necessity to Have a Developmentally Sensitive Definition. Hart, Germain, and Brassard, Garbarino and Vondra, and Navarre all stress the importance of defining psychological maltreatment in a manner that is sensitive to the

context in which the maltreating behavior occurs. The age of the child is an important component of the context. As many have pointed out, caretaker behavior that is appropriate when directed to a toddler would be inappropriate when directed to an adolescent. Navarre and Brassard and McNeill additionally suggest that vulnerability to certain types of negative experiences may vary from one developmental stage to another.

Melton and Thompson (chapter 15) tackle the issue from another perspective. They emphasize child outcomes rather than parental practices (stating that it is too difficult to predict the effect of parental practices on child outcomes). In order to define child maladaptive outcomes in age-appropriate ways, they insist that "guidelines must be framed using different criteria for children of different ages, since the expression of many psychological processes varies significantly with the developmental level of the child" (p. 18). For example, aggressive tendencies are expressed differently in a 3-year-old than they are in an 18-year-old.

Causes

There is general agreement that psychological maltreatment is multi-determined. Several possible causes have been identified. These include the following:

Denial of Basic Psychological Needs. The denial of, or the assault on, the basic psychological needs of individuals by the social, emotional and physical environment creates needy and immature individuals who are inadequate or even destructive as parents. As emotionally deprived or abused parents tend to recreate patterns of deprivation or abuse that they had experienced as children, this may result in a continuing cycle of abuse, unless the environment provides therapeutic experiences that buffer the individual from the full force of the maltreatment.

Children Are a Low Societal Priority. Paradoxical views of children are seen in the degree to which stated societal values are at odds with societal actions. Hyman (chapter 4) supports this point with examples of the low value of children in our wealthy society. This is seen in the use of physical punishment of children though unsupported in its effectiveness as a parenting or teaching tool, the low value placed on child-rearing as a full-time activity, and the severely limited funds put into health, education, nutrition, and child protection.

Institutional Abuse. Institutional abuse results from economic and social systems that are oppressive and curtail the development of individual potential. This creates aggression in some of the more frustrated members of society and fosters an ideology of inequality, selfishness, competition, and domination. Gil (chapter 12) has addressed these issues in detail.

The Influence of Negative and Limiting Models. Telzrow cites Bronfenbrenner, who has concluded that social forces (e.g., divorce, single-parent families, working mothers) have contributed to a substantial reduction in the amount of contact between parent and child, and a lessening of the parent's role in the care and development of children. Under these conditions children are subjected to increased influence by negative and limiting models via television and peers where they are exposed to sexism, violence, materialism, substance abuse, and racism.

Mediating Variables

There is an absence of the critical information needed to unravel the complex problem of maltreatment. Increased risk for maltreatment has been related primarily to caretaker characteristics (e.g., interest in the child, history of child abuse, personality characteristics), the lack of environmental support and presence of stress (e.g., unemployment, marital discord), the absence of environmental constraints (e.g., neighbors or home visitors dropping by), and to child characteristics (gender, temperament, vulnerability because of past abuse). These factors have not been investigated relative to the specific causal mechanisms by which they exert their influence. There are nonabusive families living under conditions of social stress identical to those of abusive families; nonabusive parents with developmental and/or psychiatric histories similar to abusive parents; and children with characteristics identical to those of maltreated children who do not elicit abuse. It should be our goal to search for the processes that mediate between already identified high-risk factors and maltreatment by caretakers.

Outcomes for Children

Hart, Germain and Brassard (chapter 1) review extant research on forms of psychological maltreatment that show that the psychological consequences of child maltreatment are often the most destructive of the consequences experienced by child victims. In addition, the literature indicates that child maltreatment is associated with, and in many instances causes behavior disorders in victimized children and (to a less clear extent) long term emotional distress in adults.

Schakel's (chapter 7) review identifies emotional neglect as having the most serious consequences of all forms of maltreatment, with outcomes such as attempted suicide, drug overdose, and severe medical problems. Egeland and Erickson (chapter 8) report similar findings from their longitudinal, prospective study of high-risk mothers. All children in their maltreatment groups functioned poorly from infancy through preschool. They exhibited a wide range of maladaptive behaviors. The psychologically unavailable caregiving pattern was the most devastating to a child's development. These children declined sharply in intellectual functioning and demonstrated disturbed attachment relationships and a lack of social-emotional competence. The children are at a further disadvantage in that the psychologically unavailable pattern of caregiver behavior is one of the least likely to be detected.

Interventions

There is general agreement among the authors that our current system of dealing with psychological maltreatment does not work. Melton and Thompson (chapter 15) best express the sentiment in their statement, "our approach to treating abusive families is woefully inadequate. In even the best demonstration projects, for example, the abuse recidivism rate is disturbingly high. . . . When professionals cannot eliminate even the grossest forms of physical violence against children, there is good reason to wonder about the likely success of interventions designed to change more subtle forms of 'maltreatment'" (p. 206, this volume).

In regard to the legal field, Corson and Davidson (chapter 14) think it will be some time before cases of psychological maltreatment are easily accepted and appropriately handled.

Additionally, they recognize that intervention itself may be emotionally devastating to the child. Parents are brought to court under vague statutes, and courts intervene now only when a child is suffering "serious emotional damage" *and* the parent is unwilling to seek treatment.

Macrosystem Interventions. Gil (chapter 12) forcefully argues that the only approach that promises real change is an attempt to transform society into a nonviolent, democratic one through political processes. Melton and Thompson agree, opining that a positive ideology of children as valuable in their own right (rather than in the manner in which they meet the needs of caretakers) is essential to providing for the welfare of children. They feel our society currently does not hold this view, and thus child welfare will continue to suffer. Hyman also feels that major structural changes in the attitudes, procedures and priorities of our society are in order. Political action is required to institute these changes. Hyman stresses interventions that are legislative and attitudinal in nature. For instance, he wants to eliminate the economic liabilities currently associated with family child-rearing and educational activities, and enhance family living through such social programs as full employment, improved day care and incentives for continuing education.

Exosystem Interventions. At this level, the focus is on community/societal structures which affect the experiences of the child but which do not originate within the direct experiences of the child. Practices associated with schooling, legal intervention, and cultural bias in media are good examples.

Hyman (chapter 4) and Hart, Brassard, and Germain (chapter 16) provide detailed recommendations for reducing psychological maltreatment in the schools perpetrated by school personnel and by institutional practices. Schools as a source of maltreatment have been largely ignored by researchers and mental health professionals, and interest in this topic is encouraging.

Present legal practices generally ignore psychological maltreatment cases and thus, the majority of their interventions are limited to temporary or permanent separation of victims and perpetrators. To encourage both corrective and preventative action at the child protection and court levels, a "Mental Health Neglect" model of intervention has been proposed by

Hart, Brassard, and Germain (chapter 1). Desirable components of a model law for psychological maltreatment are proposed by Corson and Davidson (chapter 14). Although the concept of such a law is controversial, there is agreement among the authors that any legal definition of psychological maltreatment needs to reflect a narrow definition of maltreatment.

Other interventions at this level are focused on reducing the negative impact of print and television media. Jones and Jones (chapter 11) recommend that racial/ethnic stereotypes be eliminated from textbooks, and Telzrow (chapter 9) supports the same recommendation for public media (television). These changes would reduce the climate of cultural bias and prejudice in our communities, and provide positive role models of women and minorities.

Microsystem Interventions. Although most authors in this volume focus primarily on interventions at the societal institution level, most agree that interventions directed to individuals and families are important. Egeland and Erickson (chapter 8) offer excellent suggestions for interventions with high-risk mothers. Based on their experience with this population they suggest intervening with high-risk mothers prior to their first child's birth. The goals of the intervention are to (a) help the mother understand her child's behavior and developmental stage; (b) help the mother become a better perspective-taker, so that her sensitivity to her infant's cues increase through observing modeled sensitive, responsive care; (c) increase the mother's understanding of her child's cues through observing her own videotaped interactions with her child while using age-appropriate toys, and then discussing with the interventionist what was going on in the videotaped interaction; (d) help the mother develop realistic expectations for her baby and obtain peer support through participating in a parent-infant group with mothers and infants of similar ages; and (e) provide an extensive outreach program for the mother, offering emotional support and concrete help with real-life problems. Schakel (chapter 7) advocates the routine assessment of mothers for risk of maltreatment at the time of the birth of their children. If high-risk status is confirmed, they would then be enrolled in a program similar to the one above and possibly receive the services of a home visitor as well.

Brassard and McNeill (chapter 5) describe

several family intervention programs designed for incestuous families, and recommend adolescence as the preferred age at which to intervene with this population. Prevention programs for children and adolescents are also described and endorsed by them.

CONTROVERSIAL ISSUES

The majority of issues associated with psychological maltreatment are subject to debate or, at the very least, in need of further clarification. In this section, unresolved issues are organized within five categories: broad versus narrow definitions, rights conflicts, nature of evidence necessary to establish psychological maltreatment, nature and levels of vulnerability, and correction and prevention.

Broad Versus Narrow Definitions

Arguments have been made in support of both broad and narrow definitions of psychological maltreatment. Presently existing definitions and standards for more concrete forms of child maltreatment (i.e., physical and sexual) are ambiguous. It is not surprising that definitions of psychological maltreatment are controversial.

Broad definitions include forms of psychological maltreatment which are direct or indirect in their attack on the victim, subtle or blatant in their observable characteristics, dependent or independent in relationships to other forms of maltreatment, and perpetrated by actors in isolation and/or collaboration at all levels of the human ecological system. Broad definitions recognize the integral and pervading nature of psychological maltreatment in all spheres of human experience. By virtue of these characteristics, broad definitions appear to be viewed by the majority of our authors as necessary to provide a comprehensive framework within which to identify directions for research, intervention, and prevention.

At the same time, broad definitions are recognized as being problematical. In a general way, the magnitude and pervasiveness of psychological maltreatment broadly defined tends to discourage researchers, practitioners, institutions, and granting agencies from dealing with it. When the focus narrows, it is primarily the implications for intervention associated with broad definitions which stimulate concern. Questions such as the following are often raised.

Are not most parents susceptible to being identified as perpetrators of such poorly defined and often unintentionally executed acts as rejection, corrupting, and exploiting? Should limited child protective service resources be diverted from more tangible and reliably identified forms of child maltreatment to deal with psychological maltreatment? Does intervention not run the risk of creating more problems than it solves, of being iatrogenic? Realistically, is there any hope of substantive intervention at the societal/institutional and child care/institutional levels where maltreatment seems to be sanctioned? Is it not likely that modal values would be unfairly applied in standards for decision making, resulting in a lack of respect for cultural diversity?

Narrow definitions of psychological maltreatment seem to hold promise for limiting these negative effects. However, they might deny recognition of its subtleties and pervasiveness, thereby leading researchers, practitioners, and policy makers to deal with it in a fragmented and ill-conceived manner. The dangers of limiting attention to the more easily recognized forms of psychological maltreatment were pointed out by several of our authors. For example, Egeland and Erickson indicated that "psychologically unavailable caretaking," the form of maltreatment found to be most devastating in their studies, is likely to be overlooked; and Gil emphasized the need to give primary importance to dealing with culturally sanctioned psychological maltreatment at the societal/institutional level, which would be completely ignored by narrow definitions. Simple and speedy resolution of divergent opinions in this area is unlikely. Levels of definition, differentiated for their appropriateness and power for application in research, intervention, and policy development, may provide part of the solution. Establishment of operational definitions and proof of child outcomes directly tied to forms of maltreatment will provide direction. Even with such clarification, the issue of values regarding the rights of children, parents, families, and society must be confronted and resolved if progress is to be made beyond action to reduce the most blatant and narrowly defined forms of psychological maltreatment.

Rights Conflicts

The difficulties our society experiences in clarifying and supporting human rights, in opposition to property and institutional rights, are multiplied when the focus is on children. The general support for children's needs and rights, which appears to be embodied in the child-protection movement, is fraught with division and conflict when translations into specific policy and action are attempted. At the root of these problems are several related conditions, including the following: our society has not articulated or committed itself to a positive ideology of children which values them as human beings in their own right; the children's rights movement has been limited almost entirely to protection rights, generally avoiding choice or empowerment rights issues; parental rights tend to be conceived as property rights rather than stewardship rights; family rights are generally formulated as expressions of parental rights; and our society has been generally ineffective in attempts to support or constructively intervene in family life.

The divisiveness and conflicts associated with the children's rights movement have been recognized as limiting the promotion of programs for healthy child development and child protection. Among those authors who have addressed rights issues, there is consensus that they are highly relevant to psychological maltreatment. Consensus does not exist, however, regarding the nature of rights issues and their influences. For example, at a fundamental level, we find that Melton judges individual rights to be well supported in the major political documents of our society, while Gil finds no guarantees for the basic needs of individuals which are comparable to property rights guarantees. In general, lack of clarity and agreement are the rule rather than the exception in dealing with more specific positions.

It is not surprising that the authors in this volume have not achieved consensus on rights issues. They reflect our society and the fields of inquiry and professional practice most relevant to them (e.g., law, child development). The rights of children to be protected from premature death by acts of commission or omission by adult caretakers, whether from abortion or denial of needed medical services after birth, continue to be debated in our communities and courts. Rights to protection from psychological maltreatment involve issues less clear and less concrete. Reaching the "age of reason" and expressing competency are no longer used as guides in determining the choice/empowerment rights available to young people. A variety of economic and social factors now keep young people in

positions of dependency until they move out of the developmental period. Our lack of knowledge regarding the potential of young people to develop competencies, justifying various balances of protection and choice rights at identifiable stages of development, deprives us of the opportunity to confront these conditions. Though there is general agreement on the nature and importance of basic psychological needs, these needs have not been translated into well-articulated rights for children.

Nature of Evidence Necessary to Establish Psychological Maltreatment

A generic definition of psychological maltreatment exists and appears to have a wide base of support. Sufficiently rigorous operational definitions and standards for decision making do not exist. Definitions and standards have been considered for the acts of psychological maltreatment, child outcomes, and interactions between the two. Acts of psychological maltreatment are generally given more attention than outcomes in discussions of definitions, while outcomes are more often considered the most crucial factors in justifying intervention in cases of psychological maltreatment.

The acts of maltreatment given major attention in this volume are rejecting, terrorizing, isolating, degrading, exploiting, corrupting, and denying emotional responsiveness. However, as a set, these acts have not yet been established (by consensus of expert opinion or empirical evidence) as accurately or sufficiently representing psychological maltreatment. With the exception of isolating, they are not found in state statutes or guidelines as defining child maltreatment, though they appear to subsume most, or possibly all, of what is found there. Research and expert opinion give the most support to rejecting and terrorizing as act categories. The remainder of the set appear logically supportable but may be expressions of rejecting or terrorizing. As examples, "denying emotional responsiveness" and "degrading" might eventually be considered as dimensions of "rejecting."

There is much disagreement on the advisability of including act categories that include common parental behaviors. The arguments for inclusion of acts such as corrupting, degrading, and denying emotional responsiveness emphasize the more insidious forms of psychological maltreatment. The arguments against inclusion of acts of this nature are described in the earlier section on broad versus narrow definitions.

The applicability of level-of-seriousness dimensions (i.e., intensity, frequency and duration) and the necessity of establishing convergence of expert and lay public opinion on categories and operational definitions are two additional issue areas requiring attention. The level-of-seriousness dimensions have been given relatively little attention (see Navarre in this volume and NCCAN standards for the National Incidence Study). The necessity of establishing the viability of categories and operational definitions through convergence of expert and lay public opinion is not clear. It has been encouraged, on the premise that a broad base of support is needed if we are to deal with such an unclear and problematical construct. Expert opinion, even though substantiated by empirical evidence, is likely to produce little impact in the realm of social events if it is not appreciated by the general public. However, there may be forms of maltreatment sanctioned by our culture (e.g., coercive discipline), the inherent destructiveness of which must be demonstrated by experts prior to the establishment of support from the general public. Neither of these issues is likely to be dealt with satisfactorily unless incorporated in rigorous attempts to develop operational definitions.

When social service or legal interventions are considered, strong support exists to limit intervention to cases in which damage to the child has already occurred. This position is not without its debatable points. Damage to the child is usually described as deviancy, which is maladaptive in the form of serious emotional or behavioral disorders. However, this point of view has not been sufficiently dealt with through empirical study to determine its power. Differences of opinion exist regarding both the necessity of establishing extant damage and the necessity of tying outcomes to perpetrator acts. The legal community appears to prefer the position that serious extant damage attributable to caretaker acts must be established to justify intervention in cases of psychological maltreatment. Associated with this position, it is recommended that mental health specialists assist in determining the existence of psychological damage due to perpetrator acts. In contrast to this emphasis on outcomes tied to acts, some acts of psychological maltreatment have been judged to be so clearly destructive in nature (e.g., exten-

sive public humiliation, grossly differential treatment of siblings) as to require legal intervention regardless of outcome. Intervention on these grounds, in a few reported cases, has been supported by court action. Additionally, an act as subtle and hard to detect as denying emotional responsiveness has been found to produce such destructive consequences as to support serious consideration for intervention before damage occurs.

Further complications are produced when the focus is primarily on outcomes. The subjective meaning given to the act by a victim may be critical in determining its impact (see Garbarino and Vondra, and Navarre in this volume). Subjective meaning may be at the core of differences between "stress-resistant" and "stress-vulnerable" subjects. Before application, the viability of this position must be established through investigation of both the influence of mediating factors and the competency of the child to accurately judge and communicate inner states. Another issue relevant to the importance of outcomes centers around the need to provide services to children who display substantial mental health problems. Most state statutes require legal intervention when caretakers refuse to provide services to the children under their care who have mental health problems, regardless of the causes of those problems. The fact that this dictum is generally ignored suggests that it is a position without sufficient support in child protective services circles and/or that practical strategies for activation have not been developed. A "mental health neglect" model which might overcome some of these obstacles has been suggested in this volume (see chapter 1 and Appendix C). It may provide a beginning point for responsible action without requiring that blame be established.

Nature and Levels of Vulnerability

Many issues have been raised regarding the nature and levels of vulnerability of victims to both acts and outcomes of psychological maltreatment. Consideration has been given to conditions associated with each of the following categories of factors: general cultural conditions, cultural subgroup status, characteristics of adult caretakers, developmental characteristics of victims, and previous history of psychological need fulfillment of victims. While there is substantial interest in these topics, there is not clear agreement on the degree to which they embody factors which influence vulnerability to various aspects of psychological maltreatment.

Existing conditions and trends in the general culture may increase the likelihood of psychological maltreatment and the magnitude of its destructive power. Of apparent relevance are conditions which limit the fulfillment of basic psychological needs for young people, making them more vulnerable to the influences of maltreatment. Examples of these conditions include less direct involvement of adults in interaction with young people, increased influences of negative media and peer models on attitudes and behavior of young people, breakdown of family structures, limited opportunities for young people to contribute to family life, increased substance abuse across all ages, increased incidence of teenage pregnancy, market manipulation of youthful consumers, and transience in geographical/community residence. These areas have not been sufficiently researched in regard to their influences on psychological maltreatment, but all seem related.

Conditions associated with cultural subgroup membership may influence vulnerability. Physical abuse and neglect appear to be more likely to occur in populations of low socioeconomic status. Whether those who are poor are more subject to psychological maltreatment is debatable, and yet it seems likely when broad conceptualizations of maltreatment are applied. Greater exposure to negative/limiting media models has been found for lower-SES populations and black children. Gil has indicated that the "have-nots" of society are much less likely than others to experience basic human needs fulfillment. The greater levels of stress and lower levels of personal satisfaction and power experienced by those living near or below the poverty level may increase the likelihood of maltreatment behavior. Egeland and Erickson have suggested that different forms of psychological maltreatment may be more likely to be accepted and manifested for different SES populations. Reschley and Graham-Clay and Jones and Jones have identified the special psychological-maltreatment conditions and influences of prejudice and bias toward minorities in our culture.

Personality and behavioral characteristics of adults vary extensively. Child maltreatment work has previously focused much attention on the possibility that personal maladjustment, poor marital adjustment, poor coping skills, and

limited or inappropriate expectations and skills for childrearing increase the likelihood that an adult will mistreat children. Available evidence for the influence of these factors is weak in regard to physical and sexual maltreatment and generally unavailable for psychological maltreatment. Egeland and Erickson and Gil suggest that adults with histories of unmet psychological needs are more likely to maltreat. Support for this position exists in research evidence indicating that psychological maltreatment of children may be produced through spillover of emotional and interpersonal difficulties of caretakers. The sex of the adult and the sex of the child may be associated differentially with various forms of psychological maltreatment perpetrated against children. To the degree that the psychological maltreatment characteristics of sexual abuse, judged to include degrading, corrupting and exploiting, are different from those of other forms of abuse, some evidence in support of this supposition presently exists. These hypothesized relationships require further research.

The developmental characteristics of the child may be related to the nature and level of vulnerability of the child to psychological maltreatment. According to Egeland and Erickson, it is of critical importance for the child to experience psychological attention and interaction in the early stages of development. Maltreatment of the infant has been found to produce behavioral and emotional maladjustment characteristics in the child, which would appear to increase the likelihood that the child will experience further maltreatment. By age 10, racial attitudes appear to be fully integrated across the thinking, feeling, and overt behavior of a child. These findings and opinions suggest that psychological maltreatment has powerful influence at early stages of development. Different forms of maltreatment may have different influences on a child according to the developmental characteristics achieved, being established, and next to be pursued for that child. Egeland and Erickson consider the denial of emotional responsiveness to be particularly destructive in infancy, due to the manner in which it frustrates the development of trust and autonomy. If biological and psychological imperatives (e.g., needs, issues, or challenges) differ in nature at different periods of development, it is reasonable to assume differential impact from various forms of maltreatment. In addition, the child's abilities to reason and develop alternative perspectives change with maturity and experience, in ways which should have substantial impact on the subjective meaning given to maltreatment. Ayalon and Van Tassel (chapter 13) indicate that quite different responses to terrorizing are expressed by young children as compared to adolescents. This may be due to developmental differences such as have been noted here. The importance of considering the developmental characteristics of young people when investigating the effects of psychological maltreatment is generally supported, often discussed, but yet to be put to rigorous testing.

To what degree does a child's previous history of psychological need fulfillment influence vulnerability to psychological maltreatment at a later point in time? Do children who have experienced a personal history of psychological maltreatment react differently to psychological maltreatment than those who have not? Navarre, in her chapter, raises this as a question in need of study. Whether or not the cumulative effects of maltreatment make recent maltreatment greater, less, or different in its impact on the victim is not known. This is an important question which has been given very little attention. Maslow has indicated that those who have not had their basic psychological needs met sufficiently are more susceptible to the impact of stress and frustration than others. Experts generally acknowledge that individuals who have not had these needs met are more likely than others to develop a negative identity, and to pursue need fulfillment in a manner destructive to themselves and others. According to Maslow, individuals who have experienced sufficient and dependable fulfillment of their psychological needs are much better able to deal responsibly with psychological stress stemming from psychological need deprivation. The investigations of "stress-resistant" children appear to support Maslow's position. Further work in this area could produce direction for the types of preventive and corrective programs necessary to deal with psychological maltreatment.

Correction and Prevention

Intervention in the forms of prevention and correction of child maltreatment have been given much attention by our society and the authors of this volume. Substantive progress, however, has been elusive. This is particularly true for psycho-logical maltreatment. Issues revolve around our culture's perspectives on and approaches to social problem solving, the relative emphasis to be given to interventions focusing on various developmental and ecological levels, and specific forms of intervention to be applied at various developmental and ecological levels. Issues in this section will be considered within these three categories.

Perspectives and approaches to child maltreatment intervention in our society are in conflict. Prevention is lauded as the most valuable and appropriate approach, while correction in the form of crisis intervention tends to be the general practice. Prevention applied to its human targets, however, has been seen as creating the risks of intrusion, interference, and error. Short-term, simple action, to correct crisis conditions which have produced verifiable demand, is standard practice. The record of success through corrective efforts of this type has been poor. Recognition of the ineffectiveness of corrective efforts, the staggering costs of child maltreatment in human suffering and loss of resources, and the promise of substantial improvement through prevention have increased the appeal of prevention. The National Committee for Prevention of Child Abuse and Neglect has focused on prevention as the major strategy for dealing with child maltreatment. The desire to emphasize prevention over correction has even resulted in the relabeling of correction as "tertiary prevention." This exemplifies the present state of affairs, in which the spirit of prevention has been translated primarily into hope and talk.

The importance of focusing intervention at particular levels of the human ecological system and at particular phases of the human development continuum is being debated. In dealing specifically with psychological maltreatment, the authors of this volume indicated the importance of intervening at the levels of the individual victim or perpetrator, the family, the school, the community, and the society (as expressed through media sources and relevant ideologies and practices). The points of debate sometimes represent strong differences of opinion about whether one or another level should be the focus of attack. As an example, Melton argues against intervention at the societal level and for intervention at the institutional child-care level, while Gil argues for intervention primarily at the societal level. Both are persuasive. While it seems logical to assume that strategies focused at each level, in proper balance, will present the most effective program of correction and prevention, this has not been established.

At the individual level the following perspectives and issues seem important. As indicated previously, it is suspected that children react differently to various types of psychological maltreatment at different stages of development. The manner and degree to which this is the case and to which differences are associated with various biological and experiential histories is yet to be clarified. It is probable that the manner and degree in which perpetrators psychologically maltreat is related to their individual and family stages of development. Even less is known in this regard. Many of our authors have indicated that we must increase our understanding of the relationships between psychological need fulfillment and psychological maltreatment, if we are to identify best directions for reducing psychological maltreatment. This position focuses most heavily at the individual level. Suggestions for correction and prevention at the child level tend to emphasize protection from maltreatment and/or reduction of the child's vulnerability. One difficulty associated with focusing preventive measures on changing child characteristics is that it tends to suggest that the child has levels of responsibility for the maltreatment or its prevention. Children should not be charged with this responsibility. At the individual adult-perpetrator level, emphasis has been on personality and behavioral change, emphasizing need fulfillment, coping strategies, and parenting knowledge. Specific to psychological maltreatment, in the form of "denying emotional responsiveness," Egeland and Erickson have recommended that preventive intervention be focused on improving the perspectives and coping skills of high-risk expectant mothers. To date, efforts at the individual level requiring involuntary participation have not proven successful for correction, and attempts at prevention have generally been without participants.

At the family level, promise has been exhibited in Giaretto's model for correction dealing with sexual abuse, but research evidence has not fully established its power, and somewhat surprisingly, the model has not been widely applied to other forms of psychological maltreatment. The "home visitor" model, using social or health service professionals and paraprofessionals as guides and resources to parents, has been identified as one of the most promising techniques for prevention of child maltreatment. While not formed specifically for psychological maltreatment, it should be applicable to it. This model is subject to the cautions generally raised about involuntarily received intrusion into family privacy and the danger of iatrogenics. Garbarino and Vondra, and Melton and Thompson, in this volume and in other writings, have presented the rationales for proscriptions and prescriptions for family intervention. Convincing arguments have been offered by Garbarino in favor of intervention and by Melton in opposition to it.

At the institutional child-care level, many recommendations have been made for correcting child maltreatment. The school has been the major institutional form given attention. Hyman has suggested that a beginning be made by eliminating corporal punishment in schools and other institutions, and thereby reducing the use of fear, intimidation, and degradation as forms of control. Hart, Brassard, and Germain have identified a broad range of corrective and preventive strategies for schooling, which could reduce psychological maltreatment in and out of schools. Melton has identified institutional child care as the most appropriate and responsible point for intervention under present conditions. While there appears to be general agreement in regard to the potential and need for intervention at this level, it is not supported by any history of general success for dealing with child maltreatment within and among schools. Educational systems have resisted social service responsibilities beyond the pursuit of narrowly defined educational development. State laws, ethical standards, and proclamations from child protection leadership and educational leadership have encouraged active participation by educators to reduce child maltreatment occurring outside of school. However, relatively little has been done and until recently, the psychological maltreatment perpetrated within schooling was almost completely ignored.

Interventions at the societal level to influence media, ideology, policy, and practice have been considered by several authors in this volume. Telzrow, Jones and Jones, and Reschley and Graham-Clay have identified the forms and negative impact of psychological maltreatment channeled through television and written material. While some progress has been made in reducing the proliferation of racial, ethnic, and sexual prejudice in media, it appears that violence is being modeled, particularly through film and video formats, at increasing levels. Our culture seems to preferentially value freedom of expression and the freedom to market products over child protection. Gil indicates that political and economic policy at the societal level must be influenced if we are to substantially reduce child maltreatment. He argues for the support of broad cultural imperatives committing us to the fulfillment of basic human needs. Melton and Thompson argue against an attack targeted at broad societal/institutional levels. Both they and Gil, along with others, have identified as a major stumbling block in this area the lack of formulation of and commitment to a positive ideology of the child in our culture.

RECOMMENDATIONS

Each chapter of this volume contains recommendations for advancing the knowledge base of psychological maltreatment and our ability to deal effectively with it. Most of these recommendations are specific to the particular issue areas given priority by the chapter author(s). The recommendations presented here are more general in form and follow logically from the points of agreement and debate which were described in the first sections of this chapter.

The first priority in psychological maltreatment work should be given to research. This social problem is fraught with ambiguities and misunderstandings. Research should initially be focused to produce and test operational definitions of the acts of psychological maltreatment; to produce assessment techniques, including standards of evidence for determining the existence and seriousness of psychological maltreatment acts; and to determine the child outcomes produced by psychological maltreatment acts. As an integral part of these stages of research, and expanding on the attention given to it, mediating variables must be investigated. Mediating variables influencing the following factors should be given attention: the likelihood for a perpetrator to maltreat in various ways, at various levels, and under various conditions; the risk that a child will be selected as the target for maltreatment during any period of childhood; and the level of vulnerability to impact of various kinds, at various levels, for various lengths of time, and under various conditions for the child victim. When these research targets have been sufficiently clarified, major attention should shift to research which will clarify the nature and power of corrective and preventive strategies. The research conducted in regard to psychological maltreatment should systematically and comprehensively investigate developmental, ecological, and holistic dimensions.

Next in priority is the recommendation that the existing child and human development knowledge base be applied in child care much more extensively than is presently the case. It is apparent that existing knowledge regarding child/human development is not being considered or applied in sufficiently powerful ways at any level of the human ecological system. Parents, educators, and others involved in protecting and encouraging the healthy development of children need to have accurate expectations for growth in cognitive, psychomotor, and affective domains. In addition, they need to be well acquainted with and skilled in the application of strategies and best practices for promoting growth and development. Particular emphasis should be given to the nature of basic psychological needs in such efforts. If caretakers are sufficiently knowledgeable and skilled in these areas, some child maltreatment will be prevented and recognition of maltreatment and its effects will be enhanced. We believe that the present state of knowledge, for example, supports the application of the "mental health neglect" model which has been proposed in chapter 1 of this volume, and that legal intervention in psychological maltreatment should be applied where clear and strong outcomes have or could be predicted to occur from caretaker acts. Enhanced awareness and application of child-development knowledge can be accomplished through a variety of channels, including parent training provided through community agencies, home visitors, churches, commercial or public television, videotape programs for home use, programs for public schools to reach both parents and students who will someday be parents, and through higher education to prepare those who will teach/influence children and parents. It is further recommended that political, economic, and public media leadership be made aware of the importance of achieving these goals, and that their specialized expertise and spheres of influence become targeted toward these ends.

Support at local, state, and national levels should be sought to provide a sense of societal emphasis on healthy child development, which can be translated into practical incentives necessary to produce changes in child rearing.

Next we recommend that our society, at each level of the human ecological system, pursue a values-clarification process focused on the ideology of children. The nature of childhood in the broader picture of human development in our culture, our work, and our religions and philosophies of life must be confronted. And it must be confronted from the perspectives of what is and what should be. It is a simple thing to recommend that children be considered and valued as human beings in their own right; and that we (in its most comprehensive sense) act as stewards of the potentials of children by assuring that their basic psychological needs are met, and that their protection and empowerment rights are balanced according to their developmental characteristics. The authors of this volume have made it clear that these recommended conditions do not exist today. There is some agreement that a positive ideology of children is prerequisite to making substantive advances in child care. In that sense, this recommendation could easily be given first-priority status. The values clarification and development we are recommending must deal with the most basic of human values and their points of conflict and compatibility. We recommend that it

be placed on the agendas of families, parent–teacher associations, legislators, media producers, and all concerned citizens at each level of the human ecological system, so that they might join in the struggle to determine what we believe and what we will commit ourselves to regarding children.

A final recommendation is offered. Psychological maltreatment work should be pursued in a systematic and comprehensive fashion which builds efficiently on each achievement of new knowledge. Efforts are presently fragmented and uncoordinated. We have limited resources to deal with a pervasive social problem of great magnitude. It is multifaceted in its generation, perpetration, and impact. It is of critical importance that concerned researchers, professionals, and lay public representatives, individually and in collective form, participate in coordinated and mutually supportive networks. This will increase the power of the contributions of each and shorten the time required to reduce psychological maltreatment. Resources for such coordination exist in the National Center for Child Abuse and Neglect, the American Humane Association, the National Committee for the Prevention of Child Abuse and Neglect, the International Society for Prevention of Child Abuse and Neglect, and the Office for the Study of the Psychological Rights of the Child. Those resources should combine their special strengths to achieve the coordination, and thus, the impact that is needed.

Appendices*

Public Law 93-247–Child Abuse Prevention and Treatment Act

For purposes of this Act the term "child abuse and neglect" means the physical or *mental injury*, sexual abuse or exploitation, negligent treatment, or maltreatment of a child under the age of 18, or the age specified by the child protection law of the state in question, by a person who is responsible for the child's welfare under circumstances which indicate that the child's health or welfare is harmed or threatened thereby as determined in accordance with regulations prescribed by the Secretary.

Model Child Protective Services Act (excerpts from draft)

An "abused or neglected child" means a child whose physical or *mental health* or welfare is harmed or threatened with harm by the acts or omission of his/her parent or other person responsible for his/her welfare.

Mental injury means an injury to the intellectual or psychological capacity of a child as evidenced by an observable and substantial impairment in his ability to function within a normal range of performance and behavior with due regard to his culture.

National Committee for the Prevention of Child Abuse

Emotional Maltreatment: excessive, aggressive, or other parental behavior that places unreasonable

demands on a child to perform beyond his or her capabilities. Examples include constant teasing, belittling or verbal attacks, and a lack of love, support, or guidance.

National Incidence Study

Emotional Abuse: verbal or emotional assault; close confinement; threatened harm

Emotional Neglect: inadequate nurturance/affection; knowingly permitting maladaptive behavior (e.g., delinquency); other refusal to provide essential care

American Humane Association

Emotional Maltreatment: A national study reporting category only. It includes behavior on the part of the caretaker which causes low self-esteem in the child, undue fear or anxiety, or other damage to the child's emotional well-being.

Emotional Abuse: Active, intentional berating, disparaging or other abusive behavior toward the child which impacts upon the well-being of the child.

Emotional Neglect: Passive or passive/aggressive inattention to the child's emotional needs, nurturing, or emotional well-being.

International Conference on Psychological Abuse

Psychological Maltreatment: Of children and youth consists of acts of omission and commission which are judged on the basis of a combination

*Appendices assembled by Mark S. Gelardo, PhD.

of community standards and professional expertise to be psychologically damaging. Such acts are committed by individuals, singly or collectively, who by their characteristics (e.g., age, status, knowledge, organizational form) are in a position of differential power that renders a child vulnerable. Examples of psychological maltreatment include acts of *rejecting, terrorizing, isolating, exploiting,* and *missocializing.* Such acts damage immediately or ultimately the behavioral, cognitive, affective, or physical functioning of the child.

APPENDIX B: POSSIBLE CONSEQUENCES OF PSYCHOLOGICAL MALTREATMENT AS COMPARED TO DIAGNOSTIC CRITERIA FOR EMOTIONAL/BEHAVIORAL DISTURBANCE

ED/BD Criteria	Possible Consequences of Psychological Maltreatment
An inability to learn which cannot be explained by intellectual, sensory or health factors	underachievement
An inability to build or maintain satisfactory interpersonal relationships with peers and teachers	inability to become independent; inability to trust others; prostitution; tendency to psychologically maltreat others
Inappropriate types of behaviors or feelings under normal circumstances	guilt; lying; stealing; violent aggression sometimes leading to homicide; juvenile delinquency; autistic-like behaviors; low frustration tolerance; emotional instability
A general pervasive mood of unhappiness or depression	low self-esteem; depression; withdrawal behaviors sometimes leading to suicide
A tendency to develop physical symptoms or fears associated with personal or school problems	failure-to-thrive syndrome; encopresis; poor appetite; school phobia

APPENDIX C: MENTAL HEALTH NEGLECT—PROPOSED DEFINITION, STANDARDS, AND PROCEDURES FOR LEGAL AND SOCIAL SERVICES INTERVENTION

Stuart N. Hart

Definition

Mental health neglect exists when a child is found to be seriously emotionally/behaviorally disordered and his/her caretaker(s) refuse(s) to apply available and recommended corrective/therapeutic procedures.

Standards for Decision Making

A finding of a serious emotional/behavioral disorder for a child must be made by a team of two or more mental health professionals including an appropriately licensed/certified psychologist and/or psychiatrist and social worker. The evaluation model utilized should give emphasis to criteria which will reliably establish the extent to which the child's condition/performance is *deviant* from age-peers in areas and directions which are known to produce *maladaptive* functioning.

A finding of refusal to apply available and recommended corrective/therapeutic services is made when the child's caretaker(s) refuse(s) to *provide or maintain* the provision of corrective/therapeutic services selected from a set of two or more prescriptive options, supplied in writing, for which scheduling, financial responsibilities, and transportation are all within a range considered reasonable for the caretaker's present circumstances.

Procedures

Suspected cases of psychological maltreatment are to be reported to child protective services units, welfare departments, or the police. Upon receipt of a report, the receiving unit is to investigate the case which may include a home/sight visit, review of educational and medical records, and interviews with the child, family members, neighbors, and relevant others. The investigation is to result in one of the following:

1. insufficient evidence to justify further consideration;
2. insufficient evidence to intervene, but sufficient evidence to periodically review the case during the year;
3. sufficient evidence to conduct a thorough evaluation.

In the event that sufficient evidence warranting a thorough investigation is found, an evaluation team is formed and an evaluation is conducted. The team is to be composed of psychological/psychiatric and social work specialists capable of making a determination of whether or not a serious emotional/behavioral disorder exists through evaluations which consider the functioning and conditions of the child and their relevance for the social systems within which s/he lives and through which s/he is influenced. The child's caretaker(s) is/are offered the opportunity to be part of this evaluation team. At the conclusion of the evaluation, the case conference team meets with the caretaker(s) and representatives of the community agency directing the case study and case disposition procedures. The findings and recommendations are reported at this meeting.

If a diagnosis of serious emotional/behavioral disorder is *not* made, the case is either closed or left open for further monitoring and review. In either case, appropriate recommendations are made to correct relevant difficulties and prevent further escalation of any problems identified.

Should a diagnosis of serious emotional/behavioral disorder result, however, prescriptive recommendations for corrective/therapeutic services are developed by the evaluation team and representatives of the community agency directing the case study and case disposition procedures. These recommendations are then given to the caretaker(s) orally (if the caretaker(s) is/are participating) and in written form. The caretaker(s), at this time or as a part of his/her/their earlier participation, is/are given the opportunity to add prescriptive alternatives to those supplied by the case conference team so that prescriptions judged to be particularly appropriate by the caretaker(s) and any specialists assisting them might be considered.

If a diagnosis of serious emotional/behavioral disorder is made and the caretaker(s) concur(s) with the findings and act(s) to apply and maintain appropriate corrective/therapeutic services as required, the case continues to be monitored by the responsible community agency. If the caretaker(s) refuse(s) to apply and maintain appropriate corrective/therapeutic services as required, or reject(s) the findings and refuse(s) to take part in any further procedures directed by the responsible community agency, the case is transferred to the court system for hearing and adjudication.

Advantages

1. The definition, standards, and procedures incorporate levels of seriousness, criteria, and practices sufficiently well established through use in mental health work, the courts, and the schools to be acceptable to the courts, child services professionals, and the lay public.

2. While psychological maltreatment may be caused by acts of terrorizing, rejecting, isolating, exploiting, corrupting, degrading, and denying emotional responsiveness, the focus is on impact or outcomes. The major focus of the impact/outcomes of psychological maltreatment under consideration is one likely to be widely understood and supported (that is, deviancy which is maladaptive at significant levels).

3. Clarification and correction are emphasized in preference to fault finding and punishment.

4. The definition is susceptible to formulations producing a continuum of levels of seriousness, including positions identifying the existence of various degrees of threat to become seriously emotionally/behaviorally disordered. All positions allow for emphasis to be given in correc-

tive or preventative prescriptions for reducing or extinguishing the act(s) of psychological maltreatment.

5. The definition falls logically within the category of "neglect to provide needed services/ treatment," which exists in many state laws but which is seldom applied to cases in which psychological maltreatment is the major or sole type of maltreatment without accompanying physical neglect of a life-threatening nature.

6. As with P.L. 94-142, due process and the present or potential integrity of the caretaker(s) and family are respected, as well as the best interests of the child.

APPENDIX D: OFFICE FOR THE STUDY OF THE PSYCHOLOGICAL RIGHTS OF THE CHILD—ADVISORY BOARD

Marla Brassard, PhD
Department of Educational Psychology
325 Aderhold Hall
University of Georgia
Athens, GA 30602
(404) 546-7300 (H)
(404) 542-4110 (W)

Area of specialization: Psychological maltreatment; sexual abuse

Howard Davidson, JD
American Bar Association
1800 M Street
Suite 200
Washington, DC 20036
(202) 331-2250 (W)

Area of specialization: Child advocacy and the law

Byron Egeland, PhD
Department of Educational Psychology
N517 Elliot Hall
75 East River Road
University of Minnesota
Minneapolis, MN 55455
(612) 373-3286 (W)

Area of specialization: Child maltreatment; developmental psychopathology

Leonard Eron, PhD
Department of Psychology
University of Illinois at Chicago
Box 4328
Chicago, IL 60680

Area of specialization: Television's impact on children's behavior; aggression

James Garbarino, PhD
Department of Individual and Family Studies
Pennsylvania State University
S 110 Henderson
Human Development Building
University Park, PA 16802
(814) 863-0267

Area of specialization: Emotional maltreatment; adolescent maltreatment

David Gil, DSW
Brandeis University
Waltham, MA 02254
(617) 736-3827 (W)
(617) 862-6037 (H)

Area of specialization: Institutional abuse; economic analysis of social problems

John Guidubaldi, PhD
1327 Sheppard Drive
Kent, OH 44240
(216) 672-2928 (W)
(616) 626-4542 (H)

Area of specialization: Divorce; child development

Stuart N. Hart, PhD
Director, Office for the Study of the
Psychological Rights of the Child
902 West New York Street
PO Box 647
Indianapolis, IN 46240
(317) 264-8296 (W)
(317) 255-5584 (H)

Area of specialization: Psychological maltreatment; children's rights

Reginald Jones, PhD

Department of Afro-American Studies
University of California at Berkeley
Berkeley, CA 74720
(415) 642-7089 (W)

Area of specialization: Cultural bias and prejudice

T. K. Li, MD

Department of Medicine
Emerson Hall, #421
Indiana University Medical School
545 Barnhill Drive
Indianapolis, IN 46227
(317) 264-8495 (W)

Area of specialization: Medical consequences of abuse

John Merrow, PhD

4403 Fessenden Street, N.W.
Washington, DC 20016
(202) 966-9080 (H/W)

Area of specialization: Investigation of children's issues through the media

Patricia Mrazek, MSW, PhD

4620 18th Avenue
Denver, CO 80220
(303) 333-2719 (H)

Area of specialization: Sexual abuse

APPENDIX E: NATIONAL/INTERNATIONAL AGENCIES CONCERNED WITH CHILD ABUSE AND NEGLECT

Legal Issues and Child Advocacy

American Bar Association
National Legal Resource Center for Child Advocacy and Protection

1880 M Street, N.W.
2nd Floor South Lobby
Washington, DC 20036
(202) 331-2250

Services provided: Technical assistance, consultation, and training for professionals in utilizing the legal system for child protection

Children's Defense Fund

122 C Street
Suite 400, N.W.
Washington, DC 20001
(202) 628-8787

Services provided: Deals with care, welfare, education, and health of children, and with advocacy affecting legislation in these areas

National Association of Counsel for Children

1205 Oneida Street
Denver, CO 80220
(303) 321-3963

Services provided: Publishes a variety of materials dealing with children's legal rights and advocacy

Resources for Parents

Big Brothers/Big Sisters of America

230 N. 13th Street
Philadelphia, PA 19107
(215) 567-2748

Services provided: Support for families or single parents under stress by working with children in need of additional attention and friendship

National Coalition Against Domestic Violence

1500 Massachusetts Avenue, NW
Suite 35
Washington, DC 20005
(202) 347-7017

Services provided: Independently operated shelters for battered women and their families as well as individuals

Parents Anonymous

Toll-free outside California: (800) 421-0353
Toll-free inside California: (800) 352-0386

Services provided: Group members provide support for each other by finding positive alternatives for their abusive behaviors

Resources for the Family

American Family Society

Washington, DC 20088
(301) 460-4455

Services provided: Assists families by providing ideas that support family unity

Family Service America

44 E. 23rd Street
Tenth Floor
New York, NY 10010
(212) 674-6100

Services provided: Agencies serve families and individuals through counseling, advocacy, and family life education. Also deals with adolescent single parents

Parents United/Daughters and Sons United

PO Box 952
San Jose, CA 95108
(408) 280-5055

Services provided: Parents United provides assistance to families involved in child sexual abuse and also sponsors groups for adults sexually abused as children. Daughters and Sons United provides help to the child victims of sexual abuse whose parents are in the Parents United program

Child Abuse Organizations

American Humane Association

9725 East Hampden Avenue
Denver, CO 80231
(303) 695-0811

Services provided: Program planning, community planning, consultation, education, and training relative to promoting and creating child protective services in every community

Family Resource Coalition

230 N. Michigan Avenue
Suite 1625
Chicago, IL 60601
(312) 762-4750

Services provided: Organization of social service agencies concerned with family issues and strengthening families through preventive services

International Society for the Prevention of Child Abuse and Neglect

1205 Oneida Street
Denver, CO 80220
(303) 321-3963

Services provided: Publishes *Child Abuse and Neglect: The International Journal* and sponsors an international congress on child abuse and neglect biennially

C. Henry Kempe National Center for the Prevention and Treatment of Child Abuse and Neglect

1205 Oneida Street
Denver, CO 80220

Services provided: Emphasizes the development of treatment programs for abused children, conducts training programs, and offers technical assistance

National Center on Child Abuse and Neglect Children's Bureau
Administration for Children, Youth, and Families
U.S. Department of Health and Human Services

PO Box 1182
Washington, DC 20013
(202) 245-2856

Services provided: Administers federal funds for child abuse prevention and treatment, research, and demonstration projects

National Child Abuse Coalition

1125 15th Street
Suite 300
Washington, DC 20005
(202) 293-7550

Services provided: Composed of national organizations interested in the field of child abuse prevention and treatment. Objective is to provide national focus on the problem of child abuse and to coordinate activities implemented by state and local groups within each organization's national network system. Also keeps member organizations informed of federal legislation relating to child abuse

National Committee for Prevention of Child Abuse

332 South Michigan Avenue
Suite 950
Chicago, IL 60604
(312) 663-3520

Services provided: Volunteer-based organization working with community, state, and national groups to disseminate information about child abuse prevention and effect community action through sound policies and prevention programs

Author Index

Subject Index

About the Editors and Contributors

Marla R. Brassard, PhD, is an Assistant Professor of Educational Psychology at the University of Georgia where she trains doctoral students in school psychology and is a faculty member in the Marriage and Family Program. She is an Associate Director for the Office for the Study of the Psychological Rights of the Child and conducts research on child maltreatment, specifically on the development of measures of psychological maltreatment and their relationships to school and family outcomes.

Robert B. Germain, PhD, is a school psychologist with Worthington, Ohio, public schools. He has been an Assistant Professor of Psychology and Director of the masters and doctoral training programs in school psychology at the University of Rhode Island. He has also served as an Associate Director of the Office for the Study of the Psychological Rights of the Child and currently works as a school psychologist with students and their families on issues of psychological maltreatment.

Stuart N. Hart, PhD, is Associate Professor of Educational Psychology in the School of Education at Indiana University–Purdue University in Indianapolis. He is Director of the Office for the Study of the Psychological Rights of the Child and coordinator for school psychology training, and he conducts research and develops projects on psychological needs, rights, and maltreatment issues.

ABOUT THE CONTRIBUTORS

Ofra Ayalon, PhD, is a psychologist and senior lecturer at the University of Haifa in Israel. She specializes in research and therapy for populations under stress of war and terrorism. Her writings include books and articles on stress and coping with family violence, divorce, adoption, handicaps, and bereavement.

Michael J. Cohn, EdD, is Clinical Administrator of Treatment Centers of Arizona–Scottsdale. He has served on advisory boards combating drug and alcohol problems at the local, state, and national levels and has lectured at the international level on teens, drugs, and suicide. He is co-author of a recent article on teens, drugs, and suicide. He is listed in *Who's Who Among Human Service Professionals in the United States* and maintains a private practice in Scottsdale, Arizona.

Janet Corson, JD, is an attorney for the Guardian Ad Litem Project in Indianapolis, where her role is that of assisting abused and neglected children through the juvenile court system. Her area of study has concentrated on state statutes dealing with mental injury as it relates to child abuse and neglect issues. Prior to earning her law degree she worked as a teacher of children with learning disabilities and emotional handicaps. She is legal advisor to the Office for the Study of the Psychological Rights of the Child.

Howard Davidson, JD, is Director of the National Legal Resource Center for Child Advocacy and Protection, Young Lawyers Division. The resource center is a national clearinghouse which provides consulting services, technical assistance, and training services and has produced many publications related to child abuse and neglect.

Byron Egeland, PhD, is Professor of Educational Psychology, Psychology and Child Development and Coordinator of the Psychology in the Schools Program at the University of Minnesota. He is Director of the Mother–Child Project, a longitudinal study of child development and factors affecting development.

Martha Farrell Erickson, PhD, is a research specialist on the Minnesota Mother–Child Project. Her research is concerned with the socio-emotional development of children in high-risk families from infancy through the early school years. She is a faculty member of the Educational Psychology Department at the University of Minnesota where she teaches courses in assessment and intervention with children with special needs. She consults with school districts and since 1984 has served as President of the Minnesota School Psychologists Association.

James Garbarino, PhD, is President of the Erikson Institute for Advanced Study in Child Development. He has served as consultant to a wide range of groups and organizations dealing with child development and child welfare including the National Committee for the Prevention of Child Abuse for whom he chairs the Board of Directors Committee on Research and Program Evaluation. The National Conference on Child Abuse and Neglect honored him in 1985 with its first C. Henry Kempe Award, in recognition of "outstanding contributions to the field of child abuse prevention and treatment." He is author or editor of nine books including *Protecting Children from Abuse and Neglect, Understanding Abusive Families, Troubled Youth Troubled Families* and *The Psychologically Battered Child*.

Mark S. Gelardo, PhD, is a Research Associate in the Department of Educational Psychology at the University of Georgia. His research efforts focus on the neurological and psychosocial sequelae of physical maltreatment and their relationships to the child's development.

David G. Gil, DSW, is Professor of Social Policy and Director of The Center for Social Change, Practice, and Theory at the Florence Heller Graduate School for Advanced Studies in Social Welfare, Brandeis University. Before coming to Brandeis in 1964 he was involved in social welfare practice, research, and administration in the United States and Israel and has worked on farms in Sweden and Israel. His teaching, research and practice are concerned with understanding and overcoming forces which obstruct human development, liberation, cooperation, and social equality. During 1981 he served as President of the Association for Humanistic Sociology. Recently he completed a study for the United Nations on social welfare policy in the

United States. His publications include *Violence Against Children, Unraveling Social Policy, The Challenge of Social Equality, Beyond the Jungle, Child Abuse and Violence, Toward Social and Economic Justice*, and *The Future of Work*. He serves on the editorial boards of several professional journals.

Susan Graham-Clay, Specialist, School Psychology, is a school psychologist for the Child Guidance Clinic of Greater Winnipeg. She has published research findings on topics of social competence in children, behavioral interventions, and fetal alcohol syndrome.

Irwin A. Hyman, EdD, is Professor of School Psychology and Director of the National Center for the Study of Corporal Punishment and Alternatives in the Schools. He is a nationally recognized expert on school discipline and corporal punishment. His latest research focuses on educator-induced post-traumatic stress disorders of school children.

James M. Jones, PhD, is Professor of Psychology at the University of Delaware where he teaches courses in social psychology and black psychology. He is Director of the Minority Fellowship Program of the American Psychological Association. His work is concerned with prejudice, racism, and the cultural aspects of discrimination, and with black motivation and achievement.

Reginald L. Jones, PhD, is Professor of Afro American Studies and Education at the University of California at Berkeley. His teaching, research, and writing are concerned with Black psychology and exceptional children. His current publications include *Psycho-educational Assessments of Minority Children: A Case Book, Handbook of Tests and Measurements for Black Populations, Black Psychology* (Third Edition), and *Advances in Black Psychology*.

Linda E. McNeill, PhD, is a staff member at the Salt Lake City Family Support Center, a center for the prevention of child abuse and neglect. Her work there includes sexual abuse evaluations and child and family therapy with abusive families. She conducts research on the behavioral effects of incest on school-age girls and factors that will predict healthy outcomes for adolescent mothers and their infants.

Gary B. Melton, PhD, is Professor of Psychology and Law and Director of the Law-Psychology

Program at the University of Nebraska at Lincoln. In 1985 he was given the American Psychological Association award for Distinguished Contributions to Psychology and the Public Interest. He serves as President of the Division of Child, Youth and Family Services of the American Psychological Association and is chairman of that organization's Committee for the Protection of Human Participants in Research. He is an officer of the American Psychology–Law Society, and is author/editor of numerous books dealing with psychological issues relating to child and family law.

Elizabeth L. Navarre, MS, is Associate Professor in the School of Social Work at Indiana University in Indianapolis where she teaches courses on family violence. She has served as Indiana Coordinator for the Region 5 Resource Center on Child Abuse and Neglect, is a member of the Indiana Chapter of the National Committee on Child Abuse and Neglect, and has served on proposal review panels for the National Center on Child Abuse and Neglect. Her research has focused on the prevention of child abuse in residential care facilities, the protection of those children from abusive home visits and school experiences. Her publications include *Sexual Abuse: Prevention, Protection and Care.*

Daniel J. Reschly, PhD, is Professor of Psychology and Director of the School Psychology graduate program at Iowa State University. He has conducted research and published extensively on non-biased assessments, mild mental retardation, and social competence. He recently served as President of the National Association of School Psychologists and is a Fellow of the American Psychological Association.

Mindy S. Rosenberg, PhD, completed her doctoral work in Clinical–Community Psychology at the University of Virginia in 1984. She is currently Assistant Professor of Psychology in the Clinical–Community Psychology program at Yale University. Her current research deals with adaptation to chronic stress, and the effects of family violence on children's socio-emotional development and on family and individual coping skills.

Jacqueline A. Schakel, MS, is Director of Preschool Resources for Alaskan Special Education, an agency funded by the Alaskan Department of

Education to provide training, technical assistance and resources to school districts throughout the state. She serves as a psychological consultant to school personnel in their efforts to provide early intervention programs for preschool children and their families. She is currently completing a doctoral thesis on the influences of early social emotional development and experiences on children's motivation to master learning tasks in school.

Cathy F. Telzrow, PhD, coordinates a regional assessment clinic for severe and multiply handicapped children in the Cleveland, Ohio, region. In her work she provides in-service training to psychologists, school administrators, parents, and other professionals on topics related to assessment and intervention with handicapped children. Particular areas of expertise include preschool children and neuropsychological assessment and intervention strategies.

Ross A. Thompson, PhD, is Associate Professor of Psychology at the University of Nebraska at Lincoln, where he is also affiliated with the Law–Psychology Program. His teaching and research are concerned with early parent-child emotional development and the application of this work to child and family policy. His writing focuses on child custody issues, grandparents' rights and child eyewitness cases. He is a former Fellow of the Bush Program in Child Development and Social Policy at the University of Michigan.

Elizabeth Van Tassel, PhD, is a Developmental Psychologist formerly associated with the Department of Pediatrics at the Indiana University School of Medicine. Currently she is re-training in clinical psychology and is an intern at the Veterans Administration Medical Center in Danville, Illinois. Her research efforts are concerned with infants and young children who are at risk for developmental and behavioral difficulties.

Joan Vondra, PhD, received her doctorate degree in Human Development and Family Studies at Pennsylvania State University and is currently engaged in a post-doctoral position in clinical research at the University of Rochester. Her research interests and publications are concerned with parental influences on child development, child maltreatment, and developmental psychopathology.

Pergamon General Psychology Series

Editors: Arnold P. Goldstein, Syracuse University
Leonard Krasner, SUNY at Stony Brook